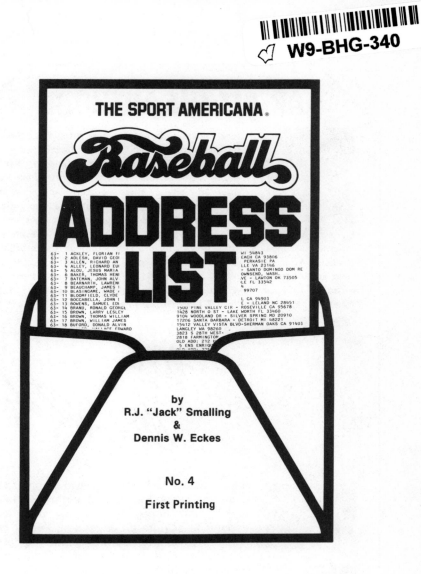

THE SPORT AMERICANA®

Baseball

ADDRESS LIST

by

R.J. "Jack" Smalling

&

Dennis W. Eckes

No. 4

First Printing

ISBN 0-937424-30-7

ABOUT THE AUTHORS

Jack Smalling has been an avid autograph collector for eighteen years and a card collector for more than thirty years. His collection of big league autographs is one of the best in the country. Reproductions of many of these signatures appear in this publication. He was educated at Iowa State University, obtaining a B.S. in Modern Languages and an M. Ed. in School Administration. His athletic activities have included officiating for twenty years—football, basketball and baseball. After a successful high school baseball career, he played thirteen years at the semi-pro level. A teaching and coaching career of fifteen years ended in 1979 when he joined the Compass Insurance Agency, Ltd., in Ames, IA, to sell commercial and personal lines of insurance. He and his wife, Marge, have four sons.

R. J. Smalling

Denny Eckes

Denny Eckes has been an avid trading card collector since the age of eight. He interrupted that hobby temporarily, only long enough to acquire an education, family, and career. He has returned with zest to the hobby over the past seven years, during which time he founded Den's Collectors Den, one of the largest and most reputable sports memorabilia establishments in the country. Mr. Eckes holds a BS in chemistry and an MBA in quantitative methods, both from the University of Maryland. Before the establishment of Den's Collectors Den, he held positions as research chemist, information analyst, scheduling engineer, and program manager for a large engineering firm. Among his other published works are *The Sport Americana Football and Basketball Card Price Guide*, *The Sport Americana Baseball Card Price Guide* and *The Sport Americana Alphabetical Baseball Card Checklist*.

THE SPORT AMERICANA
BASEBALL ADDRESS LIST
NO. 4

TABLE OF CONTENTS

iv

PREFACE

There might be nothing more distinctive and personal that a person may do throughout his life than write his own name. This signature, how it changes from childhood to senility, its thin or broad stroke, its clarity, neatness, and readability is a reflexion of the character, mood, and personality of the signer. Perhaps for these reasons, a person's signature has become his universally accepted mark for identification, acknowledgement, and legal and contractual agreement.

This book concentrates on the personal signatures or autographs of baseball players. We attempt to provide the background, explanations, and wherewithal for a collector to begin or augment his collection. Many illustrations taken from what we believe are authenic signatures are presented for your observation. Some helpful hints are provided so that your autograph hunting pursuits may be simplified and fruitful.

When reading and using this book, please keep in mind, the moral and legal rights of the ballplayers themselves. Some are more cooperative than others, some have more time to comply with your requests than others, but all are entitled to respect, privacy, and the right to affix or not affix his signature based on his own personal thoughts or moods.

As these addresses are under constant update because of the transient nature of the society in which we live, we should appreciate any information you can provide concerning the validity of the information and addresses contained herein. Please send all correspondence concerning address corrections, changes of address or death notices to:

R.J. "Jack" Smalling
2308 Van Buren Avenue
Ames, IA 50010

We hope this edition of the Sport Americana Baseball Address List provides a useful, interesting and enjoyable tool for your autograph and baseball historical pursuits.

Sincerely,

Jack Smalling
Denny Eckes

1

AUTHENTICITY

One of the enjoyable features of collecting autographs is knowing that one possesses an original mark made by another human being, a human being who for one reason or another has distinguished him or herself in the eyes of the collector. Facsimile autographs, autographs signed by someone other than the one whose name appears on the autograph, or photographs or copies of autographs do not comply with the definition of a true autograph; hence, they are of no value to the collector.

The only way one can be absolutely sure that an autograph is authentic is to personally witness the signer as he affixes his autograph. Practically speaking, were directly obtained autographs the only ones collected, logistic problems would prevent anyone from having but a modest collection. While authenticity can only be assured by directly obtaining autographs, many sources offer a high probability that an autograph is valid.

Knowing how a person's signature is supposed to look is a first step toward ascertaining authenticity. Facsimile autographs to compare with ones you are attempting to validate can be found on baseball cards, in books or magazines, or quite possibly, from the many facsimile autographs found in the text of this book. The reputation of the secondary source (dealer, friend, other collector) from whom you are obtaining the autograph is of utmost importance. Unfortunately, even the most reputable source may be unaware that he possesses a non-legitimate autograph.

Obtaining an autograph from a logical source increases the probability that an autograph is authentic. Other variables being equal, a resident of Boston is much more likely to have a valid autograph of a Red Sox player than is a resident of Butte, MT. A seventy-year old is much more likely to possess an autographed Babe Ruth ball than is a twelve-year old. Autographs obtained from the estate or from personal friends of the autographer are highly likely to be authentic. Autographs from financial or legal documents, such as cancelled checks or contracts, or any notarized communications can be considered authentic.

HOW TO OBTAIN AUTOGRAPHS

Although the text of this book is intended to provide the information necessary to obtain autographs through the mail, there are other ways to obtain autographs of ballplayers. There are basically two general categories by which you can obtain an autograph—first hand or directly, where you actually watch the ballplayer affix his signature, and second hand or indirectly, where you are not present at the time the ballplayer signs the autograph. As autograph collectors place such a high concern on authenticity, obtaining autographs first hand is preferential. Practically speaking, some autographs are impossible to obtain first hand, while many others are near impossible or at best very difficult to obtain first hand; hence, most collectors obtain a considerable portion of their collections via the indirect method.

OBTAINING AUTOGRAPHS FIRST HAND

The most obvious place to obtain a ballplayer's autograph is at the ballpark. The traditional crowd around the clubhouse awaiting the departure of their favorite players after the game, pens and papers in hands, is still perhaps the most viable means to obtain autographs. Many clubs provide special nights at the ballparks where, before the game, fans are encouraged to chat, photograph, and obtain autographs from the local team members who are available for these activities for the time periods specified.

Local merchants sometimes sponsor promotional activities at their establishments and feature a ballplayer as the guest celebrity. The ballplayer is normally available to sign autographs, and the merchants might well provide a medium (photo, postcard, etc.) for obtaining the autograph.

Other opportunities arise at hotels, airports, celebrity dinners or other public places where a ballplayer might chance to be during the course of his normal routine. However, we must emphasize again the necessity for patience and politeness when requesting an autograph in person from a ballplayer. Quite often time may allow only a few or no signatures to be signed before the ballplayer's schedule requires him to halt the autograph activities.

More and more over the past few years, the many sports collectibles conventions and shows held across the country have been featuring guest baseball players. These shows provide excellent opportunities for obtaining autographs from of the most popular ballplayers.

Each year the Baseball Hall of Fame in Cooperstown, NY, holds induction ceremonies for newly elected members. Not only do the newly elected members attend, but also many of the members who have been previously elected are in attendance. There is probably no other time or place that occurs during the year when one can obtain, in person, as many living HOFer autographs as on induction day in Cooperstown.

OBTAINING AUTOGRAPHS INDIRECTLY

Most collectors, by necessity, obtain the bulk of their collections indirectly. Trading with other collectors, purchasing from dealers, purchasing from private parties, or bidding at auction from estate liquidations, hobby paper ads, or at sports collectibles conventions are the most prevelant methods which do not involve the sports personality himself. The most common way to obtain an autograph from the sports personality without the presence of the sports personality is through the mail. It is for this purpose that the SPORT AMERICANA BASEBALL ADDRESS LIST is most useful.

Autograph collecting is a reasonably popular hobby. It is not uncommon to find other collectors with autograph interests similar to yours. It is also not uncommon to find collectors who posses more than one autograph of the same player, a duplicate which they can be convinced to part with in exchange for an autograph which they desire but do not possess— one which you yourself may have in duplicate. These conditions form the basis for trade negotiations from which both parties can obtain satisfaction. Most trading is not quite this simple; however, the underlying motives of all tradings are to obtain something you do not posses and desire to have for something you have but do not place such a high value on as you do the item you desire to obtain.

Dealers in autographed material exist just as they do for any collectible. Many specialize in particular types of autographs. In any event, these dealers have acquired autograph material and are willing to sell it at a given price(a price which may or may not be negotiable). These dealers can be found at sports collectibles conventions, at local flea markets, and from advertisements in the hobby papers or autograph oriented periodicals (including this book).

A check of your local newspapers, particular the auction section of the Sunday editions, is an excellent way to become aware of estate and private party autograph sales and auctions. The auction method offers you the opportunity to obtain autographs you desire for amounts less than you might pay to a dealer. In fact, because of the scarcity of certain autographs, the auction method may be the only available way to obtain a particular autograph. In such cases a fair market value might not be known, and the auction offers a means to arrive at a price based on the value of the autograph to the collector.

OBTAINING AUTOGRAPHS THROUGH THE MAIL

A large number of active and retired baseball players honor autograph requests made through the mail. One of the prime purposes of compiling this book is to provide the collector with the wherewithal to obtain autographs he or she desires through the mails. The authors do not profess to know all players who will comply with your autograph requests nor those who will not comply. The authors also do not promote or sanction any harassment or excessive requests on your part of the ballplayers contacted through the addresses found in this Address List. To the contrary, we emphatically suggest a polite, patient and respectful course in obtaining autographs through the mail.

Ballplayers, particularly active players during the baseball season, have schedules much tighter and more regimented than the normal 9 to 5 worker. Mail they receive may not be opened for lengthy periods. Many schedule limited time periods that they devote to autograph requests. Quite possibly, dependent on the number of autograph requests a particular player receives, your autograph request might not be answered for a considerable period of time. Be patient. The authors know of cases where years have elapsed before an autograph request was returned.

Like everyone else, ballplayers are human beings and appreciate politeness. Words such as "please" and "thank you" are as pleasantly received and as revered by ballplayers as they are by parents of teenagers (fortunately, ballplayers hear them much more often). Excessive requests, imperative tones, and impoliteness are justifiably scorned.

Some ballplayers do not honor autograph requests, either in person or through the mail. Some change their autographing philosophies over the years, becoming more liberal or conservative in their autographing habits. Whatever a player's thoughts or ideas are on accepting or rejecting autograph requests, they should be respected.

The mechanics of obtaining autographs through the mail are quite simple. Send the request, postpaid, to the ballplayer, including a politely written request outlining what you are asking of the ballplayer, any material that you wish to have autographed, and a SASE (self-addressed stamped envelope) large enough to contain the material you wish to be autographed and returned to you. Never send an autograph request postage due. To do so is presumptuous, in poor taste and completely uncalled for.

Do not send an unreasonable amount of material for autographing. A limit of three items per request has become the accepted practice of collectors. An exception to this limit is considered permissible if you have duplicates of the item you wish to have autographed, and you would like to give the ballplayer the opportunity to keep one of the duplicates for his own enjoyment. Ballplayers like most of us enjoy seeing and having interesting photos or other material concerning themselves, particularly if the item is novel or the ballplayer has never before seen it. Many collectors use this method. as a gesture of good faith and intent when requesting autographs through the mail. However, the limit of three items you wish to have signed and returned to you, exclusive of the items you wish to present to the ballplayer at his option to keep, is still the accepted standard.

It is not considered unreasonable to request a short personalization with an autograph; for example, "To John from...", or "Best Wishes to Gayle from...", etc. Requesting a two-page letter or an answer to a question that requires a dissertation is unreasonable. Do not do it.

Always include a SASE with sufficient postage to cover the material you expect might be returned to you. The SASE alleviates the need for the ballplayer to package and address your reply himself; it enables you to pay, as you should, for return postage; and it assures that the reply will be sent to the party requesting it (assuming you can competently write your own address on an envelope).

VALUES

The authors have purposely avoided any reference to price in the text of this book. Like other collectibles, there is a definite price structure for the autographs of ballplayers. Until recently, there was no price guide by which the collector could ascertain the value of his or her collection. The SPORT AMERICANA MEMORABILIA & AUTOGRAPH PRICE GUIDE, available at your local bookstore and described on the inside back cover of this book, provides the guidelines for autograph values.

Without printing prices for the autographs of specific ballplayers, we should like to present a discussion of values within a context of scarcity and desirability, which when all results are in, are the prime determinants of value for any collectible.

LIVING OR DECEASED

Like artists and martyrs, the values of whose accomplishments during their lifetimes is magnified and glorified after death, the value of a ballplayer's autograph increases considerable after his death. The deseased ballplayer can no longer, of course, sign autographs; hence, the supply of the autograph of this player ceases at this point in time. All autographs of deceased ball-players must be obtained second hand after his death, making authenticity questionable.

HALL OF FAME MEMBERS

The pinnacle of success for a ballplayer is election to baseball's Hall of Fame. This honor is limited to the most skillful and proficient players and those others who have made the most significant contributions to the game. The autographs of these men are among the most desireable and have, other factors being equal, the highest value to collectors.

POPULARITY AND NOTORIETY

While popularity can generally be measured by ballplaying skill, there are certainly exceptions. Many ballplayers whose skill on the field was limited, have achieved success and notoriety in other walks of life (William A. "Billy" Sunday, Joe Garagiola, Chuck Connors, Jim Thorpe to name but a few). The more popular the ballplayer, whether his popularity was derived by playing skill or by some other means, the higher the value placed on his autograph.

CONDITION AND TYPE OF AUTOGRAPH

Autographs, like other collectibles, exist in various physical conditions— from the weekest, broken pencil autograph to the boldest, unbroken indelable ink signature. The higher value is placed on the better condition autograph of the same person. Many types of media are available on which to obtain autographs. There are the relatively bland cuts and 3 X 5 varieties at one end of the spectrum and the most elaborate pieces of one of a kind items autographed by the player portrayed at the other end. In between there is a muriad of possible forms and designs that the autograph medium may take. The same autograph has a higher value based on the more interesting, enjoyable and attractive medium on which the autograph is written.

NEW IN THIS EDITION OF THE ADDRESS LIST

For the first time, the Address List contains over 10,000 entrees. The players new to the big leagues in 1984 and 1985 have been added with their corresponding debut years and numbers. Address corrections have been made, and obituary data has been supplied for those who have deceased since the last edition. In total, over 2,000 additions and corrections have been made.

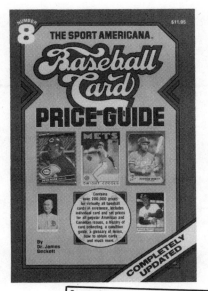

1986 SPORT AMERICANA BASEBALL CARD PRICE GUIDE

$ 11.95 plus postage & handling

"THE PRICE GUIDE"

ALL NEW 8th EDITION
Includes 1986 TOPPS, FLEER, DONRUSS

* Over 200,000 prices — current for 1986
* Well over 500 pages in length
* All Topps, Fleer, Donruss, Bowman, Play Ball, Goudey, Kellogg, Leaf, Post Cereal, Red Man, Hostess, and 100's of other national and regional issues
* Typical card front and back illustrated for each baseball card set
* History of baseball cards, card condition guide, glossary of terms, year in review and much, much more
* The ORIGINAL and AUTHORITATIVE Baseball Card PRICE GUIDE

SECOND EDITION of the SPORT AMERICANA BASEBALL CARD TEAM CHECKLIST
$ 8.95 plus postage & handling

The Sport Americana Baseball Card Team Checklist has been updated to include sets through the regular issues of 1985. For each year, the cards of the players (by name and number) who played for each Major League team are listed under that particular team. This book is a must for collectors of cards of individual teams. In addition to all regular issues of Topps, Fleer, Donruss, Bowman, Goudey and Play Ball, and the Topps and Fleer traded sets including the 1984 updates, several new items have been added to the book.

NEW IN THIS ISSUE ARE:

1934 - 1936 DIAMOND STARS
T205, T206, T207 TOBACCO ISSUES
A special section for Single Team and Regional Issues; i.e., those sets which feature players from one or a few teams only

MAJOR LEAGUE TEAM ADDRESSES

BASEBALL COMMISSIONER'S OFFICE
Peter V. Ueberroth, Commissioner
350 Park Ave
New York, NY 10022
(212) 371-7800

AMERICAN LEAGUE OFFICE
Robert W. Brown, President
350 Park Ave.
New York, NY 10022
(212) 371-7600

BALTIMORE ORIOLES
Edward Bennett Williams, Chairman & President
Memorial Stadium
Baltimore, MD 21218
(301) 243-9800

BOSTON RED SOX
Jean R. Yawkey, President
Fenway Park
Boston, MA 02215
(617) 267-9440

CALIFORNIA ANGELS
Gene Autry, Chairman & President
P.O. Box 2000
Anaheim Stadium
Anaheim, CA 92803
(714) 937-6700

CHICAGO WHITE SOX
Jerry Reinsdorf, Chairman
Eddie Einhorn, President
324 West 35th St.
Comiskey Park
Chicago, IL 60616
(312) 924-1000

CLEVELAND INDIANS
Patrick J. O'Neill, Chairman
Peter Bavasi, President
Municipal Stadium
Cleveland, OH 44114
(216) 861-1200

DETROIT TIGERS
John E. Fetzer, Chairman
James A. Campbell, President
Tiger Stadium
Detroit, MI 48216
(313) 962-4000

KANSAS CITY ROYALS
Ewing Kauffman, Chairman
Joseph Burke, President
P.O. Box 1969
Royals Stadium
Kansas City, MO 64141
(816) 921-8000

MILWAUKEE BREWERS
Allan H. (Bud) Selig, President
Milwaukee County Stadium
Milwaukee, WI 53214
(414) 933-4114

MINNESOTA TWINS
Carl R. Pohlad, Owner
Howard T. Fox, Jr., President
501 Chicago Ave. South
Hubert H. Humphrey Metrodome
Minneapolis, MN 55415
(612) 375-1366

NEW YORK YANKEES
George M. Steinbrenner III, Principal Owner
Eugene J. McHale, President
Yankee Stadium
Bronx, NY 10451
(212) 293 4300

OAKLAND A'S
Roy Eisenhardt, President
Oakland — Alameda County Coliseum
Oakland, CA 94621
(415) 638 4900

SEATTLE MARINERS
George R. Argyros, Chairman
Charles G. Armstrong, President
P.O. Box 4100
The Kingdome
Seattle, WA 98104
(206) 628-3555

TEXAS RANGERS
Eddie Chiles, Chairman
Michael H. Stone, President
P.O. Box 1111
Arlington Stadium
Arlington, TX 76010
(817) 273-5222

TORONTO BLUE JAYS
R. Howard Webster, Chairman
P.O. Box 7777, Adelaide St. Post Office
Exhibition Stadium
Toronto, Ontario
Canada M5C 2K7
(416) 595-0077

NATIONAL LEAGUE OFFICE
Charles S. (Chub) Feeney, President
350 Park Ave.
New York, NY 10022
(212) 371-7300

ATLANTA BRAVES
William C. Batholomay, Chairman
R. E. (Ted) Turner III, President
P.O. Box 4064
Atlanta — Fulton County Stadium
Atlanta, GA 30312
(404) 522-7630

CHICAGO CUBS
Dallas Green, President
1060 West Addison St.
Wrigley Field
Chicago, IL 60613
(312) 281-5050

CINCINNATI REDS
Marge Schott, President
100 Riverfront Stadium
Riverfront Stadium
Cincinnati, OH 45202
(513) 421-4510

HOUSTON ASTROS
John J. McMullen, Chairman
Richard Wagner, President
P.O. Box 288
The Astrodome
Houston, TX 77001
(713) 799-9500

LOS ANGELES DODGERS
Peter O'Malley, President
1000 Elysian Park Ave.
Dodger Stadium
Los Angeles, CA 90012
(213) 224-1500

MONTREAL EXPOS
Charles R. Bronfman, Chairman
John J. McHale, President
P.O. Box 500, Station "M"
Olympic Stadium
Montreal, Quebec
Canada H1V 3P2
(514) 253-3434

NEW YORK METS
Nelson Doubleday, Chairman
Fred Wilpon, President
William A. Shea Stadium
Flushing, NY 11368
(212) 507-METS

PHILADELPHIA PHILLIES
William Y. Giles, President
Phillies Box 7575
Veterans Stadium
Philadelphia, PA 19101
(215) 463-6000

PITTSBURGH PIRATES
Malcolm M. Prine, President
P.O. Box 7000
Three Rivers Stadium
Pittsburgh, PA 15212
(412) 323-5000

ST. LOUIS CARDINALS
August A. Busch, Jr., Chairman & President
250 Stadium Plaza
Busch Stadium
St. Louis, MO 63102
(314) 421-3060

SAN DIEGO PADRES
Mrs. Joan Kroc, Chairman
Ballard Smith, President
9449 Friars Rd.
San Diego — Jack Murphy Stadium
San Diego, CA 92108
(619) 283-7294

SAN FRANCISCO GIANTS
Bob Lurie, Chairman
Al Rosen, President
Candlestick Park
San Francisco, CA 94124
(415) 468-3700

TRIPLE A LEAGUE TEAM ADDRESSES

AMERICAN ASSOCIATION
Joseph Ryan, Presudent
P.O. Box 382
Wichita, KS 67201
(316) 267-0266

BUFFALO BISONS
Robert E. Rich, Jr., Chairman & President
P.O. Box 538, Station "G"
War Memorial Stadium
Buffalo, NY 14213
(716) 878-8215

DENVER ZEPHYRS
Robert Howsam, Jr., President
2850 West 20th Ave
Mile High Stadium
Denver, CO 80211
(303) 433-8645

INDIANAPOLIS INDIANS
Henry R. Warren, Jr., Chairman
Max B. Schumacher, President
1501 West 16th St.
Bush Stadium
Indianapolis, IN 46202
(317) 632-5371

IOWA CUBS
Ken Grandquist, President
2nd & Riverside Dr
Sec Taylor Stadium
Des Moines, Iowa 50309
(515) 243-6111

LOUISVILLE REDBIRDS
A. Ray Smith, President
P.O. Box 36407
Cardinal Stadium
Louisville, KY 40233
(502) 367-9121

NASHVILLE SOUNDS
Larry Schmittou, Chairman & Predident
P.O. Box 23290
Greer Stadium
Nashville, TN 37202
(615) 242-4371

OKLAHOMA CITY 89ers
Allie Reynolds, Chairman
Patricia Cox Hampton, President
P.O. Box 75089
All Sports Stadium
Oklahoma City, OK 73147
(405) 946-8989

OMAHA ROYALS
Irving Cherry, Chairman & President
P.O. Box 3665
Rosenblatt Stadium
Omaha, NE 68103
(402) 734-2550

INTERNATIONAL LEAGUE
Harold Cooper, President
P.O. Box 608
Grove City, OH 43123
(614) 871-1300

COLUMBUS CLIPPERS
Donald A. Borror, President
1155 West Mound St.
Cooper Stadium
Columbus, OH 43223
(614) 462-5250

MAINE GUIDES
Jordan I. Kobritz, President
P.Q Box 287
The Ballpark
Old Orchard Beach, ME 04064
(207) 934-4561

PAWTUCKET RED SOX
Bernard G. Mondor, Chairman
Mike Tamburro, President
P.O. Box 2365
McCoy Stadium
Pawtucket, RI 02860
(401) 724-7303

RICHMOND BRAVES
William C. Batholomay, Chairman
R. E. (Ted) Turner III, President
P.Q Box 6667
The Diamond
Richmond, VA 23230
(804) 359-4444

ROCHESTER RED WINGS
Anna B. Silver, Chairman
Fred Strauss, President
500 Norton St
Silver Stadium
Rochester, NY 14621
(716) 467-3000

SYRACUSE CHIEFS
Royal O'Day, Chairman
Donald R. Waful, President
MacArthur Stadium
Syracuse, NY 13208
(315) 474-7833

TIDEWATER TIDES
Richard J Davis, President
P.Q Box 12111
Met Park
Norfolk, VA 23502
(804) 461-5600

TOLEDO MUD HENS
Nel Skeldon, Chairman & President
P.Q Box 6212
Lucas County Stadium
Maumee, OH 43537
(419) 893-9483

PACIFIC COAST LEAGUE
William S. Cutler, President
2101 East Broadway, No. 35
Tempe, AZ 85282
(602) 967-7679

ALBUQUERQUE DUKES
Robert Lozinak, Chairman
Pat McKernan, President
P.O. Box 26267
Albuquerque Sports Stadium
Albuquerque, NM 87125
(505) 243-1791

CALGARY CANNONS
Russ Parker, President
P.O. Box 3690, Station "B"
Foothills Stadium
Calgary, Alberta
Canada T2M 4M4
(403) 284-1111

EDMONTON TRAPPERS
Peter Pocklington, Owner
Mel Kowalchuk, President
12315 Stony Plain Rd., No. 202
Renfrew Park
Edmonton, Alberta
Canada T5N 3N2
(403) 482- 6917

HAWAII ISLANDERS
David Elmore, Chairman & President
2255 Kuhio Ave., No. 700
Aloha Stadium
Honolulu, HI 96815
(808) 945-6300

LAS VEGAS STARS
Larry Koentopp, Chairman & President
850 Las Vegas Blvd North
Cashman Field
Las Vegas, NV 89101
(702) 386-7200

PHOENIX FIREBIRDS
Jack Singer, President
5999 East Van Buren St
Phoenix Municipal Stadium
Phoenix, AZ 85008
(602) 275-0500

PORTLAND BEAVERS
Joseph Buzas, President
P.O. Box 1659
Civic Stadium
Portland, OR 97207
(503) 233-2837

TACOMA TIGERS
E. J. Zarelli, Chairman
Stan Naccarato, President
P.O. Box 11087
Cheney Stadium
Tacoma, WA 98411
(206) 752-7707

TUCSON TOROS
William Yuill, Chairman & President
P.O. Box 27045
Hi Corbett Field
Tucson, AZ 85726
(602) 215-2621

VANCOUVER CANADIANS
Norman Seagram, Chairman & President
4601 Ontario St
Nat Bailey Stadium
Vancouver, British Columbia
Canada V5V 3H4
(604) 872-5232

HOW TO USE THE SPORT AMERICANA BASEBALL ADDRESS LIST

The Address List is composed of four sections:

1. Players in the Baseball Hall of Fame
2. Players who debuted from 1910 to 1985
3. Umpires who debuted from 1910 to 1985
4. Coaches with no big league playing experience who debuted from 1910 to 1985

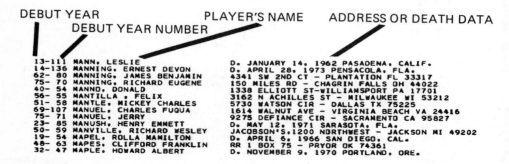

DEBUT YEAR   PLAYER'S NAME   ADDRESS OR DEATH DATA
DEBUT YEAR NUMBER

```
13-111  MANN, LESLIE                    D. JANUARY 14, 1962 PASADENA, CALIF.
14-136  MANNING, ERNEST DEVON           D. APRIL 28, 1973 PENSACOLA, FLA.
62- 80  MANNING, JAMES BENJAMIN         4341 SW 2ND CT - PLANTATION FL 33317
75- 70  MANNING, RICHARD EUGENE         150 MILES RD - CHAGRIN FALLS OH 44022
40- 54  MANNO, DONALD                   1338 ELLIOTT ST-WILLIAMSPORT PA 17701
56- 55  MANTILLA , FELIX                3162 N ACHILLES ST - MILWAUKEE WI 53212
51- 58  MANTLE, MICKEY CHARLES          5730 WATSON CIR - DALLAS TX 75225
69-107  MANUEL, CHARLES FUQUA           1614 WALNUT AVE - VIRGINIA BEACH VA 24416
75- 71  MANUEL, JERRY                   9275 DEFIANCE CIR - SACRAMENTO CA 95827
23- 85  MANUSH, HENRY EMMETT            D. MAY 12, 1971 SARASOTA, FLA.
50- 59  MANVILLE, RICHARD WESLEY        JACOBSON'S,1200 NORTHWEST - JACKSON MI 49202
19- 54  MAPEL, ROLLA MAMILTON           D. APRIL 6, 1966 SAN DIEGO, CAL.
48- 63  MAPES, CLIFFORD FRANKLIN        RR 1 BOX 75 - PRYOR OK 74361
32- 47  MAPLE, HOWARD ALBERT            D. NOVEMBER 9, 1970 PORTLAND, ORE.
```

The address portion of the listing contains the known current address of the player if the player is now living or information as follows:

> ADDRESS NOT KNOWN—An old address is given for players for whom a current address is not known. In many cases, the year the address was last valid is shown in the data. Birth information is given if no other data is available. If no information is known about a player except his name, a blank space will appear in the address portion of the listing.

> DECEASED PLAYERS—The date and place of a player's death will be listed for deceased players. Incomplete death data is given for some players because complete information is not known. The abbreviation D. with no other information in the address portion of the listing indicates that a player is reportedly deceased, but that no other data is available.

PLEASE NOTE:

> Managers who never appeared in a big league game are listed with the year they first managed in the big leagues.
> Only those coaches who never appeared in a big league game are listed in the coaches section.
> The abbreviations used for states on addresses are standard U.S. Postal Service abbreviations.
> B. indicates born, D. indicates deceased, and other abbreviations are self-explanatory as they are used in normal written communications.

As this nation is known to be a nation of transients, one can expect that the addresses of a considerable number of the ballplayers listed will become invalid over the course of the next year or two.

BASEBALL HALL OF FAME MEMBERS

HOF177	AARON, HENRY LOUIS	1611 ADAMS DR SW - ATLANTA GA 30311
HOF 14	ALEXANDER, GROVER CLEVELAND	D. NOVEMBER 4, 1950 ST. PAUL, NEB.
HOF181	ALSTON, WALTER EMMONS	D. OCTOBER 1, 1984 OXFORD, O.
HOF 17	ANSON, ADRIAN CONSTANTINE 'CAP'	D. APRIL 14, 1922 CHICAGO, ILL.
HOF185	APARICIO, LUIS ERNEST	CALLE 67 #26-82 - MARACAIBO VENEZUELA
HOF 95	APPLING, LUCIUS BENJAMIN 'LUKE'	RR 7, BRAGG RD - CUMMINGS GA 30130
HOF147	AVERILL, HOWARD EARL	D. AUGUST 16, 1983 EVERETT, WASH.
HOF 74	BAKER, JOHN FRANKLIN 'HOME RUN'	D. JUNE 28, 1963 TRAPPE, MD.
HOF119	BANCROFT, DAVID JAMES	D. OCTOBER 9, 1972 SUPERIOR, WIS.
HOF158	BANKS, ERNEST	10660 WILSHIRE #408 - WEST LOS ANGELES CA 90024
HOF 63	BARROW, EDWARD GRANT	D. DECEMBER 15, 1953 PORT CHESTER, N. Y.
HOF120	BECKLEY, JACOB PETER	D. JUNE 25, 1918 KANSAS CITY, MO.
HOF141	BELL, JAMES 'COOL PAPA'	3034 DICKSON - ST. LOUIS MO 63106
HOF 64	BENDER, CHARLES ALBERT 'CHIEF'	D. MAY 22, 1954 PHILADELPHIA, PA.
HOF127	BERRA, LAWRENCE PETER 'YOGI'	19 HIGHLAND AVE - MONTCLAIR NJ 07042
HOF142	BOTTOMLEY, JAMES LEROY	D. DECEMBER 11, 1959 SAINT LOUIS, MO.
HOF115	BOUDREAU, LOUIS	15600 ELLIS AVENUE - DOLTON IL 60419
HOF 29	BRESNAHAN, ROGER PATRICK	D. DECEMBER 4, 1944 TOLEDO, O.
HOF190	BROCK, LOUIS CLARK	12595 DURBIN DRIVE - SAINT LOUIS MO 63141
HOF 30	BROUTHERS, DENNIS 'DAN'	D. AUGUST 3, 1932 EAST ORANGE, N. J.
HOF 56	BROWN, MORDECAI PETER CENTENNIAL	D. FEBRUARY 14, 1948 TERRE HAUTE, IND.
HOF 6	BULKELEY, MORGAN G.	D. NOVEMBER 6, 1922 HARTFORD, CONN.
HOF 39	BURKETT, JESSE CAIL	D. MAY 27, 1953 WORCESTER, MASS.
HOF111	CAMPANELLA, ROY	6213 CAPISTRANO - WOODLAND HILLS CA 9167
HOF 85	CAREY, MAX GEORGE	D. MAY 30, 1976 MIAMI, FLA.
HOF 15	CARTWRIGHT, ALEXANDER JOY	D. JULY 12, 1892 HONOLULU, HAWAII
HOF 16	CHADWICK, HENRY	D. APRIL 20, 1908 BROOKLYN, N. Y,
HOF 40	CHANCE, FRANK LEROY	D. SEPTEMBER 15, 1924 LOS ANGELES, CAL.
HOF178	CHANDLER, ALBERT BENJAMIN 'HAPPY'	191 ELM STREET - VERSAILLES KY 40383
HOF152	CHARLESTON, OSCAR MCKINLEY	D. OCTOBER 11, 1954 PHILADELPHIA, PA.
HOF 41	CHESBRO, JOHN DWIGHT	D. NOVEMBER 6, 1931 CONWAY, MASS.
HOF 31	CLARKE, FRED CLIFFORD	D. AUGUST 14, 1960 WINFIELD, KAN.
HOF 91	CLARKSON, JOHN GIBSON	D. FEBRUARY 4, 1909 CAMBRIDGE, MASS.
HOF135	CLEMENTE, ROBERTO WALKER	D. DECEMBER 31,1972 SAN JUAN, P. R.
HOF 1	COBB, TYRUS RAYMOND	D. JULY 17,1961 ATLANTA, GA.
HOF 50	COCHRANE, GORDON STANLEY 'MICKEY'	D. JUNE 2, 1962 LAKE FOREST, ILL.

HOF 18	COLLINS, EDWARD TROWBRIDGE SR.	D. MARCH 25, 1951 BOSTON, MASS.
HOF 32	COLLINS, JAMES JOSEPH	D. MARCH 6, 1943 BUFFALO, N. Y.
HOF116	COMBS, EARLE BRYAN	D. JULY 21, 1976 RICHMOND, KY.
HOF 19	COMISKEY, CHARLES ALBERT	D. OCTOBER 26,1931 EAGLE RIVER, WIS.
HOF143	CONLAN, JOHN BERTRAND 'JOCKO'	7810 EAST MARIPOSA DRIVE - SCOTTSDALE1AZ 85251
HOF 65	CONNOLLY, THOMAS HENRY	D. APRIL 28, 1961 NATICK, MASS.
HOF153	CONNOR, ROGER	D. JANUARY 4, 1931 WATERBURY, CONN.
HOF112	COVELESKI, STANLEY ANTHONY	D. MARCH 20, 1984 SOUTH BEND, IND.
HOF 82	CRAWFORD, SAMUEL EARL	D. JUNE 15, 1968 HOLLYWOOD, CALIF.
HOF 80	CRONIN, JOSEPH EDWARD	D. SEPTEMBER 7, 1984 OSTERVILLE, MASS.
HOF 20	CUMMINGS, WIILLIAM ARTHUR 'CANDY'	D. MAY 17, 1924 TOLEDO, O.
HOF108	CUYLER, HAZEN SHIRLEY 'KIKI'	D. FEBRUARY 11, 1950 ANN ARBOR, MICH.
HOF 66	DEAN, JAY HANNA 'DIZZY'	D. JULY 17, 1974 RENO, NEV.

DELAHANTY   GREENBERG

HOF 33 DELAHANTY, EDWARD JAMES	D. JULY 2, 1903 FORT ERIE, ONT.
HOF 71 DICKEY, WILLIAM MALCOLM	114 E. 5TH ST - LITTLE ROCK AR 72203
HOF159 DIHIGO, MARTIN	D. MAY 22, 1971 CIENFUEGOS, CUBA
HOF 75 DIMAGGIO, JOSEPH PAUL	2150 BEACH ST - SAN FRANCISCO CA 94123
HOF194 DOERR, ROBERT PERSHING	33705 ILLAMO AGNESS RD - AGNESS OR 97406
HOF186 DRYSDALE, DONALD SCOTT	78 COLGATE - RANCHO MIRAGE CA 92270
HOF 34 DUFFY, HUGH	D. OCTOBER 19, 1954 BOSTON, MASS.
HOF136 EVANS, WILLIAM GEORGE	D. JANUARY 23, 1956 MIAMI, FLA.
HOF 42 EVERS, JOHN JOSEPH	D. MARCH 28, 1947 ALBANY, N. Y.

HOF 21 EWING, WILLIAM BUCKINGHAM 'BUCK'	D. OCTOBER 20, 1906 CINCINNATI, O.
HOF 96 FABER, URBAN CHARLES 'RED'	D. SEPTEMBER 25, 1976 CHICAGO, ILL.
HOF 87 FELLER, ROBERT WILLIAM ANDREW	BOX 157 - GATES MILLS OH 44040
HOF187 FERRELL, RICHARD BENJAMIN 'RICK'	2199 GOLFVIEW #203 - TROY MI 48084
HOF 92 FLICK, ELMER HARRISON	D. JANUARY 9, 1971 BEDFORD, O.
HOF144 FORD, EDWARD CHARLES 'WHITEY'	38 SCHOOLHOUSE LANE - LAKE SUCCESS NY 11020
HOF174 FOSTER, ANDREW "RUBE"	D. DECEMBER 9, 1930 KANKAKEE, ILL.
HOF 59 FOXX, JAMES EMORY	D. JULY 21, 1967 MIAMI, FLA.
HOF117 FRICK, FORD CHRISTOPHER	D. APRIL 8, 1978 BRONXVILLE, N. Y.
HOF 51 FRISCH, FRANK FRANCIS	D. MARCH 12, 1973 WILMINGTON, DEL.
HOF102 GALVIN, JAMES F. 'PUD'	D. MARCH 7, 1902 PITTSBURGH, PA.
HOF 22 GEHRIG, HENRY LOUIS 'LOU'	D. JUNE 2, 1941 RIVERDALE, N. Y.
HOF 57 GEHRINGER, CHARLES LEONARD	32301 LAHSER RD - BIRMINGHAM MI 48010
HOF128 GIBSON, JOSH	D. JANUARY 20, 1947 PITTSBURGH, PA.
HOF175 GIBSON, ROBERT	215 BELLEVIEW BLVD S - BELLEVIEW NE 68005
HOF167 GILES, WARREN CHRISTOPHER	D. FEBRUARY 7, 1979 CINCINNATI, O.
HOF129 GOMEZ, VERNON LOUIS	26 SAN BENITO WAY - NOVATO CA 94947
HOF109 GOSLIN, LEON ALLEN 'GOOSE'	D. MAY 15, 1971 BRIDGETON, N. J.
HOF 81 GREENBERG, HENRY BENJAMIN	1129 MIRADERO RD - BEVERLY HILLS CA 90210

GRIFFITH

HOF 43 GRIFFITH, CLARK CALVIN
HOF 97 GRIMES, BURLEIGH ARLAND
HOF 52 GROVE, ROBERT MOSES 'LEFTY'
HOF121 HAFEY, CHARLES JAMES 'CHICK'
HOF118 HAINES, JESSE JOSEPH 'POP'
HOF 86 HAMILTON, WILLIAM ROBERT
HOF130 HARRIDGE, WILLIAM
HOF148 HARRIS, STANLEY RAYMOND 'BUCKY'
HOF 76 HARTNETT, CHARLES LEO 'GABBY'
HOF 61 HEILMANN, HARRY EDWIN
HOF149 HERMAN, WILLIAM JENNINGS
HOF122 HOOPER, HARRY BARTHOLOMEW
HOF 27 HORNSBY, ROGERS
HOF113 HOYT, WAITE CHARLES
HOF154 HUBBARD, ROBERT CAL
HOF 53 HUBBELL, CARL OWEN
HOF 98 HUGGINS, MILLER JAMES
HOF137 IRVIN, MONFORD 'MONTE'
HOF179 JACKSON, TRAVIS CALVIN
HOF 35 JENNINGS, HUGH AMBROSE
HOF 7 JOHNSON, BYRON BANCROFT 'BAN'
HOF 2 JOHNSON, WALTER PERRY
HOF150 JOHNSON, WILLIAM JULIUS 'JUDY'
HOF164 JOSS, ADRIAN 'ADDIE'
HOF170 KALINE, ALBERT WILLIAM
HOF 99 KEEFE, TIMOTHY J.
HOF 23 KEELER, WILLIAM HENRY 'WEE WILLIE'
HOF182 KELL, GEORGE CLYDE
HOF123 KELLEY, JOSEPH JAMES
HOF138 KELLY, GEORGE LANGE
HOF 36 KELLY, MICHAEL JOSEPH
HOF188 KILLEBREW, HARMON CLAYTON
HOF151 KINER, RALPH MCPHERRAN
HOF171 KLEIN, CHARLES HERBERT
HOF 67 KLEM, WILLIAM J.
HOF131 KOUFAX, SANFORD
HOF 8 LAJOIE, NAPOLEON
HOF 28 LANDIS, KENESAW MOUNTAIN
HOF155 LEMON, ROBERT GRANVILLE
HOF132 LEONARD, WALTER FENNER 'BUCK'
HOF156 LINDSTROM, FRED CHARLES

MARICHAL

D. OCTOBER 27, 1955 WASHINTON, D. C.
D. DECEMBER 6, 1985 CLEAR LAKE, WIS.
D. MAY 22, 1975 NORWALK, O.
D. JULY 2, 1973 CALISTOGA, CAL.
D. AUGUST 5, 1978 DAYTON, O.
D. DECEMBER 16, 1940 WORCESTER, MASS.
D. APRIL 9, 1971 EVANSTON, ILL.
D. NOVEMBER 8, 1977 BETHESDA, MD.
D. DECEMBER 20, 1972 PARK RIDGE, ILL.
D. JULY 9, 1951 DETROIT, MICH.
3111 GARDEN E #33-PALM BEACH GARDENS FL 33410
D. DECEMBER 18, 1974 SANTA CRUZ, CALIF.
D. JANUARY 5, 1963 CHICAGO, ILL.
D. AUGUST 25, 1984 CINCINNATI, O.
D. OCTOBER 16, 1977 ST PETERSBURG, FLA.
SUNCREST APT #8,130 N LESEUER #1-MESA AZ83205
D. SEPTEMBER 25, 1929 NEW YORK, N. Y.
104 SYCAMORE CIRCLE - HOMOSASSA FL 32646
101 SOUTH OLIVE ST - WALDO AR 71770
D. FEBRUARY 1, 1928 SCRANTON, PA.
D. MARCH 28, 1931 ST. LOUIS, MO.
D. DECEMBER 10, 1946 WASHINGTON, D. C.
3701 KIAMENSI - MARSHALLTOWN DE 19808
D. APRIL 14, 1911 TOLEDO, O.
945 TIMBERLAKE DR - BLOOMFIELD HILLS MI 48013
D. APRIL 23, 1933 CAMBRIDGE, MASS.
D. JANUARY 1, 1923 BROOKLYN, N. Y.
BOX 158 - SWIFTON AR 72471
D. AUGUST 14, 1943 BALTIMORE, MD.
D. OCTOBER 13, 1984 BURLINGAME, CALIF.
D. NOVEMBER 8, 1894 BOSTON, MASS.
BOX 626 - ONTARIO OR 9798 114
17 LEGRANDE AVE #17 - GREENWICH CT 06830
D. MARCH 28, 1958 INDIANAPOLIS, IND.
D. SEPTEMBER 16, 1951 MIAMI, FLA.
P.O. BOX BB - CARPINTERIA CA 93013
D. FEBRUARY 7, 1959 DAYTONA BEACH, FLA.
D. NOVEMBER 25, 1944 CHICAGO, ILL.
1141 CLAIBORNE DR-LONG BEACH CA 90807
605 ATLANTIC AVE - ROCKY MOUNT NC 27801
D. OCTOBER 4, 1981 CHICAGO, ILL.

Billy Hamilton

HOF160 LLOYD, JOHN HENRY
HOF195 LOMBARDI, ERNEST NATALI
HOF161 LOPEZ, ALFONSO RAMON
HOF 77 LYONS, THEODORE AMAR
HOF 9 MACK, CORNELIUS ALEXANDER 'CONNIE'
HOF165 MACPHAIL, LELAND STANFORD 'LARRY'
HOF145 MANTLE, MICKEY CHARLES
HOF100 MANUSH, HENRY EMMETT 'HEINIE'
HOF 72 MARANVILLE, WALTER JAMES VINCENT
HOF183 MARICHAL, JUAN ANTONIO

D. MARCH 19, 1964
D. SEPTEMBER 26, 1977 SANTA CRUZ, CALIF.
3601 BEACH DR - TAMPA FL 33609
1401 LOREE ST - VINTON LA 70668
D. FEBRUARY 8, 1956 GERMANTOWN, PA.
D. OCTOBER 1, 1975 MIAMI, FLA.
5730 WATSON CIR - DALLAS TX 75225
D. MAY 12, 1971 SARASOTA, FLA.
D. JANUARY 5, 1954 NEW YORK, N.Y.
ED. HACHE 3, PISO ESTE, KENNEDY AVE-SANTO DOMINGO DOM REP.

HOF124 MARQUARD, RICHARD WILLIAM 'RUBE'   D. JUNE 1, 1980 BALTIMORE, MD.
HOF166 MATHEWS, EDWIN LEE   13744 RECUERDO DR - DEL MAR CA 92014
HOF 3 MATHEWSON, CHRISTOPHER   D. OCTOBER 7, 1925 SARANAC LAKE, N. Y.
HOF168 MAYS, WILLIE HOWARD   51 MT VERNON LN - ATHERTON CA 94025
HOF 83 MCCARTHY, JOSEPH VINCENT   D. JANUARY 13, 1978 BUFFALO, N. Y.
HOF 44 MCCARTHY, THOMAS FRANCIS MICHAEL   D. AUGUST 5, 1922 BOSTON, MASS.
HOF196 MCCOVEY, WILLIE LEE   220 CREST ROAD - WOODSIDE CA 94062
HOF 45 MCGINNITY, JOSEPH JEROME   D. NOVEMBER 14, 1929 BROOKLYN, N. Y.
HOF 10 MCGRAW, JOHN JOSEPH   D. FEBRUARY 25, 1934 NEW ROCHELLE, N. Y.
HOF 88 MCKECHNIE, WILLIAM BOYD   D. OCTOBER 29, 1965 BRADENTON, FLA.
HOF110 MEDWICK, JOSEPH MICHAEL   D. MARCH 21, 1975 ST. PETERSBURG, FLA.
HOF176 MIZE, JOHN ROBERT   BOX 112 - DEMOREST GA 30535
HOF114 MUSIAL, STANLEY FRANK   85 TRENT DR - LADUE MO 63124
HOF 58 NICHOLS, CHARLES AUGUSTUS 'KID'   D. APRIL 11, 1953 KANSAS CITY, MO.
HOF 37 OROURKE, JAMES HENRY   D. JANUARY 8, 1919 BRIDGEPORT, CONN.
HOF 60 OTT, MELVIN THOMAS   D. NOVEMBER 21, 1958 NEW ORLEANS, LA.
HOF125 PAIGE, LEROY 'SATCHEL'   D. JUNE 8, 1982 KANSAS CITY, MO.
HOF 54 PENNOCK, HERBERT JEFFERS   D. JANUARY 30, 1948 NEW YORK, N.Y.
HOF 46 PLANK, EDWARD STEWART   D. FEBRUARY 24, 1926 GETTYSBURG, PA.
HOF 24 RADBOURN, CHARLES 'HOSS'   D. FEBRUARY 5, 1897 BLOOMINGTON, ILL.
HOF189 REESE, HAROLD HENRY 'PEE WEE'   3211 BEALS BRANCH RD - LOUISVILLE KY 40206

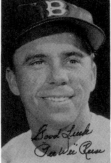

HOF 93 RICE, EDGAR CHARLES 'SAM'   D. OCTOBER 13, 1974 ROSSMOR, MD.
HOF105 RICKEY, WESLEY BRANCH   D. DECEMBER 9, 1965 COLUMBIA, MO.
HOF 94 RIXEY, EPPA   D. FEBRUARY 28, 1963 TERRACE PARK, O.
HOF157 ROBERTS, ROBIN EVAN   504 TERRACE HILL DR - TEMPLE TERRACE FL 33617
HOF184 ROBINSON, BROOKS   1506 SHERBROOK RD - LUTHERVILLE MD 21093
HOF180 ROBINSON, FRANK   15557 AQUA VERDE DR - LOS ANGELES CA 90077
HOF 89 ROBINSON, JACK ROOSEVELT   D. OCTOBER 24, 1972 STAMFORD, CONN.
HOF 38 ROBINSON, WILBERT   D. AUGUST 8, 1934 ATLANTA, GA.
HOF 90 ROUSH, EDD J.   122 39TH STREET COURT NW - BRADENTON FL 33505
HOF106 RUFFING, CHARLES HERBERT 'RED'   D. FEBRUARY 17, 1986 MAYFIELD HEIGHTS, O.
HOF162 RUSIE, AMOS WILSON   D. DECEMBER 6, 1942 SEATTLE, WASH.
HOF 4 RUTH, GEORGE HERMAN 'BABE'   D. AUGUST 16, 1948 NEW YORK, N.Y.
HOF 78 SCHALK, RAYMOND WILLIAM   D. MAY 19, 1970 CHICAGO, ILL.
HOF163 SEWELL, JOSEPH WHEELER   1618 DEARING PLACE - TUSCALOOSA ALA 35401
HOF 68 SIMMONS, ALOYSIUS HARRY   D. MAY 26, 1956 MILWAUKEE, WIS.
HOF 25 SISLER, GEORGE HAROLD   D. MARCH 26, 1973 ST. LOUIS, MO.
HOF191 SLAUGHTER, ENOS BRADSHER 'COUNTRY' RURAL ROUTE 2 - ROXBORO NC 27573
HOF172 SNIDER, EDWIN DONALD 'DUKE'   3037 LAKEMONT DR - FALLBROOK CA 92028

14

HOF139 SPAHN, WARREN EDWARD
HOF 26 SPALDING, ALBERT GOODWILL
HOF 11 SPEAKER, TRISTRAM E.
HOF103 STENGEL, CHARLES DILLON 'CASEY'
HOF 73 TERRY, WILLIAM HAROLD
HOF146 THOMPSON, SAMUEL L.
HOF 47 TINKER, JOSEPH BERT
HOF 55 TRAYNOR, HAROLD JOSEPH 'PIE'
HOF 79 VANCE, CLARENCE ARTHUR 'DAZZY'
HOF192 VAUGHAN, JOSEPH FLOYD 'ARKY'
HOF 48 WADDELL, GEORGE EDWARD 'RUBE'

RR 2 - HARTSHORNE OK 74547
D. SEPTEMBER 9, 1915 POINT LOMA, CAL.
D. DECEMBER 8, 1958 LAKE WHITNEY, TEX.
D. SEPTEMBER 29, 1975 GLENDALE, CAL.
BOX 2177 - JACKSONVILLE FL 32203
D. NOVEMBER 7, 1922 DETROIT, MICH.
D. JULY 27, 1948 ORLANDO, FLA.
D. MARCH 16, 1972 PITTSBURGH, PA.
D. FEBRUARY 16, 1961 HOMOSASSA SPRINGS, FLA.
D. AUGUST 30, 1952 EAGLEVILLE, CALIF.
D. APRIL 1, 1914 SAN ANTONIO, TEX.

HOF 5 WAGNER, JOHN PETER 'HONUS'
HOF 69 WALLACE, RHODERICK JOHN 'BOBBY'
HOF 49 WALSH, EDWARD AUGUSTIN
HOF107 WANER, LLOYD JAMES
HOF 62 WANER, PAUL GLEE
HOF101 WARD, JOHN MONTGOMERY
HOF140 WELCH, MICHAEL FRANCIS 'MICKEY'
HOF126 WEISS, GEORGE MARTIN
HOF 84 WHEAT, ZACHARY DAVIS
HOF193 WILHELM, JAMES HOYT
HOF104 WILLIAMS, THEODORE SAMUEL
HOF169 WILSON, LEWIS ROBERT 'HACK'
HOF 12 WRIGHT, GEORGE
HOF 70 WRIGHT, WILLIAM HENRY 'HARRY'
HOF133 WYNN, EARLY
HOF173 YAWKEY, THOMAS AUSTIN
HOF 13 YOUNG, DENTON TRUE
HOF134 YOUNGS, ROSS MIDDLEBROOK

D. DECEMBER 6, 1955 CARNEGIE, PA.
D. NOVEMBER 3, 1960 TORRANCE, CAL.
D. MAY 26, 1959 POMPANO BEACH, FLA.
D. JULY 22, 1982 OKLAHOMA CITY, OKLA.
D. AUGUST 29, 1965 SARASOTA, FLA.
D. MARCH 4, 1925 AUGUSTA, GA.
D. AUGUST 13, 1972 GREENWICH, CONN.
D. JULY 30, 1941 NASHUA, N. H.
D. MARCH 11, 1972 SEDALIA, MO.
BOX 2217 - SARASOTA FL 33578
BOX 481 - ISLAMORADA FL 33036
D. NOVEMBER 23, 1948 BALTIMORE, MD.
D. AUGUST 31, 1937 BOSTON, MASS.
D. OCTOBER 3, 1895 ATLANTIC CITY, N. J.
BOX 218 - NOKOMIS FL 33551
D. JULY 9, 1976 BOSTON, MASS.
D. NOVEMBER 4, 1955 NEWCOMERSTOWN, O.
D. OCTOBER 22, 1927 SAN ANTONIO, TEX.

THE SPORT AMERICANA BASEBALL MEMORABILIA
AND AUTOGRAPH PRICE GUIDE IS THE MOST RELIABLE
SOURCE FOR INFORMATION AND PRICES FOR BASE-
BALL COLLECTIBLES OTHER THAN CARDS AND FOR
AUTOGRAPHS OF BASEBALL PLAYERS.

PLAYERS DEBUTING FROM 1910 TO 1985

```
54-  1 AARON, HENRY LOUIS              1611 ADAMS DR SW - ATLANTA GA 30311
62-  1 AARON, TOMMIE LEE              D. AUGUST 16, 1984 ATLANTA, GA.
77-  1 AASE, DONALD WILLIAM           5055 VIA RICARDO - YORBA LINDA CA 92686
10-  1 ABBOTT, ODY CLEON              D. APRIL 13, 1933 WASHINGTON, D. C.
73-  1 ABBOTT, WILLIAM GLENN          4413 DAWSON - NORTH LITTLE ROCK AR 72116
50-  1 ABER, ALBERT JULIUS            7009 MEADOWBROOK AVE - CLEVELAND OH 44144
52-  1 ABERNATHIE, WILLIAM EDWARD     3395 SEPULVEDA - SAN BERNARDINO CA 92404
42-  1 ABERNATHY, TALMADGE LAFAYETTE  225 SPRING COURT - THOMASVILLE NC 27360
55-  1 ABERNATHY, THEODORE WADE       2211 ARMSTRONG PK RD - GASTONIA NC 28052
46-  1 ABERNATHY, VIRGIL WOODROW 'WOODY' 507 SOUTH KENTUCKY AVE - CHESNEE SC 29323
47-  1 ABERSON, CLIFFORD ALEXANDER    D. JUNE 23, 1973 VALLEJO, CAL.
49-  1 ABRAMS, CALVIN ROSS            BOX 974 - AMAGANSETT NY 11930
23-  1 ABRAMS, GEORGE ALLEN           701 MADISON AVE SOUTH #220 - CLEARWATER FL 33516
85-  1 ABREGO, JOHNNY RAY             563 WASATCH DRIVE - FREMONT CA 94536
42-  2 ABREU, JOSEPH LAWRENCE         26090 REGAL AVE - HAYWARD CA 94544
83-  1 ACKER, JAMES JUSTIN            BOX AA - FREER TX 78357
56-  1 ACKER, THOMAS JAMES            314 EVERS ST - WYCKOFF NJ 07481
63-  1 ACKLEY, FLORIAN FREDERICK 'FRITZ' 417 W 5TH ST - HAYWARD WI 54843
13-  1 ACOSTA, BALMADERO PEDRO 'CY'   D. NOVEMBER 17, 1963 MIAMI, FLA.
72-  1 ACOSTA, CECILIO 'CY'           AUG RAMIREZ 1420,COL GAB LEYVA-CULIACAN SINALOA MEX.
70-  1 ACOSTA, EDUARDO ELIXBET        BETANIA 6, 431 X - PANAMA CITY PAN.
20-  1 ACOSTA, JOSE                   OLD ADD: VUENA VISTA - MARIANAO CUBA
31-  1 ADAIR, JAMES AUBREY            D. DECEMBER 9, 1982 DALLAS, TEXAS
58-  1 ADAIR, KENNETH JERRY           14522 MOCKINGBIRD LN - SAND SPRINGS OK 74063
70-  2 ADAIR, MARION DANNE 'BILL'     1535 PINELLAS POINT S-ST PETERSBURG FL 33705
41-  1 ADAMS, ACE TOWNSEND            1005 SUMMETT DR-ALBANY GA 31705
46-  2 ADAMS, CHARLES DWIGHT 'RED'    1780 LAMBETH LANE - CONCORD CA 94518
14-  1 ADAMS, DANIEL LESLIE           D. OCTOBER 6, 1964 ST. LOUIS, MO.
22-  1 ADAMS, EARL JOHN 'SPARKY'      116 WASHINGTON ST - TREMONT PA 17981
39-  1 ADAMS, ELVIN CLARK 'BUSTER'    74390 ALLESANDRO #5 - PALM DESERT CA 92260
75-  1 ADAMS, GLENN CHARLES           RR 1 - SEDAN NM 88436
69-  1 ADAMS, HAROLD DOUGLAS 'DOUG'   1129 HARMONY CIR NE - JANESVILLE WI 53545
48-  1 ADAMS, HERBERT LOREN           903 S WILLISTON - WHEATON IL 60187
12-  1 ADAMS, JAMES IRVIN 'WILLIE'    D. JUNE 18, 1937 ALBANY, N.Y.
10-  2 ADAMS, JOHN BERTRAM            D. JUNE 24, 1940 LOS ANGELES, CALIF.
14-  2 ADAMS, KARL TUTWILER           D. SEPTEMBER 17, 1967 EVERETT, WASH.
47-  2 ADAMS, RICHARD LEROY           229 VIA DE AMO - FALLBROOK CA 92028
82-  1 ADAMS, RICKY LEE               10195 BOLTON - MONTCLAIR CA 91763
31-  2 ADAMS, ROBERT ANDREW           D. MARCH 6, 1970 JACKSONVILLE, FLA.
25-  1 ADAMS, ROBERT BURDETTE         105 HARVARD BLVD - WEST LAWN PA 19609
46-  3 ADAMS, ROBERT HENRY            3828 PUEBLO WAY - SCOTTSDALE AZ 85251
77-  2 ADAMS, ROBERT MELVIN JR.       7653 DESOTO AVE - CANOGA PARK CA 91304
72-  2 ADAMS, ROBERT MICHAEL 'MIKE'   3828 PUEBLO WAY - SCOTTSDALE AZ 85251
23-  2 ADAMS, SPENCER DEWEY           D. NOVEMBER 25, 1970 FT. LAUDERDALE, FLA.
67-  1 ADAMSON, JOHN MICHAEL 'MIKE'   4408 SKY GLEN CT - MOORPARK CA 93021
50-  2 ADCOCK, JOSEPH WILBUR          BOX 385 - COUSHATTA LA 71019
50-  3 ADDIS, ROBERT GORDON           7466 HOLLYCROFT LN - MENTOR OH 44060
83-  2 ADDUCI, JAMES DAVID            10429 SOUTH LAMON - OAK LAWN IL 60453
39-  2 ADERHOLT, MORRIS WOODROW       D. MARCH 18, 1955 SARASOTA, FLA.
28-  1 ADKINS, GRADY EMMETT           D. MARCH 31, 1966 LITTLE ROCK, ARK.
42-  3 ADKINS, JOHN DEWEY             2627 WESTWOOD BLVD-LOS ANGELES CA 90064
42-  4 ADKINS, RICHARD EARL           D. SEPTEMBER 12, 1955 ELECTRA, TEX.
63-  2 ADLESH, DAVID GEORGE           9770 AVENIDA MONTEREY - CYPRESS CA 90630
62-  2 AGEE, TOMMIE LEE               OLD ADD: 11208 ASTORIA BLVD - EAST ELMHURST NY 11369
54-  2 AGGANIS, HARRY                 D. JUNE 27, 1955 CAMBRIDGE, MASS.
12-  2 AGLER, JOSEPH ABRAM            D. APRIL 26, 1971 MASSILLON, O.
13-  2 AGNEW, SAMUEL LESTER           D. JULY 19, 1951 SONOMA, CALIF.
81-  1 AGOSTO, JUAN R                 VIA LETICIA 4LS8 - CAROLINA PR 00630
80-  1 AGUAYO, LUIS (MURIEL)          BOX 9036, SABANA BRANCH - VEGA BAJA PR 00764
85-  2 AGUILERA, RICHARD WARREN       1323 BAINBRIDGE AVENUE - WEST COVINA CA 91790
55-  2 AGUIRRE, HENRY JOHN            31101 SUNSET DR - FRANKLIN MI 48025
77-  3 AIKENS, WILLIE MAYS            OLD ADD: RR 4 BOX 369 - SENECA SC
79-  1 AINGE, DANIEL RAY              371 HIGHLAND ST - NEWTONVILLE MA 02160
10-  3 AINSMITH, EDWARD WILBUR        D. SEPTEMBER 6, 1981 FORT LAUDERDALE, FLA.
11-  1 AITCHISON, RALEIGH LEONIDAS    D. SEPTEMBER 26, 1958 COLUMBUS, KAN.
12-  3 AITON, GEORGE WILSON 'BILL'    D. AUGUST 16, 1976 VAN NUYS, CALIF.
64-  1 AKER, JACK DELANE              18102 E. 27TH ST - INDEPENDENCE MO 64050
12-  4 AKERS, ALBERT EARL 'JERRY'     D. MAY 15, 1979 BAY PINES, FLA.
29-  1 AKERS, THOMAS ERNEST 'BILL'    D. APRIL 13, 1962 CHATTANOOGA, TENN.
58-  2 ALBANESE, JOSEPH PETER         54 LONGFELLOW DR - COLONIA NJ 07067
78-  1 ALBERTS, FRANCIS BURT 'BUTCH'  3063 AMBERLEA LN - BALDWINSVILLE NY 13027
10-  4 ALBERTS, FREDERICK JOSEPH 'CY' D. AUGUST 27, 1917 FORT WAYNE, IND.
41-  2 ALBOSTA, EDWARD JOHN           5360 FORT RD-SAGINAW MI 48601
```

WILLIE MAYS AIKENS 1B - OF

16

8" x 10" Full Color Photos

Mickey Mantle
Yogi Berra
Ted Williams
Bob Lemon
Monte Irvin
Sandy Koufax
Bob Feller
Ernie Banks
Ralph Kiner
Whitey Ford
Roger Maris
Don Drysdale
Harmon Killebrew
Al Kaline
Brooks Robinson
Pee Wee Reese
Warren Spahn
Duke Snider
Stan Musial
Willie Mays
Bob Gibson
Eddie Mathews
Frank Robinson (Reds)
Thurmon Munson
Roberto Clemente
Carl Erskine
Lou Boudreau
Orlando Cepeda
Hank Aaron
Ted Kluzewski
Mantle & Maris
Phil Rizzuto
Lou Brock
Joe DiMaggio

Bobby Thomson
Jackie Robinson
Robin Roberts
Enos Slaughter
Frank Robinson (Orioles)
Earl Weaver
Boog Powell
Juan Marichal
Bobby Shantz
Jim Perry
Hank Bauer
Luis Aparicio (Orioles)
Bobby Richardson
Red Schoendienst
Dick Allen (Philly)
Walt Alston
Al Lopez
1961 Yankee Sluggers (Maris, Berra, Mantle, Howard, Skowron, Blanchard)
1960's Yankees Infield (Boyer, Kubek, Richardson, Pepitone)
1964 Cardinals Infield (Boyer, Groat, Javier, White)
1951 Giants (Lockman, Westrum, Mueller, Dark, Mays, Irvin)
1969 Mets (Agee, C. Jones, Swoboda)
Willie McCovey
Brooks Robinson
Elston Howard
Willie Stargell

Tony Armas
Don Baylor
Wade Boggs
George Brett
Rod Carew
Steve Carlton
Gary Carter
Andre Dawson
Carlton Fisk
Steve Garvey
Ron Guidry
Rickey Henderson
Bob Horner
Kent Hrbek
Ron Kittle
Dave Kingman
Fred Lynn
Dale Murphy
Eddie Murray
Al Oliver
Jim Palmer
Gaylord Perry
Tim Raines
Jim Rice
Dave Righetti
Cal Ripken, Jr.
Pete Rose
Nolan Ryan
Steve Sax
Mike Schmidt
Tom Seaver
Fernando Valenzuela
Dave Winfield
Carl Yastrzemski
Robin Yount

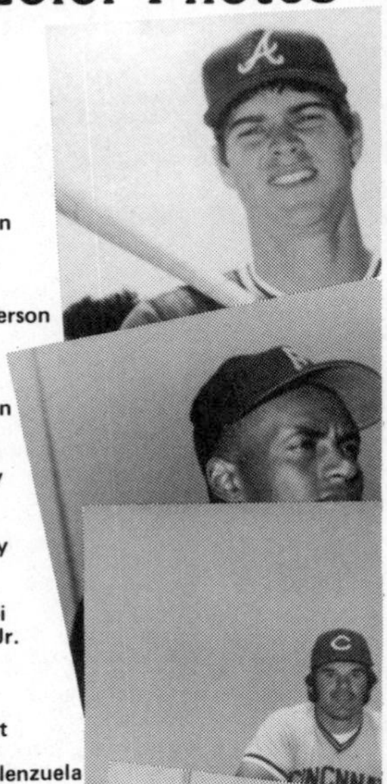

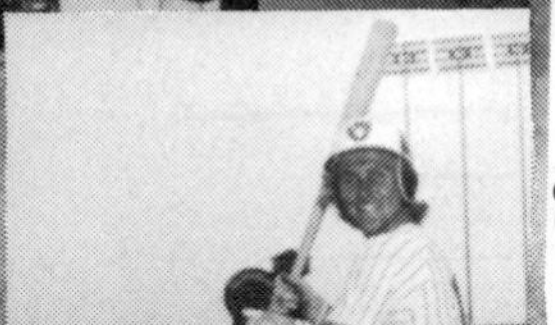

17

49-	2	ALBRECHT, EDWARD ARTHUR	D. 1979 CENTERVILLE, ILL.
47-	3	ALBRIGHT, JOHN HAROLD	5433 HEWLETT DR - SAN DIEGO CA 92115
73-	2	ALBURY, VICTOR	6205 ALCOT CT - TAMPA FL 33624
76-	1	ALCALA, SANTO	RAMON MOTA #18 - SAN PEDRO DE MACORIS DOM. REP.
67-	2	ALCARAZ, ANGEL LUIS	1968 ADD: BOX 423 - HUMACAO PR 00661
14-	3	ALCOCK, JOHN FORBES 'SCOTTY'	D. JANUARY 30, 1973 WOOSTER, O.
43-	1	ALDERSON, DALE LEONARD	D. FEBRUARY 12, 1982 GARDEN GROVE, CALIF.
17-	1	ALDRIDGE, VICTOR EDDINGTON	D. APRIL 17, 1973 TERRE HAUTE, IND.
41-	3	ALENO, CHARLES	601 MARION CT-DELAND FL 32720
29-	2	ALEXANDER, DAVID DALE	D. MARCH 2, 1979 GREENEVILLE, TENN.
71-	1	ALEXANDER, DOYLE LAFAYETTE	2801 MARQUIS CIR E - ARLINGTON TX 76016
75-	2	ALEXANDER, GARY WAYNE	5701 BOWCROFT ST - LOS ANGELES CA 90016
11-	2	ALEXANDER, GROVER CLEVELAND	D. NOVEMBER 4, 1950 ST. PAUL, NEB.
37-	1	ALEXANDER, HUGH	7211 ULMERTON RD #2159 - LARGO FL 33541
73-	3	ALEXANDER, MATTHEW	2419 STONEWALL - SHREVEPORT LA 71103
55-	3	ALEXANDER, ROBERT SOMERVILLE	350 54 EL CAMINO REAL - ENCINITAS CA 92024
12-	5	ALEXANDER, WALTER ERNEST	D. DECEMBER 29, 1978 FORT WORTH, TEXAS
79-	2	ALLARD, BRIAN MARSHALL	110 RICHARD ST - HENRY IL 61537
14-	4	ALLEN, ARTEMUS WARD 'NICK'	D. OCTOBER 16, 1939 HINES, ILL.
62-	3	ALLEN, BERNARD KEITH	9120 MOHICAN TRAIL - NEGLEY OH 44441
26-	1	ALLEN, ETHAN NATHAN	STRATFORD HILL APTS #40C-CHAPEL HIL NC 27514
10-	5	ALLEN, FLETCHER MANSON 'SLEP'	D. OCTOBER 16, 1959 LUBBOCK, TEX.
12-	6	ALLEN, FRANK LEON	D. JULY 30, 1933 GAINESVILLE, ALA.
66-	1	ALLEN, HAROLD ANDREW 'HANK'	15 STATON DR - UPPER MARLBORO MD 20870
19-	1	ALLEN, HORACE TANNER 'PUG'	D. JULY 5, 1981 CANTON, N. C.
83-	3	ALLEN, JAMES BRADLEY 'JAMIE'	1203 FOLSOM AVE - YAKIMA WA 98902
14-	5	ALLEN, JOHN MARSHALL	D. SEPTEMBER 24, 1967 HAGERSTOWN, MD.
32-	1	ALLEN, JOHN THOMAS	D. MARCH 29, 1959 ST. PETERSBURG, FLA.
80-	2	ALLEN, KIM BRYANT	1651 N. RIVERSIDE AVE #614 - RIALTO CA 92376
69-	2	ALLEN, LLOYD CECIL	OLD ADD: 1678 MARGUERITE AVE - CORONA DEL MAR CA 92625
79-	3	ALLEN, NEIL PATRICK	1402 ARMSTRONG - KANSAS CITY KS 66102
63-	3	ALLEN, RICHARD ANTHONY	3011 WEST 4TH ST - LOS ANGELES CA 90020
19-	2	ALLEN, ROBERT	B. 1896
37-	2	ALLEN, ROBERT EARL	1888 W AMES CIR-CHESAPEAKE VA 23321
61-	1	ALLEN, ROBERT GRAY	515 WOODLAWN - HENDERSON TX 75652
83-	4	ALLEN, RODERICK BERNET	1959 CLOVERFIELD BL #103-SANTA MONICA CA90405
72-	3	ALLEN, RONALD FREDRICK	917 WINONA DR - YOUNGSTOWN OH 44511
79-	4	ALLENSON, GARY MARTIN	OLD ADD: 4454 W 141ST AVE - HAWTHORNE CA
63-	4	ALLEY, LEONARD EUGENE 'GENE'	8212 NOTRE DAME DR - RICHMOND VA 23228
54-	3	ALLIE, GAIR ROOSEVELT	14122 CHURCHILL - SAN ANTONIO TX 78248
75-	3	ALLIETTA, ROBERT GEORGE	25 ROBINSON RD - FALMOUTH MA 02540
11-	3	ALLISON, MACK PENDLETON	D. MARCH 13, 1964 ST. JOSEPH, MO.
13-	3	ALLISON, MILO HENRY	D. JUNE 18, 1957 KENOSHA, WIS.
58-	3	ALLISON, WILLIAM ROBERT 'BOB'	2750 EAGANDALE BLVD - ST. PAUL MN 55121
33-	1	ALMADA, BALDOMERO MELO	OLD ADD: DICKENS 76, 201-POLANCO 5 MEXICO DF
11-	4	ALMEIDA, RAFAEL D.	D. MARCH, 1968 HAVANA, CUBA
74-	1	ALMON, WILLIAM FRANCIS	88 CLAFLIN COURT - WARWICK RI 02886
50-	4	ALOMA, LUIS BARBA	8414 N MARMORA - MORTON GROVE IL 60053
64-	2	ALOMAR, SANTOS CONDE 'SANDY'	BOX 136 - SALINAS PR 00751
58-	4	ALOU, FELIPE ROJAS	BOX 1287 - SANTO DOMINGO DOMINICAN REP.
63-	5	ALOU, JESUS MARIA ROJAS 'JAY'	CALLE 3 #5, ENS KENNEDY - SANTO DOMINGO DOMINICAN REP.
60-	1	ALOU, MATEO ROJAS	CALLE 3 #5,ENS KENNEDY - SANTO DOMINGO DOMINICAN REP.
54-	4	ALSTON, THOMAS EDISON	616 ELLWOOD DR - HIGH POINT NC 27260
36-	1	ALSTON, WALTER EMMONS 'SMOKEY'	D. OCTOBER 1, 1984 OXFORD, O.
77-	4	ALSTON, WENDELL 'DEL'	17 LAMBERT RD - WHITE PLAINS NY 10605
82-	2	ALTAMARINO, PORFIRIO	B. MAY 17, 1952 ESTELI, NICARAGUA
20-	2	ALTEN, ERNEST MATTHIAS	D. SEPTEMBER 9, 1974 NAPA, CALIF.
16-	1	ALTENBURG, JESSE HOWARD	D. MARCH 12, 1973 LANSING, MICH.
59-	1	ALTMAN, GEORGE LEE	3601 BRIAR LANE - HAZEL CREST IL 60429
55-	4	ALTOBELLI, JOSEPH	17 ADEANE DR W - ROCHESTER NY 14624
58-	5	ALUSIK, GEORGE JOSEPH	581 GARDEN AVE - WOODRIDGE NJ 07095
68-	1	ALVARADO, LUIS CESAR	BOX 853 - LAJAS PR 00667
73-	4	ALVAREZ, JESUS ORLANDO	CUMMUNIDAD DOLORES 37 - RIO GRANDE PR 00745
81-	2	ALVAREZ, JOSE LINO	7813 JAMAICA AVE - TAMPA FL 33614
58-	6	ALVAREZ, OSWALDO GONZALES 'OSSIE'	SANTUARIO 3137,COL. CHAPALITA-GUADALAJARA JALISCO MEX.
60-	2	ALVAREZ, ROGELIO	5010 NW 183RD ST - CAROL CITY FL 33055
62-	4	ALVIS, ROY MAXWELL 'MAX'	806 HUNTERWOOD DR - JASPER TX 75951
65-	1	ALYEA, GARRABRANT RYERSON 'BRANT'	330 STUYVESANT PL, 2ND FLOOR - LYNDHURST NJ 07071
54-	5	AMALFITANO, JOHN JOSEPH 'JOE'	656 10TH ST - SAN PEDRO CA 90731
58-	7	AMARO, RUBÉN	1728 BORBECK ST - PHILADELPHIA PA 19111
37-	3	AMBLER, WAYNE HARPER	913 NOBLE OAKS DR - SAVANNAH GA 31406
84-	1	AMELUNG, EDWARD ALLEN	17045 ROYAL VIEW DR - HACIENDA HEIGHTS CA 91745
55-	5	AMOR, VINCENTE ALVAREZ	OLD ADD: CONCEPCION 630 - LAWTON, HAVANA CUBA
52-	2	AMOROS, EDMUNDO ISASI 'SANDY'	2914 10TH ST - TAMPA FL 33605

15-	1	ANCKER, WALTER	D. FEBRUARY 13, 1954 ENGLEWOOD, N.J.
75-	4	ANDERSEN, LARRY EUGENE	17016 NE 2ND PL - BELLEVUE WA 98004
41-	4	ANDERSON, ALFRED WALTON	D. JUNE 23, 1985 ALBANY, GA.
48-	2	ANDERSON, ANDY HOLM	D. JULY 18, 1982 SEATTLE, WASH.
37-	4	ANDERSON, ARNOLD REVOLA 'RED'	D. AUGUST 7, 1972 SIOUX CITY, IA.
83-	5	ANDERSON, DAVID CARTER	5044 VIA DONALDO - YORBA LINDA CA 92686
71-	2	ANDERSON, DWAIN CLEAVEN	4996 LLANO DR - WOODLAND HILLS CA 91343
46-	4	ANDERSON, FERRELL JACK 'ANDY'	D. MARCH 12, 1978 JOPLIN, MO.
14-	6	ANDERSON, GEORGE ANDREW JENDRUS	D. MAY 28, 1962 CLEVELAND, O.
59-	2	ANDERSON, GEORGE LEE 'SPARKY'	4077 N VERDE VISTA DR-THOUSAND OAKS CA 91360
32-	2	ANDERSON, HAROLD	D. MAY 1, 1974 ST. LOUIS, MO.
57-	1	ANDERSON, HARRY WALTER	4823 KENNETT PIKE - GREENVILLE DE 19807
78-	2	ANDERSON, JAMES LEA	3931 CALLE VALLE VISTA-NEWBURY PARK CA 91320
58-	8	ANDERSON, JOHN CHARLES	OLD ADD: BOX 49 - BROWNING MT 59417
82-	3	ANDERSON, KARL ADAM 'BUD'	196 W CYPRUS LANE - WESTBURY NY 11590
74-	2	ANDERSON, LAWRENCE DENNIS	8037 WORTHY DR - WESTMINSTER CA 92683
71-	3	ANDERSON, MICHAEL ALLEN	RR ONE - TIMMONSVILLE SC 29161
61-	2	ANDERSON, NORMAN CRAIG	814 POPLAR RD - HELLERTOWN PA 18055
79-	5	ANDERSON, RICHARD LEE	3915 WEST 105TH ST - INGLEWOOD CA 90303

THE SPORT AMERICANA PRICE GUIDE TO THE NON—SPORTS CARDS IS THE BEST SOURCE FOR INFORMA—TION AND PRICES FOR NON—SPORTS CARDS.

57-	2	ANDERSON, ROBERT CARL	4209 EAST 104TH - TULSA OK 74137
17-	2	ANDERSON, WALTER CARL	1811 MORNINGSIDE DR SE - GRAND RAPIDS MI 49506
25-	2	ANDERSON, WILLIAM EDWARD	D. MARCH 13, 1983 MEDFORD, MASS.
10-	6	ANDERSON, WINGO CHARLIE	D. DECEMBER 19, 1950 FORT WORTH, TEX.
55-	6	ANDRE, JOHN EDWARD	D. NOVEMBER 25, 1976 CENTERVILLE, MASS.
46-	5	ANDRES, ERNEST HENRY	812 S ROSE - BLOOMINGTON IN 47403
75-	5	ANDREW, KIM DARRELL	10052 DENSMORE AVE - SEPULVEDA CA 91343
25-	3	ANDREWS, ELBERT DEVORE	D. NOVEMBER 25, 1979 GREENWOOD, S. C.
76-	2	ANDREWS, FRED	8239 SOUTH KINGSTON - CHICAGO IL 60617
47-	4	ANDREWS, HERBERT CARL	2305 2ND ST - DODGE CITY KS 67801
31-	3	ANDREWS, IVY PAUL	D. NOVEMBER 23, 1970 DORA, ALA.
73-	5	ANDREWS, JOHN RICHARD	9292 GORDON AVE - LAHABRA CA 90631
66-	2	ANDREWS, MICHAEL JAY	29 PAUL AVE - PEABODY MA 01960
37-	5	ANDREWS, NATHAN HARDY	RR 3 BOX 271 - KING NC 27021
75-	6	ANDREWS, ROBERT PATRICK	1280 MOUNTBATTEN CT - CONCORD CA 94518
39-	3	ANDREWS, STANLEY JOSEPH	3840 IRONWOOD LN #403 - BRADENTON FL 33505
31-	4	ANDRUS, WILLIAM MORGAN	D. MARCH 12, 1982 WASHINGTON, D. C.
76-	3	ANDUJAR, JOAQUIN (GARSIA)	JUAN DEACOSTA #10A-SAN PEDRO DE MARCORIS DOMR
72-	4	ANGELINI, NORMAN STANLEY	16196 E BAILS PL - AURORA CO 80012
29-	3	ANGLEY, THOMAS SAMUEL	D. OCTOBER 26, 1952 WICHITA, KAN.
36-	2	ANKENMAN, FRED NORMAN 'PAT'	4014 UNDERWOOD - HOUSTON TX 77025
44-	1	ANTOLICK, JOSEPH	723 2ND ST - CATASAUQUA PA 18032
48-	3	ANTONELLI, JOHN AUGUST	22 TOBEY WOODS - PITTSFORD NY 14534
44-	2	ANTONELLI, JOHN LAWRENCE	5539 BARFIELD RD - MEMPHIS TN 38117
53-	1	ANTONELLO, WILLIAM JAMES	4054 VALENTINE CT - ST PAUL MN 55112
56-	2	APARICIO, LUIS ERNEST	CALLE 67 #26-82 - MARACAIBO VENEZUELA S.A.
73-	6	APODACA, ROBERT JOHN	23 HIGHLAND AVE - GLENWOOD LANDING NY 11547
80-	3	APONTE, LUIS EDUARDO	CALLE BELLA VISTA 48-LA SABANITA,BOLIVAR VENE
15-	2	APPLETON, EDWARD SAMUEL	D. JANUARY 27, 1932 ARLINGTON, TEX.

```
27-  1  APPLETON, PETER WILLIAM            D. JANUARY 18, 1974 TRENTON, N.J.
30-  1  APPLING, LUCIUS BENJAMIN 'LUKE'    RR 7, BRAGG RD - CUMMINGS GA 30130
14-  7  ARAGON, ANGEL VALDES SR. 'JACK'    D. JANUARY 24, 1952 NEW YORK, N.Y.
41-  5  ARAGON, ANGEL VALDES JR. "ANGEL"   14800 WALSINGHAM #901 - LARGO FL 33544
23-  3  ARCHDEACON, MAURICE BRUCE          D. SEPTEMBER 5, 1954 ST. LOUIS, MO.
36-  3  ARCHER, FREDERICK MARVIN           D. OCTOBER 31, 1981 CHARLOTTE, N. C.
61-  3  ARCHER, JAMES WILLIAM              1414 OLEANDER DR - TARPON SPRINGS FL 33589
38-  1  ARCHIE, GEORGE ALBERT              4007 CLARKSVILLE HIGHWAY-NASHVILLE TN 37218
68-  2  ARCIA, JOSE RAIMUNDO               7325 NW 3RD ST - MIAMI FL 33125
61-  4  ARDELL, DANIEL MIERS               1966 PORT CLARIDGE - NEWPORT BEACH CA 92660
47-  5  ARDIZOIA, RINALDO JOSEPH 'RUGGER'  130 SANTA ROSA AVE - SAN FRANCISCO CA 94112
48-  4  ARFT, HENRY IRVIN                  109 SUNNYSIDE LN - BALLWIN MO 63011
59-  3  ARIAS, RODOLFO MARTINEZ 'RUDY'     3911 NW 11TH ST - MIAMI FL 33126
31-  5  ARLETT, RUSSELL LORIS 'BUZZ'       D. MAY 16, 1964 MINNEAPOLIS, MINN.
65-  5  ARLICH, DONALD LOUIS               7877 SOUTH 73RD ST - COTTAGE GROVE MN 55016
69-  3  ARLIN, STEPHEN RALPH               6338 CAMINO CORTO - SAN DIEGO CA 92120
76-  4  ARMAS, ANTONIO RAFAEL              LOS MERCEDES #37,P.PIRITU EDO. - ANZOATEGUI VENEZ
73-  7  ARMBRISTER, EDISON ROSANDER        MCQUAY ST, BOX 2003 - NASSAU BAHAMAS W.I.
34-  1  ARMBRUST, ORVILLE MARTIN           D. OCTOBER 2, 1967 MOBILE, ALA.
46-  6  ARMSTRONG, GEORGE NOBLE            16 FRANKLIN ST - EAST ORANGE NJ 07017
11-  5  ARMSTRONG, HOWARD ELMER            D. MARCH 8, 1926 CANISTEO, N.Y.
80-  4  ARMSTRONG, MICHAEL DENNIS          BOX 846 - HALIFAX VA 24558
71-  4  ARNOLD, CHRISTOPHER PAUL           2219 EL CAPITAN - ARCADIA CA 91006
36-  4  ARNOVICH, MORRIS                   D. JULY 20, 1959 SUPERIOR, WIS.
43-  2  ARNTZEN, ORIE EDGAR                D. JANUARY 28, 1970 CEDAR RAPIDS, IA.
61-  5  ARRIGO, GERALD WILLIAM             330C ST. ANDREWS DR - CINCINNATI OH 45245
75-  7  ARROYO, FERNANDO                   4917 FIRST PARKWAY - SACRAMENTO CA 95823
55-  7  ARROYO, LUIS ENRIQUE               BOX 354 - PENUELAS PR 00724
71-  5  ARROYO, RUDOLPH                    828 SIERRA VISTA - MOUNTAIN VIEW CA 94040
38-  2  ASBELL, JAMES MARION               D. JULY 6, 1967 SAN MATEO, CAL.
28-  2  ASBJORNSON, ROBERT ANTHONY         D. JANUARY 21, 1970 WILLIAMSPORT, PA.
25-  4  ASH, KENNETH LOWTHER               D. NOVEMBER 15, 1979 CLARKSBURG, W. VA.
48-  5  ASHBURN, DON RICHARD 'RICHIE'      PHILLIES ANNOUNCER - ARDMORE PA 19003
73-  8  ASHBY, ALAN DEAN                   3151 COUNTRY CLUB BLVD - SUGARLAND TX 77478
76-  5  ASHFORD, THOMAS STEVEN 'TUCKER'    502 MAPLE ST - COVINGTON TN 38019
57-  3  ASPROMONTE, KENNETH JOSEPH         % COORS, 10400 HARWIN - HOUSTON TX 77036
56-  3  ASPROMONTE, ROBERT THOMAS          29 CHARLESTON N - SUGARLAND TX 77478
76-  6  ASSELSTINE, BRIAN HANLY            1488 COUNTRY CT - SANTA YNEZ CA 93460
45-  1  ASTROTH, JOSEPH HENRY              151 SOUTH MOYER RD - CHALFONT PA 18914
83-  6  ATHERTON, KEITH ROWE               ROUTE 198 BLAKES - MATHEWS VA 23020
50-  5  ATKINS, JAMES CURTIS               3221 CLIFF RD - BIRMINGHAM AL 35205
27-  2  ATKINSON, HUBERT BURLEY 'LEFTY'    D. FEBRUARY 12, 1961 CHICAGO, ILL.
76-  7  ATKINSON, WILLIAM CECIL GLENN      RR 2 - CHATHAM ONT. N7M 5S2 CAN.
26-  2  ATTREAU, RICHARD GILBERT           D. JULY 5, 1964 CHICAGO, ILL.
52-  3  ATWELL, MAURICE DAILEY 'TOBY'      BOX 686 - PURCELLVILLE VA 22132
36-  5  ATWOOD, WILLIAM FRANKLIN           3100 EL PASO-SNYDER TX 79549
71-  4  AUERBACH, FREDERICK STEVEN 'RICK'  4724 ABARGO ST - WOODLAND HILLS CA 91364
73-  9  AUGUSTINE, DAVID RALPH             OLD ADD: 14850 SW 280TH ST #25-HOMESTEAD FL
75-  2  AUGUSTINE, GERALD LEE              569 W 13442 HALES PK CT-HALES CORNER WI 53130
33-  2  AUKER, ELDEN LEROY                 15 SAILFISH RD - VERO BEACH FL 32960
47-  6  AULDS, LEYCESTER DOYLE             YANCEY STAR RT BOX 16 - HONDO TX 78861
76-  8  AULT, DOUGLAS REAGAN               1450 23RD ST - BEAUMONT TX 77706
65-  3  AUST, DENNIS KAY                   9609 NORTH NEWPORT AVE - TAMPA FL 33612
70-  3  AUSTIN, RICK GERALD                BOX 347 - BROOKFIELD MO 64628
76-  9  AUTRY, ALBERT                      8572 FERN CREST WAY - ELK GROVE CA 95624
24-  1  AUTRY, MARTIN GORDON               D. JANUARY 26, 1950 SAVANNAH, GA.
56-  4  AVERILL, EARL DOUGLAS              1806 19TH DR NE - AUBURN WA 98002
29-  4  AVERILL, HOWARD EARL               D. AUGUST 16, 1983 EVERETT, WASH.
49-  3  AVILA, ROBERTO FRANCISCO GONZALEZ  NAVEGANTES FR-19 REFORMA - VERACRUZ VERACRUZ MEX.
77-  5  AVILES, RAMON ANTONIO              26 PADIAL ST - MANATI PR 00701
50-  6  AVREA, JAMES EPHERIUM              927 GLENSTONE - DALLAS TX 75232
74-  3  AYALA, BENIGNO 'BENNIE'            BOX 814 - BAYAMON PR 00619
47-  7  AYERS, WILLIAM OSCAR               D. SEPTEMBER 24, 1980 NEWNAN, GA.
13-  4  AYERS, YANCEY WYATT 'DOC'          D. MAY 26, 1968 PULASKI, VA.
53-  2  AYLWARD, RICHARD JOHN              D. JUNE 11, 1983 SPRING VALLEY, CALIF.
```

```
60-  3  AZCUE, JOSE JOAQUIN                10020 CRAIG - SHAWNEE MISSION KS 66212
79-  6  BABCOCK, ROBERT ERNEST             4652 OLD PITTSBURGH RD - NEW CASTLE PA 16101
52-  4  BABE,·LOREN ROLLAND                D. FEBRUARY 14, 1984 OMAHA, NEB.
34-  2  BABICH, JOHN CHARLES               6111 ROSALIND AV - RICHMOND CA 94803
15-  3  BABINGTON, CHARLES PERCY           D. MARCH 22, 1957 PROVIDENCE, R.I.
81-  5  BABITT, MACK NEAL 'SHOOTY'         2530 MATHEWS ST - BERKELEY CA 94702
80-  5  BACKMAN, WALTER WAYNE              160 SE 39TH - HILLSBORO OR 97123
17-  3  BACON, EDGAR SUTER                 D. OCTOBER 2, 1963 FRANKFORT, KY.
```

BACSIK

75-	9	BACSIK, MICHAEL JAMES
53-	3	BACZEWSKI, FREDERICK JOHN
12-	7	BADER, LORE VERNE 'KING'
29-	5	BADGRO, MORRIS HIRAM 'RED'
26-	3	BAECHT, EDWARD JOSEPH
77-	6	BAEZ, JOSE ANTONIO
12-	8	BAGBY, JAMES CHARLES JACOB SR.
38-	3	BAGBY, JAMES CHARLES JACOB
23-	4	BAGWELL, WILLIAM MALLORY
66-	3	BAHNSEN, STANLEY RAYMOND
46-	7	BAHR, EDSON GARFIELD
14-	8	BAICHLEY, GROVER CLEVELAND
19-	3	BAILEY, ABRAHAM LINCOLN
17-	4	BAILEY, ARTHUR EUGENE
16-	2	BAILEY, FRED MIDDLETON
11-	6	BAILEY, HARRY LEWIS
81-	4	BAILEY, HOWARD L
59-	4	BAILEY, JAMES HOPKINS
84-	2	BAILEY, JOHN MARK
53-	4	BAILEY, LONAS EDGAR 'ED'
62-	5	BAILEY, ROBERT SHERWOOD
67-	3	BAILEY, STEVEN JOHN
75-	10	BAILOR, ROBERT MICHAEL
45-	2	BAIN, HERBERT LOREN
80-	6	BAINES, HAROLD DOUGLAS
76-	10	BAIR, CHARLES DOUGLAS 'DOUG'
17-	5	BAIRD, ALBERT WELLS
15-	4	BAIRD, HOWARD DOUGLASS
62-	6	BAIRD, ROBERT ALLEN
64-	3	BAKENHASTER, DAVID LEE
38-	4	BAKER, ALBERT JONES
78-	3	BAKER, CHARLES JOSEPH
82-	4	BAKER, DAVID GLENN
14-	9	BAKER, DELMAR DAVID
84-	3	BAKER, DOUGLAS LEE
53-	5	BAKER, EUGENE WALTER
43-	3	BAKER, FLOYD WILSON
69-	4	BAKER, FRANK
70-	4	BAKER, FRANK WATTS
12-	9	BAKER, HOWARD FRANCIS
76-	11	BAKER, JACK EDWARD
19-	4	BAKER, JESSE EUGENE
11-	7	BAKER, JESSE ORMAND
68-	3	BAKER, JOHNNIE B. "DUSTY"
27-	3	BAKER, NEAL VERNON
78-	4	BAKER, STEVEN BYRNE
35-	1	BAKER, THOMAS CALVIN
63-	6	BAKER, THOMAS HENRY
11-	8	BAKER, TRACY LEE
40-	1	BAKER, WILLIAM PRESLEY
38-	5	BALAS, MITCHELL FRANCIS 'MIKE'
74-	4	BALAZ, JOHN LARRY
81-	5	BALBONI, STEPHEN CHARLES
56-	5	BALCENA, ROBERT RUDOLPH
61-	2	BALDSCHUN, JACK EDWARD
66-	4	BALDWIN, DAVID GEORGE
53-	6	BALDWIN, FRANK DEWITT

BANCROFT

935 GREEN RIDGE DR - DUNCANVILLE TX 75137
D. NOVEMBER 14, 1976 CULVER CITY, CALIF.
D. JUNE 2, 1973 LEROY, KAN.
1010 E TEMPERANCE ST - KENT WA 98031
D. AUGUST 15, 1957 QUARRY TWP., ILL.
27 DEFEBRERO #15 - SAN CRISTOBAL DOMINICAN REP.
D. JULY 28, 1954 MARIETTA, GA.
1910 S COBB DR #4B - MARIETTA GA 30060
D. OCTOBER 5, 1976 CHOUDRANT, LA.
780 NE 76TH ST - BOCA RATON FL 33431
OLD ADD: STAR RT 1 BOX 51 - ONALASKA WA
D. JUNE 30, 1956 SAN JOSE, CALIF.
D. SEPTEMBER 27, 1973 JOLIET, ILL.
D. NOVEMBER 14, 1973 HOUSTON, TEX.
D. AUGUST 16, 1972 HUNTINGTON, W. VA.
D. OCTOBER 27, 1967 SEATTLE, WASH.
119 SOUTH FIFTH - GRAND HAVEN MI 49417
5890 RIVERDALE RD - COLLEGE PARK GA 30349
OLD ADD: 829 SOUTH LINK - SPRINGFIELD MO 65804
642 BROOME RD - KNOXVILLE TN 37919
7065 SEAWIND DR - LONG BEACH CA 90803
1005 EUCLID AVE - LORAIN OH 44052
509 EDNA ST - CONNELLSVILLE PA 15425
OLD ADD: 1926 ARTHUR ST NE - MINNEAPOLIS MN
107 TRUSTY ST - SAINT MICHAEL MD 21663
6401 PHEASANT RD - LOVELAND OH 45140
D. NOVEMBER 27, 1976 SHREVEPORT, LA.
D. JUNE 13, 1967 THOMASVILLE, GA.
D. APRIL 11, 1974 CHATTANOOGA, TENN.
3237 MCKINLEY - COLUMBUS OH 43204
D. NOVEMBER 6, 1982 KENEDY, TEXAS
1521 CHALGROVE DR - CORONA CA 91720
RR TWO - LACONA IA 50139
D. SEPTEMBER 11, 1973 SAN ANTONIO, TEX.
19377 WINGED FOOT CIRCLE - NORTHRIDGE CA 91326
2202 E. 48TH ST - DAVENPORT IA 52807
3033 IDLEWOOD AVE-YOUNGSTOWN OH 44511
383 GIRARD AVE - SOMERSET NJ 08873
BOX 3066 - MERIDIAN MS 39301
D. JANUARY 16, 1964 BRIDGEPORT, CONN.
4536 SWALLOW PL - BIRMINGHAM AL 35213
D. JULY 25, 1960 POMONA, CALIF.
D. SEPTEMBER 26, 1972 TACOMA, WASH.
24525 PALERMO DR - CALABASAS CA 91302
D. JANUARY 5, 1982 HOUSTON, TEX.
4841 CYPRESS AVE - LAMESA CA 92041
2002 GOULD ST-FT WORTH TX 76106
D. MARCH 9, 1980 PORT TOWNSEND, WASH.
D. MARCH 14, 1975 PLACERVILLE, CAL.
412 MELROSE ST SW - LENOIR NC 28645
11 LOWELL RD - WESTFORD MA 02181
2819 WORDEN ST - SAN DIEGO CA 92110
28 CELESTE ST - MANCHESTER NH 03103
2615 CALIFORNIA AVE SW #3 - SEATTLE WA 98116
492 BADER ST - GREEN BAY WI 54302
6770 E. CARONDELET DR #206 - TUCSON AZ 85710
7298 ELKWOOD PL - WESTCHESTER OH 45069

MIKE BACSIK

Ed Bailey—Cincinnati Redlegs

GEORGE BAMBERGER

27-	4	BALDWIN, HENRY CLAY
24-	2	BALDWIN, HOWARD EDWARD 'HARRY'
78-	5	BALDWIN, REGINALD CONRAD
75-	11	BALDWIN, RICKEY ALAN
75-	12	BALDWIN, ROBERT HARVEY 'BILLY'
11-	9	BALENTI, MICHAEL RICHARD
66-	5	BALES, WESLEY OWEN 'LEE'
28-	3	BALLENGER, PELHAM ASHBY
82-	5	BALLER, JAY SCOT
71-	7	BALLINGER, MARK ALAN
25-	5	BALLOU, NOBLE WINFIELD 'WIN'
62-	7	BALSAMO, ANTHONY FRED
51-	1	BAMBERGER, GEORGE IRVIN
48-	6	BAMBERGER, HAROLD EARL
15-	5	BANCROFT, DAVID JAMES

D. FEBRUARY 24, 1964 PHILADELPHIA, PA.
D. JANUARY 23, 1958 BALTIMORE, MD.
763 LIEBOLD - DETROIT MI 48217
3304 COLONIAL DR - MODESTO CA 95350
878 PACKARD DR - AKRON OH 44320
D. AUGUST 4, 1955 ALTUS, OKLA.
7223 AUGUSTINE - HOUSTON TX 77036
D. DECEMBER 8, 1948 WEST GANTT TWP., S. C.
765 NW 12TH AVE - CANBY OR 97013
%D.BALLINGER,176 DALE - NEWBURY PARK CA 91320
D. JANUARY 30, 1963 SAN FRANCISCO, CAL.
160-15 86TH ST - HOWARD BEACH NY 11414
455 N. BATH CLUB BLVD - NORTH REDINGTON BEACH FL 33708
RR 1 BOX 317 - BIRDSBORO PA 19508
D. OCTOBER 9, 1972 SUPERIOR, WIS.

```
81-  6  BANDO, CHRISTOPHER MICHAEL          35640 BRUSHWOOD DR - SOLON OH 44139
66-  6  BANDO, SALVATORE LEONARD            104 W JUNIPER LN - MEQUON WI 53092
73- 10  BANE, EDWARD NORMAN                 BOX 50433 - PHOENIX AZ 85076
69-  5  BANEY, RICHARD LEE                  1412 DAMON AVE - ANAHEIM CA 92802
47-  8  BANKHEAD, DANIEL ROBERT             D. MAY 2, 1976 HOUSTON, TEX.
53-  7  BANKS, ERNEST                       10660 WILSHIRE #408 - WEST LOS ANGELES CA 90024
62-  8  BANKS, GEORGE EDWARD                BOX 207 - PACOLET SC 29372
15-  6  BANKSTON, WILBORN EVERETT 'BILL'    D. FEBRUARY 26, 1970 GRIFFIN, GA.
74-  5  BANNISTER, ALAN                     405 48TH ST NW - BRADENTON FL 33529
77-  7  BANNISTER, FLOYD FRANKLIN           8031 EAST DEL JOYA - SCOTTSDALE AZ 85258
47-  9  BANTA, JOHN KAY                     3215 EAST 30TH AVE - HUTCHINSON KS 67502
14- 10  BARBARE, WALTER LAWRENCE            D. OCTOBER 28, 1965 GREENVILLE, S.C.
43-  4  BARBARY, DONALD ODELL 'RED'         402 W CURTIS - SIMPSONVILLE SC 29681
26-  4  BARBEE, DAVID MONROE                D. JULY 1, 1968 ALBEMARLE, N. C.
60-  4  BARBER, STEPHEN DAVID               TOYOTA WEST,2025 S. DECATUR BL - LAS VEGAS NV 89102
70-  5  BARBER, STEVEN LEE                  1517 CUSHMAN DR - SIERRA VISTA AZ 85635
15-  7  BARBER, TYRUS TURNER                D. OCTOBER 20, 1968 MILAN, TENN.
66-  7  BARBIERI, JAMES PATRICK             13619 E 5TH AVE - SPOKANE WA 99216
57-  4  BARCLAY, CURTIS CORDELL             D. MARCH 27, 1955 MISSOULA, MONT.
72-  5  BARE, RAYMOND DOUGLAS               911 N IVY ST - JENKS OK 74037
81-  7  BARFIELD, JESSE LEE                 OLD ADD: 5700 BROOKGLEN #567 -  OUSTON TX
22-  2  BARFOOT, CLYDE RAYMOND              D. MARCH 11, 1971 HIGHLAND PARK, CAL.
83-  7  BARGAR, GREGORY ROBERT              23005 KATHRYN AVE - TORRANCE CA 90505
76- 12  BARKER, LEONARD HAROLD              1339 BEECHWOOD HILLS CT - ATLANTA GA 30324
60-  5  BARKER, RAYMOND HAROLD              % GENERAL MOTORS - MARTINSBURG WV 25401
84-  4  BARKLEY, JEFFREY CARVER             264 THIRD AVE NE - HICKORY NC 28601
37-  6  BARKLEY, JOHN DUNCAN 'RED'          1200 LAWRENCE DR - WACO TX 76710
75- 13  BARLOW, MICHAEL ROSWELL             %SHEFTIC,4524 FRANCIS RD - CAZENOVIA NY 13035
53-  8  BARMES, BRUCE RAYMOND               509 MCDONALD AVE - CHARLOTTE NC 28203
37-  7  BARNA, HERBERT PAUL 'BABE'          D. MAY 18, 1972 CHARLESTON, W. VA.
27-  5  BARNABE, CHARLES EDWARD             D. AUGUST 16, 1977 WACO, TEX.
27-  6  BARNES, EMILE DEERING 'RED'         D. JULY 3, 1959 MOBILE, ALA.
23-  5  BARNES, EVERETT DUANE 'EPPIE'       D. NOVEMBER 17, 1980 MINEOLA, N. Y.
57-  5  BARNES, FRANK                       507 COMFORT ST - GREENVILLE MS 38701
29-  6  BARNES, FRANK SAMUEL 'LEFTY'        D. SEPTEMBER 27, 1967 HOUSTON, TEX.
15-  8  BARNES, JESSE LAWRENCE              D. SEPTEMBER 9, 1961 SANTA ROSA, N.MEX.
26-  5  BARNES, JOHN FRANCIS 'HONEY'        D. JUNE 18, 1981 LOCKPORT, N. Y.
34-  3  BARNES, JUNIE SHOAF                 D. DECEMBER 31, 1963 JACKSONVILLE, N. C.
72-  6  BARNES, LUTHER OWEN 'LUTE'          3331 STIKES DR - LACEY WA 98503
82-  6  BARNES, RICHARD MONROE              4357 DAVIS ROAD - LAKE WORTH FL 33461
24-  3  BARNES, ROBERT AVERY                BOX 68 - LACON IL 61540
21-  1  BARNES, SAMUEL THOMAS               D. FEBRUARY 19, 1981 MONTGOMERY, ALA.
19-  5  BARNES, VIRGIL JENNINGS             D. JULY 24, 1958 WICHITA, KAN.
83-  8  BARNES, WILLIAM HENRY 'SKEETER'     6626 RAVENAL CT - CINCINNATI OH 45213
15-  9  BARNEY, EDMUND J.                   D. OCTOBER 4, 1967 RICE LAKE, WIS.
43-  5  BARNEY, REX EDWARD                  4601 HOLLINS FERRY RD - BALTIMORE MD 21227
20-  3  BARNHART, CLYDE LEE                 D. JANUARY 21, 1980 HAGERSTOWN, MD.
24-  4  BARNHART, EDGAR VERNON              D. SEPTEMBER 14, 1984 COLUMBIA, MO.
28-  4  BARNHART, LESLIE EARL               D. OCTOBER 7, 1971 SCOTTSDALE, ARIZ.
44-  3  BARNHART, VICTOR DEE                RR 5 - HAGERSTOWN MD 21741
39-  4  BARNICLE, GEORGE BERNARD            9981 88TH ST N - SEMINOLE FL 33543
65-  4  BARNOWSKI, EDWARD ANTHONY           6 OLIVER ST - ALBANY NY 12205
82-  7  BAROJAS, SALOME ROMERO              B. JUNE 16, 1957 COROVA, VERACRUZ, MEXICO
60-  6  BARONE, RICHARD ANTHONY             403 GLENFORD PARK CT - SAN JOSE CA 95136
71-  8  BARR, JAMES LELAND                  2129 QUEENS LN - SAN MATEO CA 94402
35-  2  BARR, ROBERT ALEXANDER              BARRINGTON MOBILE HOMES-BARRINGTON NH 03825
74-  5  BARR, STEVEN CHARLES                OLD ADD: 550 AVENUE N SE - WINTER HAVEN FL 33880
61-  7  BARRAGAN, FACUNDO ANTHONY 'CUNO'    8255 LARIVIERA DR - SACRAMENTO CA 95826
79-  7  BARRANCA, GERMAN MICHAEL            CALLE PINO SUAREZ #1642 - VERACRUZ VERACRUZ MEX.
37-  8  BARRETT, CHARLES HENRY 'RED'        410 MONTICELLO DR - WILSON NC 27893
39-  5  BARRETT, FRANCIS JOSEPH             434 N 3RD ST-LEESBURG FL 32748
42-  5  BARRETT, JOHN JOSEPH                D. AUGUST 17, 1974 SEABROOK BEACH, N. H.
82-  8  BARRETT, MARTIN GLENN               OLD ADD: 2514 72ND PL - SCOTTSDALE AZ 85257
23-  6  BARRETT, ROBERT SCHLEY              D. JANUARY 18, 1982 ATLANTA, GA.
33-  3  BARRETT, TRACEY SOUTER 'DICK'       D. NOVEMBER 7, 1966 SEATTLE, WASH.
21-  2  BARRETT, WILLIAM JOSEPH             D. JANUARY 26, 1951 CAMBRIDGE, MASS.
74-  7  BARRIOS, FRANCISCO XAVIER           D. APRIL 9, 1982 HERMOSILLO SONORA MEXICO
82-  9  BARRIOS, JOSE MANUEL                6484 SW 25TH ST - MIAMI FL 33155
29-  7  BARRON, DAVID IRENUS 'RED'          D. OCTOBER 4, 1982 ATLANTA, GA.
14- 11  BARRON, FRANK JOHN                  D. SEPTEMBER 18, 1964 PLEASANTS CO., W. VA.
12- 10  BARRY, HARDIN                       D. NOVEMBER 5, 1969 CARSON CITY, NEV.
69-  6  BARRY, RICHARD DONOVAN              47275 MIO MIO LOOP - KANEOHE HI 96744
27-  7  BARTELL, RICHARD WILLIAM            1118 ISLAND DR - ALAMEDA CA 94501
```

BARTHELSON

44-	4	BARTHELSON, ROBERT EDWARD	40 MEADOWLARK LN - NORTHFORD CT 06472
28-	5	BARTHOLOMEW, LESTER JUSTIN	D. SEPTEMBER 19, 1972 MADISON, WIS.
52-	5	BARTIROME, ANTHONY JOSEPH	1104 PALMA SOLA BLVD - BRADENTON FL 33505
43-	6	BARTLEY, BOYD OWEN	7500 NOREAST DR - FORT WORTH TX 76118
38-	6	BARTLING, IRVING HENRY	D. JUNE 12, 1973 WESTLAND, MICH.
65-	5	BARTON, ROBERT WILBUR	777 DOROTHEA AVE - SAN MARCOS CA 92069
31-	6	BARTON, VINCENT DAVID	D. SEPTEMBER 13, 1973 TORONTO, ONT.
45-	3	BARTOSCH, DAVID ROBERT	25212 AVENIDA DORENA - NEWHALL CA 91321
48-	7	BASGALL, ROMANUS 'MONTY'	1965 LAUREL LN - SIERRA VISTA AZ 85635
12-	11	BASHANG, ALBERT C.	D. JUNE 23, 1967 CINCINNATI, O.
36-	6	BASHORE, WALTER FRANKLIN	D. SEPTEMBER 26, 1984 SEBRING, FLA.
44-	5	BASINSKI, EDWIN FRANK	6585 SW 67TH ST - PORTLAND OR 97223
11-	10	BASKETTE, JAMES BLAINE	D. JULY 30, 1942 ATHENS, TENN.
82-	10	BASS, KEVIN CHARLES	1971 BYERS DR - MENLO PARK CA 94025
61-	8	BASS, NORMAN DELANEY	8814 THIRD AVE - INGLEWOOD CA 90305
77-	8	BASS, RANDY WILLIAM	RR 3 BOX 23C - LAWTON OK 73501
39-	6	BASS, RICHARD WILLIAM	P.O. BOX 291 - GREENWOOD FL 32443
18-	1	BASS, WILLIAM CAPERS 'DOC'	D. JANUARY 12, 1970 MACON, GA.
13-	5	BASSLER, JOHN LANDIS	D. JUNE 29, 1979 SANTA MONICA, CALIF.
23-	7	BATCHELDER, JOSEPH EDMUND	10 MAGNOLIA HOUSE - BEVERLY MA 01915
63-	7	BATEMAN, JOHN ALVIN	903 N. GARFIELD - SAND SPRING OK 74063
69-	7	BATES, CHARLES RICHARD 'DICK'	8601 E BONNIE ROSE AVE - SCOTTSDALE AZ 85253

BAUTA

27-	8	BATES, CHARLES WILLIAM	OLD ADD: 1257 SW COLLEGE BLVD - TOPEKA KS 66616
70-	6	BATES, DELBERT OAKLEY	8336 133RD NE - REDMOND WA 98052
39-	7	BATES, HUBERT EDGAR 'BUD'	3503 LINDEN AVE - LONG BEACH CA 90807
13-	6	BATES, RAYMOND	D. AUGUST 15, 1970 TUCSON, ARIZ.
73-	11	BATISTA, RAFAEL	BOX 15 - SAN PEDRO DE MACORIS DOM. REP.
16-	3	BATSCH, WILLIAM MCKINLEY	D. DECEMBER 31, 1963 CANTON, O.
12-	12	BATTEN, GEORGE BERNARD	D. AUGUST 4, 1972 NEW PORT RICHEY, FLA.
55-	8	BATTEY, EARL JESSE	%ALLEN, 270 JOY ST - BROOKLYN NY 11201
27-	9	BATTLE, JAMES MILTON	D. SEPTEMBER 30, 1965 CHICO, CAL.
76-	13	BATTON, CHRISTOPHER SEAN	6109 W 77TH ST - LOS ANGELES CA 90045
47-	10	BATTS, MATTHEW DANIEL	838 N ALLYSON - BATON ROUGE LA 70815
48-	8	BAUER, HENRY ALBERT	12705 W 108TH ST - OVERLAND PARK KS 66210
18-	2	BAUER, LOUIS WALTER	D. FEBRUARY 4, 1979 POMONA, N. J.
36-	7	BAUERS, RUSSELL LEE	1924 GARDNER RD-WESTCHESTER IL 60156
11-	11	BAUMANN, CHARLES JOHN 'PADDY'	D. NOVEMBER 20, 1969 INDIANAPOLIS, IND.
55-	9	BAUMANN, FRANK MATTHEW	7712 SUNRAY LN - ST LOUIS MO 63123
49-	4	BAUMER, JAMES SLOAN	303 PAOLI WOODS - PAOLI PA 19301
12-	13	BAUMGARDNER, GEORGE WASHINGTON	D. DECEMBER 13, 1970 BARBOURSVILLE, W. VA.
78-	6	BAUMGARTEN, ROSS	1020 BLUFF RD - GLENCOE IL 60022
20-	4	BAUMGARTNER, HARRY E.	D. DECEMBER 3, 1930 AUGUSTA, GA.
53-	9	BAUMGARTNER, JOHN EDWARD	705 COMER DR - BIRMINGHAM AL 35216
14-	13	BAUMGARTNER, STANWOOD FULTON	D. OCTOBER 4, 1955 PHILADELPHIA, PA.
47-	11	BAUMHOLTZ, FRANK CONRAD	4327 JENNINGS RD - CLEVELAND OH 44109
60-	7	BAUTA, EDUARDO	1087 E. JERSEY ST - ELIZABETH NJ 07201

BAXES

```
59-  5  BAXES, DIMITRIOS SPEROS 'JIM'        6211 HUNTLEY AVE - GARDEN GROVE CA 92645
56-  6  BAXES, MICHAEL                        303 WICKMAN DR - MILL VALLEY CA 94941
70-  7  BAYLOR, DONALD EDWARD                 250 TRUMAN,, BOX 476 - CRESSKILL NJ 07626
19-  6  BAYNE, WILLIAM LEAR                   D. MAY 27, 1981 ST. LOUIS, MO.
13-  7  BEALL, JOHN WOOLF                     D. JUNE 13, 1926 BELTSVILLE, MD.
75- 14  BEALL, ROBERT BROOKS                  513 BIRCHWOOD RD - HILLSBORO OR 97123
24-  5  BEALL, WALTER ESAU                    D. JANUARY 28, 1959 SUITLAND, MD.
56-  7  BEAMON, CHARLES ALONZO                1717 WOODLAND AVE #3-EAST PALO ALTO CA 94303
78-  7  BEAMON, CHARLES ALONZO                421 OAKLAND AVE #6 - OAKLAND CA 94611
30-  2  BEAN, BELVEDORE BENTON                RR 2 BOX 166 - COMANCHE TX 76442
84-  5  BEANE, WILLIAM LAMAR                  1720 KNOLL FIELD WAY - ENCINITAS CA 92024
80-  7  BEARD, CHARLES DAVID 'DAVE'           3467 REEVES ST - CHAMBLEE GA 30341
48-  9  BEARD, CRAMER THEODORE 'TED'          10517 STELOR CT - INDIANAPOLIS IN 46256
74-  8  BEARD, MICHAEL RICHARD                6200 DENHAM DR - LITTLE ROCK AR 72004
54-  6  BEARD, RALPH WILLIAM                  1367 BERKSHIRE DR - WEST PALM BEACH FL 33406
47- 12  BEARDEN, HENRY EUGENE 'GENE'          BOX 176 - HELENA AR 72342
76- 14  BEARE, GARY RAY                       2752 ELYSSEE ST - SAN DIEGO CA 92123
```

BELLIARD

```
63-  8  BEARNARTH, LAWRENCE DONALD            85-18 143RD LN - SEMINOLE FL 33542
77-  9  BEASLEY, LEWIS PAIGE 'TEX'            RR 1 BOX 65 - BOWLING GREEN VA 22427
78-  8  BEATTIE, JAMES LOUIS                  9610 SE 34TH ST - MERCER ISLAND WA 98040
14- 14  BEATTY, DESMOND A                     D. OCTOBER 6, 1969 NORWAY, ME.
63-  9  BEAUCHAMP, JAMES EDWARD               BOX 1790 - PHENIX CITY AL 36867
41-  6  BEAZLEY, JOHN ANDREW                  4304 ST. ANDREWS RD - BOYNTON BEACH FL 33436
26-  6  BECK, CLYDE EUGENE                    BOX 147 - RANDSBURG CA 93554
14- 15  BECK, GEORGE F.                       1915 ADD: 22ND AVE- MOLINE ILL
65-  6  BECK, RICHARD HENRY                   2151 HOXIE - RICHLAND WA 99352
24-  6  BECK, WALTER WILLIAM 'BOOM'BOOM'      1675 NORTH MAPLE - DECATUR IL 62526
13-  8  BECK, ZINN BERTRAM                    D. MARCH 19, 1981 WEST PALM BEACH, FLA.
11- 12  BECKER, CHARLES S.                    D. JULY 30, 1928 WASHINGTON, D.C.
43-  7  BECKER, HEINZ REINHARD                302 CLARENDON DR-DALLAS TX 75208
36-  8  BECKER, JOSEPH EDWARD                 2800 21ST PLACE - VERO BEACH FL 32960
15- 10  BECKER, MARTIN HENRY                  D. SEPTEMBER 25, 1957 CINCINNATI, O.
65-  7  BECKERT, GLENN ALFRED                 870 VIRGINA LAKE CT - PALATINE IL 60067
27- 10  BECKMAN, JAMES JOSEPH                 9763 COOPER LANE - CINCINNATI OH 45242
39-  8  BECKMANN, WILLIAM ALOYSIUS            111 FIESTA CIR-CREVE COEUR MO 63141
79-  8  BECKWITH, THOMAS JOSEPH 'JOE'         2057 COUNTRY SQUIRE RD - AUBURN AL 36830
55- 10  BECQUER, JULIO VELLEGAS               829 VINCENT AVE - MINNEAPOLIS MN 55411
62-  9  BEDELL, HOWARD WILLIAM                1187 CRESTWOOD DR - POTTSTOWN PA 19464
25-  6  BEDFORD, JAMES ELDRED                 D. JUNE 27, 1962 POUGHKEEPSIE, N. Y.
22-  3  BEDGOOD, PHILIP BURLETTE              D. NOVEMBER 8, 1927 FORT PIERCE, FLA.
12- 14  BEDIENT, HUGH CARPENTER               D. JULY 21, 1965 JAMESTOWN, N.Y.
30-  3  BEDNAR, ANDREW JACKSON                D. NOVEMBER 26, 1937 GRAHAM, TEX,
81-  8  BEDROSIAN, STEPHEN WAYNE              1923 MT. PARAN RD NW - ATLANTA GA 30327
44-  6  BEELER, JOSEPH SAM 'JODIE'            3709 NABHOLTZ - MESQUITE TX 75150
68-  4  BEENE, FREDERICK RAY                  BOX 143 - OAKHURST TX 77359
83-  9  BEENE, RAMON ANDREW 'ANDY'            7502 PINETEX DR - HUMBLE TX 77396
48- 10  BEERS, CLARENCE SCOTT                 4701 ANDERSON RD #30 - HOUSTON TX 77045
38-  7  BEGGS, JOSEPH STANLEY                 D. JULY 19, 1983 INDIANAPOLIS, IND.
24-  7  BEGLEY, JAMES LAWRENCE                D. FEBRUARY 22, 1957 SAN FRANCISCO, CAL.
21-  3  BEHAN, CHARLES FREDERICK 'PETIE'      D. JANUARY 21, 1957 BRADFORD, PA.
83- 10  BEHENNA, RICHARD KIPP                 7510 FAWNBROOK DR - HILLSBOROUGH NC 27278
70-  8  BEHNEY, MELVIN BRIAN                  241 GROVE AVE - VERONA NJ 07042
46-  8  BEHRMAN, HENRY BERNARD                1933 WOODBINE ST - RIDGEWOOD NY 11385
34-  4  BEJMA, ALOYSIUS FRANK 'OLLIE'         4510 W WASHINGTON #107 - SOUTH BEND IN 46619
65-  8  BELANGER, MARK HENRY                  2028 POT SPRING RD - TIMONIUM MD 21093
50-  7  BELARDI, CARROLL WAYNE                1467 PHANTOM AVE - SAN JOSE CA 95125
62- 10  BELINSKY, ROBERT 'BO'                 53567 KAM HWY #111 - HAUULA HI 96717
72-  7  BELL, DAVID GUS 'BUDDY'               6485 HUNTERS TRAIL - CINCINNATI OH 45243
50-  8  BELL, DAVID RUSSELL 'GUS'             MINUTEMAN, 1010 RACE ST - CINCINNATI OH 45202
85-  3  BELL, ERIC ALVIN                      1601 COUCHMAN LANE - MODESTO CA 95355
39-  9  BELL, FERN LEE                        1975 ADD: 122 W 59TH PL - LOS ANGELES CA
58-  9  BELL, GARY                            OLD ADD: 6001 E. LARKSPUR DR - SCOTTSDALE AZ 85254
24-  8  BELL, HERMAN S. 'HI'                  D. JUNE 7, 1949 GLENDALE, CAL.
71-  9  BELL, JERRY HOUSTON                   RR 3 BOX 609 - MOUNT JULIET TN 37122
81-  9  BELL, JORGE ANTONIO                   BARIO REST. CLE T #179-SAN PEDRO DE MACORIS DOM. REP.
76- 15  BELL, KEVIN ROBERT                    OLD ADD: ALGONQUIN - ROLLING MEADOWS IL
23-  8  BELL, LESTER ROWLAND                  D. NOVEMBER 26, 1985 HARRISBURG, PA.
12- 15  BELL, RALPH A.                        D. OCTOBER 18, 1959 BURLINGTON, IA.
35-  3  BELL, ROY CHESTER 'BEAU'              D. SEPTEMBER 14, 1977 COLLEGE STATION, TEXAS
52-  6  BELL, WILLIAM SAMUEL                  D. OCTOBER 11, 1962 DURHAM, N. C.
57-  6  BELLA, JOHN 'ZEKE'                    24 TAYLOR DR - COS COB CT 06807
82- 11  BELLIARD, RAFAEL LEONIDAS             DOMINGO CASTELLANO 17,GURABITO-SANTIAGO DOMINICAN REP.
```

75-	15	BELLOIR, ROBERT EDWARD	3246 WEST MANOR LN SW - ATLANTA GA 30311
67-	4	BENCH, JOHN LEE	BOX 2486 - CINCINNATI OH 45201
78-	9	BENEDICT, BRUCE EDWIN	2840 PEACHTREE RD NE #508 - ATLANTA GA 30305
31-	7	BENES, JOSEPH ANTHONY	D. MARCH 7, 1975 ELMHURST N. Y.
25-	7	BENGE, RAYMOND ADELPHIA	RR1 BOX 134A - JEWETT TX 75846
23-	9	BENGOUGH, BERNARD OLIVER	D. DECEMBER 22, 1968 PHILADELPHIA, PA.
71-	10	BENIQUEZ, JUAN JOSE	CALLE 99A BLK.87 #12 - CAROLINA PR 00630
39-	10	BENJAMIN, ALFRED STANLEY 'STAN'	46 ALLEN ST - GREENFIELD MA 01301
14-	16	BENN, HOMER OMER	D. JUNE 4, 1967 MENDOTA, WIS.
64-	4	BENNETT, DAVID HANS	408 FAIRCHILD ST - YREKA CA 96097
62-	11	BENNETT, DENNIS JOHN	630 N 5TH - KLAMATH FALLS OR 97601
27-	11	BENNETT, FRANCIS ALLEN	D. MARCH 18, 1966 WILMINGTON, DEL.
23-	10	BENNETT, HERSCHELL EMMETT	D. SEPTEMBER 9, 1964 SPRINGFIELD, MO.
28-	6	BENNETT, JAMES FRED	D. MAY 12, 1957 ATKINS, ARK.
18-	3	BENNETT, JOSEPH HARLEY	D. NOVEMBER 21, 1957 JOEL, MO.
23-	11	BENNETT, JOSEPH ROSENBLUM	CONTEMPORARY DRIVE - DANBURY CT 06811
34-	5	BENSON, ALLEN WILBERT	HURLEY SD 57036
43-	8	BENSON, VERNON ADAIR	BOX 127-GRANITE QUARRY NC 28072
13-	9	BENTLEY, JOHN NEEDLES	D. OCTOBER 24, 1969 OLNEY, MD.
78-	10	BENTON, ALFRED LEE 'BUTCH'	OLD ADD: 895 VIL LAKES#102 - ST PETERSBURG FL
34-	6	BENTON, JOHN ALTON 'AL'	D. APRIL 14, 1968 LYNWOOD, CAL.
10-	7	BENTON, JOHN CLEBON 'RUBE'	D. DECEMBER 12, 1937 DOTHAN, ALA.
23-	12	BENTON, LAWRENCE JAMES	D. APRIL 3, 1953 CINCINNATI, O.
22-	4	BENTON, SIDNEY WRIGHT	D. MARCH 8, 1977 FAYETTEVILLE, ARK.
22-	5	BENTON, STANLEY	D. JUNE 7, 1984 DALLAS, TEXAS
11-	13	BENZ, JOSEPH LOUIS	D. APRIL 23, 1957 CHICAGO, ILL.
12-	16	BERAN, DENNIS MARTIN	D. APRIL 28, 1943 BOSTON, MASS.
39-	11	BERARDINO, JOHN	1719 AMBASSADOR AVE - BEVERLY HILLS CA 90210
54-	7	BERBERET, LOUIS JOSEPH	4025 MARDON AVE - LAS VEGAS NV 89118
78-	11	BERENGUER, JUAN BAUTISTA	CALLE MALAMBO - AGUADUCLE PAN.
80-	8	BERENYI, BRUCE MICHAEL	BOX 133 - SHERWOOD OH 43556
23-	13	BERG, MORRIS 'MOE'	D. MAY 29, 1972 BELLEVILLE, N. J.
44-	7	BERGAMO, AUGUST SAMUEL	D. AUGUST 19, 1974 GROSSE POINTE CITY, MICH.
14-	17	BERGER, CLARENCE EDWARD	D. JUNE 30, 1959 WASHINGTON, D. C.
22-	6	BERGER, JOHN HENNE	D. MAY 7, 1979 LAKE CHARLES, LA.
13-	10	BERGER, JOSEPH AUGUST	D. MARCH 5, 1956 ROCK ISLAND, ILL.
32-	3	BERGER, LOUIS WILLIAM 'BOZE'	11914 RENWOOD LN - ROCKVILLE MD 20852
30-	4	BERGER, WALTER ANTONE	124 21ST ST - MANHATTAN BCH CA 90266
11-	14	BERGHAMMER, MARTIN ANDREW	D. DECEMBER 21, 1957 PITTSBURGH, PA.
16-	4	BERGMAN, ALFRED HENRY	D. JUNE 21, 1961 FORT WAYNE, IND.
75-	16	BERGMAN, DAVID BRUCE	OLD ADD: 112 PEARTREE LN - ARLINGTON HEIGHTS IL 60004
24-	9	BERLY, JOHN CHAMBERS	D. JUNE 26, 1977 HOUSTON, TEX.
18-	4	BERMAN, ROBERT LEON	105-00 SHORE FRONT PKWY-ROCKAWAY PK NY 11694
77-	10	BERNAL, VICTOR HUGO	4632 ABNER ST - LOS ANGELES CA 90032
78-	12	BERNARD, DWIGHT VERN	RURAL ROUTE 1 - BELLE RIVE IL 62810
79-	9	BERNAZARD, ANTONIO (GARCIA)	SANTA AV D-25,URB SANTA ELVIRA-CAGUAS PR00625
76-	16	BERNHARDT, JUAN RAMON	PROL. SERGIO A. BERA #13-SAN PEDRO DE MACORIS DOM REP.
18-	5	BERNHARDT, WALTER JACOB	D. JULY 26, 1958 WATERTOWN, N. Y.
53-	10	BERNIER, CARLOS RODRIGUEZ	3D5 JARDINER SANTO DOMINGO - JUANA DIAZ PR 00665
48-	11	BERO, JOHN GEORGE	D. MAY 11, 1985 GARDENA, CALIF.
77-	11	BERRA, DALE ANTHONY	19 HIGHLAND AVE - MONTCLAIR NJ 07042
46-	9	BERRA, LAWRENCE PETER 'YOGI'	19 HIGHLAND AVE - MONTCLAIR NJ 07042
34-	7	BERRES, RAYMOND	111 HAWTHORNE RD - TWIN LAKES WI 53181
62-	12	BERRY, ALLEN KENNETH 'KEN'	3421 BRIARWOOD LN - TOPEKA KS 66611

```
25-  8 BERRY, CHARLES FRANCIS              D. SEPTEMBER 6, 1972 EVANSTON, ILL.
48- 12 BERRY, CORNELIUS JOHN 'CONNIE'      407 INKSTER AVE - KALAMAZOO MI 49001
42-  6 BERRY, JONAS ARTHUR                 D. SEPTEMBER 27, 1958 ANAHEIM, CAL.
21-  4 BERRY, JOSEPH HOWARD JR             D. APRIL 29, 1976 PHILADELPHIA, PA.
64-  5 BERTAINA, FRANK LOUIS               4000 MONTGOMERY DR - SANTA ROSA CA 95405
60-  8 BERTELL, RICHARD GEORGE             25332 REMESA DR - MISSION VIEJO CA 92675
53- 11 BERTOIA, RENO PETER                 3400 ERSKINE ST #906 - WINDSOR ONTARIO CAN.
36-  9 BERTRAND, ROMAN MATHIAS             1909 MOUNT HOOD - THE DALLES OR 97058
56-  8 BESANA, FREDERICK CYRIL             222 DIAMOND OAKS DR - ROSEVILLE CA 95678
40-  2 BESSE, HERMAN                       D. AUGUST 13, 1972 LOS ANGELES, CAL.
```

```
55- 11 BESSENT, FRED DONALD 'DON'          OLD ADD: 1230 LORENTO RD - JACKSONVILLE FL 32211
83- 11 BEST, KARL JOHN                     11132 SE 129TH - KIRKLAND WA 98034
78- 13 BESWICK, JAMES WILLIAM              12519 DOMINGO RD NE - ALBUQUERQUE NM 87123
10-  8 BETCHER, FRANKLIN LYLE              D. NOVEMBER 27, 1981 WYNNEWOOD, PA.
64-  6 BETHEA, WILLIAM LAMAR               OLD ADD: RR 5 BOX 58F - AUSTIN TX 78704
65-  9 BETHKE, JAMES CHARLES               419 N OAKLEY ST - KANSAS CITY MO 64123
28-  7 BETTENCOURT, LAWRENCE JOSEPH        D. SEPTEMBER 15, 1978 NEW ORLEANS, LA.
84-  6 BETTENDORF, JEFFREY ALLEN           528 NORTH LUPINE - LOMPOC CA 93446
20-  5 BETTS, WALTER MARTIN 'HUCK'         BOX 326 - MILLSBORO DE 19966
14- 18 BETZEL, CHRISTIAN FREDERICK ALBERT  D. FEBRUARY 7, 1965 WEST HOLLYWOOD, FLA
71- 11 BEVACQUA, KURT ANTHONY              6618 GRULLA ST - CARLSBAD CA 92008
52-  7 BEVAN, HAROLD JOSEPH                D. OCTOBER 5, 1968 NEW ORLEANS, LA.
44-  8 BEVENS, FLOYD CLIFFORD 'BILL'       5067 8TH NE - SALEM OR 97303
42-  7 BEVIL, LOUIS EUGENE                 D. FEBRUARY 1, 1973 DIXON, ILL.
17-  6 BEZDEK, HUGH FRANCIS                D. SEPTEMBER 19, 1952 ATLANTIC CITY, N.J.
82- 12 BIANCALANA, ROLAND AMERICO 'BUDDY'  4120 SAN SAVERA DR N - JACKSONVILLE FL 32217
75- 17 BIANCO, THOMAS ANTHONY              OLD ADD: 4 CURVEWOOD RD - PORT WASHINGTON NY 11050
49-  5 BIASATTI, HENRY ARCADO              9024 ALLEN RD - ALLEN PARK MI 48101
72-  8 BIBBY, JAMES BLAIR                  RR 6 BOX 402 - MADISON HEIGHTS VA 24572
48- 13 BICKFORD, VERNON EDGELL             D. MAY 8, 1960 RICHMOND, VA.
48- 14 BICKNELL, CHARLES STEPHEN           6981 FORDS STATION RD - GERMANTOWN TN 38138
84-  7 BIELECKI, MICHAEL JOSEPH            1932 EASTFIELD RD - BALTIMORE MD 21222
20-  6 BIEMILLER, HARRY LEE                D. MAY 25, 1965 ORLANDO, FLA.
16-  5 BIGBEE, CARSON LEE                  D. OCTOBER 17, 1964 PORTLAND, ORE.
20-  7 BIGBEE, LYLE RANDOLPH               D. AUGUST 5, 1942 PORTLAND, ORE.
29-  8 BIGELOW, ELLIOT ALLARDICE           D. AUGUST 10, 1933 TAMPA, FLA.
32-  4 BIGGS, CHARLES ORVAL                D. MAY 24, 1954 FRENCH LICK, IND.
70-  9 BIITTNER, LARRY DAVID               169 CRESTVIEW CT - BARRINGTON IL 60010
49-  6 BILBREY, JAMES MELVIN               D. DECEMBER 26, 1985 TOLEDO, O.
37-  9 BILDILLI, EMIL                      D. SEPTEMBER 16, 1946 HARTFORD CITY, IND.
49-  1 BILKO, STEPHEN THOMAS               D. MARCH 7, 1978 WILKES-BARRE, PA.
83- 12 BILLARDELLO, DANN JAMES             810 CLUB DRIVE - PALM BEACH GARDENS FL 33418
68-  5 BILLINGHAM, JOHN EUGENE             359 ELKHORN CT - WINTER PARK FL 32789
27- 12 BILLINGS, HASKELL CLARK             D. DECEMBER 26, 1983 GREENBRAE, CALIF.
13- 11 BILLINGS, JOHN AUGUSTUS 'JOSH'      D. DECEMBER 30, 1981 SANTA MONICA, CALIF.
68-  6 BILLINGS, RICHARD ARLIN             1917 CREEKWOOD DR - ARLINGTON TX 76010
44-  9 BINKS, GEORGE EUGENE                4803 BELMONT RD - DOWNERS GROVE IL 60515
```

44- 10 BIRAS, STEPHEN ALEXANDER	D. APRIL 21, 1965 ST. LOUIS, MO.
73- 12 BIRD, JAMES DOUGLAS 'DOUG'	OLD ADD: 5542-3 MALT DR - FT MYERS FL
21- 5 BIRD, JAMES EDWARD 'RED'	D. MARCH 23, 1972 MURFREESBORO, ARK.
33- 4 BIRKOFER, RALPH JOSEPH	D. MARCH 16, 1971 CINCINNATI, O.
55- 12 BIRRER, WERNER JOSEPH 'BABE'	115 RANCH TRAIL W - WILLIAMSVILLE NY 14221
85- 4 BIRTSAS, TIMOTHY DEAN	43 ROBERTSON COURT - CLARKSTON MI 48016
42- 8 BISCAN, FRANK STEPHEN	D. MAY 22, 1959 ST. LOUIS, MO.
25- 9 BISCHOFF, JOHN GEORGE	D. DECEMBER 28, 1981 GRANITE CITY, ILL.
52- 8 BISHOP, CHARLES TULLER	2705 ADDISON DR - DORAVILLE GA 30040
23- 14 BISHOP, JAMES MORTON	D. SEPTEMBER 20, 1973 MEXICO, MO.
14- 19 BISHOP, LLOYD CLIFTON	D. JUNE 17, 1968 WICHITA, KAN.
24- 10 BISHOP, MAX FREDERICK	D. FEBRUARY 4, 1962 WAYNESBORO, PA.
83- 13 BISHOP, MICHAEL DAVID	3119 HAMPTON DR - SANTA MARIA CA 93454
21- 6 BISHOP, WILLIAM HENRY	D. FEBRUARY 14, 1956 ST. JOSEPH, MO.
12- 17 BISLAND, RIVINGTON MARTIN	D. JANUARY 11, 1973 SALZBURG, AUSTRIA
28- 8 BISSONETTE, DELPHIA LOUIS	D. JUNE 9, 1972 AUGUSTA, ME.
42- 9 BITHORN, HIRAM GABRIEL	D. JANUARY 1, 1952 EL MANTE, MEX.
35- 4 BIVIN, JAMES NATHANIEL	D. NOVEMBER 7, 1982 PUEBLO, COLO.
83- 14 BJORKMAN, GEORGE ANTON	749 E. HARVARD - ONTARIO CA 91764
14- 20 BLACK, DAVID	D. OCTOBER 27, 1936 PITTSBURGH, PA.
43- 9 BLACK, DONALD PAUL	D. APRIL 21, 1959 CUYAHOGA FALLS, O.
81- 10 BLACK, HARRY RALSTON 'BUD'	75-707 HWY 111 #C-6 - PALM DESERT CA 92260
11- 15 BLACK, JOHN FALCNOR	D. MARCH 19, 1962 RUTHERFORD, N. J.
24- 11 BLACK, JOHN WILLIAM 'BILL'	D. JANUARY 14, 1968 PHILADELPHIA, PA.
52- 9 BLACK, JOSEPH	1904 GREYHOUND TOWERS - PHOENIX AZ 85077
52- 10 BLACK, WILLIAM CARROLL	1233 MT OLIVE AVE - UNIVERSITY CITY MO 63130
62- 13 BLACKABY, ETHAN ALLEN	2308 E ORANGEWOOD - PHOENIX AZ 85020
12- 18 BLACKBURN, EARL STUART	D. AUGUST 4, 1966 MANSFIELD, O.
15- 11 BLACKBURN, FOSTER EDWIN 'BABE'	D. MARCH 9, 1984 NEWPORT RICHEY, FLA.
48- 15 BLACKBURN, JAMES RAY	D. OCTOBER 26, 1969 CINCINNATI, O.
58- 10 BLACKBURN, RONALD HAMILTON	RR 10 BOX 67 - MORGANTON NC 28655
10- 9 BLACKBURNE, RUSSELL AUBREY 'LENA'	D. FEBRUARY 29, 1968 RIVERSIDE, N. J.
28- 9 BLACKERBY, GEORGE FRANKLIN	2527 FAIN - WICHITA FALLS TX 76308
42- 10 BLACKWELL, EWELL	84 ULOQUE CT - BREVARD NC 28712
17- 8 BLACKWELL, FREDRICK WILLIAM	D. DECEMBER 8, 1975 MORGANTOWN, KY.
74- 9 BLACKWELL, TIMOTHY P	1933 MAPLEBROOK - EL CAJON CA 92021
22- 7 BLADES, FRANCIS RAYMOND	D. MAY 18, 1979 LINCOLN, ILL.
69- 8 BLADT, RICHARD ALAN	620 SOUTH WATER ST - SILVERTON OR 97381
25- 10 BLAEHOLDER, GEORGE FRANKLIN	D. DECEMBER 29, 1947 GARDEN GROVE, CALIF.
41- 7 BLAEMIRE, RAE BERTRUM	D. DECEMBER 23, 1975 CHAMPAIGN, ILL.
29- 9 BLAIR, CLARENCE VICK	D. JULY 1, 1982 TEXARKANA, TEX.
74- 10 BLAIR, DENNIS HERMAN	612 FAIRWAY - REDLANDS CA 92373
42- 11 BLAIR, LOUIS NATHAN 'BUDDY'	700 FILHOIL - MONROE LA 71203
64- 7 BLAIR, PAUL L. D.	DAMCO, 307 5TH AVE, 6TH FLOOR - NEW YORK NY 10016
51- 2 BLAKE, EDWARD JAMES	20 VIEUX CARRE DR - EAST ST LOUIS IL 62203
20- 8 BLAKE, JOHN FREDERICK 'SHERIFF'	D. OCTOBER 31, 1982 BECKLEY, W. VA.
34- 8 BLAKELY, LINCOLN HOWARD	D. SEPTEMBER 28, 1976 OAKLAND, CALIF.

55- 13 BLANCHARD, JOHN EDWIN	15541 LARKIN DR - MINNETONKA MN 55343
35- 5 BLANCHE, PROSPER ALBERT 'AL'	81 EVERETT ST - ARLINGTON MA 02174
72- 9 BLANCO, DAMASO	OLD ADD: 659 CATAMARAN ST #2 - FOSTER CITY CA
65- 10 BLANCO, GILBERT HENRY	360 E MONTE VISTA RD - PHOENIX AZ 85004
70- 10 BLANCO, OSVALDO CARLOS	OLD ADD: DE LOZADA B1 E16,SAN JOSE DE AVILAVZ
10- 10 BLANDING, FRED JAMES	D. JULY 16, 1950 SALEM, VA.
22- 8 BLANKENSHIP, HOMER	D. JUNE 22, 1974 LONGVIEW, TEX.
22- 9 BLANKENSHIP, THEODORE	D. JANUARY 14, 1945 ATOKA, OKLA.
72- 10 BLANKS, LARVELL	408 WATERS AVE - DEL RIO TX 78840
34- 9 BLANTON, DARRELL ELIJAH 'CY'	D. SEPTEMBER 13, 1945 NORMAN, OKLA.
55- 14 BLASINGAME, DONALD LEE	9795 EAST MISSION LN - SCOTTSDALE AZ 85258
63- 10 BLASINGAME, WADE ALLEN	5207 RIVERHILL RD NE - MARIETTA GA 30067
64- 8 BLASS, STEPHEN ROBERT	1756 QUIGG DR - PITTSBURGH PA 15241
71- 12 BLATERIC, STEPHEN LAWRENCE	1662 S UTICA - DENVER CO 80219
48- 16 BLATNIK, JOHN LOUIS	CHERMONT RD, BOX 427 - LANSING OH 43934
42- 12 BLATTNER, ROBERT GARNETT	RR 73 BOX 205 - LAKE OZARK MO 65049
59- 6 BLAYLOCK, GARY NELSON	BOX 395 - MALDEN MO 63860
50- 9 BLAYLOCK, MARVIN EDWARD	2200 ANDOVER CT #602 - LITTLE ROCK AR 72207
56- 9 BLAYLOCK, ROBERT EDWARD	RR 2 BOX 460 - MULDROW OK 74948
65- 11 BLEFARY, CURTIS LEROY	1850 SOUTH OCEAN DR - FORT LAUDERDALE FL 33316
60- 9 BLEMKER, RAYMOND 'BUDDY'	2363 DUNDEE DR - HENDERSON KY 42420
72- 11 BLESSITT, ISAIAH 'IKE'	19712 ANGLIN - DETROIT MI 48234
23- 15 BLETHEN, CLARENCE WALDO	D. APRIL 11, 1973 FREDERICK, MD.
42- 13 BLOCK, SEYMOUR 'CY'	4 OLDFIELD LN-LAKESUCCESS NY 11020
85- 5 BLOCKER, TERRY FENNELL	823 PINEY WOODS ROAD - COLUMBIA SC 29210

BLOMBERG   BONNELL

69- 9 BLOMBERG, RONALD MARK	11660 MOUNTAIN LAUREL DR - ROSWELL GA 30075
37- 10 BLOODWORTH, JAMES HENRY	BOX 232-APALACHICOLA FL 32320
63- 11 BLOOMFIELD, CLYDE STALCUP 'BUD'	TALE OF THE TROUT,W. NEW HOPE RD - ROGERS AR 72756
24- 12 BLOTT, JACK LEONARD	D. JUNE 11, 1964 ANN ARBOR, MICH.
21- 7 BLUE, LUZERNE ATWELL	D. JULY 28, 1958 ALEXANDRIA, VA.
69- 10 BLUE, VIDA ROCHELLE	P.O. BOX 14438 - OAKLAND CA 94614
22- 10 BLUEGE, OSWALD LOUIS	D. OCTOBER 15, 1985 EDINA, MINN.
32- 5 BLUEGE, OTTO ADAM	D. JUNE 28, 1977 CHICAGO, ILL.
14- 21 BLUEJACKET, JAMES	D. MARCH 26, 1947 PEKIN, ILL.
18- 6 BLUHM, HARVEY FRED 'RED'	D. MAY 7, 1952 FLINT, MICH.
22- 11 BLUME, CLINTON WILLIS	D. JUNE 12, 1973 ISLIP, N. Y.
70- 11 BLYLEVEN, RIKALBERT BERT	18992 CANYON DR - VILLA PARK CA 92667
53- 12 BLYZKA, MICHAEL JOHN	1615 EAST 13TH ST #1 - CHEYENNE WY 82001
60- 10 BOAK, CHESTER ROBERT "CHET"	D. NOVEMBER 28, 1983 EMPORIUM, PA.
13- 12 BOARDMAN, CHARLES LOUIS	D. AUGUST 10, 1968 SACRAMENTO, CALIF.
68- 7 BOBB, MARK RANDALL 'RANDY'	D. JUNE 13, 1982 CARNELIAN BAY, CALIF.
63- 12 BOCCABELLA, JOHN DOMINIC	1035 LEA DR - SAN RAFAEL CA 94903
33- 5 BOCEK, MILTON FRANK	2342 S 61ST CT - CICERO IL 60650
74- 11 BOCHTE, BRUCE ANTON	6475 SOUTH MAXWELTON RD - CLINTON WA 98236
78- 14 BOCHY, BRUCE DOUGLAS	115 E AVENUE B - MELBOURNE FL 32901
46- 10 BOCKMAN, JOSEPH EDWARD 'EDDIE'	1400 MILBRAE AVE #2 - MILLBRAE CA 94030
80- 9 BODDICKER, MICHAEL JAMES	BOX 21 - NORWAY IA 52318
11- 16 BODIE, FRANK STEPHAN 'PING'	D. DECEMBER 12, 1961 SAN FRANCISCO, CALIF.
17- 9 BOECKEL, NORMAN DOXIE	D. FEBRUARY 16, 1924 TORREY PINES, CALIF.
12- 19 BOEHLER, GEORGE HENRY	D. JUNE 23, 1958 LAWRENCEBURG, IND.
12- 20 BOEHLING, JOHN JOSEPH	D. SEPTEMBER 8, 1941 RICHMOND, VA.
67- 5 BOEHMER, LEONARD JOSEPH	3570 HIGHWAY P - WENTZVILLE MO 63385
32- 6 BOERNER, LAWRENCE HYER	D. OCTOBER 16, 1969 STAUNTON, VA.
85- 6 BOEVER, JOSEPH MARTIN	5141 TOWNE SOUTH ROAD - ST.LOUIS MO 63128
20- 9 BOGART, JOHN RENZIE	580 W WASHINGTON ST - GENEVA NY 14456
82- 13 BOGENER, TERRY WAYNE	411 MCCABE - PALMYRAMO 63461
28- 10 BOGGS, RAYMOND JOSEPH	1135 HILL AVE - GRAND JUNCTION CO 81501
76- 17 BOGGS, THOMAS WINSTON	8805 POINT WEST - AUSTIN TX 78759
82- 14 BOGGS, WADE ANTHONY	599 MARMORA AVE - TAMPA FL 33606
68- 8 BOGLE, WARREN FREDERICK	11605 SW 103RD AVE - MIAMI FL 33156
13- 13 BOHEN, LEO IGNATIUS 'PAT'	D. APRIL 8, 1942 NAPA, CALIF.
16- 6 BOHNE, SAMUEL ARTHUR	D. MAY 23, 1977 PALO ALTO, CALIF.
82- 15 BOHNET, JOHN KELLY	224 PANORAMA DR - BENICIA CA 94510
74- 12 BOISCLAIR, BRUCE ARMAND	29064 W. SADDLE BROOK - AGOURA CA 91301
78- 15 BOITANO, DANNY JON	15400 WINCHESTER BLVD #43-LOS GATOS CA 95030
51- 3 BOKELMANN, RICHARD WERNER	629 N BELMONT AV - ARLINGTON HEIGHTS IL 60004
33- 6 BOKEN, ROBERT ANTHONY	4011 TACOMA - LAS VEGAS NV 89121
36- 10 BOKINA, JOSEPH	1901 E 25TH ST-CHATTANOOGA TN 37404
15- 12 BOLAND, BERNARD ANTHONY	D. SEPTEMBER 12, 1973 DETROIT, MICH.
34- 10 BOLAND, EDWARD JOHN	1655 S. HIGHLAND AVE #J196 - CLEARWATER FL 33516
14- 22 BOLD, CHARLES DICKENS	D. JULY 29, 1978 CHELSEA, MASS.
19- 7 BOLDEN, WILLIAM HORACE	D. DECEMBER 8, 1966 JEFFERSON CITY, TENN.
26- 7 BOLEN, STEWART O'NEAL	D. AUGUST 30, 1969 JACKSON, ALA.
62- 14 BOLES, CARL THEODORE	18020 CASTLEWOOD CT - HAYWARD CA 94541
27- 13 BOLEY, JOHN PETER 'JOE'	D. DECEMBER 30, 1962 MAHANOY CITY, PA.
50- 10 BOLGER, JAMES CYRIL	5524 SIDNEY RD - CINCINNATI OH 45238
61- 9 BOLIN, BOBBY DONALD	BOX E - SIX MILE SC 29682
54- 8 BOLLING, FRANK ELMORE	171 FENWICK RD - MOBILE AL 36608
39- 12 BOLLING, JOHN EDWARD	BOX 9266 - PANAMA CITY BEACH FL 32407
52- 11 BOLLING, MILTON JOSEPH	2752 FONTAINEBLEAU DR S - MOBILE AL 36606
65- 12 BOLLO, GREGORY GENE	15207 REGINA ST - ALLEN PARK MI 48101
50- 11 BOLLWEG, DONALD RAYMOND	513 TIMBER RIDGE DR #206 - CAROL STREAM IL 60188
28- 11 BOLTON, CECIL GLENFORD	419 S MAIN ST - GREENVILLE MS 38701

31- 8 BOLTON, WILLIAM CLIFTON	D. APRIL 21, 1979 LEXINGTON, N. C.
78- 16 BOMBACK, MARK VINCENT	%H.BOMBACK, 87 SMITH ST - FALL RIVER MA 02721
60- 11 BOND, WALTER FRANKLIN	D. SEPTEMBER 14, 1967 HOUSTON, TEX.
68- 9 BONDS, BOBBY LEE	175 LYNDHURST - SAN CARLOS CA 94076
37- 11 BONETTI, JULIO G	D. JUNE 17, 1952 BELMONT, CAL.
27- 14 BONEY, HENRY TATE	BOX 906 - LAKE WORTH FL 33460
38- 8 BONGIOVANNI, ANTHONY THOMAS	416 ROSEWOOD AVE-SAN JOSE CA 95117
40- 3 BONHAM, ERNEST EDWARD 'TINY'	D. SEPTEMBER 15, 1949 PITTSBURGH, PA.
71- 13 BONHAM, WILLIAM GORDON	1605 SYCAMORE WAY - SOLVANG CA 93463
62- 15 BONIKOWSKI, JOSEPH PETER	5109 COTTAGE ST - PHILADELPHIA PA 19124
81- 11 BONILLA, JUAN GUILLERMO	RR 3 BOX 262 - QUINCY FL 32351
13- 14 BONIN, ERNEST LUTHER	D. JANUARY 3, 1965 SYCAMORE, O.
77- 12 BONNELL, ROBERT BARRY	2102 179TH COURT NE - REDMOND WA 98052

28

80- 10	BONNER, ROBERT AVERILL	1214 BERNICE ST - CORPUS CHRISTI TX 78412
44- 11	BONNESS, WILLIAM JOHN	D. DECEMBER 3, 1977 CLEVELAND, O.
20- 10	BONO, ADLAI WENDELL 'GUS'	D. DECEMBER 3, 1948 DEARBORN, MICH.
34- 11	BONURA, HENRY JOHN	7441 BENSON - NEW ORLEANS LA 70127
13- 15	BOE, EVERETT LITTLE	D. MAY 21, 1969 KENNEDY, TEX.
83- 15	BOOKER, GREGORY SCOTT	OLD ADD: 454 CAMP RD - BURLINGTON NC 27215
66- 8	BOOKER, RICHARD LEE	BOX 59 - BROOKNEAL VA 24528
28- 12	BOOL, ALBERT	D. SEPTEMBER 27, 1981 LINCOLN, NEB.
81- 12	BOONE, DANIEL HUGH	11424 HARVARD - NORWALK CA 90650
22- 12	BOONE, ISAAC MORGAN 'IKE'	D. AUGUST 1, 1958 NORTHPORT, ALA.
19- 8	BOONE, JAMES ALBERT 'DANNY'	D. MAY 11, 1968 TUSCALOOSA, ALA.
13- 16	BOONE, LUTE JOSEPH	D. JULY 29, 1982 PITTSBURGH, PA.
48- 17	BOONE, RAYMOND OTIS	15420 OLDE HWY 80 #137 - EL CAJON CA 92021
72- 12	BOONE, ROBERT RAYMOND	18571 VILLA DR - VILLA PARK CA 92667
62- 16	BOOZER, JOHN MORGAN	D. JANUARY 24, 1986 LEXINGTON, S. C.
69- 11	BORBON, PEDRO RODRIGUEZ	LAS PALMAS,CORRAZOND DEJESUS #2-SANTO DOMINGO DOM. REP.
34- 12	BORDAGARAY, STANLEY GEORGE 'FRENCHY'	395 CRESTWOOD AV - VENTURA CA 93003
80- 11	BORDI, RICHARD ALBERT 'RICH'	206 ARROYO DR - SOUTH SAN FRANCISCO CA 94080
80- 12	BORDLEY, WILLIAM CLARKE	25930 NARBONNE AVE - LOMITA CA 90717
72- 13	BORGMANN, GLENN DENNIS	16 LUNDY TER - BUTLER NJ 07405
82- 16	BORIS, PAUL STANLEY	12 WOODLAND DR - COLINIA NJ 07067
64- 9	BORK, FRANK BERNARD	725 FAIRWAY BLVD - COLUMBUS OH 43227
50- 12	BORKOWSKI, ROBERT VILARIAN	1031 GERHARD ST - DAYTON OH 45404
60- 12	BORLAND, THOMAS BRUCE	624 CHEROKEE DR - STILLWATER OK 74074
44- 12	BOROM, EDWARD JONES 'RED'	827 HIGHLAND OAKS - DALLAS TX 75232
57- 7	BOROS, STEPHEN	17724 VILLAMOURA DR - POWAY CA 92064
42- 14	BOROWY, HENRY LUDWIG	369 BROAD ST - BLOOMFIELD NJ 07003
12- 21	BORTON, WILLIAM BAKER 'BABE'	D. JULY 29, 1954 BERKELEY, CALIF.
66- 9	BOSCH, DONALD JOHN	1600 MCKINLEY RD - NAPA CA 94558
76- 18	BOSETTI, RICHARD ALAN 'RICK'	1233 HILL ST - ANDERSON CA 96007
77- 13	BOSLEY, THADDIS	1965 VALLEY RD - OCEANSIDE CA 92054
66- 10	BOSMAN, RICHARD ALLEN	716 N. OAKLAND ST - ARLINGTON VA 22203
28- 13	BOSS, ELMER HARLEY	D. MAY 15, 1964 NASHVILLE, TENN.
45- 4	BOSSER, MELVIN EDWARD	RR 14 BOX 291 - CROSSVILLE TN 38555
15- 13	BOSTICK, HENRY LANDERS	D. SEPTEMBER 16, 1968 DENVER, COLO.
75- 18	BOSTOCK, LYMAN WESLEY	D. SEPTEMBER 24, 1978 GARY, IND.
84- 8	BOSTON, DARYL LAMONT	1016 VALLEY LANE - CINCINNATI OH 45229
64- 10	BOSWELL, DAVID WILSON	309 ROXBURY CT - JOPPA MD 21085
67- 6	BOSWELL, KENNETH GEORGE	2301 MATTERHORN LN - AUSTIN TX 78704
82- 17	BOTELHO, DEREK WAYNE	OLD ADD: 4900 NW 5TH AVE - BOCA RATON FL 33432
37- 12	BOTTARINI, JOHN CHARLES	D. OCTOBER 8, 1976 SPRING, N. MEX.
79- 10	BOTTING, RALPH WAYNE	1154 THOMPSON AVE - GLENDALE CA 91201
22- 13	BOTTOMLEY, JAMES LEROY	D. DECEMBER 11, 1959 SAINT LOUIS, MO.
62- 17	BOTZ, ROBERT ALLEN	4592 MONCHES RD - COLGATE WI 53017
56- 10	BOUCHEE, EDWARD FRANCIS	2036 SPRUCE AVE - DES PLAINES IL 60018
14- 23	BOUCHER, ALEXANDER FRANCIS	D. JUNE 23, 1974 TORRANCE, CALIF.
14- 24	BOUCHER, MEDRIC CHARLES FRANCIS	D. MARCH 12, 1974 MARTINEZ, CALIF.

BOUDREAU   BRAGAN

```
38-  9  BOUDREAU, LOUIS                        15600 ELLIS AVENUE - DOLTON IL 60419
61- 10  BOULDIN, CARL EDWARD                   37 AUDUBON - FORT THOMAS KY 41075
80- 13  BOURJOS, CHRISTOPHER                   6323 WEST ROSCOE - CHICAGO IL 60634
71- 14  BOURQUE, PATRICK DANIEL                2013 E HARVARD DR - TEMPE AZ 85283
62- 18  BOUTON, JAMES ALAN                     6 MYRON CT - TEANECK NJ 07666
70- 12  BOWA, LAWRENCE ROBERT                  315 MAGNOLIA DR - CLEARWATER FL 33516
14- 25  BOWDEN, DAVID TIMON                    D. OCTOBER 25, 1949 EMORY UNIVERSITY, GA.
19-  9  BOWEN, EMMONS JOSEPH 'CHICK'           D. AUGUST 9, 1948 NEW HAVEN, CONN.
77- 14  BOWEN, SAMUEL THOMAS                   8 HIGH HILL DR - BRUNSWICK GA 31520
63- 13  BOWENS, SAMUEL EDWARD                  RR 4 BOX 27 NATIONAL AVE - LELAND NC 28451
49-  8  BOWERS, GROVER BILL                    P. O. BOX 401 - WYNNE AR 72396
35-  6  BOWERS, STEWART COLE                   1620 RIDGWAY RD - HAVERTOWN PA 19083
31-  9  BOWLER, GRANT TIERNEY                  D. JUNE 25, 1968 DENVER, COLO.
43- 10  BOWLES, CHARLES JAMES                  3004 N CENTER ST-HICKORY NC 28601
22- 14  BOWLES, EMMETT JEROME                  D. SEPTEMBER 3, 1959 FLAGSTAFF, ARIZ.
67-  7  BOWLIN, LOIS WELDON 'HOSS'             BOX 1026 - LIVINGSTON AL 35470
76- 19  BOWLING, STEPHEN SHADDON                1784 WEST 63RD - TULSA OK 74132
14- 26  BOWMAN, ALVAH EDSON                    D. OCTOBER 11, 1979 LONGVIEW, TEXAS
20- 11  BOWMAN, ELMER WILHELM                  846 ROBINSON ST - LOS ANGELES CA 90026
61- 11  BOWMAN, ERNEST FERRELL 'BUDDY'         ROUTE 17, EAST SHORE APT #8 - JOHNSON CITY TN 37601
32-  7  BOWMAN, JOSEPH EMIL                    2001 W 83RD ST - LEAWOOD KS 66206
39- 13  BOWMAN, ROBERT JAMES                   D. SEPTEMBER 4, 1972 BLUEFIELD, W. VA.
55- 15  BOWMAN, ROBERT LEROY                   2911 VIA CARMEN - SAN JOSE CA 95124
49-  9  BOWMAN, ROGER CLINTON                  2210 S SEPULVEDA BLVD - LOS ANGELES CA 90064
10- 11  BOWSER, JAMES H. 'RED'                 B. 1886 GREENSBURG, PA.
58- 11  BOWSFIELD, EDWARD OLIVER 'TED'         BOX 4100 - SEATTLE WA 98104
82- 18  BOYD, DENNIS RAY 'OIL CAN'             1611 20TH ST - MERIDIAN MS 39301
69- 12  BOYD, GARY LEE                         15227 CHANERA AVE - GARDENA CA 90249
10- 12  BOYD, RAYMOND C.                       D. FEBRUARY 11, 1920 HOUTONVILLE, ILL.
51-  4  BOYD, ROBERT RICHARD                   2811 N VASSAR AVE - WICHITA KS 67220
55- 16  BOYER, CLETIS LEROY                    695 CLEARWATER HARBOR DR - LARGO FL 33540
49- 10  BOYER, CLOYD VICTOR                    RR ONE BOX 231-A - WEBB CITY MO 64870
55- 17  BOYER, KENTON LLOYD                    D. SEPTEMBER 7, 1982 ST. LOUIS, MO.
78- 17  BOYLAND, DORIAN SCOTT 'DOE'            OLD ADD: 1205 SW 18TH - PORTLAND OR 97205
26-  8  BOYLE, JAMES JOHN                      D. DECEMBER 24, 1958 CINCINNATI, O.
12- 22  BOYLE, JOHN BELLEW                     D. APRIL 3, 1971 FORT LAUDERDALE, FLA.
29- 10  BOYLE, RALPH FRANCIS 'BUZZ'            D. NOVEMBER 12, 1978 CINCINNATI, O.
38- 10  BOYLES, HARRY                          101 SIOUX RD #473 - PHARR TX 78577
66- 11  BRABENDER, EUGENE MATHEW               4696 CAPITOL VIEW RD - MIDDLETON WI 53562
37- 13  BRACK, GILBERT HERMAN 'GIB'            D. JANUARY 20, 1960 GREENVILLE, TEX.
64- 11  BRADLEY, DONALD EUGENE                 OLD ADD: 3686 OAKLEY RD - WEST BLOOMFIELD MI 48033
66- 12  BRADFORD, CHARLES WILLIAM 'BUDDY'      6440 SPRING PARK AVE - LADERA HEIGHTS CA90056
43- 11  BRADFORD, HENRY VICTOR 'VIC'           RR 4-PARIS KY 40361
77- 15  BRADFORD, LARRY                        OLD ADD: 7441 S WABASH AVE - CHICAGO IL
56- 11  BRADFORD, WILLIAM D                    BOX 3043 - FAIRFIELD BAY AR 72153
48- 18  BRADLEY, FREDERICK LANGDON             4540 SOUTH LAYMAN AVE - PICO RIVERA CA 90660
46- 11  BRADLEY, GEORGE WASHINGTON             563 BRADLEY COVE - LAWRENCEBURG TN 38464
27- 15  BRADLEY, HERBERT THEODORE              D. OCTOBER 16, 1959 CLAY CENTER, KAN.
10- 13  BRADLEY, HUGH FREDERICK                D. JANUARY 26, 1949 WORCESTER, MASS.
16-  7  BRADLEY, JOHN THOMAS                   D. MARCH 18, 1969 TULSA, OKLA.
81- 13  BRADLEY, MARK ALLEN                    413 PIERCE ST - ELIZABETHTOWN KY 42701
83- 16  BRADLEY, PHILIP POOLE                  207 MEADOW DRIVE - MACOMB IL 61455
84-  9  BRADLEY, SCOTT WILLIAM                 30 ESSEX ROAD - ESSEX FALLS NJ 07021
83- 17  BRADLEY, STEVEN BERT                   RURAL ROUTE 1 - TOLEDO IL 62468
69- 13  BRADLEY, THOMAS WILLIAM                6306 WHISPERING OAKS DR - JACKSONVILLE FL 32211
17- 10  BRADSHAW, DALLAS CARL                  D. DECEMBER 11, 1939 HERRIN, ILL.
52- 12  BRADSHAW, GEORGE THOMAS                RR 2 BOX 6A - HORSE SHOE NC 28742
29- 11  BRADSHAW, JOSEPH SIAH                  42 TAMMI DR - TAVARES FL 32778
20- 12  BRADY, CLIFFORD FRANCIS                D. SEPTEMBER 25, 1974 BELLEVILLE, ILL.
15- 14  BRADY, CORNELIUS JOSEPH 'NEAL'         D. JUNE 19, 1947 FORT MITCHELL, KY.
56- 12  BRADY, JAMES JOSEPH                    6418 WHISPERING OAKS DR - JACKSONVILLE FL 32211
46- 12  BRADY, ROBERT JAY                      42 OVERLAND ST - MANCHESTER CT 06040
12- 23  BRADY, WILLIAM A.
40-  4  BRAGAN, ROBERT RANDALL                 1901 INDIAN CREEK DR - FORT WORTH TX 76107
```

30

```
14- 27  BRAINARD, FREDERICK                 D. APRIL 17, 1959 GALVESTON, TEX.
15- 15  BRAITHWOOD, ALFRED                  D. NOVEMBER 24, 1960 ROWLESBURG, W. VA.
28- 14  BRAME, ERVIN BECKHAM                D. NOVEMBER 22, 1949 HOPKINSVILLE, KY.
35-  7  BRAMHALL, ARTHUR WASHINGTON         D. SEPTEMBER 4, 1985 MADISON, WIS.
44- 13  BRANCA, RALPH THEODORE JOSEPH       791 NORTH ST - WHITE PLAINS NY 10605
39- 14  BRANCATO, ALBERT                    108 GREEN VALLEY RD-UPPER DARBY PA 19082
62- 19  BRANCH, HARVEY ALFRED               4995 JOLLY DR - MEMPHIS TN 38101
41-  8  BRANCH, NORMAN DOWNS                D. NOVEMBER 21, 1971 NAVASOTA, TEX.
79- 11  BRANCH, ROY                         5322 TERRY AVE - SAINT LOUIS MO 63120
63- 14  BRAND, RONALD GEORGE                1500 PINE VALLEY CIR - ROSEVILLE CA 95678
66- 13  BRANDON, DARRELL G                  196 OLD FARM RD - HANOVER MA 02339
28- 15  BRANDT, EDWARD ARTHUR               D. NOVEMBER 1, 1944 SPOKANE, WASH.
56- 13  BRANDT, JOHN GEORGE 'JACKIE'        611 OSAGE DR - PAPILLION NE 68046
41-  9  BRANDT, WILLIAM GEORGE              D. MAY 16, 1968 FORT WAYNE, IND.
28- 16  BRANNAN, OTIS OWEN                  D. JUNE 6, 1967 LITTLE ROCK, ARK.
27- 16  BRANOM, EDGAR DUDLEY 'DUD'          D. FEBRUARY 4, 1980 SUN CITY, ARIZ.
80- 14  BRANT, MARSHALL LEE                 301 OAK ST - PENNGROVE CA 94951
21-  8  BRATCHE, FREDERICK OSCAR            D. JANUARY 7, 1962 MASSILLON, O.
24- 13  BRATCHER, JOSEPH WARLICK            D. OCTOBER 13, 1977 FORT WORTH, TEX.
64- 12  BRAUN, JOHN PAUL                    1014 AMSTERDAM AVE - MADISON WI 53716
71- 15  BRAUN, STEPHEN RUSSELL              OLD ADD: 3108 167TH AVE NE - BELLEVUE WA 98008
69- 14  BRAVO, ANGEL ALFONSO                OLD ADD: CALLE CAMINO NUEVO #208-MARACAIBO VZ
21-  9  BRAXTON, EDGAR GARLAND              D. FEBRUARY 25, 1966 NORFLOK, VA.
41- 10  BRAY, CLARENCE WILBUR 'BUSTER'      D. SEPTEMBER 4, 1982 EVANSVILLE, IND.
21- 10  BRAZILL, FRANK LEO                  D. NOVEMBER 3, 1976 OAKLAND, CALIF.
43- 12  BRAZLE, ALPHA EUGENE                D. OCTOBER 24, 1973 GRAND JUNCTION , COL.
83- 18  BREAM, SIDNEY DAVID                 406 CHESTNUT ST - MT HOLLY SPRINGS PA 17065
69- 15  BREAZEALE, JAMES LEO                717 BOLLING LANE - HOUSTON TX 77076
40-  5  BRECHEEN, HARRY DAVID               1134 S HIGHSCHOOL - ADA OK 74820
29- 12  BRECKINRIDGE, WILLIAM ROBERTSON     D. AUGUST 23, 1958 TULSA, OKLA.
69- 16  BREEDEN, DANNY RICHARD              1000 NORTH MCKENZIE ST - FOLEY AL 36535
71- 16  BREEDEN, HAROLD NOEL                RR1 BOX 311 - LEESBURG GA 31763
60- 13  BREEDING, MARVIN EUGENE             BOX 1061 - DECATUR AL 35601
80- 15  BREINING, FRED LAWRENCE             1218 33RD AVE - SAN FRANCISCO CA 94122
37- 14  BREMER, HERBERT FREDERICK           D. NOVEMBER 28, 1979 COLUMBUS, GA.
14- 28  BRENEGAN, OLAF SELMAR               D. APRIL 20, 1956 GALESVILLE, WIS.
81- 14  BRENLY, ROBERT EARL                 936 ORANGE ST - COSHOCTON OH 43812
10- 14  BRENNAN, ADDISON FOSTER             D. JANUARY 7, 1962 KANSAS CITY, MO.
33-  7  BRENNAN, JAMES DONALD 'DON'         D. APRIL 2L, 1953 BOSTON, MASS.
81- 15  BRENNAN, THOMAS MARTIN              5500 OAK CENTER DR - OAK LAWN IL 60453
65- 13  BRENNEMAN, JAMES LEROY              OLD ADD: 16800 PFEIFFER WAY - PERRIS CA 92370
12- 24  BRENNER, DELBERT HENRY              D. APRIL 11, 1971 ST. LOUIS PARK, MINN.
13- 17  BRENTON, LYNN DAVIS                 D. OCTOBER 14, 1968 LOS ANGELES, CALIF.
32-  8  BRENZEL, WILLIAM RICHARD            D. JUNE 12, 1979 OAKLAND, CALIF.
14- 29  BRESSLER, RAYMOND BLOOM 'RUBE'      D. NOVEMBER 7, 1966 MT. WASHINGTON, O.
56- 14  BRESSOUD, EDWARD FRANCIS            10455 CRESTON DR - LOS ALTOS CA 94022
13- 18  BRETON, JOHN FREDERICK 'JIM'        D. MAY 30, 1973 BELOIT, WIS.
73- 13  BRETT, GEORGE HOWARD                3201 W 98TH - LEAWOOD KS 66206
24- 14  BRETT, HERBERT JAMES                D. NOVEMBER 25, 1974 ST PETERSBURG, FLA.
67-  8  BRETT, KENNETH ALVEN                1504 STRAND - HERMOSA BEACH CA 90254
39- 15  BREUER, MARVIN HOWARD               1106 JOYCE AVE-ROLLA MO 65401
84- 10  BREWER, ANTHONY BRUCE               2272 LATHAM #5 - MISSION VALLEY CA 94040
60- 14  BREWER, JAMES THOMAS                1101 W. HOUSTON #904 - BROKEN ARROW OK 74012
44- 14  BREWER, JOHN HERNDON                28271 WORCESTER - SUN CITY CA 92381
54-  9  BREWER, THOMAS AUSTIN               409 STATE RD - CHERAW SC 29520
43- 13  BREWSTER, CHARLES LAWRENCE          RR 2 BOX 165A - BLACKSHEAR GA 31516
61- 12  BRICE, ALAN HEALEY                  7807 16TH AVE NW - BRADENTON FL 33505
58- 12  BRICKELL, FRITZ DARRELL             D. OCTOBER 15,1965 WICHITA, KAN.
26-  9  BRICKELL, GEORGE FREDERICK 'FRED'   D. APRIL 8, 1961 WICHITA, KAN.
13- 19  BRICKLEY, GEORGE VINCENT            D. FEBRUARY 23, 1947 EVERETT, MASS.
52- 13  BRICKNER, RALPH HAROLD              3967 ROBINHILL DR - CINCINNATI OH 45211
51-  5  BRIDEWESER, JAMES EHRENFELD         24326 PARK PLACE DR - LAGUNA NIGUEL CA 92677
51-  6  BRIDGES, EVERETT LAMAR 'ROCKY'      2445 E. GATEWAY RD - COUER D'ALENE ID 83814
59-  7  BRIDGES, MARSHALL                   1908 RIDGEWAY - JACKSON MS 39206
30-  5  BRIDGES, THOMAS JEFFERSON DAVIS     D. APRIL 19, 1968 NASHVILLE, TENN.
12- 25  BRIEF, ANTHONY VINCENT 'BUNNY'      D. FEBRUARY 10, 1963 MILWAUKEE, WIS.
75- 19  BRIGGS, DANIEL LEE                  231 FRANCE ST - SONOMA CA 95476
64- 13  BRIGGS, JOHN EDWARD                 432 E. 27TH - PATERSON NJ 07514
```

RALPH BRANCA

JACK BRANDT

DAN BRIGGS 1B-OF

```
56- 15  BRIGGS, JOHN TIFT                   8724 SHERRY DR - ORANGEVALE CA 95662
58- 13  BRIGHT, HARRY JAMES                 2048 50TH AVE - SACRAMENTO CA 95827
65- 14  BRILES, NELSON KELLEY               1324 CLEARVIEW DR - GREENSBURG PA 15501
22- 15  BRILLHEART, JAMES BENSON            D. SEPTEMBER 2, 1972 RADFORD, VA.
12- 26  BRINKER, WILLIAM HUTCHINSON         D. FEBRUARY 5, 1965 ARCADIA, CAL.
```

BRINKMAN   BROWN

```
69- 17  BRINKMAN, CHARLES ERNEST           332 INGALLS ST - CINCINNATI OH 45204
61- 13  BRINKMAN, EDWIN ALBERT             7106 WYANDOTTE DR - CINCINNATI OH 45238
52- 14  BRINKOPF, LEON CLARENCE            915 S MINNESOTA - CAPE GIRARDEAU MO 63701
47- 13  BRISSIE, LELAND VICTOR 'LOU'       1908 WHITEPINE DR - NORTH AUGUSTA SC 29841
66- 14  BRISTOL, JAMES DAVID 'DAVE'        RR1 - ANDREWS NC 28901
37- 15  BRITTAIN, AUGUST SCHUSTER          D. FEBRUARY 16, 1974 WILMINGTON, N. C.
50- 13  BRITTIN, JOHN ALBERT               1036 FRANCELLA CT - SPRINGFIELD IL 62702
67-  9  BRITTON, JAMES ALAN                10455 SW 112TH ST - MIAMI FL 33176
13- 20  BRITTON, STEPHEN GILBERT           D. JUNE 20, 1983 PARSONS, KAN.
79- 12  BRIZZOLARA, ANTHONY JOHN           1638 PRINCESS CIR NE - ATLANTA GA 30345
34- 13  BROACA, JOHN JOSEPH                D. MAY 16, 1985 LAWRENCE, MASS.
71- 17  BROBERG, PETER SVEN                220 MONTEREY RD - PALM BEACH FL 33480
82- 19  BROCK, GREGORY ALLEN               427 WINDFLOWER - PLACENTIA CA 92670
17- 11  BROCK, JOHN RAY                    D. OCTOBER 27, 1951 CLAYTON, MO.
61- 14  BROCK, LOUIS CLARK                 12595 DURBIN DR - ST LOUIS MO 63141
52- 15  BRODOWSKI, RICHARD STANLEY         90 FORD ST - LYNN MA 01904
59-  8  BROGLIO, ERNEST GILBERT            2838 VIA CARMEN - SAN JOSE CA 95124
72- 14  BROHAMER, JOHN ANTHONY             1236 LEXINGTON DR - VISTA CA 92083
44- 15  BRONDELL, KENNETH LEROY            7029 DECELIS PL - VAN NUYS CA 91401
10- 15  BRONKIE, HERMAN CHARLES            D. MAY 27, 1968 SOMERS, CONN.
59-  9  BRONSTAD, JAMES WARREN             6101 KENWICK - FT WORTH TX 76116
75- 20  BROOKENS, EDWARD DWAIN             92 FIFTH AVE - FAYETTEVILLE PA 17222
79- 13  BROOKENS, THOMAS DALE              120 HILLSIDE DR - FAYETTEVILLE PA 17222
80- 16  BROOKS, HUBERT                     1502 SPRING AVE - COMPTON CA 90221
25- 11  BROOKS, JONATHAN JOSEPH 'MANDY'    D. JUNE 17, 1962 KIRKWOOD, MO.
69- 18  BROOKS, ROBERT                     1130 W 252ND ST - HARBOR CITY CA 90710
40-  6  BROSKIE, SIGMUND THEODORE          D. MAY 17, 1975 CANTON, O.
54- 10  BROSNAN, JAMES PATRICK             7742 W CHURCHILL ST - MORTON GROVE IL 60053
69- 19  BROSSEAU, FRANKLIN LEE             41 ISLAND RD - SAINT PAUL MN 55110
16-  8  BROTTEM, ANTON CHRISTIAN 'TONY'    D. AUGUST 5, 1929 CHICAGO, ILL.
80- 17  BROUHARD, MARK STEVEN              6289 JACKIE AVE - WOODLAND HILLS CA 91367
55- 18  BROVIA, JOSEPH JOHN                142 ACADIA ST - SANTA CRUZ CA 95060
20- 13  BROWER, FRANK WILLARD              D. NOVEMBER 20, 1960 BALTIMORE, MD.
31- 10  BROWER, LOUIS LESTER               308 SUNRISE RD - ROSWELL NM 88201
51-  7  BROWN, ALTON LEO                   253 CONSUL AVE - VIRGINIA BEACH VA 23462
11- 17  BROWN, CARROLL WILLIAM 'BOARDWALK' D. FEBRUARY 8, 1977 BURLINGTON, N. J.
11- 18  BROWN, CHARLES ROY 'CURLY'         D. JUNE 10, 1968 SPRING HILL, KAN.
28- 17  BROWN, CLINTON HAROLD              D. DECEMBER 31, 1955 ROCKY RIVER,O.
73- 14  BROWN, CURTIS                      3745 HAYWOOD ST - SACRAMENTO CA 95838
83- 19  BROWN, CURTIS STEVEN               104 EAST HENINWAY CIR - POMPANO BEACH FL 33063
81- 16  BROWN, DARRELL WAYNE               5843 FIFTH AVE - LOS ANGELES CA 90043
14- 30  BROWN, DELOS HIGHT                 D. DECEMBER 21, 1964 CARBONDALE, ILL.
15- 16  BROWN, DONALD G                    1917 ADD: 712 ELLAS ST - BEATRICE NE
13- 21  BROWN, DRUMMOND NICOL              D. JANUARY 27, 1927 PLATTE CO., MO.
20- 14  BROWN, EDWARD WILLIAM              D. SEPTEMBER 10, 1956 VALLEJO, CAL.
69- 20  BROWN, EDWIN RANDOLPH 'RANDY'      OLD ADD: 1119 EDMONDS ST - LEESBURG FL 32748
11- 19  BROWN, ELMER YOUNG                 D. JANUARY 23, 1955 INDIANAPOLIS, IND.
51-  8  BROWN, HECTOR HAROLD 'HAL'         BOX 1626 - GREENSBORO NC 27402
69- 21  BROWN, ISAAC 'IKE'                 LINCOLN CT #A-4 - LAKELAND FL 33805
70- 13  BROWN, JACKIE GENE                 RR 3 BOX 50B - HOLDENVILLE OK 74848
37- 16  BROWN, JAMES ROBERSON              D. DECEMBER 29, 1977 BATH, N. C.
75- 21  BROWN, JERALD RAY 'JAKE'           D. DECEMBER 18, 1981 HOUSTON, TEXAS
84- 11  BROWN, JOHN CHRISTOPHER            5015 BRIGHTON AVE - LOS ANGELES CA 90062
37- 17  BROWN, JOHN LINDSAY                D. JANUARY 1, 1967 SAN ANTONIO, TEX.
68- 10  BROWN, JOPHERY CLIFFORD            3008 W 81ST ST - INGLEWOOD CA 90305
27- 17  BROWN, JOSEPH HENRY                D. MARCH 7, 1950 LOS ANGELES, CALIF.
63- 15  BROWN, LARRY LESLEY                1428 NORTH O ST - LAKE WORTH FL 33460
76- 20  BROWN, LEON                        7537 SOUTH LAROSA - TEMPE AZ 85283
25- 12  BROWN, LLOYD ANDREW                D. JANUARY 14, 1974 OPALOCKA, FLA.
35-  8  BROWN, MACE STANLEY                305 N HOLDEN ROAD-GREENSBORO NC 27410
84- 12  BROWN, MARK ANTHONY                59 CHURCH ST - NORTH WALPOLE NH 03608
83- 20  BROWN, MICHAEL CHARLES             312 COPCO LANE - SAN JOSE CA 95123
82- 20  BROWN, MICHAEL GARY                8712 PINE NEEDLES CT - VIENNA VA 22180
22- 16  BROWN, MYRL LINCOLN                D. FEBRUARY 23, 1981 HARRISBURG, PA.
43- 14  BROWN, NORMAN                      106 E MAIN ST-BENNETTSVILLE SC 29512
65- 15  BROWN, OLLIE LEE                   8462 COUNTRY CLUB DR - BUENA PARK CA 90621
```

TOM BROOKENS

```
69- 22  BROWN, OSCAR LEE                   19113 GUNLOCK AVE - CARSON CA 90746
61- 15  BROWN, PAUL DWAYNE                 RR 4 - HOLDENVILLE OK 74848
57-  8  BROWN, RICHARD ERNEST              D. APRIL 12, 1970 BALTIMORE, MD.
14- 31  BROWN, ROBERT M.                   B. 1891
30-  6  BROWN, ROBERT MURRAY               %M.REMARD,123 RICHARD DRIVE - HANOVER MA 02339
46- 13  BROWN, ROBERT WILLIAM              1324 THOMAS PL - FT WORTH TX 76107
79- 14  BROWN, ROGERS LEE 'BOBBY'          BOX 874 - EASTVILLE VA 23307
81- 17  BROWN, SCOTT EDWARD                BOX 608 - DEQUINCY LA 70633
```

83- 21	BROWN, STEPHEN ELBERT	1203 WEST 8TH STREET - DAVIS CA 95616
78- 18	BROWN, THOMAS DALE	248 GLORIA DR - BATON ROUGE LA 70815
44- 16	BROWN, THOMAS MICHAEL	315 SHADY PL - BRENTWOOD TN 37027
63- 16	BROWN, THOMAS WILLIAM	9104 WOODLAND DR - SILVER SPRING MD 20910
25- 13	BROWN, WALTER GEORGE 'JUMBO'	D. OCTOBER 2, 1966 FREEPORT, N. Y.
47- 14	BROWN, WALTER IRVING	RR ORIENTAL PARK - BEMUS POINT NY 14712
47- 15	BROWN, WILLARD JESSE	2217 BRECKENRIDGE - HOUSTON TX 77026
63- 17	BROWN, WILLIAM JAMES 'GATES'	17206 SANTA BARBARA - DETROIT MI 48221
12- 27	BROWN, WILLIAM VERNA	D. MAY 15, 1965 LUBBOCK, TEX.
65- 16	BROWNE, BYRON ELLIS	OLD ADD: 1015 N 31ST ST - BATON ROUGE LA 7080
35- 9	BROWNE, EARL JAMES	1405 FAIR PARK BLVD - LITTLE ROCK AR 72204
62- 20	BROWNE, PRENTICE ALMONT 'PIDGE'	187-23 CASPER DR - SPRING TX 77373
60- 15	BROWNING, CALVIN DUANE	1000 CAMELOT - CLINTON OK 73601
10- 16	BROWNING, FRANK	D. MAY 19, 1948 SAN ANTONIO, TEX.
84- 13	BROWNING, THOMAS LEO	1141 CENTRAL AVE - BILLINGS MT 59102
67- 10	BRUBAKER, BRUCE ELLSWORTH	OLD ADD: 6622 RED HORSE PIKE - EVANSVILLE IN
32- 9	BRUBAKER, WILBUR LEE 'BILL'	D. APRIL 2, 1978 LAGUNA HILLS, CALIF.
59- 10	BRUCE, ROBERT JAMES	RR 4 BOX 363X - CANYON LAKE TX 78130
61- 16	BRUCKBOWER, FREDERICK JOHN	404 MCHUGH - HOLMES WI 54636
37- 18	BRUCKER, EARLE FRANCIS SR	D. MAY 8, 1981 SAN DIEGO, CALIF.
48- 19	BRUCKER, EARLE FRANCIS JR	303 S WESTWIND DR - EL CAJON CA 92020
21- 11	BRUGGY, FRANK LEO	D. APRIL 5, 1959 ELIZABETH, N. J.
78- 19	BRUHERT, MICHAEL EDWIN	143-35 95TH AVE - JAMAICA NY 11435
64- 14	BRUMLEY, TONY MIKE	2501 STARLING LN - BRADENTON FL 32707
81- 18	BRUMMER, GLENN EDWARD	RR 2 BOX 175 - MOUNTAIN GROVE MO 65711
81- 19	BRUNANSKY, THOMAS ANDREW	1319 S HILLWARD AVE - WEST COVINA CA 91791
49- 11	BRUNER, JACK RAYMOND	1641 N 76TH - LINCOLN NE 68505
39- 16	BRUNER, WALTER ROY	305 S LYNDON LN-LOUISVILLE KY 40222
56- 16	BRUNET, GEORGE STUART	2221 E. BLANCHARD - ANAHEIM CA 92806
76- 21	BRUNO, THOMAS MICHAEL	OLD ADD: 4609 LINSCOTT - DOWNERS GROVE IL
66- 15	BRUNSBERG, ARLO ADOLPH	1164 128TH AVE N - BLAINE MN 55434
77- 16	BRUSSTAR, WARREN SCOTT	3320 REDWOOD RD - NAPA CA 94558
53- 13	BRUTON, WILLIAM HARON	6122 W OUTER DR - DETROIT MI 48235
61- 17	BRYAN, WILLIAM RONALD	3313 GRACE DR - OPELIKA AL 36801
35- 10	BRYANT, CLAIBORNE HENRY	1380 NW 43RD TER #102-FORT LAUDERDALE FL33313
79- 15	BRYANT, DEREK ROSZELL	OLD ADD: C-12 COOPERSTOWN - LEXINGTON KY
66- 16	BRYANT, DONALD RAY	OLD ADD: 4023 SW 328TH - FEDERAL WAY WA 98003
85- 7	BRYANT, RALPH WENDELL	RR 4 BOX 374 - LEESBURG GA 31763
67- 11	BRYANT, RONALD RAYMOND	2318 SHIRE LN - DAVIS CA 95616
70- 14	BRYE, STEPHEN ROBERT	200 STANTONVILLE RD - OAKLAND CA 94619
22- 17	BUBSER, HAROLD FRED	D. JUNE 22, 1959 MELROSE PARK, ILL.
48- 20	BUCHA, JOHN GEORGE	1215 N MINK RD - DANIELSVILLE PA 18038
85- 8	BUCHANAN, ROBERT GORDON	4704 HIGHWAY 30 - ELY IA 52227
61- 18	BUCHEK, GERALD PETER	3950A WILMINGTON AVE - ST. LOUIS MO 63116
34- 14	BUCHER, JAMES QUINTER	RR 1 BOX 599 - PALMYRA PA 17078
18- 7	BUCKEYE, GARLAND MAIERS	D. NOVEMBER 14, 1975 STONE LAKE, WIS.
16- 9	BUCKLES, JESS ROBERT	D. AUGUST 2, 1975 WESTMINSTER, CAL.
84- 14	BUCKLEY, KEVIN JOHN	34 CALVIN ST - BRAINTREE MA 02184
69- 23	BUCKNER, WILLIAM JOSEPH	3 MCDONALD CIR - ANDOVER MA 01810
78- 20	BUDASKA, MARK DAVID	10855 BATON ROUGE - NORTHRIDGE CA 91326
56- 17	BUDDIN, DONALD THOMAS	BOX 186 - FOUNTAIN INN SC 29644
46- 14	BUDNICK, MICHAEL JOE	307 WEST BLAINE - SEATTLE WA 98119
85- 9	BUECHELE, STEVEN BERNARD	1730 MIRAMAR - FULLERTON CA 92631
13- 22	BUES, ARTHUR FREDERICK	D. NOVEMBER 7, 1954 WHITEFISH BAY, WIS.
63- 18	BUFORD, DONALD ALVIN	15412 VALLEY VISTA BLVD-SHERMAN OAKS CA 91403
53- 14	BUHL, ROBERT RAY	8550 SPACECOAST PKWY - KISSIMMEE FL 32741
45- 5	BUKER, CYRIL OWEN	108 CENTRAL AVE - GREENWOOD WI 54437
54- 11	BULLARD, GEORGE DONALD	7 DYER COURT - DANVERS MA 01923
77- 17	BULLING, TERRY CHARLES 'BUD'	OLD ADD: 15591 ASTER ST - WESTMINSTER CA
85- 10	BULLOCK, ERIC JERALD	17503 HARWICK COURT - CARSON CA 90746
36- 11	BULLOCK, MALTON JOSEPH 'RED'	BOX 727 - MOSS POINT MS 39563
72- 15	BUMBRY, ALONZO BENJAMIN	28 TREMBLANT CT - LUTHERVILLE MD 21093

TOM BRUNO

63- 19	BUNKER, WALLACE EDWARD	502 FIRST ST - LANGLEY WA 98260
55- 19	BUNNING, JAMES PAUL DAVID	30 WINSTON HILL RD - FT THOMAS KY 41075
69- 24	BURBACH, WILLIAM DAVID	BOX 3 - DICKEYVILLE WI 53808
55- 20	BURBRINK, NELSON EDWARD	9895 88TH WAY N - SEMINOLE FL 33543
69- 25	BURCHART, LARRY WAYNE	6305 SOUTH 114 EAST AVE - TULSA OK 74133
62- 21	BURDA, EDWARD ROBERT 'BOB'	8737 E KEIM DR - SCOTTSDALE AZ 85253
62- 22	BURDETTE, FREDDIE THOMASON	1200 KINGSTON CT #G5 - ALBANY GA 31707
50- 14	BURDETTE, SELVA LEWIS 'LOU'	2837 GULF OF MEXICO DR - LONGBOAT KEY FL33548
10- 17	BURG, JOSEPH PETER	D. APRIL 28, 1969 JOLIET, ILL.
49- 12	BURGESS, FORREST HARRILL 'SMOKEY'	717 CAROLEEN RD - FOREST CITY NC 28043

BURGESS   BYRD

```
54- 12  BURGESS, THOMAS ROLAND              3201 WALNUT ST NE - ST PETERSBURG FL 33704
68- 11  BURGMEIER, THOMAS HENRY             12104 WEST 100TH ST - LENEXA KS 66214
43- 15  BURGO, WILLIAM ROSS                 231 GLENWOOD ST - MORGAN LA 70380
42- 15  BURICH, WILLIAM MAX                 1175 LAMOREE RD #62 - SAN MARCOS CA 92069
10- 18  BURK, CHARLES SANFORD               D. OCTOBER 11, 1934 BROOKLYN, N.Y.
56- 18  BURK, MACK EDWIN                    4310 BRAZIL CIR - PASADENA TX 77502
15- 17  BURKAM, CHAUNCEY DEPEW              D. MAY 9, 1964 KALAMAZOO, MICH.
36- 12  BURKART, ELMER ROBERT               139 OTHRIDGE - LUTHERVILLE MD 21093
76- 22  BURKE, GLENN LAWRENCE               279 COLLINGWOOD - SAN FRANCISCO CA 94114
58- 14  BURKE, LEO PATRICK                  1417 KENSINGTON DR #301 - HAGERSTOWN MD 21740
23- 16  BURKE, LESLIE KINGSTON              D. MAY 6, 1975 DANVERS, MASS.
24- 15  BURKE, PATRICK EDWARD               D. JULY 7, 1965 ST. LOUIS, MO.
27- 18  BURKE, ROBERT JAMES                 D. FEBRUARY 8, 1971 JOLIET, ILL.
77- 18  BURKE, STEVEN MICHAEL               4656 HIBISCUS RD - STOCKTON CA 95205
85- 11  BURKE, TIMOTHY PHILIP               OLD ADD: BONSALL CA 92023
10- 19  BURKE, WILLIAM IGNATIUS             D. FEBRUARY 9, 1967 WORCESTER, MASS.
45-  6  BURKHART, WILLIAM KENNETH 'KEN'     OLD ADD: RR 27, EMORY RD - KNOXVILLE TN
74- 13  BURLESON, RICHARD PAUL 'RICK'       270 E MIRA VERDE DR - LAHABRA HEIGHTS CA 90631
27- 19  BURNETT, JOHN HENDERSON             D. AUGUST 12, 1959 TAMPA, FLA.
56- 19  BURNETTE, WALLACE HARPER            RR 1 BOX 168 - BLAIRS VA 24527
23- 17  BURNS, DENNIS                       D. MAY 21, 1969 TULSA, OKLA.
12- 28  BURNS, EDWARD JAMES                 D. JUNE 1, 1942 MONTEREY, CALIF.
14- 32  BURNS, GEORGE HENRY                 D. JANUARY 7, 1978 KIRKLAND, WASH.
11- 20  BURNS, GEORGE JOSEPH                D. AUGUST 15, 1966 GLOVERSVILLE, N.Y.
30-  7  BURNS, JOHN IRVING                  D. APRIL 18, 1975 BOSTON, MASS.
10- 20  BURNS, JOSEPH FRANCIS               98 CENTRAL ST - IPSWICH MA 01938
24- 16  BURNS, JOSEPH FRANCIS               D. JANUARY 7, 1986 TRENTON, N. J.
43- 16  BURNS, JOSEPH JAMES                 D. JUNE 24, 1974 BRYN MAWR, PA.
78- 21  BURNS, ROBERT BRITT                 912 CARLEY DR - HUNTSVILLE AL 35802
55- 21  BURNSIDE, PETER WILLITS             1945 CHESTNUT - WILMETTE IL 60091
78- 22  BURNSIDE, SHELDON JOHN              4351 BLOOR ST #34 - ETOBICKE ONT. M9C 2A4 CAN.
46- 15  BURPO, GEORGE HARVIE                8981 EAST PALMS DR - TUCSON AZ 85715
14- 33  BURR, ALEXANDER THOMSON             D. NOVEMBER 1, 1918 FRANCE
62- 23  BURRIGHT, LARRY ALLEN               1239 E PALM DR - GLENDORA CA 91740
73- 15  BURRIS, BERTRAM RAY                 4214 TICINO VALLEY DR - ARLINGTON TX 76016
48- 21  BURRIS, PAUL ROBERT                 RR 2 BOX 348 - HUNTERSVILLE NC 28078
70- 15  BURROUGHS, JEFFREY ALAN             6155 LAGUNA CT - LONG BEACH CA 90803
43- 17  BURROWS, JOHN                       RR 2 - LOWELL OH 45744
19- 10  BURRUS, MAURICE LENNON 'DICK'       D. DECEMBER 2, 1972 ELIZABETH CITY, N. C.
58- 15  BURTON, ELLIS NARRINGTON            BERTH 202 EAST BASIN - WILMINGTON CA 90744
75- 22  BURTON, JAMES SCOTT                 700 PEACH TREE LN - ROCHESTER MI 48063
50- 15  BURTSCHY, EDWARD FRANK 'MOE'        620 PEDRETTE APT A-6 - CINCINNATI OH 45238
85- 12  BURTT, DENNIS ALLEN                 1079 NORTH MALLARD STREET - ORANGE CA 92667
60- 16  BURWELL, RICHARD MATTHEW            BOX 1153 - MESA AZ 85201
20- 15  BURWELL, WILLIAM EDWIN              D. JUNE 11, 1973 ORMOND BEACH, FLA.
50- 16  BUSBY, JAMES FRANKLIN               BOX 97 - YALAHA FL 32797
41- 11  BUSBY, PAUL MILLER                  2011 35TH AVE-MERIDIAN MS 39301
72- 16  BUSBY, STEVEN LEE                   OLD ADD: BOX 783 - BLUE SPRINGS MO
43- 18  BUSCH, EDGAR JOHN                   508 E WASHINGTON-O'FALLON IL 62269
65- 17  BUSCHHORN, DONALD LEE               17804 E 26TH ST - INDEPENDENCE MO 64057
23- 18  BUSH, GUY TERRELL                   D. JULY 2, 1985 SHANNON, MISS.
12- 29  BUSH, LESLIE AMBROSE 'JOE'          D. NOVEMBER 1, 1974 FORT LAUDERDALE, FLA.
82- 21  BUSH, ROBERT RANDALL 'RANDY'        OLD ADD: 5355 NW 173RD DR - CAROL CITY FL 33055
27- 20  BUSHEY, FRANCIS CLYDE               D. MARCH 18, 1972 TOPEKA, KAN.
26- 10  BUSKEY, JOSEPH HENRY                D. APRIL 11, 1949 CUMBERLAND, MD.
77- 19  BUSKEY, MICHAEL THOMAS              315 OXFORD ST - SAN FRANCISCO CA 94134
73- 16  BUSKEY, THOMAS WILLIAM              476 ALLEGHENY DR - HARRISBURG PA 17111
71- 18  BUSSE, RAYMOND EDWARD               OLD ADD: 501 MYRTLE LN S - DAYTONA BEACH FL
36- 13  BUTCHER, ALBERT MAXWELL 'MAX'       D. SEPTEMBER 15, 1957 LOGAN, W. VA.
11- 21  BUTCHER, HENRY JOSDPH               D. DECEMBER 28, 1979 HAZEL CREST, ILL.
80- 18  BUTCHER, JOHN DANIEL                3826 SAN AUGUSTINE DR - GLENDALE CA 91206
80- 19  BUTERA, SALVATORE PHILIP            38 HILL DR- BOHEMIA NY 11716
43- 19  BUTKA, EDWARD LUKE                  131 W COLLEGE ST-CANONSBURG PA 15317
40-  7  BUTLAND, WILBURN RUE 'BILL'         2735 CRUFT-TERRE HAUTE IN 47803
11- 22  BUTLER, ARTHUR EDWARD               D. OCTOBER 7, 1984 FALL RIVER, MASS.
81- 20  BUTLER, BRETT MORGAN                2236 LUNCEFORD LN - LILBURN GA 30247
62- 24  BUTLER, CECIL DEAN                  RR4 - DALLAS GA 30132
33-  8  BUTLER, CHARLES THOMAS              D. MAY 10, 1964 BRUNSWICK, GA.
26- 11  BUTLER, JOHN STEPHEN                D. APRIL 29, 1967 LONG BEACH, CAL.
69- 26  BUTLER, WILLIAM FRANKLIN            RR 2 BOX F-13 - STEPHENS CITY VA 22655
62- 25  BUTTERS, THOMAS ARDEN               46 APPLETON PL - DURHAM NC 27705
38- 11  BUXTON, RALPH STANLEY               348 BOWLING GREEN-SAN LEANDRO CA 94577
45-  7  BUZAS, JOSEPH JOHN                  BOX 5010 - READING PA 19612
58- 16  BUZHARDT, JOHN WILLIAM              RR 2 BOX 141A - PROSPERITY SC 29127
43- 20  BYERLY, ELDRED WILLIAM 'BUD'        8611 SAPPINGTON RD-ST LOUIS MO 63126
50- 17  BYRD, HARRY GLADWIN                 D. MAY 14, 1985 DARLINGTON, S. C.
77- 20  BYRD, JEFFREY ALAN                  11085 MORNING DOVE RD - LAKESIDE CA 92040
```

34

BYRD

CANEIRA

ENOS CABELL

```
29- 13  BYRD, SAMUEL DEWEY                           D. MAY 11, 1981 MESA, ARIZ.
29- 14  BYRNE, GERALD WILFORD                        D. AUGUST 11, 1955 LANSING, MICH.
43- 21  BYRNE, THOMAS JOSEPH                         442 PINEVIEW AVE-WAKE FOREST NC 27587
43- 22  BYRNES, MILTON JOHN                          D. FEBRUARY 1, 1979 ST. LOUIS, MO.
80- 20  BYSTROM, MARTIN EUGENE                       62 BEVERLY RD - HAWTHORNE NJ 07506
44- 17  CABALLERO, RALPH JOSEPH 'PUTSY'              6773 MILNE ST - NEW ORLEANS LA 70119
72- 17  CABELL, ENOS MILTON                          7011 COUNTRY CLUB LN - ANAHEIM CA 92807
13- 23  CABRERA, ALFREDO A                           D. HAVANA, CUBA
77- 21  CACER, CRAIG THOMAS                          8916 GLORIA AVE - SEPULVEDA CA 91343
15- 18  CADORE, LEON JOSEPH                          D. MARCH 16, 1958 SPOKANE, WASH.
12- 30  CADY, FORREST LEROY 'HICK'                   D. MARCH 3, 1946 CEDAR RAPIDS, IA.
37- 19  CAFEGO, THOMAS                               D. OCTOBER 29, 1961 DETROIT, MICH.
56- 20  CAFFIE, JOSEPH CLIFFORD                      447 3RD ST - WARREN OH 44483
78- 23  CAGE, WAYNE LEVELL                           RR 1 BOX 55 - CHOUDRANT LA 71227
68- 12  CAIN, LESLIE                                 4516 CYPRESS AVE - RICHMOND CA 91804
32- 10  CAIN, MERRITT PATRICK 'SUGAR'                D. APRIL 3, 1975 ATLANTA, GA.
49- 13  CAIN, ROBERT MAX                             161 EAST 226TH ST - EUCLID ON 44123
34- 15  CAITHAMER, GEORGE THEODORE                   D. JUNE 1, 1954 CHICAGO, ILL.
84- 15  CALDERON, IVAN                               OLD ADD: 334 EST. 34 BUZON - LOIZA PR 00672
50- 18  CALDERONE, SAMUEL FRANCIS                    1000 S COOPER ST - BEVERLY NJ 08010
28- 18  CALDWELL, BRUCE                              D. FEBRUARY 15, 1959 WEST HAVEN, CONN.
25- 14  CALDWELL, CHARLES WILLIAM                    D. NOVEMBER 1, 1957 PRINCETON, N. J.
28- 19  CALDWELL, EARL WELTON                        D. SEPTEMBER 15, 1981 MISSION, TEXAS
71- 19  CALDWELL, RALPH MICHAEL 'MIKE'               1645 BROOK RUN DR - RALEIGH NC 27614
10- 21  CALDWELL, RAYMOND BENJAMIN                   D. AUGUST 17, 1967 SALAMANCA, N. Y.
84- 16  CALHOUN, JEFFREY WILTON                      1212 PARK ST - MCCOMB MS 39648
13- 24  CALHOUN, WILLIAM DAVITTE                     D. FEBRUARY 11, 1955 SANDERSVILLE, GA.
41- 12  CALIGIURI, FREDERICK JOHN                    BOX 429 - RIMERSBURG PA 16248
22- 18  CALLAGHAN, MARTIN FRANCIS                    D. JUNE 24, 1975 NORWOOD, MASS.
83- 22  CALLAHAN, BENJAMIN FRANKLIN                  BOX 676 - DOBSON NC 27017
10- 22  CALLAHAN, DAVID JOSEPH                       D. OCTOBER 28, 1969 OTTAWA, ILL.
39- 17  CALLAHAN, JOSEPH THOMAS                      D. MAY 24, 1949 SOUTH BOSTON, MASS.
13- 25  CALLAHAN, LEO DAVID                          D. MAY 2, 1982 ERIE, PA.
15- 19  CALLAHAN, RAYMOND JAMES                      D. JANUARY 23, 1973 OLYMPIA, WASH.
13- 26  CALLAHAN, WESLEY LEROY                       D. SEPTEMBER 13, 1953 DAYTON,O.
21- 12  CALLAWAY, FRANK BURNETT                      BOX 6105 - LONGBOAT KEY FL 33548
58- 17  CALLISON, JOHN WESLEY                        2316 OAKDALE ST - GLENSIDE PA 19038
63- 20  CALMUS, RICHARD LEE                          3823 S 28TH WEST AVE - TULSA OK 74107
83- 23  CALVERT, MARK                                RR 4 BOX 314J - BROKEN ARROW OK 74012
42- 16  CALVERT, PAUL LEO EMILE                      364 CHATELAINE ST #7 - SHERBROOKE QUE J1G 1Z6 CAN.
13- 27  CALVO, JACINTO 'JACK'                        D. JUNE 15, 1965 MIAMI, FLA.
80- 21  CAMACHO, ERNEST CARLOS                       OLD ADD: 746 ST REGIS - AVON LAKE OH 44012
70- 16  CAMBRIA, FREDERICK DENNIS                    12 IRIS CT - NORTHPORT NY 11768
43- 23  CAMELLI, HENRY RICHARD                       6 LARCH RD-WELLESLEY MA 02181
33-  9  CAMILLI, ADOLF LOUIS                         2831 HACIENDA ST - SAN MATEO CA 94403
60- 17  CAMILLI, DOUGLAS JOSEPH                      872 ORIOLE DRIVE SE - WINTER HAVEN FL 33880
69- 17  CAMILLI, LOUIS STEVEN                        4700 OAHU DR NE - ALBUQUERQUE NM 87111
17- 12  CAMP, HOWARD LEE                             D. MAY 8, 1950 EASTABOGA, ALA.
76- 23  CAMP, RICK LAMAR                             6 CANTEY PLACE NW - ATLANTA GA 30327
48- 22  CAMPANELLA, ROY                              6213 CAPISTRANO - WOODLAND HILLS CA 91367
64- 15  CAMPANERIS, DAGOBERTO 'BERT'                 1021 SW FIRST AVE #2 - MIAMI FL 33130
43- 24  CAMPANIS, ALEXANDER SEBASTIAN                3113 CORONADO DR - FULLERTON CA 92632
66- 17  CAMPANIS, JAMES ALEXANDER                    17082 CASCADES AVE - YORBA LINDA CA 92686
28- 20  CAMPBELL, ARCHIBALD STEWART                  OLD ADD: 800 E. NICHOLS #7 - SPARKS NV 89431
30-  8  CAMPBELL, BRUCE DOUGLAS                      4011 BAYSIDE RD - FT MYERS BEACH FL 33931
40-  8  CAMPBELL, CLARENCE                           SPARTA VA 22552
77- 22  CAMPBELL, DAVID ALLEN                        55 DUNBARTON RD - MANCHESTER NH 03102
67- 12  CAMPBELL, DAVID WILSON                       7864 HILLANDALE DR - SAN DIEGO CA 92120
70- 17  CAMPBELL, JAMES ROBERT                       RR 1 BOX 194 - LAMAR SC 29069
62- 26  CAMPBELL, JAMES ROBERT                       1924 KNOLLWOOD LN - LOS ALTOS CA 94022
33- 10  CAMPBELL, JOHN MILLARD                       100 SILVER BEACH #4-DAYTONA BEACH FL 32081
67- 13  CAMPBELL, JOSEPH EARL                        2151 SMALLHOUSE RD - BOWLING GREEN KY 42101
41- 13  CAMPBELL, PAUL MCLAUGHLIN                    BOX 1724 - FAIRFIELD GLADE TN 38555
64- 16  CAMPBELL, RONALD THOMAS                      OLD ADD: MEADOWVIEW DR - DECATUR TN 37322
33- 11  CAMPBELL, WILLIAM GILTHORPE 'GILLY'          D. FEBRUARY 21, 1973 LOS ANGELES, CAL.
73- 17  CAMPBELL, WILLIAM RICHARD                    217 BEAUMONT LN - BARRINGTON IL 60010
77- 23  CAMPER, CARDELL                              OLD ADD: BOX 1652 - AVONDALE AZ 85323
69- 28  CAMPISI, SALVATORE JOHN                      3303 LAKEWOOD DR - HOLIDAY FL 33590
51-  9  CAMPOS, FRANCISCO JOSE LOPEZ                 2840 NW 4TH ST - MIAMI FL 33125
18-  8  CANAVAN, HUGH EDWARD                         D. SEPTEMBER 4, 1967 BOSTON, MASS.
75- 23  CANDELARIA, JOHN ROBERT                      OLD ADD: 312 32ND AVE E - BRADENTON FL 33505
43- 25  CANDINI, MILO CAIN                           641 MANOR - MANTECA CA 95336
83- 24  CANDIOTTI, THOMAS CAESAR                     18081 JOSEPH DR - CASTRO VALLEY CA 94546
77- 24  CANEIRA, JOHN CASCAES                        18 SPRUCE ST - NAUGATUCK CT 06770
```

35

CANGELOSI CASH

85- 13 CANGELOSI, JOHN ANTHONY	183 SE 4TH AVENUE - HIALEAH FL 33010
60- 18 CANNIZZARO, CHRISTOPHER JOHN	576 DOLORES - SAN LEANDRO CA 94577
77- 25 CANNON, JOSEPH JEROME	6426 WAGNER RD - PENSACOLA FL 32505
85- 14 CANSECO, JOSE	2530 SW 102ND AVE - MIAMI FL 33165
25- 15 CANTRELL, DEWEY GUY	D. JANUARY 31, 1961 MCALESTER, OKLA.
27- 21 CANTWELL, BENJAMIN CALDWELL	D. DECEMBER 4, 1962 SALEM, MO.
16- 10 CANTWELL, MICHAEL JOSEPH	D. JANUARY 9, 1953 OTEEN, N.C.
76- 24 CAPILLA, DOUGLAS EDMOND	3178 MANDA DR - SAN JOSE CA 95124
81- 21 CAPPUZZELLO, GEORGE ANGELO	2345 COLLINS LN - LAKELAND FL 33803
71- 20 CAPRA, LEE WILLIAM 'BUZZ'	7112 RIVERSIDE DR - BERWYN IL 60402
82- 22 CAPRA, NICK LEE	3201 S UTICA - DENVER CO 80236
44- 18 CAPRI, PATRICK NICHOLAS	935 41ST ST - BROOKLYN NY 11219
12- 31 CAPRON, RALPH EARL	D. SEPTEMBER 19, 1980 LOS ANGELES, CALIF.
30- 9 CARAWAY, CECIL BRADFORD PATRICK 'PAT'	D. JUNE 9, 1974 EL PASO, TEX.
69- 29 CARBO, BERNARDO	908 WINCHESTER - LINCOLN PARK MI 48146
46- 16 CARDEN, JOHN BRUTON	D. FEBRUARY 8, 1949 MEXIA, TEX.
63- 21 CARDENAL, JOSE DOMEC	2219 NORTH MAIN - TULSA OK 74106
60- 19 CARDENAS, LEONARDO LAZARO 'CHICO'	11696 HINKLEY DR - FOREST PARK OH 45240
63- 22 CARDINAL, CONRAD SETH 'RANDY'	3810 VERDE WAY - NORTH LAS VEGAS NV 89030
43- 26 CARDONI, ARMAND JOSEPH 'BEN'	D. APRIL 2, 1969 JESSUP, PA.
57- 9 CARDWELL, DONALD EUGENE	BOX 474 - CLEMMONS NC 27012
67- 14 CAREW, RODNEY CLINE	5144 CRESCENT DR - ANAHEIM CA 92807
52- 16 CAREY, ANDREW ARTHUR	4411 E EMBERWOOD LN - ANAHEIM CA 92807
10- 23 CAREY, MAX GEORGE	D. MAY 30, 1976 MIAMI, FLA.
35- 11 CAREY, THOMAS FRANCIS ALOYSIUS	D. FEBRUARY 21, 1970 ROCHESTER, N. Y.
32- 11 CARLETON, JAMES OTTO 'TEX'	D. JANUARY 11, 1977 FORT WORTH, TEX.
41- 14 CARLIN, JAMES ARTHUR	1215 33RD ST-BIRMINGHAM AL 35218
67- 15 CARLOS, FRANCISCO MANUEL 'CISCO'	OLD ADD: 1229 SESMAS ST - DUARTE CA 91010
48- 23 CARLSEN, DONALD HERBERT	3600 EAST EASTER AVE - LITTLETON CO 80122
17- 13 CARLSON, HAROLD GUST	D. MAY 28, 1930 CHICAGO, ILL.
20- 16 CARLSON, LEON ALTON	D. SEPTEMBER 15, 1961 JAMESTOWN, N. Y.
11- 23 CARLSTROM, ALBIN OSCAR 'SWEDE'	D. APRIL 23, 1935 ELIZABETH, N.J.
65- 18 CARLTON, STEVEN NORMAN	16240 HOLTS LAKE DR - CHESTERFIELD MO 63017
27- 22 CARLYLE, HIRAM CLEO	D. NOVEMBER 12, 1967 LOS ANGELES, CAL.
25- 16 CARLYLE, ROY EDWARD	D. NOVEMBER 22, 1956 NORCROSS, GA.
83- 25 CARMAN, DONALD WAYNE	BOX 14 - CAMARGO OK 73885
59- 11 CARMEL, LEON JAMES 'DUKE'	10 PHEASANT VALLEY DR - CORAM NY 11727
41- 15 CARNETT, EDWIN ELLIOTT	1010 INDIAN CREEK DR - LEBANON MO 65536
43- 27 CARPENTER, LEWIS EMMETT	D. APRIL 25, 1979 MARIETTA, GA.
16- 11 CARPENTER, PAUL CALVIN	D. MARCH 14, 1968 NEWARK, O.
40- 9 CARPENTER, ROBERT LOUIS	9321 S SACRAMENTO AVE - EVERGREEN PARK IL 60642
65- 19 CARPIN, FRANK DOMINIC	5202 RIVERSIDE DR - RICHMOND VA 23225
39- 18 CARRASQUEL, ALEJANDRO ALEXANDER	D. AUGUST 19, 1969 CARACAS, VENEZUELA
50- 12 CARRASQUEL, ALFONSO COLON 'CHICO'	1432 NORTH LAWNDALE AVE - CHICAGO IL 60657
59- 12 CARREON, CAMILO GARCIA	4450 E COOPER ST - TUCSON AZ 85711
70- 18 CARRITHERS, DONALD GEORGE	1851 HARRIS AVE - SAN JOSE CA 95124
64- 17 CARROLL, CLAY PALMER	4515 26TH AVE - BRADENTON FL 33503
19- 11 CARROLL, DORSEY LEE 'DIXIE'	D. OCTOBER 13, 1984 JACKSONVILLE, FLA.
29- 15 CARROLL, EDGAR FLEISCHER	D. OCTOBER 13, 1984 ROSSVILLE, MD.
25- 17 CARROLL, OWEN THOMAS	D. JUNE 8, 1975 ORANGE, N. J.
16- 12 CARROLL, RALPH ARTHUR 'DOC'	D. JUNE 27, 1983 WORCESTER, MASS.
55- 22 CARROLL, THOMAS EDWARD	607 BAYSIDE - ROCKAWAY POINT NY 11697
74- 14 CARROLL, THOMAS MICHAEL	1447 TOWLSON RD - VIENNA VA 22180
10- 24 CARSON, ALBERT JAMES	D. NOVEMBER 26, 1962 SAN DIEGO, CALIF.
34- 16 CARSON, WALTER LLOYD 'KIT'	D. JUNE 21, 1983 LONG BEACH, CALIF.
53- 15 CARSWELL, FRANK WILLIS	3517 STANFORD - HOUSTON TX 77006
44- 19 CARTER, ARNOLD LEE	8102 PEBBLE BROOK LN - LOUISVILLE KY 40219
74- 15 CARTER, GARY EDMUND	OLD ADD:2259 CONEGO LN - FULLERTON CA 92623
26- 12 CARTER, JOHN HOWARD	430 E 86TH ST - NEW YORK NY 10028
83- 26 CARTER, JOSEPH CHRIS	1800 NE 51ST - OKLAHOMA CITY OK 73111
25- 18 CARTER, OTIS LEONARD 'BLACKIE'	D. SEPTEMBER 10, 1978 GREENVILLE, S. C.
14- 34 CARTER, PAUL WARREN 'NICK'	D. SEPTEMBER 11, 1984 LAKE PARK, GA.
31- 11 CARTER, SOLOMON MOBLEY	2402 GALE PL - EL DORADO AR 71730
63- 23 CARTY, RICARDO ADOLFO JACABO 'RICO'	5 ENS ENRIQUILLO-SAN PEDRO DE MACORIS DOM. REP.
85- 15 CARY, CHARLES DOUGLAS	3323 CASA GRANDE DRIVE - SAN RAMON CA 94583
47- 16 CARY, SCOTT RUSSELL	RR 4 - BRONSON MI 49028
58- 18 CASALE, JERRY JOSEPH	145 DURANT AVE - STATEN ISLAND NY 10306
65- 20 CASANOVA, ORTIZ PAULINO 'PAUL'	OLD ADD: 413 CHERRY - SYRACUSE NY 13210
34- 17 CASCARELLA, JOSEPH THOMAS	7111 PARK HEIGHTS AVE - BALTIMORE MD 21215
37- 20 CASE, GEORGE WASHINGTON	1108 EVERGREEN RD - MORRISVILLE PA 19067
35- 12 CASEY, HUGH THOMAS	D. JULY 3, 1951 ATLANTA, GA.
69- 30 CASH, DAVID	10471 MOORPARK ST - SPRING VALLEY CA 92078
58- 19 CASH, NORMAN DALTON	4522 ROLLING PINES CT-WEST BLOOMFIELD MI48033
73- 18 CASH, RONALD FOREST	277 EARLY PKWY SE - SMYRNA GA 30080

GARY CARTER

36

CASHION

11- 24	CASHION, JAY CARL	D. NOVEMBER 17, 1935 LAKE MILLICENT, WIS.
73- 19	CASKEY, CRAIG DOUGLAS	836 YVONNE PL - ANAHEIM CA 92801
49- 14	CASSINI, JACK DEMPSEY	1500 ROAD 1 #42 - DUNEDIN FL 33528
34- 18	CASTER, GEORGE JASPER	D. DECEMBER 18, 1955 LAKEWOOD, CAL.
42- 17	CASTIGLIA, JAMES VINCENT	5301 WESTBARD CIR #313 - WASHINGTON DC 20016
47- 17	CASTIGLIONE, PETER PAUL	1320 NE 26TH TERRACE - POMPANO BEACH FL 33062
78- 24	CASTILLO, ANTHONY BELTRAN	10300 JOYCE CT - SAN JOSE CA 95127
80- 22	CASTILLO, ESTEBAN MANUEL 'MANNY'	COSTA RICA 112,ENS. OZAMA - SANTO DOMINGO DOM. REP.
81- 22	CASTILLO, MARTIN HORACE	2669 BAYLOR ST - ANAHEIM CA 92801
82- 23	CASTILLO, MONTE CARMELO	B. JUNE 8, 1959 SAN FRANCISCO DE MACORIS, DR
77- 26	CASTILLO, ROBERT ERNIE	2837 SIERRA ST - LOS ANGELES CA 90031
79- 16	CASTINO, JOHN ANTHONY	1019 ILLINOIS RD - WILMETTE IL 60091
43- 28	CASTINO, VINCENT CHARLES	D. MARCH 6, 1967 SACRAMENTO, CAL.
73- 20	CASTLE, DONALD HARDY	RR 2 BOX 34AA - COLDWATER MS 38618
10- 25	CASTLE, JOHN FRANCIS	D. APRIL 13, 1929 PHILADELPHIA, PA.
34- 19	CASTLEMAN, CLYDELL	BOX 140601 - DONELSON TN 37214
54- 13	CASTLEMAN, FOSTER EPHRAIM	5 JUSTICIA LN - CINCINNATI OH 45218
23- 19	CASTNER, PAUL HENRY	D. MARCH 3, 1986 ST. PAUL, MINN.
74- 16	CASTRO, WILLIAMS RADHAMES	5231 RAVEN DR - GREENDALE WI 53129
64- 18	CATER, DANNY ANDERSON	1016 CAMINO LA COSTA #2606 - AUSTIN TX 78752
12- 33	CATHER, THEODORE P.	D. APRIL 9, 1945 ELKTON, MD.
42- 18	CATHEY, HARDIN	561 ELAINE DR - NASHVILLE TN 37211
83- 27	CATO, JOHN KEEFE	98 MARYTON ROAD - WHITE PLAINS NY 10603
17- 14	CATON, JAMES HOWARD 'BUSTER'	D. JANUARY 8, 1948 ZANESVILLE, O.
79- 17	CAUDILL, WILLIAM HOLLAND	1200 MANHATTAN BEACH BLVD - MANHATTAN BEACH CA 90266
46- 17	CAULFIELD, JOHN JOSEPH	557 28TH AVE - SAN FRANCISCO CA 94121
18- 9	CAUSEY, CECIL ALGERNON 'RED'	D. NOVEMBER 11, 1960 TAMPA, FLA.
55- 23	CAUSEY, JAMES WAYNE	2905 PAYNTER DR - RUSTON LA 71270
19- 12	CAVANAUGH, JOHN J.	D. JANUARY 14, 1961 NEW BRUNSWICK, N. J.
34- 20	CAVARRETTA, PHILIP JOSEPH	2206 PORTSIDE PASSAGE - PALM HARBOR FL 33563
22- 19	CAVENEY, JAMES CHRISTOPHER 'IKE'	D. JULY 6, 1949 SAN FRANCISCO, CAL.
11- 25	CAVET, TILLER 'PUG'	D. AUGUST 4, 1966 SAN LUIS OBISPO, CALIF.
55- 24	CECCARELLI, ARTHUR EDWARD	63 HALL DR - ORANGE CT 06477
44- 20	CECIL, REX HOLSTON	D. OCTOBER 30, 1966 LONG BEACH, CAL.
70- 19	CEDENO, CESAR EUGENITO	77 CARPENTER RIDGE - BLUE ASH OH 45241
42- 19	CENTER, MARVIN EARL 'PETE'	BOX 64 - CAMPTON KY 41301
58- 20	CEPEDA, ORLANDO MANUEL	1916 CHURCH ST #A - BURBANK CA 91504
75- 25	CERONE, RICHARD 'RICK'	63 EISENHOWER - CRESSKILL NJ 07626
85- 16	CERUTTI, JOHN JOSEPH	43 SOUTH MAIN AVENUE - ALBANY NY 12208
51- 10	CERV, ROBERT HENRY	2601 WINCHESTER S. - LINCOLN NE 68512
71- 21	CEY, RONALD CHARLES	22714 CREOLE RD - WOODLAND HILLS CA 91364
60- 20	CHACON, ELIO RODRIGUEZ	OLD ADD: AVE ANDALUCIA,ED. MARICAY-CARACAS VZ

CHAPMAN

29- 16	CHAGNON, LEON WILBUR	D. JULY 30, 1953 AMESBURY, MASS.
51- 11	CHAKALES, ROBERT EDWARD	206 MORELAND DR - RICHMOND VA 23229
73- 21	CHALK, DAVID LEE	6126 SUMMER CREEK CIR - DALLAS TX 75231
10- 26	CHALMERS, GEORGE W.	D. AUGUST 5, 1960 BRONX, N. Y.
79- 18	CHAMBERLAIN, CRAIG PHILIP	9057 COBBLESTONE - CYPRESS CA 90630
32- 12	CHAMBERLAIN, WILLIAM VINCENT	404 SPADARO DR - VENICE FL 33595
34- 21	CHAMBERLIN, JOSEPH JEREMIAH	D. JANUARY 28, 1983 SAN FRANCISCO, CALIF.
83- 28	CHAMBERS, ALBERT EUGENE	1303 NORTH 14TH ST - HARRISBURG PA 17103
48- 24	CHAMBERS, CLIFFORD DAY	10237 PRAIRIE RD - BOISE ID 83702
37- 21	CHAMBERS, JOHNNIE MONROE	D. MAY 11, 1977 PALATKA, FLA.
10- 27	CHAMBERS, WILLIAM CHRISTOPHER	D. MARCH 27, 1962 FORT WAYNE, IND.
71- 22	CHAMBLISS, CARROLL CHRISTOPHER 'CHRIS'	54 IVY CHASE - ATLANTA GA 30342
69- 31	CHAMPION, BUFORD BILLY	304 NE LOWER CREEK DR - LENOIR NC 28645
76- 25	CHAMPION, ROBERT MICHAEL 'MIKE'	17965 FIESTA WAY - TUSTIN CA 92680
63- 24	CHANCE, ROBERT	2258 OAK RIDGE DR - CHARLESTON WV 25311
61- 19	CHANCE, WILMER DEAN	9505 W. SMITHVILLE WESTERN - WOOSTER OH 44691
47- 18	CHANDLER, EDWARD OLIVER	5855 GREEN VALLEY CIR #109 - CULVER CITY CA 90230
37- 22	CHANDLER, SPURGEON FERDINAND 'SPUD'	1591 77TH ST N - ST PETERSBURG FL 33710
69- 32	CHANEY, DARREL LEE	5196 CLEARWATER DR - STONE MOUNTAIN GA 30087
13- 28	CHANEY, ESTEY CLEON	D. FEBRUARY 5, 1952 CLEVELAND, O.
10- 28	CHANNELL, LESTER CLARK	D. MAY 7, 1954 DENVER, COLO.
75- 24	CHANT, CHARLES JOSEPH	13426 SUNFLOWER CT - SUNNYMEAD CA 92388
20- 17	CHAPLIN, BERT EDGAR	D. AUGUST 15, 1978 SANFORD, FLA.
28- 21	CHAPLIN, JAMES BAILEY 'TINY'	D. MARCH 25, 1939 NATIONAL CITY, CAL.
35- 13	CHAPMAN, CALVIN LOUIS	D. APRIL 1, 1983 BATESVILLE, MISS.
33- 12	CHAPMAN, EDWIN VOLNEY	LAMBERT MS 38643
39- 19	CHAPMAN, FREDERICK WILLIAM	112 NORTH RIDGE AVE - KANNAPOLIS NC 28081
34- 22	CHAPMAN, GLENN JUSTICE	418 E ARBOR AVE - SUNNYVALE CA 94086
12- 34	CHAPMAN, HARRY E.	D. OCTOBER 21, 1918 NEVADA, MO.
24- 17	CHAPMAN, JOHN JOSEPH	D. NOVEMBER 3, 1953 PHILADELPHIA, PA.

37

```
79- 19 CHAPMAN, KELVIN KEITH              300 ROAD NORTH - REDWOOD VALLEY CA 94570
12- 35 CHAPMAN, RAYMOND JOHNSON           D. AUGUST 17, 1920 NEW YORK, N.Y.
38- 12 CHAPMAN, SAMUEL BLAKE              11 ANDREW DR #39 - TIBURON CA 94920
30- 10 CHAPMAN, WILLIAM BENJAMIN 'BEN'    401 SHADESWOOD CIR - BIRMINGHAM AL 35226
78- 25 CHAPPAS, HARRY PERRY               1440 NW 52ND AVE - LAUDERHILL FL 33313
13- 29 CHAPPELL, LAVERNE ASHFORD 'LARRY'  D. NOVEMBER 8, 1918 SAN FRANCISCO, CALIF.
80- 23 CHARBONEAU, JOSEPH                 44 HIGH ST - LOCKPORT NY 14094
62- 27 CHARLES, EDWIN CHARLES             8121 EAST 134TH ST - GRANDVIEW MO 64030
40- 10 CHARTAK, MICHAEL GEORGE            D. JULY 25, 1967 OAKDALE, IA.
64- 19 CHARTON, FRANK LANE "PETE"         27 VINCINDA LN - HARRIMAN TN 37748
36- 14 CHASE, KENDALL FAY                 D. JANUARY 16, 1985 ONEONTA, N. Y.
30- 11 CHATHAM, CHARLES L. 'BUSTER'       D. DECEMBER 15, 1975 WACO, TEXAS
66- 18 CHAVARRIA, OSWALDO QUIJANO 'OSSIE' 7074 INLET DR #112 - NORTH BARNEBY BRIT. COL. CAN.
67- 16 CHAVEZ, NESTOR ISAIAS SILVA        D. MARCH 16, 1969 MARACAIBO, VENEZ.
73- 22 CHEADLE, DAVID BAIRD               4236 BATTERY RD - VIRGINIA BEACH VA 23455
10- 29 CHEEK, HARRY G.                    D. JUNE 25, 1956 PARAMUS, N. J.
20- 18 CHEEVES, VIRGIL EARL 'CHIEF'       D. MAY 5, 1979 DALLAS, TEXAS
35- 14 CHELINI, ITALO VINCENT             D. AUGUST 25, 1972 SAN FRANCISCO, CAL.
11- 26 CHENEY, LAURANCE RUSSELL           D. JANUARY 6, 1969 DAYTONA BEACH, FLA.
57- 10 CHENEY, THOMAS EDGAR               607 EUGEMAR - ALBANY GA 31707
37- 23 CHERVINKO, PAUL                    D. JUNE 3, 1976 DANVILLE, ILL.
48- 25 CHESNES, ROBERT VINCENT            D. MAY 23, 1979 EVERETT, WASH.
45-  8 CHETKOVICH, MITCHELL               D. AUGUST 24, 1971 GRASS VALLEY, CAL.
77- 27 CHEVEZ, ANTONIO SILVIO             TELIA D. PTO. - LEON NICARAGUA
82- 24 CHIFFER, FLOYD JOHN                4325 LEVELSIDE AVE - LAKESIDE CA 90712
30- 12 CHILD, HARRY PATRICK               D. NOVEMBER 8, 1972 ALEXANDRIA, VA.
85- 17 CHILDRESS, RODNEY OSBORNE 'ROCKY'  5 MEADOWGLEN COURT - SANTA ROSA CA 95404
71- 23 CHILES, RICHARD FRANCIS            4501 SAN RAMON DR - DAVIS CA 95616
35- 15 CHIOZZA, DINO JOSEPH               D. APRIL 23, 1972 MEMPHIS, TENN.
34- 23 CHIOZZA, LOUIS PEO                 D. FEBRUARY 28, 1971 MEMPHIS, TENN.
41- 16 CHIPMAN, ROBERT HOWARD             D. NOVEMBER 8, 1973 HUNTINGTON, N.Y.
45-  9 CHIPPLE, WALTER JOHN               52 RAMSDELL AVE - BUFFALO NY 14216
79- 20 CHISM, THOMAS RAYMOND              1311 ELSON ROAD - CHESTER PA 19013
50- 21 CHITI, HARRY                       3897 WORDSWORTH ST - RALEIGH TN 38128
58- 21 CHITTUM, NELSON BOYD               2312 TEROVA - TROY MI 48098
70- 20 CHLUPSA, ROBERT JOSEPH             RR1 - SOUND BEACH NY 11789
60- 21 CHOATE, DONALD LEON                109 N 5TH - DESLOGE MO 63601
10- 30 CHOUINARD, FELIX GEORGE            D. APRIL 28, 1955 HINES, ILL.
10- 31 CHOUNEAU, WILLIAM 'CHIEF'          D. SEPTEMBER 17, 1948 CLOQUET, MINN.
37- 24 CHOZEN, HARRY KENNETH              2208 20TH ST - LAKE CHARLES LA 70601
79- 21 CHRIS, MICHAEL                     12437 WOODGREEN ST - LOS ANGELES CA 90066
57- 11 CHRISLEY, BARBRA O'NEIL 'NEIL'     104 WOODLAND WAY - GREENWOOD SC 29646
19- 13 CHRISTENBURY, LLOYD REID           D. DECEMBER 13, 1944 BIRMINGHAM, ALA.
71- 24 CHRISTENSEN, BRUCE RAY             BOX 178 - MORONI UT 84646
84- 17 CHRISTENSEN, JOHN LAWRENCE         2223 E. COMMONWEALTH AVE - FULLERTON CA 92631
26- 13 CHRISTENSEN, WALTER NIELS          D. DECEMBER 20, 1984 MENLO PARK, CALIF.
79- 22 CHRISTENSON, GARY RICHARD          1610 WASHINGTON AVE - NEW HYDE PARK NY 11040
73- 23 CHRISTENSON, LARRY RICHARD         4308 76TH ST NE - MARYSVILLE WA 98270
68- 13 CHRISTIAN, ROBERT CHARLES          D. FEBRUARY 20, 1974 SAN DIEGO, CAL.
84- 18 CHRISTIANSEN, CLAY C.              RURAL ROUTE 3 - COLUMBUS KS 66725
38- 13 CHRISTMAN, MARQUETTE JOSEPH        D. OCTOBER 9, 1976 ST. LOUIS, MO.
83- 29 CHRISTMAS, STEPHEN RANDALL         OLD ADD: 5860 MATTOX ST - ORLANDO FL 32809
```

Ossie Chavarria

```
59- 13 CHRISTOPHER, JOSEPH O'NEAL          1970 ADD: CALLE CHILE 108 - MAYAGUEZ PR 00708
45- 10 CHRISTOPHER, LOYD EUGENE            747 GOLDEN GATE AVE - RICHMOND CA 94801
42- 20 CHRISTOPHER, RUSSELL ORMAND         D. DECEMBER 5, 1954 POINT RICHMOND, CAL.
50- 21 CHURCH, EMORY NICHOLAS 'BUBBA'      816 NOB HILL DR #C - BIRMINGHAM AL 35209
66- 19 CHURCH, LEONARD                     BOX 832223 - RICHARDSON TX 75083
57- 12 CHURN, CLARENCE NOTTINGHAM 'CHUCK'  BOX 39 - GREENBUSH VA 23357
24- 18 CHURRY, JOHN                        D. FEBRUARY 8, 1970 ZANESVILLE, O.
51- 12 CIAFFONE, LAWRENCE THOMAS           240 LAKE ST - BROOKLYN NY 11223
83- 30 CIAS, DARRYL RICHARD                12330 LITHUANIA ST - GRANADA HILLS CA 91344
29- 17 CICERO, JOSEPH FRANCIS              D. MARCH 30, 1983 CLEARWATER, FLA.
57- 13 CICOTTE, ALVA WARREN                D. NOVEMBER 29, 1982 WESTLAND, MICH.
44- 21 CIESLAK, THADDEUS WALTER 'TED'      6244 S 20TH ST - MILWAUKEE WI 53221
45- 11 CIHOCKI, ALBERT JOSEPH              124 W GREEN - NANTICOKE PA 18634
32- 13 CIHOCKI, EDWARD JOSEPH              23 BOXWOOD AV - WILMINGTON DE 19804
65- 21 CIMINO, PETER WILLIAM               14 FILLMORE ST - BRISTOL PA 19007
56- 21 CIMOLI, GINO NICHOLAS               30 LINDA VISTA - TIBURON CA 94920
43- 29 CIOLA, LOUIS ALEXANDER              2105 8TH AVE NW-AUSTIN MN 55912
61- 20 CIPRIANI, FRANK DOMINICK            62 BARLOW - LACKAWANNA NY 14218
37- 25 CISAR, GEORGE JOSEPH                2520 S 56TH COURT-CICERO IL 60650
61- 21 CISCO, GALEN BERNARD                RR 1 BOX 150 - SAINT MARYS OH 45885
```

28- 22 CISSELL, CHALMER WILLIAM 'BILL'   D. MARCH 15, 1949 CHICAGO, ILL.
83- 31 CITARELLA, RALPH ALEXANDER   29 EAST SHERMAN AVE - COLONIA NJ 07067
26- 14 CLABAUGH, JOHN WILLIAM 'MOOSE'   D. JULY 11, 1984 TUCSON, ARIZ.
20- 19 CLAIRE, DAVID MATTHEW   D. JANUARY 7, 1956 LAS VEGAS, NEV.
11- 27 CLANCY, ALBERT HARRISON   D. OCTOBER 17, 1951 LAS CRUCES, N. MEX.
77- 28 CLANCY, JAMES   6147 ROBROY ST - OAK FOREST IL 60452
24- 19 CLANCY, JOHN WILLIAM 'BUD'   D. SEPTEMBER 26, 1968 OTTUMWA, IA.
22- 20 CLANTON, UCAL CURT   D. FEBRUARY 24, 1960 ANTLERS, OKLA.
76- 26 CLAREY, DOUGLAS WILLIAM   1126 WILSHIRE BLVD - LOS ANGELES CA 90017
47- 19 CLARK, ALFRED ALOYSIUS 'ALLIE'   250 N STEVENS AVE - SOUTH AMBOY NJ 08879
27- 23 CLARK, BAILEY EARL   D. JANUARY 16, 1938 WASHINGTON, D. C.
81- 23 CLARK, BRYAN DONALD   508 N CLARK ST - MADERA CA 93637
22- 21 CLARK, DANIEL CURRAN   D. MAY 23, 1937 MERIDIAN, MISS.
13- 30 CLARK, GEORGE MYRON   D. NOVEMBER 14, 1940 SIOUX CITY, IA.
67- 17 CLARK, GLEN ESTER   3110 E 14TH - AUSTIN TX 78702
75- 26 CLARK, JACK ANTHONY   602 CORNWALLIS - FOSTER CITY CA 94404
48- 26 CLARK, JAMES   1518 7TH ST #5 - SANTA MONICA CA 90401
71- 25 CLARK, JAMES EDWARD   1322 W ECKERMAN - WEST COVINA CA 91790
11- 28 CLARK, JAMES FRANCIS   D. MARCH 20, 1969 BEAUMONT, TEX.
38- 14 CLARK, JOHN CARROLL 'CAP'   D. FEBRUARY 16, 1957 FAYETTEVILLE, N. C.
51- 13 CLARK, MELVIN EARL   BOX 97 - WEST COLUMBIA WV 25287
52- 17 CLARK, MICHAEL JOHN   3 ASPEN AVE - BELLMAWR NJ 08030
58- 22 CLARK, PHILIP JAMES   1103 6TH ST - ALBANY GA 31701
67- 18 CLARK, RICKEY CHARLES   16132 MEADOWBROOK - DETROIT MI 48240
79- 23 CLARK, ROBERT CALE   1030 PERVISITO ST - PERRIS CA 92370
20- 20 CLARK, ROBERT WILLIAM   D. MAY 18, 1944 CARLSBAD, N. M.
66- 20 CLARK, RONALD BRUCE   700 STARKEY RD #511 - LARGO FL 33541
45- 12 CLARK, WILLIAM OTIS 'OTEY'   2735 E BASS LAKE RD - GRAND RAPIDS MN 55744
24- 20 CLARK, WILLIAM WATSON 'WATTY'   D. MARCH 4, 1972 CLEARWATER, FLA.
21- 13 CLARKE, ALAN THOMAS   D. MARCH 11, 1975 CHEVERLY, MD.
65- 22 CLARKE, HORACE MEREDITH   BOX 891 - FREDERIKSTED VI 00840
44- 22 CLARKE, RICHARD GREY   2122 GLENWOOD ST - KANNAPOLIS NC 28081
23- 20 CLARKE, RUFUS RIVERS   D. FEBRUARY 8, 1983 COLUMBIA, S. C.
83- 32 CLARKE, STANLEY MARTEN   37 EAST LAKE STREET - TOLEDO OH 43608
20- 21 CLARKE, SUMPTER MILLS   D. MARCH 16, 1962 KNOXVILLE, TENN.
55- 25 CLARKE, VIBERT ERNESTO 'WEBBO'   D. JUNE 14, 1970 CRISTOBAL, CANAL ZONE
29- 18 CLARKE, WILLIAM STUART   21252 TYEE ST - CASTRO VALLEY CA 94546
52- 18 CLARKSON, JAMES BUSTER 'BUZZ'   639 SIXTH ST - JEANETTE PA 15644
27- 24 CLARKSON, WILLIAM HENRY   D. AUGUST 27, 1971 RALEIGH, N. C.
42- 21 CLARY, ELLIS   206 W ALDEN ST-VALDOSTA GA 31603
33- 13 CLASET, GOWELL SYLVESTER   D. MARCH 8, 1981 ST. PETERSBURG, FLA.
13- 31 CLAUSS, ALBERT STANLEY   D. SEPTEMBER 13, 1952 NEW HAVEN, CONN.
43- 30 CLAY, DAIN ELMER   462 PARKWAY - CHULA VISTA CA 92010
77- 29 CLAY, KENNETH EARL   BOX 3115 - ABILENE TX 79604
79- 24 CLEAR, MARK ALAN   4005 E. ROLLING GREEN LN - ORANGE CA 92667
45- 13 CLEARY, JOSEPH CHRISTOPHER   OLD ADD: 15 JACOBUS PL - BRONX NY 10463
39- 20 CLEMENS, CHESTER SPURGEON   423 CRESPI - SAN CLEMENTE CA 92672
14- 35 CLEMENS, CLEMENT LAMBERT   D. NOVEMBER 18 1967 ST PETERSBURG, FLA.
60- 22 CLEMENS, DOUGLAS HORACE   RR 2 BOX 174 - NEW HOPE PA 18938
84- 19 CLEMENS, WILLIAM ROGER   10131 BEEKMAN PLACE DR - HOUSTON TX 77043

MARK CLEAR   RHP

39- 21 CLEMENSEN, WILLIAM MELVILLE   7555 MYRTLE VISTA AVE - SACRAMENTO CA 95831
55- 26 CLEMENTE, ROBERTO WALKER   D. DECEMBER 31,1972 SAN JUAN, P. R.
85- 18 CLEMENTS, PATRICK BRIAN   125 PARMAC ROAD #5 - CHICO CA 95926
71- 26 CLEMONS, LANCE LEVIS   1346 LODGE CIR - SPRING HILL FL 33512
14- 36 CLEMONS, ROBERT BAXTER   D. APRIL 5, 1964 LOS ANGELES, CALIF.
16- 13 CLEMONS, VERNE JAMES   D. MAY 5, 1959 BAY PINES, FLA.
61- 22 CLENDENON, DONN ALVIN   P.O. BOX 108 - INGOMAR PA 15127
69- 33 CLEVELAND, REGINALD LESLIE   OLD ADD: 1005 SPRINGFIELD - MANSFIELD TX 76063
54- 14 CLEVENGER, TRUMAN EUGENE 'TEX'   74 N CARMELITA - PORTERVILLE CA 93257
80- 24 CLIBURN, STANLEY GENE   727 NIMITZ DR - JACKSON MS 39209
84- 20 CLIBURN, STEWART WALKER   5720 MEDALLION DR - JACKSON MS 39211
34- 24 CLIFT, HARLOND BENTON   915 NORTH 15TH AVE #5 - YAKIMA WA 98902
34- 25 CLIFTON, HERMAN EARL 'FLEA'   4077 RACE RD - CINCINNATI OH 45211
60- 23 CLINE, TYRONE ALEXANDER   676 AYERS - CHARLESTON SC 29412
70- 21 CLINES, EUGENE ANTHONY   245 DARLENE ST - YORK PA 17402
60- 24 CLINTON, LUCIEAN LOUIS   330 N. ARMOUR - WICHITA KS 67206
61- 23 CLONINGER, TONY LEE   RR 2 BOX 381-A - IRON STATION NC 28080
66- 21 CLOSTER, ALAN EDWARD   CREIGHTON NE 68729
24- 21 CLOUGH, EDGAR GEORGE   D. JANUARY 30, 1944 HARRISBURG, PA.
26- 15 CLOWERS, WILLIAM PERRY   D. JANUARY 13, 1978 SWEENY, TEX.
73- 24 CLYDE, DAVID EUGENE   402 HICKORY POST - HOUSTON TX 77024
43- 31 CLYDE, THOMAS KNOX   3612 GARDEN BROOK DR - DALLAS TX 75234
46- 18 COAN, GILBERT FITZGERALD   20 E JORDAN ST - BREVARD NC 28712
56- 22 COATES, JAMES ALTON   BOX 57 - LANCASTER VA 22503

29- 19 COBB, HERBERT EDWARD	D. JANUARY 8, 1980 TARBORO, N. C.
18- 10 COBB, JOSEPH STANLEY	D. DECEMBER 24, 1947 ALLENTOWN, PA.
39- 22 COBLE, DAVID LAMAR	D. OCTOBER 15, 1971 ORLANDO, FLA.
83- 33 COCANOWER, JAMES STANLEY 'JAIME'	1609 STONEHENGE - LITTLE ROCK AR 72212
15- 20 COCHRAN, ALVAH JACKSON	D. MAY 23, 1947 ATLANTA, GA.
18- 11 COCHRAN, GEORGE LESLIE	D. MAY 21, 1960 HARBOR CITY, CALIF.
25- 19 COCHRANE, GORDON STANLEY 'MICKEY'	D. JUNE 2, 1962 LAKE FOREST, ILL.
13- 32 COCREHAM, EUGENE	D. DECEMBER 27, 1945 LULING, TEX.
82- 25 CODIROLI, CHRISTOPHER ALLEN	4851 MAUNA LOA PARK DR - FREMONT CA 94538
12- 36 COFFEY (JOHN JOSEPH SMITH) 'JACK'	D. DECEMBER 4, 1962 NEW YORK, N. Y.
37- 26 COFFMAN, GEORGE DAVID	1120 BEACON PKWY EAST #202 - BIRMINGHAM AL 35209
27- 25 COFFMAN, SAMUEL RICHARD 'DICK'	D. MARCH 24, 1972 ATHENS, ALA.
67- 19 COGGINS, FRANKLIN	106 ARMSTEDD CIR - GRIFFIN GA 30223
72- 18 COGGINS, RICHARD ALLEN	OLD ADD: 3801 PARKVIEW - IRVINE CA 92713
31- 12 COHEN, ALTA ALBERT	1 CLARIDGE DR - VERONA NJ 07044
26- 16 COHEN, ANDREW HOWARD	4341 N STANTON - EL PASO TX 79902
55- 27 COHEN, HYMAN	22610 FLAMINGO ST - WOODLAND HILLS CA 91364
34- 26 COHEN, SYDNEY HARRY	1121 RIM ROAD - EL PASO TX 79902
58- 23 COKER, JIMMIE GOODWIN	BOX TWO - THROCKMORTON TX 76083
55- 28 COLAVITO, ROCCO DOMENICO	BOX 1969 - KANSAS CITY MO 64141
78- 26 COLBERN, MICHAEL MALLOY	1059 E FAIRMONT - TEMPE AZ 85282
66- 22 COLBERT, NATHAN	17369 RUETTE ABETO - SAN DIEGO CA 92127
70- 22 COLBERT, VINCENT NORMAN	1417 'E' STREET SE - WASHINGTON DC 20003
69- 34 COLBORN, JAMES WILLIAM	2932 SOLIMAR BEACH DR - VENTURA CA 93001
21- 14 COLE, ALBERT GEORGE	D. MAY 30, 1975 SAN MATEO, CAL.
50- 22 COLE, DAVID BRUCE	30 S CONOCOCHEAGUE ST - WILLIAMSPORT MD 21795
38- 15 COLE, EDWARD WILLIAM	OLD ADD: 6853 LARMANDA - DALLAS TX 75231
51- 14 COLE, RICHARD ROY	3149 MADEIRA AVE - COSTA MESA CA 92626
61- 24 COLEMAN, CLARENCE 'CHOO-CHOO'	726 CORNELIA CT - ORLANDO FL 32807
12- 37 COLEMAN, CURTIS HANCOCK	D. JULY 1, 1980 NEWPORT, ORE.
77- 30 COLEMAN, DAVID LEE	4303 DELHI DR - DAYTON OH 45432
49- 15 COLEMAN, GERALD FRANCIS	1004 HAVENHURST DR - LAJOLLA CA 92037
59- 14 COLEMAN, GORDON CALVIN	8698 ZENITH CT - CINCINNATI OH 45231
65- 23 COLEMAN, JOSEPH HOWARD	16502 NE 46TH - REDMOND WA 98052
42- 22 COLEMAN, JOSEPH PATRICK	2422 N WESTWOOD DR - NORTH FT MYERS FL 33901
32- 14 COLEMAN, PARKE EDWARD 'ED'	D. AUGUST 5, 1964 OREGON CITY, ORE.
47- 20 COLEMAN, RAYMOND LEROY	BOX 8 - HORNBROOK CA 96044
13- 33 COLEMAN, ROBERT HUNTER	D. JULY 16, 1959 BOSTON, MASS.
85- 19 COLEMAN, VINCENT MAURICE	OLD ADD: 3810 N. CANAL ST #207 - JACKSONVILLE FL 32209

55- 29 COLEMAN, WALTER GARY	207 PAWLING AVE - TROY NY 12180
14- 37 COLES, CADWALLADER R.	D. JUNE 30, 1942 MIAMI, FLA.
58- 24 COLES, CHARLES EDWARD	BOX 32 - JEFFERSON PA 15344
83- 34 COLES, DARNELL	765 NORTH CHESTNUT - RIALTO CA 92376
72- 19 COLETTA, CHRISTOPHER MICHAEL	136 SW 38TH TER - CAPE CORAL 33914
11- 29 COLLAMORE, ALLAN EDWARD	D. AUGUST 8, 1980 BATTLE CREEK, MI.
27- 26 COLLARD, EARL CLINTON 'HAP'	D. JULY 14, 1968 JAMESTOWN, N. Y.
31- 13 COLLIER, ORLIN EDWARD	D. SEPTEMBER 9, 1944 MEMPHIS, TENN.
13- 34 COLLINS, CYRIL WILSON	D. FEBRUARY 28, 1941 KNOXVILLE, TENN.
75- 27 COLLINS, DAVID SCOTT	201 ST. CHARLES - RAPID CITY SD 57701
77- 31 COLLINS, DONALD EDWARD	3771 ROSWELL RD NE - ATLANTA GA 30305
39- 23 COLLINS, EDWARD TROWBRIDGE	BOX 206 - KENNETT SQUARE PA 19348
20- 22 COLLINS, HARRY WARREN 'RIP'	D. MAY 27, 1968 BRYAN, TEX.
31- 14 COLLINS, JAMES ANTHONY 'RIP'	D. APRIL 16, 1970 NEW HAVEN, N. Y.
14- 38 COLLINS, JOHN EDGAR "ZIP"	D. DECEMBER 19, 1983 MANASSAS, VA.
10- 32 COLLINS, JOHN FRANCIS 'SHANO'	D. SEPTEMBER 10, 1955 NEWTON, MASS.
48- 27 COLLINS, JOSEPH EDWARD	731 SUBURBAN RD - UNION NJ 07083
65- 24 COLLINS, KEVIN MICHAEL	97 W. ELMWOOD ST - CLAWSON MI 48017
23- 21 COLLINS, PHILIP EUGENE	D. AUGUST 14, 1948 CHICAGO, ILL.
40- 11 COLLINS, ROBERT JOSEPH	D. APRIL 19, 1969 PITTSBURGH, PA.
19- 14 COLLINS, THARON LESLIE 'PAT'	D. MAY 19, 1960 KANSAS CITY, KAN.
10- 33 COLLINS, WILLIAM SHIRLEY	D. JUNE 26, 1961 SAN BERNARDINO, CALIF.
51- 15 COLLUM, JACK DEAN	523 11TH AVE - GRINNELL IA 50112
42- 23 COLMAN, FRANK LOYD	D. FEBRUARY 19, 1983, LONDON, ONT.
70- 23 COLPAERT, RICHARD CHARLES	47412 ELDON - UTICA MI 48087
70- 24 COLSON, LOYD ALBERT	RR ONE - GOULD OK 73544
68- 16 COLTON, LAWRENCE ROBERT	3124 NE KNOTT - PORTLAND OR 97213
73- 25 COLUCCIO, ROBERT PASQUALI	1333 PARADISE CT SE - OLYMPIA WA 98503
80- 25 COMBE, GEOFFREY WADE	2384 E. AVENIDA OTONO - THOUSAND OAKS CA 91362
24- 22 COMBS, EARLE BRYAN	D. JULY 21, 1976 RICHMOND, KY.
47- 21 COMBS, MERRILL RUSSELL	D. JULY 8, 1981 RIVERSIDE, CALIF.
45- 14 COMELLAS, JORGE	13015 SW 50TH ST - MIAMI FL 33165
67- 20 COMER, HARRY WAYNE	RR 1 BOX 4F - SHENANDOAH VA 22849
78- 27 COMER, STEVEN MICHAEL	20500 SUMMERVILLE RD - EXCELSIOR MN 55331

Johnny Cooney

Earle Combs

54- 15 COMMAND, JAMES DALTON	1743 MATILDA ST NE - GRAND RAPIDS MI 49503
26- 17 COMORSKY, ADAM ANTHONY	D. MARCH 2, 1951 SWOYERSVILLE, PA.
11- 30 COMPTON, ANNA SEBASTIAN 'PETE'	D. FEBRUARY 3, 1978 KANSAS CITY, MO.
11- 31 COMPTON, HARRY LEROY 'JACK'	D. JULY 4, 1974 LANCASTER, O.
70- 25 COMPTON, MICHAEL LYNN	2511 N GOLDEN - ODESSA TX 79762
72- 20 COMPTON, ROBERT CLINTON	OLD ADD: 45 KENT ST - MONTGOMERY AL
84- 21 COMSTOCK, KEITH MARTIN	968 TAMARACK - SAN CARLOS CA 94070
13- 35 COMSTOCK, RALPH REMICK	D. SEPTEMBER 13, 1966 TOLEDO, O.
48- 28 CONATSER, CLINTON ASTOR	268 AVENIDA MONTALVO - SAN CLEMENTE CA 92672
70- 26 CONCEPCION, DAVID ISMAEL	URB. LOS CAOBOS BOTALON 5D, 5 PISO-MARACAY VENEZ
80- 26 CONCEPCION, ONIX (CARDONA)	PARCELA 61AA-BO.HIGUILLAR - DORADO PR 00646
62- 28 CONDE, RAMON LUIS	BOX 57 - JUANA DIAZ PR 00665
15- 21 CONE, ROBERT EARL	D. MAY 24, 1955 GALVESTON, TEX.
40- 12 CONGER, RICHARD	D. FEBRUARY 16, 1970 LOS ANGELES, CAL.
64- 20 CONIGLIARO, ANTHONY RICHARD	339 NAHANT RD - NAHANT MA 01908
69- 35 CONIGLIARO, WILLIAM MICHAEL	ROSEMARY RD - NAHANT MA 01908
20- 23 CONKWRIGHT, ALLEN HOWARD	7835 COWLES MT CT #B-2 - SAN DIEGO CA 92119
34- 27 CONLAN, JOHN BERTRAND 'JOCKO'	7810 E. MARIPOSA DR - SCOTTSDALE AZ 85251
52- 19 CONLEY, DONALD EUGENE 'GENE'	4 BIRCHTREE RD - FOXBORO MA 02035
14- 39 CONLEY, JAMES PATRICK 'SNIPE'	D. JANUARY 7, 1978 DESOTO, TEX.
58- 25 CONLEY, ROBERT BURNS	OLD ADD: 75 TOWNE SQUARE DR - NEWPORT NEWS VA 23607
23- 22 CONLON, ARTHUR JOSEPH	374 COMMONWEALTH AV - BOSTON MA 02116
83- 35 CONNALLY, FRITZIE LEE	714 CARDINAL CIRCLE - PASADENA TX 77502
21- 15 CONNALLY, GEORGE WALTER 'SARGE'	D. JANUARY 27, 1978 TEMPLE, TEXAS
25- 20 CONNALLY, MERVIN THOMAS	D. JUNE 12, 1964 BERKELEY, CAL.
31- 15 CONNATSER, BROADUS MILBURN 'BRUCE'	D. JANUARY 27, 1971 TERRE HAUTE, IND.
31- 16 CONNELL, EUGENE JOSEPH	D. AUGUST 31, 1937 WAVERLY, N. Y.
26- 18 CONNELL, JOSEPH BERNARD	D. SEPTEMBER 21, 1977 TREXLERTOWN, PA.
20- 24 CONNELLY, THOMAS MARTIN	D. FEBRUARY 18, 1941 HINES, ILL.
45- 15 CONNELLY, WILLIAM WIRT	D. NOVEMBER 27, 1980 RICHMOND, VA.
64- 21 CONNOLLY, EDWARD JOSEPH JR.	RT 49 COLONIAL ACRES - PITTSFIELD MA 01201
29- 20 CONNOLLY, EDWARD JOSEPH	D. NOVEMBER 14, 1963 PITTSFIELD, MASS.
13- 36 CONNOLLY, JOSEPH ALOYSIUS	D. SEPTEMBER 1, 1943 SPRINGFIELD, R.I.
21- 16 CONNOLLY, JOSEPH GEORGE	D. MARCH 30, 1960 SAN FRANCISCO, CALIF.
15- 22 CONNOLLY, THOMAS FRANCIS	D. MAY 14, 1966 BOSTON, MASS.
49- 16 CONNORS, KEVIN JOSEPH 'CHUCK'	STAR ROUTE BOX 4400-73 - TEHACHAPI CA 93561
37- 27 CONNORS, MERVYN JAMES	1131 ADDISON ST-BERKELEY CA 94702
66- 23 CONNORS, WILLIAM JOSEPH	895 N. VILLAGE DR #101 - ST. PETERSBURG FL 33702
78- 28 CONROY, TIMOTHY JAMES	416 LUZERNE DR - MONROEVILLE PA 15146
23- 23 CONROY, WILLIAM FREDERICK 'PEP'	D. JANUARY 23, 1970 CHICAGO, ILL.
35- 16 CONROY, WILLIAM GORDON	7194 CRAIL CT - CITRUS HEIGHTS CA 95610
53- 16 CONSOLO, WILLIAM ANGELO	1266 WILLSBROOK CT - WESTLAKE VILLAGE CA91360
56- 23 CONSTABLE, JAMES LEE	RR 14 - BOX 540 - JONESBORO TN 37659
50- 23 CONSUEGRA, SANDALIO SIMEON	CLINICA CUBANA,1200 SW 1ST ST - MIAMI FL 33135
80- 27 CONTRERAS, ARNALDO JUAN 'NARDIE'	1540 RIVER LN - TAMPA FL 33603
11- 32 CONWAY, CHARLES CONNELL	D. SEPTEMBER 12, 1968 YOUNGSTOWN, O.
41- 17 CONWAY, JACK CLEMENTS	3545 PINE - WACO TX 76708
20- 25 CONWAY, JEROME PATRICK	D. APRIL 16, 1980 HOLYOKE, MASS.
15- 23 CONWAY, OWEN SYLVESTER	D. MARCH 12, 1942 PHILADELPHIA, PA.
18- 12 CONWAY, RICHARD DANIEL 'RIP'	D. DECEMBER 3, 1971 ST PAUL, MINN.
11- 33 CONWELL, EDWARD JAMES	D. MAY 1, 1926 NORWOOD PARK, ILL.
50- 24 CONYERS, HERBERT LEROY	D. SEPTEMBER 16, 1964 CLEVELAND, O.
13- 37 CONZELMAN, JOSEPH HARRISON	D. APRIL 17, 1979 MOUNTAIN BROOK, ALA.
50- 25 COOGAN, DALE ROGER	16940 'B' STREET - HUNTINGTON BEACH CA 92647
41- 18 COOK, EARL DAVIS	RR 4 - STOUFFVILLE ONTARIO CAN.
85- 20 COOK, GLEN PATRICK	34 JOHNSON ST - TONAWQANDA NY 14150
13- 38 COOK, LUTHER ALMUS 'DOC'	D. JUNE 30, 1973 LAWRENCEBURG, TENN.
59- 15 COOK, RAYMOND CLIFFORD 'CLIFF'	605 WILLIAMSBURG MANOR - ARLINGTON TX 76014
15- 24 COOK, ROLLIN EDWARD	D. AUGUST 11, 1975 TOLEDO, O.
70- 27 COOK, RONALD WAYNE	913 FLANAGAN - LONGVIEW TX 75602
30- 13 COOKE, ALLEN LINDSEY 'DUSTY'	BOX 65 - FUQUAY VARINA NC 27526
14- 40 COOMBS, CECIL LYSANDER	D. NOVEMBER 25, 1975 FORT WORTH, TEX.
63- 25 COOMBS, DANIEL BERNARD	14130 CLEOBROOK - HOUSTON TX 77070
33- 14 COOMBS, RAYMOND FRANKLIN 'BOBBY'	BOX 782 - OGUNQUIT ME 03907
17- 15 COONEY, JAMES EDWARD	34 WOODSIA RD - SAUNDERSTOWN RI 02874
21- 17 COONEY, JOHN WALTER	818 WHITFIELD AVE - SARASOTA FL 33580
31- 17 COONEY, ROBERT DANIEL	D. MAY 4, 1976 GLEN FALLS, N. Y.
12- 38 COOPER, ARLEY WILBUR	D. AUGUST 7, 1973 ENCINO, CALIF.
48- 29 COOPER, CALVIN ASA	330 POPLAR ST - CLINTON SC 29325
71- 27 COOPER, CECIL CELESTER	BOX 213 - SEALY TX 77474
13- 39 COOPER, CLAUDE WILLIAM	D. JANUARY 21, 1974 PLAINVIEW, TEX.
81- 24 COOPER, DONALD JAMES	66-10 52ND AVE - MASPETH NY 11378
80- 28 COOPER, GARY NATHANIEL	127 OGLESBY AVE - GARDEN CITY GA 31408
14- 41 COOPER, GUY EVANS	D. AUGUST 2, 1951 SANTA MONICA, CALIF.

38- 16	COOPER, MORTON CECIL	D. NOVEMBER 17, 1958 LITTLE ROCK, ARK.
46- 19	COOPER, ORGE PATTERSON 'PAT'	4424 HOBBS HILL DR - CHARLOTTE NC 28212
40- 13	COOPER, WILLIAM WALKER	RR 1-BUCKNER MO 64016
35- 17	COPELAND, MAYS	D. NOVEMBER 29, 1982 INDIO, CALIF.
35- 18	COPPOLA, HENRY PETER	42 PLEASANT STREET-MILFORD MA 01757
80- 29	CORBETT, DOUGLAS MITCHELL	108 STONEBROOK CT - LONGWOOD FL 32779
36- 15	CORBETT, EUGENE LOUIS	BOX 904 - SALISBURY MD 21801
71- 28	CORBIN, ALTON RAY	922 LIBERTY ST - LIVE OAK FL 32060
45- 16	CORBITT, CLAUDE ELLIOTT	D. MAY 1, 1978 CINCINNATI, O.
15- 25	CORCORAN, ARTHUR ANDREW	D. JULY 27, 1958 CHELSEA, MASS.
10- 34	CORCORAN, MICHAEL JOSEPH 'MICKEY'	D. DECEMBER 9, 1950 BUFFALO, N.Y.
77- 32	CORCORAN, TIMOTHY MICHAEL	4014 N WALNUTHAVEN DR - COVINA CA 91722
18- 13	COREY, EDWARD NORMAN	D. SEPTEMBER 17, 1970 KENOSHA, WIS.
79- 25	COREY, MARK MUNDELL	OLD ADD: RR 5 BOX 686 - EVERGREEN CO 80439
25- 21	CORGAN, CHARLES HOWARD	D. JUNE 13, 1928 WAGONER, OKLA.
11- 34	CORHAN, ROY GEORGE	D. NOVEMBER 24, 1958 SAN FRANCISCO, CALIF.
69- 36	CORKINS, MICHAEL PATRICK	6354 DUCHESS DR - RIVERSIDE CA 92509
78- 29	CORNEJO, NEIVES MARDIE	321 EAST 3RD ST - WELLINGTON KS 67152
84- 22	CORNELL, JEFFERY RAY	5207 MCCOY - KANSAS CITY MO 64133
77- 33	CORNUTT, TERRY STANTON	179 W HAZEL - ROSEBURG OR 97470
64- 22	CORRALES, PATRICK	3052 BOBOLINK DR - REX GA 30273
85- 21	CORREA, EDWIN JOSUE	BUZON 749 RUTA 649 - CAROLINA PR 00630
72- 21	CORRELL, VICTOR CROSBY	9 E MOORE ST - STATESBORO GA 30458
46- 20	CORRIDEN, JOHN MICHAEL JR	5441 E 17TH ST - INDIANAPOLIS IN 46218
10- 35	CORRIDEN, JOHN MICHAEL SR. 'RED'	D. SEPTEMBER 28, 1959 INDIANAPOLIS, IND.
77- 34	CORT, BARRY LEE	OLD ADD: 8707 SEAHAWK LN - TAMPA FL
23- 24	CORTAZZO, JOHN FRANK 'SHINE'	D. MARCH 4, 1963 PITTSBURGH, PA.
51- 16	CORWIN, ELMER NATHAN 'AL'	919 REDWING DR - GENEVA IL 60134
35- 19	COSCARART, JOSEPH MARVIN	127A SPATH RD - SEQUIM WA 98382
38- 17	COSCARART, PETER JOSEPH	2808 JULINDA WAY - ESCONDIDO CA 92025
80- 30	COSEY, DONALD RAY	139 BYXBEE ST - SAN FRANCISCO CA 94132
72- 22	COSGROVE, MICHAEL JOHN	2226 W PALO VERDE DR - PHOENIX AZ 85015
66- 24	COSMAN, JAMES HARRY	6520 ROBBINS RIDGE LN - MEMPHIS TN 38119

JIM COX

13- 40	COSTELLO, DANIEL FRANCIS	D. MARCH 26, 1936 PITTSBURGH, PA.
26- 19	COTE, WARREN PETER 'PETE'	OLD ADD: 22 VENUS RD - SOUTH YARMOUTH MA 02664
26- 20	COTTER, EDWARD CHRISTOPHER	D. JUNE 14, 1959 HARTFORD, CONN.
22- 22	COTTER, HARVEY LOUIS	D. AUGUST 6, 1955 LOS ANGELES, CAL.
11- 35	COTTER, RICHARD RAPHAEL	D. APRIL 4, 1945 BROOKLYN, N. Y.
59- 16	COTTIER, CHARLES KEITH	7129 LAKE BALLINGER WAY - EDMONDS WA 98020
84- 23	COTTO, HENRY	JUAN J. GARCIA ED. 21 #201 - CAGUAS PR 00625
11- 36	COTTRELL, ENSIGN STOVER	D. FEBRUARY 27, 1947 SYRACUSE, N.Y.
17- 16	COUCH, JOHN DANIEL	D. DECEMBER 8, 1975 PALO ALTO, CALIF.
83- 36	COUCHEE, MICHAEL EUGENE	16900 CYPRESS WAY - LOS GATOS CA 95030
60- 25	COUGHTRY, JAMES MARLAN	3966 LAURAL COURT - CHINO CA 91709
69- 37	COULTER, THOMAS LEE 'CHIP'	809 TRENTON ST - TORONTO OH 43964
14- 42	COUMBE, FREDERICK NICHOLAS 'FRITZ'	D. MARCH 21, 1978 PARADISE, CALIF.
51- 17	COURTNEY, CLINTON DAWSON	D. JUNE 16, 1975 ROCHESTER, N. Y.
19- 15	COURTNEY, HENRY SEYMOUR	D. DECEMBER 11, 1954 LYME, CT.
23- 25	COUSINEAU, ED 'D'	D. JULY 14, 1951 WATERTOWN, MASS.
12- 39	COVELESKI, STANLEY ANTHONY	D. MARCH 20, 1984 SOUTH BEND, IND.
44- 23	COVINGTON, CHESTER ROGERS	D. JUNE 11, 1976 PEMBROKE PARK, FLA.
13- 41	COVINGTON, CLARENCE CALVERT 'TEX'	D. JANUARY 4, 1963 DENISON, TEX.
56- 24	COVINGTON, JOHN WESLEY 'WES'	EDMONTON SUN, 9405 50TH ST - EDMONTON ALB T6B 2Y2 CAN.
11- 37	COVINGTON, WILLIAM WILKES	D. DECEMBER 10, 1931 DENISON, TEX.
63- 26	COWAN, BILLY ROLAND	1539 VIA CORONEL-PALOS VERDES ESTATES CA90274
74- 17	COWENS, ALFRED EDWARD	5723 KENISTON AVE - LOS ANGELES CA 90043
82- 26	COWLEY, JOSEPH ALAN	146 RUGBY RD - LEXINGTON KY 40504
83- 37	COX, DANNY BRADFORD	306 FEAGIN MILL RD - WARNER ROBINS GA 31093
25- 22	COX, ELMER JOSEPH 'DICK'	D. JUNE 1, 1966 MORRO BAY, CALIF.
22- 23	COX, ERNEST THOMPSON	D. APRIL 29, 1974 BIRMINGHAM, ALA.
28- 23	COX, GEORGE MELVIN	1525 N WHARTON - SHERMAN TX 75090
55- 30	COX, GLENN MELVIN	BOX 487 - LOS MOLINOS CA 96055
73- 26	COX, JAMES CHARLES	916 SOUTH VALE - BLOOMINGTON IL 61701
80- 31	COX, JEFFREY LINDON	2727 VANDERHOOF DR - WEST COVINA CA 91791
66- 25	COX, JOSEPH CASEY	630 GRAND AVE - LONG BEACH CA 90814
73- 27	COX, LARRY EUGENE	246 VALLEY WAY - LIMA OH 45804
26- 21	COX, LESLIE WARREN	D. OCTOBER 14, 1934 SAN ANGELO, TEX.
20- 26	COX, PLATEAU REX	D. OCTOBER 15, 1984 ROANOKE, VA.
68- 15	COX, ROBERT JOE	4030 RIVER RIDGE CHASE - MARIETTA GA 30067
70- 28	COX, TERRY LEE	216 HOLLAND - CARLSBAD NM 88220
36- 16	COX, WILLIAM DONALD	45 CIRCLE DR-CHARLESTON IL 61920
41- 19	COX, WILLIAM RICHARD	D. MARCH 30, 1978 HARRISBURG, PA.
77- 35	COX, WILLIAM TED	113 W PRATT DR - MIDWEST CITY OK 73110
14- 43	COYNE, "TOOTS"	

42

45- 17	COZART, CHARLES RHUBIN	RR 2 BOX 212-A - HUDSON NC 28638
12- 40	CRABB, JAMES ROY	D. MARCH 30, 1940 LEWISTON, MONT.
10- 36	CRABLE, GEORGE E	B. 1886 BROOKLYN, N.Y.
29- 21	CRABTREE, ESTEL CRAYTON	D. JANUARY 4, 1967 LOGAN, O.
55- 31	CRADDOCK, WALTER ANDERSON	D. JULY 6, 1980 PARMA HEIGHTS OHIO
37- 28	CRAFT, HARRY FRANCIS	716 GLEN HAVEN DR - CONROE TX 77301
16- 14	CRAFT, MAURICE MONTAGUE 'MOLLY'	D. OCTOBER 25, 1978 LOS ANGELES, CALIF.
31- 18	CRAGHEAD, HOWARD OLIVER	D. JULY 15, 1962 SAN ZIELOE, CAL.
64- 23	CRAIG, PETER JOEL	801 SILVERLEAF PL - RALEIGH NC 27609
79- 26	CRAIG, RODNEY PAUL 'ROCKY'	OLD ADD: 23230 SESAME ST - TORRANCE CA
55- 32	CRAIG, ROGER LEE	2453 CANORA AVE - ALPINE CA 92331
69- 38	CRAM, GERALD ALLEN	2748 N 121ST AVE - OMAHA NE 68164
29- 22	CRAMER, ROGER MAXWELL 'DOC'.	5 HILLIARD DR - MANAHAWKIN NJ 08050
12- 41	CRAMER, WILLIAM WENDELL	D. SEPTEMBER 11, 1966 FORT WAYNE, IND.
49- 17	CRANDALL, DELMAR WESLEY	623 ROSARITA DR - FULLERTON CA 92635
14- 44	CRANE, SAMUEL BYREN	D. NOVEMBER 12, 1955 PHILADELPHIA, PA.
37- 29	CRAWFORD, CHARLES LOWRIE 'LARRY'	B. APRIL 27, 1914 SWISSVALE, PA.
29- 23	CRAWFORD, CLIFFORD RANKIN 'PAT'	1201 N QUEEN ST - KINSTON NC 28501
45- 18	CRAWFORD, GLENN MARTIN	D. JANUARY 2, 1972 SAGINAW, MICH.
73- 28	CRAWFORD, JAMES FREDERICK	OLD ADD: 48621 I-94 S'CE DR DR-BELLKEVILLE MI
15- 26	CRAWFORD, KENNETH DANIEL	D. NOVEMBER 11, 1976 PITTSBURGH, PA.
52- 20	CRAWFORD, RUFUS 'JAKE'	2928 WESTBROOK - FORT WORTH TX 76111
80- 32	CRAWFORD, STEVEN RAY	RR 1 BOX 7-8 - SALINA OK 74365
64- 24	CRAWFORD, WILLIE MURPHY	P.O. BOX 491054 - LOS ANGELES CA 90049
43- 32	CREEDEN, CORNELIUS STEPHEN	D. NOVEMBER 30, 1969 SANTA ANA, CAL.
31- 19	CREEDON, PATRICK FRANCIS	622 N MAIN ST - BROCKTON MA 02401
45- 19	CREEL, JACK DALTON	7119 OAK ARBOR - HOUSTON TX 77088
82- 27	CREEL, STEVEN KEITH	527 TRAIL RIDGE DR - DUNCANVILLE TX 75116
47- 22	CREGER, BERNARD ODELL	15 GREENWELL CT - LYNCHBURG VA 24502
27- 21	CREMINS, ROBERT ANTHONY	415 MANOR RIDGE RD - PELHAM NY 10803
38- 11	CRESPI, FRANK ANGELO JOSEPH 'CREEPY'	2647 DALTON AVE - ST LOUIS MO 63139
48- 30	CRESS, WALKER JAMES	14177 WINTERSET - GREENWELL SPRINGS LA 70739
69- 31	CRIDER, JERRY STEPHEN	821 KENSINGTON DR - ORLANDO FL 32808
51- 18	CRIMIAN, JOHN MELVIN	3012 GREEN ST - CLAYMONT DE 19703
78- 30	CRIPE, DAVID GORDON	40657 OAKLAND AVE - HEMET CA 92343
77- 36	CRISCIONE, DAVID GERALD	87 HAMLET ST - FREDONIA NY 14063
42- 24	CRISCOLA, ANTHONY PAUL	4025 BAYARD-SAN DIEGO CA 92109
10- 37	CRISP, JOSEPH SHELBY	D. FEBRUARY 5, 1939 KANSAS CITY, MO.
51- 19	CRISTANTE, LEO DANTE	D. AUGUST 24, 1977 DEARBORN, MICH.
24- 23	CRITZ, HUGH MELVILLE	D. JANUARY 10, 1980 GREENWOOD, MISS.
44- 24	CROCKER, CLAUDE ARTHUR	MERRIE OAKS - CLINTON SC 29325
74- 18	CROMARTIE, WARREN LIVINGSTON	%BOOTH,1751 NW 36TH ST - MIAMI FL 33142
37- 30	CROMPTON, HERBERT BRYAN	D. AUGUST 5, 1963 MOLINE, ILL.
54- 16	CRONE, RAYMOND HAYES	916 NW PANORAMA LOOP - WAXAHACHIE TX 75165
29- 24	CRONIN, JAMES JOHN	D. JUNE 10, 1983 RICHMOND, CALIF.
26- 22	CRONIN, JOSEPH EDWARD	D. SEPTEMBER 7, 1984 OSTERVILLE, MASS.
28- 24	CRONIN, WILLIAIM PATRICK	D. OCTOBER 26, 1966 NEWTON, MASS.
70- 29	CROSBY, EDWARD CARLTON	11463 ANTICOST WAY - CYPRESS CA 90630
75- 28	CROSBY, KENNETH STEWART	BOX 680306 - PARK CITY UT 84068
32- 15	CROSETTI, FRANK PETEREY JOSEPH	65 W MONTEREY AV - STOCKTON CA 95204
42- 25	CROSS, JOFFRE JAMES 'JEFF'	6154 LONGMONT-HOUSTON TX 77027
12- 42	CROSSIN, FRANK PATRICK	D. DECEMBER 6, 1965 KINGSPORT, PA.
30- 14	CROUCH, JACK ALBERT	D. AUGUST 25, 1972 LEESBURG, FLA.
39- 24	CROUCH, WILLIAM ELMER	D. DECEMBER 26, 1980 HOWELL, MICH.
10- 38	CROUCH, WILLIAM HENRY	D. DECEMBER 22, 1945 HIGHLAND PARK, MICH.
39- 25	CROUCHER, FRANK DONALD	D. MAY 21, 1980 HOUSTON, TEXAS
23- 26	CROUSE, CLYDE ELLSWORTH 'BUCK'	D. OCTOBER 23, 1983 MUNCIE, IND.
82- 28	CROW, DONALD LEROY	7605 WESTBROOK W - YAKIMA WA 98908
26- 23	CROWDER, ALVIN FLOYD 'GEN'	D. APRIL 3, 1972 WINSTON-SALEM, N. C.
52- 21	CROWE, GEORGE DANIEL	3820 SE 73RD ST - OCALA FL 32671
15- 27	CROWELL, MINOT JOY 'CAP'	D. SEPTEMBER 30, 1962 CENTRAL FALLS, R.I.
28- 25	CROWLEY, EDGAR JEWEL	D. APRIL 14, 1970 BIRMINGHAM, ALA.
69- 40	CROWLEY, TERRENCE MICHAEL	10626 ANGLOHILL RD - COCKEYSVILLE MD 21030
45- 20	CROWSON, THOMAS WOODROW WILSON 'WOODY'	D. AUGUST 14, 1947 MAYODAN, N. C.
14- 45	CRUISE, WALTON EDWIN	D. JANUARY 9, 1975 SYLACAUGA ALA.
17- 17	CRUM, CALVIN CARL	D. DECEMBER 7, 1945 TULSA, OKLA.
45- 21	CRUMLING, EUGENE LEON	RR 24 BOX 809 - YORK PA 17406
24- 24	CRUMP, ARTHUR ELLIOTT	D. SEPTEMBER 7, 1976 RALEIGH, N. C.
20- 27	CRUMPLER, RAY MAXTON	D. OCTOBER 6, 1969 FAYETTEVILLE, N. C.
14- 46	CRUTCHER, RICHARD LOUIS	D. JUNE 19, 1952 FRANKFORT, KY.
13- 42	CRUTHERS, CHARLES PRESTON 'PRESS'	D. DECEMBER 27, 1976 KENOSHA, WISC.
73- 29	CRUZ, CIRILO 'TOMMY'	CALLE H-E-8 - ARROYO PR 00615
73- 30	CRUZ, HECTOR LUIS	CALLE H-E-8 - ARROYO PR 00615
75- 29	CRUZ, HENRY ACOSTA	OLD ADD: MONTRE BRISAS CALLE T-O-6 - FAJARDO PR 00648
70- 30	CRUZ, JOSE DELAN	B-15 JARDINES LAFAYETTE - ARROYO PR 00615
77- 37	CRUZ, JULIO LOUIS	40 ORCAS KEY - BELLEVUE WA 98006

HEITY CRUZ

78- 31 CRUZ, TODD RUBEN	OLD ADD: 1046 20TH ST - DETROIT MI
78- 32 CRUZ, VICTOR MANUEL	ALEXANDER FLEMING NO. 67 - SANTO DOMINGO DOMINICAN REP.
74- 19 CUBBAGE, MICHAEL LEE	BOX 126 - RUCKERSVILLE VA 22968
35- 20 CUCCINELLO, ALFRED EDWARD	7 CRYSTAL ST-ELMONT NY 11003
30- 15 CUCCINELLO, ANTHONY FRANCIS	3610 BEACH DR - TAMPA FL 33629
43- 33 CUCCURULLO, ARTHUR JOSEPH 'COOKIE'	D. JANUARY 23, 1983 WEST ORANGE, N. J.
50- 26 CUELLAR, CHARLES JESUS PATRICK	3209 GRACE ST - TAMPA FL 33607
59- 17 CUELLAR, MIGUEL 'MIKE'	BLK-5 DR. VILLALOBOS ST - LEVITTOWN LAKES PR 00632
77- 38 CUELLAR, ROBERT	823 S CAMERON - ALICE TX 78332
61- 25 CUETO, DAGOBERTO CONCEPCION	EL COROJO - SAN LUIS PINAR DEL RIO CUBA
14- 47 CUETO, MANUEL MELO	D. JUNE 29, 1942 REGLA, HAVANA CUBA
43- 34 CULBERSON, DELBERT LEON 'LEE'	34 GLENRISE TER - ROME GA 30161
62- 29 CULLEN, JOHN PATRICK	164 ALEXANDER AVE - NUTLEY NJ 07110
66- 26 CULLEN, TIMOTHY LEO	789 SOLANA DR - LAFAYETTE CA 94549
38- 19 CULLENBINE, ROY JOSEPH	24638 MEADOW LN - MOUNT CLEMENS MI 48043
36- 17 CULLER, RICHARD BROADUS	D. JUNE 16, 1964 CHAPEL HILL, N. C.
26- 24 CULLOP, HENRY 'NICK'	D. DECEMBER 8, 1978 WESTERVILLE, O.
13- 43 CULLOP, NORMAN ANDREW 'NICK'	D. APRIL 15, 1961 TAZEWELL, VA.
25- 23 CULLOTON, BERNARD ALOYSIUS 'BUD'	D. NOVEMBER 9, 1976 KINGSTON, N. Y.
83- 38 CULMER, WILFRED HILLARD	BOX N9762 - NASSAU BAHAMAS W.I.
42- 26 CULP, BENJAMIN BALDY	3827 KAREN ST-PHILADELPHIA PA 19114
63- 27 CULP, RAY LEONARD	7400 WATERLINE - AUSTIN TX 78731
10- 39 CULP, WILLIAM EDWARD	D. SEPTEMBER 3, 1969 ARNOLD, PA.
66- 27 CULVER, GEORGE RAYMOND	BOX 3623 - BAKERSFIELD CA 93305
68- 16 CUMBERLAND, JOHN SHELTON	6960 COUNTY RD #95 - PALM ARBOR FL 33563
26- 25 CUMMINGS, JOHN WILLIAM	D. OCTOBER 5, 1962 WEST MIFFLIN, PA.
29- 25 CUNNINGHAM, BRUCE LEE	D. MARCH 8, 1984 HAYWARD, CALIF.
16- 15 CUNNINGHAM, GEORGE HAROLD	D. MARCH 10, 1972 CHATTANOOGA, TENN.
54- 17 CUNNINGHAM, JOSEPH ROBERT	BOX 8787 - ST.LOUIS MO 63102
31- 20 CUNNINGHAM, RAYMOND LEE	1007 CHRISTINE - HOUSTON TX 77017
21- 18 CUNNINGHAM, WILLIAM ALOYSIUS	D. SEPTEMBER 26, 1953 COLUSA, CAL.
10- 40 CUNNINGHAM, WILLIAM JAMES	D. FEBRUARY 21, 1946 SCHENECTADY, N. Y.
75- 30 CURRENCE, DELANCY LAFAYETTE	1238 STANLEY DR - ROCK HILL SC 29730
16- 16 CURRIE, MURPHY ARCHIBALD	D. JUNE 22, 1939 ASHEBORO, N.C.
55- 33 CURRIE, WILLIAM CLEVELAND	ARLINGTON GA 31713
47- 23 CURRIN, PERRY GILMORE	1967 ADD: 1615 SIGMON NW - ROANOKE VA 24017
60- 26 CURRY, GEORGE ANTHONY 'TONY'	BOX 7054 - NASSAU BAHAMAS W.I.
11- 38 CURRY, GEORGE JAMES	D. OCTOBER 5, 1963 STRATFORD, CONN.
61- 26 CURTIS, JACK PATRICK	RR 3 BOX 458 - GRANITE FALLS NC 28630
70- 31 CURTIS, JOHN DUFFIELD	858 ANDROMEDA LN - FOSTER CITY CA 94404
43- 35 CURTIS, VERNON EUGENE	724 21ST ST - CAIRO IL 62914
43- 36 CURTRIGHT, GUY PAXTON	1620 BENTWOOD DR - SUN CITY CENTER FL 33570
51- 20 CUSICK, JOHN PETER	46 NORTHWOOD AVE - DEMAREST NJ 07627
12- 43 CUTSHAW, GEORGE WILLIAM	D. AUGUST 22, 1973 SAN DIEGO, CALIF.
21- 19 CUYLER, HAZEN SHIRLEY 'KIKI'	D. FEBRUARY 11, 1950 ANN ARBOR, MICH.
22- 24 CVENGROS, MICHAEL JOHN	D. AUGUST 2, 1970 HOT SPRINGS, ARK.
14- 48 CYPERT, ALFRED BOYD	D. JANUARY 9, 1973 WASHINGTON, D.C.
73- 31 DACQUISTO, JOHN FRANCIS	3440 FIR ST - SAN DIEGO CA 92104
75- 31 DADE, LONNIE PAUL	OLD ADD: 15829 SE 171ST PL - RENTON WA 98055
43- 37 DAGENHARD, JOHN DOUGLAS	10511 HALBRENT AVE - MISSION HILLS CA 91345
32- 16 DAGLIA, PETER GEORGE	D. MARCH 11, 1952 WILLITS, CAL.
55- 34 DAGRES, ANGELO GEORGE	GREENTREE LN RFD - ROWLEY MA 01969
63- 28 DAHL, JAY STEVEN	D. JUNE 20, 1965 SALISBURY, N. C.
35- 21 DAHLGREN, ELLSWORTH TENNEY 'BABE'	17 WOODLYN LN - BRADBURY CA 91010
56- 29 DAHLKE, JEROME ALEXANDER 'JOE'	3643 HALLBROOK ST - MEMPHIS TN 38127
29- 26 DAILEY, SAMUEL LAURENCE	D. DECEMBER 2, 1979 COLUMBIA, MO.
61- 27 DAILEY, WILLIAM GARLAND	RR 1 BOX M8 - DUBLIN VA 24084
67- 21 DALCANTON, JOHN BRUCE	624 RAY DRIVE - CARNEGIE PA 15106
11- 39 DALE, EMMETT EUGENE 'GENE'	D. MARCH 20, 1958 ST. LOUIS, MO.

JOHN D'ACQUISTO

55- 35 DALEY, BUDDY LEO	RR 62-C BOX 205 - LANDER WY 82520
12- 44 DALEY, JOHN FRANCIS	470 W 3RD ST - MANSFIELD OH 44903
11- 40 DALEY, JUD LAWRENCE	D. JANUARY 26, 1967 GADSDEN, ALA.
55- 36 DALEY, PETER HARVEY	4019 CALLE MIRA MONTE - NEWBURY PARK CA 91320
37- 31 DALLESANDRO, NICHOLAS DOMINIC 'DOM'	4821 OAKKNOLL DR - INDIANAPOLIS IN 46241
60- 27 DALRYMPLE, CLAYTON ERROL	RR 3 BOX 42 - CHICO CA 95927
15- 28 DALRYMPLE, MICHAEL	B. ST. LOUIS, MO.
10- 41 DALTON, TALBOT PERCY 'JACK'	OLD ADD: 2 PROSPECT AVE - CATONSVILLE MD
13- 44 DALY, THOMAS DANIEL	D. NOVEMBER 7, 1946 MEDFORD, MASS.
63- 29 DAMASKA, JACK LLOYD	252 BLACKHAWK RD - BEAVER FALLS PA 15010
15- 29 DAMRAU, HARRY ROBERT	D. AUGUST 21, 1957 STATEN ISLAND, N. Y.
28- 26 DANEY, ARTHUR LEE	7505 SANDOWN CIR - SCOTTSDALE AZ 85253
11- 41 DANFORTH, DAVID CHARLES	D. SEPTEMBER 19, 1970 BALTIMORE, MD.
57- 14 DANIEL, CHARLES EDWARD	1640 BABS RD - MEMPHIS TN 38116
37- 32 DANIEL, HANDLEY JACOB 'JAKE'	508 SPRINGDALE DR - LAGRANGE GA 30240

57- 15 DANIELS, BENNIE	1671 E 122ND - LOS ANGELES CA 90059
10- 42 DANIELS, BERNARD ELMER 'BERT'	D. JUNE 6, 1958 CEDAR GROVE, N.J.
45- 22 DANIELS, FREDERICK CLINTON	522 SALISBURY RD - STATESVILLE NC 28677
52- 22 DANIELS, HAROLD JACK	3715 ELMRIDGE DR - EVANSVILLE IN 47711
15- 30 DANNER, HENRY FREDERICK 'BUCK'	D. SEPTEMBER 19, 1949 BOSTON, MASS.
33- 15 DANNING, HARRY	212 FOX CHAPEL COURT - VALPARAISO IN 46304
28- 27 DANNING, IKE	D. MARCH 28, 1983 SANTA MONICA, CALIF.
44- 25 DANTONIO, JOHN JAMES 'FATS'	430 S CLARK ST - NEW ORLEANS LA 70119
42- 27 DAPPER, CLIFFORD ROLAND	733 BURMA RD-FALLBROOK CA 92028
74- 20 DARCY, PATRICK LEONARD	515 S COLUMBUS BLVD - TUCSON AZ 85711
14- 49 DARINGER, CLIFFORD CLARENCE	D. DECEMBER 12, 1971 SACRAMENTO, CALIF.
14- 50 DARINGER, ROLLA HARRISON	D. MAY 23, 1974 SEYMOUR, IND.
46- 21 DARK, ALVIN RALPH	103 CRAMBERRY WAY - EASLEY SC 29640
83- 39 DARLING, RONALD MAURICE	19 WOODLAND STREET - MILLBURY MA 01527
54- 18 DARNELL, ROBERT JACK	509 MAPLE DR - SPRINGDALE AR 72764
77- 39 DARR, MICHAEL EDWARD	OLD ADD: 5862 "B" FULLERTON AVE - BUENA PARK CA 90621
34- 28 DARROW, GEORGE OLIVER	D. MARCH 24, 1983 SUN CITY, ARIZ.
62- 30 DARWIN, ARTHUR BOBBY LEE	11877 GONSALVES ST - CERRITOS CA 90701
78- 33 DARWIN, DANNY WAYNE	2218 FALL RIVER DR - ARLINGTON TX 76011
24- 25 DASHIELL, JOHN WALLACE 'WALLY'	D. MAY 20, 1972 PENSACOLA, FLA.
13- 45 DASHNER, LEE CLAIRE	D. DECEMBER 16, 1960 EL DORADO, KAN.
45- 23 DASSO, FRANCIS JOSEPH NICHOLAS	1413 MADISON - WENATCHEE WA 98801
15- 31 DAUBERT, HARRY J.	D. JANUARY 8, 1944 DETROIT, MICH.
10- 43 DAUBERT, JACOB ELSWORTH	D. OCTOBER 9, 1924 CINCINNATI, O.
76- 27 DAUER, RICHARD FREMONT	7087 TIPPICANOE - SAN BERNARDINO CA 92404
51- 21 DAUGHERTY, HAROLD RAY	66 ELDRED AVE - BEDFORD OH 44014
37- 33 DAUGHTERS, ROBERT FRANCIS	35 OLD PARISH RD - DARIEN CT 06820
83- 40 DAULTON, DARREN ARTHUR	RURAL ROUTE 3 BOX 21 - ARKANSAS CITY KS 67005
12- 45 DAUSS, GEORGE AUGUST 'HOOKS'	D. JULY 27, 1963 ST. LOUIS, MO.
53- 17 DAVALILLO, POMPEYO ANTONIO 'YO-YO'	CENTRO COMMERCIAL #8 - MAIQUETIA VENEZUELA S.A.
63- 30 DAVALILLO, VICTOR JOSE	CLE TRUJILLO 7,MARIPEREZ,Q.V.-CARACAS VENEZ
69- 41 DAVANON, FRANK GERALD	5751 CHEENA - HOUSTON TX 77096
20- 28 DAVENPORT, CLAUDE EDWIN	D. JUNE 13, 1976 CORPUS CHRISTI, TEX.
14- 51 DAVENPORT, DAVID W.	D. OCTOBER 16, 1954 EL DORADO, ARK.
58- 26 DAVENPORT, JAMES HOUSTON	1016 HEWITT DR - SAN CARLOS CA 94070
21- 20 DAVENPORT, JOUBERT LUM	D. APRIL 21, 1961 DALLAS, TEX.
77- 40 DAVEY, MICHAEL GERARD	SOUTH 5118 MADELIA - SPOKANE WA 99203
62- 31 DAVIAULT, RAYMOND JOSEPH ROBERT	12116 ONTARIO E. - POINTES AUX TREMBLES QUE CAN.
84- 24 DAVID, ANDRE ANTER	1428 CALLE LINDA - SAN DIMAS CA 91773
18- 14 DAVIDSON, CLAUDE BOUCHER	D. APRIL 18, 1956 WEYMOUTH, MASS.
65- 25 DAVIDSON, THOMAS EUGENE 'TED'	513 EAST GRANT - SANTA MONICA CA 93454
59- 18 DAVIE, GERALD LEE	14570 BALSAM - SOUTHGATE MI 48195
14- 52 DAVIES, LLOYD GARRISON 'CHICK'	D. SEPTEMBER 5, 1973 MIDDLETOWN, CONN.
84- 25 DAVIS, ALVIN GLENN	OLD ADD: 1019 EAST WEBER DR - TEMPE AZ 85281

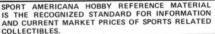

SPORT AMERICANA HOBBY REFERENCE MATERIAL IS THE RECOGNIZED STANDARD FOR INFORMATION AND CURRENT MARKET PRICES OF SPORTS RELATED COLLECTIBLES.

Pat Davey
Cincinnati Reds

65- 26 DAVIS, ARTHUR WILLARD 'BILL'	6638 KNOX AVE S - MINNEAPOLIS MN 55423
63- 31 DAVIS, BRYSHEAR BARNETT 'BROCK'	227 E 94TH ST - LOS ANGELES CA 90003
81- 25 DAVIS, CHARLES THEODORE 'CHILI'	142 EAST 85TH ST - LOS ANGELES CA 90003
34- 29 DAVIS, CURTIS BENTON	D. OCTOBER 12, 1965 COVINA, CAL.
84- 26 DAVIS, ERIC KEITH	6606 DENVER AVE #1 - LOS ANGELES CA 90044
12- 46 DAVIS, FRANK TALMADGE 'DIXIE'	D. FEBRUARY 4, 1944 RALEIGH, N.C.
12- 47 DAVIS, GEORGE ALLEN	D. JUNE 4, 1961 BUFFALO, N.Y.
82- 29 DAVIS, GEORGE EARL 'STORM'	P.O. BOX 14025 - SAVANNAH GA 31416
26- 26 DAVIS, GEORGE WILLIS 'KIDDO'	D. MARCH 4, 1983 BRIDGEPORT, CONN.
83- 41 DAVIS, GERALD EDWARD	72 THERESA STREET - TRENTON NJ 08618
84- 27 DAVIS, GLENN EARL	P.O. BOX 14025 - SAVANNAH GA 31416
32- 17 DAVIS, HARRY ALBERT	BOX 27 - SHREVEPORT LA 71161
59- 19 DAVIS, HERMAN THOMAS 'TOMMY'	9767 WHIRLAWAY - ALTA LOMA CA 91701
19- 16 DAVIS, ISAAC MARION	D. APRIL 2, 1984 TUCSON, ARIZ.
62- 32 DAVIS, JACKE SYLVESTA	1131 LYNNWOOD DR - CARTHAGE TX 75633
54- 19 DAVIS, JAMES BENNETT	3327 COUNTRYSIDE DR - SAN MATEO CA 94403
81- 26 DAVIS, JODY RICHARD	RR 1 BEN HILL DR - OAKWOOD GA 30566
85- 22 DAVIS, JOEL CLARK	7901 BAYMEADOW CIR E #482 - JACKSONVILLE FL 32216
41- 20 DAVIS, JOHN HUMPHREY	OLD ADD: HOTEL LAWRENCE - DALLAS TEX 75202
15- 32 DAVIS, JOHN WILBUR 'BUD'	D. MAY 26, 1967 LIGHTFOOT, VA.
40- 14 DAVIS, LAWRENCE COLUMBUS 'CRASH'	4767 CHAMPION CT - GREENSBORO NC 27410
80- 33 DAVIS, MARK WILLIAM	1620 READING BLVD - WYOMISSING PA 19610
80- 34 DAVIS, MICHAEL DWAYNE	3606 47TH ST - SAN DIEGO CA 92115
80- 35 DAVIS, ODIE ERNEST	1014 MONTANA ST - SAN ANTONIO TX 78203
46- 22 DAVIS, OTIS ALLEN	3078 EASTLAND BLVD #202A - CLEARWATER FL 33519
36- 18 DAVIS, RAY THOMAS 'PEACHES'	1802 BEECH ST-DUNCAN OK 73533
77- 41 DAVIS, RICHARD EARL	2415 W ALONDRA - COMPTON CA 90220
52- 23 DAVIS, ROBERT BRANDON 'BRANDY'	222 CHELTENHAM RD - NEWARK DE 19712
58- 27 DAVIS, ROBERT EDWARD	37 WEST 12TH ST - NEW YORK NY 10003

ANDRE DAWSON
Voltigeur/Outfielder

73- 32	DAVIS, ROBERT JOHN EUGENE	BOX 132 - LOCUST GROVE OK 74352
62- 33	DAVIS, RONALD EVERETTE	10811 SHAWNBROOK - HOUSTON TX 77071
78- 34	DAVIS, RONALD GENE	8103 COYTON - HOUSTON TX 77061
85- 23	DAVIS, STEVEN KENNON	802 SERENADE DRIVE - SAN ANTONIO TX 78216
79- 27	DAVIS, STEVEN MICHAEL	1377 ANTONIO LANE - SAN JOSE CA 95117
49- 18	DAVIS, THOMAS OSCAR 'TOD'	D. DECEMBER 31, 1978 WEST COVINA, CALIF.
85- 24	DAVIS, TRENCH NEAL	OLD ADD: 916 SEAGULL AVE - BALTIMORE MD 21225
28- 28	DAVIS, VIRGIL LAWRENCE 'SPUD'	D. AUGUST 14, 1984 BIRMINGHAM, ALA.
83- 42	DAVIS, WALLACE MCARTHUR 'BUTCH'	112 PRICE STREET - WILLIAMSTON NC 27892
60- 28	DAVIS, WILLIAM HENRY	4419 BUENA VISTA #203 - DALLAS TX 75202
38- 20	DAVIS, WOODROW WILSON	BOX 87-ODUM GA 31555
69- 42	DAVISON, MICHAEL LYNN	578 PROSPECT - HUTCHINSON MN 55350
83- 43	DAWLEY, WILLIAM CHESTER	RR 2, KENDALL ROAD EXT - LISBON CT 06417
76- 28	DAWSON, ANDRE NOLAN	6295 SW 58TH PL - MIAMI FL 33143
24- 26	DAWSON, RALPH FENTON 'JOE'	D. JANUARY 4, 1978 LONGVIEW, TEX.
13- 46	DAWSON, REXFORD PAUL	D. OCTOBER 20, 1958 INDIANAPOLIS, IND.
69- 43	DAY, CHARLES FREDERICK 'BOOTS'	11972 CHARTER OAK PKWY - ST. LOUIS MO 63146
24- 27	DAY, CLYDE HENRY 'PEA RIDGE'	D. MARCH 21, 1934 KANSAS CITY, MO.
83- 44	DAYETT, BRIAN KELLY	45 VILLAGE ST - DEEP RIVER CT 06417
82- 30	DAYLEY, KENNETH GRANT	1601 MOUNT HOOD ST - THE DALLES OR 97058
12- 48	DEAL, CHARLES ALBERT	D. SEPTEMBER 16, 1979 COVINA, CALIF.
47- 24	DEAL, ELLIS FERGUSON 'COT'	RR 1 BOX 456 - WELLSTON OK 74881
39- 26	DEAL, LINDSAY FRED	D. APRIL 18, 1979 LITTLE ROCK, ARK.
36- 19	DEAN, ALFRED LOVILL 'CHUBBY'	D. DECEMBER 21, 1970 RIVERSIDE, N. J.
41- 21	DEAN, JAMES HARRY	D. JUNE 1, 1960 ROCKMART, GA.
30- 16	DEAN, JAY HANNA 'DIZZY'	D. JULY 17, 1974 RENO, NEV.
34- 30	DEAN, PAUL DEE	D. MARCH 17, 1981 SPRINGDALE, ARK.
67- 22	DEAN, TOMMY DOUGLAS	RR2 - IUKA MS 38852
24- 28	DEAN, WAYLAND OGDEN	D. APRIL 10, 1930 HUNTINGTON, W. VA.
27- 28	DEAR, PAUL STANFORD 'BUDDY'	BOX 2475 - CHRISTIANSBURG VA 24073
77- 42	DEBARR, DENNIS LEE	6292 MOCK ORANGE CT - NEWARK CA 94560
16- 17	DEBERRY, JOHN HERMAN 'HANK'	D. SEPTEMBER 10, 1951 SAVANNAH, TENN.
20- 29	DEBERRY, JOSEPH GADDY	D. OCTOBER 9, 1944 SOUTHERN PINES, N. C.
17- 18	DEBUS, ADAM JOSEPH	D. MAY 13, 1977 CHICAGO, ILL.
62- 34	DEBUSSCHERE, DAVID ALBERT	90 3RD ST - GARDEN CITY NY 11530
22- 25	DECATUR, ARTHUR RUE	D. APRIL 25, 1966 TALLADEGA, ALA.
73- 33	DECINCES, DOUGLAS VERNON	9411 HAZEL CIR - VILLA PARK CA 92667
83- 45	DECKER, DEE MARTIN 'MARTY'	920 GATE LANE - PILOT HILL CA 95664
69- 44	DECKER, GEORGE HENRY "JOE"	OLD ADD: 2605 W VAN BUREN - PHOENIX AZ
16- 18	DEDE, ARTHUR RICHARD	D. SEPTEMBER 6, 1971 KEENE, N.H.
35- 22	DEDEAUX, RAOUL MARTIAL 'ROD'	1430 S EASTMAN AVE - LOS ANGELES CA 90023
83- 46	DEDMON, JEFFREY LINDEN	21102 SOUTH BROADWELL - TORRANCE CA 90502
15- 33	DEE, MAURICE LEO 'SHORTY'	D. AUGUST 12, 1971 JAMAICA PLAINS, MASS.
84- 28	DEER, ROBERT GEORGE	230 HILLCREST ST - ANAHEIM CA 92807
63- 32	DEES, CHARLES HENRY	23412 DORSET PL - HARBOR CITY CA 90710
17- 19	DEFATE, CLYDE HERBERT 'TONY'	D. SEPTEMBER 3, 1963 NEW ORLEANS, LA.
78- 35	DEFREITES, ARTURO SIMON	HERMONOS MIRABEL #21 - SAN PEDRO DE MACORIS DOM. REP.
61- 28	DEGERICK, MICHAEL ARTHUR	353 RIDGEDALE AVE - EAST HANOVER NJ 07936
74- 21	DEIDEL, JAMES LAWRENCE	OLD ADD: 2545 S PATTON CT - DENVER CO
40- 15	DEJAN, MIKE DAN	D. FEBRUARY 2, 1953 WEST LOS ANGELES, CALIF.
74- 22	DEJESUS, IVAN	758 ENEAS ST - RIO PIEDRAS PR 00926
82- 31	DEJOHN, MARK STEPHEN	21 BUNKER HILL RD - NEW BRITAIN CT 06053
45- 24	DEKONING, WILLIAM CALLAHAN	D. JULY 26, 1979 PALM HARBOR, FLA.
44- 26	DELACRUZ, TOMAS	D. SEPTEMBER 6, 1958 HAVANA, CUBA
60- 29	DELAHOZ, MIGUEL ANGEL 'MIKE'	OLD ADD: 5011 SW 127TH CT - MIAMI FL 33165
32- 18	DELANCEY, WILLIAM PINKNEY	D. NOVEMBER 28, 1946 PHOENIX, ARIZ.
24- 29	DELANEY, ARTHUR DEWEY	D. MAY 2, 1970 HAYWARD, CALIF.
75- 32	DELAROSA, JESUS	20 #28 LOS MINOS - SANTO DOMINGO DOMINICAN REP.
83- 47	DELEON, JOSE	147 GORDON ST - PERTH AMBOY NJ 08861
81- 27	DELEON, LUIS ANTONIO	SAN ANTON 120,CLE E.CABRERRA - PONCE PR 00731
77- 43	DELGADO, LUIS FELIPE	VILLA DEL CARMEN, BOX 879 - AY HATILLO PR 00659
52- 24	DELGRECO, ROBERT GEORGE	625 SOUTHVIEW DR - PITTSBURGH PA 15226

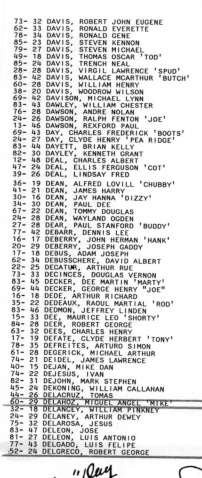

"Pea Ridge" Day

Paul "Daffy" Dean

```
12- 49  DELHI, LEE WILLIAM 'FLAME'              D. MAY 9, 1966 GREENBRAE, CALIF.
55- 37  DELIS, JUAN FRANCISCO                   1963 ADD:3A #24508, REPARTO DOLORES - HAVANA
29- 27  DELKER, EDWARD ALBERTS                  1 S FRONT ST - ST CLAIR PA 17970
12- 50  DELL, WILLIAM GEORGE 'WHEEZER'          D. AUGUST 24, 1966 INDEPENDENCE, CALIF.
33- 16  DELMAS, ALBERT CHARLES                  D. DECEMBER 4, 1979 HUNTINGTON BEACH, CALIF.
52- 25  DELOCK, IVAN MARTIN 'IKE'               147 PARKER RD - NEEDHAM MA 02194
74- 23  DELOS SANTOS, RAMON GENERO              OZAMA ESTE #13 - SANTO DOMINGO DOMINICAN REP.
43- 38  DELSAVIO, GARTON ORVILLE                48 ROOSEVELT DR-BLAUVELT NY 10913
48- 31  DELSING, JAMES HENRY                    1569 WALPOLE DR - CHESTERFIELD MO 63017
51- 22  DEMAESTRI, JOSEPH PAUL                  50 FAIRWAY - NOVATO CA 94947
12- 51  DEMAREE, ALBERT WENTWORTH               D. MAY 2, 1962 LONG BEACH, CALIF.
32- 19  DEMAREE, JOSEPH FRANKLIN                D. AUGUST 30, 1958 LOS ANGELES, CAL.
48- 32  DEMARS, WILLIAM LESTER                  661 POINSETTIA #207 - CLEARWATER FL 33515
57- 16  DEMERIT, JOHN STEPHEN                   550 W WALTER ST - PORT WASHINGTON WI 53074
74- 24  DEMERY, LAWRENCE CALVIN                 3745 0 FAIRBURN RD SW - ATLANTA GA 30331
56- 26  DEMETER, DONALD LEE                     1521 SW 56TH ST - OKLAHOMA CITY OK 73119
59- 20  DEMETER, STEVEN                         2805 MARIONCLIFF DR - PARMA OH 44134
74- 25  DEMOLA, DONALD JOHN                     500-184A PECONIC - LAKE RONKONKOMA NY 11779
10- 44  DEMOTT, BENYEW HARRISON                 D. JULY 5, 1963 SOMERVILLE, N.J.
51- 23  DEMPSEY, CORNELIUS FRANCIS 'CON'        1530 CORDILLERAS RD - REDWOOD CITY CA 94062
69- 45  DEMPSEY, JOHN RIKARD "RICK"             5641 MASON AVE - WOODLAND HILLS CA 91364
82- 32  DEMPSEY, MARK STEVEN                    OLD ADD: 30 E. LANE AVE - DAYTON OH 45406
67- 27  DENEHY, WILLIAM FRANCIS                 1520 SAYBROOK RD - MIDDLETOWN CT 06457
82- 33  DENMAN, BRIAN JOHN                      654 PARKHURST BLVD - BUFFALO NY 14223
23- 27  DENNEHEY, THOMAS FRANCIS 'TOD'          D. AUGUST 8, 1977 PHILADELPHIA, PA.
42- 28  DENNING, OTTO GEORGE                    3434 W MELROSE-CHICAGO IL 60618
```

Greetings from
DON DeMOLA

```
65- 27  DENNIS, DONALD RAY                      RR2 - UNIONTOWN KS 66779
74- 26  DENNY, JOHN ALLEN                       OLD ADD: 14551 BURNLEY ST - CHESTERFIELD MO
73- 34  DENT, RUSSELL EARL 'BUCKY'              OLD ADD: 17 WEST 544 SUTTON PL - WESTMONT IL 60559
47- 25  DENTE, SAMUEL JOSEPH                    19 REDMAN TER - WEST CALDWELL NJ 07006
43- 39  DEPHILLIPS, ANTHONY ANDREW              226 TIMBERLINE CIR - PORT JEFFERSON NY 11777
80- 36  DERNIER, ROBERT EUGENE                  9509 E 77TH ST - RAYTOWN MO 64138
10- 45  DERRICK, CLAUD LESTER                   D. JULY 15, 1974 CLAYTON, GA.
70- 32  DERRICK, JAMES MICHAEL                  1117 ONTARIO AVE - WEST COLUMBIA SC 29169
31- 21  DERRINGER, PAUL                         2017 OAK TRAIL - SARASOTA FL 33579
56- 27  DERRINGTON, CHARLES JAMES 'JIM'         10509 BRYSON AVE - SOUTH GATE CA 90281
44- 27  DERRY, ALVA RUSSELL 'RUSS'              PRINCETON MO 64673
80- 37  DESA, JOSEPH                            642D N. VINEYARD BLVD - HONOLULU HI 96817
30- 17  DESAUTELS, EUGENE ABRAHAM               2802 MANSFIELD AV - FLINT MI 48503
84- 29  DESHAIES, JAMES JOSEPH                  24 CHASE ST - MASSENA NY 13662
32- 20  DESHONG, JAMES BROOKLYN                 99 S 31ST ST - HARRISBURG PA 17109
16- 19  DESJARDIEN, PAUL RAYMOND 'SHORTY'       D. MARCH 7, 1956 MONROVIA, CALIF.
80- 38  DETHERAGE, ROBERT WAYNE                 OLD ADD: 2325 NORTH BENTON - SPRINGFIELD MO 65803
30- 18  DETORE, GEORGE FRANCIS                  RR 1 - NEW HARTFORD NY 13413
73- 35  DETTORE, THOMAS ANTHONY                 1120 MCEWEN AVE - CANONSBURG PA 15317
42- 29  DETWEILER, ROBERT STERLING 'DUCKY'      312 HOLT ST-FEDERALSBURG MD 21632
46- 23  DEUTSCH, MELVIN ELLIOTT                 RR 2 BOX 373A - CALDWELL TX 77836
32- 21  DEVENS, CHARLES                         1 POST OFFICE SQUARE #900 - BOSTON MA 02110
73- 36  DEVINE, PAUL ADRIAN                     4610 RANDALWOOD DR - STONE MOUNTAIN GA 30083
18- 15  DEVINE, WILLIAM PATRICK 'MICKEY'        D. OCTOBER 1, 1957 ALBANY, N. Y.
20- 30  DEVINEY, JOHN HAROLD 'HAL'              D. JANUARY 4, 1933 WESTWOOD, MASS.
24- 30  DEVIVEIROS, BERNARD JOHN                3520 REDDING ST - OAKLAND CA 94619
44- 28  DEVLIN, JAMES RAYMOND                   130 WORMAN ST, ESPY - BLOOMSBURG PA 17815
13- 47  DEVOGT, REX EUGENE                      D. NOVEMBER 9, 1935 ALMA, MICH.
18- 16  DEVORMER, ALBERT E.                     D. AUGUST 29, 1966 GRAND RAPIDS, MICH.
77- 44  DIAZ, BAUDILIO JOSE 'BO'                LA VEGA #40 - CUA., ESTADO MIRANDA VENEZUELA S.A.
82- 34  DIAZ, CARLOS ANTHONY                    10212 BROADACRE ST - SUN VALLEY CA 91352
83- 48  DIAZ, MICHAEL ANTHONY                   1032 BANYAN WAY - PACIFICA CA 94044
24- 31  DIBUT, PEDRO                            D. DECEMBER 4, 1979 HIALEAH, FLA.
64- 25  DICKEN, PAUL FRANKLIN                   7253 ST ANDREWS RD - LAKE WORTH FL 33460
23- 28  DICKERMAN, LEO LOUIS                    D. APRIL 30, 1982 ATKINS, ARK.
17- 20  DICKERSON, GEORGE CLARK                 D. JULY 9, 1938 LOS ANGELES, CALIF.
35- 23  DICKEY, GEORGE WILLARD 'SKEETS'         D. JUNE 16, 1976 DEWITT, ARK.
28- 29  DICKEY, WILLIAM MALCOLM                 114 E. 5TH ST - LITTLE ROCK AR 72203
36- 20  DICKMAN, GEORGE EMERSON                 D. APRIL 27, 1981 NEW YORK, N. Y.
36- 21  DICKSHOT, JOHN OSCAR                    1530 JENKINSON ST - WAUKEGAN IL 60085
63- 33  DICKSON, JAMES EDWARD                   685 FRANKLIN - ASTORIA OR 97103
39- 27  DICKSON, MURRY MONROE                   505 TERRACE RD - LEAVENWORTH KS 66048
10- 46  DICKSON, WALTER R.                      D. DECEMBER 9, 1918 ARDMORE, OKLA.
69- 46  DIDIER, ROBERT DANIEL                   1311 RUE DESIREE DR - BATON ROUGE LA 70810
42- 30  DIEHL, GEORGE KRAUSE                    717 CHIPPENDALE - KINGSPORT TN 37660
47- 26  DIERING, CHARLES EDWARD ALLEN           1 NOB HILL DR - ST LOUIS MO 63138
64- 26  DIERKER, LAWRENCE EDWARDS               9019 COLLEEN - HOUSTON TX 77035
```

33- 17	DIETRICH, WILLIAM JOHN	D. JUNE 20, 1978 PHILADELPHIA, PA.
27- 29	DIETRICK, WILLIAM ALEXANDER	D. MAY 6, 1946 BETHESDA, MD.
40- 16	DIETZ, LLOYD ARTHUR 'DUTCH'	D. OCTOBER 29, 1972 BEAUMONT, TEX.
66- 28	DIETZ, RICHARD ALLEN	P.O. BOX 724491 - ATLANTA GA 30339
54- 20	DIETZEL, LEROY LOUIS	2331 CARTWIGHT PL - CHARLOTTE NC 28208
48- 33	DIFANI, CLARENCE JOSEPH 'JAY'	808 N MILL - FESTUS MO 63028
34- 31	DIGGS, REESE WILSON	D. OCTOBER 30, 1978 BALTIMORE, MD.
69- 45	DILAURO, JACK EDWARD	168 E MOHAWK - MALVERN OH 44644
59- 21	DILLARD, DAVID DONALD 'DON'	RR1 - WATERLOO SC 29384
75- 33	DILLARD, STEPHEN BRADLEY	6217 48TH DR E - BRADENTON FL 33508
17- 21	DILLHOEFER, WILLIAM MARTIN 'PICKLES'	D. FEBRUARY 22, 1922 ST. LOUIS, MO.
14- 54	DILLINGER, HARLEY HUGH	D. JANUARY 8, 1959 CLEVELAND, O.
46- 24	DILLINGER, ROBERT BERNARD	15380 RHODODENDRON DR-CANYON COUNTY CA 91351
67- 24	DILLMAN, WILLIAM HOWARD	44 HOLLY HILL RD - RICHBORO PA 18954
63- 34	DILLON, STEPHEN EDWARD	130 W 228TH ST - BRONX NY 10463
74- 27	DILONE, MIGUEL ANGEL	CALLE EL SOL #190 - SANTIAGO DOMINICAN REP.
40- 17	DIMAGGIO, DOMINIC PAUL	162 POINT RD - MARION MA 02738
36- 22	DIMAGGIO, JOSEPH PAUL	2150 BEACH ST - SAN FRANCISCO CA 94123
37- 34	DIMAGGIO, VINCENT PAUL	7528 BECK AVE - NORTH HOLLYWOOD CA 91605
77- 45	DIMMEL, MICHAEL WAYNE	8403 MANDERVILLE LN #1091 - DALLAS TX 75231
75- 34	DINEEN, KERRY MICHAEL	702 ELDER AVE - CHULA VISTA CA 92010
45- 25	DINGES, VANCE GEORGE	274 S HIGH ST - HARRISONBURG VA 22801
73- 37	DIORIO, RONALD MICHAEL	2 WHITE OAK LN - WATERBURY CT 06705
51- 24	DIPIETRO, ROBERT LOUIS PAUL	909 CARRIAGE HILL DR - YAKIMA WA 98902
81- 28	DIPINO, FRANK MICHAEL	141 NORTHWOOD WAY - CAMILLUS NY 13031
69- 48	DISTASO, ALEC JOHN	25156 AVENIDA RONDEL - VALENCIA CA 91355
84- 30	DISTEFANO, BENITO JAMES	16 LOCUST DR - THIELLS NY 10984
18- 17	DISTEL, GEORGE ADAM 'DUTCH'	D. FEBRUARY 12, 1967 MADISON, IND.
54- 21	DITMAR, ARTHUR JOHN	13629 STARLITE DR - BROOK PARK OH 44142
52- 26	DITTMER, JOHN DOUGLAS	200 N MAIN ST - ELKADER IA 52043
53- 18	DIXON, JOHN CRAIG 'SONNY'	7920 STEELE CREEK - CHARLOTTE NC 28210
84- 31	DIXON, KENNETH JOHN	103 OTWAY DR #5 - MADISON HEIGHTS VA 24572
25- 24	DIXON, LEO MOSES	D. APRIL 11, 1984 CHICAGO, ILL.
77- 46	DIXON, THOMAS EARL	2945 S DELANEY ST - ORLANDO FL 32806
12- 52	DOAK, WILLIAM LEOPOLD	D. NOVEMBER 26, 1954 BRADENTON, FLA.
24- 32	DOBB, JOHN KENNETH	973 HAMPDEN RD - MUSKEGON MI 49441
59- 22	DOBBEK, DANIEL JOHN	4042 SE YAMHILL - PORTLAND OR 97214
29- 28	DOBENS, RAYMOND JOSEPH	D. APRIL 21, 1980 STUART, FLA.
39- 28	DOBERNIC, ANDREW JOSEPH 'JESS'	2906 MISSOURI - SAINT LOUIS MO 63118
66- 29	DOBSON, CHARLES THOMAS	2604 LACLEDE STATION RD - MAPLEWOOD MO 63143
39- 29	DOBSON, JOSEPH GORDON	BOX 1972 - COOLIDGE AZ 85228
67- 25	DOBSON, PATRICK EDWARD	6795 MAPLE HILL DR #W245S - WAUKESHA WI 53186
47- 27	DOBY, LAWRENCE EUGENE	NISHUANE RD 45 - MONTCLAIR NJ 07042
45- 26	DOCKINS, GEORGE WOODROW	BOX 3 - CLYDE KS 66938
12- 53	DODD, ORAN A. 'ONA'	D. MARCH 31, 1929 NEWPORT, ARK.
12- 54	DODGE, JOHN LEWIS	D. JUNE 19, 1916 MOBILE, ALA.
21- 21	DODGE, SAMUEL EDWARD	OLD ADD: WYALUSING, PA.
37- 35	DOERR, ROBERT PERSHING	33705 ILLAMO-AGNESS RD - AGNESS OR 97406
74- 28	DOHERTY, JOHN MICHAEL	109 WAKEFIELD ST - READING MA 01867
14- 55	DOLAN, E. L. 'BIDDY'	
30- 19	DOLJACK, FRANK JOSEPH	D. JANUARY 23, 1948 CLEVELAND, O.
35- 24	DOLL, ARTHUR JAMES	D. APRIL 28, 1978 CALUMET CITY, ILL.
23- 29	DONAHUE, JOHN FREDERICK	D. OCTOBER 3, 1949 BOSTON, MASS.
43- 40	DONAHUE, JOHN STEPHEN MICHAEL	415 N. BELMONT AVE - ARLINGTON HGTS IL 60004
38- 21	DONALD, RICHARD ATLEY	RR 2 BOX 132-CHOUDRANT LA 71227
12- 55	DONALDS, EDWARD ALEXANDER	D. JULY 3, 1950 COLUMBUS, O.

66- 30	DONALDSON, JOHN DAVID	3331 BENARD AVE - CHARLOTTE NC 28206
29- 29	DONDERO, LEONARD PETER	BOX 2224 - FREMONT CA 94536
11- 42	DONNELLY, EDWARD	D. NOVEMBER 28, 1957 RUTLAND, VT.
59- 23	DONNELLY, EDWARD VINCENT	823 ROPER - HOUSTON TX 77034
44- 29	DONNELLY, SYLVESTER URBAN 'BLIX'	D. JUNE 20, 1976 OLIVIA, MINN.
61- 29	DONOHUE, JAMES THOMAS	16 HUNTLEIGH DOWNS - ST LOUIS MO 63131
21- 22	DONOHUE, PETER JOSEPH	8713 S NORMANDALE ST #261 - FT WORTH TX 76116
79- 28	DONOHUE, THOMAS JAMES	29 RUGBY RD - WESTBURY NY 11590
55- 38	DONOSO, LINO GALATA	1971 ADD: CALLE SANTA MARIA - HAVANA CUBA
50- 27	DONOVAN, RICHARD EDWARD	61 DEEP RUN RD - COHASSET MA 02025
42- 31	DONOVAN, WILLARD EARL	1611 S 10TH AVE-MAYWOOD IL 60153
85- 25	DOPSON, JOHN ROBERT	3337 OLD GAMBER ROAD - FINKSBURG MD 21048
82- 35	DORAN, WILLIAM DONALD	OLD ADD: 5309 EASTKNOLL CT #517 - CINCINNATI OH 45239
22- 26	DORAN, WILLIAM JAMES	D. MARCH 9, 1978 SANTA MONICA, CALIF.
47- 28	DORISH, HARRY	68 ELEY ST - KINGSTON PA 18704
23- 30	DORMAN, CHARLES WILLIAM	D. NOVEMBER 15, 1928 SAN FRANCISCO, CAL.
28- 30	DORMAN, DWIGHT DEXTER	D. DECEMBER 7, 1974 ANAHEIM, CAL.

DORSETT   DUNBAR

40- 18 DORSETT, CALVIN LEAVELLE	D. OCTOBER 22, 1970 ELK CITY, OKLA.
80- 39 DORSEY, JAMES EDWARD	8010 LANGDON AVE #47 - VAN NUYS CA 91406
11- 43 DORSEY, JEREMIAH	B. 1885 OAKLAND, CALIF.
79- 29 DOTSON, RICHARD ELLIOTT	4240 PALOMINO CIR %HICKS - RENO NV 89509
61- 30 DOTTER, GARY RICHARD	1639 HURSCH - WICHITA FALLS TX 76302
57- 17 DOTTERER, HENRY JOHN 'DUTCH'	10592 DAVITT AVE - GARDEN GROVE CA 92643
21- 23 DOUGLAS, ASTYANAX SAUNDERS	D. JANUARY 26, 1975 EL PASO, TEXAS
57- 18 DOUGLAS, CHARLES WILLIAM 'WHAMMY'	135 ASH ST - HUBERT NC 28539
45- 27 DOUGLAS, JOHN FRANKLIN	D. FEBRUARY 11, 1984 MIAMI, FLA.
12- 56 DOUGLAS, PHILIPS BROOKS	D. AUGUST 1, 1952 SEQUATCHIE VALLEY, TENN.
15- 34 DOUGLASS, HOWARD LAWRENCE 'LARRY'	D. NOVEMBER 4, 1949 JELLICO, TENN.
23- 31 DOUTHIT, TAYLOR LEE	444 CENTRAL AVE #301 - FREMONT CA 94536
10- 47 DOWD, JAMES JOSEPH 'SKIP'	D. DECEMBER 20, 1960 HOLYOKE, MASS.
19- 17 DOWD, RAYMOND BERNARD 'SNOOKS'	D. APRIL 4, 1962 SPRINGFIELD, MASS.
64- 27 DOWLING, DAVID BARCLAY	1802 24TH - LONGVIEW WA 98632
61- 31 DOWNING, ALPHONSO ERWIN	2800 NEILSON WAY #412 - SANTA MONICA CA 90405
73- 38 DOWNING, BRIAN JAY	4861 SILVER SPURS - YORBA LINDA CA 92686
72- 23 DOWNS, DAVID RALPH	925 EAST 1050 NORTH - BOUNTIFUL UT 84010
78- 36 DOYLE, BRIAN REED	1310 MEADOW CIR NE - WINTER HAVEN FL 33880
43- 41 DOYLE, HOWARD JAMES	322 S PAYNE - STILLWATER OK 74074
10- 48 DOYLE, JAMES FRANCIS	D. FEBRUARY 1, 1912 SYRACUSE, N.Y.
83- 49 DOYLE, JEFFREY DONALD	28851 LINGO LANE - JUNCTION CITY OR 97448
25- 25 DOYLE, JESSE HERBERT	D. APRIL 15, 1961 BELLEVILLE, ILL.
69- 49 DOYLE, PAUL SINNOTT	5832 WOODBORO DR - HUNTINGTON BEACH CA 92649
70- 33 DOYLE, ROBERT DENNIS 'DENNY'	6756 WINTERSET GARDENS-WINTER HAVEN FL 33880
35- 25 DOYLE, WILLIAM CARL	D. SEPTEMBER 4, 1951 KNOXVILLE, TENN.
47- 29 DOZIER, WILLIAM JOSEPH 'BUZZ'	2609 BRAEMER - WACO TX 76710
56- 28 DRABOWSKY, MYRON WALTER 'MOE'	530 AUDUBON PLACE - HIGHLAND PARK IL 60035
69- 50 DRAGO, RICHARD ANTHONY	23284 DEER RUN RD - BROOKSVILLE FL 33512
11- 44 DRAKE, DELOS DANIEL	D. OCTOBER 3, 1965 FINDLAY, O.
45- 28 DRAKE, LAWRENCE FRANKLIN	OLD ADD: 1212 MAIN BLDG #750 - HOUSTON TX
22- 27 DRAKE, LOGAN GAFFNEY	D. JUNE 1, 1940
60- 30 DRAKE, SAMUEL HARRISON	6302 OVERHILL DR #2 - LOS ANGELES CA 90034
56- 29 DRAKE, SOLOMON LOUIS	1732 CORNING ST - LOS ANGELES CA 90035
39- 30 DRAKE, THOMAS KENDALL	4121 50TH AVE N-BIRMINGHAM AL 35217
82- 36 DRAVECKY, DAVID FRANCIS	5853 MENORCA RD - SAN DIEGO CA 92124
31- 22 DREESEN, WILLIAM RICHARD	D. NOVEMBER 9, 1971 MOUNT VERNON, N. Y.
44- 30 DREISEWERD, CLEMENT JOHN	45 SNIPE ST - NEW ORLEANS LA 70124
44- 31 DRESCHER, WILLIAM CLAYTON	D. MAY 15, 1968 CONGERS, N. Y.
25- 26 DRESSEN, CHARLES WALTER	D. AUGUST 10, 1966 DETROIT, MICH.
14- 56 DRESSEN, LEO AUGUST	D. JUNE 30, 1931 DILLER, NEB.
75- 35 DRESSLER, ROBERT ALAN	OLD ADD: 3002 N. 46TH ST - PHOENIX AZ 85018
44- 32 DREWS, FRANK JOHN	D. APRIL 22, 1972 BUFFALO, N. Y.
46- 25 DREWS, KARL AUGUST	D. AUGUST 15, 1963 DANIA, FLA.
73- 39 DRIESSEN, DANIEL	BOX 1001 - HILTON HEAD ISLAND SC 29928
70- 34 DRISCOLL, JAMES BERNARD	948 S ALMA SCHOOL RD #48- MESA AZ 85202
17- 22 DRISCOLL, JOHN LEO 'PADDY'	D. JUNE 28, 1968 CHICAGO, ILL.
16- 20 DRISCOLL, MICHAEL COLUMBUS	D. MARCH 21, 1953 FOXBORO, MASS.
13- 48 DROHAN, THOMAS F.	D. SEPTEMBER 17, 1926 KEWANEE, ILL.
49- 19 DROPO, WALTER	65 EAST INDIA ROW #31C - BOSTON MA 02109
57- 19 DROTT, RICHARD FRED	D. AUGUST 16, 1985 GLENDALE HEIGHTS, ILL.
78- 37 DRUMRIGHT, KEITH ALAN	825 OAK GROVE RD #12 - CONCORD CA 94518
56- 30 DRYSDALE, DONALD SCOTT	78 COLGATE - RANCHO MIRAGE CA 92270
44- 33 DUBIEL, WALTER JOHN 'MONK'	D. OCTOBER 25, 1969 HARTFORD, CONN.
63- 35 DUCKWORTH, JAMES RAYMOND	2929 GRINNELL DR - DAVIS CA 95616
29- 30 DUDLEY, ELISE CLISE	BOX 4659 - PINOPOLIS SC 29469
41- 22 DUDRA, JOHN JOSEPH	D. OCTOBER 24, 1965 PANA, ILL.
77- 47 DUES, HAL JOSEPH	DRAWER R - DICKINSON TX 77539
22- 28 DUFF, CECIL ELBA 'LARRY'	D. NOVEMBER 10, 1969 BEND, ORE.
61- 32 DUFFALO, JAMES FRANCIS	1508 DEWBERRY - LANCASTER TX 75134
67- 26 DUFFIE, JOHN BROWN	3453 GLEN RD - DECATUR GA 30032
13- 49 DUFFY, BERNARD ALLEN	D. FEBRUARY 9, 1962 ABILENE, TEX.
70- 35 DUFFY, FRANK THOMAS	1044 DANBURY DR - SAN JOSE CA 95129
28- 31 DUGAN, DANIEL PHILLIP	D. JUNE 25, 1968 GREEN BROOK, N. J.
17- 23 DUGAN, JOSEPH ANTHONY	D. JULY 7, 1982 NORWOOD, MASS.
30- 20 DUGAS, AUGUSTIN JOSEPH	46 SOUTH "A" ST - TAFTVILLE CT 06380
13- 50 DUGEY, OSCAR JOSEPH	D. JANUARY 1, 1966 DALLAS, TEX.
11- 45 DUGGAN, JAMES ELMER	D. DECEMBER 5, 1951 INDIANAPOLIS, IND.
69- 51 DUKES, JAN NOBLE	3189 AGATE DR - SANTA CLARA CA 95051
67- 27 DUKES, THOMAS EARL	325 MONTE VISTA RD - ARCADIA CA 91007
59- 24 DULIBA, ROBERT JOHN	113 GROVE ST - EXETER PA 18643
15- 35 DUMONT, GEORGE HENRY	D. OCTOBER 13, 1956 MINNEAPOLIS, MINN.
77- 48 DUMOULIN, DANIEL LYNN	304 IVY DR - KOKOMO IN 46902
23- 32 DUMOVICH, NICHOLAS	D. DECEMBER 12, 1979 LAGUNA HILLS, CALIF.
83- 50 DUNBAR, THOMAS JEROME	117 CHURCH STREET - GRANITEVILLE SC 29829

HAL DUES
Lanceur/Pitcher

TOMMY DUNBAR

64- 28	DUNCAN, DAVID EDWIN	455 WEST RAPA - TUCSON AZ 85704
15- 36	DUNCAN, LOUIS BAIRD 'PAT'	D. JULY 17, 1960 COLUMBUS, O.
85- 26	DUNCAN, MARIANO	INGENIO ANGELINA #137 - SAN PEDRO DE MACORIS DOM REP.
77- 49	DUNCAN, TAYLOR MCDOWELL	176 SHILOH RD - ASHEVILLE NC 28803
13- 51	DUNCAN, VERNON VAN DYKE	D. JUNE 1, 1954 DAYTONA BEACH, FLA.
70- 36	DUNEGAN, JAMES WILLIAM	1405 S 12TH ST - BURLINGTON IA 52601
26- 27	DUNHAM, LELAND HUFFIELD	D. MAY 11, 1961 ATLANTA, ILL.
53- 19	DUNLAP, GRANT LESTER	1881 CAMPUS RD - LOS ANGELES CA 90041
29- 31	DUNLAP, WILLIAM JAMES	D. NOVEMBER 29, 1980 READING, PA.
13- 52	DUNLOP, GEORGE HENRY	D. DECEMBER 12, 1972 MERIDEN, CONN.
52- 27	DUNN, JAMES WILLIAM	1656 SUMMIT DR - GADSDEN AL 35901
74- 29	DUNN, RONALD RAY	OLD ADD: 236 E. CALIMYRNA ST - FRESNO CA 93726
70- 37	DUNNING, STEVEN JOHN	23 PLYMOUTH - IRVINE CA 92714
85- 27	DUNSTON, SHAWON DONNELL	OLD ADD: 945 42ND ST - BROOKLYN NY 11219
76- 29	DUPREE, MICHAEL DENNIS	5164 E. ASHLAN #129 - FRESNO CA 93727
81- 29	DURAN, DANIEL JAMES	201 DEL NORTE - SUNNYVALE CA 94086
54- 22	DUREN, RINOLD GEORGE	2371 WILLIAMS POINT DR - STOUGHTON WI 53589
72- 24	DURHAM, DONALD GARY	BOX 31 - YOSEMITE KY 42566
29- 32	DURHAM, EDWARD FANT	D. APRIL 27, 1976 CHESTER, S. C.
54- 23	DURHAM, JOSEPH VANN	9715 MENDOZA RD - RANDALLSTOWN MD 21133
80- 40	DURHAM, LEON	3932 DICKSON AVE - CINCINNATI OH 45229
57- 20	DURNBAUGH, ROBERT EUGENE	1638 N CENTRAL DR - DAYTON OH 45432
25- 27	DURNING, GEORGE DEWEY	10007 NEBRASKA AVE #1 - TAMPA FL 33612
17- 24	DURNING, RICHARD KNOTT	D. SEPTEMBER 23, 1948 CASTLE POINT, N. Y.
25- 28	DUROCHER, LEO ERNEST	1400 E PALM CANYON #210-PALM SPRINGS CA 92262
44- 34	DURRETT, ELMER CHARLES 'RED'	RR 3 BOX 93 - WAXAHACHIE TX 75165
22- 29	DURST, CEDRIC MONTGOMERY	D. FEBRUARY 16, 1971 SAN DIEGO, CAL.
41- 23	DUSAK, ERVIN FRANK	241 E PRAIRIE AVE - LOMBARD IL 60148
56- 31	DUSER, CARL ROBERT	3021 CORNWALL RD - BETHLEHEM PA 18017
63- 36	DUSTAL, ROBERT ANDREW	4919 CACHET BLVD - LAKELAND FL 33806
73- 40	DWYER, JAMES EDWARD	7607 W 159TH PL - TINLEY PARK IL 60477
37- 36	DWYER, JOSEPH MICHAEL	56 HIGH ST - WEST ORANGE NJ 07052
80- 41	DYBZINSKI, JEROME MATTHEW	89 245 DEBY - NAPERVILLE IL 60540
51- 25	DYCK, JAMES ROBERT	1704 SECOND STREET - CHENEY WA 99004
14- 57	DYER, BENJAMIN FRANKLIN	D. AUGUST 7, 1959 KENOSHA, WIS.
68- 17	DYER, DONALD ROBERT 'DUFFY'	742 W LAS PALMARITAS - PHOENIX AZ 85021
22- 30	DYER, EDWIN HAWLEY	D. APRIL 20, 1964 HOUSTON, TEX.
18- 18	DYKES, JAMES JOSEPH	D. JUNE 15, 1976 PHILADELPHIA, PA.
85- 28	DYKSTRA, LEONARD KYLE	2701 SHENANDOAH DR - LAGUNA HILLS CA 92653
59- 25	EADDY, DONALD JOHNSON	%J.EADDY,3440 POINSETTIA-GRAND RAPIDS MI49508
15- 37	EAKLE, CHARLES EMORY	D. JUNE 15, 1959 BALTIMORE, MD.
84- 32	EARL, WILLIAM SCOTT	BOX 63 - NORTH VERNON IN 47265
60- 31	EARLEY, ARNOLD CARL	4341 CAPTAINS LN - FLINT MI 48507
38- 22	EARLEY, THOMAS FRANCIS ALOYSIUS	51 CEDAR ST - NEW BRITAIN CT 06052
39- 31	EARLY, JACOB WILLARD	D. MAY 31, 1985 MELBOURNE, FLA.
28- 32	EARNSHAW, GEORGE LIVINGSTON	D. DECEMBER 1, 1976 LITTLE ROCK, ARK.
73- 41	EASLER, MICHAEL ANTHONY	14901 MILVERTON - CLEVELAND OH 44120
15- 38	EAST, CARLTON WILLIAM	D. JANUARY 15, 1953 WHITESBURG, GA.
41- 24	EAST, GORDON HUGH	D. NOVEMBER 2, 1981 CHARLESTON, S. C.
49- 20	EASTER, LUSCIOUS LUKE	D. MARCH 29, 1979 EUCLID, O.
28- 33	EASTERLING, PAUL	% TATTNALL, BOX 860 - REIDSVILLE GA 30453
74- 30	EASTERLY, JAMES MORRIS 'JAMIE'	1306 PLANTATION - CROCKETT TX 75835
44- 35	EASTERWOOD, ROY CHARLES	BUNGER RD - GRAHAM TX 76046
55- 39	EASTON, JOHN DAVID	SCOTCH RD BOX 418 RR1 - PENNINGTON NJ 08534
74- 31	EASTWICK, RAWLINS JACKSON	10 SODEN ST #27 - CAMBRIDGE MA 02139
79- 30	EATON, CRAIG	3307 BALTUSROL LN - LAKE WORTH FL 33467
44- 36	EATON, ZEBULON VANCE	131 LINCOLN BLVD - KENMORE NY 14217
35- 26	EAVES, VALLIE ENNIS	D. APRIL 19, 1960 NORMAN, OKLA.
13- 53	EAYRS, EDWIN	D. NOVEMBER 30, 1969 WARWICK, R.I.
15- 39	ECCLES, HARRY JOSIAH	D. JUNE 28, 1955 JAMESTOWN, N.Y.
39- 32	ECHOLS, JOHN GRESHAM	D. NOVEMBER 13, 1972 ATLANTA, GA.
75- 36	ECKERSLEY, DENNIS LEE	263 MORSE RD - SUDBURY MA 01776
30- 21	ECKERT, ALBERT GEORGE	D. APRIL 20, 1974 MILWAUKEE, WIS.
19- 18	ECKERT, CHARLES WILLIAM	4936 RIDGE AVE - TREVOSE PA 19047
32- 22	ECKHARDT, OSCAR GEORGE 'OX'	D. APRIL 22, 1951 YORKTOWN, TEX.

70- 38	EDDY, DONALD EUGENE	BOX 537 - ROCKWELL IA 50469
79- 31	EDDY, STEVEN ALLEN	OLD ADD: 2332 14TH AVE - MOLINE IL 61265
81- 30	EDELEN, BENNY JOE	BOX 13 - GRACEMONT OK 73042
32- 23	EDELEN, EDWARD JOSEPH	D. FEBRUARY 1, 1982 LAPLATA, MD.
55- 40	EDELMAN, JOHN ROGERS	922 MONTE VISTON DR - WEST CHESTER PA 19380
76- 30	EDEN, EDWARD MICHAEL 'MIKE'	OLD ADD: 6705 NORTH HINES AVE - TAMPA FL 33614
79- 32	EDGE, CLAUDE LEE 'BUTCH'	1561 BREWERTON DR - SACRAMENTO CA 95833
66- 31	EDGERTON, WILLIAM ALBERT	56339 NORTH CEDAR - MISHAWAKA IN 46544

12- 57	EDINGTON, JACOB FRANK 'STUMP'	D. NOVEMBER 29, 1969 BASTROP, LA.
80- 42	EDLER, DAVID DELMAR	1504 S 34TH AVE - YAKIMA W A 98902
13- 54	EDMONDSON, EDWARD EARL	D. MAY 10, 1971 LEESBURG, FLA.
22- 31	EDMONDSON, GEORGE HENDERSON	D. JULY 11, 1973 WACO, TEX.
69- 52	EDMONDSON, PAUL MICHAEL	D. FEBRUARY 13, 1970 SANTA BARBARA, CALIF.
15- 40	EDWARDS, ALBERT	B. 1896 FREEPORT, N.Y.
46- 26	EDWARDS, CHARLES BRUCE	D. APRIL 25, 1975 SACRAMENTO, CALIF.
78- 38	EDWARDS, DAVID LEONARD	3216 WADSWORTH AVE - LOS ANGELES CA 90011
25- 29	EDWARDS, FOSTER HAMILTON	D. JANUARY 4, 1980 ORLEANS, MASS.
41- 25	EDWARDS, HENRY ALBERT	1815 W CERRITOS-ANAHEIM CA 92804
62- 35	EDWARDS, HOWARD RODNEY 'DOC'	3660 2ND AVE - PALM BAY FL 32905
22- 32	EDWARDS, JAMES CORBETTE 'JIM JOE'	D. JANUARY 19, 1965 CALHOUN COUNTY, MISS.
61- 33	EDWARDS, JOHN ALBAN	10118 SPRINGWOOD FOREST DR - HOUSTON TX 77055
81- 31	EDWARDS, MARSHALL LYNN	3216 WADSWORTH AVE - LOS ANGELES CA 90011
77- 50	EDWARDS, MICHAEL LEWIS	3216 WADSWORTH AVE - LOS ANGELES CA 90011
34- 32	EDWARDS, SHERMAN STANLEY	1223 W 1ST - ELDORADO AR 71730
63- 37	EGAN, RICHARD WALLIS	OLD ADD: 969 CASEY LN - GARDNERVILLE NV
65- 28	EGAN, THOMAS PATRICK	16318 E HALBURTON RD-HACIENDA HEIGHTS CA91745
27- 30	EGGERT, ELMER ALBERT	D. APRIL 9, 1971 ROCHESTER, N. Y.
15- 41	EHMKE, HOWARD JONATHAN	D. MARCH 17, 1959 PHILADELPHIA, PA.
24- 33	EHRHARDT, WELTON CLAUDE 'RUBE'	D. APRIL 27, 1980 CHICAGO HEIGHTS, ILL.
12- 58	EIBEL, HENRY HACK	D. OCTOBER 16, 1945 MACON, GA.
78- 39	EICHELBERGER, JUAN TYRONE	14674 SILVERSET ST - POWAY CA 92064
82- 37	EICHHORN, MARK ANTHONY	85 KERR RD - WATSONVILLE CA 95076
25- 30	EICHRODT, FREDERICK GEORGE	D. JULY 14, 1965 INDIANAPOLIS, IND.
64- 29	EILERS, DAVID LOUIS	1500 LEE - BRENHAM TX 77833
44- 37	EISENHART, JACOB HENRY 'HANK'	HCR-61 BOX 354 - MILL CREEK PA 17060
82- 38	EISENREICH, JAMES MICHAEL	OLD ADD: 3333 HARBOR LN N - PLYMOUTH MN 55441
35- 27	EISENSTAT, HARRY	3333 WARRENSVILLE CTR. RD-SHAKER HTS OH 44122
49- 21	ELDER, GEORGE REZIN	40200 BROOKSIDE AVE - CHERRY VALLEY CA 92223
13- 55	ELDER, HENRY KNOX 'HEINIE'	D. NOVEMBER 13, 1958 LONG BEACH, CALIF.
66- 32	ELIA, LEE CONSTANTINE	1201 NORWOOD AVE - CLEARWATER FL 33516
43- 42	ELKO, PETER	133 MADISON ST -WILKES BARRE PA 18702
17- 25	ELLER, HORACE OWEN 'HOD'	D. JULY 18, 1961 INDIANAPOLIS, IND.
19- 19	ELLERBE, FRANCIS ROGERS	LATTA SC 29565
74- 32	ELLINGSEN, HAROLD BRUCE	5873 DANELAND - LAKEWOOD CA 90713
62- 36	ELLIOT, LAWRENCE LEE	13278 STONE CANYON RD #B - POWAY CA 92064
23- 33	ELLIOTT, ALLEN CLIFFORD	D. MAY 6, 1979 ST. LOUIS, MO.
21- 24	ELLIOTT, CARTER WARD	D. MAY 21, 1959 PALM SPRINGS, CAL.
11- 46	ELLIOTT, EUGENE BIRMINGHOUSE	D. JANUARY 5, 1976 HUNTINGDON, PA.
10- 49	ELLIOTT, HAROLD B. 'ROWDY'	D. FEBRUARY 12, 1934 SAN FRANCISCO, CALIF.
29- 33	ELLIOTT, HAROLD WILLIAM	D. APRIL 25, 1963 HONOLULU, HAW.
53- 20	ELLIOTT, HARRY LEWIS	1154 RANDOM - EL CAJON CA 92020
47- 30	ELLIOTT, HERBERT GLENN	D. JULY 27, 1969 PORTLAND, ORE.
23- 34	ELLIOTT, JAMES THOMPSON	D. JANUARY 7, 1970 TERRE HAUTE, IND.
72- 25	ELLIOTT, RANDY LEE	P.O. BOX 834 - SOMIS CA 93066
39- 33	ELLIOTT, ROBERT IRVING	D. MAY 4, 1966 SAN DIEGO, CAL.
68- 18	ELLIS, DOCK PHILIP	121 E. 139TH ST - LOS ANGELES CA 90061
67- 28	ELLIS, JAMES RUSSELL	13608 AVE 224 - TULARE CA 93274
69- 53	ELLIS, JOHN CHARLES	15 WHITNEY LN - EAST LYME CT 06333
71- 29	ELLIS, ROBERT WALTER	OLD ADD: 13210 LAKEWOOD DR NE - AURORA OR 97002
62- 37	ELLIS, SAMUEL JOSEPH	6111 WHITEWAY - TEMPLE TERRACE FL 33617
20- 31	ELLISON, GEORGE RUSSELL	D. JANUARY 20, 1978 SAN FRANCISCO, CALIF.
16- 21	ELLISON, HERBERT SPENCER 'BABE'	D. AUGUST 11, 1955 SAN FRANCISCO, CALIF.
58- 28	ELLSWORTH, RICHARD CLARK	1099 W MORRIS - FRESNO CA 93705
24- 34	ELMORE, VERDO WILSON	D. AUGUST 5, 1969 BIRMINGHAM, ALA.
23- 35	ELSH, EUGENE ROY	D. NOVEMBER 12, 1978 PHILADELPHIA, PA.
53- 21	ELSTON, DONALD RAY	2436 MAPLE ST - NORTHBROOK IL 60062
41- 26	EMBREE, CHARLES WILLIAM 'RED'	5500 N. BANK RD - CRESCENT CITY CA 95531
23- 36	EMBRY, CHARLES AKIN 'SLIM'	D. OCTOBER 10, 1947 NASHVILLE, TENN.
11- 47	EMERSON, CHESTER ARTHUR	D. JULY 2, 1971 AUGUSTA, ME.
63- 38	EMERY, CALVIN WAYNE	8232 EAST WILSHIRE - SCOTTSDALE AZ 85257
24- 35	EMERY, HERRICK SMITH 'SPOKE'	D. JUNE 2, 1975 CAPE CANAVERAL, FLA.
16- 22	EMMER, FRANK WILLIAM	D. OCTOBER 18, 1963 HOMESTEAD, FLA.
23- 37	EMMERICH, ROBERT G.	D. NOVEMBER 22, 1948 BRIDGEPORT, CONN.
45- 29	EMMERICH, WILLIAM PETER 'SLIM'	257 EAST FAIRVIEW ST - ALLENTOWN PA 18103
46- 27	ENDICOTT, WILLIAM FRANKLIN	BOX 48, 5 MILE LANDING - TOPOCK AZ 86436
12- 59	ENGEL, JOSEPH WILLIAM	D. JUNE 12, 1969 CHATTANOOGA, TENN.
85- 29	ENGEL, STEVEN MICHAEL	1657 TRILLIUM COURT - READING OH 45215
25- 31	ENGLE, CHARLES AUGUST	D. OCTOBER 12, 1983 SAN ANTONIO, TEX.
81- 32	ENGLE, RALPH DAVID 'DAVE'	1024 N. MORNINGSIDE DR - MANHATTAN BEACH CA 90266
81- 33	ENGLE, RICHARD DOUGLAS	2634 JACKSON PIKE - BATAVIA OH 45103
32- 24	ENGLISH, CHARLES DEWIE	1600 S. BALDWIN AVE #32 - ARCADIA CA 91006

```
27- 31  ENGLISH, ELWOOD GEORGE           14 N ELEVENTH ST - NEWARK OH 43055
31- 23  ENGLISH, GILBERT RAYMOND         RR 2 - TRINITY NC 27370
46- 28  ENNIS, DELMAR                    712 WOODSIDE RD - JENKINTOWN PA 19046
26- 28  ENNIS, RUSSELL ELWOOD            D. JANUARY 29, 1949 SUPERIOR, WIS.
76- 31  ENRIGHT, GEORGE ALBERT           6046 LAKE WORTH RD #969-LAKE WORTH FL 33463
17- 26  ENRIGHT, JOHN PERCY              D. AUGUST 18, 1975 POMPANO BEACH, FLA.
12- 60  ENS, ANTON 'MUTZ'                D. JUNE 28, 1950 ST. LOUIS, MO.
22- 33  ENS, JEWEL WINKLEMEYER           D. JANUARY 17, 1950 SYRACUSE, N. Y.
74- 33  ENYART, TERRY GENE               520 SEAL AVE - PIKETON OH 45661
14- 58  ENZENROTH, CLARENCE HERMAN 'JACK' D. FEBRUARY 21, 1944
14- 59  ENZMANN, JOHN                    D. MARCH 14, 1984 RIVERHEAD, N. Y.
38- 23  EPPERLY, ALBERT PAUL             2621 IOWA ST - DAVENPORT IA 52803
35- 28  EPPS, AUBREY LEE                 D. NOVEMBER 13, 1984 ACKERMAN, MISS.
38- 24  EPPS, HAROLD FRANKLIN            8121 GARLAND DR-HOUSTON TX 77017
66- 33  EPSTEIN, MICHAEL PETER           7775 SOUTH BISCAY ST - AURORA CO 80016
77- 51  ERARDI, JOSEPH GREGORY           204 HANOVER AVE - LIVERPOOL NY 13088
47- 31  ERAUTT, EDWARD LORENZ            7252 WAITE DR - LAMESA CA 92041
50- 28  ERAUTT, JOSEPH MICHAEL           D. OCTOBER 6, 1976 PORTLAND, ORE.
58- 29  ERICKSON, DON LEE                2717 INTERLACHEN - SPRINGFIELD IL 62704
14- 60  ERICKSON, ERIC GEORGE ADOLPH     D. MAY 19, 1965 JAMESTOWN, N. Y.
53- 22  ERICKSON, HAROLD JAMES           333 BAYSHORE DR - OSPREY FL 33559
35- 29  ERICKSON, HENRY NELS             D. DECEMBER 13, 1964 LOUISVILLE, KY.
41- 27  ERICKSON, PAUL WALFORD           363 BOYD ST - FOND DU LAC WI 54935
29- 34  ERICKSON, RALPH LEIF             5770 WINFIELD BLVD #153 - SAN JOSE CA 95123
78- 40  ERICKSON, ROGER FARRELL          2647 DELAWARE DR - SPRINGFIELD IL 62702
47- 32  ERMER, CALVIN COOLIDGE           1009 PANORAMA DR - CHATTANOOGA TN 37421
57- 21  ERNAGA, FRANK JOHN               50 N ROOP ST - SUSANVILLE CA 96130
38- 25  ERRICKSON, RICHARD MERRIWELL     2976 DOUGLAS LANE - VINELAND NJ 08360
48- 34  ERSKINE, CARL DANIEL             6214 S MADISON AVE - ANDERSON IN 46013
83- 51  ESASKY, NICHOLAS ANDREW          1779 STARLIGHT DR NE - MARIETTA GA 30062
54- 24  ESCALERA, SATURNINO CUADRADO 'NINO' COND-LAGUNA GARDEN 4 #1E-ISLA VERDE PR 00913
82- 39  ESCARREGA, ERNESTO (ACOSTA)      APATADO POSTAL 48G - LOS MOCHIS SINOLOA MEX.
15- 42  ESCHEN, JAMES GODRICH            D. SEPTEMBER 27, 1960 SLOATSBURG, N.Y.
42- 32  ESCHEN, LAWRENCE EDWARD          OLD ADD: 5540 ROSWELL RD #B212 - ATLANTA GA 30342
11- 48  ESMOND, JAMES J.                 D. JUNE 26, 1948 TROY, N.Y.
82- 40  ESPINO, JUAN                     EUGENIO M. DE CESTOS #50 - BONAO DOMINICAN REP.
74- 34  ESPINOSA, ARNULFO ACEVEDO 'NINO' 27 DE BEBRERO #9 - VILLA ALTAGRACIA DOMINICAN REP.
84- 33  ESPINOZA, ALVARO ALBERTO         URB. MICHELENA C/93 #86-74 - VALENCIA VENEZUELA S.A.
52- 28  ESPOSITO, SAMUEL                 ATH DEPT N. C. ST U - RALEIGH NC 27607
83- 52  ESPY, CECIL EDWARD               P.O. BOX 14464 - SAN DIEGO CA 92114
58- 30  ESSEGIAN, CHARLES ABRAHAM        144 N HOBART BLVD - LOS ANGELES CA 90004
79- 33  ESSER, MARK GERALD               4 JACKSON DR - POUGHKEEPSIE NY 12603
73- 42  ESSIAN, JAMES SARKIS             22959 GAUKLER - ST CLAIR SHORES MI 48080
35- 30  ESTALELLA, ROBERTO MENDEZ        3297 W 14TH LN - HIALEAH FL 33012
64- 30  ESTELLE, RICHARD HARRY           2221 TAYLOR AVE - POINT PLEASANT NJ 08742
51- 26  ESTOCK, GEORGE JOHN              595 RAY STREET - SEBASTIAN FL 32958
60- 32  ESTRADA, CHARLES LEONARD         BOX 186 - SANTA MARGARITA CA 93453
71- 30  ESTRADA, FRANCISCO (SOTO)        MANUEL DOBLADO PTE 605-A - NAVAJOA SONORA MEX.
29- 35  ESTRADA, OSCAR                   D. JANUARY 2, 1978 HAVANA, CUBA
62- 38  ETCHEBARREN, ANDREW AUGUSTE      15851 DODRILL DR - HACIENDA HEIGHTS CA 91745
43- 43  ETCHISON, CLARENCE HAMPTON 'BUCK' D. JANUARY 24, 1980 EAST NEW MARKET, MD.
67- 29  ETHERIDGE, BOBBY LAMAR           OLD ADD: 103 LOTUS ST - GREENVILLE MS 38701
38- 26  ETTEN, NICHOLAS RAYMOND TOM      21 SPINNING WHEEL RD - HINSDALE IL 60521
22- 34  EUBANKS, UEL MELVIN              D. NOVEMBER 21, 1954 DALLAS, TEX.
85- 30  EUFEMIA, FRANK ANTHONY           71 DELFORD AVENUE - BERGENFIELD NJ 07621
17- 27  EUNICK, FERNANDES BOWEN          D. DECEMBER 9, 1959 BALTIMORE, MD.
39- 34  EVANS, ALFRED HUBERT             D. APRIL 6, 1979 WILSON, N. C.
78- 41  EVANS, BARRY STEVEN              143 COLLEGE ST - MCDONOUGH GA 30253
69- 54  EVANS, DARRELL WAYNE             354 PROVENCAL - DETROIT MI 48231
72- 26  EVANS, DWIGHT MICHAEL            3 JORDAN RD - LYNNFIELD MA 01940
15- 43  EVANS, JOSEPH PATTON             D. AUGUST 9, 1953 GULFPORT, MISS.
36- 23  EVANS, RUSSELL EDISON 'RED'      D. JUNE 14, 1982 LAKEVIEW, ARK.
32- 25  EVANS, WILLIAM ARTHUR            D. JANUARY 8, 1952 WICHITA, KANS.
16- 23  EVANS, WILLIAM JAMES             D. DECEMBER 21, 1946 BURLINGTON, N. C.
49- 22  EVANS, WILLIAM LAWRENCE          D. NOVEMBER 30, 1983 GRAND JUNCTION, COLO.
69- 55  EVERITT, EDWARD LEON             RR 1 BOX 417 - MARSHALL TX 75670
13- 56  EVERS, JOSEPH FRANCIS            D. JANUARY 4, 1949 ALBANY, N.Y.
41- 28  EVERS, WALTER ARTHUR 'HOOT'      637 S RIPPLE CREEK - HOUSTON TX 77057
21- 25  EWING, REUBEN                    D. OCTOBER 5, 1970 WEST HARTFORD, CONN.
73- 43  EWING, SAMUEL JAMES              RR 4, POWELL RD - LEWISBURG TN 37091
19- 20  EWOLDT, ARTHUR LEE               D. DECEMBER 8, 1977 DES MOINES, IA.
43- 44  EYRICH, GEORGE LINCOLN           565 S 15TH ST-READING PA 19602
23- 38  EZZELL, HOMER ESTELL             D. AUGUST 3, 1976 SAN ANTONIO, TEX.
```

Nino Escalera-Cincinnati Redlegs

FABER   FERRARA

14- 61	FABER, URBAN CHARLES 'RED'	D. SEPTEMBER 25, 1976 CHICAGO, ILL.
16- 24	FABRIQUE, ALBERT LAVERNE 'BUNNY'	D. JANUARY 10, 1960 ANN ARBOR, MICH.
53- 23	FACE, ELROY LEON	608 DELLA DR #5F - NORTH VERSAILLES PA 15137
80- 43	FAEDO, LEONARDO LAGO 'LENNY'	2920 COLLINS ST - TAMPA FL 33607
19- 21	FAETH, ANTHONY JOSEPH	D. DECEMBER 22, 1982 ST. PAUL, MINN.
43- 45	FAGAN, EVERETT JOSEPH	D. FEBRUARY 16, 1983 MORRISTOWN, N.J.
18- 19	FAHEY, FRANCIS RAYMOND	D. MARCH 19, 1954 UXBRIDGE, MASS.
12- 61	FAHEY, HOWARD SIMPSON	D. OCTOBER 24, 1971 CLEARWATER, FLA.
71- 31	FAHEY, WILLIAM ROGER	19467 MACARTHUR - DETROIT MI 48240
51- 27	FAHR, GERALD WARREN 'RED'	816 WEST PARK ST - PARAGOULD AR 72450
14- 62	FAHRER, CLARENCE WILLIE 'PETE'	D. JUNE 10, 1967 FREMONT, MICH.
47- 33	FAIN, FERRIS ROY	BOX 1357 - GEORGETOWN CA 95634
19- 22	FAIRCLOTH, JAMES LAMAR 'RAGS'	D. OCTOBER 5, 1953 TUCSON, ARIZ.
68- 19	FAIREY, JAMES BURKE	218 STRAWBERRY LN - CLEMSON SC 29361
58- 31	FAIRLY, RONALD RAY	23140 PARK SORRENTO - CALABASAS CA 91302
75- 37	FALCONE, PETER FRANK	3179 BOLERO DR - ATLANTA GA 30341
20- 32	FALK, BIBB AUGUST	4213 AVE 'D ' - AUSTIN TX 78751
25- 32	FALK, CHESTER EMANUEL	5924 HIGHLAND HILLS DR - AUSTIN TX 78731
31- 24	FALLENSTIN, EDWARD JOSEPH	D. NOVEMBER 24, 1971 ORANGE, N.J.
37- 32	FALLON, GEORGE DECATUR	71 PLAINVIEW DR - STRATFORD CT 06497
84- 34	FALLON, ROBERT JOSEPH	2114 NORTH 44TH AVE - HOLLYWOOD FL 33021
14- 63	FALSEY, PETER JAMES	D. MAY 23, 1976 LOS ANGELES, CALIF.
45- 30	FANNIN, CLIFFORD BRYSON	D. DECEMBER 11, 1966 SANDUSKY, O.
54- 25	FANNING, WILLIAM JAMES 'JIM'	BOX 500 STATION M - MONTREAL QUEBEC H1V 3P2 CAN.
63- 39	FANOK, HARRY MICHAEL	16 FANOK RD - WHIPPANY NJ 07981
49- 23	FANOVICH, FRANK JOSEPH	7 BLOSSOM RD - SUFFERN NY 10901
10- 50	FANWELL, HARRY CLAYTON	D. JULY 15, 1965 BALTIMORE, MD.
70- 39	FANZONE, CARMEN	4147 SHADYGLADE - STUDIO CITY CA 91604
61- 34	FARLEY, ROBERT JACOB	RR 3 - MONTOURSVILLE PA 17754
71- 32	FARMER, EDWARD JOSEPH	16213 HAMLIN - VAN NUYS CA 91406
16- 25	FARMER, FLOYD HASKELL 'JACK'	D. MAY 21, 1970 COLUMBIA, LA.
82- 41	FARR, JAMES ALFRED	RR 1 BOX 98 - ATHENS PA 18810
84- 35	FARR, STEVEN MICHAEL	RR 2 BOX 2365CC - LAPLATA MD 20646
25- 33	FARRELL, EDWARD STEPHEN 'DOC'	D. DECEMBER 20, 1966 LIVINGSTON, N. J.
14- 64	FARRELL, JOHN J.	D. MARCH 24, 1918 CHICAGO, ILL.
43- 46	FARRELL, MAJOR KERBY	D. DECEMBER 17, 1975 NASHVILLE, TENN.
56- 32	FARRELL, RICHARD JOSEPH	D. JUNE 11, 1977 GREAT YARMOUTH, ENGLAND
68- 20	FAST, DARCY RAE	OLD ADD: 7241 RIDGEMONT DR SE - LACEY WA 98503
53- 24	FASZHOLZ, JOHN EDWARD	7108 GENEVA - AUSTIN TX 78723
62- 39	FAUL, WILLIAM ALVAN	RR1 BOX 7 - PLEASANT PLAIN OH 45162
27- 32	FAULKNER, JAMES LEROY	D. JUNE 2, 1962 WEST PALM BEACH, FLA.
44- 38	FAUSETT, ROBERT SHAW	503 SOUTHWEST PARKWAY #711 - COLLEGE STATION TX 77840
11- 49	FAUST, CHARLES VICTOR	D. JUNE 18, 1915 FORT STEILACOOM, WASH.
16- 26	FAUTSCH, JOSEPH ROAMON	D. MARCH 16, 1971 NEW HOPE, MINN.
62- 40	FAZIO, ERNEST JOSEPH	2626 NICHOLSON ST - SAN LEANDRO CA 94577
52- 29	FEAR, LUVERN CARL	D. SEPTEMBER 6, 1976 SPENCER, IA.
51- 28	FEDEROFF, ALFRED	10150 MORTONVIEW - TAYLOR MI 48080
34- 33	FEHRING, WILLIAM PAUL 'DUTCH'	1735 POPPY AVE - MENLO PARK CA 94023
38- 27	FEINBERG, EDWARD	9200 N. H'BROOK LAKE BLD-8,#209 - HOLLYWOOD FL 33025
85- 31	FELDER, MICHAEL OTIS	322 SOUTH 17TH STREET - RICHMOND CA 94804
42- 33	FELDERMAN, MARVIN WILFRED	4342 W 177TH ST-TORRANCE CA 90504
41- 29	FELDMAN, HARRY	D. MARCH 16, 1962 FORT SMITH, ARK.
23- 39	FELIX, AUGUST GUENTHER	D. MAY 12, 1960 MONTGOMERY, ALA.
58- 32	FELLER, JACK LELAND	111 GREENLEAF - ONSTED MI 49265
36- 24	FELLER, ROBERT WILLIAM ANDREW	BOX 157 - GATES MILLS OH 44040
15- 44	FELSCH, OSCAR EMIL 'HAPPY'	D. AUGUST 17, 1964 MILWAUKEE, WIS.
68- 21	FELSKE, JOHN FREDRICK	600 LIVINGSTON - MCHENRY IL 60050
79- 34	FELTON, TERRY LANE	BOX 533 - BAKER LA 70714
21- 26	FENNER, HORACE ALFRED 'HOD'	D. NOVEMBER 20, 1954 DETROIT, MICH.
72- 27	FENWICK, ROBERT RICHARD	1223 FIFTH AVE SOUTH - ANOKA MN 55303
42- 34	FERENS, STANLEY	BOX 261-YUKON PA 15698
18- 20	FERGUSON, JAMES ALEXANDER	D. APRIL 28, 1976 SEPULVEDA, CALIF.
70- 40	FERGUSON, JOSEPH VANCE	1041 BRET COVE COURT - SAN JOSE CA 95120
44- 39	FERGUSON, ROBERT LESTER	RR 1 BOX 235 - WETUMPKA AL 36092
40- 19	FERNANDES, EDWARD PAUL	D. NOVEMBER 27, 1968 HAYWARD, CAL.
83- 53	FERNANDEZ, CHARLES SIDNEY 'SID'	992C AWAAWAANOA PLACE - HONOLULU HI 96825
67- 30	FERNANDEZ, FRANK	37 COUGHLAN AVE - STATEN ISLAND NY 10310
42- 35	FERNANDEZ, FROILAN 'NANNY'	26229 MONTE VISTA-LOMITA CA 90717
56- 33	FERNANDEZ, HUMBERTO PEREZ 'CHICO'	3322 24TH ST - DETROIT MI 48208
68- 22	FERNANDEZ, LORENZO MARTO	1310 SW 97TH AVE - MIAMI FL 33175
83- 54	FERNANDEZ, OCTAVIO ANTONIO 'TONY'	CALLE N#3,B.RESTAURACION-SAN PEDRO DE MACORIS DOM. REP.
63- 40	FERRARA, ALFRED JOHN	BOX 69263 - LOS ANGELES CA 90069

55- 41	FERRARESE, DONALD HUGH	14140 GAYHEAD RD - APPLE VALLEY CA 92307
66- 34	FERRARO, MICHAEL DENNIS	6195-B LAUREL LANE - TAMARAC FL 33319
35- 31	FERRAZZI, WILLIAM JOSEPH	RR 1 BOX 46-HAWTHORNE FL 32640
85- 32	FERREIRA, ANTHONY ROSS	3756 LOFTON PLACE - RIVERSIDE CA 92501
29- 36	FERRELL, RICHARD BENJAMIN 'RICK'	2199 GOLFVIEW #203 - TROY MI 48084
27- 33	FERRELL, WESLEY CHEEK	D. DECEMBER 9, 1976 SARASOTA, FLA.
74- 35	FERRER, SERGIO	P.AREILAGE NX-8,LEVITTOWN LAKES - TOA BAJA PR 00632
41- 30	FERRICK, THOMAS JEROME	517 HARRINGTON RD-HAVERTOWN PA 19083
79- 35	FERRIS, ROBERT EUGENE	9718 IRONMASTER DR - BURKE VA 22015
45- 31	FERRISS, DAVID MEADOW 'BOO'	510 ROBINSON DR - CLEVELAND MS 38732
10- 51	FERRY, JOHN FRANCIS	D. AUGUST 29, 1954 PITTSFIELD, MASS.
37- 38	FETTE, LOUIS HENRY WILLIAM	D. JANUARY 3, 1981 WARRENSBURG, MO.
17- 28	FEWSTER, WILSON LLOYD 'CHICK'	D. APRIL 16, 1945 BALTIMORE, MD.
81- 34	FIALA, NEIL STEPHEN	3715 ANDORA - ST.LOUIS MO 63125
44- 40	FICK, JOHN RALPH	D. JUNE 9, 1958 SOMERS POINT, N. J.
76- 32	FIDRYCH, MARK STEVEN	259 CRAWFORD - NORTHBOROUGH MA 01532
32- 26	FIEBER, CLARENCE THOMAS 'LEFTY'	D. AUGUST 20, 1985 REDWOOD CITY, CALIF.
85- 33	FIELDER, CECIL GRANT	17066 EAST MAIN ST - LAPUENTE CA 91744
73- 44	FIFE, DANNY WAYNE	5037 TIMBER RIDGE - CLARKSTON MI 48016
74- 36	FIGUEROA, EDUARDO	CALLE 41 A-N15 - SANTA JUANITA PR 00619
80- 44	FIGUEROA, JESUS MARIA	SANTA CRUZ VILLA MELLA KM 8 - SANTO DOMINGO DOM. REP.
40- 20	FILE, LAWRENCE SAMUEL	171/2 W ROLAND RD-CHESTER PA 19015
82- 42	FILER, THOMAS CARSON	9748 SUSAN RD - PHILADELPHIA PA 19115
44- 41	FILIPOWICZ, STEPHEN CHARLES	D. FEBRUARY 21, 1975 WILKES-BARRE, PA.
34- 34	FILLEY, MARCUS LUCIUS	43 FIRST ST - TROY NY 12180
15- 45	FILLINGIM, DANA	D. FEBRUARY 3, 1961 TUSKEGEE, ALA.
82- 43	FILSON, WILLIAM PETER 'PETE'	1034 10TH AVE - FOLSOM PA 19033
83- 55	FIMPLE, JOHN JOSEPH	930 8TH ST - EUREKA CA 95501
79- 36	FINCH, JOEL D	68571 OAK SPRING RD - EDWARDSBURG MI 49112
16- 27	FINCHER, WILLIAM ALLEN	D. MAY 7, 1946 SHRFVEPORT, LA.
47- 34	FINE, THOMAS MORGAN	159 KING GEORGE CT - JACKSONVILLE NC 28540
68- 23	FINGERS, ROLAND GLEN	1268 HIDDEN MOUNTAIN DR - EL CAJON CA 92020
54- 26	FINIGAN, JAMES LEROY	D. MAY 16, 1981 QUINCY, ILL.
35- 32	FINK, HERMAN ADAM	D. AUGUST 24, 1980 SALISBURY, N. C.
43- 47	FINLEY, ROBERT EDWARD	D. JANUARY 2, 1986 WEST COVINA, CALIF.
30- 22	FINN, CORNELIUS FRANCIS 'MICKEY'	D. JULY 7, 1933 ALTOONA, PA.
12- 62	FINNERAN, JOSEPH IGNATIUS 'HAPPY'	D. FEBRUARY 3, 1942 ORANGE, N.J.
31- 25	FINNEY, HAROLD WILSON	RR 2 BOX 195 - LAFAYETTE AL 36862
31- 26	FINNEY, LOUIS KLOPSCHE	D. APRIL 22, 1966 LAFAYETTE, ALA.
68- 24	FIORE, MICHAEL GARY JOSEPH	17 SILVER ST - MALVERNE NY 11565

81- 35	FIREOVID, STEPHEN JOHN	RR 5 - BRYAN OH 43506
81- 36	FIROVA, DANIEL MICHAEL	202 ST JOHN - REFUGIO TX 78377
19- 23	FISBURN, SAMUEL	D. APRIL 11, 1965 BETHLEHEM, PA.
30- 23	FISCHER, CHARLES WILLIAM 'CARL'	D. DECEMBER 10, 1963 MEDINA, N. Y.
62- 41	FISCHER, HENRY WILLIAM	3304 PEBBLE BEACH DR - LAKE WORTH FL 33467
41- 31	FISCHER, REUBEN WALTER	2453 DORN DR - GREEN BAY WI 54301
13- 57	FISCHER, WILLIAM CHARLES	D. SEPTEMBER 4, 1945 RICHMOND, VA.
56- 34	FISCHER, WILLIAM CHARLES	604 BROUGHTON DR - BEVERLY MA 01915
77- 52	FISCHLIN, MICHAEL THOMAS	9523 COLTON AVE - ELK GROVE CA 95624
11- 50	FISHER, AUGUSTUS HARRIS	D. APRIL 8, 1972 PORTLAND, ORE.
85- 34	FISHER, BRIAN KEVIN	629 JASPER ST - AURORA CO 80011
19- 24	FISHER, CLARENCE HENRY	D. NOVEMBER 2, 1965 POINT PLEASANT, W. VA.
45- 32	FISHER, DONALD RAYMOND	D. JULY 29, 1973 MAYFIELD HEIGHTS, O.
59- 26	FISHER, EDDIE GENE	408 CARDINAL CIRCLE S - ALTUS OK 73521
64- 31	FISHER, FREDERICK BROWN 'FRITZ'	OLD ADD: 11730 ECKEL JUNCTION - PERRYSBURG OH 43551
23- 40	FISHER, GEORGE ALOYS 'SHOWBOAT'	BARACUDA AVE S. (BOX 203) - AVON MN 56310
51- 29	FISHER, HARRY DEVEREAUX	D. SEPTEMBER 20, 1981 WATERLOO, ONT.
10- 52	FISHER, JOHN GUS 'RED'	D. JANUARY 1, 1940 LOUISVILLE, KY.
59- 27	FISHER, JOHN HOWARD	611 HAMILTON ST - EASTON PA 18042
55- 42	FISHER, MAURICE WAYNE	15920 LUCERNE RD - FREDERICKTOWN OH 43019
10- 53	FISHER, RAYMOND LYLE	D. NOVEMBER 3, 1982 ANN ARBOR, MICH.
12- 63	FISHER, ROBERT TAYLOR	D. AUGUST 4, 1963 JACKSONVILLE, FLA.
67- 31	FISHER, THOMAS GENE	8233 HUMMINGBIRD CT - INDIANAPOLIS IN 46256
16- 28	FISHER, WILBUR MCCULLOUGH	D. OCTOBER 24, 1960 WELCH, W. VA.
69- 56	FISK, CARLTON ERNEST	16612 CATAWBA RD - LOCKPORT IL 60441
14- 65	FISKE, MAXIMILIAN PATRICK	D. MAY 15, 1928 CHICAGO, ILL.
14- 66	FITTERY, PAUL CLARENCE	D. JANUARY 28, 1974 CARTERSVILLE, GA.
28- 34	FITZBERGER, CHARLES CASPAR	D. JANUARY 25, 1965 BALTIMORE, MD.
48- 35	FITZGERALD, EDWARD RAYMOND	431 CHRISTOPHER ST - FOLSOM CA 95630
22- 35	FITZGERALD, HOWARD CHUMNEY	D. FEBRUARY 26, 1959 EAGLE FALLS, TEX.
58- 33	FITZGERALD, JOHN FRANCIS	RR 1 BOX 351 - WESTTOWN NY 10998
11- 51	FITZGERALD, JUSTIN HOWARD 'MIKE'	D. JANUARY 17, 1945 SAN MATEO, CALIF.
83- 56	FITZGERALD, MICHAEL ROY	3641 MANOR DR - LAKEWOOD CA 90712
31- 27	FITZGERALD, RAYMOND FRANCIS	D. SEPTEMBER 6, 1977 WESTFIELD, MASS.

```
24- 36 FITZKE, PAUL FREDERICK HERMAN      D. JUNE 30, 1950 SACRAMENTO, CAL.
66- 35 FITZMAURICE, SHAUN EARLE           6253 NICOLET RD - RICHMOND VA 23225
69- 57 FITZMORRIS, ALAN JAMES             3545 MOUNT EVEREST AVE - SAN DIEGO CA 92111
15- 46 FITZPATRICK, EDWARD HENRY          D. OCTOBER 23, 1965 BETHLEHEM, PA.
25- 34 FITZSIMMONS, FREDERICK LANDIS      D. NOVEMBER 18, 1979 YUCCA VALLEY, CALIF.
19- 25 FITZSIMMONS, THOMAS WILLIAM        D. DECEMBER 20, 1971 OAKLAND, CALIF.
14- 67 FLACK, MAX JOHN                    D. JULY 31, 1975 BELLEVILLE, ILL.
45- 33 FLAGER, WALTER LEONARD             3087 PORTLAND RD NE #1 - SALEM OR 97303
17- 29 FLAGSTEAD, IRA JAMES               D. MARCH 13, 1940 OLYMPIA, WASH.
41- 32 FLAIR, ALBERT DELL                 2538 CALHOUN ST-NEW ORLEANS LA 70118
75- 38 FLANAGAN, MICHAEL KENDALL          35 EAGLE ROCK - AMHERST NH 03031
13- 58 FLANIGAN, CHARLES JAMES            D. JANUARY 8, 1930 SAN FRANCISCO, CALIF.
46- 29 FLANIGAN, RAYMOND ARTHUR           1416 GLENDALE RD - BALTIMORE MD 21239
54- 27 FLANIGAN, THOMAS ANTHONY           5845 CADILLAC DR - INDEPENDENCE KY 41015
77- 53 FLANNERY, JOHN MICHAEL 'MIKE'      9652 LENORE DR - GARDEN GROVE CA 92641
79- 37 FLANNERY, TIMOTHY EARL             1835 BEL AIR TER - ENCINITAS CA 92024
27- 34 FLASKAMPER, RAYMOND HAROLD         D. FEBRUARY 3, 1978 SAN ANTONIO, TEX.
64- 32 FLAVIN, JOHN THOMAS                5744 NORTH BOND - FRESNO CA 93710
48- 36 FLEITAS, ANGEL FELIX HUSTA         OLD ADD: 101 SW 52ND COURT - MIAMI FL 33134
40- 21 FLEMING, LESLIE FLETCHERD 'BILL'   2750 WEST HOLCOMB LN - RENO NV 89511
39- 35 FLEMING, LESLIE HARVEY             D. MARCH 5, 1980
34- 35 FLETCHER, ELBURT PRESTON           131 OTIS AVE - MILTON MA 02186
14- 68 FLETCHER, OLIVER FRANK             D. OCTOBER 7, 1974 ST. PETERSBURG, FLA.
81- 37 FLETCHER, SCOTT BRIAN              2063 PANOLA RD,%O.BELLAMY - ELLENWOOD GA 30049
62- 42 FLETCHER, THOMAS WAYNE             RR 1 BOX 408 - OAKWOOD IL 61858
```

DEE FONDY
Cincinnati Redlegs

Greetings from
BARRY FOOTE

```
55- 43 FLETCHER, VANOIDE                  YADKINVILLE NC 27055
43- 48 FLICK, LEWIS MILLER                1712 ECHO DR - KINGSPORT TN 37665
17- 30 FLINN, DON RAPHIEL                 D. MARCH 9, 1959 WACO, TEX.
78- 42 FLINN, JOHN RICHARD                173 RIVO ALTO CANAL - LONG BEACH CA 90803
42- 36 FLITCRAFT, HILDRETH MILTON 'HILLY' WOODSTOWN NJ 08098
34- 36 FLOHR, MORITZ HERMAN 'MORT'        ORDWAY LANE - CANISTEO NY 14823
56- 35 FLOOD, CURTIS CHARLES              2368 MONTICELLO AVE - OAKLAND CA 94611
26- 29 FLORENCE, PAUL ROBERT              1740 SW 38TH PLACE - GAINESVILLE FL 32608
77- 54 FLORES, GILBERTO                   BDA SALAZAR 1 #38 - PONCE PR 00731
42- 37 FLORES, JESSE SANDOVAL             1930 EL PORTAL DR - LAHABRA CA 90632
51- 30 FLOWERS, BENNETT                   901 TREMONT RD - WILSON NC 27895
40- 22 FLOWERS, CHARLES WESLEY            1622 DODD DR - WYNNE AR 72396
23- 41 FLOWERS, D'ARCY RAYMOND 'JAKE'     D. DECEMBER 27, 1962 CLEARWATER, FLA.
44- 42 FLOYD, LESLIE ROE 'BUBBA'          OLD ADD: 7731 MEADOW PARK DR - DALLAS TX
68- 25 FLOYD, ROBERT NATHAN               OLD ADD: 10112 E. 72ND ST - RAYTOWN MD 64133
15- 47 FLUHRER, JOHN L.                   D. JULY 17, 1946 COLUMBUS, O.
10- 54 FLYNN, JOHN ANTHONY                D. MARCH 23, 1935 PROVIDENCE, R.I.
75- 39 FLYNN, ROBERT DOUGLAS              428 MCKENNA CT - LEXINGTON KY 40505
36- 25 FLYTHE, STUART MCGUIRE             D. OCTOBER 18, 1963 DURHAM, N. C.
58- 34 FODGE, EUGENE ARLEN                1505 N CHICAGO ST - SOUTH BEND IN 46628
53- 25 FOILES, HENRY LEE                  BOX 1021 - VIRGINIA BEACH VA 23451
78- 43 FOLEY, MARVIS EDWIN                5212 LAKE VILLAGE - SARASOTA FL 33580
28- 35 FOLEY, RAYMOND KIRWIN              D. MARCH 22, 1980 VERO BEACH, FLA.
83- 57 FOLEY, THOMAS MICHAEL              OLD ADD: 8131 SW 124TH ST - MIAMI FL 33156
70- 41 FOLI, TIMOTHY JOHN                 105 WILLOW ROAD LN - ORMOND BEACH FL 32074
70- 42 FOLKERS, RICHARD NEVIN             2215 W VINA DEL MAR - ST PETERSBURG FL 33706
51- 31 FONDY, DEE VIRGIL                  1422 BELLA VISTA CIR - REDLANDS CA 92373
21- 27 FONSECA, LEWIS ALBERT              525 HAWTHORNE PL #904 - CHICAGO IL 60657
83- 58 FONTENOT, SILTON RAY               904 LAKE RIDGE LN - LAKE CHARLES LA 70605
71- 33 FOOR, JAMES EMERSON                42 S SCHLUETER - ST LOUIS MO 63135
73- 45 FOOTE, BARRY CLIFTON               5300 CASTLEBROOK DR - RALEIGH NC 27604
85- 35 FORD, CURTIS GLENN                 5255 QUEEN ELEANOR LANE - JACKSON MS 39209
75- 40 FORD, DARNELL GLENN 'DANNY'        7080 E. COLUMBUS DR - ANAHEIM CA 92807
78- 44 FORD, DAVID ALAN                   OLD ADD: 3585 WEST 49TH ST - CLEVELAND OH 44102
50- 29 FORD, EDWARD CHARLES 'WHITEY'      38 SCHOOLHOUSE LANE - LAKE SUCCESS NY 11020
36- 26 FORD, EUGENE MATTHEW               D. SEPTEMBER 7, 1970 EMMETSBURG, IA.
19- 26 FORD, HORACE HILLS 'HOD'           D. JANUARY 29, 1977 WINCHESTER, MASS.
73- 46 FORD, PERCIVAL EDMUND WENTWORTH    D. JULY 8, 1980 NASSAU BAHAMAS
70- 43 FORD, THEODORE HENRY               769 SOUTHWEST AVE - VINELAND NJ 08360
24- 37 FOREMAN, AUGUST                    D. FEBRUARY 13, 1953 NEW YORK, N. Y.
52- 30 FORNIELES, JOSE MIGUEL 'MIKE'      29 OAK SQUARE AVE - BRIGHTON MA 02135
70- 44 FORSCH, KENNETH ROTH               7445 STONE CREEK LN - ANAHEIM CA 92807
74- 37 FORSCH, ROBERT HERBERT             428 HICKORY GLEN LN - ST LOUIS MO 63141
71- 34 FORSTER, TERRY JAY                 7690 TREERIDGE CT - DUNWOODY GA 30338
15- 48 FORSYTHE, CLARENCE D               B. ST. LOUIS, MO.
16- 29 FORTUNE, GARRETT REESE             D. SEPTEMBER 23, 1955 WASHINGTON, D. C.
64- 33 FOSNOW, GERALD EUGENE 'JERRY'      253 WHOOPING LOOP - ALTAMONTE SPRINGS FL 32701
21- 28 FOSS, GEORGE DUEWARD               D. NOVEMBER 10, 1969 MIAMI, FLA.
61- 35 FOSS, LAWRENCE CURTIS              125 N BELMONT ST - WICHITA KS 67211
```

```
67- 32  FOSSE, RAYMOND EARL                      7950 W BATES RD - TRACY CA 95376
67- 33  FOSTER, ALAN BENTON                      1515 STALKER CT - EL CAJON CA 92020
10- 55  FOSTER, EDWARD CUNNINGHAM                D. JANUARY 15, 1937 WASHINGTON, D.C.
13- 59  FOSTER, GEORGE 'RUBE'                    D. MARCH 1, 1976 BOKOSHE, OKLA.
69- 58  FOSTER, GEORGE ARTHUR                    BOX 11098 - GREENWICH CT 06830
63- 41  FOSTER, LARRY LYNN                       BOX 97 - WHITEHALL MI 49461
71- 35  FOSTER, LEONARD NORRIS                   36 JACOB PRICE APTS - COVINGTON KY 41012
70- 45  FOSTER, ROY                              RR 5 - BROKEN ARROW OK 74012
22- 36  FOTHERGILL, ROBERT ROY 'FATTY'           D. MARCH 20, 1938 DETROIT, MICH.
73- 47  FOUCAULT, STEVEN RAYMOND                 1512 HORSEWAY DR #1602 - ARLINGTON TX 76012
12- 64  FOURNIER, JOHN FRANK                     D. SEPTEMBER 5, 1973 TACOMA, WASH.
24- 38  FOWLER, JESSE                            D. SEPTEMBER 23, 1973 COLUMBIA, S. C.
54- 28  FOWLER, JOHN ARTHUR 'ART'                3046 E MAIN EXTENSION - SPARTANBURG SC 29301
23- 42  FOWLER, JOSEPH CHESTER 'BOOB'            5757 PRESTON VIEW BLVD #135 - DALLAS TX 75240
41- 33  FOWLER, RICHARD JOHN                     D. MAY 22, 1972 ONEONTA, N. Y.
82- 44  FOWLKES, ALAN KIM                        OLD ADD: 1333 N. 68TH ST #224 - SCOTTSDALE AZ 85257
42- 38  FOX, CHARLES FRANCIS                     5721 N. 20TH ST - PHOENIX AZ 85016
33- 18  FOX, ERVIN 'PETE'                        D. JULY 5, 1966 DETROIT, MICH.
44- 43  FOX, HOWARD FRANCIS                      D. OCTOBER 9, 1955 SAN ANTONIO, TEX.
47- 35  FOX, JACOB NELSON 'NELLIE'               D. DECEMBER 1, 1975 BALTIMORE, MD.
60- 33  FOX, TERRENCE EDWARD                     STAR ROUTE A BOX 196-D - NEW IBERIA LA 70560
25- 35  FOXX, JAMES EMORY                        D. JULY 21, 1967 MIAMI, FLA.
66- 36  FOY, JOSEPH ANTHONY                      1655 UNDERCLIFF DR - BRONX NY 10453
53- 26  FOYTACK, PAUL EUGENE                     5590 TADWORTH PL - WEST BLOOMFIELD MI 48033
72- 28  FRAILING, KENNETH DOUGLAS                4137 PRESCOTT - SARASOTA FL 33582
60- 34  FRANCIS, EARL COLEMAN                    28 QUAIL HILL RD - PITTSBURGH PA 15214
22- 37  FRANCIS, RAY JAMES                       D. JULY 14, 1932 ATLANTA, GA.
84- 36  FRANCO, JOHN ANTHONY                     OLD ADD: 2227 STILLWELL AVE - BROOKLYN NY 11223
82- 45  FRANCO, JULIO CESAR                      CF 16 B.LIBRE ING CONS-SAN PEDRO DE MACORIS DOM. REP.
56- 36  FRANCONA, JOHN PATSY 'TITO'              2206 MERCER RD - NEW BRIGHTON PA 15066
81- 38  FRANCONA, TERRY JON                      2206 MERCER RD - NEW BRIGHTON PA 15066
27- 35  FRANKHOUSE, FREDRICK MELOY               BOX 297 - PORT ROYAL PA 17082
44- 44  FRANKLIN, JAMES WILFORD 'JACK'           1128 SOUTH GAY ST #E - PANAMA CITY FL 32404
```

JOHN PATSY FRANCONA

```
71- 36  FRANKLIN, JOHN WILLIAM 'JAY'             OLD ADD: 2305 STRYKER AVE - VIENNA VA
41- 34  FRANKLIN, MURRAY ASHER                   D. MARCH 16, 1978 HARBOR CITY, CALIF.
39- 36  FRANKS, HERMAN LOUIS                     2745 COMANCHE DR-SALT LAKE CITY UT 84108
31- 28  FRASIER, VICTOR PATRICK                  D. JANUARY 10, 1977 JACKSONVILLE, TEX.
78- 45  FRAZIER, GEORGE ALLEN                    1235 S. 120TH EAST AVE #1B - TULSA OK 74128
47- 36  FRAZIER, JOSEPH FILMORE                  519 FAIRWAY DR - BROKEN ARROW OK 74012
29- 37  FREDERICK, JOHN HENRY                    D. JUNE 18, 1977 TIGARD, ORE.
42- 39  FREED, EDWIN CHARLES                     840 MCDOW DR-ROCK HILL SC 29730
70- 46  FREED, ROGER VERNON                      1329 S WILLOW AVE - WEST COVINA CA 91790
61- 36  FREEHAN, WILLIAM ASHLEY                  4248 SUNNINGDALE - BLOOMFIELD HILLS MI 48013
21- 29  FREEMAN, ALEXANDER VERNON 'BUCK'         D. FEBRUARY 21, 1953 FORT SAM HOUSTON, TEXAS
21- 30  FREEMAN, HARVEY BAYARD                   D. JANUARY 10, 1970 KALAMAZOO, MICH.
52- 31  FREEMAN, HERSHELL BASKIN                 5437 SAN MARINO PL - ORLANDO FL 32807
72- 29  FREEMAN, JIMMY LEE                       2164 S URBANA - TULSA OK 74114
27- 36  FREEMAN, JOHN EDWARD                     D. APRIL 14, 1958 WASHINGTON, D. C.
59- 28  FREEMAN, MARK PRICE                      6 BROOKSIDE DR - LITTLETON CO 80120
55- 44  FREESE, EUGENE LEWIS                     6504 GLENDALE - METAIRIE LA 70003
53- 27  FREESE, GEORGE WALTER                    3341 SW MARIGOLD ST - PORTLAND OR 97219
25- 36  FREEZE, CARL ALEXANDER 'JAKE'            D. APRIL 9, 1983 SAN ANGELO, TEX.
61- 37  FREGOSI, JAMES LOUIS                     18772 WINNWOOD LN - SANTA ANA CA 92705
41- 35  FREIBURGER, VERNON DONALD                15490 DEVONSHIRE CIR - WESTMINSTER CA 92683
22- 38  FREIGAU, HOWARD EARL                     D. JULY 18, 1932 CHATTANOOGA, TENN.
74- 38  FREISLEBEN, DAVID JAMES                  2119 PEACH LN - PASADENA TX 77502
32- 27  FREITAS, ANTONIO                         5648 GREENACRES WAY - ORANGEVALE CA 95662
17- 31  FRENCH, FRANK ALEXANDER 'PAT'            D. JULY 13, 1969 BATH, ME.
29- 38  FRENCH, LAWRENCE ROBERT                  3128 ORLEANS E - SAN DIEGO CA 92110
20- 33  FRENCH, RAYMOND EDWARD                   D. APRIL 3, 1978 ALAMEDA, CALIF.
65- 29  FRENCH, RICHARD JAMES 'JIM'              6960 GLORIA DR - PENNGROVE CA 94951
23- 43  FRENCH, WALTER EDWARD                    D. MAY 13, 1984 MOUNTAIN HOME, ARK.
29- 39  FREY, BENJAMIN RUDOLPH                   D. NOVEMBER 1, 1937 JACKSON, MICH.
80- 45  FREY, JAMES GOTTFRIED                    1805 REUTER RD - TIMONIUM MD 21093
33- 19  FREY, LINUS REINHARD 'LONNY'             14424 127TH AVE SE - SNOHOMISH WA 98290
73- 48  FRIAS, JESUS MARIA 'PEPE'                CALLE 4 #9 - SAN PEDRO DE MACORIS DOM. REP.
19- 27  FRIBERG, AUGUSTAF BERNHARD 'BARNEY'      D. DECEMBER 8, 1958 SWAMPSCOTT, MASS.
52- 32  FRICANO, MARION JOHN                     D. MAY 18, 1976 TIJUANA, MEX.
23- 44  FRIDAY, GRIER WILLIAM 'SKIPPER'          D. AUGUST 25, 1962 GASTONIA, N. C.
52- 33  FRIDLEY, JAMES RILEY                     540 JOSMINE NW AVE - PORT CHARLOTTE FL 33952
20- 34  FRIED, ARTHUR EDWIN 'CY'                 D. OCTOBER 10, 1970 SAN ANTONIO, TEX.
32- 28  FRIEDRICHS, ROBERT GEORGE                2091 NEEB ROAD - CINCINNATI OH 45238
49- 24  FRIEND, OWEN LACEY                       2917 HALSTED - WICHITA KS 67204
51- 32  FRIEND, ROBERT BARTMESS                  4 SALEM CIR - FOX CHAPEL PA 15238
```

```
41- 36  FRIERSON, ROBERT LAWRENCE              OLD ADD: RR 1 - ARTHUR CITY TX 7541
10- 56  FRILL, JOHN EDMUND                     D. SEPTEMBER 28, 1918 WESTERLY, R. I.
34- 37  FRINK, FREDERICK FERDINAND             OLD ADD: 2150 NE 169TH ST - NORTH MIAMI BEACH FL 33162
19- 28  FRISCH, FRANK FRANCIS                  D. MARCH 12, 1973 WILMINGTON, DEL.
67- 34  FRISELLA, DANIEL VINCENT               D. JANUARY 1, 1977 PHOENIX, ARIZ.
13- 60  FRITZ, HARRY KOCH                      D. NOVEMBER 4, 1974 COLUMBUS, O.
75- 41  FRITZ, LAURENCE JOSEPH                 2632 SCHRAGE AVE - WHITING IN 46394
55- 45  FROATS, WILLIAM JOHN                   OLD ADD: 16 ASHTON RD - YONKERS NY 10705
82- 46  FROBEL, DOUGLAS STEPHEN                63 GLENRIDGE RD - OTTAWA ONT. K2G 2Z8 CAN.
77- 55  FROST, CARL DAVID 'DAVE'               2206 OCANA DR - LONG BEACH CA 90815
78- 46  FRY, JERRY RAY                         405 E MULBERRY #12 - CHATHAM IL 62629
23- 45  FRY, JOHNSON                           D. APRIL 7, 1959 CARMI, ILL.
40- 23  FRYE, CHARLES ANDREW                   D. MAY 25, 1945 HICKORY, N. C.
66- 37  FRYMAN, WOODROW THOMPSON               RR 1 BOX 21 - EWING KY 41039
42- 40  FUCHS, CHARLES RUDOLPH                 D. JUNE 10, 1969 WEEHAWKEN, N. J.
29- 40  FUCHS, EMIL EDWIN                      D. DECEMBER 5, 1961 BOSTON, MASS.
83- 59  FUENTES, MICHAEL JAY                   6001 CELLINI STREET - CORAL GABLES FL 33146
69- 59  FUENTES, MIGUEL                        D. JANUARY 29, 1970 LOIZA ALDEA, P. R.
65- 30  FUENTES, RIGOBERTO PEAT 'TITO'         4 MORTON COURT - DALY CITY CA 94015
21- 31  FUHR, OSCAR LAWRENCE                   D. MARCH 27, 1975 DALLAS, TEX.
22- 39  FUHRMAN, ALFRED GEORGE 'OLLIE'         D. JANUARY 11, 1969 PEORIA, ILL.
21- 32  FULGHUM, JAMES LAVOISIER 'DOT'         D. NOVEMBER 11, 1947 MIAMI, FLA.
79- 38  FULGHUM, JOHN THOMAS                   OLD ADD: 2703 ARROW HEIGHTS - MARYLAND HEIGHTS MO 63043
15- 49  FULLER, FRANK EDWARD                   D. OCTOBER 29, 1965 WARREN, MICH.
73- 49  FULLER, JAMES H                        2844 POINSETTIA DR - SAN DIEGO CA 92106
74- 39  FULLER, JOHN EDWARD                    33022 CHRISTINA - DANA POINT CA 92629
64- 34  FULLER, VERNON GORDON                  OLD ADD: EXECUTIVE HOUSE - DENVER CO 80301
21- 33  FULLERTON, CURTIS HOOPER               D. JANUARY 2, 1975 WINTHROP, MASS.
```

LINUS
FREY

```
28- 36  FULLIS, CHARLES PHILIP 'CHICK'         D. MARCH 28, 1946 ASHLAND, PA.
81- 39  FUNDERBURK, MARK CLIFFORD              6924 OLD PROVIDENCE RD - CHARLOTTE NC 28226
29- 41  FUNK, ELIAS CALVIN 'LIZ'               D. JANUARY 17, 1968 OKLAHOMA CITY, OKLA.
60- 35  FUNK, FRANKLIN RAY                     4452 E BELLVIEW ST - PHOENIX AZ 85008
46- 30  FURILLO, CARL ANTHONY                  1415 CARSONIA AVE - STONY CREEK MILLS PA19606
22- 40  FUSSELL, FREDERICK MORRIS              D. OCTOBER 23, 1966 SYRACUSE, N. Y.
52- 34  FUSSELMAN, LESTER LEROY                D. MAY 21, 1970 CLEVELAND, O.
35- 33  GABLER, FRANK HAROLD                   D. NOVEMBER 1, 1967 LONG BEACH, CAL.
59- 29  GABLER, JOHN RICHARD                   8606 W 81ST ST - OVERLAND PARK KS 66204
58- 35  GABLER, WILLIAM LOUIS                  722 POPE - ST LOUIS MO 63147
45- 34  GABLES, KENNETH HARLIN                 D. JANUARY 2, 1960 WALNUT GROVE, MO.
60- 36  GABRIELSON, LEONARD GARY               24230 HILLVIEW DR - LOS ALTOS HILLS CA 94022
39- 37  GABRIELSON, LEONARD HILBOURNE          1387 GLEN DR - SAN LEANDRO CA 94577
38- 28  GADDY, JOHN WILSON                     D. MAY 3, 1966 ALBEMARLE, N. C.
51- 33  GAEDEL, EDWARD CARL                    D. JUNE 19, 1961 CHICAGO, ILL.
81- 40  GAETTI, GARY JOSEPH                    1420 JONQUIL ST - CENTRALIA IL 62801
82- 47  GAFF, BRENT ALLEN                      CHURUBUSCO IN 46723
36- 27  GAFFKE, FABIAN SEBASTIAN               4305 S PENNSYLVANIA AVE-MILWAUKEE WI 53207
63- 42  GAGLIANO, PHILIP JOSEPH                723 GARLYN CT - ST LOUIS MO 63123
65- 31  GAGLIANO, RALPH MICHAEL                845 DICKINSON ST - MEMPHIS TN 38107
83- 60  GAGNE, GREGORY CARPENTER               8318 17TH AVE SOUTH - BLOOMINGTON MN 55420
14- 69  GAGNIER, EDWARD J.                     D. SEPTEMBER 13, 1946 DETROIT, MICH.
22- 41  GAGNON, HAROLD DENNIS 'CHICK'          D. APRIL 30, 1970 WILMINGTON, DEL.
60- 37  GAINES, ARNESTA JOE                    4759 MELDON AVE - OAKLAND CA 94619
21- 34  GAINES, WILLARD ROLAND 'NEMO'          D. JANUARY 26, 1979 WARRENTON, VA.
85- 36  GAINEY, TELMANCH 'TY'                  131 JERICHO ST - CHERAW SC 29520
34- 38  GALAN, AUGUST JOHN                     1345 NOB HILL - PINOLE CA 94564
85- 37  GALARRAGA, ANDRES JOSE PADOVANI        BARRIO NUEVO CHAPELLIN CLEJON SOLEDAD #5-CARACAS VENEZ
77- 56  GALASSO, ROBERT JOSE                   RR 1 BOX 493-A - CONNELLSVILLE PA 15425
33- 20  GALATZER, MILTON                       D. JANUARY 29, 1976 SAN FRANCISCO, CALIF.
78- 47  GALE, RICHARD BLACKWELL                FOX RIDGE RD - LITTLETON NH 03561
34- 39  GALEHOUSE, DENNIS WARD                 121 HUFFMAN AVE - DOYLESTOWN OH 44230
70- 47  GALLAGHER, ALAN MITCHELL               1852 BEVERLY AVE - CLOVIS CA 93612
62- 43  GALLAGHER, DOUGLAS EUGENE              1690 MAPLE LN - FREMONT OH 43420
32- 29  GALLAGHER, EDWARD MICHAEL              D. DECEMBER 22, 1981 HYANNIS PORT, MASS.
15- 50  GALLAGHER, JOHN C.                     B. 1894 PITTSBURGH, PA.
23- 46  GALLAGHER, JOHN LAURENCE               D. SEPTEMBER 10, 1984 GLADWYN, PA.
39- 38  GALLAGHER, JOSEPH EMMETT               CUSHING TX 75760
22- 42  GALLAGHER, LAWRENCE KIRBY 'GIL'        D. JANUARY 6, 1957 WASHINGTON, D. C.
72- 30  GALLAGHER, ROBERT COLLINS              315 FAIR AVE - SANTA CRUZ CA 95060
42- 41  GALLE, STANLEY JOSEPH                  7 N REED AVE - MOBILE AL 36604
85- 38  GALLEGO, MICHAEL ANTHONY               17041 WHEATLEY DRIVE - WHITTIER CA 90603
12- 65  GALLIA, MELVIN ALLYS 'BERT'            D. MARCH 19, 1976 DEVINE, TEX.
31- 29  GALLIVAN, PHILIP JOSEPH                D. NOVEMBER 24, 1969 ST. PAUL, MINN.
```

```
19- 29 GALLOWAY, CLARENCE EDWARD 'CHICK'   D. NOVEMBER 7, 1969 CLINTON, S. C.
12- 66 GALLOWAY, JAMES CATO 'BAD NEWS'     D. MAY 3, 1950 FORT WORTH, TEX.
30- 24 GALVIN, JAMES JOSEPH                D. SEPTEMBER 30, 1969 MARIETTA, GA.
72- 31 GAMBLE, JOHN ROBERT                 3740 AMADOR WAY - RENO NV 89502
35- 34 GAMBLE, LEE JESSE                   237 JENKS AVE-PUNXATAWNEY PA 15767
69- 60 GAMBLE, OSCAR CHARLES               108 TENSAW RD - MONTGOMERY AL 36117
10- 57 GANDIL, CHARLES ARNOLD 'CHICK'      D. DECEMBER 12, 1970 CALISTOGA, CALIF.
16- 30 GANDY, ROBERT BRINKLEY              D. JUNE 19, 1945 JACKSONVILLE, FLA.
39- 39 GANTENBEIN, JOSEPH STEPHEN          535 ORANGE AVE - SOUTH SAN FRANCISCO CA 94080
76- 33 GANTNER, JAMES ELMER                BOX 156 - EDEN WI 53019
27- 37 GANZEL, FOSTER PIRIE 'BABE'         D. FEBRUARY 6, 1978 JACKSONVILLE  FLA.
46- 31 GARAGIOLA, JOSEPH HENRY             6221 EAST HUNTRESS DR - PARADISE VALLEY AZ 85253
34- 40 GARBARK, NATHANIEL MICHAEL          2321 CHARLOTTE DR - CHARLOTTE NC 28203
44- 45 GARBARK, ROBERT MICHAEL             267 JEFFERSON ST - MEADVILLE PA 16335
69- 61 GARBER, HENRY EUGENE 'GENE'         OLD ADD: RR 1 BOX 331 - ELIZABETHTOWN PA 17022
56- 37 GARBER, ROBERT MITCHELL             101 ACACIA LN - REDWOOD CITY CA 94062
84- 37 GARBEY, BARBARO GARBEY              OLD ADD: 181-10 NW 56TH ST - MIAMI FL 33178
52- 35 GARBOWSKI, ALEXANDER                110 ELLIOTT ST - YONKERS NY 10705
76- 34 GARCIA, ALFONSO RAFAEL              526A N CIVIC DR - WALNUT CREEK CA 94596
78- 48 GARCIA, DAMASO DOMINGO              SANCHEZ NO. 104 - MOCA DOMINICAN REP.
81- 41 GARCIA, DANIEL RAPHAEL              OLD ADD: 90-64 184TH PL - HOLLIS NY 11423
77- 57 GARCIA, DAVID                       15420 OLDE HWY 80 #129 - EL CAJON CA 92021
48- 37 GARCIA, EDWARD MIGUEL 'MIKE'        D. JANUARY 13, 1986 FAIRVIEW PARK, O.
73- 50 GARCIA, PEDRO MODESTO               OLD ADD: BARRIOS PUENTO DE JOBOS-GUAYAMA PR
72- 32 GARCIA, RALPH                       725 EL CENTAURO DR - EL PASO TX 79922
48- 38 GARCIA, RAMON GARCIA                FALGUERAS 256 - HAVANA CUBA
54- 29 GARCIA, VINICIO UZCANGA 'CHICO'     R CAMPOAMOR 805 COL ANAHUAC-MONTERREY NUEVO LAREDO MEX.
45- 35 GARDELLA, ALFRED STEVE              OLD ADD: 3160 BERN LN DW #93 - ROANOKE VA 24018
44- 46 GARDELLA, DANIEL LEWIS              16 MORSEMERE PL - YONKERS NY 10701
81- 42 GARDENHIRE, RONALD CLYDE            7701 QUAIL - WICHITA KS 67212
23- 47 GARDINER, ARTHUR CECIL              D. OCTOBER 21, 1954 COPIAGUE, N. Y.
75- 42 GARDNER, ARTHUR JUNIOR              RR 2 BOX 41 - WALNUT GROVE MS 39189
45- 36 GARDNER, GLENN MILESO               D. JULY 7, 1964 ROCHESTER, N. Y.
11- 52 GARDNER, HARRY RAY                  D. AUGUST 2, 1961 CANBY, ORE.
29- 42 GARDNER, RAYMOND VINCENT            D. MAY 3, 1968 FREDERICK, MD.
65- 32 GARDNER, RICHARD FRANK 'ROB'        OLD ADD: 129 CHAPIN ST - BINGHAMTON NY 13905
84- 38 GARDNER, WESLEY BRIAN               305 RUTH ST - BENTON AR 72015
54- 30 GARDNER, WILLIAM FREDERICK          35 DAYTON RD - WATERFORD CT 06385
36- 28 GARIBALDI, ARTHUR EDWARD            D. OCTOBER 20, 1967 SACRAMENTO, CAL.
62- 44 GARIBALDI, BOB ROY                  2443 OREGON AVE - STOCKTON CA 95204
31- 30 GARLAND, LOUIS LYMAN                BOX 492 - IDAHO FALLS ID 83401
73- 51 GARLAND, MARCUS WAYNE               7123 CEDAR RD - CHESTERLAND OH 44026
69- 62 GARMAN, MICHAEL DOUGLAS             3806 AIRPORT AVE - CALDWELL ID 83605
32- 30 GARMS, DEBS C.                      D. DECEMBER 16, 1984 GLEN ROSE, TEXAS
73- 52 GARNER, PHILIP MASON                BOX 288 - HOUSTON TX 77001
68- 26 GARR, RALPH ALLAN                   7819 CHASEWAY DR - MISSOURI CITY TX 77459
82- 48 GARRELTS, SCOTT WILLIAM             206 EAST ELM - BUCKLEY IL 60918
15- 51 GARRETT, CLARENCE RAYMOND           D. FEBRUARY 11, 1977 MOUNDSVILLE, W. VA.
70- 48 GARRETT, GREGORY                    14963 SANDRA - SAN FERNANDO CA 91340
66- 38 GARRETT, HENRY ADRIAN 'ADE'         BOX 201 - MANCHACA TX 78652
69- 63 GARRETT, RONALD WAYNE               5221 NORTH SHADE AVE - SARASOTA FL 33580
64- 35 GARRIDO, GIL GONZALO                556 N. MCDONOUGH ST - DECATUR GA 30030
46- 32 GARRIOTT, CECIL VIRGIL              31750 MACHADO #71 - LAKE ELSINORE CA 92330
28- 37 GARRISON, CLIFFORD WILLIAM          815 CAPAY ST - ESPARTO CA 95627
43- 49 GARRISON, ROBERT FORD               5075 65TH AVE N - PINELLAS PARK FL 33565
31- 31 GARRITY, FRANCIS JOSEPH 'HANK'      D. SEPTEMBER 3, 1962 BOSTON, MASS.
48- 39 GARVER, NED FRANKLIN                BOX 114 - NEY OH 43549
69- 64 GARVEY, STEVEN PATRICK              4320 LAJOLLA VILLAGE DR - SAN DIEGO CA 92122
77- 58 GARVIN, THEODORE JARED 'JERRY'      2090 NORTH WINERY - FRESNO CA 93703
69- 65 GASPAR, RODNEY EARL                 27632 RUISENOR - MISSION VIEJO CA 92692
44- 47 GASSAWAY, CHARLES CASON             10925 WESTWOOD LAKE DR - MIAMI FL 33165
55- 46 GASTALL, THOMAS EVERETT             D. SEPTEMBER 20, 1956 CHESAPEAKE BAY, MD.
20- 35 GASTON, ALEXANDER NATHANIEL         D. FEBRUARY 8, 1979 SANTA MONICA, CALIF.
67- 35 GASTON, CLARENCE EDWIN 'CITO'       65 HILTON AVE - TORONTO ONTARIO N5R 3E5 CAN.
24- 39 GASTON, NATHANIEL MILTON 'MILT'     5064 WHITE OAK CT - BRADENTON FL 33507
78- 49 GATES, JOSEPH DANIEL                1517 EAST NINETEENTH AVE - GARY IN 46407
81- 43 GATES, MICHAEL GRANT                8149 GARDEN GROVE - RESEDA CA 91335
63- 43 GATEWOOD, AUBREY LEE                1807 SANFORD DR - LITTLE ROCK AR 72207
78- 50 GAUDET, JAMES JENNINGS              1264-G WOODSMILL DR SE - MARIETTA GA 30067
25- 37 GAUTREAU, WALTER PAUL 'DOC'         D. AUGUST 23, 1970 SALT LAKE CITY, UTAH
36- 29 GAUTREAUX, SIDNEY ALLEN             D. APRIL 19, 1980 MORGAN CITY, LA.
20- 36 GAW, GEORGE JOSEPH 'CHIPPY'         D. MAY 26, 1968 BOSTON, MASS.
23- 48 GAZELLA, MICHAEL                    D. SEPTEMBER 11, 1978 ODESSA, TEX.
47- 37 GEARHART, LLOYD WILLIAM             206 HOME AVE - XENIA OH 45385
```

WAYNE GARLAND

23- 49 GEARIN, DENNIS JOHN 'DINTY'	D. MARCH 11, 1959 PROVIDENCE, R. I.
42- 42 GEARY, EUGENE FRANCIS JOSEPH 'HUCK'	D. JANUARY 27, 1981 CUBA, N. Y.
18- 21 GEARY, ROBERT NORTON	D. JANUARY 31, 1980 CINCINNATI, O.
71- 37 GEBHARD, ROBERT HENRY	117 MARQUETTE AVE -NORTH MANKATO MN 56001
47- 38 GEBRIAN, PETER	103 RIVER RD #E-4 - NUTLEY NJ 07110
72- 33 GEDDES, JAMES LEE	4129 ZUBER RD - ORIENT OH 43146
39- 40 GEDEON, ELMER JOHN	D. APRIL 15, 1944 FRANCE
13- 61 GEDEON, ELMER JOSEPH	D. MAY 19, 1941 SAN FRANCISCO, CALIF.
80- 46 GEDMAN, RICHARD LEO	32 LAFAYETTE - WORCESTER MA 01608
39- 41 GEE, JOHN ALEXANDER	71 HICKORY PARK RD - CORTLAND NY 13045
23- 50 GEHRIG, HENRY LOUIS	D. JUNE 2, 1941 RIVERDALE, N. Y.
24- 40 GEHRINGER, CHARLES LEONARD	32301 LAHSER RD - BIRMINGHAM MI 48010
37- 39 GEHRMAN, PAUL ARTHUR	1535 AWBREY RD-BEND OR 97701
58- 36 GEIGER, GARY MERLE	7327 S 69TH E CT - TULSA OK 74133
78- 51 GEISEL, JOHN DAVID 'DAVE'	59 COSHWAY PLACE - TONAWANDA NY 14150
69- 66 GEISHERT, VERNON WILLIAM	RR 4 - RICHLAND CENTER WI 53581
29- 43 GELBERT, CHARLES MAGNUS	D. JANUARY 13, 1967 EASTON, PA.
64- 36 GELNAR, JOHN RICHARD	312 S ROBINSON - MANGUM OK 73554
22- 43 GENEWICH, JOSEPH EDWARD	D. DECEMBER 21, 1985 LOCKPORT, N. Y.
50- 30 GENOVESE, GEORGE MICHAEL	11474 ERWIN ST - HOLLYWOOD CA 91606
57- 22 GENTILE, JAMES EDWARD	1016 NEPTUNE - EDMOND OK 73034
43- 50 GENTILE, SAMUEL CHRISTOPHER	123 CENTRAL AVE-EVERETT MA 02149
69- 67 GENTRY, GARY EDWARD	205 STAR ROUTE 2 - CAVE CREEK AZ 85333
54- 31 GENTRY, HARVEY WILLIAM	109 EATON LN - BRISTOL TN 37620
43- 51 GENTRY, JAMES RUFFUS	4929 FULP ST - WINSTON SALEM NC 27105
55- 47 GEORGE, ALEX THOMAS	1001 ROMANY ROAD - KANSAS CITY MO 64113
35- 35 GEORGE, CHARLES PETER 'GREEK'	RR 2 BOX 39E - BRUNSWICK GA 31520
11- 53 GEORGE, THOMAS EDWARD 'LEFTY'	D. MAY 13, 1955 YORK, PA.
38- 29 GEORGY, OSCAR JOHN	6878 VICKSBURG ST-NEW ORLEANS LA 70124
36- 30 GERAGHTY, BENJAMIN RAYMOND	D. JUNE 18, 1963 JACKSONVILLE, FLA.
62- 45 GERARD, DAVID FREDERICK	318 DOONE PL - FAIRLESS HILLS PA 19030
85- 39 GERBER, CRAIG STUART	4297 PERSHING AVENUE - SAN BERNARDINO CA 92407
14- 70 GERBER, WALTER	D. JUNE 19 , 1951 COLUMBUS, O.
62- 46 GERBERMAN, GEORGE ALOIS	1501 MICHAEL - EL CAMPO TX 77437
74- 40 GERHARDT, ALLEN RUSSELL 'RUSTY'	2931 HISS AVE - PARKVILLE MD 21234
43- 52 GERHEAUSER, ALBERT	D. MAY 28, 1972 SPRINGFIELD, MO.
27- 38 GERKEN, GEORGE HERBERT	D. OCTOBER 23, 1977 ARCAIDA, CALIF.
45- 37 GERKIN, STEPHEN PAUL	D. NOVEMBER 8, 1978 BAY PINES, FLA.
38- 30 GERLACH, JOHN GLENN	5721 DOGWOOD PL - MADISON WI 53705
19- 30 GERNER, EDWIN FREDERICK	D. MAY 15, 1970 PHILADELPHIA, PA.
52- 36 GERNERT, RICHARD EDWARD	1420 ROSE VIRGINIA RD - READING PA 19615
69- 68 GERONIMO, CESAR FRANCISCO	TEFADA FLO. #56 - SANTO DOMINGO DOMINICAN REP.
13- 62 GERVAIS, LUCIEAN EDWARD 'LEFTY'	D. OCTOBER 19, 1950 LOS ANGELES, CALIF.
45- 38 GETTEL, ALLEN JONES	5620 PARLIAMENT DR - VIRGINIA BEACH VA 23452
10- 58 GEYER, JACOB BOWMAN 'RUBE'	D. OCTOBER 12, 1962 WAHKON, MINN.
24- 41 GEYGAN, JAMES EDWARD 'CHAPPIE'	D. MARCH 16, 1966 COLUMBUS, O.
16- 31 GHARRITY, EDWARD PATRICK 'PATSY'	D. OCTOBER 10, 1966 BELOIT, WIS.
83- 61 GHELFI, ANTHONY PAUL	3522 EAST AVE SOUTH #D - LACROSSE WI 54601
58- 37 GIALLOMBARDO, ROBERT PAUL	1340 E FIFTH - BROOKLYN NY 11230
11- 54 GIANNINI, JOSEPH FRANCIS	D. SEPTEMBER 26, 1942 SAN FRANCISCO, CALIF.
25- 38 GIARD, JOSEPH OSCAR	D. JULY 10, 1956 WORCESTER, MASS.
60- 38 GIBBON, JOSEPH CHARLES	RR 2 - NEWTON MS 39345
84- 39 GIBBONS, JOHN MICHAEL	12411 LA ALBADA - SAN ANTONIO TX 78233
62- 47 GIBBS, JERRY DEAN 'JAKE'	219 ST. ANDREWS CIR - OXFORD MS 38655
24- 42 GIBSON, CHARLES GRIFFIN	408 RIDLEY AVE - LAGRANGE GA 30241
13- 63 GIBSON, FRANK GILBERT	D. APRIL 27, 1961 AUSTIN, TEX.
67- 36 GIBSON, JOHN RUSSELL 'RUSS'	495 GARDNERS NOOK RD - SWANSEA MA 02777
79- 39 GIBSON, KIRK HAROLD	1082 OAK POINTE DR - PONTIAC MI 48054
59- 30 GIBSON, ROBERT	215 BELLEVIEW BLVD S - BELLEVIEW NE 68005
83- 62 GIBSON, ROBERT LOUIS	261 POWELL ROAD - SPRINGFIELD PA 19064
26- 30 GIBSON, SAMUEL BRAXTON	D. JANUARY 31, 1983 HIGH POINT, N. C.
37- 40 GICK, GEORGE EDWARD	3 BRADY CT - LAFAYETTE IN 47905
75- 42 GIDEON, JAMES LESLIE	5623 BRAESVALLEY - HOUSTON TX 77035
13- 64 GIEBEL, JOSEPH HENRY	D. MARCH 17, 1981 SILVER SPRING, MD.
39- 42 GIEBELL, FLOYD GEORGE	RR 1 BOX 111, LAURELWOOD DR - WILKESBORO NC 28697
54- 32 GIEL, PAUL ROBERT	13400 MCGINTZ RD - MINNEAPOLIS MN 55343
59- 31 GIGGIE, ROBERT THOMAS	89 MCANDREW RD - BRAINTREE MA 02184
67- 37 GIGON, NORMAN PHILLIP	205 PAXINOSA RD E - EASTON PA 18042
67- 38 GIL, TOMAS GUSTAVO 'GUS'	URB. URDAVETA,VEREDA 15#1 - CARACAS VENEZUELA S.A.
42- 43 GILBERT, ANDREW	803 WALNUT DR-LATROBE PA 15650
40- 24 GILBERT, CHARLES MADER	D. AUGUST 13, 1983 NEW ORLEANS, LA.
59- 32 GILBERT, DREW EDWARD 'BUDDY'	1913 BELCARO DR - KNOXVILLE TN 37918
50- 31 GILBERT, HAROLD JOSEPH 'TOOKIE'	D. JUNE 23, 1967 NEW ORLEANS, LA.

Lou Gehrig

George Gerken

72- 34 GILBERT, JOE DENNIS   1952 N BOWIE ST - JASPER TX 75951
14- 71 GILBERT, LAWRENCE WILLIAM   D. FEBRUARY 17, 1965 NEW ORLEANS, LA.
85- 40 GILBERT, MARK DAVID   OLD ADD: 3151 N. COURSE LN #201 - POMPANO BEACH FL 3306
28- 38 GILBERT, WALTER JOHN   D. SEPTEMBER 8, 1959 DULUTH, MINN.
72- 35 GILBREATH, RODNEY JOE   1438 RIDGELAND WAY - LILBURN GA 30247
71- 38 GILBRETH, WILLIAM FREEMAN   690 E N 16TH ST - ABILENE TX 79601
59- 33 GILE, DONALD LOREN   3145 PORTER DR - PALO ALTO CA 94304
81- 44 GILES, BRIAN JEFFREY   8607 GLEN HAVEN ST - SAN DIEGO CA 92125
20- 37 GILHAM, GEORGE LEWIS   D. APRIL 25, 1937 LANSDOWNE, PA.
11- 55 GILHOOLEY, FRANK PATRICK   D. JULY 11, 1959 TOLEDO, O.
19- 31 GILL, EDWARD JAMES   27 FEDERICO CIR - STOUGHTON MA 02072
37- 41 GILL, GEORGE LLOYD   RAYMOND MS 39154
23- 51 GILL, HAROLD EDWARD   D. AUGUST 1, 1932 BROCKTON, MASS.
27- 39 GILL, JOHN WESLEY   D. DECEMBER 26, 1984 NASHVILLE, TENN.
40- 25 GILLENWATER, CARDEN EDISON   66 COUNTRY CLUB DR - LARGO FL 33543
23- 52 GILLENWATER, CLARAL LEWIS   D. FEBRUARY 26, 1978 PENSACOLA, FLA.
22- 44 GILLESPIE, JOHN PATRICK   D. FEBRUARY 15, 1954 VALLEJO, CAL.
42- 44 GILLESPIE, PAUL ALLEN   D. AUGUST 11, 1970 ANNISTON, ALA.
44- 48 GILLESPIE, ROBERT WILLIAM   123 CAROL RD - WINSTON SALEM NC 27106
53- 28 GILLIAM, JAMES WILLIAM 'JUNIOR'   D. OCTOBER 8, 1978 INGLEWOOD, CALIF.
67- 39 GILLIFORD, PAUL GANT   7 WOODLAND DR - MALVERN PA 19355
27- 40 GILLIS, GRANT   D. FEBRUARY 4, 1981 THOMASVILLE, ALA.
14- 72 GILMORE, ERNEST GROVER   D. NOVEMBER 25, 1919 SIOUX CITY, IA.
44- 49 GILMORE, LEONARD PRESTON   RR 2 BOX 213C - JONES OK 73049
68- 27 GILSON, HAROLD   OLD ADD: 1509 JULIE ST #B - BERKELEY CA 94703
15- 52 GINGRAS, JOSEPH ELZEAD JOHN   D. SEPTEMBER 6, 1947 JERSEY CITY, N.J.
14- 73 GINN, TINSLEY RUCKER   D. AUGUST 30, 1931 ATLANTA, GA.
48- 40 GINSBERG, MYRON NATHAN 'JOE'   24247 BASHION DR - NOVI MI 48050
44- 50 GIONFRIDDO, ALBERT FRANCIS   64 BRISTOL PLACE - GOLETA CA 93117
53- 29 GIORDANO, THOMAS ARTHUR   1026 CARLL DR - BAYSHORE NY 11706
10- 59 GIRARD, CHARLES AUGUST   D. AUGUST 6, 1936 BROOKLYN, N. Y.
36- 31 GIULIANI, ANGELO JOHN   1985 NORFOLK AVE - ST PAUL MN 55116
62- 48 GIUSTI, DAVID JOHN   524 CLAIR DR - PITTSBURGH PA 15241
46- 33 GLADD, JAMES WALTER   D. NOVEMBER 8, 1977 LONG BEACH, CALIF.
83- 63 GLADDEN, CLIFTON DANIEL 'DAN'   888 BROOK GROVE LN - CUPERTINO CA 95014
61- 38 GLADDING, FRED EARL   4721 MACMONT CIR - POWELL TN 37819
44- 51 GLADU, ROLAND EDWIN   4368 BERRIE - MONTREAL QUEBEC CAN.
20- 38 GLAISER, JOHN BURKE   D. MARCH 7, 1959 HOUSTON, TEX.
25- 39 GLASS, THOMAS JOSEPH   D. DECEMBER 15, 1981 GREENSBORO, N. C.
13- 65 GLAVENICH, LUKE FRANK   D. MAY 22, 1935 STOCKTON, CALIF.
49- 25 GLAVIANO, THOMAS GIATANO   23905 HITCHING POST RD - SONORA CA 95370
20- 39 GLAZNER, CHARLES FRANKLIN   850 MAURY RD BOX 4 - ORLANDO FL 32804
20- 40 GLEASON, JOSEPH PAUL   18 EXCHANGE - PHELPS NY 14532
63- 44 GLEASON, ROY WILLIAM   1115 WILCOX AVE - MONTEREY PARK CA 91754
16- 32 GLEASON, WILLIAM PATRICK   D. JANUARY 9, 1957 HOLYOKE, MASS.
79- 40 GLEATON, JERRY DON   121 GARMAN DR - EARLY TX 76801
36- 32 GLEESON, JAMES JOSEPH   545 E 129TH TER - KANSAS CITY MO 64145
19- 32 GLEICH, FRANK ELMER   D. MARCH 27, 1949 COLUMBUS, O.
20- 41 GLENN, BURDETTE 'BOB'   D. JUNE 3, 1977 RICHMOND, CALIF.
15- 53 GLENN, HARRY MELVILLE   D. OCTOBER 12, 1918 ST. PAUL, MINN.
60- 39 GLENN, JOHN   32 EDGEWATER BEACH APTS - BEVERLY NJ 08010
32- 31 GLENN, JOSEPH CHARLES   D. MAY 6, 1985 TUNKHANNOCK, PA.
30- 25 GLIATTO, SALVADOR MICHAEL   6031 D. ARBOLEDA WAY - DALLAS TX 75248
14- 74 GLOCKSON, NORMAN STANLEY   D. AUGUST 5, 1955 MAYWOOD, ILL.
39- 43 GLOSSOP, ALBAN   907 WEST MONROE ST - BELLEVILLE IL 62220

75- 44 GLYNN, EDWARD PAUL   16205 45TH AVE - FLUSHING NY 11355
49- 26 GLYNN, WILLIAM VINCENT   6916 51ST - SAN DIEGO CA 92120
74- 41 GODBY, DANNY RAY   RR 2 BOX 28A - CHAPMANVILLE WV 25508
72- 36 GODDARD, JOSEPH HAROLD   302 RIIDGE PARK DR - BECKLEY WV 25801
22- 45 GOEBEL, EDWIN   D. AUGUST 12, 1959 BROOKLYN, N. Y.
60- 40 GOETZ, JOHN HARDY   3253 MYDDLETON - TROY MI 48084
72- 37 GOGGIN, CHARLES FRANCIS   6008 ROBERT E. LEE DR - NASHVILLE TN 37215
70- 49 GOGOLEWSKI, WILLIAM JOSEPH   1522 GRAHAM AVE - OSHKOSH WI 54901
60- 41 GOLDEN, JAMES EDWARD   8630 SW 10TH - TOPEKA KS 66606
10- 60 GOLDEN, ROY KRAMER   D. OCTOBER 4, 1961 NORWOOD, O.
28- 39 GOLDMAN, JONAH JOHN   D. AUGUST 17, 1980 PALM BEACH, FLA.
49- 27 GOLDSBERRY, GORDON FREDERICK   22772 BAY FRONT LN - LAKE FOREST CA 92630
26- 31 GOLDSMITH, HAROLD EUGENE   %GENE GOLDSMITH,8 GRANDVIEW TER - ESSEX CT 06426
32- 32 GOLDSTEIN, ISADORE   944 FLANDERS T - DELRAY BEACH FL 33446
43- 53 GOLDSTEIN, LESLIE ELMER 'LONNIE'   6516 SABROSA CT W - FORT WORTH TX 76133
62- 49 GOLDY, PURNAL WILLIAM   1318 CHERRYVILLE RD - LITTLETON CO 80120
41- 37 GOLETZ, STANLEY   RR 2 BOX 598 - JONES OK 73049
49- 28 GOLIAT, MIKE MITCHEL   2650 GREEN LAWN DR - SEVEN HILLS OH 44131
72- 38 GOLTZ, DAVID ALLAN   RR 6 BOX 230 - FERGUS FALLS MN 56537
22- 46 GOLVIN, WALTER GEORGE   D. JUNE 11, 1973 GARDENA, CALIF.

```
35- 36 GOMEZ, JOSE LUIS RODRIGUEZ 'CHILE'      GONZALEZ DE COSIO 359-3 - MEXICO CITY D.F. MEX.
74- 42 GOMEZ, LUIS JOSE                        BOX 4064 - ATLANTA GA 30303
44- 52 GOMEZ, PEDRO MARTINEZ 'PRESTON'         5991 AVENUE LAVIDA - ANAHEIM CA 92807
84- 40 GOMEZ, RANDALL SCOTT 'ROCKY'            801 BARNESON AVE - SAN MATEO CA 94402
53- 30 GOMEZ, RUBEN                            T2-8 IGUAZA PARK GARDENS-RIO PIEDRAS PR 00928
30- 26 GOMEZ, VERNON LOUIS 'LEFTY'             26 SAN BENITO WAY - NOVATO CA 94947
60- 42 GONDER, JESSE LEMAR                     5937 WHITNEY ST - OAKLAND CA 94609
79- 41 GONZALES, DANIEL DAVID                  OLD ADD: 12319 CULLMAN AVE-WHITTIER CA 90604
18- 22 GONZALES, EUSEBIO MIGUEL                D. FEBRUARY 14, 1976 HAVANA, CUBA
37- 42 GONZALES, JOE MADRID                    30715 COCOS PALM AVE - HOMELAND CA 92348
77- 59 GONZALES, JULIO CESAR                   BO. RIO CANAS, BOX 86 - CAGUAS PR 00625
49- 29 GONZALES, JULIO ENRIQUE                 OLD ADD: CALIXTO GARCIA 37 - ORIENTE CUBA
84- 41 GONZALES, RENE ADRIAN                   755 ORANGEWOOD - COVINA CA 91723
55- 48 GONZALES, WENCESLAO O'REILLY 'VINCE'    D. MARCH 11, 1981 CIUDAD DEL CARMEN,CAMP.MEX
60- 43 GONZALEZ, ANDRES ANTONIO 'TONY'         8011 SW 196TH TER - MIAMI FL 33189
84- 42 GONZALEZ, DENIO MARIANO                 CALLE SAN LUIS #131, GUALEY - SANTO DOMINGO DOM. REP.
72- 39 GONZALEZ, JOSE FERNANDO                 URB VISTA ANGEL CALLE 4-A-48-ARECIBO PR 00612
85- 41 GONZALEZ, JOSE RAFAEL                   CALLE ANTERA MOTA #35 - PUERTO PLATA DOMINICAN REP.
12- 67 GONZALEZ, MIGUEL ANGEL CORDERO 'MIKE'   D. FEBRUARY 19, 1977 HAVANA, CUBA
76- 35 GONZALEZ, ORLANDO EUGENE                OLD ADD: 2352 SW 26TH LN - MIAMI FL
63- 45 GONZALEZ, PEDRO                         104 GEN CABRAL - SAN PEDRO DE MACORIS DOM. REP.
29- 44 GOOCH, CHARLES FURMAN                   D. MAY 30, 1982 LANHAM, MD.
21- 35 GOOCH, JOHN BEVERLEY                    D. MAY 15, 1975 NASHVILLE, TENN.
15- 54 GOOCH, LEE CURRIN                       D. MAY 18, 1966 RALEIGH, N.C.
10- 61 GOOD, RALPH NELSON                      D. NOVEMBER 24, 1965 WATERVILLE, ME.
28- 40 GOODELL, JOHN HENRY WILLIAM 'BILL'      10 LITTLE DRIVE, BELLA VISTA - BENTONVILLE AR 72714
84- 43 GOODEN, DWIGHT EUGENE                   3101 EAST ELM ST - TAMPA FL 33610
35- 37 GOODMAN, IVAL RICHARD                   D. NOVEMBER 25, 1984 CINCINNATI, O.
47- 39 GOODMAN, WILLIAM DALE                   D. OCTOBER 1, 1984 SARASOTA, FLA.
70- 50 GOODSON, JAMES EDWARD 'ED'              RR 2 BOX 12-0 - INDEPENDENCE VA 24348
14- 75 GOODWIN, CLAIRE VERNON 'PEP'            D. FEBRUARY 15, 1972 OAKLAND, CALIF.
75- 45 GOODWIN, DANNY KAY                      2001 N BOURLAND - PEORIA IL 61601
48- 41 GOODWIN, JAMES PATRICK                  11533 FRANCETTA LN - ST. LOUIS MO 63138
16- 33 GOODWIN, MARVIN MARDO                   D. OCTOBER 21, 1925 HOUSTON, TES.
46- 34 GOOLSBY, RAYMOND DANIEL                 OLD ADD: 1101 LEE RD #3 - WINTER PARK FL
65- 33 GOOSSEN, GREGORY BRYANT                 12321 BLIX ST - NORTH HOLLYWOOD CA 91607
55- 49 GORBOUS, GLEN EDWARD                    1511 CAYUGA DR NW - CALGARY ALBERTA P2L 0N1 CAN.
38- 31 GORDON, JOSEPH LOWELL                   D. APRIL 14, 1978 SACRAMENTO, CALIF.
77- 60 GORDON, MICHAEL WILLIAM                 161 BISHOP ST - BROCKTON MA 02401
41- 38 GORDON, SIDNEY                          D. JUNE 17, 1975 NEW YORK, N.Y.
21- 36 GORDONIER, RAYMOND CHARLES              D. NOVEMBER 15, 1960 ROCHESTER, N. Y.
54- 33 GORIN, CHARLES PERRY                    2617 FISET DR - AUSTIN TX 78731
77- 61 GORINSKI, ROBERT JOHN                   BOX 133 - CALUMET PA 15621
52- 37 GORMAN, HERBERT ALLEN                   D. APRIL 5, 1953 SAN DIEGO, CAL.
37- 43 GORMAN, HOWARD PAUL                     D. APRIL 29, 1984 HARRISBURG, PA.
52- 38 GORMAN, THOMAS ALOYSIUS                 474 W VLY STRM BLVD - VALLEY STREAM NY 11581
39- 44 GORMAN, THOMAS DAVID                    697 CLOSTER DOCK RD - CLOSTER NJ 07624
81- 45 GORMAN, THOMAS PATRICK                  2523 N BOONES FERRY RD - WOODBURN OR 97071
41- 39 GORNICKI, FRANK T. 'HANK'               5510 TAMBERLANE DR-PALM BCH GARDENS FL 33480
40- 26 GORSICA, JOHN JOSEPH PERRY              BOX 1518 - BECKLEY WV 25801
57- 22 GORYL, JOHN ALBERT                      3282 YOTHERS RD - APOPKA FL 32703
63- 46 GOSGER, JAMES CHARLES                   729 DELAWARE - MARYSVILLE MI 48040
21- 37 GOSLIN, LEON ALLEN 'GOOSE'              D. MAY 15, 1971 BRIDGETON, N.J.
62- 50 GOSS, HOWARD WAYNE                      11511 SANTA GERTRUDES #20 - WHITTIER CA 90604
72- 40 GOSSAGE, RICHARD MICHAEL 'GOOSE'        10565 VIACHA WAY - SAN DIEGO CA 92124
13- 66 GOSSETT, JOHN STAR 'DICK'               D. OCTOBER 6, 1962 MASSILLON, O.
60- 44 GOTAY, JULIO ENRIQUE                    JUAN JOSE CARTAGENA ST #L34 - PONCE PR 00731
82- 49 GOTT, JAMES WILLIAM                     1840 LOS ROBLES AVE - SAN MARINO CA 91108
12- 68 GOULAIT, THEODORE LEE                   D. JULY 15, 1936 ST. CLAIR, MICH.
16- 34 GOULD, ALBERT FRANK                     D. AUGUST 8, 1982 SAN JOSE, CALIF.
44- 53 GOULISH, NICHOLAS EDWARD                D. MAY 15, 1984 YOUNGSTOWN, O.
10- 62 GOWDY, HARRY 'HANK'                      D. AUGUST 1, 1966 COLUMBUS, O.
72- 41 GOWELL, LAWRENCE CLYDE                  45 SEVENTH ST - AUBURN ME 04210
69- 69 GRABARKEWITZ, BILLY CORDELL             BOX 30635 - DALLAS TX 75230
58- 38 GRABER, RODNEY BLAINE                   4674 MOUNT ARMET DR - SAN DIEGO CA 92117
29- 45 GRABOWSKI, ALFONS FRANCIS               D. OCTOBER 29, 1966 MEMPHIS, N. Y.
24- 43 GRABOWSKI, JOHN PATRICK                 D. MAY 23, 1946 ALBANY, N. Y.
32- 33 GRABOWSKI, REGINALD JOHN                D. APRIL 2, 1955 SYRACUSE, N. Y.
38- 32 GRACE, JOSEPH LAVERNE                   D. SEPTEMBER 18, 1969 MURPHYSBORO, ILL.
78- 52 GRACE, MICHAEL LEE                      3514 SHELBY - PONTIAC MI 48054
29- 46 GRACE, ROBERT EARL                      D. DECEMBER 22, 1980 PHOENIX, ARIZ.
13- 67 GRAF, FREDERICK GOTTLIEB                D. OCTOBER 4, 1979 CHATTANOOGA, TENN.
57- 24 GRAFF, MILTON EDWARD                    249 MAGNOLIA PL - PITTSBURGH PA 15225
34- 41 GRAHAM, ARTHUR WILLIAM 'SKINNY'         D. JULY 10, 1967 ARLINGTON, MASS.
```

GRAHAM   GRIFFIN

10- 63 GRAHAM, BERT	D. JUNE 17, 1971 COTTONWOOD, ARIZ.
79- 42 GRAHAM, DANIEL JAY	BOX 728 - WINKELMAN AZ 85298
14- 76 GRAHAM, DAWSON FRANK 'TINY'	D. DECEMBER 29, 1962 NASHVILLE, TENN.
46- 35 GRAHAM, JOHN BERNARD	1521 INTERLACHEN #258K - SEAL BEACH CA 90740
24- 44 GRAHAM, KYLE	D. DECEMBER 1, 1973 OAK GROVE, ALA.
83- 64 GRAHAM, LEE WILLIAM	OLD ADD: BOX 1012 - BELLEVIEW FL 32620
22- 47 GRAHAM, ROY VINCENT	D. APRIL 26, 1933 MANILLA, PHILLIPINES
63- 47 GRAHAM, WAYNE LEON	ATH. DEPT. SAN JACINTO COL N - HOUSTON TX 77049
66- 39 GRAHAM, WILLIAM ALBERT	RR 2 BOX 275 - FLEMINGSBURG KY 41041
68- 28 GRAMLY, BERT THOMAS 'TOM'	16485 REDWOOD CIR, RR 1 - MCKINNEY TX 75069
54- 34 GRAMMAS, ALEXANDER PETER	3432 OAKDALE DR - BIRMINGHAM AL 35223
27- 41 GRAMPP, HENRY ECKHARDT	D. MARCH 24, 1986 NEW YORK, N. Y.
68- 29 GRANGER, WAYNE ALLEN	BOX 134, ALDRICH AVE - HUNTINGTON MA 01050
23- 53 GRANT, GEORGE ADDISON	RR 2 BOX 445 - PRATTVILLE AL 36067
42- 45 GRANT, JAMES CHARLES	D. JULY 8, 1970 ROCHESTER, MINN.
23- 54 GRANT, JAMES RONALD	304 NORTH LOCUST - MADRID IA 50156
58- 39 GRANT, JAMES TIMOTHY 'MUDCAT'	1020 SOUTH DUNSMUIR - LOS ANGELES CA 90019
84- 44 GRANT, MARK ANDREW	123 FAIRLANE DR - JOLIET IL 60435
83- 65 GRANT, THOMAS RAYMOND	BOX 113 - MENDON MA 01756
22- 48 GRANTHAM, GEORGE FARLEY	D. MARCH 16, 1954 KINGMAN, ARIZ.
83- 66 GRAPENTHIN, RICHARD RAY	RURAL ROUTE 1 - LINN GROVE IA 51033
48- 42 GRASMICK, LOUIS JUNIOR	6715 QUAD AVE - BALTIMORE MD 21237
46- 36 GRASSO, NEWTON MICHAEL 'MICKEY'	D. OCTOBER 15, 1975 MIAMI FLA.
45- 39 GRATE, DONALD	1245 NW 203RD ST - MIAMI FL 33169
26- 32 GRAVES, JOSEPH EBENEZER	D. DECEMBER 22, 1980 SALEM, MASS.
27- 42 GRAVES, SAMUEL SIDNEY 'SID'	D. DECEMBER 26, 1983 BIDDEFORD, ME.
64- 37 GRAY, DAVID ALEXANDER	539 BRINKER AVE - OGDEN UT 84404
77- 62 GRAY, GARY GEORGE	BOX 98 - LAPLACE LA 70068
54- 35 GRAY, JOHN LEONARD	6320 SW 138TH COURT #206 - MIAMI FL 33183
82- 50 GRAY, LORENZO	3263 PALM AVE #A - LYNWOOD CA 90262
37- 40 GRAY, MILTON MARSHALL	D. JUNE 30, 1969 QUINCY, FLA.
45- 40 GRAY, PETER	203 PHILLIPS ST - NANTICOKE PA 18634
58- 40 GRAY, RICHARD BENJAMIN	503 S HAMPTON - ANAHEIM CA 92804
24- 45 GRAY, SAMUEL DAVID	D. APRIL 16, 1953 MCKINNEY, TEX.
12- 69 GRAY, STANLEY OSCAR	D. OCTOBER 11, 1964 SNYDER, TEX.
46- 37 GRAY, THEODORE GLENN	21 E WASHINGTON - CLARKSTON MI 48016
59- 34 GRBA, ELI	332 E. 17TH - VANCOUVER BC V7L 2V9 CAN.
54- 36 GREASON, WILLIAM HENRY	4536 HILLMAN DR SW - BIRMINGHAM AL 35221
84- 45 GREEN, CHRISTOPHER DEWAYNE	3740 59TH AVE WEST - BRADENTON FL 33507
81- 46 GREEN, DAVID ALEJANDRO	COLINIA MANAGUA GRUPO H#47 - MANAGUA NICARAGUA C.A.
59- 35 GREEN, ELIJAH JERRY 'PUMPSIE'	BERKELEY H.S. 2246 MILVA-BERKELEY CA 94704

59- 36 GREEN, FRED ALLAN	BOX 161 - TITUSVILLE NJ 08560
57- 25 GREEN, GENE LEROY	D. MAY 23, 1981 ST. LOUIS, MO.
60- 45 GREEN, GEORGE DALLAS	1060 W. ADDISON ST - CHICAGO IL 60613
35- 38 GREEN, HARVEY GEORGE	D. JULY 24, 1970 FRANKLIN, LA.
24- 46 GREEN, JOSEPH HENRY	D. FEBRUARY 4, 1972 BRYN MAWR, PA.
28- 41 GREEN, JULIUS FOUST 'JUNE'	D. MARCH 19, 1974 GLENDORA, CALIF.
57- 26 GREEN, LEONARD CHARLES	18693 SUNSET ST - DETROIT MI 48234
63- 48 GREEN, RICHARD LARRY	525 38TH - RAPID CITY SD 57701
30- 27 GREENBERG, HENRY BENJAMIN	1129 MIRADERO RD - BEVERLY HILLS CA 90210
79- 43 GREENE, ALTAR ALPHONSE	18294 MARLOWE - DETROIT MI 48235
24- 47 GREENE, NELSON GEORGE	D. APRIL 6, 1983 LEBANON, PA.
24- 48 GREENFIELD, KENT	D. MARCH 14, 1978 GUTHRIE, KY.
52- 39 GREENGRASS, JAMES RAYMOND	2930 OCTAVIA CIR - MARIETTA GA 30062
85- 42 GREENWELL, MICHAEL LEWIS	954 EAST HYACINTH ST - NORTH FORT MYERS FL 33903
54- 37 GREENWOOD, ROBERT CHANDLER	35800 MOLINA CT - FREMONT CA 94536
77- 63 GREER, BRIAN KEITH	914 CARLSON DR - BREA CA 92621
13- 68 GREGG, DAVID CHARLES	D. NOVEMBER 12, 1965 CLARKSTON, WASH.
43- 54 GREGG, HAROLD DANA	17952 MANN ST - IRVINE CA 92664
11- 56 GREGG, SYLVEANUS AUGUSTUS 'VEAN'	D. JULY 29, 1964 ABERDEEN, WASH.
12- 70 GREGORY, FRANK ERNST	D. NOVEMBER 5, 1955 BELOIT, WIS.
64- 38 GREGORY, GROVER LEROY 'LEE'	6456 N TEILMAN - FRESNO CA 93705
11- 57 GREGORY, HOWARD WATTERSON	D. MAY 30, 1970 TULSA, OKLA.
32- 34 GREGORY, PAUL EDWIN	ATH. DEPT. MISSISSIPPI ST - STATE COLLEGE MS 39762
71- 39 GREIF, WILLIAM BRILEY	807 E 31ST - AUSTIN TX 78705
40- 27 GREMP, LOUIS EDWARD 'BUDDY'	205 FLOYD AVENUE #2 - MODESTO CA 95350
19- 33 GREVELL, WILLIAM	D. JUNE 21, 1923 SPRINGFIELD TWP., PA.
70- 51 GRICH, ROBERT ANTHONY	206 PROSPECT AVE - LONG BEACH CA 90803
20- 42 GRIESENBECK, CARLOS PHILIPPE TIMOTHY	D. MARCH 25, 1953 SAN ANTONIO, TEX.
70- 52 GRIEVE, THOMAS ALAN	3206 HERITAGE CT - ARLINGTON TX 76016
46- 38 GRIFFETH, LEON CLIFFORD	BOX 335 - PATTERSON NY 12563
73- 53 GRIFFEY, GEORGE KENNETH 'KEN'	5385 CROSS BRIDGE DR - WESTCHESTER OH 45069
76- 36 GRIFFIN, ALFREDO CLAUDINO	B#3 B HATOMAYOR ING CONS-SAN PEDRO DE MACORIS DOM. REP.
70- 53 GRIFFIN, DOUGLAS LEE	15811 EL SONETO DR - WHITTIER CA 90603

GRIFFIN　　　　　　　　　　　　GULLIVER

17- 32 GRIFFIN, FRANCIS ARTHUR 'PUG'　　D. OCTOBER 12, 1951 COLORADO SPRINGS COLO.
19- 34 GRIFFIN, IVY MOORE　　　　　　　D. AUGUST 25, 1957 GAINESVILLE, FLA.
11- 58 GRIFFIN, JAMES LINTON 'HANK'　　D. FEBRUARY 11, 1950 TERRELL, TEX.
28- 42 GRIFFIN, MARTIN JOHN　　　　　　D. NOVEMBER 19, 1951 LOS ANGELES, CAL.
79- 44 GRIFFIN, MICHAEL LEROY　　　　　1620 GROVE AVE - WOODLAND CA 95695
14- 77 GRIFFIN, PATRICK RICHARD　　　　D. JUNE 7, 1927 YOINGSTOWN, O.
69- 70 GRIFFIN, THOMAS JAMES　　　　　　OLD ADD: 13147 AVE LAVELENCIA-POWAY CA 92064
22- 49 GRIFFITH, BARTHOLOMEW JOSEPH　　D. MAY 5, 1973 BISHOP, CALIF.
63- 49 GRIFFITH, ROBERT DERRELL　　　　515 1/2 WEST TEXAS - ANADARKO OK 73005
13- 69 GRIFFITH, THOMAS HERMAN　　　　　D. APRIL 13, 1967 CINCINNATI, O.
56- 38 GRIGGS, HAROLD LLOYD　　　　　　1100 NE 4TH ST - POMPANO BEACH FL 33060
23- 55 GRIGSBY, DENVER CLARENCE　　　　D. NOVEMBER 10, 1973 SAPULPA, OKLA.
66- 40 GRILLI, GUIDO JOHN　　　　　　　4636 LORECE - MEMPHIS TN 38117
75- 46 GRILLI, STEPHEN JOSEPH　　　　　3040 WALPOLE LN - BALDWINSVILLE NY 13027
54- 38 GRIM, ROBERT ANTON　　　　　　　7118 CODY - OVERLAND PARK KS 66203
16- 35 GRIMES, BURLEIGH ARLAND　　　　　D. DECEMBER 6, 1985 CLEAR LAKE, WIS.
31- 32 GRIMES, EDWARD ADELBERT　　　　　D. OCTOBER 4, 1974 CHICAGO, ILL.
38- 33 GRIMES, OSCAR RAY JR.　　　　　　25151 BROOKPARD RD #203 - NORTH OLMSTED OH 44070
20- 43 GRIMES, OSCAR RAY SR.　　　　　　D. MAY 25, 1953 MINERVA, O.
20- 44 GRIMES, ROY AUSTIN　　　　　　　D. SEPTEMBER 13, 1954 HANOVERTON, O.
16- 36 GRIMM, CHARLES JOHN　　　　　　　D. NOVEMBER 15, 1983 SCOTTSDALE, ARIZ.
71- 40 GRIMSLEY, ROSS ALBERT II　　　　39 JUDGES LN - TOWSON MD 21204
51- 34 GRIMSLEY, ROSS ALBERT　　　　　　1538 FRAYSER BLVD - MEMPHIS TN 38127
12- 71 GRINER, DONALD DEXTER 'DAN'　　　D. JUNE 3, 1950 BISHOPVILLE, S.C.
34- 42 GRISSOM, LEE THEO　　　　　　　BOX 875 - CORNING CA 96021
46- 39 GRISSOM, MARVIN EDWARD　　　　　13975 NOBLE WAY - RED BLUFF CA 96080
52- 40 GROAT, RICHARD MORROW　　　　　　320 BEACH ST - PITTSBURGH PA 15218
56- 39 GROB, CONRAD GEORGE　　　　　　　5047 ENCHANTED VALLEY RD - CROSS PLAINS WI 53528
41- 40 GRODZICKI, JOHN　　　　　　　　RR 2 BOX 346 - DAYTONA BEACH FL 32019
12- 72 GROH, HENRY KNIGHT 'HEINIE'　　　D. AUGUST 22, 1968 CINCINNATI,O.
19- 35 GROH, LEWIS CARL　　　　　　　　D. OCTOBER 20, 1960 ROCHESTER, N. Y.
41- 41 GROMEK, STEPHEN JOSEPH　　　　　21455 CORSAUT - BIRMINGHAM MI 48010
55- 50 GROSS, DONALD JOHN　　　　　　　6918 WEST SHORE DR - WEIDMAN MI 48893
25- 40 GROSS, EWELL 'TURKEY'　　　　　　D. JANUARY 22, 1936 DALLAS, TEX.
73- 54 GROSS, GREGORY EUGENE　　　　　　556 WOODLEA LN - BERWYN PA 19312

83- 67 GROSS, KEVIN FRANK　　　　　　　402 FOURTH ST - FILLMORE CA 93015
76- 37 GROSS, WAYNE DALE　　　　　　　45 LEONARD COURT - DANVILLE CA 94526
30- 28 GROSSKLOS, HOWARD HOFFMAN 'HOWDIE'　310 LLWYD'S LANE - VERO BEACH FL 32960
52- 41 GROSSMAN, HARLEY JOSEPH　　　　　1032 OAKWOOD LN - EVANSVILLE IN 47710
63- 50 GROTE, GERALD WAYNE　　　　　　148-26 WILLOW BEND - SAN ANTONIO TX 78232
47- 40 GROTH, ERNEST WILLIAM　　　　　　BLACKHAWK-NEGLY RD - BEAVER FALLS PA 15010
46- 40 GROTH, JOHN THOMAS　　　　　　　177 QUEENS LN - PALM BEACH FL 33480
40- 28 GROVE, ORVAL LEROY　　　　　　　2743 POPE AVE - SACRAMENTO CA 95821
25- 41 GROVE, ROBERT MOSES 'LEFTY'　　　D. MAY 22, 1975 NORWALK, O.
13- 70 GROVER, CHARLES BERT　　　　　　D. MAY 24, 1971 EMMETT TWP., CALHOUN CO.,MICH
16- 37 GROVER, ROY ARTHUR　　　　　　　D. FEBRUARY 7, 1978 MILWAUKIE, ORE.
12- 73 GRUBB, HARVEY HARRISON　　　　　D. JANUARY 25, 1970 CORPUS CHRISTI, TEX.
72- 42 GRUBB, JOHN MAYWOOD　　　　　　　3920 COGBILL RD - RICHMOND VA 23234
20- 45 GRUBBS, THOMAS DILLARD　　　　　N MAYSVILLE LN - MT STERLING KY 40353
31- 33 GRUBE, FRANKLIN THOMAS　　　　　D. JULY 2, 1945 NEW YORK, N. Y.
84- 46 GRUBER, KELLY WAYNE　　　　　　　1205 FALCON LEDGE - AUSTIN TX 78746
55- 51 GRUNWALD, ALFRED HENRY　　　　　7120 BOTHWELL RD - RESEDA CA 91335
38- 34 GRYSKA, SIGMUND STANLEY　　　　　4527 S DRAKE-CHICAGO IL 60632
61- 39 GRZENDA, JOSEPH CHARLES　　　　　GOULDSBORO PA 18424
82- 51 GUANTE, CECILIO (MAGALLANE)　　　JALISCO 67 SIMON BOLIVAR-SANTO DOMINGO DOMINICAN REP.
84- 47 GUBICZA, MARK STEVEN　　　　　　593 MONASTERY AVE - PHILADELPHIA PA 19128
29- 47 GUDAT, MARVIN JOHN　　　　　　　D. MARCH 2, 1954 LOS ANGELES, CAL.
37- 45 GUERRA, FERMIN ROMERO 'MIKE'　　　4025 NW 3RD ST - MIAMI FL 33126
73- 55 GUERRERO, MARIO MIGUEL　　　　　CALLE DUARTE #450 - SANTO DOMINGO DOMINICAN REP.
78- 53 GUERRERO, PEDRO　　　　　　　　535 S. PLYMOUTH BLVD - LOS ANGELES CA 90020
84- 48 GUETTERMAN, ARTHUR LEE　　　　　OLD ADD: 6002 BROADMEADOWS - MILLINGTON TN 38053
75- 47 GUIDRY, RONALD AMES　　　　　　　109 CONWAY - LAFAYETTE LA 70507
85- 43 GUILLEN, OSWALDO JOSE　　　　　　CLE SAN JOSE #52,EL RODEO DEL TUY-MIRANDO VENEZ
64- 39 GUINDON, ROBERT JOSEPH　　　　　THORNHILL INN - JACKSON NH 03846
68- 30 GUINN, DRANNON EUGENE 'SKIP'　　　5270 ESTRADE LN - SAN JOSE CA 95118
46- 41 GUINTINI, BENJAMIN JOHN　　　　　1231 CALIFORNIA ST - LOS BANOS CA 93635
40- 29 GUISE, WITT ORISON　　　　　　　D. AUGUST 13, 1968 NORTH LITTLE ROCK, ARK.
16- 38 GUISTO, LOUIS JOSEPH　　　　　　2037 WAVERLY - NAPA CA 94558
78- 54 GULDEN, BRADLEY LEE　　　　　　　BOX 254 (LIME STREET) - CARVER MN 55315
70- 54 GULLETT, DONALD EDWARD　　　　　130 MEADOW AVE - RACELAND KY 41169
23- 56 GULLEY, THOMAS JEFFERSON　　　　D. NOVEMBER 24, 1966 ST. CHARLES, ARK.
30- 29 GULLIC, TEDD JOSEPH　　　　　　　BOX 703 - WEST PLAINS MO 65775
79- 45 GULLICKSON, WILLIAM LEE　　　　　OLD ADD: BOX 6263 - CHAMPAIGN IL 61820
82- 52 GULLIVER, GLENN JAMES　　　　　　8123 CORTLAND - ALLEN PARK MI 48101

63

35- 39 GUMBERT, HARRY EDWARD	BOX 377 - WIMBERLEY TX 78676
82- 53 GUMPERT, DAVID LAWRENCE	921 CHAMBERS ST - SOUTH HAVEN MI 49090
36- 33 GUMPERT, RANDALL PENNINGTON	MONOCACY STATION PA 19542
16- 39 GUNKEL, WOODROW WILLIAM 'RED'	D. APRIL 19, 1954 NORTH CHICAGO, ILL.
11- 59 GUNNING, HYLAND	D. MARCH 28, 1975 TOGUS, ME.
70- 55 GURA, LARRY CYRIL	9 NW CIRCLE DR - JOLIET IL 60432
11- 60 GUST, ERNEST HERMAN FRANK	D. OCTOBER 26, 1945 MAUPIN, ORE.
39- 45 GUSTINE, FRANK WILLIAM	1130 GREENTREE RD - PITTSBURGH PA 15220
72- 43 GUTH, CHARLES HENRY 'BUCKY'	202 MORRIS DR - SALISBURY MD 21801
67- 40 GUTIERREZ, CESAR DARIO	PINTO A MISERIA #100 - CARACAS VENEZUELA S.A.
83- 68 GUTIERREZ, JOAQUIN FERNANDO	AMBERES 3ER CALLEJON # 29-35-CARTAGENA COL.
36- 34 GUTTERIDGE, DONALD JOSEPH	804 LAKEVIEW DR - PITTSBURG KS 66762
85- 44 GUZMAN, JOSE ALBERTO	BO. PLAYA #28 - SANTA ISABEL PR 00757
69- 71 GUZMAN, SANTIAGO DONOVAN	ENS RESTAUROSIN M4TA#12-SAN PEDRO DE MACORIS DOM. REP.
81- 47 GWOSDZ, DOUGLAS WAYNE	14503 ROYAL HILL DR - HOUSTON TX 77083
82- 54 GWYNN, ANTHONY KEITH	3524 DELTA - LONG BEACH CA 90810
33- 21 GYSELMAN, RICHARD RENALD	5212 54TH AV S - SEATTLE WA 98118
37- 46 HAAS, BERTHOLD JOHN	4604 KENSINGTON AVE - TAMPA FL 33629
15- 55 HAAS, BRUNO PHILIP	D. JUNE 5, 1952 SARASOTA, FLA.
76- 38 HAAS, BRYAN EDMOND 'MOOSE'	5 WENGATE RD - OWINGS MILLS MD 21117
57- 27 HAAS, GEORGE EDWIN 'EDDIE'	100 HILLMONT DR, RR 10 - PADUCAH KY 42001
25- 42 HAAS, GEORGE WILLIAM 'MULE'	D. JUNE 30, 1974 NEW ORLEANS, LA.
51- 35 HABENICHT, ROBERT JULIUS	D. DECEMBER 24, 1980 RICHMOND, VA.
85- 45 HABYAN, JOHN GABRIEL	122 PLUNKETT ST - BRENTWOOD NY 11717
32- 35 HACK, STANLEY CAMFIELD	D. DECEMBER 15, 1979 DIXON, ILL.
71- 41 HACKER, RICHARD WARREN	930 E MAIN - BELLEVILLE IL 62220
48- 43 HACKER, WARREN LOUIS	BOX 41 - LENZBURG IL 62255
52- 42 HADDIX, HARVEY	4001 VERNON ASHBURY RD-SOUTH VIENNA OH 45369
26- 33 HADLEY, IRVING DARIUS 'BUMP'	D. FEBRUARY 15,1963 LYNN, MASS.
58- 41 HADLEY, KENT WILLIAM	549 HYDE - POCATELLO ID 83201
15- 56 HAEFFNER, WILLIAM BERNHARD	D. JANUARY 27, 1982 DELAWARE CO., PA.
43- 55 HAEFNER, MILTON ARNOLD 'MICKEY'	504 JACKSON-NEW ATHENS IL 62264
24- 49 HAFEY, CHARLES JAMES 'CHICK'	D. JULY 2, 1973 CALISTOGA, CAL.
35- 40 HAFEY, DANIEL ALBERT 'BUD'	BOX 701-SIERRA CITY CA 96125
39- 46 HAFEY, THOMAS FRANCIS	7747 TERRACE DR - EL CERRITO CA 94532
11- 61 HAGEMAN, KURT MORITZ 'CASEY'	D. APRIL 1, 1964 NEW BEDFORD, MA.
83- 69 HAGEN, KEVIN EUGENE	15232 SE 272ND #15 - KENT WA 98031
68- 31 HAGUE, JOE CLARENCE	14027 FAIRWAY OAKS - SAN ANTONIO TX 78217
69- 72 HAHN, DONALD ANTONE	1046 BOISE DR - CAMPBELL CA 95008
52- 43 HAHN, FREDERICK ALOYS	D. AUGUST 16, 1984 VALHALLA, N.Y.
40- 30 HAHN, RICHARD FREDERICK	1616 ORIOLE AVE - ORLANDO FL 32803
19- 36 HAID, HAROLD AUGUSTINE	D. AUGUST 13, 1952 LOS ANGELES, CAL.
23- 57 HAINES, HENRY LUTHER 'HINKEY'	D. JANUARY 9, 1979 SHARON HILL, PA.
18- 23 HAINES, JESSE JOSEPH 'POP'	D. AUGUST 5, 1978 DAYTON, O.
73- 56 HAIRSTON, JERRY WAYNE	900 CARLSON COURT - NAPERVILLE IL 60540
69- 73 HAIRSTON, JOHN LOUIS	3612 4TH ST W - BIRMINGHAM AL 35207
51- 35 HAIRSTON, SAMUEL	3800 CENTERPLACE WEST - BIRMINGHAM AL 35207
13- 71 HAISLIP, JAMES CLIFTON	D. JANUARY 22, 1970 DALLAS, TEX.
41- 42 HAJDUK, CHESTER	6838 CONCORD LN-NILES IL 60648
19- 37 HALAS, GEORGE STANLEY	D. OCTOBER 31, 1983 CHICAGO, ILL.
31- 34 HALE, ARVEL ODELL	D. JUNE 9, 1980 EL DORADO, ARK.
14- 78 HALE, GEORGE WAGNER	D. NOVEMBER 1, 1945 WICHITA, KAN.
74- 43 HALE, JOHN STEVEN	2309 9TH ST - WASCO CA 93280
55- 52 HALE, ROBERT HOUSTON	2919 W. SIBLEY - PARK RIDGE IL 60068
20- 46 HALE, SAMUEL DOUGLAS	D. SEPTEMBER 6, 1974 WHEELER, TEX.
15- 57 HALEY, RAYMOND TIMOTHY	D. OCTOBER 8, 1973 BRADENTON, TEX.
74- 44 HALICKI, EDWARD LOUIS	273 HICKORY ST - KEARNEY NJ 07032
81- 48 HALL, ALBERT	1628 SPAULDING RD - BIRMINGHAM AL 35211
11- 62 HALL, HERBERT ERNEST	D. JULY 18, 1948 SEATTLE, WASH.
18- 24 HALL, HERBERT SILAS	D. JULY 1, 1970 FRESNO, CAL.
43- 56 HALL, IRVIN GLADSTONE	1153 DEANWOOD RD - BALTIMORE MD 21234
63- 51 HALL, JIMMIE RANDOLPH	OLD ADD: BOX 342 - MOUNT HOLLY NC 28120
48- 44 HALL, JOHN SYLVESTER	300 BELL DR - MIDWEST CITY OK 73110
10- 64 HALL, MARCUS	D. FEBRUARY 24, 1915 JOPLIN, MO.
81- 49 HALL, MELVIN	RR 1 ROUTE 90 - CAYAGA NY 13034
52- 44 HALL, RICHARD WALLACE	2131 FOLKSTONE RD - TIMONIUM MD 21093
49- 30 HALL, ROBERT LEWIS	D. MARCH 12, 1983 ST. PETERSBURG, FLA.
68- 32 HALL, THOMAS EDWARD	3592 LILLIAN AVE - RIVERSIDE CA 92504
13- 72 HALL, WILLIAM BERNARD	D. AUGUST 15, 1947 NEWPORT, KY.
54- 39 HALL, WILLIAM LEMUEL	RR1 - HARTSFIELD GA 31756
25- 43 HALLAHAN, WILLIAM ANTHONY	D. JULY 8, 1981 BINGHAMTON, N. Y.
61- 40 HALLER, THOMAS FRANK	745 COLUMBIA DR - SAN MATEO CA 94402
40- 31 HALLETT, JACK PRICE	D. JUNE 11, 1982 TOLEDO, O.
16- 40 HALLIDAY, NEWTON REESE	D. APRIL 6, 1918 GREAT LAKES, ILL.
11- 63 HALLINAN, EDWARD S	D. AUGUST 24, 1940 SAN FRANCISCO, CALIF.
14- 79 HALT, ALVA WILLIAM	D. JANUARY 22, 1973 SANDUSKY, O.

DON GUTTERIDGE

WARREN HACKER
CINCINNATI REDLEGS

22- 50	HAMANN, ELMER JOSEPH 'DOC'	D. JANUARY 11, 1973 MILWAUKEE, WIS.
71- 42	HAMBRIGHT, ROGER DEE	OLD ADD: 523 N 39 TH ST - SPRINGFIELD OR
26- 34	HAMBY, JAMES SANFORD	1117 S 11TH ST - SPRINGFIELD IL 62703
72- 44	HAMILTON, DAVID EDWARD	9464 CHERRY HILLS LN - SAN RAMON CA 94583
11- 64	HAMILTON, EARL ANDREW	D. NOVEMBER 17, 1968 ANAHEIM, CALIF.
62- 51	HAMILTON, JACK EDWIN	MORNING SUN IA 52640
61- 41	HAMILTON, STEVE ABSHER	RR 5 - MOREHEAD KY 40351
52- 45	HAMILTON, THOMAS BALL	D. NOVEMBER 29, 1973 TYLER, TEX.
57- 28	HAMLIN, KENNETH LEE	TALL TIMBERS - CLIMAX MI 49034
33- 22	HAMLIN, LUKE DANIEL	D. FEBRUARY 18,1978 CLARE, MICH.
70- 56	HAMM, PETER WHITFIELD	525 LOCKHART BULCH RD - SANTA CRUZ CA 95060
81- 55	HAMMAKER, CHARLTON ATLEE	2739 STUBB BLUFF RD - KNOXVILLE TN 37932
82- 55	HAMMOND, STEVEN BEN	OLD ADD: 2555 FOX HALL LN - COLLEGE PARK GA 30349
15- 58	HAMMOND, WALTER CHARLES 'JACK'	D. MARCH 4, 1942 KENOSHA, WIS.
44- 54	HAMNER, GRANVILLE WILBUR	OLD ADD: 50 ROYAL WAY - CLEARWATER FL 33515
46- 42	HAMNER, RALPH CONANT	BOX 236 - BRADLEY AR 71826
45- 41	HAMNER, WESLEY GARVIN 'GAR'	%J.LOVING,6512 HALL COURT - MECHANICSVILLE VA 23111
74- 43	HAMPTON, ISAAC BERNARD 'IKE'	1604 LEE ST - CAMDEN SC 29020
55- 53	HAMRIC, ODBERT HERMAN 'BERT'	D. AUGUST 8, 1984 SPRINGBORO, O.
43- 57	HAMRICK, RAYMOND BERNARD	3125 SHANE DR-RICHMOND CA 94806
40- 32	HANCKEN, MORRIS MEDLOCK 'BUDDY'	BOX 288 - HOUSTON TX 77001
49- 31	HANCOCK, FRED JAMES	D. MARCH 12, 1986 CLEARWATER, FLA.
78- 55	HANCOCK, RONALD GARRY	OLD ADD: 15806 ASHBURY PL - TAMPA FL
70- 57	HAND, RICHARD ALLEN	2103 OAKWOOD LN - ARLINGTON TX 76012
11- 65	HANDIBOE, ALOYSIUS JAMES 'MIKE'	D. JANUARY 31, 1953 SAVANNAH, GA.
46- 42	HANDLEY, EUGENE LOUIS	8656 FRESNO DR #506A - HUNTINGTON BEACH CA 92646
36- 35	HANDLEY, LEE ELMER	D. APRIL 8, 1970 PITTSBURGH, PA.
64- 40	HANDRAHAN, JAMES VERNON 'VERN'	36 NEWLAND CRESCENT - CHARLOTTETOWN PEI C1A 4H5 CAN.
65- 34	HANDS, WILLIAM ALFRED	WILLOW TERRACE - ORIENT NY 11957
53- 31	HANEBRINK, HARRY ALOYSIUS	10400 RENFREW DR - ST LOUIS MO 63137
22- 51	HANEY, FRED GIRARD	D. NOVEMBER 9, 1977 BEVERLY HILLS, CALIF.
66- 41	HANEY, WALLACE LARRY	BOX 97 - BARBOURSVILLE VA 22923
14- 80	HANFORD, CHARLES JOSEPH	D. JULY 19, 1963 TRENTON, N.J.
27- 43	HANKINS, DONALD WAYNE	D. MAY 16, 1963 WINSTON-SALEM, N. C.
61- 42	HANKINS, JAY NELSON	9309 E 84TH TER - RAYTOWN MO 64138
13- 73	HANLEY, JOSEPH PATRICK	D. MAY 1, 1961 ELMHURST, N. Y.
75- 48	HANNA, PRESTON LEE	5555 MAYFAIR DR - PENSACOLA FL 32506
18- 25	HANNAH, JAMES HARRISON 'TRUCK'	D. APRIL 27, 1982 FOUNTAIN VALLEY, CALIF.
76- 39	HANNAHS, GERALD ELLIS	26 LORNA DR - LITTLE ROCK AR 72205
62- 52	HANNAN, JAMES JOHN	3907 CHERRY HILL WAY - ANNADALE VA 22003
39- 47	HANNING, LOY VERNON	RR 2 BOX 256B - SAINT CLAIR MO 63077
44- 55	HANSEN, ANDREW VIGGO	362 YORKTOWN CIR - ATLANTIS FL 33462
51- 37	HANSEN, DOUGLAS WILLIAM	OLD ADD: 4126 W. SLAUSON AVE - LOS ANGELES CA 90043
74- 46	HANSEN, ROBERT JOSEPH	19 N KELSEY AVE - EVANSVILLE IN 47711
58- 42	HANSEN, RONALD LAVERN	13602 ALLISTON DR - BALDWIN MD 21013
30- 30	HANSEN, ROY EMIL FREDERICK 'SNIPE'	D. SEPTEMBER 11, 1978 CHICAGO, ILL.
18- 26	HANSEN, ROY INGLOF	D. FEBRUARY 9, 1977 BELOIT, WIS.

GERALD HANNAHS
Lanceur/Pitcher

LARRY HARLOW

43- 58	HANSKI, DONALD THOMAS	D. SEPTEMBER 2, 1957 WORTH, ILL.
21- 38	HANSON, EARL SYLVESTER 'OLLIE'	D. AUGUST 19, 1951 CLIFTON, N.J.
13- 74	HANSON, HARRY	B. ST. LOUIS, MO.
42- 46	HANYZEWSKI, EDWARD MICHAEL	RR 1 BOX 120 - VERGAS MN 56587
23- 58	HAPPENNY, JOHN CLIFFORD	4421 NE 15TH AVE - FORT LAUDERDALE FL 33334
28- 43	HARDER, MELVIN LEROY	130 CENTER ST #6A - CHARDON OH 44024
18- 27	HARDGROVE, WILLIAM HENRY 'PAT'	D. JANUARY 26, 1973 JACKSON, MISS.
67- 41	HARDIN, JAMES WARREN	OLD ADD: 10340 SW 102ND AVE - MIAMI FL 33156
52- 46	HARDIN, WILLIAM EDGAR	8135 ENCINO AVE - NORTHRIDGE CA 91324
13- 75	HARDING, CHARLES HAROLD	D. OCTOBER 30, 1971 BOLD SPRINGS, TENN.
58- 43	HARDY, CARROLL WILLIAM	213 VAQUERO DR - BOULDER CO 80302
51- 38	HARDY, FRANCIS JOSEPH 'RED'	5620 N 12TH ST - PHOENIX AZ 85014
74- 47	HARDY, HOWARD LAWRENCE 'LARRY'	2402 DRAWBRIDGE RD - ARLINGTON TX 76012
65- 35	HARGAN, STEVEN LOWELL	2502 MORANGO TRAIL - PALM SPRINGS CA 92262
80- 43	HARGESHEIMER, ALAN ROBERT	7400 W MYRTLE - CHICAGO IL 60631
79- 46	HARGIS, GARY LYNN	157 GEMINI AVE - LOMPOC CA 93436
13- 76	HARGRAVE, EUGENE FRANKLIN 'BUBBLES'	D. FEBRUARY 23, 1969 CINCINNATI, O.
23- 59	HARGRAVE, WILLIAM MCKINLEY 'PINKY'	D. OCTOBER 3, 1942 FT. WAYNE, IND.
23- 60	HARGREAVES, CHARLES RUSSELL	D. MAY 9, 1979 NEPTUNE, N. J.
74- 48	HARGROVE, DUDLEY MICHAEL 'MIKE'	RR 3 BOX 94C - PERRYTON TX 79070
10- 65	HARKNESS, FREDERICK HARVEY 'SPECS'	D. MAY 18, 1952 COMPTON, CALIF.
61- 43	HARKNESS, THOMAS WILLIAM 'TIM'	222 PEARSON #42 - OSHAWA ONTARIO CAN.
75- 49	HARLOW, LARRY DUANE	OLD ADD: 1002 TOWNSEND AVE - AZTEC NM
41- 43	HARMAN, WILLIAM BELL	9 GUYENNE RD - WILMINGTON DE 19807
54- 41	HARMON, CHARLES BYRON	6035A RIDGEACRE DR - CINCINNATI OH 45237
67- 42	HARMON, TERRY WALTER	OAKWOOD DR - MEDFORD NJ 08055
79- 47	HARPER, BRIAN DAVID	6 SILVERLEAF DR - ROLLING HILLS CA 90274
16- 41	HARPER, GEORGE WASHINGTON	D. AUGUST 18, 1978 MAGNOLIA, ARK.

```
13- 77 HARPER, HARRY CLAYTON                       D. APRIL 23, 1963 LAYTON, N.J.
15- 59 HARPER, JOHN WESLEY                         D. JUNE 18, 1927 HALSTEAD, KAN.
80- 48 HARPER, TERRY JOE                           1685 DORRIS RD - DOUGLAS GA 30134
62- 53 HARPER, THOMAS                              3 CHRISTOPHER DR - STOUGHTON MA 02072
11- 66 HARPER, WILLIAM HOMER                       D. JUNE 17, 1951 SOMERVILLE, TENN.
69- 74 HARRAH, COLBERT DALE 'TOBY'                 824 CHAPARRAL - BEDFORD TX 76021
69- 75 HARRELL, JOHN ROBERT                        756 ERIE CIR - MILPITAS CA 95035
12- 74 HARRELL, OSCAR MARTIN 'SLIM'                D. APRIL 30, 1971 HILLSBORO, TEX.
35- 41 HARRELL, RAYMOND JAMES                      D. JANUARY 28, 1984 ALEXANDRIAS, LA.
55- 54 HARRELL, WILLIAM                            128 OAKWOOD AVE - TROY NY 12180
65- 36 HARRELSON, DERRELL MCKINLEY 'BUD'           31 FALCON DR - HAUPPAUGE NY 11787
63- 52 HARRELSON, KENNETH SMITH 'HAWK'             WMAQ RADIO STATION - CHICAGO IL 60601
68- 33 HARRELSON, WILLIAM CHARLES                  580N FAIR OAKS DR - BAKERSFIELD CA 93306
13- 78 HARRINGTON, ANDREW FRANCIS                  D. NOVEMBER 12, 1938 MALDEN, MASS.
25- 44 HARRINGTON, ANDREW MATTHEW                  D. JANUARY 26, 1979 BOISE, IDAHO
63- 53 HARRINGTON, CHARLES MICHAEL 'MIKE'          RR 7 BOX 626 - HATTIESBURG MS 39401
53- 52 HARRINGTON, WILLIAM WOMBLE                  RR1 - GARNER NC 27529
67- 43 HARRIS, ALONZO                              7753 S. HOOPER - LOS ANGELES CA 90001
25- 46 HARRIS, ANTHONY SPENCER                     D. JULY 3, 1982 MINNEAPOLIS, MINN.
14- 81 HARRIS, BENJAMIN FRANKLIN                   D. APRIL 29, 1927 ST. LOUIS, MO.
55- 55 HARRIS, BOYD GAIL                           7583 MARGATE CT #004 - MANASSAS VA 22110
41- 44 HARRIS, CHALMER LUMAN 'LUM'                 RR 1 BOX 280 - VINCENT AL 35178
48- 45 HARRIS, CHARLES 'BUBBA'                     P. O. BOX 159 - NOBLETON FL 34263
25- 45 HARRIS, DAVID STANLEY                       D. SEPTEMBER 18, 1973 ATLANTA, GA.
81- 51 HARRIS, GREG ALLEN                          11248 BARBI LANE - LOS ALAMITOS CA 90720
36- 36 HARRIS, HERBERT BENJAMIN                    545 WOODMAR TER - CRYSTAL LAKE IL 60014
68- 34 HARRIS, JAMES WILLIAM 'BILLY'               OLD ADD: 1404 PRINCESS ST - WILMINGTON NC
79- 48 HARRIS, JOHN THOMAS                         3609 LINKWOOD - CLOVIS NM 88101
14- 82 HARRIS, JOSEPH                              D. DECEMBER 10, 1959 RENTON, PA.
40- 33 HARRIS, MAURICE CHARLES 'MICKEY'            D. APRIL 15, 1971 FARMINGTON, MICH.
38- 35 HARRIS, ROBERT ARTHUR                       BOX 492 - NORTH PLATTE NE 69101
41- 45 HARRIS, ROBERT NED                          D. DECEMBER 18, 1976 WEST PALM BEACH, FLA.
19- 38 HARRIS, STANLEY RAYMOND 'BUCKY'             D. NOVEMBER 8, 1977 BETHESDA, MD.
72- 45 HARRIS, VICTOR LANIER                       6329 GREEN VALLEY CIR - CULVER CITY CA 90230
70- 58 HARRIS, WALTER FRANCIS 'BUDDY'              2305 CAROL LN - NORRISTOWN PA 19403
23- 61 HARRIS, WILLIAM MILTON                      D. AUGUST 21, 1965 INDIAN TRAIL, N. C.
57- 29 HARRIS, WILLIAM THOMAS                      322 S REED - KENNEWICK WA 99336
65- 37 HARRISON, CHARLES WILLIAM                   1958 WILLOW DR - ABILENE TX 79602
55- 56 HARRISON, ROBERT LEE                        253 BRIERLEY WAY - INDIANAPOLIS IN 46032
72- 46 HARRISON, RORIC EDWARD                      4333 N. SCOTTSDALE RD - SCOTTSDALE AZ 85251
65- 38 HARRISON, THOMAS JAMES                      6822 SHERMAN WAY - BELL CA 90203
20- 47 HARRISS, WILLIAM JENNINGS BRYAN 'SLIM       D. SEPTEMBER 19, 1963 TEMPLE, TEXAS
45- 42 HARRIST, EARL                               BOX 238 - SIMSBORO LA 71275
37- 47 HARSHANEY, SAMUEL                           419 THELMA DR-SAN ANTONIO TX 78212
48- 46 HARSHMAN, JOHN ELVIN                        2227 COMMONWEALTH - SAN DIEGO CA 92104
15- 60 HARSTAD, OSCAR THEANDER                     D. NOVEMBER 14, 1985 CORVALLIS, ORE.
80- 49 HART, JAMES MICHAEL 'MIKE'                  409 LARKSPUR - PORTAGE MI 49081
63- 54 HART, JAMES RAYMOND                         OLD ADD: 4041 GEARY - SAN FRANCISCO CA
84- 49 HART, MICHAEL LAWRENCE                      16552 WEST CRESCENT DR - NEW BERLIN WI 53151
43- 59 HART, WILLIAM WOODROW                       D. JULY 29, 1968 LYKINS, PA.
65- 39 HARTENSTEIN, CHARLES OSCAR                  6815 DEPAUL COVE - AUSTIN TX 78723
12- 75 HARTER, FRANKLIN PIERCE                     D. APRIL 14, 1959 BREESE, ILL.
14- 83 HARTFORD, BRUCE DANIEL                      D. MAY 25, 1975 LOS ANGELES, CAL.
39- 48 HARTJE, CHRISTIAN HENRY                     D. JUNE 26, 1946 SEATTLE, WASH.
11- 67 HARTLEY, GROVER ALLEN                       D. OCTOBER 19, 1964 DAYTONA BEACH, FLA.
62- 54 HARTMAN, J. C.                              3425 ROSEDALE ST - HOUSTON TX 77004
59- 37 HARTMAN, ROBERT LOUIS                       19880 CLAREMONT LN - HUNTINGTON BEACH CA 92646
22- 52 HARTNETT, CHARLES LEO 'GABBY'               D. DECEMBER 20, 1972 PARK RIDGE, ILL.
13- 79 HARTRANFT, RAYMOND CHARLES                  D. FEBRUARY 10, 1955 CHESTER CO., PA.
73- 57 HARTS, GREGORY RUDOLPH                      OLD ADD: 160 WOODARD AVE SE - ATLANTA GA
50- 32 HARTSFIELD, ROY THOMAS                      150 HUNTERS COVE - ROSWELL GA 30076
47- 41 HARTUNG, CLINTON 'HONDO'                    1018 EAST FULTON - SINTON TX 78387
76- 40 HARTZELL, PAUL FRANKLIN                     610 NEWPORT CENTER RD #1290 - NEWPORT BEACH CA 92660
28- 44 HARVEL, LUTHER RAYMOND                      D. APRIL 10, 1986 KANSAS CITY, MO.
16- 42 HASBROOK, ROBERT LYNDON 'ZIGGY'             D. FEBRUARY 9, 1976 GARLAND, TEX.
45- 43 HASENMAYER, DONALD IRVIN                    12 BARBARA ST - HATBORO PA 19040
40- 34 HASH, HERBERT HOWARD                        BOSTON VA 22713
33- 23 HASLIN, MICHAEL JOSEPH 'MICKEY'             171 GEORGE AV - PLAINS PA 18705
36- 37 HASSETT, JOHN ALOYSIUS 'BUDDY'              114 STONY RIDGE DR-HILLSDALE NJ 07642
78- 56 HASSEY, RONALD WILLIAM                      OLD ADD: 3849 CALLE ALTAR - TUCSON AZ
71- 43 HASSLER, ANDREW EARL                        OLD ADD: BOX 17101 - TUCSON AZ
28- 45 HASSLER, JOSEPH FREDERICK                   D. SEPTEMBER 4, 1971 DUNCAN, OKLA.
37- 48 HASSON, CHARLES EUGENE 'GENE'               830 E KINGSLEY AVE #63 - POMONA CA 91767
```

19- 39	HASTY, ROBERT KELLER	D. MAY 28, 1972 DALLAS, GA.
79- 49	HATCHER, MICHAEL VAUGHN 'MICKEY'	720 SOUTH DOBSON #59 - MESA AZ 85202
84- 50	HATCHER, WILLIAM AUGUSTUS	P.O. BOX 207 - WILLIAMS AZ 86046
50- 33	HATFIELD, FRED JAMES	STAR ROUTE 1 BOX 3025 - TALLAHASSEE FL 32304
45- 44	HATHAWAY, RAY WILSON	25 LEISURE MOUNT RD - ASHEVILLE NC 28804
46- 44	HATTEN, JOSEPH HILARIAN	RR 2 BOX 678 - SHINGLETOWN CA 96088
35- 42	HATTER, CLYDE MELNO	D. OCTOBER 16, 1937 YOSEMITE, KY.
46- 45	HATTON, GRADY EDGEBERT	BOX 97 - WARREN TX 77664
12- 76	HAUGER, JOHN ARTHUR	D. AUGUST 2, 1944 REDWOOD CITY, CALIF.
43- 60	HAUGHEY, CHRISTOPHER FRANCIS	4737 THORTON #28 - FREMONT CA 94536
47- 42	HAUGSTAD, PHILIP DONALD	RR 4 BOX 180 - BLACK RIVER FALLS WI 54615
10- 66	HAUSER, ARNOLD GEORGE	D. MAY 22, 1956 AURORA, ILL.
22- 53	HAUSER, JOSEPH JOHN	914 N. 5TH ST #14 - SHEBOYGAN WI 53081
75- 50	HAUSMAN, THOMAS MATTHEW	3165 WESTFIELD CIR - LAS VEGAS NV 89121
44- 56	HAUSMANN, CLEMENS RAYMOND	D. AUGUST 29, 1972 BAYTOWN, TEX.
44- 57	HAUSMANN, GEORGE JOHN	218 FAWN VALLEY - BOERNE TX 78006
81- 52	HAVENS, BRADLEY DAVID	1526 EAST WOODLAWN - ROYAL OAK MI 48073
51- 39	HAWES, ROY LEE	BOX 912 - RINGGOLD GA 30736
11- 68	HAWK, EDWARD	D. MARCH 26, 1936 NEOSHO, MO.
82- 56	HAWKINS, MELTON ANDREW 'ANDY'	9101 LARK - WACO TX 76710
60- 46	HAWKINS, WYNN FIRTH	5326 COTTAGE LN - CORTLAND OH 44410
21- 39	HAWKS, NELSON LOUIS 'CHICK'	D. MAY 26, 1973 SAN RAFAEL, CAL.
15- 61	HAWORTH, HOMER HOWARD	D. JANUARY 28, 1953 TROUTDALE, ORE.
70- 59	HAYDEL, JOHN HAROLD 'HAL'	304 LYNWOOD DR - HOUMA LA 70360
58- 44	HAYDEN, EUGENE FRANKLIN	1597 ALAMO DR #188 - VACAVILLE CA 95688
82- 57	HAYES, BEN JOSEPH	3501 10TH ST NE - ST PETERSBURG FL 33704
33- 24	HAYES, FRANKLIN WITMAN	D. JUNE 22, 1955 POINT PLEASANT, N. J.
35- 43	HAYES, JAMES MILLARD	6180 ROCKLAND RD - LITHONIA GA 30058
27- 44	HAYES, MINTER CARNEY'JACKIE'	D. FEBRUARY 9, 1983 BIRMINGHAM, ALA.
81- 53	HAYES, VON FRANCIS	129 WHITBURN CT - STOCKTON CA 95210
80- 50	HAYES, WILLIAM ERNEST	8 SOUTH ASH ST - NORTH PLATTE NE 69101
39- 49	HAYNES, JOSEPH WALTER	D. JANUARY 6, 1967 HOPKINS, MINN.
68- 35	HAYWOOD, WILLIAM KIERNAN	2143 EAST FAIRFIELD - MESA AZ 85203
44- 58	HAYWORTH, MYRON CLAUDE 'RED'	507 OAK VIEW RD - HIGH POINT NC 27260
26- 35	HAYWORTH, RAYMOND HALL	RR 1 BOX 160 - HIGH POINT NC 27260
80- 51	HAZEWOOD, DRUNGO LARUE	5130 DEL NORTE BLVD - SACRAMENTO CA 95820
55- 57	HAZLE, ROBERT SIDNEY	164 DORSET DR - COLUMBIA SC 29210
40- 35	HEAD, EDWARD MARVIN	D. JANUARY 31, 1980 BASTROP, LA.
23- 62	HEAD, RALPH	D. OCTOBER 8, 1962 MUSCADINE, ALA.
30- 31	HEALEY, FRANCIS XAVIER PAUL	13 SCHOOL ST - HOLYOKE MA 01040
69- 76	HEALY, FRANCIS XAVIER	1 PRIMROSE LN - HOLYOKE MA 01040
15- 62	HEALY, THOMAS FITZGERALD	D. JANUARY 15, 1974 CLEVELAND, O.
54- 41	HEARD, JEHOSIE	6465 3RD AVE SOUTH - BIRMINGHAM AL 35212
10- 67	HEARN, BUNN 'BUNNY'	D. OCTOBER 11, 1959 WILSON, N.C.
10- 68	HEARN, EDMUND	D. SEPTEMBER 8, 1952 SAWTELLE, CALIF.
26- 36	HEARN, ELMER LAFAYETTE 'BUNNY'	D. MARCH 31, 1974 VENICE, FLA.
47- 43	HEARN, JAMES TOLBERT	1678 BEVERLY WOOD CT - CHAMBLEE GA 30341
85- 46	HEARRON, JEFFREY VERNON	13176 EAST HEDDA DR - CERRITOS CA 90701
36- 38	HEATH, JOHN GEOFFREY 'JEFF'	D. DECEMBER 9, 1975 SEATTLE, WASH.
82- 58	HEATH, KELLY MARK	202 WOODSTOCK DR - GREENVILLE NC 27834
78- 57	HEATH, MICHAEL THOMAS	505 CENTERBROOK DR - BRANDON FL 33511
31- 35	HEATH, MINOR WILSON 'MICKEY'	30652 LA SONORA - MALIBU CA 90265
20- 48	HEATH, SPENCER PAUL	D. JANUARY 25, 1930 CHICAGO, ILL.
35- 44	HEATH, THOMAS GEORGE	D. FEBRUARY 26, 1967 LOS GATOS, CAL.
65- 40	HEATH, WILLIAM CHRIS	2111 PLANTATION DR - RICHMOND TX 77469
83- 70	HEATHCOCK, RONALD JEFFREY 'JEFF'	12861 ASPENWOOD LN - GARDEN GROVE CA 92640
18- 28	HEATHCOTE, CLIFTON EARL	D. JANUARY 19, 1939 YORK, PA.
82- 59	HEATON, NEAL	611 BLUE POINT RD - HOLTSVILLE NY 11742
75- 51	HEAVERLO, DAVID WALLACE	3720 WEST LAKESHORE DR - MOSES LAKE WA 98837
31- 36	HEBERT, WALLACE ANDREW	3408 WESTWOOD RD - WEST LAKE LA 70665
68- 36	HEBNER, RICHARD JOSEPH	510 NATHAN ST - NORWOOD MA 02062
12- 77	HECHINGER, MICHAEL VINCENT	D. AUGUST 13, 1967 CHICAGO, ILL.
13- 80	HEDGEPETH, HARRY MALCOLM	D. JULY 30, 1966 RICHMOND, VA.
65- 41	HEDLUND, MICHAEL DAVID	2412 KLINGER RD - ARLINGTON TX 76016
79- 50	HEEP, DANIEL WILLIAM	327 TEAKWOOD LN - SAN ANTONIO TX 78216
34- 43	HEFFNER, DONALD HENRY	816 SOUTHVIEW - ARCADIA CA 91006
63- 55	HEFFNER, ROBERT FREDERIC	1817 LIBERTY - ALLENTOWN PA 18104
45- 45	HEFLIN, RANDOLPH RUTHERFORD	509 HANSON AVE - FREDERICKSBURG VA 22401
41- 46	HEGAN, JAMES EDWARD	D. JUNE 17, 1984 SWAMPSCOTT, MASS.
64- 41	HEGAN, JAMES MICHAEL 'MIKE'	9648 OLD BARN RD - MEQUON WI 53092
85- 47	HEGMAN, ROBERT HILMER	617 FOURTH AVE NORTH - SAUK RAPIDS MN 56379
18- 29	HEHL, HERMAN JACOB 'JAKE'	D. JULY 4, 1961 BROOKLYN, N. Y.
69- 77	HEIDEMANN, JACK SEALE	2710 W. OBISPO CIR - MESA AZ 85202
14- 84	HEILMANN, HARRY EDWIN	D. JULY 9, 1951 SOUTHFIELD, MICH.
42- 47	HEIM, VAL RAYMOND	1050 LOUDON - SUPERIOR NE 68978

HEIMACH

HERNANDEZ

HERNANDEZ

HILL

```
77- 65 HERNANDEZ, GUILLERMO 'WILLIE'        BO ESPINA CALLE C BOX 125 - AGUADA PR 00602
65- 43 HERNANDEZ, JACINTO 'JACKIE'          OLD ADD: 1391 NW 95TH ST - MIAMI FL 33147
74- 51 HERNANDEZ, KEITH                     1300 CHRISTMAS VALLEY - CHESTERFIELD MO 63017
82- 61 HERNANDEZ, LEONARDO JESUS            URB. EL MILAGRO,CALLE SUCRE 38 - EDO MIRANDA VENEZ
79- 52 HERNANDEZ, PEDRO JULIO               JULIO A. GARCIA #43 - LA ROMANA DOMINICAN REP.
67- 46 HERNANDEZ, RAMON GONZALEZ            REPARTO, ROSAMARIA CLE 5F-19-CAROLINA PRO0630
72- 47 HERNANDEZ, RODOLFO 'RUDY'            CARVAJAL #1802 NORTE - MAZATLAN SINOLOA MEX.
60- 48 HERNANDEZ, RUDOLPH ALBERT            8 CALLE RODRIGUEZ SERRA - CONDADO PR 00907
42- 48 HERNANDEZ, SALVADOR JOSE RAMOS       D. JANUARY 3, 1986 HAVANA, CUBA
84- 52 HERNANDEZ, TOBIAS RAFAEL            IRA CALLE GUAMACHITO #47-49 - CALABOZO, GUARICO VENE.
74- 52 HERNDON, LARRY DARNELL               6915 SKYLINE BLVD - HILLSBOROUGH CA 94010
79- 53 HERR, THOMAS MITCHELL                1077 OLDE FORGE CROSSING - LANCASTER PA 17601
11- 72 HERRELL, WALTER WILLIAM              D. JANUARY 23, 1949 FRONT ROYAL, VA.
67- 47 HERRERA, JOSE CONCEPCION             MARAVEN ADRI 12,CEN.COM. LAGUNILLAS - E. ZULIA VENEZ
58- 45 HERRERA, JUAN FRANCISCO 'PANCHO'     2930 NW 21ST AVE - MIAMI FL 33142
51- 40 HERRERA, PROCOPIO RODRIGUEZ 'TITO'   APDO POSTAL 257-CIUDAD SATELITE, EDO MEX.
25- 47 HERRERA, RAMON 'MIKE'                D. FEBRUARY 3, 1978 HAVANA, CUBA
56- 42 HERRIAGE, WILLIAM TROY               3400 KINGSWOOD #16 - MODESTO CA 95355
54- 44 HERRIN, THOMAS EDWARD                BOX 550 - SAN JOSE CA 95125
29- 48 HERRING, ARTHUR L.                   296 HIGHWAY DR - MARION IN 46952
12- 78 HERRING, HERBERT LEE                 D. APRIL 22, 1964 TUCSON, ARIZ.
15- 65 HERRING, WILLIAM FRANCIS             D. SEPTEMBER 10, 1962 HONESDALE, PA.
67- 48 HERRMANN, EDWARD MARTIN              16935 ALONDRA DR - SAN DIEGO CA 92128
32- 36 HERRMANN, LEROY GEORGE               D. JULY 3, 1972 LIVERMORE, CAL.
18- 31 HERRMANN, MARTIN JOHN                D. SEPTEMBER 11, 1956 CINCINNATI, O.
62- 55 HERRNSTEIN, JOHN ELLETT              603 SEMINOLE RD - CHILLICOTHE OH 45602
62- 56 HERRSCHER, RICHARD FRANKLIN 'RICK'   4024 DRUID - DALLAS TX 75205
56- 43 HERSH, EARL WALTER                   3201 MURKLE RD - WESTMINSTER MD 21157
61- 48 HERSHBERGER, NORMAN MICHAEL 'MIKE'   4130 MEADOWVIEW DR - CANTON OH 44709
38- 37 HERSHBERGER, WILLARD MCKEE           D. AUGUST 3, 1940 BOSTON, MASS.
83- 72 HERSHISER, OREL LEONARD QUINTON      549 LYONS WAY - PLACENTIA CA 92670
52- 48 HERTWECK, NEAL CHARLES               3030 ST CLAIRE RD - WINSTON SALEM NC 27106
64- 43 HERTZ, STEVE ALLAN                   10211 SW 96TH TER - MIAMI FL 33156
56- 44 HERZOG, DORREL HORMAN ELVERT 'WHITEY' 3613 S FOREST - INDEPENDENCE MO 64052
84- 53 HESKETH, JOSEPH THOMAS               3690 SALISBURY AVE - BLASDELL NY 14219
16- 43 HESSELBACHER, GEORGE EDWARD          D. FEBRUARY 18, 1980 RYDAL, PA.
45- 47 HETKI, JOHN EDWARD                   4004 STARY DR - PARMA OH 44134
35- 46 HEUSSER, EDWARD BURLETON             D. MARCH 1, 1956 AURORA, COLO.
20- 50 HEVING, JOHN ALOYSIUS                D. DECEMBER 24, 1968 SALISBURY, N. C.
30- 33 HEVING, JOSEPH WILLIAM               D. APRIL 11, 1970 COVINGTON, KY.
73- 60 HEYDEMAN, GREGORY GEORGE             61 VIA PARAISO - MONTEREY CA 93940
64- 44 HIATT, JACK E                        26825 W PICO CANYON RD - NEWHALL CA 91321
67- 49 HIBBS, JAMES KERR                    2821 SOUTH MAIN ST - VENTURA CA 93003
42- 49 HICKEY, JAMES ROBERT                 163 CHESTER ST - EAST HARTFORD CT 06108
81- 55 HICKEY, KEVIN JOHN                   5715 SOUTH MASON - CHICAGO IL 60638
15- 66 HICKMAN, DAVID JAMES                 D. DECEMBER 30, 1958 BROOKLYN, N. Y.
62- 57 HICKMAN, JAMES LUCIUS                BOX  355 - HENNING TN 38041
65- 44 HICKMAN, JESSE OWENS                 114 MYRTLEWOOD DR - PINEVILLE LA 71360
56- 45 HICKS, CLARENCE WALTER 'BUDDY'       7600 COOLGROVE DR - DOWNEY CA 90240
64- 45 HICKS, JAMES EDWARD                  3717 EUCLID AVE - EAST CHICAGO IN 46312
59- 38 HICKS, WILLIAM JOSEPH 'JOE'          2707 BROOKMERE RD - CHARLOTTESVILLE VA 22901
37- 52 HIGBE, WALTER KIRBY                  D. MAY 6, 1985 COLUMBIA, S. C.
```

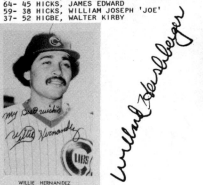

WILLIE HERNANDEZ

```
22- 55 HIGBEE, MAHLON JESSE                 D. APRIL 7, 1968 DEPAUW, IND.
49- 33 HIGDON, WILLIAM TRAVIS               117 KENTWOOD DR - GULFPORT MS 39503
66- 44 HIGGINS, DENNIS DEAN                 2204 ANDERSON DR - JEFFERSON CITY MO 65101
30- 34 HIGGINS, MICHAEL FRANKLIN 'PINKY'    D. MARCH 21, 1969 DALLAS, TEX.
22- 56 HIGH, ANDREW AIRD                    D. FEBRUARY 22, 1981 TOLEDO, O.
19- 41 HIGH, CHARLES EDWIN                  D. SEPTEMBER 11, 1960 PORTLAND, ORE.
13- 83 HIGH, HUGH JENKEN                    D. NOVEMBER 16, 1962 ST. LOUIS CO., MO.
85- 48 HIGUERA, TEODORO VALENZUELA          OLD ADD: CIUDAD DE JUAREZ CHIHUAHUA MEX.
31- 38 HILCHER, WALTER FRANK                D. NOVEMBER 21, 1962 MINNEAPOLIS, MINN.
31- 39 HILDEBRAND, ORAL CLYDE               D. SEPTEMBER 8, 1977 SOUTHPORT, IND.
13- 84 HILDEBRAND, PALMER MARION            D. JANUARY 25, 1960 NORTH CANTON, O.
69- 79 HILGENDORF, THOMAS EUGENE            BOX 1131 - COTTAGE GROVE OR 97424
15- 67 HILL, CARMEN PROCTOR                 2913 BROADWAY - INDIANAPOLIS IN 46205
17- 33 HILL, CLIFFORD JOSEPH 'RED'          D. AUGUST 11, 1938 EL PASO, TEX.
57- 32 HILL, DAVID BURNHAM                  OLD ADD: 11206 CROWN POINT DR - KNOXVILLE TN 37923
83- 73 HILL, DONALD EARL                    5607 E. NAPLES CANAL ST - LONG BEACH CA 90803
69- 80 HILL, GARRY ALTON                    3538 BACK CREEK CHURCH RD - CHARLOTTE NC 28213
15- 68 HILL, HERBERT LEE                    D. SEPTEMBER 2, 1970 FARMERS BRANCH, TEX.
69- 81 HILL, HERMAN ALEXANDER               D. DECEMBER 14, 1970 MAGALLANES, VEN.
35- 47 HILL, JESSE TERRILL                  1616 FAIROAKS AVE #11-SOUTH PASADENA CA 91030
39- 50 HILL, JOHN CLINTON                   D. SEPTEMBER 20, 1970 DECATUR, GA.
73- 61 HILL, MARC KEVIN                     804 LINCOLN - ELSBERRY MO 63343
```

HILLER   # HOLBOROW

61- 49 HILLER, CHARLES JOSEPH	6425 JET PILOT TRAIL - TALLAHASSEE FL 32308
46- 46 HILLER, FRANK WALTER	222 CHANDLER DR - WEST CHESTER PA 19380
20- 51 HILLER, HARVEY MAX 'HOB'	D. DECEMBER 27, 1956 LEHIGHTON, PA.
65- 45 HILLER, JOHN FREDERICK	STAR ROUTE 1 BOX 176 - IRON MOUNTAIN MI 49801
24- 51 HILLIS, MALCOLM DAVID 'MACK'	D. JUNE 16, 1961 CAMBRIDGE, MASS.
55- 58 HILLMAN, DARIUS DUTTON 'DAVE'	849 MIMOSA DR - KINGSPORT TN 37660
14- 88 HILLY, WILLIAM EDWARD	D. JULY 25, 1953 EUREKA, MO.
72- 48 HILTON, JOHN DAVID	5205 CAMDEN LANE - PEARLAND TX 77581
61- 50 HIMSL, AVITUS BERNARD 'VEDIE'	1060 W ADDISON ST - CHICAGO IL 60613
77- 66 HINDS, SAMUEL RUSSELL	6394 TOWNSEND - FRESNO CA 93727
34- 45 HINKLE, DANIEL GORDON 'GORDIE'	D. MARCH 19, 1972 HOUSTON, TEX.
51- 41 HINRICHS, PAUL EDWIN	1100 E CLAYTON RD - BALLWIN MO 63011
10- 71 HINRICHS, WILLIAM LOUIS	D. AUGUST 18, 1972 SELMA, CALIF.
82- 62 HINSHAW, GEORGE ADDISON	1927 N SLATER AVE - COMPTON CA 90220
64- 46 HINSLEY, JERRY DEAN	OLD ADD: RR 1 BOX 908 #32 - LAS CRUCES NM 88001
28- 47 HINSON, JAMES PAUL	D. SEPTEMBER 23, 1960 MUSKOGEE, OKLA.
61- 51 HINTON, CHARLES EDWARD	6330 16TH ST NW - WASHINGTON DC 20011
71- 46 HINTON, RICHARD MICHAEL	OLD ADD: 730 AGAVE PLACE - TUCSON AZ 85718
66- 45 HIPPAUF, HERBERT AUGUST	1781 KIMBERLY DR - SUNNYVALE CA 94087
71- 47 HISER, GENE TAYLOR	1107 LITCHFIELD RD - BALTIMORE MD 21239
68- 38 HISLE, LARRY EUGENE	P.O. BOX 84 %FERGUSON - PORTSMOUTH OH 45662
51- 42 HISNER, HARLEY PARNELL	RR 2 BOX 253A - MONROEVILLE IN 46773
38- 38 HITCHCOCK, JAMES FRANKLIN	D. JUNE 23, 1959 MONTGOMERY, ALA.
42- 50 HITCHCOCK, WILLIAM CLYDE	1117 W COLLINWOOD CIR-OPELIKA AL 36801
17- 34 HITT, BRUCE SMITH	D. NOVEMBER 10, 1973 PORTLAND, ORE.
49- 34 HITTLE, LLOYD ELDON	2031 WEST ELM ST - LODI CA 95240
31- 40 HOAG, MYRIL OLIVER	D. JULY 28, 1971 HIGH SPRINGS, FLA.
54- 45 HOAK, DONALD ALBERT	D. OCTOBER 9, 1969 PITTSBURGH, PA.
61- 52 HOBAUGH, EDWARD RUSSELL	527 5TH AVE - FORD CITY PA 16226
57- 33 HOBBIE, GLEN FREDERICK	RR 2, NORTHWOOD HEIGHTS - HILLSBORO IL 62049
81- 56 HOBBS, JOHN DOUGLAS	3 WADE DR - CHERRY HILL NJ 08034
13- 85 HOBBS, WILLIAM LEE	D. JANUARY 5, 1945 HAMILTON, O.
75- 52 HOBSON, CLELL LAVERN 'BUTCH'	1422 CLARENDON AVE - BESSEMER AL 35020
20- 52 HOCK, EDWARD FRANCIS	D. NOVEMBER 21, 1963 PORTSMOUTH, O.
75- 53 HOCKENBERY, CHARLES MARION	1112 PIERCE ST - ONALASKA WI 54650
38- 39 HOCKETT, ORIS LEON	D. MARCH 23, 1969 HAWTHORNE, CAL.
34- 46 HOCKETTE, GEORGE EDWARD	D. JANUARY 20, 1974 PLANTATION, FLA.
25- 48 HODAPP, URBAN JOHN	D. JUNE 14, 1980 CINCINNATI, O.
51- 43 HODERLEIN, MELVIN ANTHONY	535 CINTI BATAVIA PIKE - CINCINNATI OH 45244
20- 53 HODGE, CLARENCE CLEMET 'SHOVEL'	D. DECEMBER 31, 1967 FORT WALTON BEACH, FLA.
84- 54 HODGE, ED OLIVER	12043 LEMMING ST - LAKEWOOD CA 90715
42- 51 HODGE, EDWARD BURTON 'BERT'	RR 19-KNOXVILLE TN 37920
71- 48 HODGE, HAROLD MORRIS 'GOMER'	RR 5 BOX 206 - RUTHERFORDTON NC 28139
43- 63 HODGES, GILBERT RAYMOND	D. APRIL 2, 1972 WEST PALM BEACH, FLA.
73- 62 HODGES, RONALD WRAY	LAKE VIEW DR - ROCKY MOUNT VA 24157
39- 51 HODGIN, ELMER RALPH	3203 FARMINGTON DR-GREENSBORO NC 27407
80- 52 HODGSON, PAUL JOSEPH DENIS	5 MCGLOIN ST - FREDERICTON NEW BRUNSWICK E3A 4J9 CAN.
46- 47 HODKEY, ALOYSIUS JOSEPH 'ELI'	5163 BROADWAY - LORAIN OH 44052
52- 49 HOEFT, WILLIAM FREDERICK	36427 SHERWOOD - LIVONIA MI 48154
63- 57 HOERNER, JOSEPH WALTER	6344 TIDEWATER DR - FLORISSANT MO 63033
40- 36 HOERST, FRANK JOSEPH	31 VILLAGE LANE - MOUNT LAUREL NJ 08054
11- 73 HOFF, CHESTER CORNELIUS 'RED'	133 LAURIE DR - ORMOND BEACH FL 32074
44- 60 HOFFERTH, STEWART EDWARD	BOX 283 - KOUTS IN 46347
29- 49 HOFFMAN, CLARENCE CASPER 'DUTCH'	D. DECEMBER 6, 1962 BELLEVILLE, ILL.
15- 69 HOFFMAN, EDWARD ADOLPH 'TEX'	D. MAY 19, 1947 NEW ORLEANS, LA.
80- 53 HOFFMAN, GLENN EDWARD	217 N DALE ST - ANAHEIM CA 92801
79- 54 HOFFMAN, GUY ALAN	1109 GLENWOOD AVE - PEORIA IL 61606
64- 47 HOFFMAN, JOHN EDWARD	2315 NW 85TH - SEATTLE WA 98117

CHUCK HOCKENBERY P

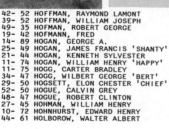

42- 52 HOFFMAN, RAYMOND LAMONT	10562 GULFSHORE #402 - NAPLES FL 33963
39- 52 HOFFMAN, WILLIAM JOSEPH	3234 N 25TH ST-PHILADELPHIA PA 19129
49- 35 HOFMAN, ROBERT GEORGE	14 BROOK HOLLOW - OAKLAND NJ 07436
19- 42 HOFMANN, FRED	D. NOVEMBER 19, 1964 ST. HELENA, CAL.
14- 89 HOGAN, GEORGE A.	D. FEBRUARY 28, 1922 BARTLESVILLE, OKLA.
25- 49 HOGAN, JAMES FRANCIS 'SHANTY'	D. APRIL 7, 1967 BOSTON, MASS.
21- 44 HOGAN, KENNETH SYLVESTER	D. JANUARY 2, 1980 CLEVELAND, O.
11- 74 HOGAN, WILLIAM HENRY 'HAPPY'	D. SEPTEMBER 28, 1974 SAN JOSE, CALIF.
11- 75 HOGG, CARTER BRADLEY	D. APRIL 2, 1935 BUENA VISTA, GA.
34- 47 HOGG, WILBERT GEORGE 'BERT'	D. NOVEMBER 5, 1973 DETROIT, MICH.
29- 50 HOGSETT, ELON CHESTER 'CHIEF'	115 W 16TH ST - HAYS KS 67601
52- 50 HOGUE, CALVIN GREY	1050 BERKSHIRE RD - DAYTON OH 45419
48- 47 HOGUE, ROBERT CLINTON	2514 SW 25TH TER - MIAMI FL 33133
27- 45 HOHMAN, WILLIAM HENRY	D. OCTOBER 29, 1968 BALTIMORE, MD.
10- 72 HOHNHURST, EDWARD HENRY	D. MARCH 26, 1916 COVINGTON, KY.
44- 61 HOLBOROW, WALTER ALBERT	11720 SW 11TH ST - FORT LAUDERDALE FL 33325

35- 48	HOLBROOK, JAMES MARBURY 'SAMMY'	1215 21ST AVE - MERIDIAN MS 39301
45- 48	HOLCOMBE, KENNETH EDWARD	32 BOTANY DR - ASHEVILLE NC 28805
34- 48	HOLDEN, JOSEPH FRANCIS	424 S 2ND ST - ST CLAIR PA 17970
13- 86	HOLDEN, WILLIAM PAUL	D. SEPTEMBER 14, 1971 PENSACOLA, FLA.
72- 49	HOLDSWORTH, FREDRICK WILLIAM	47300 W MAIN ST - NORTHVILLE MI 48167
14- 90	HOLKE, WALTER HENRY	D. OCTOBER 12, 1954 ST LOUIS, MO.
20- 54	HOLLAHAN, WILLIAM JAMES	D. NOVEMBER 27, 1965 NEW YORK, NEW YORK
77- 67	HOLLAND, ALFRED WILLIS	6 ALLUVIUM LAKES DR - WEST BERLIN NJ 08091
26- 38	HOLLAND, HOWARD ARTHUR 'MUL'	D. FEBRUARY 16, 1969 WESTCHESTER, VA.
32- 37	HOLLAND, ROBERT CLYDE 'DUTCH'	D. JUNE 16, 1967 LUMBERTON, N.C.
39- 53	HOLLAND, WILLIAM DAVID	504 CASHWELL PL - GOLDSBORO NC 27530
79- 55	HOLLE, GARY CHARLES	820 FIFTH AVE - WATERVLIET NY 12189
28- 48	HOLLEY, EDWARD EDGAR	SUPERIOR CARE HOME,3100 CLAY-PADUCAH KY 42001
21- 45	HOLLING, CARL	D. JULY 28, 1962 SONOMA, CAL.
35- 49	HOLLINGSWORTH, ALBERT WAYNE	8901 BISSONNET #69 - HOUSTON TX 77074
22- 57	HOLLINGSWORTH, JOHN BURNETT 'BONNIE'	801 VANOSDALE RD #203 - KNOXVILLE TN 37919
49- 36	HOLLMIG, STANLEY ERNEST	D. DECEMBER 4, 1981 SAN ANTONIO, TEXAS
18- 32	HOLLOCHER, CHARLES JACOB	D. AUGUST 14, 1940 STRATMAN, MO.
53- 33	HOLLOMAN, ALVA LEE 'BOBO'	650 RIVERMONT RD - ATHENS GA 30601
29- 51	HOLLOWAY, JAMES MADISON	RR 1 BOX 3285 - MARINGOUIN LA 70757
22- 58	HOLLOWAY, KENNETH EUGENE	D. SEPTEMBER 25, 1968 THOMASVILLE, GA.
77- 68	HOLLY, JEFFREY OWEN	2601 ALVORD ST - REDONDO BEACH CA 90278
24- 52	HOLM, ROSCOE ALBERT 'WATTIE'	D. MAY 19, 1950 EVERLY, IA.
43- 64	HOLM, WILLIAM FRED	D. JULY 27, 1977 EAST CHICAGO, IND.
68- 39	HOLMAN, GARY RICHARD	800 E DATE - BREA CA 92621
80- 54	HOLMAN, RANDY SCOTT	OLD ADD: 750 MOBILE AVE #48 - CAMARILLO CA 93010
18- 33	HOLMES, ELWOOD MARTER	D. APRIL 15, 1954 CAMDEN, N. J.
42- 53	HOLMES, THOMAS FRANCIS	1 PINE DR-WOODBURY NY 11797
30- 35	HOLSHAUSER, HERMAN ALEXANDER	90 WINECOFF NE - CONCORD NC 28025
25- 50	HOLT, JAMES EMMETT MADISON 'RED'	D. FEBRUARY 2, 1961 BIRMINGHAM, ALA.
68- 40	HOLT, JAMES WILLIAM	RR 3 BOX 335 - GRAHAM NC 27253
80- 55	HOLT, ROGER BOYD	1615 SAILFISH AVE - FRUITLAND PARK FL 32731
65- 46	HOLTGRAVE, LAVERN GEORGE 'VERN'	389 N 8TH ST - BREESE IL 62230
85- 49	HOLTON, BRIAN JOHN	114 ELWAY ST - BUENA VISTA PA 15018
65- 47	HOLTZMANN, KENNETH DALE	933 PROVIDENCE - BUFFALO GROVE IL 60089
77- 69	HONEYCUTT, FREDERICK WAYNE 'RICK'	2237 VALLE DR - LAHABRA HEIGHTS CA 90631
25- 51	HOOD, ALBIE LARRISON 'ABE'	1126 HAZEL AVE - CHESAPEAKE VA 23324
73- 63	HOOD, DONALD HARRIS	708 FIRESTONE DR - FLORENCE SC 29501
49- 37	HOOD, WALLACE JAMES JR.	966 EILINITA AVE - GLENDALE CA 91208
20- 55	HOOD, WALLACE JAMES SR.	D. MAY 2, 1965 HOLLYWOOD, CAL.
57- 34	HOOK, JAMES WESLEY 'JAY'	768 SUFFIELD - BIRMINGHAM MI 48009
35- 50	HOOKS, ALEXANDER MARCUS	BOX 123-EDGEWOOD TX 75117
50- 35	HOOPER, ROBERT NELSON	D. MARCH 17, 1980 NEW BRUNSWICK, N. J.
74- 53	HOOTEN, MICHAEL LEON	461 N 11TH ST - COOS BAY OR 97420
71- 49	HOOTON, BURT CARLTON	726 HILLVIEW DR - ARLINGTON TX 76011
52- 51	HOOVER, RICHARD LLOYD	D. APRIL 12, 1981 LAKE PLACID, FLA.
43- 65	HOOVER, ROBERT JOE	D. SEPTEMBER 2, 1965 LOS ANGELES, CAL.
75- 54	HOPKINS, DONALD	BOX 39081 - CINCINNATI OH 45230
68- 41	HOPKINS, GAIL EASON	745 SOUTH HAWTHORNE - ELMHURST IL 60126
34- 49	HOPKINS, MEREDITH HILLIARD 'MARTY'	D. NOVEMBER 20, 1963 DALLAS, TEX.
27- 46	HOPKINS, PAUL HENRY	131 MAIN ST - DEEP RIVER CT 06417
39- 54	HOPP, JOHN LEONARD	715 E 5TH ST-HASTINGS NE 68901
46- 48	HOPPER, JAMES MCDANIEL	D. JANUARY 23, 1982 CHARLOTTE, N. C.
13- 87	HOPPER, WILLIAM BOOTH	D. JANUARY 14, 1965 ALLEN PARK, MICH.
24- 53	HORAN, JOSEPH PATRICK 'SHAGS'	D. FEBRUARY 13, 1969 LOS ANGELES, CAL.
61- 53	HORLEN, JOEL EDWARD	3718 CHARTWELL DR - SAN ANTONIO TX 78230
29- 52	HORNE, BERLYN DALE 'TRADER'	D. FEBRUARY 3, 1983 FRANKLIN, O.
78- 58	HORNER, JAMES ROBERT 'BOB'	1660 CHEVRON WAY - DUNWOODY GA 30338
15- 70	HORNSBY, ROGERS	D. JANUARY 5, 1963 CHICAGO, ILL.
12- 79	HORSEY, HANSON	D. DECEMBER 1, 1949 MILLINGTON, MD.
17- 35	HORSTMAN, OSCAR THEODORE	D. MAY 11, 1977 SALINA, KAN.
64- 48	HORTON, ANTHONY DARRIN	17001 LIVORNO DR - PACIFIC PALISADES CA 90272
84- 55	HORTON, RICKY NEAL	OLD ADD: 18 LAWRENCE RD - HYDE PARK NY 12538
63- 58	HORTON, WILLIAM WATTERSON 'WILLIE'	19312 STEEL ST - DETROIT MI 48235
53- 34	HOSKINS, DAVID TAYLOR	D. APRIL 2, 1970 FLINT, MICH.
70- 60	HOSLEY, TIMOTHY KENNETH	401 W HENRY ST - SPARTANBURG SC 29301
56- 46	HOST, EUGENE EARL	1415 FULTON ST - NASHVILLE TN 37206
44- 62	HOSTETLER, CHARLES CLOYD	D. FEBRUARY 18, 1971 FORT COLLINS, COLO.
81- 57	HOSTETLER, DAVID ALAN	918 FORRESTAL DR - ARLINGTON TX 76010
71- 50	HOTTMAN, KENNETH ROGER	7960 BAR DU LN - SACRAMENTO CA 95828
12- 80	HOUCK, BYRON SIMON	D. JUNE 17, 1969 SANTA CRUZ, CALIF.
70- 61	HOUGH, CHARLES OLIVER	2266 SHADE TREE CIR - BREA CA 92621
47- 44	HOUK, RALPH GEORGE 'MAJOR'	2941 NE 23RD CT - POMPANO BEACH FL 33062
50- 36	HOUSE, HENRY FRANKLIN 'FRANK'	2570 ACTON RD #105 - BIRMINGHAM AL 35243
67- 50	HOUSE, PATRICK LORY	4205 GREEN MEADOWS DR - MERIDIAN ID 83642

PITCHER   CHARLIE HUDSON   TEXAS RANGERS

71- 51	HOUSE, THOMAS ROSS	12794 VIA FELINO - DEL MAR CA 92014
13- 88	HOUSE, WILLARD EDWIN	D. NOVEMBER 16, 1923 KANSAS CITY, MO.
80- 56	HOUSEHOLDER, PAUL WESLEY	BOX 236 - NORTH MONMOUTH ME 04265
10- 73	HOUSER, BENJAMIN FRANKLIN	D. JANUARY 15, 1952 AUGUSTA, ME.
14- 91	HOUSER, JOSEPH WILLIAM	D. JANUARY 3, 1953 ORLANDO, FLA.
45- 49	HOUTTEMAN, ARTHUR JOSEPH	1755 W BUELL RD - LAKE ORION MI 48035
69- 82	HOVLEY, STEPHEN EUGENE	1400 MCANDREW RD #11 - OJAI CA 93023
18- 34	HOVLIK, EDWARD C.	D. MARCH 20, 1955 PAINESVILLE, O.
63- 59	HOWARD, BRUCE ERNEST	3114 BOUGAINVILLEA - SARASOTA FL 33579
12- 81	HOWARD, DAVID AUSTIN	D. JANUARY 26, 1956 DALLAS, TEX.
72- 50	HOWARD, DOUGLAS LYNN	OLD ADD: 352 SOUTH 1200 EAST - SALT LAKE CITY
18- 35	HOWARD, EARL NYCUM	D. APRIL 4, 1937 EVERETT, PA.
55- 59	HOWARD, ELSTON GENE	D. DECEMBER 14, 1980 NEW YORK, N. Y.
58- 46	HOWARD, FRANK OLIVER	560 ST MARYS BLVD - GREEN BAY WI 54301
79- 56	HOWARD, FRED IRVING	88 SCAMMAN ST - SOUTH PORTLAND ME 04106.
14- 92	HOWARD, IVAN CHESTER	D. MARCH 30, 1967 MEDFORD, ORE.
70- 62	HOWARD, LARRY RAYFORD	OLD ADD: 2201 BROOKHOLLOW - ABILENE TX 79605
46- 49	HOWARD, LEE VINCENT	570 S ROSEMEAD BLVD - PASADENA CA 91107
81- 58	HOWARD, MICHAEL FREDRIC	OLD ADD: 4981 46TH ST - SACRAMENTO CA 95820
73- 64	HOWARD, WILBUR LEON	OLD ADD: 12500 DUNLAP #423 - HOUSTON TX 77031
71- 52	HOWARTH, JAMES EUGENE	606 SANTINI ST - BILOXI MS 39530
74- 54	HOWE, ARTHUR HENRY	806 DAVIA - HOUSTON TX 77079
52- 52	HOWE, CALVIN EARL	1104 MAYBELLE NE - GRAND RAPIDS MI 49503
23- 65	HOWE, LESTER CURTIS	D. JULY 16, 1976 WOODMERE, N. Y.
80- 57	HOWE, STEVEN ROY	28844 GARNET HILL CT - AGOURA CA 91301
47- 45	HOWELL, HOMER ELLIOTT 'DIXIE'	216 STONEHENGE DR - LOUISVILLE KY 40207
85- 50	HOWELL, JACK ROBERT	OLD ADD: 5353 E. 22ND ST #405 - TUCSON AZ 85711
80- 58	HOWELL, JAY CANFIELD	2920 WASHINGTON ST - MIAMI FL 33133
84- 56	HOWELL, KENNETH	16845 PLAINVIEW - DETROIT MI 48219
40- 37	HOWELL, MILLARD FILLMORE 'DIXIE'	D. MARCH 18, 1960 HOLLYWOOD, FLA.
41- 47	HOWELL, MURRAY DONALD 'RED'	OCTOBER 1, 1950 GREENVILLE, S. C.
12- 82	HOWELL, ROLAND BOATNER	D. MARCH 31, 1973
74- 55	HOWELL, ROY LEE	9812 OSCAR CIR - FOUNTAIN VALLEY CA 92708
49- 38	HOWERTON, WILLIAM RAY	1430 BUCKINGHAM WAY - HAYWARD CA 94544
13- 89	HOWLEY, DANIEL PHILIP	D. MARCH 10, 1944 EAST WEYMOUTH, MASS.
61- 54	HOWSER, RICHARD DALTON	215 NE BAYVIEW ST - LEES SUMMIT MO 64063
52- 53	HOYLE, ROLAND EDISON 'TEX'	695 CHURCH ST - CARBONDALE PA 18407
79- 57	HOYT, DEWEY LAMARR	146 MIOT ST - COLUMBIA SC 29204
18- 36	HOYT, WAITE CHARLES	D. AUGUST 25, 1984 CINCINNATI, O.
70- 63	HRABOSKY, ALAN THOMAS	8800 PLEASANT HILL RD - LITHONIA GA 30058
81- 59	HRBEK, KENT ALAN	9109 4TH AVE S - BLOOMINGTON MN 55420
68- 42	HRINIAK, WALTER JOHN	44 BARNSDALE RD - NATICK MA 01762
78- 59	HUBBARD, GLENN DEE	712 WEST 24TH ST - OGDEN UT 84401
28- 59	HUBBELL, CARL OWEN	SUNCREST APT #8,130 N LESEUER #1-MESA AZ83205
19- 43	HUBBELL, WILBERT WILLIAM 'BILL'	D. AUGUST 3, 1980 LAKEWOOD, CO.
61- 55	HUBBS, KENNETH DOUGLASS	D. FEBRUARY 15, 1964 UTAH LAKE, UTAH
20- 56	HUBER, CLARENCE BILL	D. FEBRUARY 22, 1965 LAREDO, TEX.
39- 52	HUBER, OTTO	225 MIDLAND AVE - GARFIELD NJ 07026
35- 51	HUCKLEBERRY, EARL EUGENE	RR 2-MAUD OK 74854
83- 74	HUDGENS, DAVID MARK	OLD ADD: 735 EAST APACHE #22 - TEMPE AZ 85257
23- 66	HUDGENS, JAMES PRICE	D. AUGUST 26, 1955 ST. LOUIS, MO.
84- 57	HUDLER, REX ALLEN	503 EAST MENLO - FRESNO CA 93710
26- 39	HUDLIN, GEORGE WILLIS	14 BETSEY LN - LITTLE ROCK AR 72205
72- 51	HUDSON, CHARLES	RR 5 BOX 50 - COALGATE OK 74538
83- 75	HUDSON, CHARLES LYNN	2124 HEATHER GLEN - DALLAS TX 75232
52- 54	HUDSON, HAL CAMPBELL	15 FARMER ST - NEWNAN GA 30263
69- 83	HUDSON, JESSIE JAMES	1101 ELOISE - MANSFIELD LA 71052
36- 40	HUDSON, JOHN WILSON	D. NOVEMBER 7, 1970 BRYAN, TEX.
74- 56	HUDSON, REX HAUGHTON	1604 WEST DENGAR - MIDLAND TX 79701
40- 38	HUDSON, SIDNEY CHARLES	1309 WESTWOOD DR - WACO TX 76710
14- 93	HUENKE, ALBERT A.	D. SEPTEMBER 20, 1974 SAINT MARYS, O.
37- 53	HUFFMAN, BENJAMIN FRANKLIN	2 CEDAR LN-LURAY VA 22835
79- 58	HUFFMAN, PHILLIP LEE	334 CALADIUM ST - LAKE JACKSON TX 77566
74- 57	HUGHES, JAMES MICHAEL	7526 EL MANOR AVE - LOS ANGELES CA 90045
52- 55	HUGHES, JAMES ROBERT	4521 W 83RD ST - CHICAGO IL 60652
66- 46	HUGHES, RICHARD HENRY	BOX 598 - STEPHENS AR 71764
35- 52	HUGHES, ROY JOHN	4730 BRANDT PIKE-DAYTON OH 45424
70- 64	HUGHES, TERRY WAYNE	432 PIERPONT AVE EXT - SPARTANBURG SC 29303
59- 39	HUGHES, THOMAS EDWARD	OLD ADD: 5921 SOUTHCREST ST - HOUSTON TX
30- 36	HUGHES, THOMAS FRANKLIN	790 19TH ST - BEAUMONT TX 77706
41- 48	HUGHES, THOMAS OWEN	RR 4-MOUNTAINTOP PA 18707
14- 94	HUGHES, VERNON ALEXANDER	D. SEPTEMBER 26, 1961 SEWICKLEY, PA.
21- 46	HUGHES, WILLIAM NESBERT	D. FEBRUARY 25, 1963 BIRMINGHAM, ALA.
41- 49	HUGHSON, CECIL CARLTON 'TEX'	RR 2 BOX 343 - SAN MARCOS TX 78666

15- 71 HUHN, EMIL HUGO	D. SEPTEMBER 5, 1925 CAMDEN, S.C.
83- 76 HUISMAN, MARK LAWRENCE	1711 F STREET - SCHUYLER NE 68661
83- 77 HULETT, TIMOTHY CRAIG	OLD ADD: 2018 LINDBERG BLVD - SPRINGFIELD IL 62704
22- 59 HULIHAN, HARRY JOSEPH	D. SEPTEMBER 11, 1980 RUTLAND, VT.
23- 67 HULVEY, JAMES HENSEL 'HANK'	D. APRIL 9, 1982 MOUNT SIDNEY, VA.
77- 70 HUME, THOMAS HUBERT	1803 W 7TH ST - PALMETTO FL 33561
11- 76 HUMPHREY, ALBERT	D. MAY 13, 1961 ASHTABULA, O.
38- 40 HUMPHREY, BYRON WILLIAM 'BILL'	3248 SOUTH CLAY - SPRINGFIELD MO 65807
71- 53 HUMPHREY, TERRYAL GENE	21 ENSUENO WEST - IRVINE CA 92701
62- 58 HUMPHREYS, ROBERT WILIIAM	ATH DEPT, VIRGINIA TECH-BLACKSBURG VA 24061
10- 74 HUMPHRIES, ALBERT	D. SEPTEMBER 21, 1945 ORLANDO, FLA.
38- 41 HUMPHRIES, JOHN WILLIAM	D. JUNE 24, 1965 NEW ORLEANS, LA.
64- 49 HUNDLEY, CECIL RANDOLPH 'RANDY'	122 E FOREST LN - PALATINE IL 60067
22- 60 HUNGLING, BERNARD HERMAN	D. MARCH 30, 1968 DAYTON, O.
26- 40 HUNNEFIELD, WILLIAM FENTON	D. AUGUST 28, 1976 NANTUCKET, MASS.
10- 75 HUNT, BENJAMIN FRANKLIN	OLD ADD: 730 K ST - SACRAMENTO CA
85- 51 HUNT, JAMES RANDALL 'RANDY'	117 DESTIN ST - MONTGOMERY AL 36110
59- 40 HUNT, KENNETH LAWRENCE	1464 W 170TH ST - GARDENA CA 90247
61- 56 HUNT, KENNETH RAYMOND	268 EAST 300 NORTH - MORGAN UT 84050
31- 41 HUNT, OLIVER JOEL	D. JULY 24, 1978 TEAGUE, TEXAS
63- 60 HUNT, RONALD KENNETH	2806 JACKSON RD - WENTZVILLE MO 63385
33- 28 HUNTER, EDISON FRANKLIN	D. MARCH 14, 1967 COLERAIN TWP., O.
11- 77 HUNTER, FREDERICK CREIGHTON 'NEWT'	D. OCTOBER 26, 1963 COLUMBUS, O.
53- 35 HUNTER, GORDON WILLIAM 'BILLY'	104 E SEMINARY AVE - LUTHERVILLE MD 21093
71- 54 HUNTER, HAROLD JAMES 'BUDDY'	5407 S 15TH ST - OMAHA NE 68107
16- 44 HUNTER, HERBERT HARRISON	D. JULY 26, 1970 ORLANDO, FLA.
65- 48 HUNTER, JAMES AUGUSTUS 'CATFISH'	RR ONE BOX 895 - HERTFORD NC 27944
62- 59 HUNTER, WILLARD MITCHELL	2562 POPPLETON AVE - OMAHA NE 68105
12- 83 HUNTER, WILLIAM ELLSWORTH	D. APRIL 10, 1934 BUFFALO, N.Y.
67- 51 HUNTZ, STEPHEN MICHAEL	4425 FAIRVIEW PKWY - CLEVELAND OH 44126
23- 68 HUNTZINGER, WALTER HENRY	D. AUGUST 11, 1981 UPPER DARBY, PA.
83- 78 HUPPERT, DAVID BLAINE	OLD ADD: 7524 BRADLEY DR - BUENA PARK CA 90620
54- 46 HURD, THOMAS CARR	D. SEPTEMBER 5, 1982 WATERLOO, IOWA
77- 71 HURDLE, CLINTON MERRICK	515 MARGARET ST - MERRITT ISLAND FL 32952
80- 59 HURST, BRUCE VEE	539 CHURCHILL DR - ST. GEORGE UT 84770

FRED HUTCHINSON
Cincinnati Reds

HERB HUTSON

28- 50 HURST, FRANK O'DONNELL 'DON'	D. DECEMBER 6, 1952 LOS ANGELES, CAL.
25- 52 HUSTA, CARL LAWRENCE	D. NOVEMBER 6, 1951 KINGSTON, N. Y.
37- 54 HUSTON, WARREN LLEWELLYN	29 ROBINWOOD RD - BUZZARDS BAY MA 02532
33- 27 HUTCHESON, JOSEPH JOHNSON	2400 BELL AVE - DENTON TX 76201
40- 39 HUTCHINGS, JOHN RICHARD JOSEPH	D. APRIL 27, 1963 INDIANAPOLIS, IND.
39- 56 HUTCHINSON, FREDERICK CHARLES	D. NOVEMBER 12, 1964 BRADENTON, FLA.
33- 28 HUTCHINSON, IRA KENDALL	D. AUGUST 21, 1973 CHICAGO, ILL.
74- 58 HUTSON, GEORGE HERBERT	7203 WEST SUGARTREE CT - SAVANNAH GA 31410
25- 53 HUTSON, ROY LEE	D. MAY 20, 1957 LAMESA, CAL.
70- 65 HUTTO, JAMES NEAMON	SILVER STADIUM - ROCHESTER NY 14621
66- 47 HUTTON, THOMAS GEORGE	1713 LYNDON ST - SOUTH PASADENA CA 91030
55- 60 HYDE, RICHARD ELDE	1506 CAMBRIDGE - CHAMPAIGN IL 61820
73- 65 IGNASIAK, GARY RAYMOND	9656 SPRINGBORN DR - ANCHORVILLE MI 48004
13- 90 IMLAY, HARRY MILLER 'DOC'	D. OCTOBER 7, 1948 BORDENTOWN, N.J.
14- 95 INGERSOLL, ROBERT RANDOLPH	D. JANUARY 13, 1927 MINNEAPOLIS, MINN.
11- 78 INGERTON, WILLIAM JOHN 'SCOTTY'	D. JUNE 15, 1956 CLEVELAND, O.
29- 53 INGRAM, MELVIN DAVID	D. OCTOBER 28, 1979 MEDFORD, ORE.
77- 72 IORG, DANE CHARLES	730 EAST 950 NORTH - OREM UT 84057
78- 60 IORG, GARTH RAY	515 CALIFORNIA ST - ARCATA CA 95521
41- 50 IOTT, CLARENCE EUGENE 'HOOKS'	D. AUGUST 17, 1980 ST. PETERSBURG, FLA.
14- 96 IRELAN, HAROLD	D. JULY 16, 1944 CARMEL, IND.
81- 60 IRELAND, TIMOTHY NEAL	20932 TIMES AVE - HAYWARD CA 94541
49- 39 IRVIN, MONFORD MERRILL 'MONTE'	104 SYCAMORE CIR - HOMOSASSA FL 32646
12- 84 IRVIN, WILLIAM EDWARD	D. FEBRUARY 18, 1916 PHILADELPHIA, PA.
38- 42 IRWIN, THOMAS ANDREW	508 50TH ST-ALTOONA PA 16602
21- 47 IRWIN, WALTER KINGSLEY	D. AUGUST 18, 1976 SPRING LAKE, MICH.
80- 60 ISALES, ORLANDO	OLD ADD: 1171 16TH SE CAPARRA TER - HATO REY PR 00921
71- 55 IVIE, MICHAEL WILSON	534 MIDLAND PARK DR - STONE MOUNTAIN GA 30083
67- 52 IZQUIERDO, ENRIQUE ROBERTO 'HANK'	6011 SW 97TH AVE - MIAMI FL 33173
53- 36 JABLONSKI, RAYMOND LEO	4457 S SACRAMENTO AVE - CHICAGO IL 60632
59- 41 JACKSON, ALVIN NEIL	ONE SAINT MARKS PL - DIX HILLS NY 11746
15- 72 JACKSON, CHARLES HERBERT	D. MAY 27, 1968 RATFORD, VA.
83- 79 JACKSON, DANNY LYNN	31 NEWARK #C - AURORA CO 80012
78- 61 JACKSON, DARRELL PRESTON	1310 JARVIS AVE - LOS ANGELES CA 90061
85- 52 JACKSON, DARRIN JAY	11238 HANNUM AVE - CULVER CITY CA 90230
11- 79 JACKSON, GEORGE CHRISTOPHER	D. NOVEMBER 25, 1972 CLEBURNE, TEX.
65- 49 JACKSON, GRANT DWIGHT	212 MESA CIRCLE - UPPER SAINT CLAIR PA 15241
33- 29 JACKSON, JOHN LEWIS	D. OCTOBER 24, 1956 SOMERS POINT, N. J.

55- 61	JACKSON, LAWRENCE CURTIS	1661 SHORELINE DR #110 - BOISE ID 83706
58- 47	JACKSON, LOUIS CLARENCE	D. MAY 27, 1969 TOKYO, JAPAN
70- 66	JACKSON, MICHAEL WARREN	626 N. 13TH ST - HUMBOLDT TN 38343
50- 37	JACKSON, RANSOM JOSEPH 'RANDY'	250 HUNNICUT DR - ATHENS GA 30601
67- 53	JACKSON, REGINALD MARTINEZ	22 YANKEE HILL - OAKLAND CA 94616
63- 61	JACKSON, ROLAND THOMAS 'SONNY'	3377 BOBOLINK DR - ATLANTA GA 30311
54- 47	JACKSON, RONALD ALLEN	2828 SPRINGBROOK DR - KALAMAZOO MI 49004
75- 55	JACKSON, RONNIE D	2944 PEMBROKE CT - FULLERTON CA 92631
77- 73	JACKSON, ROY LEE	711 DOGWOOD AVE - OPELIKA AL 36801
22- 61	JACKSON, TRAVIS CALVIN	101 SOUTH OLIVE ST - WALDO AR 71770
14- 97	JACKSON, WILLIAM RILEY	D. SEPTEMBER 26, 1958 PEORIA, ILL.
48- 48	JACOBS, ANTHONY ROBERT	D. DECEMBER 21, 1980 NASHVILLE, TENN.
39- 57	JACOBS, ARTHUR EVAN	D. JUNE 8, 1967 INGLEWOOD, CAL.
54- 48	JACOBS, FORREST VANDERGRIFT 'SPOOK'	BOX 66 - MILFORD DE 19963
60- 49	JACOBS, LAMAR GARY 'JAKE'	BOX 340 - CANFIELD OH 44406
37- 55	JACOBS, NEWTON SMITH 'BUCKY'	1437 GREYCOURT AVE-RICHMOND VA 23227
18- 37	JACOBS, OTTO ALBERT	D. NOVEMBER 19, 1955 CHICAGO, ILL.
28- 51	JACOBS, RAYMOND F.	D. APRIL 5, 1952 LOS ANGELES, CAL.
14- 98	JACOBS, WILLIAM ELMER	D. FEBRUARY 10, 1958 SALEM , MO.
15- 73	JACOBSON, MERWIN JOHN WILLIAM	D. JANUARY 13, 1978 BALTIMORE, MD.
15- 74	JACOBSON, WILLIAM CHESTER 'BABY DOLL'	D. JANUARY 16, 1977 ORION, ILL.
18- 38	JACOBUS, STUART LOUIS 'LARRY'	D. AUGUST 19, 1965 NORTH COLLEGE HILL, OHIO
81- 61	JACOBY, BROOK WALLACE	2383 SCOTER AVE - VENTURA CA 93003
71- 56	JACQUEZ, PATRICK THOMAS	8351 COLONIAL - STOCKTON CA 95209
64- 50	JAECKEL, PAUL HENRY	250 S ROSE DR #141 - PLACENTIA CA 92690
20- 57	JAEGER, JOSEPH PETER	D. DECEMBER 13, 1963 HAMPTON, IA.
25- 54	JAHN, ARTHUR CHARLES	D. JANUARY 9, 1948 LITTLE ROCK, ARK.
36- 41	JAKUCKI, SIGMUND	D. MAY 28, 1979 GALVESTON, TEXAS

JESSE JEFFERSON

24- 54	JAMERSON, CHARLEY DEWEY	D. AUGUST 4, 1980 MOCKSVILLE, N. C.
75- 56	JAMES, ARTHUR	4531 GARLAND AVE - DETROIT MI 48214
60- 50	JAMES, CHARLES WESLEY	104 COLLIER ST - FULTON MO 65221
68- 43	JAMES, CLEO JOEL	6020 KITTYHAWK DR - RIVERSIDE CA 92504
83- 80	JAMES, DION	804 NINTH AVENUE - SACRAMENTO CA 95818
68- 44	JAMES, JEFFREY LYNN	38310 UPPER CAMP CREEK RD - SPRINGFIELD OR 97478
58- 48	JAMES, JOHN PHILLIP	6037 E LARKSPUR - SCOTTSDALE AZ 85254
77- 74	JAMES, PHILIP ROBERT 'SKIP'	7716 W. 72ND TER - OVERLAND PARK KS 66204
67- 54	JAMES, RICHARD LEE	2358 FOXWORTH DR - PANAMA CITY FL 32405
29- 54	JAMES, ROBERT BYRNE 'BERNIE'	8425 AHERN #407 - SAN ANTONIO TX 78216
78- 62	JAMES, ROBERT HARVEY	7838 KYLE - SUNLAND CA 91040
12- 85	JAMES, WILLIAM A. 'LEFTY'	D. MAY 3, 1933 PORTSMOUTH, O.
11- 80	JAMES, WILLIAM HENRY	D. MAY 24, 1942 VENICE, CALIF.
13- 91	JAMES, WILLIAM LAWRENCE	D. MARCH 10, 1971 OROVILLE, CALIF.
15- 75	JAMIESON, CHARLES DEVINE	D. OCTOBER 27, 1969 PATERSON, N.J.
70- 67	JANESKI, GERALD JOSEPH	317 N MISSION DR - SAN GABRIEL CA 91711
53- 37	JANOWICZ, VICTOR FELIX	1966 JERVIS RD - COLUMBUS OH 43221
47- 46	JANSEN, LAWRENCE JOSEPH	RR 2 BOX 413A - FOREST GROVE OR 97116
10- 76	JANSEN, RAYMOND WILLIAM	D. MARCH 19, 1934 ST. LOUIS, MO.
12- 86	JANTZEN, WALTER C. 'HEINIE'	D. APRIL 1, 1948 HINES, ILL.
11- 81	JANVRIN, HAROLD CHANDLER	D. MARCH 2, 1962 BOSTON, MASS.
44- 63	JARVIS, LEROY GILBERT	2605 NORTH HUDSON - OKLAHOMA CITY OK 73103
69- 84	JARVIS, RAYMOND ARNOLD	OLD ADD: 266 FRUITHILL AVE - NORTH PROVIDENCE RI 02911
66- 48	JARVIS, ROBERT PATRICK 'PAT'	4425 E KINGSPOINTS CIR - DUNWOOD GA 30338
14- 99	JASPER, HARRY W. 'HI'	D. MAY 22, 1937 ST. LOUIS, MO.
65- 50	JASTER, LARRY EDWARD	1306 WHITEHOUSE DR-COLORADO SPRINGS CO 80904
72- 52	JATA, PAUL	35-25 34TH ST - LONG ISLAND CITY NY 11101
40- 40	JAVERY, ALVA WILLIAM	D. SEPTEMBER 13, 1977 WOODSTOCK, CONN.
76- 41	JAVIER, IGNACIO ALFREDO	BARRIO LIBRE #96 ING CON-SAN PEDRO DE MACORIS DOM. REP.
60- 51	JAVIER, MANUEL JULIAN	B/#12 URB. PINA - SAN FRANCISCO DE MACORIS DOM REP
84- 58	JAVIER, STANLEY JULIAN ANTONIO	B/#12 URB. PINA-SAN FRANCISCO DE MACORIS DOMINICAN REP.
53- 38	JAY, JOSEPH RICHARD	OLD ADD: 3660 STATE ROAD 580 - CLEARWATER FL 33519
21- 48	JEANES, ERNEST LEE 'TEX'	D. APRIL 5, 1973 LONGVIEW, TEX.
36- 42	JEFFCOAT, GEORGE EDWARD	D. OCTOBER 13, 1978 LEESVILLE, S. C.
48- 49	JEFFCOAT, HAROLD BENTLEY	4016 WISCONSIN AVE - TAMPA FL 33616
83- 81	JEFFCOAT, JAMES MICHAEL 'MIKE'	RURAL ROUTE 1 BOX 289 - PINE BLUFF AR 71603
73- 66	JEFFERSON, JESSE HARRISON	1421 RAILROAD AVE - MIDLOTHIAN VA 23113
30- 37	JEFFRIES, IRVINE FRANKLIN	D. JUNE 8, 1982 LOUISVILLE, KY.
41- 51	JELINCICH, FRANK ANTHONY	526 PINEWOOD CT - LOS GATOS CA 95030
83- 82	JELTZ, LARRY STEVEN 'STEVE'	615 WEST 28TH PLACE - LAWRENCE KS 66044
65- 51	JENKINS, FERGUSON ARTHUR	BOX 275 - BLENHEIM ONTARIO CAN.
22- 62	JENKINS, JOHN ROBERT	D. AUGUST 3, 1968 COLUMBIA, MO.
14-100	JENKINS, JOSEPH DANIEL	D. JUNE 21, 1974 FRESNO, CALIF.
25- 55	JENKINS, THOMAS GRIFFIN	D. MAY 3, 1979 WEYMOUTH, MASS.
62- 60	JENKINS, WARREN WASHINGTON 'JACK'	3810 OBISPO - TAMPA FL 33609

```
51- 44  JENNINGS, WILLIAM LEE              7065 FOXCROFT DR - AFFTON MO 63123
50- 38  JENSEN, JACK EUGENE                D. JULY 14, 1982 CHARLOTTESVILLE, VA.
12- 87  JENSEN, WILLIAM CHRISTIAN          D. MARCH 27, 1917 PHILADELPHIA, PA.
29- 55  JESSEE, DANIEL EDWARD              D. APRIL 30, 1970 VENICE, FLA.
69- 85  JESTADT, GARRY ARTHUR              825 PARNELL PL - SUNNYVALE CA 94087
52- 56  JESTER, VIRGIL MILTON              8130 RALEIGH PL - WESTMINSTER CO 80030
69- 86  JETER, JOHN                        OLD ADD: ROBSON - SHREVEPORT LA 71109
50- 39  JETHROE, SAMUEL                    340 E 14TH ST - ERIE PA 16503
83- 83  JIMENEZ, ALFONSO 'HOUSTON'         OLD ADD: NAVOJOA MEXICO
64- 51  JIMENEZ, FELIX ELVIO               SIMON BOLIVAR #24 - SAN PEDRO DE MACORIS DOM. REP.
62- 61  JIMENEZ, MANUEL EMILIO             24 SIMON BOLIVAR - SAN PEDRO DE MACORIS DOM. REP.
74- 59  JIMINEZ, JUAN ANTONIO              CALLE 9,CASA 1N EL ENSUENO - SANTIAGO DOMINICAN REP.
63- 62  JOHN, THOMAS EDWARD                3133 N. 16TH ST - TERRE HAUTE IN 47804
26- 41  JOHNS, AUGUSTUS FRANCIS            D. SEPTEMBER 12, 1975 SAN ANTONIO, TEX.
15- 76  JOHNS, WILLIAM R. 'PETE'           D. AUGUST 9, 1964 CLEVELAND, O.
14-101  JOHNSON, ADAM RANKIN SR            D. JULY 2, 1972 WILLIAMSPORT, PA.
41- 52  JOHNSON, ADAM RANKIN JR            1306 WARREN AVE-WILLIAMSPORT PA 17706
64- 52  JOHNSON, ALEXANDER                 OLD ADD: 19474 BIRWOOD - DETROIT MI 48221
81- 62  JOHNSON, ANTHONY CLAIR             4446 JANSSEN DR - MEMPHIS TN 38128
27- 47  JOHNSON, ARTHUR GILBERT            D. JUNE 7, 1982 SARASOTA, FLA.
40- 41  JOHNSON, ARTHUR HENRY              23 HEMLOCK DR-HOLDEN MA 01520
59- 42  JOHNSON, BENJAMIN FRANKLIN         112 LOCKSLEY DR - GREENWOOD SC 29646
81- 63  JOHNSON, BOBBY EARL                OLD ADD: 3432 SOUTH LOOP 12 - DALLAS TX 75224
46- 50  JOHNSON, CHESTER LILLIS            D. APRIL 10, 1983 SEATTLE, WASH.
69- 87  JOHNSON, CLAIR BARTH 'BART'        7519 SUSSEX CREEK DR #109 - DARIEN IL 60559
72- 53  JOHNSON, CLIFFORD                  318 GLEN OAK - SAN ANTONIO TX 78220
53- 39  JOHNSON, CLIFFORD 'CONNIE'         1900 E 54TH ST - KANSAS CITY MO 64130
52- 57  JOHNSON, DARRELL DEAN              913 ELM DR - RODEO CA 94572
65- 52  JOHNSON, DAVID ALLEN               4245 BEAR GULLEY RD - WINTER PARK FL 32789
74- 60  JOHNSON, DAVID CHARLES             2402 MARCHALL ST - ABILENE TX 79605
60- 52  JOHNSON, DERON ROGER               13847 TWIN PEAKS RD - POWAY CA 92064
47- 47  JOHNSON, DONALD ROY                1509 NE 10TH AVE #207 - PORTLAND OR 97232
43- 66  JOHNSON, DONALD SPORE              580 BROOKS - LAGUNA BEACH CA 92651
40- 42  JOHNSON, EARL DOUGLAS              9541 25TH AVE NW-SEATTLE WA 98107
20- 58  JOHNSON, EDWIN CYRIL               D. JULY 3, 1975 MORGANFIELD, KY.
12- 88  JOHNSON, ELLIS WATT                D. JANUARY 14, 1965 MINNEAPOLIS, MINN.
14-102  JOHNSON, ELMER ELLSWORTH           D. OCTOBER 31, 1966 HOLLYWOOD, FLA.
12- 89  JOHNSON, ERNEST RUDOLPH            D. MAY 1, 1952 MONROVIA, CALIF.
50- 40  JOHNSON, ERNEST THORWALD           500 DORRIS RD - ALPHARETTA GA 30201
66- 49  JOHNSON, FRANK HERBERT             568 N CENTER ST - MESA AZ 85201
22- 63  JOHNSON, FREDERICK EDWARD          D. JUNE 14, 1973 KERRVILLE, TEX.
13- 92  JOHNSON, GEORGE HOWARD 'CHIEF'     D. JUNE 12, 1922 DES MOINES, IA.
25- 56  JOHNSON, HENRY WARD                D. AUGUST 20, 1982 BRADENTON, FLA.
82- 63  JOHNSON, HOWARD MICHAEL            141-17 11TH AVE - WHITESTON NY 11357
70- 68  JOHNSON, JAMES BRIAN               1459 MADISON ST - MUSKEGON MI 49442
68- 45  JOHNSON, JERRY MICHAEL             4566 DEL MAR AVE - SAN DIEGO CA 92107
44- 64  JOHNSON, JOHN CLIFFORD             BOX 1271 - VALRICO FL 33594
78- 63  JOHNSON, JOHN HENRY                7578 YOUNG CIR - RENO NV 89511
85- 53  JOHNSON, JOSEPH RICHARD            14 EVERGREEN RD - PLAINVILLE MA 02762
58- 49  JOHNSON, KENNETH TRAVIS            121 MYRTLEWOOD DR - PINEVILLE LA 71360
47- 48  JOHNSON, KENNETH WANDERSEE         326 BROOKFIELD - WICHITA KS 67206
74- 61  JOHNSON, LAMAR                     6010 AMBERWOOD CT - ARLINGTON TX 76016
72- 54  JOHNSON, LARRY DOBY                3115 E 98TH ST - CLEVELAND OH 44104
34- 50  JOHNSON, LLOYD WILLIAM             D. OCTOBER 8, 1980 STOCKTON, CALIF.
60- 53  JOHNSON, LOUIS BROWN               5830 GREEN VALLEY CIR - CULVER CITY CA 90230
74- 62  JOHNSON, MICHAEL NORTON            OLD ADD: RR 1 - FARIBAULT MN 55021
11- 82  JOHNSON, OTIS L.                   D. NOVEMBER 9, 1915 JOHNSON CITY, N. Y.
20-136  JOHNSON, PAUL OSCAR                D. FEBRUARY 14, 1973 MCALLEN, TEX.
82- 64  JOHNSON, RANDALL GLENN             852 W 11TH AVE - ESCONDIDO CA 92025
80- 61  JOHNSON, RANDALL STUART            40 W 64TH ST - HIALEAH FL 33012
58- 50  JOHNSON, RICHARD ALLAN             808-B N BEELINE - PAYSON AZ 85541
69- 88  JOHNSON, ROBERT DALE               12862 MALENA DR - SANTA ANA CA 92705
33- 30  JOHNSON, ROBERT LEE                D. JULY 6, 1982 TACOMA, WASH.
60- 54  JOHNSON, ROBERT WALLACE            1474 BARCLAY ST - ST PAUL MN 55106
82- 65  JOHNSON, RONALD DAVID              11371 KATHY LN - GARDEN GROVE CA 92640
29- 56  JOHNSON, ROY CLEVELAND             D. SEPTEMBER 10, 1973 TACOMA, WASH.
82- 66  JOHNSON, ROY EDWARD                902 N ST. LOUIS - CHICAGO IL 60651
18- 40  JOHNSON, ROY J. 'HARDROCK'         D. JANUARY 10, 1986 SCOTTSDALE, ARIZ.
16- 45  JOHNSON, RUSSELL CONWELL 'JING'    D. DECEMBER 6, 1950 POTTSTOWN, PA.
28- 52  JOHNSON, SILAS KENNETH             BOX 291 - SHERIDAN IL 60551
60- 55  JOHNSON, STANLEY LUCIUS            56 MORNINGSIDE DR - DALY CITY CA 94015
22- 64  JOHNSON, SYLVESTER                 D. FEBRUARY 20, 1985 PORTLAND, ORE.
73- 67  JOHNSON, TIMOTHY EVALD             3016 HAMPSHIRE DR - SACRAMENTO CA 95821
```

74- 63	JOHNSON, TIMOTHY RAYMOND	2117 WORRINGTON ST - SARASOTA FL 33581
44- 65	JOHNSON, VICTOR OSCAR	1515 DRURY AVE - EAU CLAIRE WI 54701
81- 64	JOHNSON, WALLACE DARNELL	2512 ADAMS ST - GARY IN 46407
83- 84	JOHNSON, WILLIAM CHARLES	OLD ADD: 1701 N. LINCOLN ST - WILMINGTON DE 19806
16- 46	JOHNSON, WILLIAM LAWRENCE	D. NOVEMBER 5, 1950 LOS ANGELES, CALIF.
43- 67	JOHNSON, WILLIAM RUSSEL	2903 LAKE FOREST DR-AUGUSTA GA 30904
79- 59	JOHNSTON, GREGORY BERNARD	20528 BUCKLAND AVE - WALNUT CA 91789
11- 83	JOHNSTON, JAMES HARLE	D. FEBRUARY 14, 1967 CHATTANOOGA, TENN.
13- 93	JOHNSTON, JOHN THOMAS	D. MARCH 7, 1940 SAN DIEGO, CALIF.
64- 53	JOHNSTON, REX DAVID	15117 ILLINOIS ST - PARAMOUNT CA 90723
24- 55	JOHNSTON, WILFRED IVEY 'FRED'	D. JULY 14, 1959 TYLER, TEX.
66- 50	JOHNSTONE, JOHN WILLIAM 'JAY'	1365 ST ALBANS - SAN MARINO CA 91108
34- 51	JOINER, ROY MERRILL	BOX 153 - VINA CA 96092
54- 49	JOK, STANLEY EDWARD	D. MARCH 6, 1972 BUFFALO, N. Y.
30- 38	JOLLEY, SMEAD POWELL	2020 SANTA CLARA AVE #402 - ALAMEDA CA 94501
53- 40	JOLLY, DAVID	D. MAY 27, 1963 DURHAM, N. C.
83- 85	JONES, ALFORNIA	RURAL ROUTE 1 BOX 63 - CHARLESTON MS 38921
32- 38	JONES, ARTHUR LENOX	D. NOVEMBER 25, 1980 COLUMBIA, S. C.
16- 47	JONES, CARROLL ELMER 'DEACON'	D. DECEMBER 28, 1952 PITTSBURG, KAN.
85- 54	JONES, CHRISTOPHER DALE	1821 WESTWARD HO CIR - EL CAJON CA 92021
67- 55	JONES, CLARENCE WOODROW	OLD ADD: 214 HIGH - ZANESVILLE OH 43701
63- 63	JONES, CLEON JOSEPH	751 EDWARD ST - MOBILE AL 36610
28- 53	JONES, COBURN DYAS	D. JUNE 3, 1969 DENVER, COLO.
41- 53	JONES, DALE ELDON	D. NOVEMBER 8, 1980 ORLANDO, FLA.
79- 60	JONES, DARRYL LEE	BOX 175 - HARMONSBURG PA 16422
26- 42	JONES, DECATUR POINDEXTER 'DICK'	125 MCAULEY DR - VICKSBURG MS 39180
82- 67	JONES, DOUGLAS REID	3107 FAITH - WEST COVINA CA 91792
45- 50	JONES, EARL LESLIE	4054 MONTECITO AVE - FRESNO CA 93702
70- 69	JONES, GARY HOWELL	475 S. WESTRIDGE CIR - ANAHEIM HILLS CA 92807
54- 50	JONES, GORDON BASSETT	53 MOONLIT CIR - SACRAMENTO CA 95831
62- 62	JONES, GROVER WILLIAM 'DEACON'	1015 GOLDFINCH - SUGARLAND TX 77478
61- 57	JONES, HAROLD MARION	4125 PALMYRA RD - LOS ANGELES CA 90008
21- 49	JONES, HOWARD	D. JULY 15, 1972 JEANNETTE, PA.
64- 54	JONES, JAMES DALTON	6914 OAK CLUSTER DR - GREENWELL SPRINGS LA 70739
41- 54	JONES, JAMES MURRELL 'JAKE'	BOX 156-EPPS LA 71237
83- 86	JONES, JEFFERY RAYMOND	311 WHITE HORSE PL - HADDON HEIGHTS NJ 08035
80- 62	JONES, JEFFREY ALLEN	15626 DRAKE - SOUTHGATE MI 48198
23- 69	JONES, JESSE F. 'BROADWAY'	D. SEPTEMBER 7, 1977 LEWES, DEL.
24- 56	JONES, JOHN JOSEPH 'BINKY'	D. MAY 13, 1961 ST. LOUIS, MO.
19- 44	JONES, JOHN PAUL	D. JUNE 5, 1980 RUSTON, LA.
23- 70	JONES, JOHN WILLIAM	D. NOVEMBER 3, 1956 BALTIMORE, MD.
24- 57	JONES, KENNETH FREDERICK	4 RIDGE ROAD - SIMSBURY CT 06070
79- 61	JONES, LYNN MORRIS	BOX 175 - HARMONSBURG PA 16422
61- 58	JONES, MACK	184 NATHAN RD - ATLANTA GA 30331
80- 63	JONES, MICHAEL CARL	6182 HILLVIEW CT - JACKSONVILLE FL 32210
40- 43	JONES, MORRIS E. 'RED'	D. JUNE 30, 1975 LINCOLN, NEB.
75- 57	JONES, ODELL	17800 LYSANDER DR - CARSON CA 90746
20- 59	JONES, PERCY LEE	OLD ADD: 606 CLERMONT AVE - DALLAS TX 75223
73- 68	JONES, RANDALL LEO	15358 MIDLAND RD - POWAY CA 92064
74- 64	JONES, ROBERT OLIVER	2107 ABEYTA CT - LOVELAND CO 80537
17- 36	JONES, ROBERT WALTER	D. AUGUST 30, 1964 SAN DIEGO, CAL.
84- 59	JONES, ROSS A.	5371 WEST 12TH AVE - HIALEAH FL 33012
76- 42	JONES, RUPPERT SANDERSON	P.O. BOX 1149 - POWAY CA 92064
51- 45	JONES, SAMUEL	D. NOVEMBER 5, 1971 MORGANTOWN, W. VA.
14-103	JONES, SAMUEL POND 'SAD SAM'	D. JULY 6, 1966 BARNESVILLE, O.
46- 51	JONES, SHELDON LESLIE	1700 N ELM #1E - GREENSBORO NC 27408
60- 56	JONES, SHERMAN JARVIS 'ROADBLOCK'	WYANDOTTE COUNTY POLICE DEPT. - KANSAS CITY KS 66101
67- 56	JONES, STEVEN HOWELL	8116 KINGSDALE DR - KNOXVILLE TN 37919
76- 43	JONES, THOMAS FREDERICK 'TIM'	4835 MANVILLE CIR - JACKSONVILLE FL 32210
77- 75	JONES, TIMOTHY BYRON	6204 GREENEYES WAY - ORANGEVALE CA 95662
46- 52	JONES, VERNAL LEROY 'NIPPY'	7322 ALCEDO CIR - SACRAMENTO CA 95823
11- 84	JONES, WILLIAM DENNIS	D. OCTOBER 10, 1946 BOSTON, MASS.
11- 85	JONES, WILLIAM RODERICK 'TEX'	D. FEBRUARY 26, 1938 WICHITA, KAN.
47- 49	JONES, WILLIE EDWARD	D. OCTOBER 18, 1983 CINCINNATI, O.
20- 60	JONNARD, CLARENCE JAMES 'BUBBER'	D. AUGUST 23, 1977 NEW YORK, N. Y.
21- 57	JONNARD, CLAUDE ALFRED	D. AUGUST 27, 1959 NASHVILLE, TENN.
36- 43	JOOST, EDWIN DAVID	245 BELGREEN PLACE - SANTA ROSA CA 95405
27- 48	JORDAN, BAXTER BYERLY 'BUCK'	2004-D LINCOLNTON RD - SALISBURY NC 28144
33- 31	JORDAN, JAMES WILLIAM	D. DECEMBER 4, 1957 CHARLOTTE, N. C.
53- 41	JORDAN, MILTON MIGNOT	57 LAKESHORE RD - LANSING NY 14881
51- 46	JORDAN, NILES CHAPMAN	1114 METCALF - SEDRO WOOLLEY WA 98284
12- 90	JORDAN, RAYMOND WILLIS 'RIP'	D. JUNE 5, 1960 MERIDEN, CONN.
44- 66	JORDAN, THOMAS JEFFERSON	BOX 148 - MOUNT ENTERPRISE TX 75681
29- 57	JORGENS, ARNDT LUDWIG 'ART'	D. MARCH 1, 1980 WILMETTE, ILL.
35- 53	JORGENS, ORVILLE EDWARD	129 S SPRUCE ST-WOOD DALE IL 60191
47- 50	JORGENSEN, JOHN DONALD 'SPIDER'	8267 KIRKWOOD CT - CUCAMONGA CA 91730
68- 46	JORGENSEN, MICHAEL	1604 LILLIAN AVE - ARLINGTON TX 76013
37- 56	JORGENSON, CARL 'PINKY'	119 MINNIE ST - SANTA CRUZ CA 95062
64- 55	JOSEPH, RICARDO EMELINDO	D. SEPTEMBER 8, 1979 SANTIAGO DOM REP
65- 53	JOSEPHSON, DUANE CHARLES	RR 1 BOX 58A - NEW HAMPTON IA 50659
69- 89	JOSHUA, VON EVERETT	1896 REDDING AVE - UPLAND CA 91786
16- 48	JOURDAN, THEODORE CHARLES	D. SEPTEMBER 23, 1961 NEW ORLEANS, LA.
62- 63	JOYCE, MICHAEL LEWIS	1609 WHITMAN LN - WHEATON IL 60187
65- 54	JOYCE, RICHARD EDWARD	20 HILLSIDE AVE - UPPER SADDLE RIVER NJ 07458
39- 58	JOYCE, ROBERT EMMETT	D. DECEMBER 10, 1981 SAN FRANCISCO, CALIF.
27- 49	JUDD, RALPH WESLEY	D. MAY 6, 1957 LAPEER, MICH.
41- 55	JUDD, THOMAS WILLIAM OSCAR	CATERBURY ST 64 - INGERSOLL ONTARIO CAN.
15- 77	JUDGE, JOSEPH IGNATIUS	D. MARCH 11, 1963 WASHINGTON, D.C.
40- 44	JUDNICH, WALTER FRANKLIN	D. JULY 12, 1971 GLENDALE, CAL.
48- 50	JUDSON, HOWARD KOLLS	12107 MCKINLEY - HEBRON IL 60034
35- 54	JUDY, LYLE LEROY	410 FLAGLER BLVD - SAINT AUGUSTINE FL 32084
39- 59	JUELICH, JOHN WALTER	D. DECEMBER 25, 1970 ST. LOUIS, MO.
40- 45	JUMONVILLE, GEORGE BENEDICT	5507 WILLIAM & MARY - MOBILE AL 36608
37- 57	JUNGELS, KENNETH PETER	D. SEPTEMBER 9, 1975 WEST BEND, WIS.
82- 68	JURAK, EDWARD JAMES	3650 S WALKER AVE - SAN PEDRO CA 90731
65- 55	JUREWICZ, MICHAEL ALLEN	17826 IXONIA AVE W - LAKEVILLE MN 55044
31- 42	JURGES, WILLIAM FREDERICK	7001 142ND AVE #74 - LARGO FL 33541

Curt Kaufman

31- 43	JURGES, WILLIAM FREDERICK	2048 BEL OMBRE CIR - LAKE WALES FL 33853
44- 67	JURISICH, ALVIN JOSEPH	D. NOVEMBER 3, 1981 NEW ORLEANS, LA.
44- 68	JUST, JOSEPH ERWIN	7708 W KANGAROO LAKE-BAILEYS HARBOR WI 54202
72- 55	JUTZE, ALFRED HENRY 'SKIP'	3395 ZEPHYR CT - WHEAT RIDGE CO 80033
14-104	JUUL, EARL HERBERT	D. JANUARY 4, 1942 CHICAGO, ILL.
11- 86	JUUL, HERBERT VICTOR	D. NOVEMBER 14, 1928 CHICAGO, ILL.
59- 43	KAAT, JAMES LEE	BOX 86 - GLEN MILLS PA 19342
10- 77	KADING, JOHN FREDERICK	D. JUNE 2, 1964 CHICAGO, ILL.
13- 94	KAFORA, FRANK JACOB 'JAKE'	D. MARCH 23, 1928 CHICAGO, ILL.
22- 65	KAHDOT, ISAAC LEONARD 'IKE'	2218 NW 42ND - OKLAHOMA CITY OK 73112
38- 43	KAHLE, ROBERT WAYNE	5311 GLASGOW CT-LOS ANGELES CA 90045
10- 78	KAHLER, GEORGE RANNELS	D. FEBRUARY 14, 1924 BATTLE CREEK, MICH.
30- 39	KAHN, OWEN EARLE	D. JANUARY 17, 1981 RICHMOND, VA.
80- 64	KAINER, DONALD WAYNE	10 DARNELL - CONROE TX 77301
11- 87	KAISER, ALFRED EDWARD	D. APRIL 11, 1969 CINCINNATI, O.
55- 62	KAISER, CLYDE DONALD 'DON'	2901 EAST 12TH - ADA OK 74820
85- 55	KAISER, JEFFREY PATRICK	15324 DUMAY - SOUTHGATE MI 48195
71- 57	KAISER, ROBERT THOMAS	272 VASSAR AVE - ELYRIA OH 44035
14-105	KAISERLING, GEORGE	D. MARCH 2, 1918 STEUBENVILLE, O.
37- 58	KALFASS, WILLIAM PHILIP	D. SEPTEMBER 8, 1968 BROOKLYN, N. Y.
40- 46	KALIN, FRANK BRUNO	D. JANUARY 12, 1975 WEIRTON, W. VA.
53- 42	KALINE, ALBERT WILLIAM	945 TIMBERLAKE DR - BLOOMFIELD HILLS MI 48013
18- 41	KALLIO, RUDOLPH	D. APRIL 6, 1979 NEWPORT, ORE.
23- 71	KAMM, WILLIAM EDWARD 'WILLIE'	2021 DEVEREUX DRIVE - BURLINGAME CA 94011
78- 64	KAMMEYER, ROBERT LYNN	4711 DEL RIO RD - SACRAMENTO CA 95822
24- 58	KAMP, ALPHONSE FRANCIS 'IKE'	D. FEBRUARY 26, 1955 BOSTON, MASS.
34- 52	KAMPOURIS, ALEX WILLIAM	2776 17TH ST - SACRAMENTO CA 95818
15- 78	KANE, FRANCIS THOMAS	D. DECEMBER 2, 1962 BROCKTON, MASS.
25- 57	KANE, JOHN FRANCIS	D. JULY 25, 1956 CHICAGO, ILL.
38- 44	KANE, THOMAS JOSEPH	D. NOVEMBER 26, 1973 CHICAGO, ILL.
62- 64	KANEHL, RODERICK EDWIN	617 EAST WILLIAM - WICHITA KS 67202
14-106	KANTLEHNER, ERVINE LESLIE	66-2 BARRANCE AVE - SANTA BARBARA CA 93109
36- 44	KARDOW, PAUL OTTO	D. APRIL 27, 1968 SAN ANTONIO, TEXAS
43- 68	KARL, ANTON ANDREW	RR 3, HOLLYWYLE PARK - NEW FAIRFIELD CT 06812
30- 40	KARLON, WILLIAM JOHN	D. DECEMBER 7, 1964 MONSON, MASS.
27- 50	KAROW, MARTIN GREGORY	RR 3 BOX 428 - BRYAN TX 77801
46- 53	KARPEL, HERBERT	6922 BABCOCK AVE - NORTH HOLLYWOOD CA 91605
20- 61	KARR, BENJAMIN JOYCE	D. DECEMBER 8, 1968 MEMPHIS, TENN.
15- 79	KARST, JOHN GOTTLIEB	D. MAY 21, 1976 CAPE MAY COURT HOUSE, N. J.
57- 35	KASKO, EDWARD MICHAEL	317 BURNWICK RD - RICHMOND VA 23227
52- 58	KATT, RAYMOND FREDERICK	711 RUDELOFF RD - SEGUIN TX 78155
44- 69	KATZ, ROBERT CLYDE	D. DECEMBER 14, 1962 ST. JOSEPH, MICH.
12- 91	KAUFF, BENJAMIN MICHAEL	D. NOVEMBER 17, 1961 COLUMBUS, O.
14-107	KAUFFMAN, HOWARD RICHARD 'DICK'	D. APRIL 17, 1948 LEWISBURG, PA.
21- 51	KAUFMAN, ANTHONY CHARLES	D. JUNE 4, 1982 ELGIN, ILL.
82- 69	KAUFMAN, CURT GERRARD	RR 3 BOX 33 - HARLAN IA 51537
14-108	KAVANAGH, CHARLES HUGH	D. SEPTEMBER 6, 1973 REEDSBURG, WIS.
14-109	KAVANAGH, LEO DANIEL	D. AUGUST 10, 1950 CHICAGO, ILL.
14-110	KAVANAGH, MARTIN JOSEPH	D. JULY 28, 1960 TAYLOR, MICH.
48- 51	KAZAK, EDWARD TERRANCE	802 NEWMAN DR - AUSTIN TX 78703
53- 43	KAZANSKI, THEODORE STANLEY	40008 CROSSWIND - NOVI MI 48050
68- 47	KEALEY, STEVEN WILLIAM	RR 1 BOX 6 - HILLSBORO KS 67063
61- 59	KEANE, JOHN JOSEPH	D. JANUARY 6, 1967 HOUSTON, TEX.
79- 62	KEARNEY, ROBERT HENRY	OLD ADD: 7839 GALLOP - SAN ANTONIO TX
24- 59	KEARNS, EDWARD PAUL 'TED'	D. DECEMBER 21, 1949 TRENTON, N. J.
42- 54	KEARSE, EDWARD PAUL	D. JULY 15, 1968 EUREKA, CALIF.
12- 92	KEATING, RAYMOND HERBERT	D. DECEMBER 28, 1963 SACRAMENTO, CALIF.
13- 95	KEATING, WALTER FRANCIS 'CHICK'	D. JULY 13, 1959 PHILADELPHIA, PA.
81- 65	KEATLEY, GREGORY STEVEN	120 LONGITUDE LN - LEXINGTON SC29072
22- 66	KECK, FRANK JOSEPH 'CACTUS'	D. FEBRUARY 6, 1981 ST. LOUIS, MO.
85- 56	KEEDY, CHARLES PATRICK 'PAT'	OLD ADD: RR 20 BOX 548 - BIRMINGHAM AL 35214
17- 37	KEEFE, DAVID EDWIN	D. FEBRUARY 4, 1978 KANSAS CITY, MO.
59- 44	KEEGAN, EDWARD CHARLES	BOX 71-A, HARRISONVILLE RD - MULLICA HILL NJ 08067
53- 44	KEEGAN, ROBERT CHARLES	101 SANDSTONE DR - ROCHESTER NY 14616
44- 70	KEELY, ROBERT WILLIAM	313 BRYN MAWR ISLAND - BRADENTON FL 33507
18- 42	KEEN, HOWARD VICTOR	D. DECEMBER 10, 1976 SALISBURY, MD.
11- 88	KEEN, WILLIAM BROWN	D. JULY 16, 1947 SOUTH POINT, O.
20- 62	KEENAN, JAMES WILLIAM	D. JUNE 5, 1980 SEMINOLE, FLA.
82- 70	KEENER, JEFFREY BRUCE	RR 3 BOX 150 - ALBION IL 62806
76- 44	KEENER, JOSEPH DONALD	STAR ROUTE 79 - ADELANTO CA 92301
25- 58	KEESEY, JAMES WARD	D. SEPTEMBER 5, 1951 BOISE, IDA.
80- 65	KEETON, RICKEY	3433 STATHEM AVE - CINCINNATI OH 45211
42- 55	KEHN, CHESTER LAURENCE	D. APRIL 5, 1984 SAN DIEGO, CALIF.
14-111	KEIFER, SHERMAN C. 'KATIE'	B. 1892

77

65- 56 KEKICH, MICHAEL DENNIS	OLD ADD: 15121 NE 84TH ST #182-REDMOND WA
11- 89 KELIHER, MAURICE MICHAEL	D. SEPTEMBER 7, 1930 WASHINGTON, D.C.
52- 59 KELL, EVERETT LEE 'SKEETER'	4918 STEVENS DR - PINE BLUFF AR 71605
43- 69 KELL, GEORGE CLYDE	BOX 158 - SWIFTON AR 72471
16- 49 KELLEHER, ALBERT ALOYSIUS 'DUKE'	D. SEPTEMBER 28, 1947 STATEN ISLAND, N. Y.
42- 56 KELLEHER, FRANCIS EUGENE	D. APRIL 13, 1979 STOCKTON, CALIF.
35- 55 KELLEHER, HAROLD JOSEPH	220 23RD ST - AVALON NJ 08202
12- 93 KELLEHER, JOHN PATRICK	D. AUGUST 21, 1960 BOSTON, MASS.
72- 56 KELLEHER, MICHAEL DENNIS	2429 ANACAPA ST - SANTA BARBARA CA 93105
39- 60 KELLER, CHARLES ERNEST	8238 YELLOW SPRING RD - FREDERICK MD 21701
49- 40 KELLER, HAROLD KEFAUVER	620 MELROSE - SEGUIN TX 78155
66- 51 KELLER, RONALD LEE	4280 ROLAND RD - INDIANAPOLIS IN 46208
53- 45 KELLERT, FRANK WILLIAM	D. NOVEMBER 19, 1976 OKLAHOMA CITY, OKLA.
23- 72 KELLETT, ALFRED HENRY	D. JULY 14, 1960 NEW YORK, N. Y.
34- 53 KELLETT, DONALD STAFFORD 'RED'	D. NOVEMBER 5, 1970 FT. LAUDERDALE, ALA.
25- 59 KELLEY, HARRY LEROY	D. MARCH 23, 1958 PARKIN, ARK.
64- 56 KELLEY, RICHARD ANTHONY	13630 ADDISON ST - SHERMAN OAKS CA 91423
64- 57 KELLEY, THOMAS HENRY	2933 FINCH DR - DANVILLE VA 24540
19- 45 KELLIHER, FRANCIS MORTIMER	D. MARCH 4, 1956 SOMERVILLE, MASS.
48- 52 KELLNER, ALEXANDER RAYMOND	3716 N JACKSON AVE - TUCSON AZ 85719
52- 60 KELLNER, WALTER JOSEPH	3737 N TUCSON BLVD - TUCSON AZ 85716
14-112 KELLOGG, WILLIAM DEARSTYNE	D. DECEMBER 12, 1971 BALTIMORE, MD.
10- 79 KELLY, ALBERT MICHAEL 'RED'	D. JANUARY 29, 1961 ZEPHYRHILLS, FLA.
80- 66 KELLY, DALE PATRICK 'PAT'	5176 SAN SIMEON DR - SANTA BARBARA CA 93111
14-113 KELLY, EDWARD LEO	D. NOVEMBER 4, 1928 RED LODGE, MONT.
15- 80 KELLY, GEORGE LANGE	D. OCTOBER 13, 1984 BURLINGAME, CALIF.
67- 57 KELLY, HAROLD PATRICK 'PAT'	836 E HAINES ST - PHILADELPHIA PA 19138
14-114 KELLY, HERBERT BARRETT	D. MAY 18, 1973 TORRANCE, CALIF.
14-115 KELLY, JAMES ROBERT	D. APRIL 10, 1961 KINGSPORT, TENN.
75- 58 KELLY, JAY THOMAS 'TOM'	173 PULASKI AVE - SAYREVILLE NJ 08872
14-116 KELLY, JOSEPH HENRY	D. AUGUST 16, 1977 ST. JOSEPH, MO.
26- 43 KELLY, JOSEPH JAMES	D. NOVEMBER 24, 1967 LYNBROOK, N. Y.
26- 44 KELLY, MICHAEL J.	OLD ADD: 5853 VON VESSEN AVE - ST LOUIS MO
23- 73 KELLY, REYNOLDS JOSEPH 'REN'	D. AUGUST 24, 1963 MILLBRAE, CAL.
51- 47 KELLY, ROBERT EDWARD	9 MOHAWK DR - NIENTIC CT 06359
69- 90 KELLY, VAN HOWARD	11 BEAUREGARD DR - SPENCER NC 28159
20- 63 KELLY, WILLIAM HENRY	37 QUEENS WAY - CAMILLUS NY 13031
10- 80 KELLY, WILLIAM JOSEPH	D. JUNE 3, 1940 DETROIT, MICH.
64- 58 KELSO, WILLIAM EUGENE	OLD ADD: 5316 NW 33RD TER - KANSAS CITY MO
37- 59 KELTNER, KEN FREDERICK	3220 KING ARTHURS CT W - GREENFIELD WI 53221
54- 51 KEMMERER, RUSSELL PAUL	RR 4, HICKORY HILLS - NORTH VERNON IN 47265
29- 58 KEMNER, HERMAN JOHN 'DUTCH'	301 N. 8TH ST #201 - QUINCY IL 62301
77- 76 KEMP, STEVEN F	32151 SEA ISLAND #1 - LAGUNA NIGUEL CA 92677
69- 91 KENDALL, FRED LYNN	1219 HICKORY AVE - TORRANCE CA 90503
61- 60 KENDERS, ALBERT DANIEL GEORGE	8744 MATILIJA AVE - VAN NUYS CA 91402
28- 54 KENNA, EDWARD ALOYSIUS	D. AUGUST 21, 1972 SAN FRANCISCO, CALIF.
70- 70 KENNEDY, JAMES EARL	OLD ADD: 2573 NW NORTHRUP - PORTLAND OR 97210
62- 65 KENNEDY, JOHN EDWARD	2 RODNEY ROAD - WEST PEABODY MA 01960
57- 36 KENNEDY, JOHN IRVIN	%E.WHITE,4166 LOCKHART-JACKSONVILLE FL 32209
74- 65 KENNEDY, JUNIOR RAYMOND	OLD ADD: 25459 JUDITH ST - ARVIN CA 93203

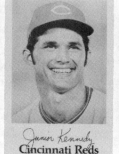

Junior Kennedy
Cincinnati Reds

34- 54 KENNEDY, LLOYD VERNON 'VERN'	RR 1 BOX 164 - MENDON MO 64660
46- 54 KENNEDY, MONTIA CALVIN	5735 BERRYWOOD - RICHMOND VA 23224
16- 50 KENNEDY, RAYMOND LINCOLN	D. JANUARY 18, 1969 CASSELBERRY, FLA.
39- 61 KENNEDY, ROBERT DANIEL	3708 E OMEGA CIR - MESA AZ 85205
78- 65 KENNEDY, TERRENCE EDWARD	2411-1 ADIRONDACK ROW - SAN DIEGO CA 92139
48- 53 KENNEDY, WILLIAM AULTON	D. APRIL 8, 1983 SEATTLE, WASH.
42- 57 KENNEDY, WILLIAM GORMAN	BOX 16244 - ALEXANDRIA VA 22302
38- 45 KENNEY, ARTHUR JOSEPH	#3 TIMBER LANE - NORTH READING MA 01864
67- 58 KENNEY, GERALD T	1980 HARRISON - BELOIT WI 53511
12- 94 KENT, MAURICE ALLEN	D. APRIL 19, 1966 IOWA CITY, IA.
62- 66 KENWORTHY, RICHARD LEE	3745 TADE LN - INDIANAPOLIS IN 46234
12- 95 KENWORTHY, WILLIAM JENNINGS 'DUKE'	D. SEPTEMBER 21, 1950 EUREKA, CALIF.
68- 48 KEOUGH, JOSEPH WILLIAM	4198 SHARAB CT - PLEASANTON CA 94566
77- 77 KEOUGH, MATTHEW LON	6281 FRONT SOUTH RD - LIVERMORE CA 94550
56- 47 KEOUGH, RICHARD MARTIN 'MARTY'	BOX 12-COTO - TRABUCO CANYON CA 92678
84- 60 KEPSHIRE, KURT DAVID	OLD ADD: 296 SOUNDVIEW AVE - BRIDGEPORT CT 06606
85- 57 KERFELD, CHARLES PATRICK	1001 SONOMA ST - CARSON CITY NV 89701
50- 41 KERIAZAKOS, CONSTANTINE NICHOLAS 'GUS'	6 SUMMIT RD - BROOKSIDE NJ 07926
39- 62 KERKSIECK, WAYMAN WILLIAM 'BILL'	D. MARCH 11, 1970 LITTLE ROCK, ARK.
15- 81 KERLIN, ORIE MILTON	D. OCTOBER 29, 1974 SHREVEPORT, LA.
74- 66 KERN, JAMES LESTER	6009 AMBERWOOD CT - ARLINGTON TX 76016
62- 67 KERN, WILLIAM GEORGE	625 GREEN ST - ALLENTOWN PA 18102
65- 57 KERNEK, GEORGE BOYD	210 NORTH GULF - HOLDENVILLE OK 74848
20- 64 KERNS, DANIEL P	B. PHILADELPHIA, PA.

KERNS

```
45- 51  KERNS, RUSSELL ELDON
23- 74  KERR, JOHN FRANCIS
14-117  KERR, JOHN JONAS 'DOC'
43- 70  KERR, JOHN JOSEPH 'BUDDY'
25- 60  KERR, JOHN MELVILLE 'MEL'
19- 46  KERR, RICHARD HENRY
76- 45  KERRIGAN, JOSEPH THOMAS
64- 59  KESSINGER, DONALD EULON
68- 49  KESTER, RICHARD LEE
22- 67  KETCHUM, AUGUSTUS FRANKLIN
12- 96  KETTER, PHILIP
14-118  KEUPPER, HENRY J.
84- 61  KEY, JAMES EDWARD
85- 58  KHALIFA, SAM
25- 61  KIBBIE, HORACE KENT 'HOD'
12- 97  KIBBLE, JOHN WESTLY
20- 65  KIEFER, JOSEPH WILLIAM
84- 62  KIEFER, STEVEN GEORGE
51- 48  KIELY, LEO PATRICK
17- 38  KILDUFF, PETER JOHN
14-119  KILHULLEN, JOSEPH ISADORE 'PAT'
69- 92  KILKENNY, MICHAEL DAVID
54- 52  KILLEBREW, HARMON CLAYTON
59- 45  KILLEEN, EVANS HENRY
11- 90  KILLILAY, JOHN WILLIAM
37- 60  KIMBALL, NEWELL W. 'NEWT'
36- 45  KIMBERLIN, HARRY LYDLE
45- 52  KIMBLE, RICHARD LOUIS
20- 66  KIME, HAROLD LEE
76- 46  KIMM, BRUCE EDWARD
19- 47  KIMMICK, WALTER LYONS
29- 59  KIMSEY, CLYDE ELIAS 'CHAD'
56- 48  KINDALL, GERALD DONALD
46- 55  KINDER, ELLIS RAYMOND
46- 56  KINER, RALPH MCPHERRAN
54- 53  KING, CHARLES GILBERT
44- 71  KING, CLYDE EDWARD
16- 52  KING, EDWARD LEE
16- 51  KING, EDWARD LEE
67- 59  KING, HAROLD
55- 63  KING, JAMES HUBERT
35- 56  KING, LYNN PAUL
54- 54  KING, NELSON JOSEPH
32- 39  KINGDON, WESCOTT WILLIAM
79- 63  KINGMAN, BRIAN PAUL
71- 58  KINGMAN, DAVID ARTHUR
14-120  KINGMAN, HENRY LEES
```

KLAERNER

```
22000 LAWRENCE RD - FIDDLETOWN CA 95629
2812 E 220TH PL - LONG BEACH CA 90810
D. JUNE 9, 1937 BALTIMORE, MD.
341 GROVE ST-ORADELL NJ 07649
D. AUGUST 9, 1980 VERO BEACH, FLA.
D. MAY 4, 1963 HOUSTON, TEX.
490 MARINERS ISLAND BLVD #323 - SAN MATEO CA 94404
2771 CLARK ROAD - MEMPHIS TN 38115
BOX 623 - GARDNERVILLE NV 89410
OLD ADD: 4409 NW 16TH PL-OKLAHOMA CITY OK
B. HUTCHINSON, KAN.
D. AUGUST 14  1960 MARION, ILL.
3301 AVERY AVE SW - HUNTSVILLE AL 35805
8825 EAST SECOND PLACE - TUCSON AZ 85710
D. OCTOBER 19, 1975 FORT WORTH, TEX.
D. DECEMBER 13, 1969 ROUNDUP, MONT.
D. JULY 5, 1975 UTICA, N. Y.
11822 OLD FASHION - GARDEN GROVE CA 92640
D. JANUARY 18, 1984 GLEN RIDGE, N. J.
D. FEBRUARY 14, 1930 PITTSBURG, KAN.
D. NOVEMBER 2, 1922 OAKLAND, CALIF.
274 HOLLAND ST W - BRADFORD ONTARIO CAN.
BOX 626 - ONTARIO OR 97914
123 MAIN ST - WESTHAMPTON NY 11978
D. OCTOBER 21, 1968 TULSA, OKLA.
1425 GRIFFITH AVE - LAS VEGAS NV 89104
1028 KINZER ST #201B - POPLAR BLUFF MO 63901
3733 LARCHMONT PARKWAY - TOLEDO OH 43613
D. MAY 16, 1939 COLUMBUS, O.
RR 1 BOX 13A - AMANA IA 52203
401 WOODSIDE RD - PITTSBURGH PA 15221
D. DECEMBER 3, 1942 PRYOR, OKLA.
ATH DEPT, UNIV OF ARIZONA - TUCSON AZ 85721
D. OCTOBER 16, 1968 JACKSON, TENN.
17 LEGRANDE AVE #17 - GREENWICH CT 06830
BOX 741 - PARIS TN 38242
103 STRATFORD RD - GOLDSBORO NC 27530
D. SEPTEMBER 7, 1938 CHELSEA, MASS.
D. SEPTEMBER 16, 1967 SHINNSTOWN, W. VA.
1027 WEST SOUTH ST - ORLANDO FL 32805
RR 2 BOX 15 - ELKINS AR 72727
D. MAY 11, 1972 ATLANTIC, IA.
126 JAMES PL - PITTSBURGH PA 15228
D. APRIL 19, 1975 CAPISTRANO, CALIF.
11 TOKENEKE TRAIL - DARIEN CT 06820
818 W BUSSE AVE - MOUNT PROSPECT IL 60056
D. DECEMBER 27, 1982 OAKLAND, CALIF.
```

```
78- 66  KINNEY, DENNIS PAUL
18- 43  KINNEY, WALTER WILLIAM
80- 67  KINNUNEN, MICHAEL JOHN
19- 48  KINSELLA, ROBERT FRANCIS
34- 55  KINZY, HENRY HENSEL 'HARRY'
57- 37  KIPP, FRED LEO
85- 59  KIPPER, ROBERT WAYNE
53- 46  KIPPER, THORNTON JOHN
14-121  KIPPERT, EDWARD AUGUST
69- 93  KIRBY, CLAYTON LAWS
49- 41  KIRBY, JAMES HERSCHEL
12- 98  KIRBY, LARUE
19- 49  KIRCHER, MICHAEL ANDREW
47- 51  KIRK, THOMAS DANIEL
61- 61  KIRK, WILLIAM PARTHEMORE
10- 81  KIRKE, JUDSON FABIAN 'JAY'
58- 51  KIRKLAND, WILLIE CHARLES
62- 68  KIRKPATRICK, EDGAR LEON
12- 99  KIRKPATRICK, ENOS CLAIRE
74- 67  KIRKWOOD, DONALD PAUL
50- 42  KIRRENE, JOSEPH JOHN
10- 82  KIRSCH, HARRY LOUIS
45- 53  KISH, ERNEST ALEXANDER
71- 59  KISON, BRUCE EUGENE
54- 55  KITSOS, CHRISTOPHER ANESTOS
82- 71  KITTLE, RONALD DALE
34- 56  KLAERNER, HUGO EMIL
```

```
7440 CROESSCREEKS #3 - TEMPERANCE MI 48182
D. JULY 1, 1971 ESCONDIDO, CAL.
5818 MCKINLEY PL N - SEATTLE WA  98103
D. DECEMBER 30, 1951 LOS ANGELES, CALIF.
3721 ARROYO RD - FT WORTH TX 76109
6510 W 69TH ST - OVERLAND PARK KS 66204
2145 BILTER ROAD - AURORA IL 60505
8780 E MCKELLOPS #340 - SCOTTSDALE AZ 85257
D. JUNE 3, 1960 DETROIT, MICH.
949 N POTOMAC ST - ARLINGTON VA 22205
729 DOVER RD - NASHVILLE TN 37211
D. JUNE 10, 1961 LANSING, MICH.
D. JUNE 26, 1972 ROCHESTER, N. Y.
D. AUGUST 1, 1974 PHILADELPHIA, PA.
365 FOLKSTONE WAY - YORK PA 17402
D. AUGUST 31, 1968 NEW ORLEANS, LA.
OLD ADD: 16549 PARKSIDE ST - DETROIT MI 48221
24791 VIA LARGA - LAGUNA NIGUEL CA 92677
D. APRIL 14, 1964 PITTSBURGH, PA.
455 W ELMWOOD - CLAWSON MI 48017
2340 MARSHALL WAY - SACRAMENTO CA 95819
D. DECEMBER 25, 1925 PITTSBURGH, PA.
6619 S.O.M. CENTER RD - SOLON OH 44139
2509 NIGHTINGALE LANE #61 - BRADENTON FL 33529
1219 ANCHOR DR - MOBILE AL 36609
8080 E. 109TH - CROWN POINT IN 46307
D. JANUARY 3, 1982 FREDERICKSBURG, TEXAS
```

KLAGES

KOMMINSKI

66- 52 KLAGES, FRED ANTHONY	OLD ADD: 261 BERRY ST - BADEN PA 15005
64- 60 KLAUS, ROBERT FRANCIS	10661 GABACHO DR - SAN DIEGO CA 92124
52- 61 KLAUS, WILLIAM JOSEPH	1655 SOUTH DR - SARASOTA FL 33579
85- 60 KLAWITTER, THOMAS CARL	2506 KENWOOD - JANESVILLE WI 53545
25- 62 KLEE, OLLIE CHESTER	D. FEBRUARY 9, 1977 TOLEDO, O.
28- 55 KLEIN, CHARLES HERBERT	D. MARCH 28, 1958 INDIANAPOLIS, IND.
44- 72 KLEIN, HAROLD JOHN	D. DECEMBER 10, 1957 ST. LOUIS, MO.
43- 71 KLEIN, LOUIS FRANK	D. JUNE 20, 1976 METAIRIE, LA.
34- 57 KLEINHANS, THEODORE OTTO	D. JULY 24, 1985 REDINGTON BEACH, FLA.
35- 57 KLEINKE, NORBERT GEORGE 'NUB'	D. MARCH 16, 1950 MARIN, CAL.
11- 91 KLEPFER, EDWARD LLOYD	D. AUGUST 9, 1950 TULSA, OKLA.
76- 47 KLEVEN, JAY ALLEN	118 VIA BOLSA - SAN LORENZO CA 94580
43- 72 KLIEMAN, EDWARD FREDERICK	D. NOVEMBER 15, 1979 HOMOS ASSA, FLA.
58- 52 KLIMCHOCK, LOUIS STEPHEN	1913 EAST MYRNA LANE - TEMPE AZ 85284
69- 94 KLIMKOWSKI, RONALD BERNARDO	791 EDGEWOOD DR - WESTBURY NY 11590
55- 64 KLINE, JOHN ROBERT 'BOBBY'	5924 47TH AVE N -ST PETERSBURG FL 33703
30- 41 KLINE, ROBERT GEORGE	7513 RIVERSIDE DR - POWELL OH 43065
52- 62 KLINE, RONALD LEE	MAIN ST BOX 155 - CALLERY PA 16024
70- 71 KLINE, STEVEN JACK	BOX 429 - CHELAN WA 98816
27- 51 KLINGER, JOSEPH JOHN	D. JULY 31, 1960 LITTLE ROCK, ARK.
38- 46 KLINGER, ROBERT HAROLD	D. AUGUST 19, 1977 VILLA RIDGE, MO.
50- 43 KLIPPSTEIN, JOHN CALVIN	1176 ABERDEEN RD - PALATINE IL 60067
44- 73 KLOPP, STANLEY HAROLD	D. MARCH 11, 1980 ROBESONIA, PA.
31- 44 KLOZA, JLHN CLARENCE 'NAP'	D. JUNE 11, 1962 MILWAUKEE, WIS.
21- 52 KLUGMANN, JOSIE	D. JULY 18, 1951 MOBERLY, MO.
34- 58 KLUMPP, ELMER EDWARD	N67 W27085 HWY 74 - SUSSEX WI 53089
47- 52 KLUSZEWSKI, THEODORE BERNARD	8353 ISLAND LN - MAINEVILLE OH 45039
76- 48 KLUTTS, GENE ELLIS "MICKEY"	20701 BECH BLVD #259-HUNTINGTON BCH CA 92648
42- 58 KLUTTZ, CLYDE FRANKLIN	D. MAY 12, 1979 SALISBURY, N. C.

Ted Kluszewski—Cincinnati Redlegs

75- 59 KNAPP, ROBERT CHRISTIAN 'CHRIS'	1415 CASTLE CT - ST JOSEPH MI 49085
10- 83 KNAUPP, HENRY ANTONE 'COTTON'	D. JULY 6, 1967 NEW ORLEANS, LA.
26- 45 KNEISCH, RUDOLPH FRANK	D. APRIL 6, 1965 BALTIMORE, MD.
76- 49 KNEPPER, ROBERT WESLEY	2045 OAKHILL RD - ROSEBURY OR 97470
45- 54 KNERR, WALLACE LUTHER 'LOU'	D. MARCH 23, 1980 LANCASTER, P A.
79- 64 KNICELY, ALAN LEE	BOX 433 - DAYTON VA 22821
47- 53 KNICKERBOCKER, AUSTIN JAY	CLINTON CORNERS NY 12514
33- 32 KNICKERBOCKER, WILLIAM HART	D. SEPTEMBER 8, 1963 SEBASTOPOL, CALIF.
74- 68 KNIGHT, CHARLES RAY	RR2 BOX 380C - ALBANY GA 31707
22- 68 KNIGHT, ELMA RUSSELL 'JACK'	D. JULY 30, 1976 SAN ANTONIO, TEX.
12-100 KNISELY, PETER C.	D. JULY 1, 1948 BROWNSVILLE, PA.
20- 67 KNODE, KENNETH THOMSON 'MIKE'	D. DECEMBER 20, 1980 SOUTH BEND, IND.
23- 75 KNODE, ROBERT TROXELL 'RAY'	D. APRIL 13, 1982 BATTLE CREEK, MICH.
64- 61 KNOOP, ROBERT FRANK	1910 W. PALMYRA #110 - ORANGE CA 92668
32- 40 KNOTHE, GEORGE BERTRAM	D. JULY 3, 1981 DOVER, N. J.
32- 41 KNOTHE, WILFRED EDGAR 'FRITZ'	D. MARCH 22, 1963 PASSAIC, N. J.
33- 33 KNOTT, JOHN HENRY	D. OCTOBER 13, 1981 BROWNWOOD, TEXAS
65- 58 KNOWLES, DAROLD DUANE	2513 LYNN LAKE CIRCLE SOUTH - ST. PETERSBURG FL 33712
15- 82 KNOWLSON, THOMAS HERBERT	D. APRIL 11, 1943 MIAMI SHORES, FLA.
20- 68 KNOWLTON, WILLIAM YOUNG	D. FEBRUARY 25, 1944 PHILADELPHIA, PA.
24- 60 KNOX, CLIFFORD HIRAM 'BUD'	D. SEPTEMBER 24, 1965 OSKALOOSA, IA.
72- 57 KNOX, JOHN CLINTON	OLD ADD: 492 TROUTWOOD DR - PITTSBURGH PA
85- 61 KNUDSON, MARK RICHARD	881 WEST 100TH AVE - NORTHGLENN CO 80221
53- 47 KOBACK, NICHOLAS NICHOLIA	52 STONEHEDGE DR - NEWINGTON CT 06111
73- 69 KOBEL, KEVIN RICHARD	EDDY RD - COLDEN NY 14033
63- 64 KOCH, ALAN GOODMAN	1517 RIDGELAND RD EAST - MOBILE AL 36609
44- 74 KOCH, BARNETT	6448 19TH ST W #48B - TACOMA WA 98466
12-101 KOCHER, BRADLEY WILSON	D. JANUARY 13, 1965 WHITE HAVEN, PA.
46- 57 KOECHER, RICHARD FINLAY	2000 VALLEY FORGE CIR-KING OF PRUSSIA PA19406
70- 72 KOEGEL, PETER JOHN	OLD ADD: 1205 N 48TH - PHOENIX AZ 85008
25- 63 KOEHLER, HORACE LEVERING 'PIP'	1018 S SPRAGUE AVE - TACOMA WA 98405
32- 42 KOENECKE, LEONARD GEORGE	D. SEPTEMBER 17, 1935 TORONTO, ONT.
25- 64 KOENIG, MARK ANTHONY	4295 WARM SPRINGS - GLEN ELLEN CA 95442
19- 50 KOENIGSMARK, WILLIS THOMAS	D. JULY 1, 1972 WATERLOO, ILL.
10- 84 KOESTNER, ELMER JOSEPH	D. OCTOBER 27, 1959 FAIRBURY, ILL.
37- 61 KOHLMAN, JOSEPH JAMES	D. MARCH 16, 1974 PHILADELPHIA, PA.
48- 54 KOKOS, RICHARD JEROME	D. APRIL 9, 1986 CHICAGO, ILL.
60- 57 KOLB, GARY ALAN	154 CIRCLE DRIVE - CHARLESTON WV 25314
40- 47 KOLLOWAY, DONALD MARTIN	2236 W 121ST STREET PL - BLUE ISLAND IL 60406
21- 53 KOLP, RAYMOND CARL	D. JULY 29, 1967 NEW ORLEANS, LA.
15- 83 KOLSETH, KARL DICKEY	D. MAY 3, 1956 CUMBERLAND, MD.
62- 69 KOLSTAD, HAROLD EVERETTE	15149 BEL ESCOU DR - SAN JOSE CA 95124
13- 96 KOMMERS, FRED RAYMOND	D. JUNE 14, 1943 CHICAGO, ILL.
83- 87 KOMMINSK, BRAD LYNN	2987 HANOVER DRIVE - LIMA OH 45805

80

73- 70	KONIECZNY, DOUGLAS JAMES	40304 SPITZ DR- STERLING HEIGHTS MI 48078
48- 55	KONIKOWSKI, ALEXANDER JAMES	OLD ADD: BANK ST - SEYMOUR CT 06483
42- 59	KONOPKA, BRUCE BRUNO	3212 S ADAMS - DENVER CO 80210
44- 75	KONSTANTY, CASIMIR JAMES 'JIM'	D. JUNE 11, 1976 ONEONTA, N. Y.
15- 84	KOOB, ERNEST GERALD	D. NOVEMBER 12, 1941 LEMAY, MO.
62- 70	KOONCE, CALVIN LEE	3646 GOLFVIEW DR - HOPE MILLS NC 28348
67- 60	KOOSMAN, JERRY MARTIN	RR 2 BOX 67E - CHASKA MN 55318
66- 53	KOPACZ, GEORGE FELIX	4120 S RICHMOND - CHICAGO IL 60623
21- 54	KOPF, WALTER HENRY	D. APRIL 30, 1979 CINCINNATI, O.
13- 97	KOPF, WILLIAM LORENZ 'LARRY'	5 WEST 4TH ST #310 - CINCINNATI OH 45202
61- 62	KOPLITZ, HOWARD DEAN	623 BOYD ST - OSHKOSH WI 54901
15- 85	KOPP, MERLIN HENRY	D. MAY 7, 1960 SACRAMENTO, CALIF.
58- 53	KOPPE, JOSEPH	7887 BEATRICE ST - WESTLAND MI 48185
23- 76	KOPSHAW, GEORGE KARL	D. DECEMBER 26, 1934 LYNCHBURG, VA.
54- 56	KORCHECK, STEPHEN JOSEPH	8018 WILLOW AVE - SARASOTA FL 33580
15- 86	KORES, ARTHUR EMIL	D. MARCH 26, 1974 MILWAUKEE, WIS.
66- 54	KORINCE, GEORGE EUGENE	OLD ADD: 83 SHORELINE DR - ST. CATHERINES ONT. L2N 5N7
65- 59	KOSCO, ANDREW JOHN	9329 NEW SPRINGFIELD RD - POLAND OH 44514
52- 63	KOSHOREK, CLEMENT JOHN	3951 AMHERST - ROYAL OAK MI 48072
51- 49	KOSKI, WILLIAM JOHN	2656 EL GRECO DR - MODESTO CA 95351
41- 56	KOSLO, GEORGE BERNARD 'DAVE'	D. DECEMBER 1, 1975 MENASHA, WIS.
44- 76	KOSMAN, MICHAEL THOMAS	2110 S. 6TH - LAFAYETTE IN 47904
31- 45	KOSTER, FREDERICK CHARLES	D. APRIL 24, 1979 SAINT MATTHEWS, KY.
62- 71	KOSTRO, FRANK JERRY	36 STEELE ST #200- DENVER CO 80206
55- 65	KOUFAX, SANFORD	P.O. BOX BB - CARPINTERIA CA 93013
25- 65	KOUPAL, LOUIS LADDIE	D. DECEMBER 8, 1961 SAN GABRIEL, CAL.
32- 43	KOWALIK, FABIAN LORENZ	D. AUGUST 14, 1954 KARNES CITY, TEX.
38- 47	KOY, ERNEST ANYZ	BOX 476 1047 S OAK-BELLVILLE TX 77418
48- 56	KOZAR, ALBERT KENNETH	3004 VINCENT RD - WEST PALM BEACH FL 33405
39- 63	KRACHER, JOSEPH PETER	D. DECEMBER 25, 1981 SAN ANGELO, TEXAS
14-122	KRAFT, CLARENCE OTTO	D. MARCH 26, 1958 FORT WORTH, TEX.
37- 62	KRAKAUSKAS, JOSEPH VICTOR LAWRENCE	D. DECEMBER 8, 1960 HAMILTON, ONT.
59- 46	KRALICK, JOHN FRANCIS	BOX 3006 - SOLDOTNA AK 99669
53- 48	KRALY, STEVEN CHARLES	2246 SCHRAGE - WHITING IN 46354
39- 64	KRAMER, JOHN HENRY	2126 PAULINE ST-NEW ORLEANS LA 70117
62- 72	KRANEPOOL, EDWARD EMIL	133-09 BLOSSOM AVE - FLUSHING NY 11355
11- 92	KRAPP, EUGENE H.	D. APRIL 13, 1923 DETROIT, MICH.
43- 73	KRAUS, JOHN WILLIAM 'TEX'	D. JANUARY 2, 1976 SAN ANTONIO, TEX.
31- 46	KRAUSSE, LEWIS BERNARD SR.	3680 EDGERTON CIR - SARASOTA FL 33581
61- 63	KRAUSSE, LOUIS BERNARD JR	RR 1 BOX 572C - HOLT MO 64048
75- 60	KRAVEC, KENNETH PETER	13599 MOHAWK TRAIL - MIDDLEBURG HGTS OH 44130
56- 49	KRAVITZ, DANIEL	RR1 - DUSHORE PA 18614
84- 63	KRAWCZYK, RAYMOND ALLEN	10032 RIDGLEY DR - GARDEN GROVE CA 92643
31- 47	KREEVICH, MICHAEL ANDREAS	3S637 TERRACE DR - AURORA IL 60504
43- 74	KREITNER, ALBERT JOSEPH	313 CHURCH ST - NASHVILLE TN 37201
11- 93	KREITZ, RALPH WESLEY	D. JULY 20, 1941 PORTLAND, ORE.
24- 61	KREMER, REMY PETER 'RAY'	D. FEBRUARY 8, 1965 PINOLE, CAL.
73- 71	KREMMEL, JAMES LOUIS	2704 S BLAKE RD - SPOKANE WA 99216
79- 65	KRENCHICKI, WAYNE RICHARD	53 FARRELL AVE - TRENTON NJ 08618
47- 54	KRESS, CHARLES STEVEN	3102 DUNCAN - SAINT JOSEPH MO 64507
27- 52	KRESS, RALPH 'RED'	D. NOVEMBER 29, 1962 LOS ANGELES, CALIF.
46- 58	KRETLOW, LOUIS HENRY	3302 GOLDFINCH - ENID OK 73701
75- 61	KREUGER, RICHARD ALAN	1143 POWERS NW - GRAND RAPIDS MI 49504
62- 73	KREUTZER, FRANKLIN JAMES	21 SILVERWOOD CIR - ANNAPOLIS MD 21403
11- 94	KRICHELL, PAUL BERNARD	D. JUNE 4, 1957 NEW YORK, N. Y.
49- 42	KRIEGER, KURT FERDINAND	D. AUGUST 16, 1970 ST. LOUIS, MO.
37- 63	KRIST, HOWARD WILBUR	44 GROVE ST - DELAVAN NY 14042
78- 67	KROL, JOHN THOMAS	3012 FLEET ST - WINSTON SALEM NC 27107
64- 62	KROLL, GARY MELVIN	9038 E 40TH ST - TULSA OK 74145
35- 58	KRONER, JOHN HAROLD	D. AUGUST 26, 1968 ST. LOUIS, MO.
60- 58	KRSNICH, MICHAEL	4361 NW 12TH AVE - POMPANO BEACH FL 33064
49- 43	KRSNICH, ROCCO PETER	9221 HARVERS LN - WICHITA KS 67207
13- 98	KRUEGER, ERNEST GEORGE	D. APRIL 22, 1976 WAUKEGAN, ILL.
83- 88	KRUEGER, WILLIAM CULP	1844 HARVEST RD - PLEASANTON CA 94566
65- 60	KRUG, EVERETT BEN 'CHRIS'	4125 ALLOTT AVE - SHERMAN OAKS CA 91423
81- 66	KRUG, GARY EUGENE	1327 BAYLOR DR - COLORADO SPRINGS CO 80909
12-102	KRUG, MARTIN JOHN	D. JUNE 27, 1966 GLENDALE, CALIF.
76- 50	KRUKOW, MICHAEL EDWARD	317 W FAIRVIEW AVE - SAN GABRIEL CA 91776
49- 44	KRYHOSKI, RICHARD DAVID	18855 WARWICK RD - BIRMINGHAM MI 48009
57- 38	KUBEK, ANTHONY CHRISTOPHER	3311 N MCDONALD - APPLETON WI 54911
67- 61	KUBIAK, THEODORE ROGER	196 CALDECOTT LN #303 - OAKLAND CA 94618
61- 64	KUBISZYN, JACK JOSEPH	2306 UNIVERSITY BLVD - TUSCALOOSA AL 35401
80- 68	KUBSKI, GILBERT THOMAS	1565 SUNRISE CIR - CARLSBAD CA 92008

50- 44	KUCAB, JOHN ALBERT	D. MAY 26, 1977 YOUNGSTOWN, O.
74- 69	KUCEK, JOHN ANDREW CHARLES	1219 WARREN RD - NEWTON FALLS OH 44444
55- 66	KUCKS, JOHN CHARLES	15 OAKLAND ST - HILLSDALE NJ 07642
49- 45	KUCZEK, STANISLAW LEO 'STEVE'	769 SACANDAGA RD - SCOTIA NY 12302
43- 75	KUCZYNSKI, BERNARD CARL 'BERT'	RR 4 - ALLENTOWN PA 18103
76- 51	KUEHL, KARL OTTO	8218 VIA DE LA ESCUELA - SCOTTSDALE AZ 85258
52- 64	KUENN, HARVEY EDWARD	17406 COUNTRY CLUB - SUN CITY AZ 85373
77- 78	KUHAULUA, FRED MAHELE	89-203 NALAKAHIKI PL - NANAKULI HI 96792
30- 42	KUHEL, JOSEPH ANTHONY	D. FEBRUARY 26, 1984 KANSAS CITY, KAN.
24- 62	KUHN, BERNARD DANIEL 'BUB'	D. NOVEMBER 20, 1956 LANSING, MICH.
55- 67	KUHN, KENNETH HAROLD	OLD ADD: CLAYBROOK & MAINE - DOVER MA 02030
12-103	KUHN, WALTER CHARLES	D. JUNE 14, 1935 FRESNO, CALIF.
74- 70	KUIPER, DUANE EUGENE	5507-A SUTTON LN - WILLOUGHBY OH 44094
55- 68	KUME, JOHN MIKE	RR2 WOODARD RD - ANDOVER OH 44003
84- 64	KUNKEL, JEFFREY WILLIAM	1 NAUTILUS DR - LEONARDO NJ 07737
61- 65	KUNKEL, WILLIAM GUSTAVE JAMES	D. MAY 4, 1985 RED BANK, N. J.
79- 66	KUNTZ, RUSSELL JAY 'RUSTY'	1254 LANA ST - PASO ROBLES CA 93446
23- 77	KUNZ, EARL DEWEY	D. APRIL 14, 1963 SACRAMENTO, CAL.
75- 62	KUROSAKI, RYAN YOSHITOMO	1324 HIGH VIEW PL - HONOLULU HI 96816
41- 57	KUROWSKI, GEORGE JOHN 'WHITEY'	310 SPRINGSIDE DR-SHILLINGTON PA 19607
68- 50	KURTZ, HAROLD JAMES	BELLE POINT - QUEENSTOWN MD 21658
41- 58	KUSH, EMIL BENEDICT	D. NOVEMBER 26, 1969 RIVER GROVE, ILL.
73- 72	KUSICK, CRAIG ROBERT	%D.BAERTSCHY,RR 1 - ST GERMAIN WI 54558
70- 73	KUSNYER, ARTHUR WILLIAM	4316 MEADOWLAND CIR - SARASOTA FL 33583
11- 95	KUTINA, JOSEPH PETER	D. APRIL 13, 1945 CHICAGO, ILL.
59- 47	KUTYNA, MARION JOHN 'MARTY'	2711 EAST CAMBRIA ST - PHILADELPHIA PA 19134
46- 59	KUZAVA, ROBERT LEROY	1118 VINEWOOD ST - WYANDOTTE MI 48192
42- 60	KVASNAK, ALEXANDER	3265 HEMPSTEAD AVE-ARCADIA CA 91006
12-104	KYLE, ANDREW EWING	D. SEPTEMBER 6, 1971 TORONTO, ONT.
37- 64	LAABS, CHESTER PETER	D. JANUARY 26, 1983 WARREN, MICH.
50- 45	LABINE, CLEMENT WALTER	BOX 643 - WOONSOCKET RI 02895
69- 95	LABOY, JOSE ALBERTO 'COCO'	CALLE TRUBIA, BLDG 29 #26 - CAROLINA PR 00630
77- 79	LACEY, ROBERT JOSEPH	2525 E FOUNTAIN - MESA AZ 85201
69- 96	LACHEMANN, MARCEL ERNEST	1449 BOOKMAN AVE - WALNUT CA 91789
65- 61	LACHEMANN, RENE GEORGE	2736 W PLATA AVE - MESA AZ 85202
83- 89	LACHOWICZ, ALLEN ROBERT	310 ROOSEVELT AVE - MCKEES ROCK PA 15136
14-128	LACLAIRE, GEORGE LEWIS	D. OCTOBER 10, 1918 FARNHAM, QUE.
72- 58	LACOCK, RALPH PIERRE 'PETE'	9725 RIGGS - OVERLAND PARK KS 66212
75- 63	LACORTE, FRANK JOSEPH	751 GARY ST - GILROY CA 95020
78- 68	LACOSS, MICHAEL JAMES	4110 LAVIDA - VISALIA CA 93277
72- 59	LACY, LEONDAUS 'LEE'	4450 PARK ALISAL - CALABASAS CA 91302
26- 46	LACY, OSCEOLA GUY	D. NOVEMBER 19, 1953 CLEVELAND, TENN.
79- 67	LADD, PETER LINWOOD	5665 GROVE TER - GREENDALE WI 53129
46- 60	LADE, DOYLE MARION	445 N 12TH ST - GENEVA NE 68361
47- 55	LAFATA, JOSEPH JOSEPH	29321 BRITTANY CT W - ROSEVILLE MI 48066
45- 55	LAFOREST, BYRON JOSEPH 'TY'	D. MAY 5, 1947 ARLINGTON, MASS.
82- 72	LAFRANCOIS, ROGER VICTOR	28 ASPINOOK ST - JEWETT CITY CT 06351
82- 73	LAGA, MICHAEL RUSSELL	27 CENTER ST - RAMSEY NJ 07446
34- 59	LAGGER, EDWIN JOSEPH	D. NOVEMBER 10, 1981 JOLIET, ILL.
70- 74	LAGROW, LERRIN HARRIS	12271 E TURQUOISE - SCOTTSDALE AZ 85259
68- 51	LAHOUD, JOSEPH MICHAEL	HUT HILL ROAD - BRIDGEWATER CT 06752
82- 74	LAHTI, JEFFREY ALLEN	OLD ADD: 90 SW SIXTH AVE - ONTARIO OR 97914
46- 61	LAJESKIE, RICHARD EDWARD	D. AUGUST 15, 1976 RAMSEY, N. J.
39- 65	LAKE, EDWARD ERVING	1840 NELSON ST - SAN LEANDRO CA 94579
83- 90	LAKE, STEVEN MICHAEL	OLD ADD: 10916 1/2 LARCH AVE - LENNOX CA 90304
42- 61	LAKEMAN, ALBERT WESLEY	D. MAY 25, 1976 SPARTANBURG, S. C.
62- 74	LAMABE, JOHN ALEXANDER	16224 ANTIETAM AVE - BATON ROUGE LA 70816
43- 76	LAMACCHIA, ALFRED ANTHONY	13515 VISTA BONITA - SAN ANTONIO TX 78216
40- 48	LAMANNA, FRANK	D. SEPTEMBER 1, 1980 SYRACUSE, N. Y.
41- 59	LAMANNO, RAYMOND SIMON	827 POLK ST-ALBANY CA 94706
35- 59	LAMANSKE, FRANK JAMES	D. AUGUST 4, 1971 OLNEY,ILL.
17- 39	LAMAR, WILLIAM HARMONG	D. MAY 24, 1970 ROCKPORT, MASS.
37- 65	LAMASTER, WAYNE LEE	2525 E ELM ST NEW-ALBANY IN 47150
70- 75	LAMB, JOHN ANDREW	SHARON VALLEY RD - SHARON CT 06069
20- 69	LAMB, LAYMAN RAYMOND	D. OCTOBER 5, 1955 FAYETTEVILLE, ARK.
69- 97	LAMB, RAYMOND RICHARD	1741 TUSTIN AVE #17C - COSTA MESA CA 92627
46- 62	LAMBERT, CLAYTON PATRICK	D. APRIL 3, 1981 OGDEN, UTAH
41- 60	LAMBERT, EUGENE MARION	268 MONTELO-MEMPHIS TN 38117
16- 53	LAMBETH, OTIS SAMUEL	D. JUNE 5, 1976 MORAN, KAN.
12-105	LAMLINE, FREDERICK ARTHUR	D. SEPTEMBER 20, 1970 PORT HURON, MICH.
70- 76	LAMONT, GENE WILLIAM	4110 TONGA - SARASOTA FL 33583
20- 70	LAMOTTE, ROBERT EUGENE	D. NOVEMBER 2, 1970 CHATHAM, GA.
77- 80	LAMP, DENNIS PATRICK	12100 MONTECITO RD #161-LOS ALAMITOS CA 90720
69- 98	LAMPARD, CHRISTOPHER KEITH	842 NE 74TH AVE - PORTLAND OR 97213

35- 60 LANAHAN, RICHARD ANTHONY	D. MARCH 12, 1975 ROCHESTER, MINN.
77- 81 LANCE, GARY DEAN	1802 OMEGA DR - COLUMBIA SC 29206
82- 75 LANCELOTTI, RICHARD ANTHONY 'RICK'	5 CIRCLE LN - CHERRY HILL NJ 08003
29- 60 LAND, WILLIAM GILBERT 'DOC'	BOX 964 -LIVINGSTON AL 35470
52- 65 LANDENBERGER, KENNETH HENRY	D. JULY 28, 1960 CLEVELAND, O.
77- 82 LANDESTOY, RAFAEL SIVIALDO CAMILO	KM 8 1/2 CARRET SANCHEZ,CLE#1 - SANTO DOMINGO DOM REP.
57- 39 LANDIS, JAMES HENRY	2439 STONEHOUSE CT - NAPA CA 94558
63- 65 LANDIS, WILLIAM HENRY	525 SYCAMORE - HANFORD CA 93230
77- 83 LANDREAUX, KENNETH FRED	1840 S. MARENGO #56 - ALHAMBRA CA 91803
76- 52 LANDRETH, LARRY ROBERT	5 BURRITT ST - STRATFORD ONT. N5A 4W6 CAN.
50- 46 LANDRITH, HOBERT NEAL	1462 NOME CT - SUNNYVALE CA 94087
57- 40 LANDRUM, DONALD LEROY	19 BARRIE COURT - PITTSBURG CA 94565
38- 48 LANDRUM, JESSE GLENN	D. JUNE 27, 1983 BEAUMONT, TEX.
50- 47 LANDRUM, JOSEPH BUTLER	RR 5 BOX 339 - COLUMBIA SC 29203
80- 69 LANDRUM, TERRY LEE 'TITO'	1121 KENTUCKY SE - ALBUQUERQUE NM 87108
24- 63 LANE, JAMES HUNTER	5720 HERALD SQUARE - MEMPHIS TN 38119
53- 49 LANE, JERALD HAL	7306 ELAINE DR - CHATTANOOGA TN 37421
71- 60 LANE, MARVIN	17191 ARDMORE - DETROIT MI 48235
49- 46 LANE, RICHARD HARRISON	26609 ACADEMY DR-PALOS VERDES PENIN CA 90274
41- 61 LANFRANCONI, WALTER OSWALD	NORTH BARRE MANOR #405 - BARRE VT 05641
38- 49 LANG, DONALD CHARLES	5700 KIRKSIDE DR #F - BAKERSFIELD CA 93309
30- 43 LANG, MARTIN JOHN	D. JANUARY 13, 1968 LAKEWOOD, COLO.
75- 64 LANG, ROBERT DAVID	985 HOMER AVE - PITTSBURGH PA 15237
14-123 LANGE, ERWIN HENRY	D. APRIL 24, 1971 MAYWOOD, ILL.
10- 85 LANGE, FRANK HERMAN	D. DECEMBER 26, 1945 MADISON, WIS.
72- 60 LANGE, RICHARD OTTO	3387 BROOKS RD, RR 2 - FREELAND MI 48623
26- 47 LANGFORD, ELTON L. 'SAM'	1003 OAKLAND ST - PLAINVIEW TX 79072
76- 53 LANGFORD, JAMES RICK	1119 59TH ST NW - BRADENTON FL 33505
84- 65 LANGSTON, MARK EDWARD	2935 MARIETTA DR - SANTA CLARA CA 95051
64- 63 LANIER, HAROLD CLIFTON	2365 WOODLAWN CIR E - ST PETERSBURG FL 33704
38- 50 LANIER, HUBERT MAX	RR 1 BOX 487 - DUNNELLON FL 32630
71- 61 LANIER, LORENZO	2928 WOODHILL AVE - CLEVELAND OH 44104
36- 46 LANNING, JOHN YOUNG	28 DEANWOOD CIR - ASHEVILLE NC 28803
16- 54 LANNING, LESTER ALFRED	D. JUNE 13, 1962 BRISTOL, CONN.
38- 51 LANNING, THOMAS NEWTON	D. NOVEMBER 4, 1967 MARIETTA, GA.
78- 69 LANSFORD, CARNEY RAY	821 REDWOOD DR - DANVILLE CA 94526
82- 76 LANSFORD, JOSEPH DALE 'JODY'	RR TWO - EUFAULA OK 74432
22- 69 LANSING, EUGENE HEWETT	D. JANUARY 18, 1945 RENSSELAER, N. Y.
51- 50 LAPALME, PAUL EDMORE	167 MITH ST - LEOMINSTER MA 01453
22- 70 LAPAN, PETER NELSON	D. JANUARY 5, 1953 NORWALK, CAL.
42- 62 LAPIHUSKA, ANDREW	900 MULBERRY STREET-MILLVILLE NJ 08332
80- 70 LAPOINT, DAVID JEFFREY	21 WINDYHILL RD - GLENS FALLS NY 12801
47- 56 LAPOINTE, RALPH JOHN	D. SEPTEMBER 13, 1967 BURLINGTON, VT.
58- 54 LARKER, NORMAN HOWARD	2500 EAST 4TH ST #306 - LONG BEACH CA 90814
83- 91 LARKIN, PATRICK CLIBURN	1101 GREENFIELD AVENUE - ARCADIA CA 91006
34- 60 LARKIN, STEPHEN PATRICK	D. MAY 2, 1969 NORRISTOWN, PA.
18- 44 LARMORE, ROBERT MCCAHAN	D. JANUARY 15, 1964 ST. LOUIS, MO.
70- 77 LAROCHE, DAVID EUGENE	36 HARBOR SIGHT DR - ROLLING HILLS ESTATES CA 90274
78- 70 LAROSE, HENRY JOHN	99 ROLAND - CUMBERLAND RI 02864
68- 52 LAROSE, VICTOR RAYMOND	2908 E SYLVIA ST - PHOENIX AZ 85028
14-124 LAROSS, HARRY RAYMOND	D. MARCH 22, 1954 HINES, ILL.
53- 50 LARSEN, DONALD JAMES	17090 COPPER HILL DR - MORGAN HILL CA 95037
36- 47 LARSEN, ERLING ADELI	3154 EAST DREXEL RD - TUCSON AZ 85706
76- 54 LARSON, DANIEL JAMES	1616 MONTEREY AVE - HERMOSA BEACH CA 90254
63- 66 LARUSSA, ANTHONY	2620 OAK GROVE CIR - SARASOTA FL 33580
54- 57 LARY, ALFRED ALLEN	RR 8 BOX 139 - NORTHPORT AL 35476
54- 58 LARY, FRANK STRONG	RR 8 BOX 142 - NORTHPORT AL 35476
29- 61 LARY, LYNFORD HOBART	D. JANUARY 9, 1973 DOWNEY, CAL.
63- 67 LASHER, FREDERICK WALTER	HIGHWAY E - MERRILLAN WI 54754
82- 77 LASKEY, WILLIAM ALAN	311 E WEBER ST - TOLEDO OH 43608
24- 64 LASLEY, WILLARD ALMOND	2565 DEXTER AVE N #201 - SEATTLE WA 98109
54- 59 LASORDA, THOMAS CHARLES	1473 W MAXZIM - FULLERTON CA 92633
57- 41 LASSETTER, DONALD O'NEAL	406 GORDY ST - PERRY GA 31069
85- 62 LATHAM, WILLIAM CAROL	1312 BAROSWOOD TER - BIRMINGHAM AL 35235
10- 86 LATHERS, CHARLES TEN EYCK 'CHICK'	D. JULY 26, 1971 PETOSKEY, MICH.
13- 99 LATHROP, WILLIAM GEORGE	D. NOVEMBER 20, 1958 JANESVILLE, WIS.
57- 42 LATMAN, ARNOLD BARRY	18316 HATTERAS ST #34 - TARZANA CA 91356
56- 50 LAU, CHARLES RICHARD	D. MARCH 18, 1984 KEY COLONY BEACH, FLA.
81- 67 LAUDNER, TIMOTHY JON	1801 PEARSON PKWY - MINNEAPOLIS MN 55444
67- 62 LAUZERIQUE, GEORGE ALBERT	3471 CUMBERLAND GAP CT - PLEASANTO CA 94566
34- 61 LAVAGETTO, HARRY ARTHUR 'COOKIE'	46 TARA RD - ORINDA CA 94563
84- 66 LAVALLIERE, MICHAEL EUGENE	12 SCOTT AVE - HOCKSETT NH 03106
13-100 LAVAN, JOHN LEONARD 'DOC'	D. MAY 29, 1952 DETROIT, MICH.
74- 71 LAVELLE, GARY ROBERT	1015 E LINDEN ST - ALLENTOWN PA 18103

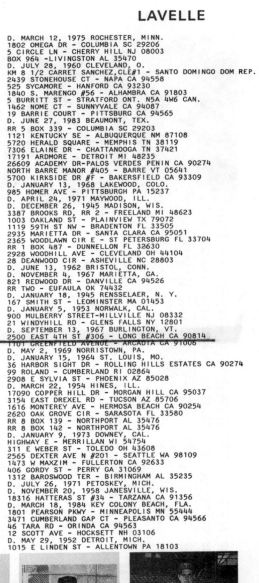

Greetings from   vous salut!
CHIP LANG

CHARLIE LAU

LAVENDER   LEINHAUSER

12-106	LAVENDER, JAMES SANFORD	D. JANUARY 12, 1960 CARTERSVILLE, GA.
14-125	LAVIGNE, ARTHUR DAVID	D. JULY 18, 1950 WORCESTER, MASS.
69- 99	LAW, RONALD DAVID	OLD ADD: 9000 YUCCA WAY - THORNTON CO
78- 71	LAW, RUDY KARL	10712 FELTON ST - INGLEWOOD CA 90304
80- 71	LAW, VANCE AARON	1760 WILLOWBROOK DR - PROVO UT 84601
50- 48	LAW, VERNON SANDERS	3885 N LITTLE ROCK DR - PROVO UT 84601
46- 63	LAWING, GARLAND FREDERICK	5710 ORR RD #20 - CHARLOTTE NC 28213
82- 78	LAWLESS, THOMAS JAMES	1736 W 25TH ST - ERIE PA 16502
54- 60	LAWRENCE, BROOKS ULYSSES	720C NORTHLAND RD - CINCINNATI OH 45240
63- 68	LAWRENCE, JAMES ROSS	BOX 851 - CALEDONIA ONTARIO NOA 1AO CAN.
24- 65	LAWRENCE, ROBERT ANDREW	%FRANCES LAWRENCE,RR 2 BOX 304 - GOSHEN NY 10924
32- 44	LAWRENCE, WILLIAM HENRY	135 GRAND ST - REDWOOD CITY CA 94062
16- 55	LAWRY, OTIS CARROLL	D. OCTOBER 23, 1965 CHINA, ME.
30- 44	LAWSON, ALFRED VOYLE 'ROXIE'	D. APRIL 9, 1977 STOCKPORT, IA.
72- 61	LAWSON, STEVEN GEORGE	3013 LIVE OAK CT - DANVILLE CA 94526
70- 78	LAXTON, WILLIAM HARRY	261 MANSION AVE - AUDUBON NJ 08106
15- 87	LAYDEN, EUGENE FRANCIS	D. DECEMBER 12, 1984 PITTSBURGH, PA.
48- 57	LAYDEN, PETER JOHN	D. JULY 18, 1982 EDNA, TEXAS
27- 53	LAYNE, HERMAN	D. AUGUST 27, 1973 GALLIPOLIS, O.
41- 62	LAYNE, IVORIA HILLIS 'HILLY'	4623 DORISA AVE-CHATTANOOGA TN 37411
48- 58	LAYTON, LESTER LEE	8780 E MCKELLIPS RD #27 - SCOTTSDALE AZ 85257
68- 53	LAZAR, JOHN DAN	8444 OAKWOOD AVE - MUNSTER IN 46321
43- 77	LAZOR, JOHN PAUL	8054 S. 116TH ST - SEATTLE WA 98178
84- 67	LAZORKO, JACK THOMAS	742 FIFTH AVE - RIVER EDGE NJ 07661
26- 48	LAZZERI, ANTHONY MICHAEL	D. AUGUST 6, 1946 SAN FRANCISCO, CAL.
80- 72	LEA, CHARLES WILLIAM	4237 FAIRMONT AVE - MEMPHIS TN 38108
23- 78	LEACH, FREDERICK M	D. DECEMBER 10, 1981 HAGERMAN, ID.
81- 68	LEACH, RICHARD MAX 'RICK'	4033 WEST COURT - FLINT MI 48504
81- 69	LEACH, TERRY HESTER	603 HOWELL AVE - SELMA AL 36701
80- 73	LEAL, LUIS ENRIQUE	CALLE 28 #30-60 - BARQUISMETO,EDO. LARA VENEZ
14-126	LEAR, CHARLES BERNARD 'KING'	D. OCTOBER 31, 1976 GREENCASTLE, PA.
15- 88	LEAR, FREDERICK FRANCIS	D. OCTOBER 13, 1955 EAST ORANGE, N.J.
17- 40	LEARD, WILLIAM WALLACE	D. JANUARY 15, 1970 SAN FRANCISCO, CAL.
14-127	LEARY, JOHN LOUIS	D. AUGUST 18, 1961 WALTHAM, MASS.
81- 70	LEARY, TIMOTHY JAMES	201 OCEAN AVE #1801B - SANTA MONICA CA 90402
20- 71	LEATHERS, HAROLD LANGFORD	D. APRIL 12, 1977 MODESTO, CALIF.
19- 51	LEBOURVEAU, DEWITT WILEY 'BEVO'	D. DECEMBER 19, 1947 NEVADA CITY, CAL.
15- 89	LEDBETTER, RALPH OVERTON 'RAZOR'	D. FEBRUARY 1, 1969 WEST PALM BEACH, FLA.
19- 52	LEE, CLIFFORD WALKER	D. AUGUST 25, 1980 DENVER, COLO.
57- 43	LEE, DONALD EDWARD	9101 PALM TREE DR - TUCSON AZ 85710
20- 72	LEE, ERNEST DUDLEY 'DUD'	D. JANUARY 7, 1971 DENVER, COLO.
30- 45	LEE, HAROLD BURNHAM	4118 RIVER RD - MOSS POINT MS 39563
69-100	LEE, LERON	111 SOUTH AVE - SACRAMENTO CA 95838
85- 63	LEE, MANUEL LEE	3RA #86 VILLA MAGDALENA - SAN PEDRO DE MACORIS DOM REP.
78- 72	LEE, MARK LINDEN	RT VIGO BOX 89 -TULIA TX 79088
60- 59	LEE, MICHAEL RANDALL	2511 BUENA FLORES - FALLBROOK CA 92028
64- 64	LEE, ROBERT DEAN	207 WEST A STREET - TEHACHAPI CA 93561
45- 56	LEE, ROY EDWIN	D. NOVEMBER 11, 1985 ST. LOUIS, MO.
33- 34	LEE, THORNTON STARR	509 W VIRGINIA AV - PHOENIX AZ 85003
34- 62	LEE, WILLIAM CRUTCHER	D. JUNE 15, 1977 PLAQUEMINE, LA.
69-101	LEE, WILLIAM FRANCIS	OLD ADD: MONCTON NEW BRUNSWICK
15- 90	LEE, WILLIAM JOSEPH	D. JANUARY 6, 1984 WEST HAZELTON, PA.
59- 48	LEEK, EUGENE HAROLD	3327 BANCROFT ST - SAN DIEGO CA 92104
84- 68	LEEPER, DAVID DALE	1922 FERN - ORANGE CA 92667
21- 55	LEES, GEORGE EDWARD	D. JANUARY 2, 1980 MECHANICSBURG, PA.
65- 62	LEFEBVRE, JAMES KENNETH	1114 6TH ST - SANTA MONICA CA 90403
80- 74	LEFEBVRE, JOSEPH HENRY	19 RIVER RD - PENCOOK NH 03301
38- 52	LEFEBVRE, WILFRID HENRY 'BILL'	7200 ULMERTON RD #1379 - LARGO FL 33541
20- 73	LEFEVRE, ALFREDO MODESTO	D. JANUARY 21, 1982 GLEN COVE, N. Y.
83- 92	LEFFERTS, CRAIG LINDSAY	6320 CAMINO ARCO - TUCSON AZ 85718
24- 66	LEFLER, WADE HAMPTON	D. MARCH 6, 1981 HICKORY, N. C.
74- 72	LEFLORE, RONALD	5126 IROQUOIS - DETROIT MI 48213
29- 62	LEGETT, LOUIS ALFRED	20 SNIPE ST - NEW ORLEANS LA 70124
32- 45	LEHENY, REGIS FRANCIS	D. NOVEMBER 2, 1976 PITTSBURGH, PA.
61- 66	LEHEW, JAMES ANTHONY	398 ARMSTRONG LN - BALTIMORE MD 21221
52- 66	LEHMAN, KENNETH KARL	447 COIN LAKE RD -SEDRO WOOLLEY WA 98284
46- 64	LEHNER, PAUL EUGENE	D. DECEMBER 27, 1967 BIRMINGHAM, ALA.
11- 96	LEHR, CLARENCE EMANUEL	D. JANUARY 31, 1948 DETROIT, MICH.
26- 49	LEHR, NORMAN CARL MICHAEL	D. JULY 17, 1968 CONESUS LAKE, N. Y.
33- 35	LEIBER, HENRY EDWARD	RR 2 BOX 811 - TUCSON AZ 85749
13-101	LEIBOLD, HARRY LORAN 'NEMO'	D. FEBRUARY 4, 1977 DETROIT, MICH.
79- 68	LEIBRANDT, CHARLES LOUIS	1424 OVERLOOK DR - GOLF IL 60029
21- 56	LEIFER, ELMER EDWIN	D. SEPTEMBER 26, 1948 EVERETT, WASH.
12-107	LEINHAUSER, WILLIAM CHARLES	D. APRIL 14, 1978 ELKINS PARK, PA.

39- 66	LEIP, EDGAR ELLSWORTH	D. NOVEMBER 24, 1983 ZEPHYRHILLS, FLA.
84- 69	LEIPER, DAVID PAUL	1421 HURON TRAIL - PLANO TX 75075
54- 61	LEJA, FRANK JOHN	118 WILSON RD - NAHANT MA 01908
11- 97	LEJEUNE, SHELDON ALDENBERT 'LARRY'	D. APRIL 21, 1952 CHATTANOOGA, TENN.
65- 63	LEJOHN, DONALD EVERETT	154 EDWARDS ST - BROWNSVILLE PA 15417
73- 73	LEMANCZYK, DAVID LAWRENCE	24 LEHIGH CT - ROCKVILLE CENTRE NY 11570
62- 75	LEMASTER, DENVER CLAYTON	4424 RIVERCLIFF DR - LILBURN GA 30247
75- 65	LEMASTER, JOHNNIE LEE	372 4TH ST - PAINTSVILLE KY 41240
61- 67	LEMAY, RICHARD PAUL	4821 S FLORENCE AVE - TULSA OK 74105
50- 49	LEMBO, STEPHEN NEAL	133-22 124TH ST - SOUTH OZONE PARK NY 11420
75- 66	LEMON, CHESTER EARL 'CHET'	4124 LAKE RIDGE LN - BLOOMFIELD HILLS MI 48013
50- 50	LEMON, JAMES ROBERT	6824 PINEWAY - HYATTSVILLE MD 20782
41- 63	LEMON, ROBERT GRANVILLE	1141 CLAIBORNE DR-LONG BEACH CA 90807
69-102	LEMONDS, DAVID LEE	207 JACKSON DR - CHARLOTTE NC 28213
76- 55	LEMONGELLO, MARK	OLD ADD: 251 ATLANTIC ST #30A - KEYPORT NJ 07735
50- 51	LENHARDT, DONALD EUGENE	13317 WOODLAKE VILLAGE CT - ST LOUIS MO 63141
28- 56	LENNON, EDWARD FRANCIS	D. SEPTEMBER 13, 1947 PHILADELPHIA, PA.
54- 62	LENNON, ROBERT ALBERT	8 DUDLEY LANE - DIX HILLS NY 11746
78- 73	LENTINE, JAMES MATTHEW	1901 EAST LAHABRA BLVD - LAHABRA CA 90631
68- 54	LEON, EDUARDO ANTONIO	5616 N. CALLE DE LA REINA - TUCSON AZ 85718
45- 57	LEON, ISIDORO JUAN	CALLE O NO. 260, APT 5 - VADARO HAVANA CUBA
73- 74	LEON, MAXIMINO (MEDINA)	DOMICILIO CONOCIDO - VILLA ACULA VERACRUZ MEX.
74- 73	LEONARD, DENNIS PATRICK	4102 EVERGREEN LN - BLUE SPRINGS MO 64015
11- 98	LEONARD, ELMER ELLSWORTH	D. MAY 27, 1981 NAPA, CALIF.
33- 36	LEONARD, EMIL JOHN "DUTCH"	D. APRIL 17, 1983 SPRINGFIELD, ILL.
13-102	LEONARD, HUBERT BENJAMIN 'DUTCH'	D. JULY 11, 1952 FRESNO, CALIF.
77- 84	LEONARD, JEFFREY N	1626 N FELTON ST - PHILADELPHIA PA 19151
14-129	LEONARD, JOSEPH HOWARD	D. MAY 1, 1920 WASHINGTON, D.C.
67- 63	LEONHARD, DAVID PAUL	87 CORNING ST - BEVERLY MA 01915
28- 57	LEOPOLD, RUDOLPH MATAS	D. SEPTEMBER 3, 1965 BATON ROUGE, LA.
41- 64	LEOVICH, JOHN JOSEPH	3531 NORTH REEF DR - LINCOLN CITY OR 97367
52- 67	LEPCIO, THADDEUS STANLEY 'TED'	263 GREENLODGE ST - DEDHAM MA 02026
55- 69	LEPPERT, DON EUGENE	5130 DURANT - MEMPHIS TN 38116
61- 68	LEPPERT, DONALD GEORGE	ROAD #1 BOX AA-7 - NINEVAH IN 46164
75- 67	LERCH, RANDY LOUIS	1253 LARGE OAK DR - PLACERVILLE CA 95667
10- 87	LERCHEN, BERTRAM ROE	D. JANUARY 7, 1962 DETROIT, MICH.
52- 68	LERCHEN, GEORGE EDWARD	354 EAST ROSE - GARDEN CITY MI 48135
28- 58	LERIAN, WALTER IRVIN	D. OCTOBER 22, 1929 BALTIMORE, MD.
69-103	LERSCH, BARRY LEE	OLD ADD: 1617 1/2 PALMER ST - PUEBLO CO 81004
72- 62	LESHNOCK, DONALD LEE	464 LORA AVE - YOUNGSTOWN OH 44504
82- 79	LESLEY, BRADLEY JAY	BOX 1012 - TURLOCK CA 95381
17- 41	LESLIE, ROY REID	D. APRIL 9, 1972 SHERMAN, TEX.
29- 63	LESLIE, SAMUEL ANDREW	D. JANUARY 21, 1979 PASCAGOULA, MISS.
39- 67	LETCHAS, CHARLIE	1121 HIGHLAND ST - THOMASVILLE GA 31792
47- 57	LEVAN, JESSE ROY	255 LINCOLN RD - READING PA 19606
13-103	LEVERENZ, WALTER FRED	D. MARCH 19, 1973 ATASCADERO, CALIF.
22- 71	LEVERETT, GORHAM VANCE 'DIXIE'	D. FEBRUARY 20, 1957 BEAVERTON, ORE.
20- 74	LEVERETTE, HORACE WILBUR 'HOD'	D. APRIL 10, 1958 ST. PETERSBURG, FLA.
30- 46	LEVEY, JAMES JULIUS	D. MARCH 14, 1970 DALLAS, TEX.
23- 79	LEVSEN, EMIL HENRY 'DUTCH'	D. MARCH 12, 1972 MINNEAPOLIS, MINN.
40- 49	LEVY, EDWARD CLARENCE	%E.WHITNER,505 RIDGECREST RD - LAGRANGE GA 30240
75- 68	LEWALLYN, DENNIS DALE	2900 BRECKENRIDGE DR - PENSACOLA FL 32506
51- 51	LEWANDOWSKI, DANIEL WILLIAM	OLD ADD: 61 MAYBERRY - BUFFALO NY 14227
67- 64	LEWIS, ALLAN SYDNEY	PUERTO ARMUELLAS - CHIRIQUI GRANDE PAN.
10- 88	LEWIS, GEORGE EDWARD 'DUFFY'	D. JUNE 17, 1979 SALEM, N. H.
79- 69	LEWIS, JAMES MARTIN	16049 NE 8TH AVE - NORTH MIAMI BEACH FL 33162
11- 99	LEWIS, JOHN DAVID	D. FEBRUARY 25, 1956 STEUBENVILLE, O.
35- 61	LEWIS, JOHN KELLY 'BUDDY'	BOX 788-GASTONIA NC 28052
64- 65	LEWIS, JOHNNY JOE	OLD ADD: 1133 URSULA ST - UNIVERSITY CITY MO
24- 67	LEWIS, WILLIAM BURTON	D. MARCH 24, 1950 TONAWANDA, N. Y.

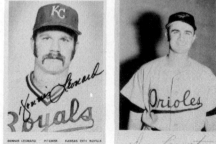

DENNIS LEONARD PITCHER   KANSAS CITY ROYALS

33- 37	LEWIS, WILLIAM HENRY	D. OCTOBER 24, 1977 MEMPHIS, TENN.
71- 62	LEY, TERRENCE RICHARD	4443 NE PRESCOTT ST - PORTLAND OR 97218
80- 75	LEZCANO, CARLOS MANUEL	962 ALAMEDA VILLA-GRANADA,RIO PIEDRAS PR00923
74- 74	LEZCANO, SIXTO JOAQUIN	OLD ADD: 437 S HAWLEY RD #69-MILWAUKEE WI
45- 58	LIBKE, ALBERT WALTER	1117 SOUTH APPELAND DR - WENATCHEE WA 98801
69-104	LIBRAN, FRANCISCO	CALLE DR ESCADE #202 - MAYAGUEZ PR 00708
81- 71	LICKERT, JOHN WILBUR	922 WILHELM ST - PITTSBURGH PA 15220
53- 51	LIDDLE, DONALD EUGENE	1022 NORTH CHERRY ST - MOUNT CARMEL IL 62863
35- 62	LIEBER, CHARLES EDWIN 'DUTCH'	D. DECEMBER 31, 1961 LOS ANGELES, CAL.
30- 47	LIEBHARDT, GLENN IGNATIUS	2460 TANTELON PL - WINSTON SALEM NC 27107
10- 89	LIESE, FREDERICK RICHARD	D. JUNE 30, 1967 LOS ANGELES, CALIF.
36- 48	LILLARD, ROBERT EUGENE 'GENE'	5676 ENCINA RD - GOLETA CA 93117
39- 68	LILLARD, WILLIAM BEVERLY	5290 PAREJO DR - SANTA BARBARA CA 93111
58- 55	LILLIS, ROBERT PERRY	12506 ELLA LEE - HOUSTON TX 77077
51- 52	LIMMER, LOUIS	100-11 DEBS PL - BRONX NY 10475

85

81- 72 LINARES, RUFINO DELACRUZ	QUIS QUEYA,LA LOMA 14 #23-SAN PEDRO DE MACORIS DOM REP.
27- 54 LIND, HENRY CARL	D. AUGUST 2, 1946 NEW YORK, N. Y.
74- 75 LIND, JACKSON HUGH	718 N. LINDEN CIR - MESA AZ 85203
60- 60 LINDBECK, EMERIT DESMOND	347 E GARFIELD ST - KEWANNEE IL 61443
65- 64 LINDBLAD, PAUL AARON	6203 LAKE RIDGE RD - ARLINGTON TX 76016
47- 58 LINDE, LYMAN GILBERT	607 W BURNETT ST - BEAVER DAM WI 53916
41- 65 LINDELL, JOHN HARLAN	D. AUGUST 27, 1985 NEWPORT BEACH, CALIF.
50- 52 LINDEN, WALTER CHARLES	4432 HARVEY AVE - WESTERN SPRINGS IL 60558
43- 78 LINDQUIST, CARL EMIL	RR 1 BOX 185A - EMPORIUM PA 15834
11-100 LINDSAY, WILLIAM GIBBONS	D. JULY 14, 1963 GREENSBORO, N.C.
22- 72 LINDSEY, JAMES KENDRICK	D. OCTOBER 25, 1963 JACKSON, LA.
16- 56 LINDSTROM, AXEL OLAF	D. JUNE 25, 1940 ASHEVILLE, N. C.
58- 56 LINDSTROM, CHARLES WILLIAM	220 PARK PLACE - LINCOLN IL 62656
24- 63 LINDSTROM, FRED CHARLES	D. OCTOBER 4, 1981 CHICAGO, ILL.
66- 55 LINES, RICHARD GEORGE	OLD ADD: 4220 N. FEDERAL HWY - FT LAUDERDALE FL 33306
52- 69 LINHART, CARL JAMES	2647 DELMAR AVE - GRANITE CITY IL 62040
10- 90 LINK, FREDERICK THEODORE	D. MAY 22, 1939 HOUSTON, TEXAS
33- 38 LINKE, EDWARD KARL	4830 N MULLIGAN AVE - CHICAGO IL 60630
54- 63 LINT, ROYCE JAMES	6814 SE JACK RD - MILWAUKIE OR 97222
29- 64 LINTON, CLAUD CLARENCE 'BOB'	D. APRIL 3, 1980 DESTIN, FLA.
73- 75 LINTZ, LARRY	71 LACONIA CT - SAN JOSE CA 95139
62- 76 LINZ, PHILIP FRANCIS	1189 FIRST AVE - NEW YORK NY 10021
63- 69 LINZY, FRANK ALFRED	RR 2 BOX 395 - COWETA OK 74429
56- 51 LIPIETRI, MICHAEL ANGELO	150 YOAKUM AVE - FARMINGDALE NY 11735
42- 63 LIPON, JOHN JOSEPH	13315 ALCHESTER - HOUSTON TX 77079
37- 66 LIPSCOMB, GERARD 'NIG'	D. FEBRUARY 27, 1978 HUNTERSVILLE, N. C.
63- 70 LIPSKI, ROBERT PETER	1 SNOOK ST - SCRANTON PA 18505
70- 79 LIS, JOSEPH ANTHONY	107 KIMBERLY RD - SOMERVILLE NJ 08876
27- 55 LISENBEE, HORACE MILTON 'HOD'	872 DOVER RD - CLARKSVILLE TN 37042
81- 81 LISI, RICCARDO PATRICK EMILIO	OLD ADD: 32 RIVERVIEW W. APTS#2-PITTSFIELD MA
29- 65 LISKA, ADOLPH JAMES	3831 NE WASCO - PORTLAND OR 97232
73- 76 LITTELL, MARK ALAN	BOX 35 - DEFIANCE MO 63341
80- 76 LITTLE, DONALD JEFFREY 'JEFF'	5550 C. R. 44 - WOODVILLE OH 43469
82- 80 LITTLE, RICHARD BRYAN	1003 MAGNOLIA - HEARNE TX 77859
12-108 LITTLE, WILLIAM ARTHUR 'JACK'	D. JULY 27, 1961 DALLAS, TEX.
80- 77 LITTLEFIELD, JOHN ANDREW	1214 N. ALAMEDA ST - AZUSA CA 91702
50- 53 LITTLEFIELD, RICHARD BERNARD	14838 KENTFIELD - DETROIT MI 48223
27- 56 LITTLEJOHN, CHARLES CARLISLE	D. OCTOBER 27, 1977 KANSAS CITY, MO.
78- 74 LITTLEJOHN, DENNIS GERALD	OLD ADD: 2244 W FREMONT DR - TEMPE AZ
81- 74 LITTLETON, LARRY MARVIN	2318 ARMAND RD NE - ATLANTA GA 30324
52- 70 LITTRELL, JACK NAPIER	7510 FLOYDSBURG RD - CRESTWOOD KY 40014
40- 50 LITWHILER, DANIEL WEBSTER	2696 TERI TERRACE - EAST LANSING MI 48823
47- 59 LIVELY, EVERETT ADRIAN 'BUD'	8605 ESSLINGER CT - HUNTSVILLE AL 35802
11-101 LIVELY, HENRY EVERETT 'JACK'	D. DECEMBER 5, 1967 ARAB, ALA.
39- 63 LIVENGOOD, WESLEY AMOS	2220 ELGIN RD - WINSTON SALEM NC 27103
38- 53 LIVINGSTON, THOMPSON ORVILLE 'MICKEY'	D. APRIL 3, 1983 HOUSTON, TEXAS
68- 55 LLENAS, WINSTON ENRIQUILLO	APARTADO #92 - SANTIAGO DOMINICAN REP.
22- 73 LLEWELLYN, CLEMENT MANLEY	D. NOVEMBER 27, 1969 CHARLOTTE, N. C.
12-109 LOAN, WILLIAM JOSEPH 'MIKE'	D. NOVEMBER 12, 1966 SPRINGFIELD, PA.
39- 70 LOANE, ROBERT KENNETH	BOX 246 - COOL CA 95614
14-130 LOBERT, FRANK JOHN	D. MAY 29, 1932 PITTSBURGH, PA.
62- 77 LOCK, DONALD WILSON	1330 N WALNUT - KINGMAN KS 67068
55- 70 LOCKE, CHARLES EDWARD	1718 BIG BEND RD - POPLAR BLUFF MO 63901
59- 49 LOCKE, LAWRENCE DONALD 'BOBBY'	RR 1 BOX 400 - DUNBAR PA 15431
64- 66 LOCKE, RONALD THOMAS	LEWISTON AVE - KENYON RI 02836
65- 65 LOCKER, ROBERT AWTRY	735 SILVERCREST CT - LAFAYETTE CA 94549
73- 77 LOCKLEAR, GENE	RR1 BOX 213 - PEMBROKE NC 28382
55- 71 LOCKLIN, STUART CARLTON	1823 S BOUTEN - APPLETON WI 54911
45- 59 LOCKMAN, CARROLL WALTER 'WHITEY'	8234 N 75TH ST - SCOTTSDALE AZ 85253
65- 66 LOCKWOOD, CLAUDE EDWARD 'SKIP'	131 BUCKSKIN DR - WESTON MA 02193
38- 54 LODIGIANI, DARIO ANTHONY	745 LATHROP ST - NAPA CA 94558
28- 59 LOEPP, GEORGE HERBERT	D. SEPTEMBER 4, 1967 LOS ANGELES, CAL.
50- 54 LOES, WILLIAM 'BILLY'	33-08 84TH ST - JACKSON HEIGHTS NY 11372
26- 50 LOFTUS, FRANCIS PATRICK	D. OCTOBER 27, 1980 BELCHERTOWN, MASS.
24- 69 LOFTUS, RICHARD JOSEPH	D. JANUARY 21, 1972 CONCORD, MASS.
51- 53 LOGAN, JOHN	6115 W CLEVELAND AVE - MILWAUKEE WI 53219
35- 63 LOGAN, ROBERT DEAN	D. MAY 20, 1978 INDIANAPOLIS, IND.
14-131 LOHR, HOWARD SYLVESTER	D. JUNE 9, 1977 PHILADELPHIA, PA.
47- 60 LOHRKE, JACK WAYNE 'LUCKY'	2817 LUCENA DR - SAN JOSE CA 95132
34- 63 LOHRMAN, WILLIAM LEROY	250 ROUTE 208 - NEW PALTZ NY 12561
78- 75 LOIS, ALBERTO	INGENIO CONSUELO CALLE 5-SAN PEDRO DE MACORIS DOM. REP.
63- 71 LOLICH, MICHAEL STEPHEN 'MICKEY'	6252 ROBINHILL - WASHINGTON MI 48094
71- 63 LOLICH, RONALD JOHN	OLD ADD: 2436 N. SAVIER - PORTLAND OR 97210

LOLLAR   LUKON

46- 65 LOLLAR, JOHN SHERMAN 'SHERM' D. SEPTEMBER 24, 1977 SPRINGFIELD, MO.
80- 78 LOLLAR, WILLIAM TIMOTHY 'TIM' 316 N JEFFERSON - FARMINGTON MO 63640
84- 70 LOMAN, DOUGLAS EDWARD 4308 CHADBOURN ST - BAKERSFIELD CA 93309
31- 48 LOMBARDI, ERNEST NATALI D. SEPTEMBER 26, 1977 SANTA CRUZ, CALIF.
45- 60 LOMBARDI, VICTOR ALVIN 5164 E ASHLAN #103 - FRESNO CA 93727
48- 59 LOMBARDO, LOUIS 1551 FIRST STREET SOUTH - JACKSONVILLE FL 32250
85- 64 LOMBARDOZZI, STEPHEN PAUL 2 HAND HEWN WAY - MANLIUS NY 13104
65- 67 LONBORG, JAMES REYNOLD 498 FIRST PARISH RD - SCITUATE MA 02066
11-102 LONERGAN, WALTER E. D. JANUARY 23, 1958 LEXINGTON, MASS.
22- 74 LONG, JAMES ALBERT D. SEPTEMBER 14, 1970 FORT DODGE, IA.
63- 72 LONG, JEOFFREY KEITH 11 FLOWER CT - LAKESIDE PARK KY 41017
11-103 LONG, LESTER 'LEP' D. OCTOBER 21, 1958 BIRMINGHAM, ALA.
51- 54 LONG, RICHARD DALE 7 CLOVERDALE CT S - PALM COAST FL 32037
81- 75 LONG, ROBERT EARL 3560 MOHAVE DR - GRANDVILLE MI 49418
11-104 LONG, THOMAS AUGUSTUS D. JUNE 15, 1972 MOBILE, ALA.
24- 70 LONG, THOMAS FRANCIS D. SEPTEMBER 16, 1973 LOUISVILLE, KY.
85- 65 LONG, WILLIAM DOUGLAS 7699 DIMMICK ROAD - CINCINNATI OH 45241
56- 52 LONNETT, JOSEPH PAUL 126 DUNCAN CIR - BEAVER PA 15009
68- 56 LOOK, BRUCE MICHAEL 3863 HEMMINGWAY - OKEMOS MI 48864
61- 69 LOOK, DEAN ZACHARY 2103 BUTTERNUT - OKEMOS MI 48864
44- 77 LOPAT, EDMUND WALTER 99 OAK TRAIL RD - HILLSDALE NJ 07642
48- 60 LOPATA, STANLEY EDWARD 1518 ELKINS AVE - ABINGTON PA 19001
45- 61 LOPATKA, ARTHUR JOSEPH 7310 N HARLEM - CHICAGO IL 60648
72- 63 LOPES, DAVID EARL 'DAVEY' 16984 AVE DE SANTA YNEZ-PACIFIC PALISADES CA 90272
28- 60 LOPEZ, ALFONSO RAMON 3601 BEACH DR - TAMPA FL 33609
65- 68 LOPEZ, ARTURO 57 WALNUT ST - OAKLAND NJ 07436
74- 76 LOPEZ, AURELIO RIOS 5 PONIENTE #8 - TEXAMACHALCO PUEBLA MEX.
76- 56 LOPEZ, CARLOS ANTONIO MEXICI #33A, POINTE - MAZATLAN SINALOA MEX.
55- 72 LOPEZ, HECTOR HEADLEY 666 JANOS LN - WEST HEMPSTEAD NY 11552
66- 56 LOPEZ, JOSE RAMON D. SEPTEMBER 4, 1982 MIAMI, FLA.
63- 73 LOPEZ, MARCELINO PONS 841 NW LITTLE RIVER DR - MIAMI FL 33150
23- 80 LORD, WILLIAM CARLTON 'CARL' D. AUGUST 15, 1947 CHESTER, PA.
13-104 LORENZEN, ADOLPH ANDREAS 'LEFTY' D. MARCH 5, 1963 DAVENPORT, IA.
16- 57 LOTZ, JOSEPH PETER D. JANUARY 1, 1971 HAYWARD, CAL.
80- 79 LOUCKS, SCOTT GREGORY 1801 VIOLA DR - SIERRA VISTA AZ 85635
10- 91 LOUDELL, ARTHUR D. FEBRUARY 19, 1961 KANSAS CITY, MO.
67- 65 LOUGHLIN, LAWRENCE JOHN 410 S 57TH - TACOMA WA 98408
64- 67 LOUN, DONALD NELSON 9095 WEXFORD DR - VIENNA VA 22180
13-105 LOVE, EDWARD HAUGHTON 'SLIM' D. NOVEMBER 30, 1942 MEMPHIS, TENN.
22- 75 LOVELACE, THOMAS RIVERS D. JULY 12, 1979 DALLAS, TEX.
55- 73 LOVENGUTH, LYNN RICHARD 13565 SW HART RD - BEAVERTON OR 97005
33- 39 LOVETT, MERRITT MARWOOD 'MEM' 407 ASHLAND AVE #1H - RIVER FOREST IL 60305
80- 80 LOVIGLIO, JOHN PAUL 'JAY' 96 COUNTRY VILLAGE LN - EAST ISLIP NY 11730
72- 64 LOVITTO, JOSEPH 3803 SHADY CREEK NORTH - ARLINGTON TX 76013
63- 74 LOVRICH, PETER 19626 BEECHNUT DR - MOKENA IL 60448
15- 91 LOW, FLETCHER D. JUNE 6, 1973 HANOVER, N.H.
11-105 LOWDERMILK, LOUIS BAILEY D. DECEMBER 27, 1975 CENTRALIA, ILL.
20- 75 LOWE, GEORGE WESLEY D. SEPTEMBER 2, 1981 SOMERS POINT, N. J.
70- 80 LOWENSTEIN, JOHN LEE 1208 STARKY - AUGUSTA KS 67010
51- 55 LOWN, OMAR JOSEPH 'TURK' 1106 VAN BUREN - PUEBLO CO 81004
42- 64 LOWREY, HARRY LEE 'PEANUTS' 802 EDGEWOOD ST #3 - INGLEWOOD CA 90302
84- 71 LOWRY, DWIGHT RR 2 BOX 225 - PEMBROKE NC 28372
42- 65 LOWRY, SAMUEL JOSEPH OLD ADD: 4716 FOWLER - PHILADELPHIA PA 19127
84- 72 LOZADO, WILLIAM 551 EUCLID AVE - BROOKLYN NY 11208
81- 76 LUBRATICH, STEVEN GEORGE 910 CASTLE - SAN LEANDRO CA 94578
36- 49 LUBY, HUGH MAX 1730 W 28TH AVE-EUGENE OR 97405
38- 55 LUCADELLO, JOHN 103 OAKWOOD DR-SAN ANTONIO TX 78228
23- 81 LUCAS, CHARLES FRED 'RED' 1124 GREENFIELD AV - NASHVILLE TN 37216
35- 64 LUCAS, FREDERICK WARRINGTON 711 MARYLAND - CAMBRIDGE MD 21613
80- 81 LUCAS, GARY PAUL 3356 AVENIDA SIERRA - ESCONDIDO CA 92025
31- 49 LUCAS, JOHN CHARLES D. OCTOBER 31, 1970 MARYVILLE, ILL.
29- 66 LUCAS, RAY WESLEY D. OCTOBER 9, 1969 HARRISON, MICH.
70- 81 LUCCHESI, FRANK JOSEPH 3027 GLASGOW DR - ARLINGTON TX 76013
23- 82 LUCE, FRANK EDWARD D. FEBRUARY 3, 1942 MILWAUKEE, WIS.
20- 76 LUCEY, JOSEPH EARL D. JULY 30, 1980 HOLYOKE, MASS.
43- 79 LUCIER, LOUIS JOSEPH 579 HIGHLAND ST - NORTHBRIDGE MA 01534
24- 71 LUDOLPH, WILLIAM FRANCIS D. APRIL 8, 1952 OAKLAND, CAL.
25- 66 LUEBBE, ROY JOHN D. AUGUST 21, 1985 PAPILLION, NEB.
71- 64 LUEBBER, STEPHEN LEE RR 1 BOX 252 - CARL JUNCTION MO 64834
62- 78 LUEBKE, RICHARD RAYMOND D. DECEMBER 4, 1974 SAN DIEGO, CALIF.
85- 66 LUGO, URBANO RAFAEL ROOEVELT RES. TIUNA ENT BPH 44 ROSALES - CARACAS VENEZ
13-106 LUHRSEN, WILLIAM FERDINAND D. AUGUST 15, 1973 NORTH LITTLE ROCK, ARK.
41- 66 LUKON, EDWARD PAUL RR 3, CHERRY VALLEY RD - BURGETTSTOWN PA15021

CARLOS LOPEZ

87

67- 66 LUM, MICHAEL KEN-WAI	3476 COCHISE DR NW - ATLANTA GA 30339
57- 44 LUMENTI, RALPH ANTHONY	9 TOMASSO - MILFORD MA 01757
56- 53 LUMPE, JERRY DEAN	732 PEARSON DR - SPRINGFIELD MO 65801
54- 64 LUNA, GUILLERMO ROMERO "MEMO"	CARDENAS 50 OTE. - LOS MOCHIS SINOLOA MEX.
45- 62 LUND, DONALD ANDREW	1000 S STATE ST - ANN ARBOR MI 48109
67- 67 LUND, GORDON T	1717 ROBBIE LN - MOUNT PROSPECT IL 60056
24- 72 LUNDGREN, EBIN DELMAR 'DEL'	423 N 3RD ST - LINDSBORG KS 67456
73- 78 LUNDSTEDT, THOMAS ROBERT	8645 HUNTERS WAY - ST. PAUL MN 55124
19- 53 LUNTE, HARRY AUGUST	D. JULY 27, 1965 ST. LOUIS, MO.
40- 51 LUPIEN, ULYSSES JOHN 'TONY'	BOX 351 - NORWICH VT 05055
61- 70 LUPLOW, ALVIN DAVID	2450 STARLITE DR - SAGINAW MI 48603
14-132 LUQUE, ADOLFO	D. JULY 3, 1957 HAVANA, CUBA
10- 92 LUSH, ERNEST BENJAMIN	D. FEBRUARY 26, 1937 DETROIT, MICH.
56- 54 LUTTRELL, LYLE KENNETH	D. JULY 11, 1984 CHATTANOOGA, TENN.
22- 76 LUTZ, LOUIS WILLIAM	D. FEBRUARY 22, 1984 CINCINNATI, O.
51- 56 LUTZ, ROLLIN JOSEPH 'JOE'	1411 QUAIL DR - SARASOTA FL 33581
23- 83 LUTZKE, WALTER JOHN 'RUBE'	D. MARCH 6, 1938 MILWAUKEE, WIS.
70- 82 LUZINSKI, GREGORY MICHAEL	84 SWEETBRIER CT - MEDFORD NJ 08055
67- 68 LYLE, ALBERT WALTER 'SPARKY'	107 PINE TERRACE DR - DEMAREST NJ 07627
25- 67 LYLE, JAMES CHARLES	D. OCTOBER 10, 1977 WILLIAMSPORT, PA.
20- 77 LYNCH, ADRIAN RYAN	D. MARCH 16, 1934 DAVENPORT, IA.
80- 82 LYNCH, EDWARD FRANCIS	5940 SW 120TH ST - MIAMI FL 33156
54- 65 LYNCH, GERALD THOMAS	RR 1 BOX 285 - BOLIVAR PA 15923
48- 61 LYNCH, MATT DANNY 'DUMMY'	D. JUNE 30, 1978 PLANO, TEXAS
22- 77 LYNCH, WALTER EDWARD	D. DECEMBER 21, 1976 DAYTONA BEACH, CALIF.
16- 58 LYNN, BYRD	D. FEBRUARY 5, 1940 NAPA, CAL.
74- 77 LYNN, FREDRIC MICHAEL	6961 E VIA EL ESTRIBO-ANAHEIM HILLS CA 92807
39- 71 LYNN, JAPHET MONROE 'RED'	D. OCTOBER 27, 1977 BELLVILLE, TEX.
37- 67 LYNN, JEROME EDWARD	D. SEPTEMBER 25, 1972 SCRANTON, PA.
44- 78 LYON, RUSSELL MAYO	BOX 366 - CALHOUN FALLS SC 29629
44- 79 LYONS, ALBERT HAROLD	D. DECEMBER 20, 1965 INGLEWOOD, CAL.
47- 61 LYONS, EDWARD HOYT	1466 EBERT ST - WINSTON SALEM NC 27103
20- 78 LYONS, GEORGE TONY	D. AUGUST 12, 1981 NEVADA, MO.
41- 67 LYONS, HERSCHEL E	7900 DUNBARTON AVE-LOS ANGELES CA 90045
85- 67 LYONS, STEPHEN JOHN	8475 SW PARKVIEW LOOP - BEAVERTON OR 97005
29- 67 LYONS, TERENCE HILBERT	D. SEPTEMBER 9, 1959 DAYTON, O.
23- 84 LYONS, THEODORE AMAR	1401 LOREE ST - VINTON LA 70668
83- 93 LYONS, WILLIAMS ALLEN	2621 GRANDVIEW AVENUE - ALTON IL 62002
80- 83 LYSANDER, RICHARD EUGENE	225 FLORENCE ST #1 - SUNNYVALE CA 94086
69-105 LYTTLE, JAMES LAWRENCE	998 SW 21ST ST - BOCA RATON FL 33432
55- 74 MAAS, DUANE FREDRICK 'DUKE'	D. DECEMBER 7, 1976 MOUNT CLEMENS, MICH.
58- 57 MABE, ROBERT LEE	90 BISHOP AVE - DANVILLE VA 24541
76- 57 MACCORMACK, FRANK LOUIS	2 SCHMIDT PL - SECAUCUS NJ 07094
28- 61 MACDONALD, HARVEY FORSYTH	D. OCTOBER 4, 1965 MANOA, PA.
50- 55 MACDONALD, WILLIAM PAUL	RR 1 BOX 13 - BELLEVUE ID 83313
26- 51 MACFAYDEN, DANIEL KNOWLES	D. AUGUST 26, 1972 BRUNSWICK, ME.
74- 78 MACHA, KENNETH EDWARD	876 PATTON ST - MONROEVILLE PA 15146
79- 70 MACHA, MICHAEL WILLIAM	117 PERTH - VICTORIA TX 77901
71- 65 MACHEMEHL, CHARLES WALTER	RR 5 BOX 234 - BRENHAM TX 77833
78- 76 MACHEMER, DAVID RITCHIE	1359 ST. JOSEPH CIR - ST. JOSEPH MI 49085
10- 93 MACK, EARLE THADDEUS	D. FEBRUARY 4, 1967 UPPER DARBY, PA.
22- 78 MACK, FRANK GEORGE	D. JULY 2, 1971 CLEARWATER, FLA.
45- 63 MACK, JOSEPH JOHN	OLD ADD: 2038 MULBERRY LN - ARLINGTON HEIGHTS IL 60004
38- 56 MACK, RAYMOND JAMES	D. MAY 7, 1969 BUCYRUS, O.
85- 68 MACK, TONY LYNN	3304 MONTA VESTA RD #E32 - LEXINGTON KY 40502
73- 79 MACKANIN, PETER	6500 N. UNIVERSITY #208 - PEORIA IL 61614
55- 75 MACKENZIE, ERIC HUGH	1224 EMILY ST - MOORETOWN ONTARIO CAN.
61- 71 MACKENZIE, HENRY GORDON 'GORDY'	RR1 BOX 411C - LEESBURG FL 32748
60- 61 MACKENZIE, KENNETH PURVIS	232 YORK ST - NEW HAVEN CT 06520
41- 68 MACKIEWICZ, FELIX THADDEUS	33 NANTUCKET LN-OLIVETTE MO 63132
53- 52 MACKINSON, JOHN JOSEPH	17934 HATTON ST - RESEDA CA 91335
79- 71 MACKO, STEVEN JOSEPH	D. NOVEMBER 15, 1981 ARLINGTON, TEX.
62- 79 MACLEOD, WILLIAM DANIEL	6 FRANKLIN ST #2 - MARBLEHEAD MA 01945
38- 57 MACON, MAX CULLEN	825 WEST CENTER ST #16B - JUPITER FL 33458
22- 79 MACPHEE, WALTER SCOTT 'WADDY'	D. JANUARY 20, 1980 CHARLOTTE, N. C.
44- 80 MACPHERSON, HARRY WILLIAM	GAGE HILL RD - PELHAM NH 03076
80- 84 MACWHORTER, KEITH	86B VILLAGE GREEN NORTH - EAST PROVIDENCE RI 02915
14-133 MADDEN	B. PITTSBURGH, PA.
16- 59 MADDEN, EUGENE	D. APRIL 6, 1949 UTICA, N. Y.
12-110 MADDEN, LEONARD JOSEPH	D. SEPTEMBER 9, 1949 TOLEDO, O.
83- 94 MADDEN, MICHAEL ANTHONY	4733 FRANKFORT WAY - DENVER CO 80239
46- 66 MADDERN, JAMES CLARENCE	BOX 1656 - BISBEE AZ 85603
70- 83 MADDOX, ELLIOTT	109 HILTON AVE - VAUXHALL NJ 07088
72- 65 MADDOX, GARRY LEE	OLD ADD: 26 BRIARWOOD - BERLIN NJ 08091
78- 77 MADDOX, JERRY GLENN	15513 DOMART - NORWALK CA 90650
85- 69 MADISON, CHARLES SCOTT 'SCOTTIE'	STAR ROUTE BOX 1605 - LILLIAN AL 36549
50- 56 MADISON, DAVID PLEDGER	D. DECEMBER 9, 1985 MACON, MISS.
32- 46 MADJESKI, EDWARD WILLIAM	47 DE HART - ELIZABETH NJ 07202
73- 80 MADLOCK, BILL	453 E DECATUR ST - DECATUR IL 62521
47- 62 MADRID, SALVADOR	D. FEBRUARY 24, 1977 FORT WAYNE, IND.
60- 62 MAESTRI, HECTOR ANIBAL	OLD ADD: 2360 SW 3RD ST - MIAMI FL 33135
11-106 MAGEE, LEO CHRISTOPHER	D. MARCH 14, 1966 COLUMBUS, O.
38- 58 MAGGERT, HARL WARREN	240 EDITH AVE #242 - CORNING CA 96021
45- 64 MAGLIE, SALVATORE ANTHONY	77 MORNINGSIDE DR - GRAND ISLAND NY 14072
11-107 MAGNER, EDMUND BURKE 'STUBBY'	D. SEPTEMBER 9, 1956 CHILLICOTHE, O.
70- 84 MAGNUSON, JAMES ROBERT	641 STATE ST - MARINETTE WI 54143
66- 57 MAGRINI, PETER ALEXANDER	2402 RANCHO CABEZA DR - SANTA ROSA CA 95404
22- 80 MAGUIRE, FRED EDWARD	D. NOVEMBER 3, 1961 BRIGHTON, MASS.
50- 57 MAGUIRE, JACK	BOX 13947 - GAINESVILLE FL 32604
21- 57 MAHADY, JAMES BERNARD	D. AUGUST 9, 1936 CORTLAND, N. Y.
60- 63 MAHAFFEY, ARTHUR	3545 RHOADS AVE - NEWTOWN SQUARE PA 19073
26- 52 MAHAFFEY, LEE ROY	D. JULY 23, 1969 ANDERSON, S. C.
40- 52 MAHAN, ARTHUR LEO	1002 KENWYN ST-PHILADELPHIA PA 19124
12-111 MAHARG, WILLIAM JOSEPH	D. NOVEMBER 20, 1953 PHILADELPHIA, PA.
78- 78 MAHLBERG, GREGORY JOHN	5100 N. PLACITA DEL LAZO - TUCSON AZ 85715
77- 85 MAHLER, MICHAEL JAMES	7911 QUIRT DR - SAN ANTONIO TX 78227
79- 72 MAHLER, RICHARD KEITH 'RICK'	7911 QUIRT DR - SAN ANTONIO TX 78227
30- 48 MAHON, ALFRED GWINN	D. DECEMBER 26, 1977 NEW HAVEN, CONN.
10- 94 MAHONEY, CHRISTOPHER JOHN	D. JULY 15, 1954 VISALIA, CALIF.

11-108 MAHONEY, DANIEL JOSEPH	D. SEPTEMBER 28, 1960 UTICA, N.Y.
59- 50 MAHONEY, JAMES THOMAS	150 SYCAMORE TER - GLEN ROCK NJ 07452
51- 57 MAHONEY, ROBERT PAUL	6901 LYNN - LINCOLN NE 68505
45- 65 MAIER, ROBERT PHILIP	334 DUNELLEN AVE - DUNELLAN NJ 08812
36- 50 MAILHO, EMIL PIERRE	566 SCOTT ST - FREMONT CA 94538
15- 92 MAILS, JOHN WALTER 'DUSTER'	D. JULY 5, 1974 SAN FRANCISCO, CALIF.
48- 62 MAIN, FORREST HARRY 'WOODY'	563 CAMINO DE TEODORO - WALNUT CA 91789
14-134 MAIN, MILES GRANT 'ALEX'	D. DECEMBER 29, 1965 ROYAL OAK, MICH.
43- 80 MAINS, JAMES ROYAL	D. MARCH 17, 1969 BRIDGTON, ME.
15-105 MAISEL, CHARLES LOUIS	D. AUGUST 25, 1953 BALTIMORE, MD.
13-107 MAISEL, FREDERICK CHARLES 'FRITZ'	D. APRIL 22, 1967 BALTIMORE, MD.
13-108 MAISEL, GEORGE JOHN	D. NOVEMBER 20, 1968 BALTIMORE, MD.
39- 72 MAJESKI, HENRY	12 ROOSEVELT ST - STATEN ISLAND NY 10304
37- 68 MAKOSKY, FRANK	7001 142ND AVE NORTH #45 - LARGO FL 33541
75- 69 MAKOWSKI, THOMAS ANTHONY	195 ROESCH AVE - BUFFALO NY 14201
33- 40 MALAY, JOSEPH CHARLES	233 SUCCESS PARK - BRIDGEPORT CT 06610
81- 77 MALDONADO, CANDIDO	BUZON G-27, BO. DOMINGUITO-ARECIBO PR 00612
81- 78 MALER, JAMES MICHAEL	14408 SW 143RD CT - MIAMI FL 33186
37- 69 MALINOSKY, ANTHONY JOSEPH	5540 W FIFTH ST #60 - OXNARD CA 93030
34- 64 MALIS, CYRUS SOL	D. JANUARY 12, 1971 NORTH HOLLYWOOD, FLA.
57- 45 MALKMUS, ROBERT EDWARD	400 WALLINGFORD TER - UNION NJ 07083
59- 51 MALLETT, GERALD GORDON	7610 FOREST PARK DR - BEAUMONT TX 77707
50- 58 MALLETTE, MALCOLM FRANCIS	2419 SILVER FOX LN - RESTON VA 22091
31- 50 MALLON, LESLIE CLYDE	702 CIMMARON TRAIL - GRANBURY TX 76048
21- 58 MALLONEE, HOWARD BENNETT 'BEN'	D. FEBRUARY 19, 1978 BALTIMORE, MD.
25- 68 MALLONEE, JULIUS NORRIS	D. DECEMBER 26, 1934 CHARLOTTE, N. C.
40- 53 MALLORY, JAMES BAUGH	1905 FOREST HILLS DR - GREENVILLE NC 27834
77- 86 MALLORY, SHELDON	17604 S. OAKWOOD - HAZELCREST IL 60429
10- 95 MALLOY, ARCHIBALD ALEXANDER	D. MARCH 1, 1961 FERRIS, TEX.
43- 81 MALLOY, ROBERT PAUL	3850 KIRKUP AVE-CINCINNATI OH 45213
55- 76 MALMBERG, HARRY WILLIAM	D. OCTOBER 29, 1976 SAN FRANCISCO, CALIF.
49- 47 MALONE, EDWARD RUSSELL	224 AVENIDA MAJORCA #A - LAGUNA HILLS CA 92653
15- 93 MALONE, LEWIS ALOYSIUS	D. FEBRUARY 17, 1972 BROOKLYN, N.Y.
28- 62 MALONE, PERCE LEIGH 'PAT'	D. MAY 13, 1943 ALTOONA, PA.
60- 64 MALONEY, JAMES WILLIAM	2217 W KEATS - FRESNO CA 93705
12-112 MALONEY, PATRICK WILLIAM	D. JUNE 27, 1979 PAWTUCKET, R. I.
13-109 MALOY, PAUL AUGUSTUS	D. MARCH 18, 1976 SANDUSKY, O.
43- 82 MALTZBERGER, GORDON RALPH	D. DECEMBER 11, 1974 RIALTO, CALIF.
55- 77 MALZONE, FRANK JAMES	16 ALETHA RD - NEEDHAM MA 02192
13-110 MAMAUX, ALBERT LEON	D. JANUARY 2, 1963 SANTA MONICA, CALIF.
28- 63 MANCUSO, AUGUST RODNEY 'GUS'	D. OCTOBER 26, 1984 HOUSTON, TEXAS
44- 81 MANCUSO, FRANK OCTAVIUS	5126 CRIPPLE CREEK - HOUSTON TX 77017
14-135 MANDA, CARL ALAN	D. MARCH 9, 1983 ARTESIA, N. MEX.
41- 69 MANDERS, HAROLD CARL	BOX 149 - DALLAS CENTER IA 50063
52- 71 MANGAN, JAMES DANIEL	6878 TRINIDAD - SAN JOSE CA 95120
69-106 MANGUAL, ANGEL LUIS	LAS DELICIAS R10,ROD.DEL VALLE-PONCE PR 00731
72- 66 MANGUAL, JOSE MANUEL 'PEPE'	CALLE 41,AC19 LOS CAOBOS - PONCE PR 00731
24- 73 MANGUM, LEON ALLEN	D. JULY 9, 1974 LIMA, O.
12-113 MANGUS, GEORGE GRAHAM	D. AUGUST 10, 1933 RUTLAND. MASS.

PEPE MANGUAL

20- 79 MANION, CLYDE JENNINGS	D. SEPTEMBER 4, 1967 DETROIT, MICH.
76- 58 MANKOWSKI, PHILIP ANTHONY	204 ROSEWOOD TER - CHEEKTOWAGA NY 14225
44- 82 MANN, BEN GARTH	RR 1 BOX 14 - ITALY TX 76651
28- 64 MANN, JOHN LEO	D. MARCH 31, 1977 TERRE HAUTE, IND.
13-111 MANN, LESLIE	D. JANUARY 14, 1962 PASADENA, CALIF.
14-136 MANNING, ERNEST DEVON	D. APRIL 28, 1973 PENSACOLA, FLA.
62- 80 MANNING, JAMES BENJAMIN	4341 SW 2ND CT - PLANTATION FL 33317
75- 70 MANNING, RICHARD EUGENE 'RICK'	150 MILES RD - CHAGRIN FALLS OH 44022
40- 54 MANNO, DONALD	1338 ELLIOTT ST-WILLIAMSPORT PA 17701
81- 79 MANRIQUE, FRED ELOI	CARRERA 6 #21 SANTE FE - CIUDAD BOLIVAR VENEZ
56- 55 MANTILLA, FELIX	6973 N TACOMA ST - MILWAUKEE WI 53224
51- 58 MANTLE, MICKEY CHARLES	5730 WATSON CIR - DALLAS TX 75225
69-107 MANUEL, CHARLES FUQUA	4930 BOWER RD SW - ROANOKE VA 24018
75- 71 MANUEL, JERRY	9275 DEFIANCE CIR - SACRAMENTO CA 95827
23- 85 MANUSH, HENRY EMMETT 'HEINIE'	D. MAY 12, 1971 SARASOTA, FLA.
50- 59 MANVILLE, RICHARD WESLEY	JACOBSON'S, 255 W. MICHIGAN AVE - JACKSON MI 49201
19- 54 MAPEL, ROLLA MAMILTON	D. APRIL 6, 1966 SAN DIEGO, CAL.
48- 63 MAPES, CLIFFORD FRANKLIN	BOX 872 - PRYOR OK 74362
32- 47 MAPLE, HOWARD ALBERT	D. NOVEMBER 9, 1970 PORTLAND, ORE.
60- 65 MARANDA, GEORGES HENRI	13 THIBEAULT #1 - LEVIS QUEBEC G6V 2J6 CAN.
12-114 MARANVILLE, WALTER JAMES VINCENT	D. JANUARY 5, 1954 NEW YORK, N.Y.
23- 86 MARBERRY, FREDRICK 'FIRPO'	D. JUNE 30, 1976 MEXIA, TEX.
13-112 MARBET, WALTER WILLIAM	D. SEPTEMBER 24, 1956 HOHENWALD, TENN.
40- 55 MARCHILDON, PHILIP JOSEPH	3 COURTWRIGHT RD - ETOBICOKE ONTARIO CAN.
33- 41 MARCUM, JOHN ALFRED	D. SEPTEMBER 10, 1984 LOUISVILLE, KY.

65- 69	MARENTETTE, LEO JOHN	4000 SYLVANIA #66 - TOLEDO OH 43623
56- 56	MARGONERI, JOSEPH EMANUEL	RR 1 BOX 177 - WEST NEWTON PA 15089
60- 66	MARICHAL, JUAN ANTONIO	ED.HACHE 3,PISO ESTE,KENNEDY AVE-SANTO DOMINGO DOM REP.
14-137	MARION, DONALD G. 'DAN'	D. JANUARY 18, 1933 MILWAUKEE, WIS.
35- 65	MARION, JOHN WYETH 'RED'	D. MARCH 13, 1975 SAN JOSE, CALIF.
40- 56	MARION, MARTIN WHITEFORD 'SLATS'	8 FORCEE LANE - ST.LOUIS MO 63124
57- 46	MARIS, ROGER EUGENE	D. DECEMBER 14, 1985 HOUSTON, TEX.
51- 59	MARKELL, HARRY DUQUESNE 'DUKE'	D. JUNE 14, 1984 FORT LAUDERDALE, FLA.
50- 60	MARKLAND, CLENETH EUGENE 'GENE'	613 E OLEANDER CIR - SEBASTIAN FL 32958
15- 94	MARKLE, CLIFFORD MONROE	D. MAY 24, 1974 TEMPLE CITY, CALIF.
51- 60	MARLOWE, RICHARD BURTON	D. DECEMBER 30, 1968 TOLEDO, O.
40- 57	MARNIE, HARRY SYLVESTER 'HAL'	2715 S SMETLEY-PHILADELPHIA PA 19145
53- 53	MAROLEWSKI, FRED DANIEL	298 BENSLEY - CALUMET CITY IL 60409
69-108	MARONE, LOUIS STEPHEN	663 TYRONE ST - EL CAJON CA 92020
31- 51	MARQUARDT, ALBERT LUDWIG 'OLLIE'	D. FEBRUARY 7, 1968 PORT CLINTON, O.
72- 67	MARQUEZ, GONZALO	D. DECEMBER 20, 1984 VALENCIA, VENEZUELA
51- 61	MARQUEZ, LUIS ANGEL	113 MERCADO ST - AGUADILLO PR 00603
25- 69	MARQUIS, JAMES MILBURN	BOX F - WEST POINT CA 95255
53- 54	MARQUIS, ROBERT RUDOLPH	2075 LONGFELLOW DR - BEAUMONT TX 77706
55- 78	MARQUIS, ROGER J	5 LINDBERGH AVE - HOLYOKE MA 01040
50- 61	MARRERO, CONRADO EUGENIO RAMOS	205 AVONTAMIENTO #1 - CERRO HAVANA CUBA
17- 42	MARRIOTT, WILLIAM EARL	D. AUGUST 11, 1969 BERKELEY, CALIF.
32- 48	MARROW, CHARLES KENNON 'BUCK'	D. NOVEMBER 21, 1982 NEWPORT NEWS, VA.
11-109	MARSANS, ARMANDO	D. SEPTEMBER 3, 1960 HAVANA, CUBA
49- 48	MARSH, FRED FRANCIS	RR4 - CORRY PA 16407
41- 70	MARSHALL, CHARLES ANDREW	1 RADCLIFF CT-WILMINGTON DE 19804
46- 67	MARSHALL, CLARENCE WESTLY 'CUDDLES'	2732 N LICIA PL - SIMA CA 93065
67- 69	MARSHALL, DAVID LEWIS	4433 CHARLEMAGNE - LONG BEACH CA 90808
29- 68	MARSHALL, EDWARD HARBERT 'DOC'	1840 FAIRWAY CIR CR - SAN MARCOS CA 92069
58- 58	MARSHALL, JIM RUFE	5761 N. CASA BLANCA - SCOTTSDALE AZ 85253
73- 81	MARSHALL, KEITH ALAN	113 DURLAND AVE - ELMIRA NY 14905
81- 80	MARSHALL, MICHAEL ALLEN	4641 FULTON AVE #105 - SHERMAN OAKS CA 92423
67- 70	MARSHALL, MICHAEL GRANT	25360 BIRCH BLUFF RD - SHOREWOOD MN 55331
42- 66	MARSHALL, MILO MAX	4794 BOLIVAR CT - SALEM OR 97301
12-115	MARSHALL, ROY DEVERNE 'RUBE'	D. JUNE 11, 1980 DOVER, O.
42- 67	MARSHALL, WILLARD WARREN	204 MAIN ST-FORT LEE NJ 07024
31- 52	MARSHALL, WILLIAM HENRY	D. MAY 5, 1977 SACRAMENTO, CALIF.
50- 62	MARTIN, ALFRED MANUEL 'BILLY'	417 SOUTH BROAD ST - NEW ORLEANS LA 70119
53- 55	MARTIN, BARNEY ROBERT	1617 TALL PINES CIR - COLUMBIA SC 29205
44- 83	MARTIN, BORIS MICHAEL 'BABE'	323 FAWN MEADOWS - BALLWIN MO 63011
79- 73	MARTIN, DONALD RENIE	504 FAIRVIEW AVE - DOVER DE 19901
17- 43	MARTIN, ELWOOD GOOD 'SPEED'	D. JUNE 14, 1983 LEMON GROVE, CALIF.
46- 68	MARTIN, FRED TURNER	D. JUNE 11, 1979 CHICAGO, ILL.
37- 70	MARTIN, HERSHEL RAY	D. NOVEMBER 17, 1980 CUBA, MO.
74- 79	MARTIN, JERRY LINDSEY	918 S BONHAM RD - COLUMBIA SC 29205
12-116	MARTIN, JOHN CHRISTOPHER	D. JULY 4, 1980 BRONX, N. Y.
28- 65	MARTIN, JOHN LEONARD ROOS. 'PEPPER'	D. MARCH 5, 1965 MCALESTER, OKLA.
80- 85	MARTIN, JOHN ROBERT	1901 WASHYENAW - YPSILANTI MI 48197
59- 52	MARTIN, JOSEPH CLIFTON	19 SHERWOOD PL - WHEATON IL 60187
49- 49	MARTIN, MORRIS WEBSTER	244 POTTERY RD - WASHINGTON MO 63090
19- 55	MARTIN, PATRICK FRANCIS	D. FEBRUARY 4, 1949 BROOKLYN, N. Y.
55- 79	MARTIN, PAUL CHARLES	OLD ADD: BOX 221 - FAYETTE CITY PA
43- 83	MARTIN, RAYMOND JOSEPH	107 PELLANA RD-NORWOOD MA 02062
36- 51	MARTIN, STUART JOSEPH	BOX 184 - SEVERN NC 27877
68- 57	MARTIN, THOMAS EUGENE 'GENE'	110 STANLEY DR - LEESBURG GA 31763
14-138	MARTIN, WILLIAM GLOYD	D. SEPTEMBER 15, 1949 WASHINGTON, D.C.
36- 52	MARTIN, WILLIAM JOSEPH 'JOE'	D. SEPTEMBER 28, 1960 BUFFALO, N. Y.
24- 74	MARTINA, JOSEPH JOHN	D. MARCH 22, 1962 NEW ORLEANS, LA.
80- 86	MARTINEZ, ALFREDO	2346 THOMAS - LOS ANGELES CA 90031
83- 95	MARTINEZ, CARMELO (SALGADO)	BUZON 1297 - DORADO PR 00646
74- 80	MARTINEZ, FELIX ANTHONY 'TIPPY'	1524 DELLSWAY RD - TOWSON MD 21204
63- 75	MARTINEZ, GABRIEL ANTONIO 'TONY'	OLD ADD: 4599 NW 9TH ST - MIAMI FL 33126
69-109	MARTINEZ, JOHN ALBERT 'BUCK'	6213 VISTA AVE - SACRAMENTO CA 95824
69-110	MARTINEZ, JOSE AZCUIZ	11813 E 59TH TER CIR - KANSAS CITY MO 64133
76- 59	MARTINEZ, JOSE DENNIS 'DENNY'	3 BROOK FARM COURT - COCKEYSVILLE MD 21030
62- 82	MARTINEZ, ORLANDO OLIVO 'MARTY'	748 N 23RD WEST AVE - TULSA OK 74127
62- 81	MARTINEZ, RODOLFO HECTOR	OLD ADD: MARIANOA - HAVANA CUBA

50- 63	MARTINEZ, ROGELIO ULLOA	9118 5TH AVE - BROOKLYN NY 11209
77- 87	MARTINEZ, SILVIO RAMON	CARLOS DELORA 25,BELLE VISTA - SANTIAGO DOMINICAN REP.
70- 85	MARTINEZ, TEODORE NOEL	CALLE ABREU 150 - SANTO DOMINGO DOMINICAN REP.
35- 66	MARTINI, GUIDO JOE 'WEDO'	D. OCTOBER 28, 1970
37- 71	MARTY, JOSEPH ANTON	D. OCTOBER 4, 1984 SACRAMENTO, CALIF.
57- 47	MARTYN, ROBERT GORDON	3365 SW 123RD - BEAVERTON OR 97005
75- 72	MARTZ, GARY ARTHUR	E 8003 EUCLID - SPOKANE WA 99212

80- 87	MARTZ, RANDY CARL	901 NATCHEZ DR - ST. CHARLES MO 63303
69-111	MASHORE, CLYDE WAYNE	14680 MARSH CREEK RD - CLAYTON CA 94517
39- 73	MASI, PHILIP SAMUEL	1 NORTH MAIN STREET - MOUNT PROSPECT IL 60056
66- 58	MASON, DONALD STETSON	1572 ROBERTA DR - SAN MATEO CA 94403
58- 59	MASON, HENRY	1136 S LINCOLN - MARSHALL MO 65340
71- 66	MASON, JAMES PERCY	RR 1 BOX 308 - THEODORE AL 36582
82- 81	MASON, MICHAEL PAUL	5955 STONEYBROOK DR - MINNETONKA MN 55343
84- 73	MASON, ROGER LEROY	5955 STONEYBROOK DR - MINNETONKA MN 55343
57- 48	MASSA, GORDON RICHARD	5905 KIMBERLY AVE - CINCINNATI OH 45213
18- 45	MASSEY, ROY HARDEE	D. JUNE 23, 1954 ATLANTA, GA.
17- 44	MASSEY, WILLIAM HERBERT 'MIKE'	D. OCTOBER 17, 1971 SHREVEPORT, LA.
31- 53	MASTERS, WALTER THOMAS	151 METCALFE ST #404 - OTTAWA ONTARIO K2P 1N8 CAN.
40- 58	MASTERSON, PAUL NICKALIS	3003 W 53RD ST-CHICAGO IL 60632
39- 74	MASTERSON, WALTER EDWARD	4515 CARTERET DR - NEW BERN NC 28560
84- 74	MATA, VICTOR JOSE	AVE DE LOS MARTIRES 131 - SANTO DOMINGO DOMINICAN REP.
52- 72	MATARAZZO, LEONARD	2715 CARLISLE ST - NEW CASTLE PA 16105
67- 71	MATCHICK, JOHN THOMAS 'TOM'	126 MASTERS CT - MAUMEE OH 43537
12-117	MATHES, JOSEPH JOHN	D. DECEMBER 21, 1978 ST. LOUIS, MO.
52- 73	MATHEWS, EDWIN LEE	13744 RECUERDO DR - DEL MAR CA 92014
60- 67	MATHEWS, NELSON ELMER	211 CRESTVIEW - COLUMBIA IL 62236
60- 68	MATHIAS, CARL LYNWOOD	RR 2 - OLEY PA 19567
85- 70	MATHIS, RONALD VANCE	OLD ADD: 10326 BON OAK DR - ST. LOUIS MO 63136
70- 86	MATIAS, JOHN ROY	98-1616 HOOLAUAE ST - AIEA HI 96701
71- 67	MATLACK, JONATHAN TRUMPBOUR	8100 SHELTON DR - FORT WORTH TX 76112
14-139	MATTESON, HENRY EDSON	D. AUGUST 31, 1943 BROCTON, N.Y.
72- 68	MATTHEWS, GARY NATHANIEL	13215 MERCER ST - PACOIMA CA 91331
22- 81	MATTHEWS, JOHN JOSEPH	D. FEBRUARY 8, 1968 HAGERSTOWN, MD.
23- 87	MATTHEWS, WID CURRY	D. OCTOBER 5, 1965 WINCHESTER, CAL.
43- 84	MATTHEWSON, DALE WESLEY	D. FEBRUARY 20, 1984 BLAIRSVILLE, GA.
38- 59	MATTICK, ROBERT JAMES	1721 159TH PLACE NE - BELLEVUE WA 98008
12-118	MATTICK, WALTER JOSEPH	D. NOVEMBER 5, 1968 LOS ALTOS, CALIF.
82- 82	MATTINGLY, DONALD ARTHUR	BOX 110 BROWNING RD - EVANSVILLE IN 47711
31- 54	MATTINGLY, LAURENCE EARL	4007 BEDFORD PL - SUITLAND MD 20023
14-140	MATTIS, RALPH L.	D. SEPTEMBER 13, 1960 WILLIAMSPORT, PA.
29- 69	MATTOX, CLOY MITCHELL	D. AUGUST 3, 1985 DANVILLE, VA.
22- 82	MATTOX, JAMES POWELL	D. OCTOBER 12, 1973 MYRTLE BEACH, S. C.
79- 74	MATULA, RICHARD CARLTON	1817 CHAPEL HEIGHTS DR - WHARTON TX 77488
81- 81	MATUSZEK, LEONARD JAMES	1875 BARCELONA DR - DUNEDIN FL 33528
34- 65	MATUZAK, HARRY GEORGE	D. NOVEMBER 26, 1978 HOPE, ALA.
44- 84	MAUCH, EUGENE WILLIAM	46 LA RONDA DR - RANCHO MIRAGE CA 92270
34- 66	MAULDIN, MARSHALL REESE 'MARK'	6545 HANEN ST - UNION CITY GA 30291
24- 75	MAUN, ERNEST GERALD	RR 1 BOX 129 - FALFURRIAS TX 78355
45- 66	MAUNEY, RICHARD	D. FEBRUARY 6, 1970 ALBEMARLE, N. C.
58- 60	MAURIELLO, RALPH	23644 DEL CER CIR - CANOGA PARK CA 91304
48- 64	MAURO, CARMEN LOUIS	536 STANFORD DR - SAN LUIS OBISPO CA 93401
49- 50	MAVIS, ROBERT HENRY	300 MARKWOOD DR - LITTLE ROCK AR 72205
69-112	MAXIE, LARRY HANS	BOX 814 - UPLAND CA 91786
62- 83	MAXVILL, CHARLES DALLAN 'DAL'	6745 RYAN CREST RD - FLORISSANT MO 63031
50- 54	MAXWELL, CHARLES RICHARD	RR2 MAPLE LAKE - PAW PAW MI 49079
68- 58	MAY, CARLOS	5533 HILL AND DALE DR - CINCINNATI OH 45213
67- 72	MAY, DAVID LAFRANCE	915 GRAY ST - NEW CASTLE DE 19720
17- 45	MAY, FRANK SPRUIELL 'JAKIE'	D. JUNE 3, 1970 WENDELL, N.C.
64- 68	MAY, JERRY LEE	RR 2 BOX 318 - BRIDGEWATER VA 22812
65- 70	MAY, LEE ANDREW	5533 HILL & DALE DR - CINCINNATI OH 45213
39- 75	MAY, MERRILL GLEND 'PINKY'	122 52ND ST - HOLMES BEACH FL 33510
70- 87	MAY, MILTON SCOTT	2424 MANATEE AVE W - BRADENTON FL 33505
65- 71	MAY, RUDOLPH	BOX 1078 - NORTH FORK CA 93643
24- 76	MAY, WILLIAM HERBERT 'BUCKSHOT'	D. MARCH 15, 1984 BAKERSFIELD, CALIF.
68- 59	MAYBERRY, JOHN CLAIBORN	20061 ORLEANS - DETROIT MI 48203
59- 53	MAYE, ARTHUR LEE	OLD ADD: 867 E. 52ND ST - LOS ANGELES CA 90011
57- 49	MAYER, EDWIN DAVID	440 OAKDALE AVE - CORTE MADERA CA 94925
12-119	MAYER, ERSKINE JOHN	D. MARCH 10, 1957 LOS ANGELES, CALIF.
15- 95	MAYER, SAMUEL FRANKEL	D. JULY 1, 1962 ATLANTA, GA.
11-110	MAYER, WALTER A.	D. NOVEMBER 18, 1951 MINNEAPOLIS, MINN.
11-111	MAYES, ADAIR BUSHYHEAD 'PADDY'	D. MAY 28, 1962 FAYETTEVILLE, ARK.
40- 59	MAYNARD, JAMES WALTER	D. SEPTEMBER 7, 1977 DURHAM, N. C.
22- 83	MAYNARD, LEROY EVANS 'CHICK'	D. JANUARY 31, 1957 BANGOR, ME.
36- 53	MAYO, EDWARD JOSEPH	825 OCEAN PINES - BERLIN MD 21811
48- 65	MAYO, JOHN LEWIS 'JACKIE'	719 MAPLERIDGE DR - YOUNGSTOWN OH 44512
15- 96	MAYS, CARL WILLIAM	D. APRIL 4, 1971 EL CAJON, CALIF.
51- 62	MAYS, WILLIE HOWARD	51 MT VERNON LN - ATHERTON CA 94025
56- 57	MAZEROSKI, WILLIAM STANLEY	RR6 BOX 130 - GREENSBURG PA 15601
35- 67	MAZZERA, MELVIN LEONARD	6 WEST DUNMAR LN - STOCKTON CA 95207
76- 60	MAZZILLI, LEE LOUIS	12 CARPENTERS DRK RD - GREENWICH CT 06830

MCADAMS   MCDERMOTT

11-112	MCADAMS, GEORGE D. 'JACK'	D. MAY 21, 1937 SAN FRANCISCO, CALIF.
30- 49	MCAFEE, WILLIAM FORT	D. JULY 8, 1958 CULPEPPER, VA.
13-113	MCALLESTER, WILLIAM LUSK	D. MARCH 3, 1970 CHATTANOOGA, TENN.
71- 68	MCANALLY, ERNEST LEE	RR 4 BOX 61-A - MOUNT PLEASANT TX 75455
58- 61	MCANANY, JAMES	11066 RHODA WAY - CULVER CITY CA 90230
68- 60	MCANDREW, JAMES CLEMENT	5749 N STETSON CT - PARKER CO 80134
14-141	MCARTHUR, OLAND ALEXANDER 'DIXIE'	2602 MCARTHUR DR - COLUMBUS MS 39701
14-142	MCAULEY, JAMES EARL 'IKE'	D. APRIL 6, 1928 DES MOINES, IA.
60- 69	MCAULIFFE, RICHARD JOHN	BOX 211 - WEST SIMSBURY CT 06092
14-143	MCAVOY, GEORGE H	OLD ADD: ARDMORE OK 73401
13-114	MCAVOY, JAMES EUGENE 'WICKEY'	D. JULY 5, 1973 ROCHESTER, N. Y.
59- 54	MCAVOY, THOMAS JOHN	CLINTON COURT - STILLWATER NY 12118
61- 72	MCBEAN, ALVIN O'NEAL	BOX 4475 - ST THOMAS VI 00801
26- 53	MCBEE, PRYOR EDWARD	D. APRIL 19, 1963 ROSEVILLE, CALIF.
73- 82	MCBRIDE, ARNOLD RAY "BAKE"	5210 N HWY 67 - FLORISSANT MO 63033
59- 55	MCBRIDE, KENNETH FAYE	2138 DAVENPORT AVE - CLEVELAND OH 44114
43- 85	MCBRIDE, THOMAS RAYMOND	2100 SANTE FE - WICHITA FALLS TX 76309
64- 69	MCCABE, JOE ROBERT	1001 CRESCENT DR - GREENCASTLE IN 46135
46- 69	MCCABE, RALPH HERBERT	D. MAY 4, 1974 WINDSOR, ONT.
18- 46	MCCABE, RICHARD JAMES	D. APRIL 11, 1950 BUFFALO, N. Y.
15- 97	MCCABE, TIMOTHY	D. APRIL 12, 1977 IRONTON, MO.
18- 47	MCCABE, WILLIAM FRANCIS	D. SEPTEMBER 2, 1966 CHICAGO, ILL.
46- 70	MCCAHAN, WILLIAM GLENN	8 PENINSULA DR - GRANBURY TX 76048

THE SPORT AMERICANA FOOTBALL, HOCKEY, BAS—
KETBALL & BOXING CARD PRICE IS THE AUTHORI—
TATIVE SOURCE FOR INFORMATION AND CURRENT
PRICES FOR CARDS OF THESE SPORTS.

62- 84	MCCALL, BRIAN ALLEN	105 UNION ST - ALEXANDRIA VA 22314
48- 66	MCCALL, JOHN WILLIAM	2959 PALMER DR - SIERRA VISTA AZ 85635
77- 88	MCCALL, LARRY STEPHEN	RR 5 BOX 354 - CANDLER NC 28715
48- 67	MCCALL, ROBERT LEONARD 'DUTCH'	2600 ASHLEY #A107-NORTH LITTLE ROCK AR 72114
27- 57	MCCALLISTER, JOHN	D. OCTOBER 18, 1946 COLUMBUS, O.
14-144	MCCANDLESS, SCOTT COOK 'JOHN'	D. AUGUST 17, 1961 PITTSBURGH, PA.
20- 80	MCCANN, ROBERT EMMETT	D. APRIL 15, 1937 PHILADELPHIA, PA.
59- 56	MCCARDELL, ROGER MORTON	16 W MAIN ST - RISING SUN MD 21911
23- 88	MCCARREN, WILLIAM JOSEPH	D. SEPTEMBER 11, 1983 DENVER, COLO.
10- 96	MCCARTHY, ALEXANDER GEORGE	D. MARCH 12, 1978 SALISBURY, MD.
48- 68	MCCARTHY, JEROME FRANCIS	D. OCTOBER 3, 1965 OCEANSIDE, N. Y.
34- 67	MCCARTHY, JOHN JOSEPH	D. SEPTEMBER 13, 1973 MUNDELEIN, ILL.
26- 54	MCCARTHY, JOSEPH VINCENT	D. JANUARY 13, 1978 BUFFALO, N. Y.
85- 71	MCCARTHY, THOMAS MICHAEL	5 CAROLYN DR, RR 8 - PLYMOUTH MA 02360
13-115	MCCARTY, GEORGE LEWIS	D. JUNE 9, 1930 READING, PA.
59- 57	MCCARVER, JAMES TIMOTHY 'TIM'	1518 YOUNGFORD RD - GLADWYNNE PA 19035
85- 72	MCCASKILL, KIRK EDWARD	15226 N. 51ST ST - SCOTTSDALE AZ 85254
77- 89	MCCATTY, STEVEN EARL	692 TENNYSON - ROCHESTER MI 48063
61- 73	MCCLAIN, JOE FRED	RR 8 BOX 109 - JOHNSON CITY TN 37601
31- 55	MCCLANAHAN, PETE	BOX 157 - MONT BELVIOU TX 77580
19- 56	MCCLELLAN, HERVEY MCDOWELL	D. NOVEMBER 6, 1925 CYNTHIANA, KY.
13-116	MCCLESKEY, JEFFERSON LAMAR	D. MAY 11, 1971 AMERICUS, GA.
36- 54	MCCLOSKEY, JAMES ELLWOOD	D. AUGUST 18, 1971 JERSEY CITY, N. J.
10- 97	MCCLURE, LAWRENCE LEDWITH	D. AUGUST 31, 1948 HUNTINGTON, W. VA.
75- 73	MCCLURE, ROBERT CRAIG	1301 CANYONWOOD CT - WALNUT GROVE CA 94595
15- 98	MCCLUSKEY, HARRY ROBERT	D. JUNE 7, 1962 TOLEDO, O.
33- 42	MCCOLL, ALEXANDER BOYD	1203 SHERMAN ST - GENEVA OH 44041
14-145	MCCONNAUGHEY, RALPH J.	D. JUNE 4, 1966 DETROIT, MICH.
15- 99	MCCONNELL, SAMUEL FAULKNER	D. JUNE 27, 1981 PHOENIXVILLE, PA.
64- 70	MCCOOL, WILLIAM JOHN	863 FERNSHIRE DR - CENTERVILLE OH 45459
80- 88	MCCORMACK, DONALD ROSS	RR 2 BOX 93 - OMAK WA 98841
34- 68	MCCORMICK, FRANK ANDREW	D. NOVEMBER 21, 1982 MANHASSET, N. Y.
56- 58	MCCORMICK, MICHAEL FRANCIS	464 CHESLEY - MOUNTAIN VIEW CA 94040
40- 60	MCCORMICK, MYRON WINTHROP 'MIKE'	D. APRIL 14, 1976 LOS ANGELES, CALIF.
39- 76	MCCOSKY, WILLIAM BARNEY	33 PINE ARBOR LN #102 - VERO BEACH FL 32962
59- 58	MCCOVEY, WILLIE LEE	220 CREST ROAD - WOODSIDE CA 94062
38- 60	MCCOY, BENJAMIN JENISON	3932 E OMAHA DR SW-GRANDVILLE MI 49418
39- 77	MCCRABB, LESTER WILLIAM	412 S CHURCH ST - QUARRYVILLE PA 17566
63- 76	MCCRAW, TOMMY LEE	2225 CLYDE #1 - LOS ANGELES CA 90016
25- 70	MCCREA, FRANCIS WILLIAM	D. FEBRUARY 25, 1981 DOVER, N. J.
14-146	MCCREERY, ESLEY PORTERFIELD	D. OCTOBER 19, 1960 SACRAMENTO, CALIF.
22- 84	MCCUE, FRANK ALOYSIUS	D. JULY 5, 1953 EVERGREEN PARK, ILL.
85- 73	MCCULLERS, LANCE GRAYE	5853 MENORCA DRIVE - SAN DIEGO CA 92124
40- 61	MCCULLOUGH, CLYDE EDWARD	D. SEPTEMBER 18, 1982 SAN FRANCISCO, CALIF.
29- 70	MCCULLOUGH, PAUL WILLARD	D. NOVEMBER 7, 1970 NEWCASTLE, PA.
42- 68	MCCULLOUGH, PHILIP LAMAR	25 EXETER RD-AVONDALE ESTATES GA 30002
22- 85	MCCURDY, HARRY HENRY	D. JULY 21, 1972 HOUSTON, TEX.
55- 80	MCDANIEL, LYNDALL DALE	5024 SOUTH OSAGE - KANSAS CITY MO 64133
57- 50	MCDANIEL, MAX VON	33202 ROLLING WOOD - PINEHURST TX 77361
12-120	MCDERMOTT, FRANK A. 'RED'	D. SEPTEMBER 11, 1964 PHILADELPHIA, PA.
48- 69	MCDERMOTT, MAURICE JOSEPH 'MICKEY'	4950 BRILL - PHOENIX AZ 85008

92

93

Cincinnati Reds

72- 69	MCDERMOTT, TERRENCE MICHAEL	407 N VILLAGE AVE - ROCKVILLE CENTRE NY 11552
57- 51	MCDEVITT, DANIEL EUGENE	2991 SALEM RD SE - CONYERS GA 30207
12-121	MCDONALD, CHARLES E. 'TEX'	D. MARCH 31, 1943 HOUSTON, TEX.
69-113	MCDONALD, DAVID BRUCE	714 RIDGEVIEW DR - SHELBY NC 28150
11-113	MCDONALD, EDWARD C.	D. MARCH 11, 1946 ALBANY, N.Y.
31- 56	MCDONALD, HENRY MONROE	D. OCTOBER 17, 1982 HEMET, CALIF.
50- 65	MCDONALD, JIMMIE LEROY	3012 KNOXVILLE AVE - LONG BEACH CA 90808
10- 98	MCDONALD, MALCOLM JOSEPH	D. MAY 30, 1963 BAYTOWN, TEXAS
43- 86	MCDONNELL, JAMES WILLIAM	OLD ADD: 14238 SEYMOUR - DETROIT MI 48205
51- 63	MCDOUGALD, GILBERT JAMES	10 WARREN AVE - SPRING LAKE NJ 07762
85- 74	MCDOWELL, ODDIBE	5240 SW 18TH ST - HOLLYWOOD FL 33023
85- 75	MCDOWELL, ROGER ALAN	OLD ADD: 1385 WEST GALBRAITH #B2 - CINCINNATI OH 45231
61- 74	MCDOWELL, SAMUEL EDWARD	7727 ST LAWRENCE AVE - PITTSBURGH PA 15218
16- 60	MCELWEE, LELAND STANFORD	D. FEBRUARY 8, 1957 UNION, ME.
42- 69	MCELYEA, FRANK	722 E MARYLAND ST - EVANSVILLE IN 47711
74- 81	MCENANEY, WILLIAM HENRY 'WILL'	OLD ADD: 1038 ROYAL PALM DR - ELLENTON FL 33532
30- 50	MCEVOY, LOUIS ANTHONY	D. DECEMBER 16, 1953 WEBSTER GROVE, MO.
68- 61	MCFADDEN, LEON	15110 MARQUETTE #C - MOORPARK CA 92021
45- 67	MCFARLAND, HOWARD ALEXANDER	8321 WILLOWBROOK - WICHITA KS 67207
62- 85	MCFARLANE, ORLANDO DE JESUS	OLD ADD: 33 TAFT AVE - ASHEVILLE NC 28803
81- 82	MCGAFFIGAN, ANDREW JOSEPH	356 SWEET BRIAR LN - LAKELAND FL 33803
17- 46	MCGAFFIGAN, MARK ANDREW 'PATSY'	D. DECEMBER 22, 1940 CARLYLE, ILL.
46- 71	MCGAH, EDWARD JOSEPH	1070 GREEN ST #1900 - SAN FRANCISCO CA 94133
62- 86	MCGAHA, FRED MELVIN 'MEL'	3220 JUNIOR PLACE - SHREVEPORT LA 71109
12-122	MCGARR, JAMES VINCENT	D. JULY 21, 1981 MIAMI, FLA.
12-123	MCGARVEY, DANIEL FRANCIS	D. MARCH 7, 1947 PHILADELPHIA, PA.
34- 69	MCGEE, DANIEL ALOYSIUS	252 BUTTRICK AVE - BRONX NY 10465
25- 71	MCGEE, FRANCIS D. 'TUBBY'	D. JANUARY 30, 1934 COLUMBUS, O.
35- 68	MCGEE, WILLIAM HENRY	RR 1 BOX 16 - HARDIN IL 62047
82- 83	MCGEE, WILLIE DEAN	2081 LUPINE RD - HERCULES CA 94547
11-114	MCGEEHAN, DANIEL DESALES	D. JULY 12, 1955 HAZELTON, PA.
12-124	MCGEHEE, PATRICK HENRY	D. DECEMBER 30, 1946 PADUCAH, KY.
50- 66	MCGHEE, WARREN FRANK 'ED'	D. FEBRUARY, 1986
44- 85	MCGHEE, WILLIAM MAC	1775 TILDEN AVE - JONESBORO GA 30326
77- 90	MCGILBERRY, RANDALL KENT	OLD ADD: NORTHPOINT APTS #23 - SARALAND AL 36571
44- 86	MCGILLEN, JOHN JOSEPH	1214 5TH AVE - WOODLYN PA 19094
68- 62	MCGINN, DANIEL MICHAEL	1340 S 163RD ST - OMAHA NE 68120
72- 70	MCGLOTHEN, LYNN EVERATT	D. AUGUST 14, 1984 DUBACH, LA.
49- 51	MCGLOTHIN, EZRA MAC 'PAT'	2317 COREFIELD RD - KNOXVILLE TN 37919
65- 72	MCGLOTHLIN, JAMES MILTON	D. DECEMBER 23, 1975 UNION, KY.
22- 86	MCGOWAN, FRANK BERNARD 'BEAUTY'	D. MAY 6, 1982 HAMDEN, CONN.
48- 70	MCGOWAN, TULLIS EARL 'MICKEY'	618 SPRATT ST - WAYCROSS GA 31501
12-125	MCGRANER, HOWARD	D. OCTOBER 22, 1952 ZALESKI, O.
65- 73	MCGRAW, FRANK EDWIN "TUG"	COLESHILL ROSE VALLEY RD - MEDIA PA 19063
14-147	MCGRAW, JOHN	D. NOVEMBER 14, 1918 CLEVELAND, O.
17- 47	MCGRAW, ROBERT EMMETT	D. JUNE 2, 1978 BOISE, ID.
76- 61	MCGREGOR, SCOTT HOUSTON	641 W SYCAMORE - EL SEGUNDO CA 90245
22- 87	MCGREW, WALTER HOWARD 'SLIM'	D. AUGUST 21, 1967 PORT ARTHUR, TEX.
62- 87	MCGUIRE, M C ADOLFUS 'MICKEY'	4326 DORSET DR - DAYTON OH 45405
14-148	MCGUIRE, THOMAS PATRICK	D. DECEMBER 8, 1959 PHOENIX, AZ.
43- 87	MCHALE, JOHN JOSEPH	BOX 500 STATION "M" - MONTREAL QUEBEC H1V 3P2 CAN.
10- 99	MCHALE, MARTIN JOSEPH	D. MAY 7, 1979 HEMPSTEAD, N. Y.
18- 48	MCHENRY, AUSTIN BUSH	D. NOVEMBER 27, 1922 MT. OREB, O.
81- 83	MCHENRY, VANCE LOREN	2396 BROWN ST--DURHAM CA 95938
21- 59	MCILREE, VANCE ELMER	D. MAY 6, 1959 KANSAS CITY, MO.
57- 52	MCILWAIN, WILLIAM STOVER	D. JANUARY 15, 1966 BUFFALO, N. Y.
74- 82	MCINTOSH, JOSEPH ANTHONY	1002 PARKHILL - BILLINGS MT 59102
11-115	MCIVER, EDWARD OTTO	D. MAY 4, 1954 DALLAS, TEX.
37- 72	MCKAIN, ARCHIE RICHARD	D. MAY 21, 1985 SALINA, KAN.
27- 58	MCKAIN, HAROLD LEROY	D. JANUARY 24, 1970 SACRAMENTO, CAL.
75- 74	MCKAY, DAVID LAWRENCE	6102 EAST SURREY AVE - SCOTTSDALE AZ 85254
15-100	MCKAY, REEVE STEWART	D. JANUARY 18, 1946 DALLAS, TEX.
72- 71	MCKEE, JAMES MARION	31 SOUTH HAMILTON - COLUMBUS OH 43213
13-117	MCKEE, RAY 'RED'	D. AUGUST 5, 1972 SAGINAW, MICH.
43- 88	MCKEE, ROGERS HORNSBY	BOX 61-SHELBY NC 28150
32- 49	MCKEITHAN, EMMETT JAMES 'TIM'	D. AUGUST 20, 1969 FOREST CITY, N. C.
15-101	MCKENRY, FRANK GORDON 'LIMB'	D. NOVEMBER 1, 1956 FRESNO, CALIF.
73- 83	MCKEON, JOHN ALOYSIUS 'JACK'	6525 DECANTURE ST - SAN DIEGO CA 92120
70- 88	MCKINNEY, CHARLES RICHARD 'RICH'	2393 EAST PETERSON - TROY OH 45373
60- 70	MCKNIGHT, JAMES ARTHUR	RR2 - BEE BRANCH AR 72013
63- 77	MCLAIN, DENNIS DALE	0400-018 BOX PMB - TALLADEGA, AL 35160
32- 50	MCLARNEY, ARTHUR JAMES	D. DECEMBER 20, 1984 SEATTLE, WASH.
12-126	MCLARRY, HOWARD ZELL 'POLLY'	D. NOVEMBER 4, 1971 BONHAM, TEX.

77- 91	MCLAUGHLIN, BYRON SCOTT	3464 SWEETWATER MESA - MALIBU CA 92154
14-149	MCLAUGHLIN, JAMES ANSON 'KID'	D. NOVEMBER 13, 1934 ALLEGANY, N.Y.
32- 51	MCLAUGHLIN, JAMES ROBERT	D. DECEMBER 18, 1968 MOUNT VERNON, ILL.
77- 92	MCLAUGHLIN, JOEY RICHARD	1611 S TROOST - TULSA OK 74120
31- 57	MCLAUGHLIN, JUSTIN THEODORE 'JUD'	D. SEPTEMBER 27, 1964 CAMBRIDGE, MASS.
76- 62	MCLAUGHLIN, MICHAEL DUANE 'BO'	3708 OAKWOOD - AMELIA OH 45102
37- 73	MCLAUGHLIN, PATRICK ELMER	1535 CHANTILLY LN - HOUSTON TX 77018
35- 69	MCLEAN, ALBERT ELDON	B. SEPTEMBER 20, 1912 CHICAGO, ILL.
51- 64	MCLELAND, WAYNE GAFFNEY	6622 BELDART - HOUSTON TX 77017
38- 61	MCLEOD, RALPH ALTON	30 ACTON ST - WOLLASTON MA 02170
30- 51	MCLEOD, SOULE JAMES 'JIM'	D. AUGUST 3, 1981 LITTLE ROCK, ARK.
44- 87	MCLISH, CALVIN COOLIDGE	700 TIMBER RIDGE RD - EDMOND OK 73034
56- 59	MCMAHAN, JACK WALLY	BOX O - ALEXANDER AR 72002
57- 53	MCMAHON, DONALD JOHN	11131 FRALEY ST - GARDEN GROVE CA 92641
60- 71	MCMANUS, JAMES MICHAEL	OLD ADD: 1238 BOYLSTON ST - CHESTNUT HILL MA 02167
13-118	MCMANUS, JOAB LOGAN	D. DECEMBER 23, 1955 SKELTON, W. VA.
20- 81	MCMANUS, MARTIN JOSEPH	D. FEBRUARY 18, 1966 ST. LOUIS, MO.
68- 63	MCMATH, JIMMY LEE	3321 22ND ST - TUSCALOOSA AL 35401
22- 88	MCMILLAN, NORMAN ALEXIS	D. SEPTEMBER 28, 1969 LATTA, S. C.
51- 65	MCMILLAN, ROY DAVID	1200 E 9TH ST - BONHAM TX 75418
77- 93	MCMILLAN, THOMAS ERWIN	3810 W COOPER LAKE DR - SMYRNA GA 30080
25- 72	MCMULLEN, HUGH RAPHAEL	1051 SITE DR #42 - BREA CA 92621
62- 88	MCMULLEN, KENNETH LEE	10 ESTABAN - CAMARILLO CA 93010
14-150	MCMULLIN, FREDERICK WILLIAM	D. NOVEMBER 21, 1952 LOS ANGELES, CALIF.
83- 96	MCMURTRY, JOE CRAIG	55 ROSE DRIVE - TROY TX 76579
45- 68	MCNABB, CARL MAC	BOX 203 - JASPER TN 37347
29- 71	MCNAIR, DONALD ERIC	D. MARCH 11, 1949 MERIDIAN, MISS.
62- 89	MCNALLY, DAVID ARTHUR	3305 RAMADA DR - BILLINGS MT 59102
15-102	MCNALLY, MICHAEL JOSEPH	D. MAY 29, 1965 BETHLEHEM, PA.
22- 89	MCNAMARA, GEORGE FRANCIS	111 OLD CREEK RD - PALOS PARK IL 60464
69-114	MCNAMARA, JOHN FRANCIS	158 STILL MEADOW DR - CINCINNATI OH 45245
27- 59	MCNAMARA, JOHN RAYMOND 'DINNY'	D. DECEMBER 20, 1963 LEXINGTON, MASS.
39- 78	MCNAMARA, ROBERT MAXEY	23810 BARONA MESA RD - RAMONA CA 92065
22- 90	MCNAMARA, THOMAS HENRY	D. MAY 5, 1974 DANVERS, MASS.
22- 91	MCNAMARA, TIMOTHY AUGUSTINE	21 SUMMIT AV - WOONSOCKET RI 02895
32- 52	MCNAUGHTON, GORDON JOSEPH	D. AUGUST 6, 1942 CHICAGO, ILL.
83- 97	MCNEALY, ROBERT LEE	3301 BOZEMAN STREET - SACRAMENTO CA 95838
24- 77	MCNEELY, GEORGE EARL	D. JULY 16, 1971 SACRAMENTO, CAL.
19- 57	MCNEIL, NORMAN FRANCIS	D. APRIL 11, 1942 BUFFALO, N. Y.
64- 71	MCNERTNEY, GERALD EDWARD	1719 GRAND AVENUE - AMES IA 50010
22- 92	MCNULTY, PATRICK HOWARD	D. MAY 4, 1963 HOLLYWOOD, CAL.
69-115	MCNULTY, WILLIAM FRANCIS	5408 TIBURON WAY - SACRAMENTO CA 95841
23- 89	MCQUAID, HERBERT GEORGE	D. APRIL 5, 1966 RICHMOND, CAL.
34- 70	MCQUAIG, GERALD JOSEPH	110 SCHOOL DR - BUFORD GA 30518
69-116	MCQUEEN, MICHAEL ROBERT	3206 CAMEO DR - HOUSTON TX 77055
18- 49	MCQUILLAN, HUGH A.	D. AUGUST 26, 1947 NEW YORK, N. Y.
38- 62	MCQUILLEN, GLENN RICHARD	4400 ANNTANA AVE - BALTIMORE MD 21206
36- 55	MCQUINN, GEORGE HARTLEY	D. DECEMBER 24, 1978 ALEXANDRIA, VA.
68- 64	MCRAE, HAROLD ABRAHAM	1312 63RD ST NW - BRADENTON FL 33505
69-117	MCRAE, NORMAN	OLD ADD: 1009 LAURA ST - ELIZABETH NJ 07206
83- 98	MCREYNOLDS, WALTER KEVIN	CAMP ROBINSON - NORTH LITTLE ROCK AR 72118
11-116	MCTIGUE, WILLIAM PATRICK	D. MAY 11, 1920 NASHVILLE, TENN.
21- 60	MCWEENY, DOUGLAS LAWRENCE	D. JANUARY 1, 1953 MELROSE PARK, ILL.
78- 79	MCWILLIAMS, LARRY DEAN	736 HENSON DR - HURST TX 76053
31- 58	MCWILLIAMS, WILLIAM HENRY	OLD ADD: 559 SURF ST - CHICAGO IL 60651
83- 99	MEACHAM, ROBERT ANDREW	15982 PLUMWOOD ST - WESTMINSTER CA 92683
43- 89	MEAD, CHARLES RICHARD	16350 FREMONTIA - HESPERIA CA 92345
20- 82	MEADOR, JOHN DAVIS	D. APRIL 11, 1970 WINSTON-SALEM, N. C.
15-103	MEADOWS, HENRY LEE	D. JANUARY 29, 1963 DAYTONA BEACH, FLA.
26- 55	MEADOWS, RUFUS RIVERS	D. MAY 10, 1970 WICHITA, KAN.
12-127	MEANEY, PATRICK	D. OCTOBER 20, 1922 PHILADELPHIA, PA.
14-151	MEARA, CHARLES EDWARD	D. FEBRUARY 8, 1962 KINGSBRIDGE, N. Y.
45- 69	MEDEIROS, RAY ANTON	313 SAN MIGUEL WAY - SAN MATEO CA 94403
72- 72	MEDICH, GEORGE FRANCIS 'DOC'	2332 LINDEN AVE - ALIQUIPPA PA 15001
49- 52	MEDLINGER, IRVING JOHN	D. SEPTEMBER 3, 1975 WHEELING, ILL.
32- 53	MEDWICK, JOSEPH MICHAEL	D. MARCH 21, 1975 ST. PETERSBURG, FLA.
10-100	MEE, THOMAS WILLIAM	D. MAY 16, 1981 CHICAGO, ILL.
15-104	MEEHAN, WILLIAM THOMAS	D. OCTOBER 8, 1982 DOUGLAS, WYO.
23- 90	MEEKER, CHARLES ROY	D. MARCH 25, 1929 ORLANDO, FLA.
48- 71	MEEKS, SAMUEL MACK	4963 HELENE - MEMPHIS TN 38117
72- 73	MEELER, CHARLES PHILLIP 'PHIL'	OLD ADD: 108 HAWTHORNE LN - LENOIR NC 28645
41- 71	MEERS, RUSSELL HARLAN	207 IVYWOOD LANE - ROSWELL GA 30076
84- 75	MEIER, DAVID KEITH	523 WEST STUART - FRESNO CA 93704
22- 93	MEINE, HENRY WILLIAM 'HEINIE'	D. MARCH 18, 1968 ST. LOUIS, MO.

Jerry McNertney

THE SPORT AMERICANA FOOTBALL, HOCKEY, BAS-
KETBALL & BOXING CARD PRICE IS THE AUTHORI-
TATIVE SOURCE FOR INFORMATION AND CURRENT
PRICES FOR CARDS OF THESE SPORTS.

```
13-119 MEINERT, WALTER HENRY              D. NOVEMBER 9, 1958 DECATUR, ILL.
10-101 MEINKE, ROBERT BERNARD             D. DECEMBER 29, 1952 CHICAGO, ILL.
13-120 MEISTER, KARL DANIEL               D. AUGUST 15, 1967 MARIETTA, O.
12-128 MEIXELL, MERTON MERRILL 'MOXIE'    D. AUGUST 17, 1982 LOS ANGELES, CALIF.
55- 81 MEJIAS, ROMAN GEORGE               3242 W 59TH ST - LOS ANGELES CA 90043
76- 63 MEJIAS, SAMUEL ELIAS               AVE ENRIQUILLO 31 - SANTIAGO DOMINICAN REP.
37- 74 MELE, ALBERT ERNEST 'DUTCH'        D. FEBRUARY 12, 1975 HOLLYWOOD, FLA.
47- 63 MELE, SABATH ANTHONY 'SAM'         340 ADAMS ST - QUINCY MA 02169
84- 76 MELENDEZ, FRANCISCO                OLD ADD: RR 3 BOX 590 - RIO PIEDRAS PR 00928
70- 89 MELENDEZ, LUIS ANTONIO             OLD ADD: EXT SAN JOSE #D2 - AIBONITO PR 00609
26- 56 MELILLO, OSCAR DONALD              D. NOVEMBER 14, 1963 CHICAGO, ILL.
27- 60 MELLANA, JOSEPH PETER              D. NOVEMBER 1, 1969 SAN RAFAEL, CALIF.
10-102 MELOAN, PAUL                       D. FEBRUARY 11, 1950 TAFT, CALIF.
37- 75 MELTON, CLIFFORD GEORGE            1525 ARGONNE DR - BALTIMORE MD 21218
56- 60 MELTON, DAVID OLIN                 10253 RICHWOOD DR - CUPERTINO CA 95014
41- 72 MELTON, REUBEN FRANKLIN            D. SEPTEMBER 11, 1971 GREER, S. C.
68- 65 MELTON, WILLIAM EDWIN              285 BEVERLY - LAGUNA BEACH CA 92651
85- 76 MELVIN, ROBERT PAUL                350 LINFIELD DR - MENLO PARK CA 94025
70- 90 MENDOZA, CRISTOBAL RIGOBERTO 'MINNIE' 4110 BROADVIEW DR - CHARLOTTE NC 28210
74- 83 MENDOZA, MARIO                     LATERAL DE PACUAL OROZEO #1123 - CHIHUAHUA CHI. MEX.
79- 75 MENDOZA, MICHAEL JOSEPH            12812 ELMFIELD LN - POWAY CT 92064
62- 90 MENKE, DENIS JOHN                  780 MAPLE RIDGE RD - PALM HARBOR FL 33563
14-152 MENOSKY, MICHAEL WILLIAM           D. APRIL 11, 1983 DETROIT, MICH.
12-129 MENSOR, EDWARD                     D. APRIL 20, 1970 SALEM, ORE.
18- 50 MENZE, THEODORE CHARLES            D. DECEMBER 23, 1969 ST. LOUIS, MO.
33- 43 MEOLA, EMILE MICHAEL 'MIKE'        D. SEPTEMBER 1, 1976 FAIR LAWN, N. J.
71- 69 MEOLI, RUDOLPH BARTHOLOMEW         3233 EAST GREENLEAF DR - BREA CA 92621
82- 84 MERCADO, ORLANDO (RODRIGUEZ)       BOX 6145 - ARECIBO PR 00613
10-103 MERCER, JOHN
12-224 MERCER, JOHN LOCKE                 D. DECEMBER 22, 1982 SHREVEPORT, LA, 71106
81- 84 MERCER, MARK KENNETH               OLD ADD: 1465 THIRD ST - MINNEAPOLIS MN 55404
75- 75 MERCHANT, JAMES ANDERSON           716 EUCLID AVE - MOBILE AL 36601
34- 71 MERENA, JOHN JOSEPH 'SPIKE'        D. MARCH 8, 1977 BRIDGEPORT, CONN.
22- 94 MEREWETHER, ARTHUR FRANCIS         37-02 222ND ST - BAYSIDE NY 11361
84- 77 MERIDITH, RONALD KNOX              501 SYDNOR - RIDGECREST CA 93555
49- 53 MERRIMAN, LLOYD ARCHER             6691 N DEWOLF - CLOVIS CA 93612
21- 61 MERRITT, HERMAN G.                 D. MAY 26, 1927 KANSAS CITY, MO.
65- 74 MERRITT, JAMES JOSEPH              12530 OAK CREEK - CERRITOS CA 90701
13-121 MERRITT, JOHN HOWARD               D. NOVEMBER 3, 1955 TUPELO, MISS.
57- 54 MERRITT, LLOYD WESLEY              206 MARY AVE - PITTSBURGH PA 15209
51- 66 MERSON, JOHN WARREN                6264 OLD WASHINGTON RD - ELK RIDGE MD 21227
43- 90 MERTZ, JAMES VERLIN                5116 EMORY CIR - JACKSONVILLE FL 32207
41- 73 MERULLO, LEONARD RICHARD           159 SUMMER AVE - READING MA 01867
38- 63 MESNER, STEPHEN MATHIAS            D. APRIL 6, 1981 SAN DIEGO, CALIF.
24- 78 MESSENGER, ANDREW WARREN 'BUD'     D. NOVEMBER 4, 1971 LANSING, MICH.
68- 66 MESSERSMITH, JOHN ALEXANDER 'ANDY' 200 LAGUNITA DR - SOQUEL CA  95073
63- 78 METCALF, THOMAS JOHN               1390 WISCONSIN RIVER DR-PORT EDWARDS WI 54469
40- 62 METHA, FRANK JOSEPH 'SCAT'         D. MARCH 2, 1975 FOUNTAIN VALLEY, CALIF.
43- 91 METHENY, ARTHUR BEAUREGARD 'BUD'   2424 N SANDPIPER RD - VIRGINIA BEACH VA 23456
22- 95 METIVIER, GEORGE DEWEY             D. MARCH 2, 1947 CAMBRIDGE, MASS.
43- 92 METKOVICH, GEORGE MICHAEL 'CATFISH' 18191 DEVONWOOD CIR-FOUNTAIN VALLEY CA 92708
43- 93 METRO, CHARLES                     7890 INDIANA ST-GOLDEN CO 80401
23- 91 METZ, LEONARD RAYMOND              D. FEBRUARY 24, 1953 DENVER, COLO.
74- 84 METZGER, CLARENCE EDWARD 'BUTCH'   6808 STARBOARD WAY - SACRAMENTO CA 95831
70- 91 METZGER, ROGER HENRY               OLD ADD: 202 WESTMORELAND - SAN ANTONIO TX
44- 88 METZIG, WILLIAM ANDREW             2129 57TH ST - LUBBOCK TX 79412
25- 73 METZLER, ALEXANDER                 D. NOVEMBER 30, 1973 FRESNO, CAL.
14-154 MEUSEL, EMIL FREDERICK 'IRISH'     D. MARCH 1, 1963 LONG BEACH, CALIF.
20- 83 MEUSEL, ROBERT WILLIAM             D. NOVEMBER 28, 1977 DOWNEY, CALIF.
13-122 MEYER, BENJAMIN                    D. FEBRUARY 6, 1974 FESTUS, MO.
74- 85 MEYER, DANIEL THOMAS               222 REMINGTON LOOP - DANVILLE CA 94526
38- 64 MEYER, GEORGE FRANCIS              537 S WARREN - PALATINE IL 60067
55- 82 MEYER, JOHN ROBERT                 D. MARCH 9, 1967 PHILADELPHIA, PA.
37- 76 MEYER, LAMBERT DALTON 'DUTCH'      2205 PARK HILL DR - FORT WORTH TX 76101
64- 72 MEYER, ROBERT BERNARD             24721 TARZANA - MISSION VIEJO CA 92690
46- 72 MEYER, RUSSELL CHARLES             334 ELM ST - OGLESBY IL 61348
78- 80 MEYER, SCOTT WILLIAM               OLD ADD: 15243 S HAMLIN AVE - MIDLOTHIAN IL
13-123 MEYER, WILLIAM ADAM                D. MARCH 31, 1957 KNOXVILLE, TENN.
54- 66 MICELOTTA, ROBERT PETER            295 SAVILLE RD - MINEOLA NY 11501
66- 59 MICHAEL, GENE RICHARD              30 FARRINGTON ST - CLOSTER NJ 07624
43- 94 MICHAELS, CASIMIR EUGENE           D. NOVEMBER 12, 1982 GROSSE POINTE, MICH.
32- 54 MICHAELS, JOHN JOSEPH              3190 NW 63RD ST - FORT LAUDERDALE FL 33309
24- 79 MICHAELS, RALPH JOSEPH             123 LOCUST ST - PITTSBURGH PA 15223
```

MICHAELSON   MILLIES

21- 62 MICHAELSON, JOHN AUGUST	D. APRIL 16, 1968 WOODRUFF, WIS.
50- 67 MICKELSON, EDWARD ALLEN	12620 FEE FEE RD - CREVE COUER MO 63141
53- 56 MICKENS, GLENN ROGER	7241 WHITE OAK AVE BOX 583 - RESEDA CA 91335
17- 48 MIDDLETON, JAMES BLAINE	D. JANUARY 12, 1974 ARGOS, IND.
22- 96 MIDDLETON, JOHN WAYNE	2026 ONG ST - AMARILLO TX 79109
12-223 MIDKIFF, EZRA MILLINGTON	D. MARCH 21, 1957 HUNTINGTON, W. VA.
38- 65 MIDKIFF, RICHARD JAMES	D. OCTOBER 30, 1956 TEMPLE, TEX.
45- 70 MIERKOWICZ, EDWARD FRANK	7530 MACOMB #1-A - GROSSE ILE MI 48138
48- 72 MIGGINS, LAWRENCE EDWARD	2405 KINGSTON DR - HOUSTON TX 77019
35- 70 MIHALIC, JOHN MICHAEL	120 BELLE MEADE BLVD - NASHVILLE TN 37205
64- 73 MIKKELSEN, PETER JAMES	RR 1 BOX 1667 - PROSSER WA 99350
44- 89 MIKLOS, JOHN JOSEPH	19701 S 115TH AVE - MOKENA IL 60448
44- 90 MIKSIS, EDWARD THOMAS	3906 WHITMAN RD - HUNTINGDON VALLEY PA 19006
15-106 MILAN, HORACE ROBERT	D. JUNE 29, 1955 TEXARKANA, TEX.
74- 86 MILBOURNE, LAWRENCE WILLIAM	11228 83RD PL NE - KIRKLAND WA 98033
40- 63 MILES, CARL THOMAS	806 AUSTIN RD - HORSESHOE BEND AR 72512
58- 62 MILES, DONALD RAY	25326 ELM CREEK - SPRING TX 77380
68- 67 MILES, JAMES CHARLIE	RR2 - BATESVILLE MS 38606
35- 71 MILES, WILSON DANIEL 'DEE'	D. NOVEMBER 2, 1976 BIRMINGHAM, ALA.
75- 76 MILEY, MICHAEL WILFRED	D. JANUARY 6, 1977 BATON ROUGE, LA.
15-107 MILJUS, JOHN KENNETH	D. FEBRUARY 11, 1976 POLSON, MONT.
66- 60 MILLAN, FELIX BERNARDO	CALLE 13R-14, EL CONQUISTADOR - TRUJILLO ALTO PR 00760
73- 84 MILLER, CHARLES BRUCE	2126 PARKLAND DR - FORT WAYNE IN 46825
12-130 MILLER, CHARLES ELMER	D. APRIL 23, 1972 WARRENSBURG, MO.
15-108 MILLER, CHARLES HESS	D. JANUARY 13, 1951 MILLERSVILLE, PA.
13-124 MILLER, CHARLES MARION	D. JUNE 16, 1961 HOUSTON, TEX.
84- 78 MILLER, DARRELL KEITH	6246 PROMONTORY LN - RIVERSIDE CA 92506
75- 77 MILLER, DYAR K	RR 9 BOX 421A - GREENSBURG IN 47240
21- 63 MILLER, EDMUND JOHN 'BING'	D. MAY 7, 1966 PHILADELPHIA, PA.
77- 94 MILLER, EDWARD LEE	5014 HARTNETT - RICHMOND CA 94804
36- 56 MILLER, EDWARD ROBERT	19 CANONICUS AVE - NEWPORT RI 02840
12-131 MILLER, EDWIN	D. APRIL 17, 1980 LEBANON, PA.
12-132 MILLER, ELMER	D. NOVEMBER 28, 1944 BELOIT, WIS.
29- 72 MILLER, ELMER LEROY	OLD ADD: 15920 23 MILE RD - MOUNT CLEMENS MI 48043
13-125 MILLER, FRANK LEE	D. FEBRUARY 19, 1974 ALLEGAN, MICH.
10-104 MILLER, FREDERICK HOLMAN	D. MAY 2, 1953 BROOKVILLE, IND.
11-117 MILLER, HUGH STANLEY	D. DECEMBER 24, 1945 JEFFERSON BARRACKS, MO.
22- 97 MILLER, JACOB GEORGE	D. AUGUST 24, 1974 TOWSON, MD.
44- 91 MILLER, JAMES ELDRIDGE 'HACK'	D. NOVEMBER 21, 1966 DALLAS, TEX
66- 61 MILLER, JOHN ALLEN	5105 RIVER AVE - NEWPORT BEACH CA 92660
43- 95 MILLER, JOHN ANTHONY 'OX'	STAR RT - GEORGE WEST TX 78022
62- 91 MILLER, JOHN ERNEST	1216 REDCLIFFE RD - BALTIMORE MD 21228
44- 92 MILLER, KENNETH ALBERT	9344 RAMBLER DR - AFFTON MO 63123
64- 74 MILLER, LARRY DON	442 NORTH OHIO - TOPEKA KS 66616
16- 61 MILLER, LAWRENCE H. 'HACK'	D. SEPTEMBER 17, 1971 OAKLAND, CAL.
84- 79 MILLER, LEMMIE EARL	1245 PHILLIPS LN #99 - SAN LUIS OBISPO CA 93401
23- 92 MILLER, LEO ALPHONSO 'RED'	D. OCTOBER 20, 1973 ORLANDO, FL.
10-105 MILLER, LOWELL OTTO	D. MARCH 29, 1962 BROOKLYN, N.Y.
65- 75 MILLER, NORMAN CALVIN	OLD ADD: 3006 BROADMOOR - SUGARLAND TX 77478
27- 61 MILLER, OTIS LOUIS 'OTTO'	D. JULY 26, 1959 BELLEVILLE, ILL.
21- 64 MILLER, RALPH HENRY	D. FEBRUARY 18, 1967 WHITE BEAR LAKE, MINN.
20- 84 MILLER, RALPH JOSEPH	D. MARCH 18, 1939 FORT WAYNE, IND.
77- 95 MILLER, RANDALL SCOTT	321 E. PEDREGOSA - SANTA BARBARA CA 93101
17- 49 MILLER, RAYMOND PETER	D. APRIL 7, 1927 PITTSBURGH, PA.
85- 77 MILLER, RAYMOND ROGER	P. O. BOX 41 - NEW ATHENS OH 43981
71- 70 MILLER, RICHARD ALAN	130 DRAPER RD - WAYLAND MA 01778
53- 57 MILLER, ROBERT GERALD	104 LAKEWOOD CIR - BURR RIDGE IL 60521
49- 54 MILLER, ROBERT JOHN	17397 GLENMORE - DETROIT MI 48240
57- 55 MILLER, ROBERT LANE	7215 LINDEN TERR - CARLSBAD CA 92008
57- 56 MILLER, RODNEY CARTER	8459 SOUTHGATE AVE - SOUTH GATE CA 90280
74- 87 MILLER, ROGER WESLEY	RR 1 BOX 130 - MILL RUN PA 15464
41- 74 MILLER, ROLLAND ARTHUR 'RONNIE'	OLD ADD: 3827-A HUMPHREY - ST. LOUIS MO 63116
10-106 MILLER, ROY OSCAR 'DOC'	D. JULY 31, 1938 JERSEY CITY, N. J.
29- 73 MILLER, RUDEL CHARLES	2246 TIPPERARY RD - KALAMAZOO MI 49001
27- 62 MILLER, RUSSELL LEWIS	D. AUGUST 30, 1962 BUCYRUS, O.
52- 74 MILLER, STUART LEONARD	252 DEVONSHIRE BLVD - SAN CARLOS CA 94070
18- 51 MILLER, THOMAS ROYALL	D. AUGUST 13, 1980 RICHMOND, VA.
24- 80 MILLER, WALTER JACOB 'JAKE'	D. AUGUST 20, 1975 VENICE, FLA.
11-118 MILLER, WALTER W.	D. MARCH 1, 1956 MARION, IND.
37- 77 MILLER, WILLIAM FRANCIS	D. FEBRUARY 26, 1982 HANNIBAL, MO.
52- 75 MILLER, WILLIAM PAUL	501 EXTON RD - HATBORO PA 19040
34- 72 MILLIES, WALTER LOUIS	5312 W 96TH ST - OAK LAWN IL 60453

28- 66 MILLIGAN, JLHN ALEXANDER   D. MAY 15, 1972 FORT PIERCE, FLA.
53- 58 MILLIKEN, ROBERT FOGLE   1875 SOUTHWOOD LN - CLEARWATER FL 33516
11-119 MILLS, ABBOTT PAIGE 'JACK'   D. JUNE 3, 1973 WASHINGTON, D.C.
27- 63 MILLS, ARTHUR GRANT   D. JULY 23, 1975 UTICA, N. Y.
34- 73 MILLS, COLONEL BUSTER   BOX 13081 - ARLINGTON TX 76016
14-155 MILLS, FRANK LEMOYNE   D. AUGUST 31, 1983 YOUNGSTOWN, O.
34- 74 MILLS, HOWARD ROBINSON 'LEFTY'   D. SEPTEMBER 23, 1982 RIVERSIDE, CALIF.
80- 89 MILLS, JAMES BRADLEY 'BRAD'   BOX 54 - LEMONCOVE CA 93244
70- 92 MILLS, RICHARD ALAN   OLD ADD: 44 WOOD AVE - SCITUATE MA 02060
15-109 MILLS, RUPERT FRANK   D. JULY 20, 1929 LAKE HOPATCONG, N. J.
44- 93 MILLS, WILLIAM HENRY   BOX 43 - EL JOBEAN FL 33927
36- 57 MILNAR, ALBERT JOSEPH   19520 SHAWNEE AVE-CLEVELAND OH 44119
48- 73 MILNE, WILLIAM JAMES 'PETE'   BOX 160566 - MOBILE AL 36616
78- 81 MILNER, BRIAN TATE   1401 CAIRN CIR - FORT WORTH TX 76134
80- 90 MILNER, EDDIE JAMES   49: STAMBAUGH - COLUMBUS OH 43207
71- 71 MILNER, JOHN DAVID   1821 CAVENDISH PL - PITTSBURGH PA 15220
44- 94 MILOSEVICH, MICHAEL   D. FEBRUARY 3, 1966 EAST CHICAGO, IND.
24- 81 MILSTEAD, GEORGE EARL   D. AUGUST 9, 1977 CLEBURNE, TEX.
55- 83 MINARCIN, RUDY ANTHONY   37 N FIRST ST - NORTH VANDERGRIFT PA 15690
60- 72 MINCHER, DONALD RAY   BOX 120 - MERIDIANVILLE AL 35759
21- 65 MINER, RAYMOND THEADORE   D. SEPTEMBER 15, 1963 GLENRIDGE SAN., N. Y.
78- 82 MINETTO, CRAIG STEPHEN   206 W MONTEREY - STOCKTON CA 95204
70- 93 MINGORI, STEPHEN BERNARD   7710 WEST 86TH ST - OVERLAND PARK KS 66212
46- 73 MINNER, PAUL EDISON   115 GREEN LANE DR - CAMP HILL PA 17011
57- 57 MINNICK, DONALD ATHEY   FRANKLIN HGTS - ROCKY MOUNT VA 24151
49- 55 MINOSO, SATURNINO ORESTES 'MINNIE'   4250 MARIN DR - CHICAGO IL 60613
74- 88 MINSHALL, JAMES EDWARD   3607 27TH AVE W - BRADENTON FL 33505
75- 78 MINTON, GREGORY BRIAN   256 PULIDO RD - DANVILLE CA 94526
78- 83 MIRABELLA, PAUL THOMAS   550 KNOLL RD - BOONTON MANOR NJ 07005
51- 67 MIRANDA, GUILLERMO PEREZ 'WILLIE'   5502 WHITWOOD RD - BALTIMORE MD 21206
14-156 MISSE, JOHN BEVERLY   D. MARCH 18, 1970 ST. JOSEPH, MO.
10-107 MITCHELL, ALBERT ROY   D. SEPTEMBER 8, 1959 TEMPLE, TEX.
84- 80 MITCHELL, CHARLES ROSS   5017 HASTY DR - NASHVILLE TN 37211
11-120 MITCHELL, CLARENCE ELMER   D. NOVEMBER 6, 1963 GRAND ISLAND, NEB.
75- 79 MITCHELL, CRAIG SETON   BOX 174 - ELK CA 95432
21- 66 MITCHELL, JOHN FRANKLIN   D. NOVEMBER 4, 1965 OAKLAND CO., MICH.
84- 81 MITCHELL, KEVIN DARRELL   4812 LOGAN AVE - SAN DIEGO CA 92113
46- 74 MITCHELL, LOREN DALE   3434 E 75TH PL S - TULSA OK 74136
23- 93 MITCHELL, MONROE BARR   D. SEPTEMBER 4, 1976 VALDOSTA, GA.
75- 80 MITCHELL, PAUL MICHAEL   7 WABASH AVE - WORCESTER MA 0160J
70- 94 MITCHELL, ROBERT VANCE   38 E ELM ST - NORRISTOWN PA 19401
80- 91 MITCHELL, ROBERT VAN   25691 LUPITA DR - VALENCIA OH 91355
16- 62 MITTERLING, RALPH   D. JANUARY 22, 1956 PITTSBURGH, PA.
66- 62 MITTERWALD, GEORGE EUGENE   1721 MURDOCK BLVD - ORLANDO FL 32807
36- 58 MIZE, JOHN ROBERT   BOX 112 - DEMOREST GA 30535
52- 76 MIZELL, WILMER DAVID 'VINEGAR BEND'   RR 5 BOX 333 - WINSTON SALEM NC 27107
83-100 MIZEROCK, JOHN JOSEPH   RR 1 BOX 140 - ROCHESTER MILLS PA 15771
23- 94 MIZEUR, WILLIAM FRANCIS   D. AUGUST 27, 1976 DANVILLE, ILL.
74- 89 MOATES, DAVID ALLAN   6401 35TH AVE NW - BRADENTON FL 33529
45- 71 MODAK, MICHAEL JOSEPH ALOYSIUS   235 COITSVILLE - CAMPBELL OH 44405
62- 92 MOELLER, JOSEPH DOUGLAS   2512 OCEAN DR - MANHATTAN BEACH CA 90266
56- 61 MOELLER, RONALD RALPH   3560 GAILYNN DR - CINCINNATI OH 45211
72- 74 MOFFITT, RANDALL JAMES   675 RIVERMONT RD - ATHENS GA 30606
55- 84 MOFORD, HERBERT   RR 1 - DOVER KY 41034
11-121 MOGRIDGE, GEORGE ANTHONY   D. MARCH 4, 1962 ROCHESTER, N.Y.
22- 98 MOHARDT, JOHN HENRY   D. NOVEMBER 24, 1961 SAN DIEGO, CAL.
20- 85 MOHART, GEORGE BENJAMIN   D. OCTOBER 2, 1970 SILVER CREEK, N.Y.
53- 59 MOISAN, WILLIAM JOSEPH   BOX 41 - NEWTON NH 03858
21- 67 MOKAN, JOHN LEE   D. FEBRUARY 10, 1985 BUFFALO, N. Y.
49- 56 MOLE, FENTON LEROY   349 ALOHA DR - SAN LEANDRO CA 94578
75- 81 MOLINARO, ROBERT JOSEPH   6 DUNN RD - WEST ORANGE NJ 07052
78- 84 MOLITOR, PAUL LEO   OLD ADD: 924 EAST JUNEAU - MILWAUKEE WI 53202
14-157 MOLLENKAMP, FREDERICK HENRY   D. NOVEMBER 1, 1948 CINCINNATI, O.
13-126 MOLLWITZ, FREDERICK AUGUST 'FRITZ'   D. OCTOBER 3, 1967 BRADENTON, FLA.
70- 95 MOLONEY, RICHARD HENRY   125 MALLARD WAY - WALTHAM MA 02154
17- 50 MOLYNEAUX, VINCENT LEO   D. MAY 4, 1950 STAMFORD, CONN.
37- 78 MONACO, BLAS   410 FROST DR - SAN ANTONIO TX 78201
53- 60 MONAHAN, EDWARD FRANCIS   165 83RD ST - BROOKLYN NY 11209
58- 63 MONBOUQUETTE, WILLIAM CHARLES   271 CLARK HILL RD - NEW BOSTON NH 03070
28- 67 MONCEWICZ, FRED ALFRED   D. APRIL 23, 1969 BROCKTON, MASS.
40- 64 MONCHAK, ALEX   2404 BRANCH PIKE-RIVERTON NJ 08077
66- 63 MONDAY, ROBERT JAMES 'RICK'   1056 RASHFORD DR - PLACENTIA CA 92670
68- 68 MONEY, DONALD WAYNE   282 OLD FOREST RD - VINELAND NJ 08360
75- 82 MONGE, ISIDRO PEDROZA 'SID'   9722 AVIARY DR - SAN DIEGO CA 92131

GUILLERMO MIRANDA
(WILLY)

DALE MITCHELL

PAUL MITCHELL

RANDY MOFFITT

MONROE

17- 51 MONROE, EDWARD OLIVER	D. APRIL 29
21- 68 MONROE, JOHN ALLEN	D. JUNE 19
76- 64 MONROE, LAWRENCE JAMES	1846 WELL'
58- 64 MONROE, ZACHARY CHARLES	10 SANDA'
28- 68 MONTAGUE, EDWARD FRANCIS	396 EL F
73- 85 MONTAGUE, JOHN EVANS	3313A F
66- 64 MONTANEZ, GUILLERMO NARANJO 'WILLIE'	ZONA F
63- 79 MONTEAGUDO, AURELIO FAUNTINI	BOX
38- 66 MONTEAGUDO, RENE MIRANDA	D. SL
74- 90 MONTEFUSCO, JOHN JOSEPH	24 DOWN
61- 75 MONTEJO, MANUEL	LEONCIO V
53- 61 MONTEMAYOR, FELIPE ANGEL	TORREON #308
41- 75 MONTGOMERY, ALVIN ATLAS	D. APRIL 26, 19
71- 72 MONTGOMERY, MONTY BRYSON	BOX 1314 - ALBEMAR
70- 96 MONTGOMERY, ROBERT EDWARD	2 PARKWAY DR - SAUGU
72- 75 MONTREUIL, ALLAN ARTHUR	2016 LAUREL ST - GRETNA
54- 67 MONZANT, RAMON SEGUNDO	CALLE 87 NRO 2A-33 - MARAC
72- 76 MONZON, DANIEL FRANCISCO	912 OLMSTEAD AVE - BRONX NY
67- 73 MOOCK, JOSEPH GEOFFREY	12432 PECOS AVE - GREENWELL LA
32- 55 MOON, LEO	D. AUGUST 25, 1970 NEW ORLEANS, L
54- 68 MOON, WALLACE WADE	JOE COURTNEY INS. BOX 10088 - COLLEC
31- 59 MOONEY, JAMES IRVING	D. APRIL 27, 1979 JOHNSON CITY, TENN.
25- 74 MOORE, ALBERT JAMES	D. NOVEMBER 29, 1974 ATLANTIC OCEAN
76- 65 MOORE, ALVIN EARL 'JUNIOR'	3728 WALL AVE - RICHMOND CA 94804
46- 75 MOORE, ANSELM WINN	245 MARILYN DR - JACKSON MS 39208
64- 75 MOORE, ARCHIE FRANCIS	69 TOWNSEND DR - FLORHAM PARK NJ 07932
70- 97 MOORE, BALOR LILBON	3107 EDMONTON - PASADENA TX 77503
30- 52 MOORE, CARLOS WHITMAN	D. JULY 2, 1958 NEW ORLEANS, LA.
12-133 MOORE, CHARLES WESLEY	D. JULY 29, 1970 PORTLAND, ORE.
73- 86 MOORE, CHARLES WILLIAM	1636 CIRCLEWOOD DR - BIRMINGHAM AL 35214
36- 59 MOORE, D C 'DEE'	2600 UNIVERSITY - WILLISTON ND 58801
75- 83 MOORE, DONNIE RAY	RR 1 BOX 776B - LUBBOCK TX 79401
34- 75 MOORE, EUEL WALTON	307 EAST 20TH - TISHOMINGO OK 73460
31- 60 MOORE, EUGENE JR.	D. MARCH 12, 1978 JACKSON, MISS.
14-158 MOORE, FERDINAND DEPAGE	D. MAY 6, 1947 ATLANTIC CITY, N.J.
70- 98 MOORE, GARY DOUGLAS	OLD ADD: 5018 AIRLINE - DALLAS TX 75205
23- 95 MOORE, GRAHAM EDWARD 'EDDIE'	D. FEBRUARY 10, 1976 FORT MYERS, FLA.
65- 76 MOORE, JACKIE EARLY	509 CHAFFEE - ARLINGTON TX 76010
28- 69 MOORE, JAMES STANFORD	D. MAY 19, 1973 SEATTLE, WASH.
30- 53 MOORE, JAMES WILLIAM	475 N HIGHLAND ST #10B - MEMPHIS TN 38122
28- 70 MOORE, JOHN FRANCIS	4-A SWAN LAKE VLG - BRADENTON FL 33507
30- 54 MOORE, JOSEPH GREGG	BOX 65 - GAUSE TX 77857
81- 85 MOORE, KELVIN ORLANDO	RR 1 BOX 132 - LEROY AL 36548
36- 60 MOORE, LLOYD ALBERT 'WHITEY'	144 WASHINGTON AVE-UHRICHSVILLE OH 44683
82- 85 MOORE, MICHAEL WAYNE	2020 RIDGEWAY - WEATHERFORD OK 73096
27- 64 MOORE, RANDOLPH EDWARD	BOX 757 - OMAHA TX 75571
52- 77 MOORE, RAYMOND LEROY	BOX 4214 - UPPER MARLBORO MD 20870
65- 77 MOORE, ROBERT BARRY	RR1 BOX 174 - CLEVELAND NC 27013
85- 78 MOORE, ROBERT DEVELL	15543 NORDHOFF ST #24 - SEPULVEDA CA 91343
20- 86 MOORE, ROY DANIEL	D. APRIL 5, 1951 SEATTLE, WASH.
35- 72 MOORE, TERRY BLUFORD	501 RIDGEMONT DR - COLLINSVILLE IL 62234
72- 77 MOORE, TOMMY JOE	OLD ADD: RR 1 - DEKALB TX 75559
17- 52 MOORE, WILLIAM ALLEN 'SCRAPPY'	D. OCTOBER 13, 1964 LITTLE ROCK, ARK.
29- 74 MOORE, WILLIAM AUSTIN 'CY'	D. MARCH 28, 1972 AUGUSTA, GA.
25- 75 MOORE, WILLIAM CHRISTOPHER	D. JANUARY 24, 1984 CORNING, N. Y.
26- 57 MOORE, WILLIAM HENRY	D. MAY 24, 1972 KANSAS CITY, MO.
27- 65 MOORE, WILLIAM WILCY	D. MARCH 29, 1963 HOLLIS, OKLA.
62- 93 MOORHEAD, CHARLES ROBERT 'BOB'	747 STATE STREET - LEMOYNE PA 17043
67- 74 MOOSE, ROBERT RALPH	D. OCTOBER 9, 1976 MARTINS FERRY, O.
36- 61 MOOTY, J. T. 'JAKE'	D. APRIL 20, 1970 FORT WORTH, TEX.

76- 66 MORA, ANDRES (IBARRA)	GALEANO 567, PTE. - LOS MOCHIS SINOLOA MEX.
73- 87 MORALES, JOSE MANUEL	BOX 3450 - MAYAGUEZ PR 00709
69-118 MORALES, JULIO RUBEN 'JERRY'	VILLA NUEVA CALLE 16-C5 - CAGUAS PR 00625
67- 75 MORALES, RICHARD ANGELO	1650 ROSITA RD - PACIFICA CA 94044
38- 67 MORAN, ALBERT THOMAS	88 CONGRESS ST #109 - SARATOGA SPRINGS NY 12866
74- 91 MORAN, CARL WILLIAM 'BILL'	200 SHORE DR - PORTSMOUTH VA 23701
12-134 MORAN, HARRY EDWIN	D. NOVEMBER 28, 1962 BECKLEY, W VA
63- 80 MORAN, RICHARD ALAN 'AL'	OLD ADD: 24236 LEEWIN - DETROIT MI 48219
12-135 MORAN, ROY ELLIS	D. JULY 18, 1966 ATLANTA, GA.
58- 65 MORAN, WILLIAM NELSON	8245 GLEDSTONE WAY - FAIRBURN GA 30213
24- 82 MOREHART, RAYMOND ANDERSON	5939 VANDERBILT - DALLAS TX 75206
63- 81 MOREHEAD, DAVID MICHAEL	1342 TIKI CIR - TUSTIN CA 92680
57- 58 MOREHEAD, SETH MARVIN	8675 GROVER PLACE - SHREVEPORT LA 71115

99

ON, DANIEL TORRES	OLD ADD: 4401 SW 117TH AVE - MIAMI FL 33165
LAND, BOBBY KEITH	1815 MONTGOMERY CT - DEERFIELD IL 60015
ENO, ANGEL	GOMEZ FARIAZ #604 - AGUASCALIENTES AGUAS. MEX.
RENO, JOSE DE LOS SANTOS	CORREA Y CIDRON 9 - SANTO DOMINGO DOM. REP.
ORENO, JULIO GONZALES	1000 SW 96TH AVE - MIAMI FL 33144
MORENO, OMAR RENAN	APTD. #5 BALBOA, NCON - PANAMA CITY PAN.
MORET, ROGELIO 'ROGER'	OLD ADD: BARRIO PUERTO JOBOS - GUAYAMA PR 00654
MOREY, DAVID BEALE	D. JANUARY 4, 1986 OAK BLUFF, MASS.
3 MORGAN, CHESTER COLLINS	602 ORIOLE LA-PASADENA TX 77502
69 MORGAN, CYRIL ARLON	D. SEPTEMBER 11, 1946 LAKEVILLE, MASS.
71 MORGAN, EDWARD CARRE	D. APRIL 9, 1980 NEW ORLEANS, LA.
62 MORGAN, EDWIN WILLIS	D. JUNE 27, 1982 LAKEWOOD, O.
63 MORGAN, JOHN P	
63- 82 MORGAN, JOSEPH LEONARD	5588 FERNHOFF RD - OAKLAND CA 94619
59- 59 MORGAN, JOSEPH MICHAEL	15 OAK HILL DRIVE - WALPOLE MA 02081
78- 86 MORGAN, MICHAEL THOMAS	2008 JANSEN ST - LAS VEGAS NV 89101
11-122 MORGAN, RAYMOND CARYLL	D. FEBRUARY 15, 1940 BALTIMORE, MD.
50- 69 MORGAN, ROBERT NORRIS	2212 BARCLAY RD - OKLAHOMA CITY OK 73120
51- 68 MORGAN, TOM STEPHEN	2724 CLE AVENTURA-RANCHO PALOS VERDE CA 90274
54- 69 MORGAN, VERNON THOMAS	D. NOVEMBER 8, 1975 MINNEAPOLIS, MINN.
61- 76 MORHARDT, MEREDITH GOODWIN 'MOE'	182 WILLIAMS AVE - WINSTED CT 06098
35- 74 MORIARTY, EDWARD JEROME	485 SOUTH ST #322 - HOLYOKE MA 01040
73- 88 MORLAN, JOHN GLEN	2348 SALEM AVE - GROVE CITY OH 43123
13-128 MORLEY, (WILLIAM MORLEY JENNINGS)	D. MAY 14, 1985 LUBBOCK, TEXAS
83-101 MOROGIELLO, DANIEL JOSEPH	2365 EAST 72ND ST - BROOKLYN NY 11234
84- 82 MORONKO, JEFFREY ROBERT	OLD ADD: 3637 S. SHAVER #309 - PASADENA TX 77504
26- 58 MORRELL, WILLARD BLACKMER	D. AUGUST 5, 1975 BIRMINGHAM, ALA.
68- 69 MORRIS, DANNY WALKE	216 WILSON ST - GREENVILLE KY 42345
37- 79 MORRIS, DOYT THEODORE	D. JULY 4, 1984 GASTONIA, N. C.
77- 96 MORRIS, JOHN SCOTT	OLD ADD: 304 OAK ST - MANISTEE MI 49660
66- 65 MORRIS, JOHN WALLACE	5538 E. PARADISE LN - SCOTTSDALE AZ 85254
22-100 MORRIS, WALTER EDWARD	D. MARCH 3, 1932 CENTURY, FLA.
15-110 MORRISETTE, WILLIAM LEE	D. MARCH 25, 1966 VIRGINIA BEACH, VA.
77- 97 MORRISON, JAMES FOREST	OLD ADD: 505 S. MATUBBA ST - ABERDEEN MS 39730
20- 87 MORRISON, JOHN DEWEY	D. MARCH 20, 1966 LEXINGTON, KY.
21- 70 MORRISON, PHILIP MELVIN	D. JANUARY 18, 1955 LEXINGTON, KY.
27- 66 MORRISON, WALTER GUY	D. AUGUST 14, 1934 GRAND RAPIDS, MICH.
32- 56 MORRISSEY, JOSEPH ANSELM 'JO-JO'	D. MAY 2, 1950 WORCESTER, MASS.
29- 75 MORSE, NEWELL OBEDIAH 'BUD'	2015 IVES AVE - RENO NV 89503
11-123 MORSE, PETER RAYMOND 'HAP'	D. JUNE 19, 1974 ST. PAUL, MINN.
69-119 MORTON, CARL WENDLE	D. APRIL 12, 1983 TULSA, OKLA.
54- 70 MORTON, GUY JR.	969 BLACKLEYVILLE RD - WOOSTER OH 44691
14-159 MORTON, GUY SR.	D. OCTOBER 18, 1934 SHEFFIELD, ALA.
61- 72 MORTON, WYCLIFFE NATHAN 'BUBBA'	3332 MONACO PARKWAY - DENVER CO 80207
54- 71 MORYN, WALTER JOSEPH	545 CHARLES ST - GLENDALE HEIGHTS IL 60137
65- 78 MOSCHITTO, ROSAIRO ALLEN 'ROSS'	32 MORTON ST - GARNERSVILLE NY 10923
80- 93 MOSEBY, LLOYD ANTHONY	3400 KINGMONT DR - LOOMIS CA 95650
13-129 MOSELEY, EARL VICTOR	D. JULY 1, 1963 ALLIANCE, O.
37- 80 MOSER, ARNOLD ROBERT	7714 ANTOINE - HOUSTON TX 77088
65- 79 MOSES, GERALD BRAHEEN	111 WALDEMAR AVE - SOUTH BOSTON MA 02128
82- 86 MOSES, JOHN WILLIAM	5343 E LAFAYETTE - PHOENIX AZ 85018
35- 75 MOSES, WALLACE	777 W. GERMANTOWN PIKE - PLYMOUTH MEETING PA 19462
77- 98 MOSKAU, PAUL RICHARD	4152 E SECOND ST - TUCSON AZ 85711
10-108 MOSKIMAN, WILLIAM BANKHEAD 'DOC'	D. JANUARY 11, 1953 SAN LEANDRO, CALIF.
29- 76 MOSOLF, JAMES FREDERICK	D. DECEMBER 28, 1979 DALLAS, ORE.
34- 76 MOSS, CHARLES CROSBY	2400 40TH AVE - MERIDIAN MS 39304
30- 55 MOSS, CHARLES MALCOLM 'MAL'	D. FEBRUARY 5, 1983 SAVANNAH, GA.
42- 70 MOSS, HOWARD GLENN	3805 KIMBLE RD-BALTIMORE MD 21218
46- 76 MOSS, JOHN LESTER 'LES'	420 TULLIS AVE - LONGWOOD FL 32750
26- 59 MOSS, RAYMOND EARL	3734 KINGS RD - CHATTANOOGA TN 37416
54- 72 MOSSI, DONALD LOUIS	1340 SANFORD RANCH RD - UKIAH CA 95482
51- 69 MOSSOR, EARL DALTON	652 MARIETTA - CINCINNATI OH 45245
18- 52 MOSTIL, JOHN ANTHONY	D. DECEMBER 10, 1970 MIDLOTHIAN, ILL.
62- 94 MOTA, MANUEL RAFAEL	27 DE FABRERO #445 - SANTA DOMINGO DOMINICAN REP.
81- 87 MOTLEY, DARRYL DEWAYNE	2717 NE 12TH - PORTLAND OR 97212
45- 52 MOTT, ELISHA MATTHEW 'BITSY'	806 EAST EMMA ST - TAMPA FL 33603
67- 76 MOTTON, CURTELL HOWARD	1522 25TH AVE - OAKLAND CA 94601
46- 77 MOULDER, GLEN HUBERT	2946 LAVISTA CT - DECATUR GA 30083
11-124 MOULTON, ALBERT THEODORE 'OLLIE'	D. JULY 10, 1968 PEABODY, MASS.
13-130 MOWE, RAYMOND BENJAMIN	D. AUGUST 14, 1968 SARASOTA, FLA.
33- 44 MOWRY, JOSEPH ALOYSIUS	6321 BANCROFT - ST LOUIS MO 63109
10-109 MOYER, CHARLES EDWARD	D. NOVEMBER 18, 1962 JACKSONVILLE, FLA.
54- 73 MROZINSKI, RONALD FRANK	WASH. ARMS BLDG 100 #D2 - WASHINGTON NJ 07882

63- 83 MUDROCK, PHILIP RAY — 2548 EAST 6600 SOUTH-SALT LAKE CITY UT 84121
20- 88 MUELLER, CLARENCE FRANCIS 'HEINIE' — D. JANUARY 23, 1975 DESOTO, MO.
48- 74 MUELLER, DONALD FREDERICK — 11224 MUELLER LN - MARYLAND HEIGHTS MO 63042
38- 68 MUELLER, EMMETT JEROME 'HEINIE' — 6057 WINDHOVER DR - ORLANDO FL 32819
50- 70 MUELLER, JOSEPH GORDON 'GORDY' — 1404 CHESAPEAKE AVE - MIDDLE RIVER MD 21220
41- 76 MUELLER, LESLIE CLYDE — RR 2 BOX 294 - MILLSTADT IL 62260
35- 76 MUELLER, RAY COLEMAN — 1021 S. PROGRESS AVE #D-1 - HARRISBURG PA 17111
22-101 MUELLER, WALTER JOHN — D. AUGUST 16, 1971 ST. LOUIS, MO.
78- 87 MUELLER, WILLARD LAWRENCE 'WILLIE' — 1246 WALLACE LAKE - WEST BEND WI 53095
42- 71 MUELLER, WILLIAM LAWRENCE — 318 NORRISTOWN CT, BAYWOOD - CHESTERFIELD MO 63017
57- 59 MUFFETT, BILLY ARNOLD — 706 BAYOU SHORE DRIVE - MONROE LA 71203
24- 83 MUICH, IGNATIUS ANDREW 'JOE' — 9244 LODGE POLE LN - ST LOUIS MO 63126
51- 70 MUIR, JOSEPH ALLEN — D. JUNE 25, 1980 BALTIMORE, MD.
35- 77 MULCAHY, HUGH NOYES — 175 WAYNE ST - BEAVER PA 15009
30- 56 MULLEAVY, GREGORY THOMAS — D. FEBRUARY 1, 1980 ARCADIA, CALIF.
10-110 MULLEN, CHARLES GEORGE — D. JUNE 6, 1963 SEATTLE, WASH.
44- 95 MULLEN, FORD PARKER — 7127 MULLEN RD SE - OLYMPIA WA 98503
20- 89 MULLEN, WILLIAM JOHN — D. MAY 4, 1971 ST. LOUIS, MO.
33- 45 MULLER, FREDERICK WILLIAM — D. OCTOBER 20, 1976 DAVIS, CALIF.
15-111 MULLIGAN, EDWARD JOSEPH — D. MARCH 15, 1982 SAN RAFAEL, CALIF.
34- 77 MULLIGAN, JOSEPH IGNATIUS — 441 W ROXBURY PARKWAY - BOSTON MA 02132
41- 77 MULLIGAN, RICHARD CHARLES — 1205 E WALNUT AVE - VICTORIA TX 77901
40- 65 MULLIN, PATRICK JOSEPH — 320 CHURCH ST - BROWNSVILLE PA 15417
77- 99 MULLINIKS, STEVEN RANCE — 707 TEPIC - EL PASO TX 79932
80- 94 MULLINS, FRANCIS JOSEPH — 6180 BROADWAY TER - OAKLAND CA 94618
21- 71 MULRENAN, DOMINICK JOSEPH — D. JULY 27, 1964 MELROSE, MASS.
30- 57 MULRONEY, FRANCIS JOSEPH — 205 W 8TH - ABERDEEN WA 98520
74- 92 MUMPHREY, JERRY WAYNE — 3913 SILVERWOOD - TYLER TX 75701
18- 53 MUNCH, JACOB FERDINAND — D. JUNE 8, 1966 LANSDOWNE, PA.
37- 81 MUNCRIEF, ROBERT CLEVELAND — 731 RIDGE CREST - DUNCANVILLE TX 75116
13-131 MUNDY, WILLIAM EDWARD — D. SEPTEMBER 23, 1958 KALAMAZOO, MICH.
43- 96 MUNGER, GEORGE DAVID 'RED' — 8101 LEONORA #407 - HOUSTON TX 77061
31- 61 MUNGO, VAN LINGLE — D. FEBRUARY 12, 1985 PAGELAND, S. C.
71- 73 MUNIZ, MANUEL — CALLE 23-R-12 VILLA NUEVA - CAGUAS PR 00626
80- 95 MUNNINGHOFF, SCOTT ANDREW — 3418 SAYBROOK AVE - CINCINNATI OH 45208
34- 78 MUNNS, LESLIE ERNEST — 236 E 5TH - WAHOO NE 68066
25- 76 MUNSON, JOSEPH MARTIN NAPOLEON — 7274 LAMPORT RD - UPPER DARBY PA 19082
69-120 MUNSON, THURMAN LEE — D. AUGUST 2, 1979 AKRON-CANTON AIRPORT, O.
78- 88 MURA, STEPHEN ANDREW — 1300 GIUFFRIAS AVE - METAIRIE LA 70001
64- 76 MURAKAMI, MASANORI — NIPPON HOSC,3-20-5 YAKUMO - MEGURO KU TOKYO 152, JAPAN
65- 80 MURCER, BOBBY RAY — OLD ADD: 3244 WHIPPOORWILL - OKLAHOMA CITY OK
17- 53 MURCHISON, THOMAS MALCOM 'TIM' — D. OCTOBER 20, 1962 LIBERTY, N. C.
56- 62 MURFF, JOHN ROBERT "RED" — 1005 LAWNDALE - BRENHAM TX 77833
76- 67 MURPHY, DALE BRIAN — 12055 HOUZE ROAD - ROSWELL GA 30076
60- 73 MURPHY, DANIEL FRANCIS — 56 LOTHROP ST #5 - BEVERLY MA 01915
78- 89 MURPHY, DWAYNE KEITH — 1132 "W" AVENUE #H6 - LANCASTER CA 93534
42- 72 MURPHY, EDWARD JOSEPH — 1317 JEFFERSON ST-JOLIET IL 60435
14-160 MURPHY, HERBERT COURTLAND 'DUMMY' — D. AUGUST 10, 1962 TALLAHASSEE, FLA.
12-136 MURPHY, JOHN EDWARD — D. FEBRUARY 20, 1969 DUNMORE, PA.
32- 57 MURPHY, JOHN JOSEPH — D. JANUARY 14, 1970 NEW YORK, N. Y.
15-112 MURPHY, LEO JOSEPH — D. AUGUST 12, 1960 RACINE, WIS.
12-137 MURPHY, MICHAEL JEROME — D. OCTOBER 26, 1952 JOHNSON CITY, N.Y.
54- 74 MURPHY, RICHARD LEE — 7114 MIAMI HILLS DR - CINCINNATI OH 45243
85- 79 MURPHY, ROBERT ALBERT — 7520 SW 72ND COURT - MIAMI FL 33143
18- 54 MURPHY, ROBERT R. 'BUZZ' — D. MAY 11, 1938 DENVER, COLO.
68- 70 MURPHY, THOMAS ANDREW — 26566 CALLE LORENZO - SAN JUAN CAPISTRANO CA 92675
31- 62 MURPHY, WALTER JOSEPH — 16123 AMBERWOOD - DALLAS TX 75248
66- 66 MURPHY, WILLIAM EUGENE — 10214 88TH AVE SW - TACOMA WA 98498
23- 97 MURRAY , ROBERT HAYES — D. JANUARY 4, 1979 NASHUA, N. H.
36- 63 MURRAY, AMBROSE JOSEPH — 8297 SE COCONUT ST - HOBO SOUND FL 33455
23- 96 MURRAY, ANTHONY JOHN — D. MARCH 19, 1974 CHICAGO, ILL.
74- 93 MURRAY, DALE WAYNE — MIDDLETOWN RD - CUERO TX 77954
77-100 MURRAY, EDDIE CLARENCE — 711 40TH ST #450 - BALTIMORE MD 21211
17- 54 MURRAY, EDWARD FRANCIS — D. NOVEMBER 8, 1970 CHEYENNE, WYO.
22-102 MURRAY, GEORGE KING — D. OCTOBER 18, 1955 MEMPHIS, TENN.
22-103 MURRAY, JAMES FRANCIS — D. JULY 15, 1973 NEW YORK , N. Y.
50- 71 MURRAY, JOSEPH AMBROSE — 2719 VIA SANTA TOMAS - SAN CLEMEMTE CA 92672
74- 94 MURRAY, LARRY — OLD ADD: 3544 SOUTH CALUMET AVE - CHICAGO IL 60653
19- 58 MURRAY, PATRICK JOSEPH — D. NOVEMBER 5, 1983 ROCHESTER, N. Y.
48- 75 MURRAY, RAYMOND LEE — BOX 453 - KENNEDALE TX 76060
80- 96 MURRAY, RICHARD DALE — 435 E 108TH ST - LOS ANGELES CA 90061
17- 55 MURRAY, WILLIAM ALLENWOOD — D. SEPTEMBER 14, 1943 BOSTON, MASS.
63- 84 MURRELL, IVAN AUGUSTO — OLD ADD: 4840 ZION ST - SAN DIEGO CA 92120
41- 78 MURTAUGH, DANIEL EDWARD — D. DECEMBER 2, 1976 CHESTER PA.
69-121 MUSER, ANTHONY JOSEPH — 11222 MARYHA ANN DR - LOS ALAMITOS CA 90720
65- 81 MUSGRAVES, DENNIS EUGENE — RR FOUR - CENTRALLIA MO 65240
41- 79 MUSIAL, STANLEY FRANK — 85 TRENT DR - LADUE MO 63124
82- 87 MUSSELMAN, RALPH RICHARD — 5313 AUTUMN DR - WILMINGTON NC 28401
12-138 MUSSER, PAUL — D. JULY 7, 1973 STATE COLLEGE, PA.
32- 58 MUSSER, WILLIAM DANIEL 'DANNY' — 1062 HOMEWOOD CT - DECATUR GA 30033
44- 96 MUSSILL, BERNARD JAMES 'BARNEY' — 912 MOORLAND DR -GROSSE POINTE WOODS MI 48236
40- 66 MUSTAIKIS, ALEXANDER DOMINICK — D. JANUARY 17, 1970 SCRANTON, PA.
38- 69 MYATT, GEORGE EDWARD — 1623 CANTON AVE-ORLANDO FL 32803
20- 90 MYATT, GLENN CALVIN — D. AUGUST 9, 1969 HOUSTON, TEX.
25- 77 MYER, CHARLES SOLOMON 'BUDDY' — D. OCTOBER 31, 1974 BATON ROUGE, LA.
15-113 MYERS, ELMER GLENN — D. JULY 29, 1976 COLLINGSWOOD, N. J.
38- 70 MYERS, LINNWOOD LINCOLN — 1111 YVERDON DR #C1 - CAMP HILL PA 17011
10-111 MYERS, RALPH EDWARD 'HAP' — D. JUNE 30, 1967 SAN FRANCISCO, CALIF.
85- 80 MYERS, RANDALL KIRK — P.O. BOX 9900 SUITE 155 - VANCOUVER WA 98668
56- 63 MYERS, RICHARD — 5400 SAMPSON BLVD - SACRAMENTO CA 95820
35- 78 MYERS, WILLIAM HARRISON — 204 SALT RD-ENOLA PA 17025
76- 68 MYRICK, ROBERT HOWARD — 1923 ADELINE ST - HATTIESBURG MS 39401
15-114 NABORS, HERMAN JOHN 'JACK' — D. OCTOBER 29, 1923 WILTON, ALA.
39- 79 NAGEL, WILLIAM TAYLOR — OLD ADD: 4025 CAMELOT LN - MEMPHIS TN 38118
12-139 NAGELSON, LOUIS MARCELLUS — D. OCTOBER 22, 1965 FORT WAYNE, IND.
68- 71 NAGELSON, RUSSELL CHARLES — ONE POWDERHORN CT - LITTLE ROCK AR 72212
11-125 NAGLE, WALTER HAROLD 'JUDGE' — D. MAY 27, 1971 SANTA ROSA, CALIF.
69-122 NAGY, MICHAEL TIMOTHY — 8 INDIAN TRAIL - BRONX NY 10465

47- 64 NAGY, STEPHEN — 3435 63RD AVE SW - SEATTLE WA 98116
38- 71 NAHEM, SAMUEL RALPH — 624 VINCENTE - BERKELEY CA 94704
76- 69 NAHORODNY, WILLIAM GERARD — 204 S COMET - CLEARWATER FL 33515
36- 64 NAKTENIS, PETER ERNEST — 125 ADELAIDE RD - MANCHESTER CT 06041
24- 84 NALEWAY, FRANK — D. JANUARY 28, 1949 CHICAGO, ILL.
12-140 NAPIER, SKELTON LEROY 'BUDDY' — D. MARCH 29, 1968 DALLAS, TEX.
49- 57 NAPLES, ALOYSIUS FRANCIS — 52 RODGER CT - WYCKOFF NJ 07481
65- 82 NAPOLEON, DANIEL — OLD ADD: 116 OLIVE AVE - TRENTON NJ
51- 71 NARAGON, HAROLD RICHARD — 1521 HAGEY DR - BARBERTON OH 44203
56- 64 NARANJO, LAZARO RAMON GONZALO — D #270, 10 Y 11 - LAWTON, HAVANA CUBA
54- 75 NARLESKI, RAYMOND EDMOND — 1183 CHEWS LANDING RD-LAUREL SPRINGS NJ 08021
29- 77 NARLESKI, WILLIAM EDWARD — D. JULY 22, 1964 LAUREL SPRINGS, N. J.
79- 76 NARRON, JERRY AUSTIN — 232 HILLCREST DR - GOLDSBORO NC 27530
35- 79 NARRON, SAMUEL — RR 1 BOX 125 - MIDDLESEX NC 27557
63- 85 NARUM, LESLIE FERDINAND 'BUSTER' — 324 S GLENWOOD AVE - CLEARWATER FL 33515
67- 77 NASH, CHARLES FRANCIS 'COTTON' — 600 SUMMERSHADE CIR - LEXINGTON KY 40502
66- 67 NASH, JAMES EDWIN — 37 REGINA DR NE - MARIETTA GA 30067
12-141 NASH, KENNETH LELAND — D. FEBRUARY 16, 1977 EPSOM, N. H.
78- 90 NASTU, PHILIP — 119 AUSTIN ST - BRIDGEPORT CT 06604
53- 62 NATON, PETER ALPHONSUS — 4136 SPLIT ROCK RD - CAMILLUS NY 13031
62- 95 NAVARRO, JULIO VENTURA — CALLE 3, BLOQUE 10, #32 - SANTA ROSA, BAYAMON PR 00619
42- 73 NAYLOR, EARL EUGENE — 616 IDAHO AVE E-ST PAUL MN 55117
17- 56 NAYLOR, ROLEINE CECIL — D. JUNE 18, 1966 FORT WORTH, TEX.
39- 80 NAYMICK, MICHAEL JOHN — 8334 BERWICK WAY - STOCKTON CA 95210
56- 65 NEAL, CHARLES LEONARD — 7724 RYAN RIDGE - DALLAS TX 75232
16- 64 NEALE, ALFRED EARLE 'GREASY' — D. NOVEMBER 2, 1973 LAKE WORTH, FL.
52- 78 NECCIAI, RONALD ANDREW — 201 ROSEWOOD DR - MONONGAHELA PA 15063
57- 60 NEEMAN, CALVIN AMANDUS — 93 CHAMPAGNE - LAKE ST. LOUIS MO 63367

14-161 NEFF, DOUGLAS WILLIAM — D. MAY 23, 1932 CAPE CHARLES, VA.
52- 79 NEGRAY, RONALD ALVIN — 587 WEST NIMISLIA RD - AKRON OH 44319
12-142 NEHER, JAMES GILMORE — D. NOVEMBER 11, 1951 BUFFALO, N.Y.
15-115 NEHF, ARTHUR NEUKOM — D. DECEMBER 18, 1960 PHOENIX, ARIZ.
69-123 NEIBAUER, GARY WAYNE — 7110 VAN DORN #89 - LINCOLN NE 68506
60- 74 NEIGER, ALVIN EDWARD — 213 PINEHURST RD - WILMINTON DE 19803
39- 81 NEIGHBORS, ROBERT OTIS — D. AUGUST 8, 1952 NORTH KOREA
46- 78 NEILL, THOMAS WHITE — OLD ADD: 1526 HIDDEN HILL - HOUSTON TX 77064
20- 91 NEIS, BERNARD EDMUND — D. NOVEMBER 29, 1972 INVERNESS, FLA.
29- 78 NEKOLA, FRANCIS JOSEPH 'BOTS' — 13 DEVONSHIRE DR - NEW HYDE PARK NY 11044
10-112 NELSON, ALBERT FRANCIS 'RED' — D. OCTOBER 26, 1956 ST PETERSBURG, FLA.
68- 72 NELSON, DAVID EARL — 850 NORTH STATE ST #8G - CHICAGO IL 60610
35- 80 NELSON, GEORGE EMMETT — D. AUGUST 25, 1967 SIOUX FALLS, S. D.
49- 58 NELSON, GLENN RICHARD 'ROCKY' — BOX 35 - PORTSMOUTH OH 45662
70-100 NELSON, JAMES LORIN — 8648 LODESTONE CIR - ELK GROVE CA 95624
83-102 NELSON, JAMES VICTOR — 9692 READING AVENUE - GARDEN GROVE CA 92644
19- 59 NELSON, LUTHER MARTIN 'LUKE' — BOX 14 - MATHERVILLE ILL 61263
30- 58 NELSON, LYNN BERNARD — D. FEBRUARY 15, 1955 KANSAS CITY, MO.
60- 75 NELSON, MELVIN FREDERICK — 27420 FISHER ST - HIGHLAND CA 92346
83-103 NELSON, RICKY LEE — 7250 SOUTH 46TH ST - PHOENIX AZ 85040
55- 85 NELSON, ROBERT SIDNEY — 10830 WALLBROOK - DALLAS TX 75238
67- 78 NELSON, ROGER EUGENE — OLD ADD: 533 WINDSOR - ARCADIA CA 91006
45- 73 NELSON, TOM COUSINEAU — D. SEPTEMBER 24, 1973 SAN DIEGO, CAL.
81- 88 NELSON, WAYLAND EUGENE 'GENE' — BOX 458 - LACOOCHIE FL 33537
63- 86 NEN, RICHARD LEROY — 4124 BIRCHWOOD - SEAL BEACH CA 90740
11-126 NESS, JOHN CHARLES — D. DECEMBER 3, 1957 DELAND, FLA.
67- 79 NETTLES, GRAIG — 13 NORTH LANE - DEL MAR CA 92014
70-101 NETTLES, JAMES WILLIAM — 4632 DARIEN DR - TACOMA WA 98407
74- 95 NETTLES, MORRIS — 551 1/2 SAN JUAN - VENICE CA 90291
17- 58 NEU, OTTO ADAM — D. SEPTEMBER 19, 1932 KENTON, O.
25- 78 NEUBAUER, HAROLD CHARLES — D. SEPTEMBER 9, 1949 PROVIDENCE, R. I.
72- 78 NEUMEIER, DANIEL GEORGE — RR 3 BOX 438E - LODI WI 53555
25- 79 NEUN, JOHN HENRY — 3501 ST PAUL ST #718 - BALTIMORE MD 21218
50- 72 NEVEL, ERNIE WYRE — 615 MADDUX ST - BRANSON MO 65616
26- 60 NEVERS, ERNEST ALONZO — D. MAY 3, 1976 SAN RAFAEL, CALIF.
49- 59 NEWCOMBE, DONALD — 22507 PEALE DR - WOODLAND HILLS CA 91364
72- 79 NEWHAUSER, DONALD LOUIS — 321 SHERYL DR - DELTONA FL 32738
39- 82 NEWHOUSER, HAROLD — 2584 MARCY-BLOOMFIELD HILLS MI 48013
34- 79 NEWKIRK, FLOYD ELMO — D. APRIL 15, 1976 CLAYTON, MO.
19- 60 NEWKIRK, JOEL IVAN — D. JANUARY 22, 1966 ELDORADO, ILL.
40- 67 NEWLIN, MAURICE MILTON — D. AUGUST 14, 1978 HOUSTON, TEXAS
85- 81 NEWMAN, ALBERT DWAYNE — 1044 LARODA - ONTARIO CA 91761
62- 96 NEWMAN, FREDERICK WILLIAM — 17 ELDA RD - FRAMINGHAM MA 01704
76- 70 NEWMAN, JEFFREY LYNN — 537 QUIVIRA CT - DANVILLE CA 94526
71- 74 NEWMAN, RAYMOND FRANCIS — 1361 HOWARD - MUSKEGON MI 49442
10-113 NEWNAM, PATRICK HENRY — D. JUNE 20, 1938 SAN ANTONIO, TEX.

```
29- 79 NEWSOM, NORMAN LOUIS 'BOBO'        D. DECEMBER 7, 1962 ORLANDO, FLA.
41- 80 NEWSOME, HEBER HAMPTON 'DICK'      D. DECEMBER 15, 1965 AHOSKIE, N. C.
35- 81 NEWSOME, LAMAR ASHBY 'SKEETER'     1626 17TH AVE-COLUMBUS GA 31901
46- 79 NIARHOS, CONSTANTINE GREGORY 'GUS' 244 MONUMENT AVE - HARRISONBURG VA 22801
52- 80 NICHOLAS, DONALD LEIGH             12311 CHASE - GARDEN GROVE CA 92645
26- 61 NICHOLS, CHESTER RAYMOND SR.       D. JULY 11, 1982 PAWTUCKET, R. I.
51- 72 NICHOLS, CHESTER RAYMOND JR        18 COLONIAL DR - LINCOLN RI 02865
58- 67 NICHOLS, DOLAN LEVON               OLD ADD: 1351 OLD HICKORY RD - MEMPHIS TN
44- 97 NICHOLS, ROY                       104 ARIAS WAY - HOT SPRINGS VILLAGE AR 71901
80- 97 NICHOLS, THOMAS REID               501 MARSHALL AVE - BIRMINGHAM AL 35215
60- 76 NICHOLSON, DAVID LAWRENCE          527 SPRINGINGSGUTH - ROSELLE IL 60172
12-143 NICHOLSON, FRANK COLLINS           D. NOVEMBER 11, 1972 JERSEY SHORE, PA.
17- 57 NICHOLSON, FREDERICK               BOX 510 - KILGORE TX 75662
12-144 NICHOLSON, OVID EDWARD             D. MARCH 24, 1968 SALEM, IND.
36- 65 NICHOLSON, WILLIAM BECK            RR 3 - CHESTERTOWN MD 21620
78- 91 NICOSIA, STEVEN RICHARD            11822 SW 44TH ST - DAVIE FL 33330
21- 73 NIEBERGALL, CHARLES ARTHUR         D. AUGUST 29, 1982 HOLIDAY, FLA.
81- 89 NIEDENFUER, THOMAS EDWARD          974 THISTLEGATE RD - AGOURA CA 91301
25- 80 NIEHAUS, ALBERT BERNARD            D. OCTOBER 14, 1931 CINCINNATI, O.
13-132 NIEHAUS, RICHARD J.                D. MARCH 12, 1957 ATLANTA, GA.
13-133 NIEHOFF, JOHN ALBERT               D. DECEMBER 8, 1974 INGLEWOOD, CALIF.
67- 80 NIEKRO, JOSEPH FRANKLIN            214 ASH LN - LAKELAND FL 33801
64- 77 NIEKRO, PHILIP HENRY               4781 CASTLEWOOD DR - LILBURN GA 30247
49- 60 NIELSON, MILTON ROBERT             824 MCGILL - ST PETER MN 56082
43- 97 NIEMAN, ELMER LEROY 'BUTCH'        1324 BOSWELL AVE-TOPEKA KS 66604
51- 73 NIEMAN, ROBERT CHARLES             D. MARCH 10, 1985 CORONA, CALIF.
```

```
79- 77 NIEMANN, RANDY HAROLD              233 VALLEY AVE - FORTUNA CA 95540
43- 98 NIEMES, JACOB LELAND      'JACK'   D. MARCH 4, 1966 HAMILTON, O.
34- 80 NIEMIEC, ALFRED JOSEPH             BOX 467 - KIRKLAND WA 98033
64- 78 NIESON, CHARLES BASSETT            3209 W HIGHLAND DR - BURNSVILLE MN 55374
84- 83 NIETO, THOMAS ANDREW               18002 HORST AVE - ARTESIA CA 90701
21- 72 NIETZKE, ERNEST FREDRICH           D. APRIL 27, 1977 SYLVANIA, O.
38- 72 NIGGELING, JOHN ARNOLD             D. SEPTEMBER 16, 1963 LEMARS, IA.
83-104 NIPPER, ALBERT SAMUEL              5105 VILLE MARIA LANE - HAZELWOOD MO 63042
62- 97 NIPPERT, MERLIN LEE                1015 N MICHIGAN ST - MANGUM OK 73554
61- 78 NISCHWITZ, RONALD LEE              6790 GARBER RD - DAYTON OH 45415
45- 74 NITCHOLAS, OTHO JAMES              1500 ERWIN - MCKINNEY TX 75069
15-116 NIXON, ALBERT RICHARD              D. NOVEMBER 9, 1960 OPELOUSAS, LA.
83-105 NIXON, OTIS JUNIOR                 BOX 23 HIGHWAY 74 - EVERGREEN NC 28438
57- 61 NIXON, RUSSELL EUGENE              BOX 557 - WILLIAMSBURG OH 45176
50- 73 NIXON, WILLARD LEE                 335 REECEBURG SE - SILVER CREEK GA 30173
51- 74 NOBLE, RAFAEL MIGUEL 'RAY'         698 CHAUNCEY ST - BROOKLYN NY 11207
84- 84 NOBOA, MILCIADES ARTURO 'JUNIOR'   OLD ADD: EVA MARIA PELLERANO,CASTRO #1-SANTO DOMINGO DR
85- 82 NOKES, MATTHEW DODGE               5692 LINFIELD AVE - SAN DIEGO CA 92120
67- 81 NOLAN, GARY LYNN                   MGM GRAND,3645 LAS VEGAS BLVD S - LAS VEGAS NV 89109
72- 80 NOLAN, JOSEPH WILLIAM              9515 ALIX DR - MEHLVILLE MO 63123
67- 82 NOLD, RICHARD LOUIS                121 PARK PLAZA DR #6 - DALY CITY CA 94015
79- 78 NOLES, DICKIE RAY                  OLD ADD: 1109 OPAL ST - CHARLOTTE NC
33- 46 NONNENKAMP, LEO WILLIAM 'RED'      1 OAKWOOD RD - LITTLE ROCK AR 72202
74- 96 NORDBROOK, TIMOTHY CHARLES         302 LORI DR #L - GLEN BURNIE MD 21061
76- 71 NORDHAGEN, WAYNE OREN              25896 RAMILLO WAY - VALENCIA CA 91355
50- 74 NOREN, IRVING ARNOLD               2281 VALLEY RD - OCEANSIDE CA 92056
69-124 NORIEGA, JOHN ALAN                 2 EAST 900 SOUTH - KAYSVILLE UT 84037
77-101 NORMAN, DANIEL EDMUND              1336 MESA DR - BARSTOW CA 92311
62- 98 NORMAN, FREDIE ROBERT              6560 BAYWOOD LN - CINCINNATI OH 45224
31- 63 NORMAN, HENRY WILLIS PATRICK 'BILL' D. APRIL 21, 1962 MILWAUKEE, WIS.
78- 92 NORMAN, NELSON AUGUSTO             ING CONSUELO CALLE D5 - SAN PEDRO DE MACORIS DOM. REP.
77-102 NORRIS, JAMES FRANCIS              5524 MANSFIELD RD - ARLINGTON TX 76017
36- 66 NORRIS, LEO JOHN                   ZACHARY HOME, DRAWER C - ZACHARY LA 70791
75- 85 NORRIS, MICHAEL KELVIN             1003 IMPERIAL DR - HAYWARD CA 94541
13-134 NORTH, LOUIS ALEXANDER             D. MAY 16, 1974 SHELTON, CONN.
71- 75 NORTH, WILLIAM ALEX                3303 E MADISON - SEATTLE WA 98102
10-114 NORTHEN, HUBBARD ELWIN             D. OCTOBER 1, 1947 SHREVEPORT, LA.
42- 74 NORTHEY, RONALD JAMES              D. APRIL 16, 1971 PITTSBURGH, PA.
69-125 NORTHEY, SCOTT RICHARD             OLD ADD: 481 RIVIERA BLVD W - NAPLES FL
18- 55 NORTHROP, GEORGE HOWARD 'JAKE'     D. NOVEMBER 16, 1945 MONROETON, PA.
64- 79 NORTHRUP, JAMES THOMAS             1326 OTTER DR - PONTIAC MI 48054
72- 81 NORTON, THOMAS JOHN                4900 SOUTHWOOD - SHEFFIELD LAKES OH 44054
77-103 NORWOOD, WILLIE                    18324 LAURELBROOK CIR - CERRITOS CA 90701
64- 80 NOSSEK, JOSEPH RUDOLPH             437 TERRA LN - AMHERST OH 44001
60- 77 NOTTEBART, DONALD EDWARD           5442 LYMBAR - HOUSTON TX 77035
41- 81 NOVIKOFF, LOUIE ALEXANDER          D. SEPTEMBER 30, 1970 SOUTH GATE, CAL.
49- 61 NOVOTNEY, RALPH JOSEPH 'RUBE'      2311 W 165TH ST - TORRANCE CA 90504
13-135 NOYES, WINFIELD CHARLES            D. APRIL 8, 1969 CASHMERE, WASH.
```

11-127	NUNAMAKER, LESLIE GRANT	D. NOVEMBER 14, 1938 HASTINGS, NEB.
82- 88	NUNEZ, EDWIN (MARTINEZ)	BO. RIO ABAJO, BUZON 2762 - HUMACAO PR 00661
59- 60	NUNN, HOWARD RALPH	RR1 - WESTFIELD NC 27053
19- 61	NUTTER, EVERETT CLARENCE 'DIZZY'	D. JULY 25, 1958 BATTLE CREEK, MICH.
44- 98	NUXHALL, JOSEPH HENRY	5706 LINDENWOOD LN - FAIRFIELD OH 45014
66- 68	NYE, RICHARD RAYMOND	1923 S. MANNHEIM RD - WESTCHESTER IL 60153
82- 89	NYMAN, CHRISTOPHER CURTIS	2992 SHADOW CREEK DR #34 - BOULDER CO 80301
68- 73	NYMAN, GERALD SMITH	2627 N. 16TH E. - LOGAN UT 84321
74- 97	NYMAN, NYLS WALLACE REX	300 KEOKUK - LINCOLN IL 62656
34- 81	OANA, HENRY KAUHANE 'PRINCE'	D. JUNE 19, 1976 AUSTIN, TEX.
70-102	OATES, JOHNNY LANE	1704 LAKE AVE - WILMETTE IL 60091
77-104	OBERKFELL, KENNETH RAY	305 S DONK ST - MARYVILLE IL 62062
79- 79	OBERRY, PRESTON MICHAEL 'MIKE'	1100 DEARING DOWNS DR - HELENA AL 35017
78- 93	OBRADOVICH, JAMES THOMAS	1212 MAIN AVE #V - NITRO WV 25143
85- 83	OBRIEN, CHARLES HUGH	4932 EAST 38TH PLACE - TULSA OK 74135
78- 94	OBRIEN, DANIEL JOGUES	8104 VALLEY GLEN DR #2022 - DALLAS TX 75228
53- 63	OBRIEN, EDWARD JOSEPH	3414 108TH PL NE #1 - BELLEVUE WA 98004
23- 98	OBRIEN, FRANK ALOYSIUS 'MICKEY'	D. NOVEMBER 4, 1971 MONTEREY PARK, CAL.
15-117	OBRIEN, GEORGE JOSEPH	D. MARCH 24, 1966 COLUMBUS, O.

When Lefty O'Doul was a Giant

53- 64	OBRIEN, JOHN THOMAS	938 21ST ST E - SEATTLE WA 98112
82- 90	OBRIEN, PETER MICHAEL	BOX 1037 - PEBBLE BEACH CA 93953
16- 65	OBRIEN, RAYMOND JOSEPH	D. MARCH 31, 1942 ST. LOUIS, MO.
71- 76	OBRIEN, ROBERT ALLEN	3628 N SHIRLEY - FRESNO CA 93727
69-126	OBRIEN, SYDNEY LLOYD	4576 EVEREST CIR - CYPRESS CA 90630
43- 99	OBRIEN, THOMAS EDWARD	D. NOVEMBER 5, 1978 ANNISTON, ALA.
11-128	OBRIEN, THOMAS JOSEPH 'BUCK'	D. JULY 25, 1959 DORCHESTER, MASS.
35- 82	OCK, HAROLD DAVID 'WHITEY'	D. MARCH 18, 1975 MOUNT KISCO, N. Y.
44- 99	OCKEY, WALTER ANDREW	D. DECEMBER 4, 1971 STATEN ISLAND, N.Y.
50- 75	OCONNELL, DANIEL FRANCIS	D. OCTOBER 2, 1969 CLIFTON, N. J.
23- 99	OCONNELL, JAMES JOSEPH	D. NOVEMBER 11, 1976 BAKERSFIELD, CALIF.
28- 72	OCONNELL, JOHN CHARLES	1611 19TH ST NE - CANTON OH 44714
81- 90	OCONNOR, JACK WILLIAM	BOX 430 - YUCCA VALLEY CA 92284
16- 66	OCONNOR, JOHN CHARLES	D. MAY 30, 1982 BONNER SPRINGS, KAN.
35- 83	ODEA, JAMES KENNETH 'KEN'	D. DECEMBER 17, 1985 LIMA, N. Y.
44-100	ODEA, PAUL	D. DECEMBER 11, 1978 CLEVELAND, O.
54- 76	ODELL, WILLIAM OLIVER	RR 1 BOX 60 - NEWBERRY SC 29108
21- 74	ODENWALD, THEODORE JOSEPH	D. OCTOBER 23, 1965 SHAKOPEE, MINN.
43-100	ODOM, DAVID EVERETT	BOX 7564 DUNES STA. - MYRTLE BEACH SC 29577
25- 81	ODOM, HERMAN BOYD 'HEINIE'	D. AUGUST 31, 1970 RUSK, TEXAS
64- 81	ODOM, JOHN LEE 'BLUE MOON'	10337 SLATER AVE #206 - FOUNTAIN VALLEY CA 92708
54- 77	ODONNELL, GEORGE DANA	121 HIGH STREET - WINCHESTER IL 62694
27- 67	ODONNELL, HARRY HERMAN	D. JANUARY 31, 1958 PHILADELPHIA, PA.
63- 87	ODONOGHUE, JOHN EUGENE	500 S CEDAR - INDEPENDENCE MO 64053
19- 62	ODOUL, FRANCIS JOSEPH 'LEFTY'	D. DECEMBER 7, 1969 SAN FRANCISCO, CAL.
12-145	ODOWD (JOHN LEO DOWD)	D. JANUARY 31, 1981 FORT LAUDERDALE, FLA.
83-106	OELKERS, BRYAN ALOIS	2700 LINK - OVERLAND MO 63114
58- 68	OERTEL, CHARLES FRANK	BOX 90 - PONTIAC MI 48055
14-162	OESCHGER, JOSEPH CARL	29 FRANCIS CIR - ROHNERT PARK CA 94928
78- 95	OESTER, RONALD JOHN	3971 HAMBLER DR - CINCINNATI OH 45230
15-118	OFARRELL, ROBERT ARTHUR	27 SOUTH WEST - WAUKEGAN ILL 60085
72- 82	OFFICE, ROWLAND JOHNIE	3212 HARBOR VIEW CT - DECATUR GA 30034
18- 56	OGDEN, JOHN MAHLON	D. NOVEMBER 9, 1977 PHILADELPHIA, PA.
22-104	OGDEN, WARREN HARVEY 'CURLY'	D. AUGUST 6, 1964 CHESTER, PA.
36- 67	OGLESBY, JAMES DORN	D. SEPTEMBER 1, 1955 TULSA, OKLA.
71- 77	OGLIVIE, BENJAMIN AMBROSIO	917 BODARK LANE - AUSTIN TX 78745
36- 68	OGRODOWSKI, AMBROSE FRANCIS 'BRUSIE'	D. MARCH 5, 1956 SAN FRANCISCO, CAL.
25- 82	OGRODOWSKI, JOSEPH ANTHONY	D. JUNE 24, 1959 ELMIRA, N. Y.
80- 98	OJEDA, ROBERT MICHAEL	14884 ROAD 312 - VISALIA CA 93277
20- 92	OKRIE, FRANK ANTHONY	D. OCTOBER 16, 1959 DETROIT, MICH.
48- 76	OKRIE, LEONARD JOSEPH	4603 STRATHMORE - FAYETTEVILLE NC 28304
14-163	OLDHAM, JOHN CYRUS 'RED'	D. JANUARY 28,1961 COSTA MESA, CALIF.
56- 66	OLDHAM, JOHN HARDIN	1845 ANNE WAY - SAN JOSE CA 95124
53- 65	OLDIS, ROBERT CARL	306 VIRGINIA DR - IOWA CITY IA 52240
62- 99	OLIVA, PEDRO 'TONY'	212 SPRING VALLEY DR - BLOOMINGTON MN 55420
60- 78	OLIVARES, EDWARD BALZAC	CARRO 330 KIH2 BUZON 427-SAN GERMAN PR 00750
68- 74	OLIVER, ALBERT	OLD ADD: 1320 KINNEY ST - PORTSMOUTH OH 45662
77-105	OLIVER, DAVID JACOB	3604 NEWTON RD - STOCKTON CA 95205
59- 61	OLIVER, EUGENE GEORGE	2805 35TH ST - ROCK ISLAND IL 61201
63- 88	OLIVER, NATHANIEL	1320 104TH AVE - OAKLAND CA 94603
65- 83	OLIVER, ROBERT LEE	4329 EIGHTH AVE - SACRAMENTO CA 95817
30- 59	OLIVER, THOMAS NOBLE	BOX 1701 - MONTGOMERY AL 36104
60- 79	OLIVO, DIOMEDES ANTONIO	D. FEBRUARY 15, 1977 SANTO DOMINGO, DOM. REP.
61- 79	OLIVO, FEDERICO EMILIO 'CHI-CHI'	D. FEBRUARY 3, 1977 GUAYUBIN, DOMINICAN REP.
66- 69	OLLOM, JAMES DONALD	OLD ADD: 8601 9TH SE - EVERETT WA 98205

COACH REGGIE OTERO
Cincinnati Reds

OTTEN   PARKER

74-100 OTTEN, JAMES EDWARD	BOX 242 - KALISPELL MT 59901
33- 47 OULLIBER, JOHN ANDREW	D. DECEMBER 26, 1980 NEW ORLEANS, LA.
33- 48 OUTEN, WILLIAM AUSTIN 'CHICK'	D. SEPTEMBER 11, 1961 DURHAM, N. C.
37- 82 OUTLAW, JAMES PAULUS	118 JAMES ST - JACKSON AL 36545
43-107 OVERMIRE, FRANK 'STBBY'	D. MARCH 3, 1977 LAKELAND, FLA.
76- 72 OVERY, HARRY MICHAEL	101 FAIRVIEW PL - CLINTON IL 61727
11-131 OVITZ, ERNEST GAYHART	D. SEPTEMBER 11, 1980 GREEN BAY, WISC.
76- 73 OWCHINKO, ROBERT DENNIS	-11317 SARASOTA - REDFORD TWP. MI 48239
37- 83 OWEN, ARNOLD MALCOLM 'MICKEY'	2731 E.LOMBARD - SPRINGFIELD MO 65802
83-109 OWEN, DAVE	RURAL ROUTE 5 BOX 281 - CLEBURNE TX 76031
81- 91 OWEN, LAWRENCE THOMAS	804 WHITE PINE ST - NEW CARLISLE OH 45344
31- 65 OWEN, MARVIN JAMES	42 HAWTHORNE WAY - SAN JOSE CA 95110
83-110 OWEN, SPIKE DEE	RURAL ROUTE 5 BOX 281 - CLEBURNE TX 76031
35- 86 OWENS, FURMAN LEE 'JACK'	D. NOVEMBER 14, 1958 GREENVILLE, S. C.
55- 87 OWENS, JAMES PHILIP	1761 CROTON DR - VENICE FL 33595
72- 84 OWENS, PAUL FRANCIS	RR 3 BOX 251 - SEWELL NJ 08080
82- 93 OWNBEY, RICHARD WAYNE	2752 W STOCKTON AVE - ANAHEIM CA 92801
65- 85 OYLER, RAYMOND FRANCIS	D. JANUARY 26, 1981 REDMOND, WASH.
73- 92 OZARK, DANIEL LEONARD	BOX 6666 - VERO BEACH FL 32960
23-100 OZMER, HORACE ROBERT 'DOC'	D. DECEMBER 28, 1970 ATLANTA, GA.
77-106 PACELLA, JOHN LEWIS	6586 SUNBURY RD - WESTERVILLE OH 43081
63- 89 PACIOREK, JOHN FRANCIS	8400 HUNTINGTON DR - SAN GABRIEL CA 91775
70-103 PACIOREK, THOMAS MARTIN	2872 NORTH DESHON RD - STONE MOUNTAIN GA 30087
49- 62 PACK, FRANKIE	BOX 1623 - HENDERSONVILLE NC 28739
12-151 PACKARD, EUGENE MILO	D. MAY 19, 1959 RIVERSIDE, CALIF.
75- 87 PACTWA, JOSEPH MARTIN	232 154TH PL - CALUMET CITY IL 60409
32- 59 PADDEN, THOMAS FRANCIS	D. JUNE 11, 1973 MANCHESTER, N. H.
12-152 PADDOCK, DELMAR HAROLD	D. FEBRUARY 6, 1952 REMER, MINN.
37- 84 PADGETT, DON WILSON	D. DECEMBER 9, 1980 HIGH POINT, N. C.
23-101 PADGETT, ERNEST KITCHEN	D. APRIL 15, 1957 EAST ORANGE, N. J.
69-130 PAEPKE, DENNIS RAY	DRAWER #CE - CRESTLINE CA 92325
43-108 PAFKO, ANDREW	1420 BLACKHAWK DR - MOUNT PROSPECT IL 60056
73- 93 PAGAN, DAVID PERCY	BOX 1819 - NIPAWIN SASK. SOE 1EO CAN.
59- 63 PAGAN, JOSE ANTONIO	CALLE JASPE #15 - CAGUAS PR 00625
44-103 PAGE, JOSEPH FRANCIS	D. APRIL 21, 1980 LATROBE, PA.
68- 75 PAGE, MICHAEL RANDY	BOX 334 - WOODRUFF SC 29388
77-107 PAGE, MITCHELL OTIS	125 E 93RD ST - LOS ANGELES CA 90003
39- 86 PAGE, SAMUEL WALTER	BOX 204-WOODRUFF SC 29388
38- 73 PAGE, VANCE LINWOOD	D. JULY 14, 1951 WILSON, N. C.
28- 74 PAGE,PHILIP RAUSAC	D. JUNE 26, 1958 SPRINGFIELD, MASS.
78- 96 PAGEL, KARL DOUGLAS	6241 NORTH SIXTEENTH AVE - PHOENIX AZ 85015
55- 88 PAGLIARONI, JAMES VINCENT	10388 PARTRIDGE DR - GRASS VALLEY CA 95945
84- 86 PAGLIARULO, MICHAEL TIMOTHY	254 WILLIS AVE - MEDFORD MA 02155
11-132 PAIGE, GEORGE LYNN 'PAT'	D. JUNE 8, 1939 BERLIN, WIS.
48- 78 PAIGE, LEROY "SATCHEL"	D. JUNE 8, 1982 KANSAS CITY, MO.
51- 76 PAINE, PHILLIPS STEERE	D. FEBRUARY 19, 1978 LEBANON, PA.
39- 87 PALAGYI, MICHAEL RAYMOND	167 14TH ST-CONNEAUT OH 44030
45- 76 PALICA, ERVIN MARTIN	D. MAY 29, 1982 HUNTINGTON BEACH, CALIF.
48- 79 PALM, RICHARD PAUL 'MIKE'	63 NICHOLS RD - COHASSET MA 02025
78- 97 PALMER, DAVID WILLIAM	61 SHERMAN AVE - GLENS FALLS NY 12801
17- 59 PALMER, EDWIN HENRY	D. JANUARY 9, 1983 MARLOW, OKLA.
65- 86 PALMER, JAMES ALVIN	BOX 145 - BROOKLANDVILLE MD 21022
69-131 PALMER, LOWELL RAYMOND	4057 STEPHEN DR - NORTH HIGHLANDS CA 95660
15-119 PALMERO, EMILIO ANTONIO	D. JULY 15, 1970 TOLEDO, O.
31- 66 PALMISANO, JOSEPH	D. NOVEMBER 5, 1971 ALBUQUERQUE, N. M.
60- 81 PALMQUIST, EDWIN LEE	128 W.MARIPOSA ST - SAN CLEMENTE CA 92672
53- 66 PALYS, STANLEY FRANCIS	RR ONE - MOSCOW PA 18444
84- 87 PANKOVITS, JAMES FRANKLIN	9419 BONNIE DALE RD - RICHMOND VA 23229
71- 78 PANTHER, JAMES EDWARD	1125 SHARI LN - LIBERTYVILLE IL 60048
61- 81 PAPA, JOHN PAUL	29 PHILLIPS DR - SHELTON CT 06484
48- 80 PAPAI, ALFRED THOMAS	2553 S 7TH ST - SPRINGFIELD IL 62703
76- 74 PAPE, KENNETH WAYNE	2714 OAK FIRE - SAN ANTONIO TX 78217
74-101 PAPI, STANLEY GERARD	1111 WEST SIERRA MADRE - FRESNO CA 93705
45- 77 PAPISH,-FRANK RICHARD	D. AUGUST 30, 1965 PUEBLO, COLO.
57- 64 PAPPAS, MILTON STEPHEN	205 THOMPSON DR - WHEATON ILL 60187
85- 86 PARDO, ALBERTO JUDAS	614 WEST BUFFALO AVE - TAMPA FL 33603
82- 94 PARIS, KELLY JAY	OLD ADD: 19961 SANTA RITA ST - WOODLAND HILLS CA 91364
43-109 PARISSE, LOUIS PETER	D. JUNE 2, 1956 PHILADELPHIA, PA.
15-120 PARK, JAMES	D. DECEMBER 17, 1970 LEXINGTON, KY.
37- 85 PARKER, CLARENCE MCKAY 'ACE'	210 SNEAD'S FAIRWAY-PORTSMOUTH VA 23701
15-121 PARKER, CLARENCE PERKINS 'PAT'	D. MARCH 21, 1967 CLAREMONT, N.H.
73- 94 PARKER, DAVID GENE	OLD ADD: 1854 WESTLAND GARDEN - TOLEDO OH 43615
23-102 PARKER, DOUGLAS WOOLLEY 'DIXIE'	D. MAY 15, 1972 GREEN POND, ALA.

MILT PAPPAS
Cincinnati Reds

36- 70	PARKER, FRANCIS JAMES 'SALTY'	9201 CLAREWOOD #121 - HOUSTON TX 77036
70-104	PARKER, HARRY WILLIAM	RR 1 BOX 123 - BEGGS OK 74421
64- 82	PARKER, MAURICE WESLEY 'WES'	2140 COLORADO AVE - SANTA MONICA CA 90404
19- 64	PARKER, ROY W.	B. 1897
71- 79	PARKER, WILLIAM DAVID	4825 SOUTH MILL AVE - TEMPE AZ 85282
21- 76	PARKINSON, FRANK JOSEPH	D. JULY 4, 1960 TRENTON, N.J.
37- 86	PARKS, ARTIE WILLIAM	127 S HARVEY-GREENVILLE MS 38701
21- 77	PARKS, VERNON HENRY 'SLICKER'	D. FEBRUARY 21, 1978 ROYAL OAK, MICH.
29- 81	PARMELEE, LEROY EARL	D. AUGUST 31, 1981 MONROE, MICH.
47- 65	PARNELL, MELVIN LLOYD	700 TURQUOISE ST - NEW ORLEANS LA 70124
16- 67	PARNHAM, JAMES ARTHUR 'RUBE'	D. NOVEMBER 25, 1963 MCKEESPORT, PA.
70-105	PARRILLA, SAMUEL	33 WYCKOFF ST - BROOKLYN NY 11201
77-108	PARRISH, LANCE MICHAEL	960 WEST HARDSALE - BLOOMFIELD HILLS MI 48013
74-102	PARRISH, LARRY ALTON	4989 E STATE RD #544 - HAINES CITY FL 33844
77-109	PARROTT, MICHAEL EVERETT ARCH	2784 MAGNOLIA ST - CAMARILLO CA 93010
10-115	PARSON, WILLIAM EDWIN 'JIGGS'	D. MAY 19, 1967 INGLEWOOD, CALIF.
81- 92	PARSONS, CASEY ROBERT	EAST 12124 25TH - SPOKANE WA 99206
39- 88	PARSONS, EDWARD DIXON 'DIXIE'	4723 W MARSHALL ST - LONGVIEW TX 75601
63- 90	PARSONS, THOMAS ANTHONY	LINCOLN CITY ROAD - LAKEVILLE CT 06039
71- 80	PARSONS, WILLIAM RAYMOND	2725 S AZALEA - TEMPE AZ 85281
43-110	PARTEE, ROY ROBERT	DRAWER AJ - TRINIDAD CA 95570
13-137	PARTENHEIMER, HAROLD PHILIP 'STEVE'	D. JUNE 16, 1971 MANSFIELD, O.
44-104	PARTENHEIMER, STANWOOD WENDELL	117 BEAVER RD - SEWICKLEY PA 15143
27- 69	PARTRIDGE, JAMES BUGG 'JAY'	D. JANUARY 4, 1974 NASHVILLE, TENN.
15-122	PASCHAL, BENJAMIN EDWIN	D. NOVEMBER 10, 1974 CHARLOTTE, N. C.
78- 98	PASCHALL, WILLIAM HERBERT	OLD ADD: 4557 PRINCESS ANNE RD - VIRGINIA BEACH VA 2346
54- 79	PASCUAL, CAMILO ALBERTO	7741 SW 32ND ST - MIAMI FL 33155
50- 76	PASCUAL, CARLOS LUIS	2540 SW 92ND CT - MIAMI FL 33165
33- 49	PASEK, JOHN PAUL	D. MARCH 13, 1976 NIAGARA FALLS, N. Y.
82- 95	PASHNICK, LARRY JOHN	506 HIGHLAND - WYANDOTTE MI 48192
74-103	PASLEY, KEVIN PATRICK	1 PARKVIEW CT - FARMINGDALE NY 11735
85- 87	PASQUA, DANIEL ANTHONY	3 GEORGE STREET - HARRINGTON PARK NJ 07640
19- 65	PASQUELLA, MICHAEL JOHN	D. APRIL 5, 1965 BRIDGEPORT, CONN.
35- 87	PASSEAU, CLAUDE WILLIAM	113 LONDON ST - LUCEDALE MS 39452
79- 81	PASTORE, FRANK ENRICO	1542 N FRAMIS WAY - UPLAND CA 91786
83-111	PASTORNICKY, CLIFFORD SCOT	15078 SE 44TH TERRACE - BELLEVUE WA 98006
26- 63	PATE, JOSEPH WILLIAM	D. DECEMBER 26, 1948 FORT WORTH, TEX.
80-100	PATE, ROBERT WAYNE	17509 NAUSET CT - CARSON CA 90746
68- 76	PATEK, FREDERICK JOSEPH	965 E WEINERT ST - SEQUIN TX 78155
41- 84	PATRICK, ROBERT LEE	107 N 18TH-FORT SMITH AR 72901
68- 77	PATTERSON, DARYL ALAN	20145 TOLLHOUSE RD - CLOVIS CA 93612
79- 82	PATTERSON, DAVID GLENN	15669 VELOUR DR - CHINO CA 91710
77-110	PATTERSON, GILBERT THOMAS	8185 NW 8 MANOR - PLANT FL 33324
32- 60	PATTERSON, HENRY JOSEPH	D. SEPTEMBER 30, 1970 PANORAMA CITY, CAL.
81- 93	PATTERSON, MICHAEL LEE	2419 RIDGELEY DR #9 - LOS ANGELES CA 90016
81- 94	PATTERSON, REGINALD ALLEN	2900 ARLINGTON AVE - BESSEMER AL 35020
85- 88	PATTERSON, ROBERT CHANDLER	201 CHEROKEE DRIVE - GREENVILLE SC 29615
21- 78	PATTERSON, WILLIAM JENNINGS BRYAN	D. OCTOBER 1, 1977 ST. LOUIS, MO.
68- 78	PATTIN, MARTIN WILLIAM	1520 ALVAMAR DR - LAWRENCE KS 66044
29- 82	PATTISON, JAMES WELLS	142 BILLIAR AVE NE - PALM BAY FL 32907
44-105	PATTON, GENE TUNNEY	60 S 17TH AVE - COATESVILLE PA 19320
35- 88	PATTON, GEORGE WILLIAM 'BILL'	1604 CHERRY LN-FLOURTOWN PA 19031
10-116	PATTON, HARRY C.	B. DAVENPORT, IA.
57- 65	PATTON, THOMAS ALLEN	RR 4 BOX 335 - HONEY BROOK PA 19344
68- 79	PAUL, MICHAEL GEORGE	4441 CAMINO DEL REY - TUCSON AZ 85718
54- 80	PAULA, CARLOS (CONNILL)	D. FEBRUARY 8, 1966 LITTLE ROCK, ARK.
11-133	PAULETTE, EUGENE EDWARD	2022 8TH ST NE - PUYALLUP WA 98371
25- 85	PAULSEN, GUILFORD PAUL HANS 'GIL'	11934 W HAYES AVE - WEST ALLIS WI 53227
57- 66	PAVLETICH, DONALD STEPHEN	D. FEBRUARY 12, 1964 CHICAGO HEIGHTS, ILL.
46- 81	PAWELEK, THEODORE JOHN	1013 GORMAN ST - PHILADELPHIA PA 19116
55- 89	PAWLOSKI, STANLEY WALTER	OLD ADD: 345 LINCOLN #10 - BOSTON MA 02111
77-111	PAXTON, MICHAEL DEWAYNE	D. JANUARY 24, 1959 BELLFLOWER, CALIF.
20- 95	PAYNE, GEORGE WASHINGTON	BOX 712 - WILLISTON FL 32696
84- 88	PAYNE, MICHAEL EARL	9205 KIRKDALE - BETHESDA MD 20817
75- 88	PAZIK, MICHAEL JOSEPH	D. OCTOBER 17, 1981 WILSON, N. C.
37- 87	PEACOCK, JOHN GASTON	D. SEPTEMBER 3, 1950 VAN BUREN, N. Y.
33- 50	PEARCE, FRANKLIN THOMAS	D. OCTOBER 11, 1935 JOLIET, ILL.
12-153	PEARCE, GEORGE THOMAS	D. JANUARY 8, 1942 PHILADELPHIA, PA.
17- 60	PEARCE, HARRY JAMES	RR 5 BOX 404 - ZEBULON NC 27597
49- 63	PEARCE, JAMES MADISON	BOX E-3 - MAMMOTH LAKE CA 93546
58- 70	PEARSON, ALBERT GREGORY	D. MARCH 17, 1985 SARASOTA, FLA.
39- 89	PEARSON, ISSAC OVERTON	D. JANUARY 27, 1978 FRESNO, CALIF.
32- 61	PEARSON, MONTGOMERY MARCELLUS	D. DECEMBER 27, 1948 SAN FRANCISCO, CALIF.
10-117	PEASLEY, MARVIN WARREN	

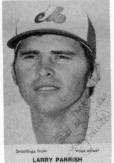

LARRY PARRISH

15-123 PECHOUS, CHARLES EDWARD	D. SEPTEMBER 13, 1980 KENOSHA, WIS.
43-111 PECK, HAROLD ARTHUR	RR 2 BOX 334 - FORT ATKINSON WI 53538
10-118 PECKINPAUGH, ROGER THORPE	D. NOVEMBER 17, 1977 CLEVELAND, O.
53- 67 PEDEN, LESLIE EARL	17293 HOLMES MILL AVE - JACKSONVILLE FL 32226
85- 89 PEDERSON, STUART RUSSELL	24848 SKYLAND - LOS GATOS CA 95030
41- 85 PEEK, STEPHEN GEORGE	204 W HAMILTON AVE-SHERRILL NY 13461
27- 70 PEEL, HOMER HEFNER	3757 GREENWAY - SHREVEPORT LA 71105
35- 89 PEERSON, JACK CHILES	D. OCTOBER 23, 1966 FT. WALTON BEACH, FLA.
27- 71 PEERY, GEORGE A. 'RED'	144 W UTAH AVE - PAYSON UT 84651
56- 67 PEETE, CHARLES	D. NOVEMBER 27, 1956 CARACAS, VENEZ.
46- 82 PELLAGRINI, EDWARD CHARLES	103 WEBB ST - WEYMOUTH MA 02188
74-104 PEMBERTON, BROCK	1012 S FLORENCE - TULSA OK 74104
81- 95 PENA, ADALBERTO	19-2-0-5, BAIROA MIRABEL-CAGUAS PR 00625
81- 96 PENA, ALEJANDRO	1713 GERMAIN DR - MONTEBELLO CA 90640
80-101 PENA, ANTONIO FRANCISCO	COMP HAB 30 DEMARZO,MAN #1 ED 14-SANTIAGO DOM. REP.
69-132 PENA, JOSE	A.FLORES #1116 NTE,C.JIQUILPAN-LOS MOCHIS SINOLOA MEX.
58- 71 PENA, ORLANDO GREGORY	1750 WEST 46TH ST #543 - MIAMI FL 33012
65- 87 PENA, ROBERTO CESAR	F-28,URBAN.,LAS COLISHA - SANTIAGO DOMINICAN REP.
22-108 PENCE, ELMER CLAIR	D. SEPTEMBER 17, 1968 SAN FRANCISCO, CAL.
21- 79 PENCE, RUSSELL WILLIAM	D. AUGUST 11, 1971 HOT SPRINGS, ARK.
53- 68 PENDLETON, JAMES EDWARD	6622 HARTWICK - HOUSTON TX 77016
84- 89 PENDLETON, TERRY LEE	512 N. VENTURA RD - PORT HUENEME CA 93041
16- 68 PENNER, KENNETH WILLIAM	D. MAY 28, 1959 SACRAMENTO, CAL.
17- 61 PENNINGTON, GEORGE LOUIS 'KEWPIE'	D. MAY 5, 1953 NEWARK, N. J.
12-154 PENNOCK, HERBERT JEFFERIS	D. JANUARY 30, 1948 NEW YORK, N.Y.
54- 81 PENSON, PAUL EUGENE	711 LAKE OF THE FOREST-BONNER SPGS KS 66012
75- 89 PENTZ, EUGENE DAVID	919 PARSON ST - JOHNSTOWN PA 15902
62-102 PEPITONE, JOSEPH ANTHONY	OLD ADD: LIGHTHOUSE RD - SAUGERTIES NY 12477
29- 83 PEPLOSKI, HENRY STEPHEN	D. JANUARY 28, 1982 DOVER, N. J.
13-139 PEPLOSKI, JOSEPH ANTHONY 'PEPPER'	D. 1946 OR 1947
66- 70 PEPPER, DONALD HOYTE	RR2 - GANSEVOORT NY 12831
54- 82 PEPPER, HUGH MCLAURIN 'LAURIN'	123 HOLCOMB BLVD - OCEAN SPRINGS MS 39564
32- 62 PEPPER, RAYMOND WATSON	BOX 40 - MOORESVILLE AL 35649
15-124 PEPPER, ROBERT ERNEST	D. APRIL 8, 1968 FORD CLIFF, PA.
69-133 PERAZA, LUIS	CALLE 6 C.F. 13 RES. BAIROA-CAGUAS PR 00625
80-102 PERCONTE, JOHN PATRICK	1016 JOHN ST - JOLIET IL 60435
11-134 PERDUE, HERBERT RODNEY 'HUB'	D. OCTOBER 31, 1968 GALLATIN, TENN.
64- 83 PEREZ, ATANASIO RIGAL 'TONY'	LOS FLORES 113 - SANTURCE PR 00911
58- 72 PEREZ, GEORGE THOMAS	39646 87TH ST W - LEONA VALLEY CA 93550
69-134 PEREZ, MARTIN ROMAN	30 WILLOWICK DR - DECATUR GA 30034
80-103 PEREZ, PASCUAL (GROSS)	SALVADOR, CUCURULO #105 - SANTIAGO DOMINICAN REP.
78- 99 PERKINS, BRODERICK PHILLIP	2110 BURTON AVE - PITTSBURG CA 94565
67- 84 PERKINS, CECIL BOYCE	RR 1 BOX 100-P - MARTINSBURG WV 25401
30- 60 PERKINS, CHARLES SULLIVAN	OLD ADD: 249 MURRAY AVE - RIDGEWOOD NJ
15-125 PERKINS, RALPH FOSTER 'CY'	D. OCTOBER 2, 1963 PHILADELPHIA, PA.
50- 77 PERKOVICH, JOHN JOSEPH	16 ATHENA CT - LITTLE ROCK AR 72207
47- 66 PERKOWSKI, HAROLD WALTER	211 MCGINNIS - BECKLEY WV 25801
85- 90 PERLMAN, JONATHAN SAMUEL	1019 FORREST LANE - CARTHAGE TX 75633
77-112 PERLOZZO, SAMUEL BENEDICT	42 SCOTT COURT - CUMBERLAND MD 21502
42- 75 PERME, LEONARD JOSEPH	3350 D ST - HAYWARD CA 94541
10-119 PERNOLL, HENRY HUBBARD	D. FEBRUARY 18, 1944 GRANTS PASS, ORE.
61- 82 PERRANOSKI, RONALD PETER	18731 MARTHA ST - TARZANA CA 91356
21- 80 PERRIN, JOHN STEPHENSON	D. JUNE 24, 1969 DETROIT, MICH.
34- 83 PERRIN, WILLIAM JOSEPH	D. JUNE 30, 1974 NEW ORLEANS, LA.
12-155 PERRITT, WILLIAM DAYTON 'POL'	D. OCTOBER 15, 1947 SHREVEPORT, LA.
41- 86 PERRY, BOYD GLENN	RR 1 - SNOW CAMP NC 27349
62-103 PERRY, GAYLORD JACKSON	RR 3 BOX 565 - WILLIAMSTON NC 27892
83-112 PERRY, GERALD JUNE	BOX 1403 - HILTON HEAD SC 29928
15-126 PERRY, HERBERT SCOTT	D. OCTOBER 27, 1959 KANSAS CITY, MO.
59- 64 PERRY, JAMES EVAN	5744 DUNCAN LANE - MINNEAPOLIS MN 55436
63- 91 PERRY, MELVIN GAY "BOB"	621 HOLIDAY CITY - NEW BERN NC 28562
12-156 PERRY, WILLIAM HENRY 'HANK'	D. JULY 18, 1956 PONTIAC, MICH.
85- 91 PERRY, WILLIAM PATRICK 'PAT'	1115 WEST FRANKLIN - TAYLORVILLE IL 62568
15-127 PERRYMAN, EMMETT KEY 'PARSON'	D. SEPTEMBER 12, 1966 STARKE, FLA.
18- 57 PERTICA, WILLIAM ANDREW	D. DECEMBER 28, 1967 LOS ANGELES, CAL.
71- 81 PERZANOWSKI, STANLEY	3250 173RD ST - HAMMOND IN 46323
42- 76 PESKY, JOHN MICHAEL	25 PARSONS DR-SWAMPSCOTT MA 01907
42- 77 PETERMAN, WILLIAM DAVID	9823 WISTERIA ST - PHILADELPHIA PA 19115
59- 65 PETERS, GARY CHARLES	2626 ESPANOLA AVE - SARASOTA FL 33580
15-128 PETERS, JOHN WILLIAM	D. FEBRUARY 21, 1932 KANSAS CITY, MO.
12-157 PETERS, OSCAR C. 'RUBE'	B. MARCH 15, 1886 GRAND FORK, ILL.
70-106 PETERS, RAYMOND JAMES	OLD ADD: 6542 NORTH FOOTHILLS DR - TUCSON AZ 85218
79- 83 PETERS, RICHARD DEVIN 'RICKY'	12601 HALO DRIVE - COMPTON CA 90221

36- 71 PETERS, RUSSELL DIXON 'RUSTY'	BOX 751 - BEDFORD VA 24523
55- 90 PETERSON, CARL FRANCIS 'BUDDY'	8665 FLORIN RD #101 - SACRAMENTO CA 95828
62-104 PETERSON, CHARLES ANDREW 'CAP'	D. MAY 16, 1980 TACOMA WA
66- 71 PETERSON, FRED INGELS 'FRITZ'	BOX 141 - WHEATON IL 60189
55- 91 PETERSON, HARDING WILLIAM 'PETE'	348 ORCHARD DR - PITTSBURGH PA 15228
31- 67 PETERSON, JAMES NIELS	D. APRIL 8, 1975 PALM BEACH, FLA.
44-106 PETERSON, KENT FRANKLIN	P.O. BOX 164 - PROVO UT 84603
43-112 PETERSON, SIDNEY HERBERT	4503 INGLESIDE - WICHITA FALLS TX 76308
34- 84 PETOSKEY, FREDERICK LEE 'TED'	RR 4 BOX 109 - HOPKINS SC 29061
82- 96 PETRALLI, EUGENE JAMES 'GENO'	1324 SAN AUGUSTINE WAY - SACRAMENTO CA 95831
63- 92 PETROCELLI, AMERICO PETER 'RICO'	19 TOWNSEND RD - LYNNFIELD MA 01940
79- 84 PETRY, DANIEL JOSEPH	1808 CARTLEN DRIVE - PLACENTIA CA 92670
83-113 PETTIBONE, HARRY JONATHAN 'JAM'	1261 WEST CATALPA - ANAHEIM CA 92801
14-165 PETTIGREW, JIM NED	D. AUGUST 20, 1952 DUNCAN, OKLA.
80-104 PETTINI, JOSEPH PAUL	BOX 37 - WINDSOR HEIGHTS WV 26075
82- 97 PETTIS, GARY GEORGE	927 BLENHEIM ST - OAKLAND CA 94603
51- 77 PETTIT, GEORGE WILLIAM PAUL	25313 WOODWARD - LOMITA CA 90717
35- 90 PETTIT, LEON ARTHUR	D. NOVEMBER 21, 1974 COLUMBIA, TENN.
21- 81 PETTY, JESSE LEE	D. OCTOBER 23, 1971 ST. PAUL, MINN.
14-166 PEZOLD, LORENZ JOHANNES 'LARRY'	D. OCTOBER 22, 1957 BATON ROUGE, LA.
35- 91 PEZZULLO, JOHN 'PRETZELS'	3127 W LEDBETTER-DALLAS TX 75233
11-135 PFEFFER, EDWARD JOSEPH 'JEFF'	D. AUGUST 15, 1972 CHICAGO, ILL.
13-138 PFEFFER, MONTE	D. SEPTEMBER 27, 1941 NEW YORK, N. Y.
69-135 PFEIL, ROBERT RAYMOND	840 BENJAMIN HALT DR - STOCKTON CA 95207
61- 83 PFISTER, DANIEL ALBIN	3600 NW 91ST AVE - WEST HOLLYWOOD FL 33024
41- 87 PFISTER, GEORGE EDWARD	215 JOHN ST - BOUND BROOK NJ 08805
45- 78 PFUND, LEROY HERBERT	ATH. DEPT., WHEATON COLLEGE - WHEATON IL 60188
36- 72 PHEBUS, RAYMOND WILLIAM 'BILL'	930 LAKEVIEW AVE-BARTOW FL 33830
10-120 PHELAN, ARTHUR THOMAS	D. DECEMBER 27, 1964 FORT WORTH, TEX.
31- 68 PHELPS, ERNEST GORDON 'BABE'	1417 HALE ST - ODENTON MD 21113
80-105 PHELPS, KENNETH ALLEN	7531 E TURQUOISE AVE - SCOTTSDALE AZ 85258
30- 61 PHELPS, RAYMOND CLIFFORD	D. JULY 7, 1971 FT. PIERCE, FLA.
41- 88 PHILLEY, DAVID EARL	1336 E POLK ST-PARIS TX 75460
64- 84 PHILLIPS, ADOLFO EMILIO	APARTADO 6109 CHORILLA - PANAMA CITY PAN.
30- 62 PHILLIPS, ALBERT ABERNATHY 'BUZZ'	D. NOVEMBER 6, 1964 BALTIMORE, MD.
34- 85 PHILLIPS, CLARENCE LEMUEL 'RED'	2111 S ESTELLE - WICHITA KS 67211
42- 78 PHILLIPS, DAMON RUSSELL	BOX 805 - HENDERSON TX 75652
24- 85 PHILLIPS, EDWARD DAVID	D. JANUARY 26, 1968 BUFFALO, N.Y.
69-136 PHILLIPS, HAROLD ROSS 'LEFTY'	D. JUNE 12, 1972 FULLERTON, CAL.
53- 69 PHILLIPS, HOWARD EDWARD 'ED'	WEST ELY - HANNIBAL MO 63401
47- 67 PHILLIPS, JACK DORN	MAY RD #2 - POTSDAM NY 13676
45- 79 PHILLIPS, JOHN	D. JUNE 16, 1958 ST. LOUIS, MO.
55- 92 PHILLIPS, JOHN MELVIN 'BUBBA'	2704 MIMOSA LN - HATTIESBURG MS 39401
82- 98 PHILLIPS, KEITH ANTHONY 'TONY'	P.O. BOX 602 - ROSWELL GA 30075
73- 95 PHILLIPS, MICHAEL DWAINE	3322 RIDGEFIELD - IRVING TX 75060
70-107 PHILLIPS, NORMAN EDWIN 'EDDIE'	2207 EDGEHILL RD - LOUISVILLE KY 40205
62-105 PHILLIPS, RICHARD EUGENE	6280 MARLBOROUGH #302 - BURNABY BRIT. COL. V5H 3L8 CAN.
15-129 PHILLIPS, THOMAS GERALD	D. APRIL 12, 1929 PHILIPSBURG, PA.
56- 68 PHILLIPS, WILLIAM TAYLOR	BOX 13 - AUSTELL GA 30001
66- 72 PHOEBUS, THOMAS HAROLD	207 146TH ST NW - BRADENTON FL 33505
77-113 PICCIOLO, ROBERT MICHAEL 'ROB'	6421 FIREBRAND ST - LOS ANGELES CA 90045
45- 80 PICCIUTO, NICHOLAS THOMAS	261 ELMWOOD AVE - MAPLEWOOD NJ 07040
60- 82 PICHE, RONALD JACQUES	100 DE GASPE #1208 - NUNS ISLAND QUEBEC H3E 1E5 CAN.
16- 69 PICINICH, VALENTINE JOHN	D. DECEMBER 5, 1942 NOBLEBORO, ME.
14-167 PICK, CHARLES THOMAS	D. JUNE 26, 1954 LYNCHBURG, VA.
23-103 PICK, EDGAR EVERETT	D. MAY 13, 1967 WEST LOS ANGELES, CAL.
31- 69 PICKERING, URBANE HENRY 'DICK'	D. MAY 13, 1970 MODESTO, CALIF.
10-121 PICKETT, CHARLES ALBERT	D. MAY 20, 1969 SPRINGFIELD, O.
33- 51 PICKREL, CLARENCE DOUGLAS	D. NOVEMBER 4, 1983 ROCKY MOUNT, VA.
18- 58 PICKUP, CLARENCE WILLIAM 'TY'	D. AUGUST 2, 1974 PHILADELPHIA, PA.
47- 68 PICONE, MARIO PETER	8876 BAY 16 - BROOKLYN NY 11214
40- 68 PIECHOTA, ALOYSIUS EDWARD	1656 N MAYFIELD AVE-CHICAGO IL 60639
13-140 PIEH, EDWIN JOHN 'CY'	D. SEPTEMBER 12, 1945 JACKSONVILLE, FLA.
73- 96 PIERCE, LAVERN EDWARD	454 N 9TH ST - SAN JOSE CA 95112
24- 86 PIERCE, RAYMOND LESTER	D. MAY 4, 1963 DENVER, COLO.
67- 85 PIERCE, TONY MICHAEL	5002 WILLOWBROOK DR - COLUMBUS GA 31909
45- 81 PIERCE, WALTER WILLIAM 'BILLY'	9000 SOUTH FRANCISCO - EVERGREEN PARK IL60642
17- 62 PIERCY, WILLIAM BENTON	D. AUGUST 28, 1951 LONG BEACH, CAL.
45- 82 PIERETTI, MARINO PAUL	D. JANUARY 30, 1981 SAN FRANCISCO, CALIF.
20- 96 PIEROTTI, ALBERT FELIX	D. FEBRUARY 12, 1964 REVERE, MASS.
50- 78 PIERRO, WILLIAM LEONARD	1751 74TH ST - BROOKLYN NY 11204
50- 79 PIERSALL, JAMES ANTHONY	1105 OAKVIEW DR - WHEATON IL 60187
18- 59 PIERSON, WILLIAM MORRIS	D. FEBRUARY 20, 1959 ATLANTIC CITY, N. J.

31- 70 PIET, ANTHONY FRANCIS
14-168 PIEZ, CHARLES WILLIAM 'SANDY'
57- 67 PIGNATANO, JOSEPH BENJAMIN
46- 83 PIKE, JAMES WILLARD
56- 69 PIKTUZIS, GEORGE RICHARD
56- 70 PILARCIK, ALFRED JAMES
49- 64 PILLETTE, DUANE XAVIER
17- 63 PILLETTE, HERMAN POLYCARP
15-130 PILLION, CECIL RANDOLPH 'SQUIZ'
36- 73 PILNEY, ANDREW JAMES
68- 80 PINA, HORACIO GARCIA
18- 60 PINELLI, RALPH ARTHUR 'BABE'
84- 85 PINIELLA, LOUIS VICTOR
64- 85 PINIELLA, LOUIS VICTOR
58- 73 PINSON, VADA EDWARD
22-109 PINTO, WILLIAM LERTON
32- 63 PIPGRAS, EDWARD JOHN
23-104 PIPGRAS, GEORGE WILLIS
13-141 PIPP, WALTER CHARLES
36- 74 PIPPEN, HENRY HAROLD 'COTTON'
78-100 PIRTLE, GERALD EUGENE
53- 70 PISONI, JAMES PETE
38- 74 PITKO, ALEXANDER
17- 64 PITLER, JACOB ALBERT
70-108 PITLOCK, LEE PATRICK THOMAS 'SKIP'
85- 92 PITTARO, CHRISTOPHER FRANCIS
21- 82 PITTENGER, CLARKE ALONZO 'PINKY'
81- 97 PITTMAN, JOSEPH WAYNE
74-105 PITTS, GAYLEN RICHARD
57- 68 PITULA, STANLEY
57- 69 PIZARRO, JUAN CORDOVA
79- 85 PLADSON, GORDON CECIL
31- 71 PLANETA, EMIL JOSEPH
78-101 PLANK, EDWARD ARTHUR
55- 93 PLARSKI, DONALD JOSEPH
62-106 PLASKETT, ELMO ALEXANDER
42- 79 PLATT, MIZELL GEORGE 'WHITEY'
13-142 PLATTE, ALFRED FREDERICK JOSEPH
61- 84 PLEIS, WILLIAM
56- 71 PLESS, RANCE
56- 72 PLEWS, HERBERT EUGENE
18- 61 PLITT, NORMAN WILLIAM
72- 85 PLODINEC, TIMOTHY ALFRED
68- 81 PLUMMER, WILLIAM FRANCIS
42- 80 POAT, RAYMOND WILLIAM
75- 90 POCOROBA, BIFF BENEDICT
49- 65 PODBIELAN, CLARENCE ANTHONY 'BUD'
40- 69 PODGAJNY, JOHN SIGMUND
53- 71 PODRES, JOHN JOSEPH
75- 91 POEPPING, MICHAEL HAROLD
26- 64 POETZ, JOSEPH FRANK
40- 70 POFAHL, JAMES WILLARD

D. DECEMBER 1, 1981 HINSDALE, ILL.
D. DECEMBER 29, 1930 ATLANTIC CITY, N.J.
150 78TH STREET - BROOKLYN NY 11209
D. MARCH 28, 1984 SAN DIEGO, CALIF.
12051 PARAMOUNT BLVD #9 - DOWNEY CA 90242
BOX 185 - ST JOHN IN 46373
165 BLOSSOM HILL RD #404 - SAN JOSE CA 95123
D. APRIL 30, 1960 SACRAMENTO, CAL.
D. SEPTEMBER 30, 1962 PITTSBURGH, PA.
3309 RIDGEWAY DR-METAIRIE LA 70002
OLD ADD: VENUSTIANA CARRANZA 207-COAHUILA MEX
D. OCTOBER 22, 1984 DALY CITY, CALIF.
103 MACINTYRE LN - ALLENDALE NJ 07401
57 SHERI DR - ALLENDALE NJ 07401
710 31ST ST - OAKLAND CA 94609
D. MAY 13, 1983 OXNARD, CALIF.
D. APRIL 13, 1964 CURRIE, MINN.
205 NORTH TROUT AVE - INVERNESS FL 32650
D. JANUARY 11, 1965 GRAND RAPIDS, MICH.
D. FEBRUARY 15, 1981 WILLIAMS, CALIF.
9403 S 236TH E AVE - BROKEN ARROW OK 74012
10832 MUELLER RD - ST. LOUIS MO 63123
8001 E. BROADWAY #6512 - MESA AZ 85208
D. FEBRUARY 3, 1968 BINGHAMTON, N. Y.
11335 S HOOPER AVE - LOS ANGELES CA 90059
42 PINTINALLI DRIVE - TRENTON NJ 08619
D. NOVEMBER 4, 1977 FT LAUDERDALE, FLA.
809 MCKINNON DR - COLUMBUS GA 31907
101 PINE FOREST DR #29 - MAUMELLE AR 72118
D. AUGUST 16, 1965 HACKENSACK, N. J.
278 DEL RIO - SANTURCE PR 00912
OLD ADD: 11375 84TH AVE - DELTA BC
D. FEBRUARY 2, 1963 ROCKY HILL, CONN.
1468 W JUANITA - MESA AZ 85202
D. DECEMBER 29, 1981 ST. LOUIS, MO.
BOX 1764 - FREDERIKSTED VI 00840
D. JULY 27, 1970 WEST PALM BEACH, FLA.
D. AUGUST 29, 1976 GRAND RAPIDS, MICH.
5 MARNE DR - LAKE SAINT LOUIS MO 63367
RR 4 BOX 210 - GREENEVILLE TN 37743
1460 NORTHWESTERN RD - LONGMONT CO 80501
D. FEBRUARY 1, 1954 NEW YORK, N. Y.
2201 MCMINN - ALIQUIPPA PA 15001
2170 RHONDA RD - COTTONWOOD CA 96022
4833 W 109TH ST - OAK LAWN IL 60453
23238 DOLOROSA ST - WOODLAND HILLS CA 91364
D. OCTOBER 26, 1982 SYRACUSE, N. Y.
D. MARCH 2, 1971 CHESTER, PA.
1 COLONIAL COURT - GLENS FALLS NY 12801
RR 2 - PIERZ MN 56364
D. FEBRUARY 7, 1942 ST. LOUIS, MO.
D. SEPTEMBER 14, 1984 OWATONNA, MINN.

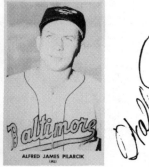

ALFRED JAMES PILARCIK
(AL)

79- 86 POFF, JOHN WILLIAM
37- 88 POFFENBERGER, CLETUS ELWOOD 'BOOTS'
50- 80 POHOLSKY, THOMAS GEORGE
36- 75 POINDEXTER, CHESTER JENNINGS 'JINKS'
63- 93 POINTER, AARON ELTON
43-113 POLAND, HUGH REID
73- 97 POLE, RICHARD HENRY
85- 93 POLIDOR, GUSTAVO ADOLFO
47- 69 POLIVKA, KENNETH LYLE
41- 89 POLLET, HOWARD JOSEPH
32- 64 POLLI, LOUIS AMERICO
37- 89 POLLY, NICHOLAS JOSEPH
77-114 POLONI, JOHN PAUL
34- 86 POMORSKI, JOHN LEON
85- 94 PONCE, CARLOS ANTONIO
10-122 POND, RALPH BENJAMIN
17- 65 PONDER, CHARLES ELMER
34- 87 POOL, HARLIN WELTY
25- 86 POOLE, JAMES RALPH
41- 90 POOLE, RAYMOND HERMAN
52- 81 POPE, DAVID

78 BROWNS LN - FAIRFIELD CT 06430
13 1/2 N CONOCOCHEAGUE-WILLIAMSPORT MD 21795
177 HORSESHOE DR - KIRKWOOD MO 63122
D. MARCH 3, 1983 NORMAN, OKLA.
4406 ARBORDALE AVE W - TACOMA WA 98466
D. MARCH 30, 1984 GUTHRIE, KY.
246 VALLEY WAY - LIMA OH 45804
LA AV.DE PRO-PATRIA BLOQ.3 PATRIA B#9-CARACAS VENEZ
1532 SUNNYBROOK DR - NAPERVILLE IL 60540
D. AUGUST 8, 1974 HOUSTON, TEX.
BOX 45 - GRANITEVILLE VT 05654
2331 N LEAVITT AVE-CHICAGO IL 60647
3205 ELLIS - CHANDLER AZ 85224
D. DECEMBER 6, 1977 BRAMPTON, ONTARIO
51-15 44TH ST,VILLA CAROLINA - CAROLINA PR 00630
D. SEPTEMBER 8, 1947 CLEVELAND, O.
D. APRIL 20, 1974 ALBUQUERQUE, N. M.
D. FEBRUARY 15, 1963 RODEO, CAL.
D. JANUARY 2, 1975 HICKORY, N. C.
RR 10 BOX 655-SALISBURY NC 28144
9020 PARMELEE AVE - CLEVELAND OH 44108

64- 86 POPOVICH, PAUL EDWARD	2501 PARTRIDGE - NORTHBROOK IL 60062
69-137 POPOWSKI, EDWARD JOSEPH	BOX 5 CRESTVIEW APTS - SAYREVILLE NJ 08872
73- 98 POQUETTE, THOMAS ARTHUR	3404 RIDGEWAY RD - EAU CLAIRE WI 54701
14-169 PORRAY, EDMUND JOSEPH	D. JULY 13, 1954 LACKAWAXEN, PA.
81- 98 PORTER, CHARLES WILLIAM	9321 SNYDER LN - PERRY HALL MD 21128
51- 78 PORTER, DANIEL EDWARD	7360 COWLES MT BLVD - SAN DIEGO CA 92119
71- 82 PORTER, DARRELL RAY	OLD ADD: 3833 WEST 73RD ST - MILWAUKEE WI 53216
14-170 PORTER, IRVING MARBLE	D. FEBRUARY 20, 1971 LYNN, MASS.
52- 82 PORTER, J. W. 'JAY'	9677 HEATHER CIR W-PALM BCH GARDENS FL 33410
26- 65 PORTER, NED SWINDELL	D. JUNE 30, 1968 GAINESVILLE, FLA.
29- 84 PORTER, RICHARD TWILLEY	D. SEPTEMBER 24, 1974 PHILADELPHIA, PA.
81- 99 PORTER, ROBERT LEE	1222 RIVER PARK - NAPA CA 94559
48- 81 PORTERFIELD, ERWIN COOLIDGE 'BOB'	D. APRIL 28, 1980 CHARLOTTE, N. C.
48- 82 PORTO, ALFRED	4117 AVENUE S-4 - PALMDALE CA 93550
54- 83 PORTOCARRERO, ARNOLD MARIO	5208 PARISH - ROELAND PARK KS 66205
85- 95 PORTUGAL, MARK STEVEN	14008 CROSSDALE - NORWALK CA 90650
60- 83 POSADA, LEOPOLDO JESUS	385 NW 77TH AVE - MIAMI FL 33126
38- 75 POSEDEL, WILLIAM JOHN	179 HAUS AVE - SAN LEANDRO CA 94577
32- 65 POSER, JOHN FALK 'BOB'	551 W SCHOOL - COLUMBUS WI 53925
46- 84 POSSEHL, LOUIS THOMAS	3536 N NEW ENGLAND - CHICAGO IL 60634
22-110 POST, SAMUEL GILBERT	D. MARCH 31, 1971 PORTSMOUTH, VA.
49- 66 POST, WALTER CHARLES	D. JANUARY 6, 1982 SAINT HENRY, O.
22-111 POTT, NELSON ADOLPH	D. DECEMBER 3, 1963 MACK,O.
38- 76 POTTER, MARYLAND DYKES	RR 5 BOX 476 - ASHLAND KY 41101
76- 75 POTTER, MICHAEL GARY	21582 ARCHER CIR - HUNTINGTON BEACH CA 92646
36- 76 POTTER, NELSON THOMAS	RR 1-MT MORRIS IL 61054
23-105 POTTER, SQUIRE	D. JANUARY 27, 1983 ASHLAND, KY.
14-171 POTTS, JOHN FREDERICK	D. SEPTEMBER 5, 1962 CLEVELAND, O.
67- 86 POULSEN, KEN STERLING	684 E WEAVER - SIMI VALLEY CA 93065
30- 63 POWELL, ALVIN JACOB 'JAKE'	D. NOVEMBER 4, 1948 WASHINGTON. D. C.
85- 96 POWELL, DENNIS CLAY	P. O. BOX 133 - NORMAN PARK GA 31771
63- 94 POWELL, GROVER DAVID	D. MAY 21, 1985 RALEIGH, N. C.
78-102 POWELL, HOSKEN	115 MEMORY LANE - PENSACOLA FL 32503
61- 85 POWELL, JOHN WESLEY 'BOOG'	U. S. ANGLERS MARINE - KEY WEST FL 33040
71- 83 POWELL, PAUL RAY	810 N MYERS - ELOY AZ 85231
13-143 POWELL, RAYMOND REATH	D. OCTOBER 16, 1962 CHILLICOTHE, O .
13-144 POWELL, REGINALD BERTRAND 'JACK'	D. MARCH 12, 1930 MEMPHIS, TENN.
55- 94 POWELL, ROBERT LEROY	5366 STAMPA ST - LAS VEGAS NV 89102
81-100 POWER, TED HENRY	10310 NW 18TH PL - PEMBROKE FL 33026
54- 84 POWER, VICTOR PELLOT	CONDOMINEO TORRE,MOLINOS 703-GUAYNABO PR00657
32- 66 POWERS, ELLIS FOREE 'MIKE'	D. DECEMBER 2, 1983 LOUISVILLE, KY.
55- 95 POWERS, JOHN CALVIN	6727 FIRST AVE S - BIRMINGHAM AL 35206
27- 72 POWERS, JOHN LLOYD 'IKE'	D. DECEMBER 22, 1968 HANCOCK, MD.
38- 77 POWERS, LESLIE EDWIN	OLD ADD: 11928 DARLINGTON #106 - LOS ANGELES
57- 70 POWIS, CARL EDGAR	8502 EASTON COMMONS #104 - HOUSTON TX 77095
75- 92 PRALL, WILFRED ANTHONY 'WILLIE'	351 TERHUNE AVE - PASSAIC NJ 07055
49- 67 PRAMESA, JOHN STEVEN	4324 SUNBURST LN - CINCINNATI OH 45238
12-158 PRATT, DERRILL BURNHAM 'DEL'	D. SEPTEMBER 30, 1977 TEXAS CITY, TEX.
21- 83 PRATT, FRANCIS BRUCE	D. APRIL 8, 1974 CENTREVILLE, ALA.
14-172 PRATT, LESTER JOHN 'LARRY'	D. JANUARY 8, 1969 PEORIA, ILL.
63- 95 PREGENZER, JOHN ARTHUR	6314 104TH ST E - PUYALLUP WA 98373
40- 71 PREIBISCH, MELVIN ADOLPHUS	D. APRIL 12, 1980 SEALY, TEXAS
48- 83 PRENDERGAST, JAMES BARTHOLOMEW	330 FAIRFIELD AVE - BUFFALO NY 14223
14-173 PRENDERGAST, MICHAEL THOMAS	D. NOVEMBER 18, 1967 OMAHA, NEB.
61- 86 PRESCOTT, GEORGE BERTRAND 'BOBBY'	ESTAFETA PARQUE LEFEVRE - PANAMA CITY 10, PAN.
51- 79 PRESKO, JOSEPH EDWARD	1024 NE 42ND TERRACE - KANSAS CITY MO 64116
84- 90 PRESLEY, JAMES ARTHUR	OLD ADD: 720 N. FAIRFIELD DR - PENSACOLA FL 32506
38- 78 PRESSNELL, FOREST CHARLES 'TOT'	329 E LIMA ST-FINDLAY OH 45840
67- 87 PRICE, JIMMIE WILLIAM	3365 BUCKINGHAM TR - WEST BLOOMFIELD MI 48033
46- 85 PRICE, JOHN THOMAS REID 'JACKIE'	D. OCTOBER 2, 1967 SAN FRANCISCO, CAL.
28- 75 PRICE, JOSEPH PRESTON	D. JANUARY 15, 1961 WASHINGTON. D. C.
80-106 PRICE, JOSEPH WALTER	BOX 1696 - LAKESIDE CA 92040
39- 90 PRICHARD, ROBERT ALEXANDER	BOX 1205-STAMFORD TX 79553
41- 91 PRIDDY, GERALD EDWARD	D. MARCH 3, 1980 NORTH HOLLYWOOD, CALIF.
62-107 PRIDDY, ROBERT SIMPSON	OLD ADD: 519 N CASCADE TER-SUNNYVALE CA94087
11-136 PRIEST, JOHN GOODING	D. NOVEMBER 4, 1979 WASHINGTON, D. C.
33- 52 PRIM, RAYMOND LEE	11553 E BEVERLY BLVD - WHITTIER CA 90601
62-108 PRINCE, DONALD MARK	5 BAHAMA DR - WRIGHTSVILLE BEACH NC 28480
57- 71 PRITCHARD, HAROLD WILLIAM 'BUDDY'	507 E SUNNY HILL RD - FULLERTON CA 92635
59- 66 PROCTOR, JAMES ARTHUR	609 COUNT FLEET CT - NAPERVILLE IL 60540
23-106 PROCTOR, NOAH RICHARD 'RED'	D. DECEMBER 17, 1954 RICHMOND, VA.
76- 76 PROLY, MICHAEL JAMES	2585 FRISCO DR - CLEARWATER FL 33519
23-107 PROPST, WILLIAM JACOB 'JAKE'	D. FEBRUARY 24, 1967 COLUMBUS, MISS.
20- 97 PROTHRO, JAMES THOMPSON 'DOC'	D. OCTOBER 14, 1971 MEMPHIS, TENN.

Wally Post - Cincinnati Redlegs

PROUGH

RAMIREZ

12-160 PROUGH, HERSCHEL CLINTON 'BILL'	D. NOVEMBER 29, 1936 RICHMOND, IND.
29- 85 PRUDHOMME, JOHN OLGUS	5935 FAIRFIELD AVE - SHREVEPORT LA 71106
20- 98 PRUESS, EARL HENRY	D. AUGUST 28, 1979 BRANSON, MO.
22-112 PRUETT, HUBERT SHELBY	D. JANUARY 28, 1982 LADUE, MO.
44-107 PRUETT, JAMES CALVIN	1906 MADERA ST - WAUKESHA WI 53186
75- 93 PRUITT, RONALD RALPH	1510 SKYLAND DR - HINCKLEY OH 44223
76- 77 PRYOR, GRDGORY RUSSELL	1135 GULF OF MEXICO #602-LONGBOAT KEY FL33548
30- 64 PUCCINELLI, GEORGE LAWRENCE	D. APRIL 16, 1956 SAN FRANCISCO, CAL.
84- 91 PUCKETT, KIRBY	OLD ADD: 7921 SOUTH WOLCOTT - CHICAGO IL 60620
11-137 PUCKETT, TROY LEVI	D. APRIL 13, 1971 WINCHESTER, IND.
70-109 PUENTE, MIGUEL ANTONIO	COBRE 106,COL MORALES-SAN LUIS POTOSI SAN LUIS POT MEX.
77-115 PUHL, TERRENCE STEPHEN	3523 GOLDEN TEE LN - MISSOURI CITY TX 77459
74-106 PUIG, RICHARD GERALD	16708 FOOTHILL DR - TAMPA FL 33624
77-116 PUJOLS, LUIS BIENVENIDO	NICOLAS HEREDIA - BANI DOMINICAN REP.
81-101 PULEO, CHARLES MICHAEL	44 EDISON ST - BLOOMFIELD NJ 07003
83-114 PULIDO, ALFONSO (MANZO)	OLD ADD: EL FRAYLE VERACRUZ MEXICO
25- 87 PUMPELLY, SPENCER ARMSTRONG	D. DECEMBER 5, 1973 SAYRE, PA.
64- 87 PURDIN, JOHN NOLAN	4748 GEORGE AVE - SARASOTA FL 33583
26- 66 PURDY, EVERETT VIRGIL 'PID'	D. JANUARY 16, 1951 BEATRICE, NEB.
54- 85 PURKEY, ROBERT THOMAS	5767 KING SCHOOL RD - BETHEL PARK PA 15102
76- 78 PUTMAN, EDDY WILLIAM	819 CALLE ARROYO - SAN DIMAS CA 91773
77-117 PUTNAM, PATRICK EDWARD	309 MORSE PLAZA - TICE FL 33905
55- 96 PYBURN, JAMES EDWARD	RR 13 BOX 265 - JASPER AL 35501
54- 86 PYECHA, JOHN NICHOLAS	7015 FALCONBRIDGE RD - CHAPEL HILL NC 27514
28- 76 PYLE, HARLAN ALBERT	BOX 307 - LIBERTY NE 68381
39- 91 PYLE, HERBERT EWALD	538 HALLIDAY AVE-DUQUOIN IL 62832
32- 67 PYTLAK, FRANK ANTHONY	D. MAY 8, 1977 BUFFALO, N. Y.
69-138 QUALLS, JAMES ROBERT	STAR RT - WARSAW IL 62379
53- 72 QUALTERS, THOMAS FRANCIS	RR 2 BOX 39 - SOMERSET PA 15501
64- 88 QUEEN, MELVIN DOUGLAS	2130 NORTH MAIN - MORRO BAY CA 93442
42- 81 QUEEN, MELVIN JOSEPH	D. APRIL 4, 1982 FORT SMITH, ARK.
54- 87 QUEEN, WILLIAM EDDLEMAN	1616 E PERCY ST - GASTONIA NC 28052
31- 72 QUELLICH, GEORGE WILLIAM	D. AUGUST 31, 1958 JOHNSVILLE, CALIF.
39- 92 QUICK, JAMES HAROLD	D. MARCH 9, 1974 SWANSEA, ILL.
65- 88 QUILICI, FRANK RALPH	BOX 3017 - NORTHBROOK IL 60062
13-145 QUINLAN, THOMAS ALOYSIUS 'FINNERS'	D. FEBRUARY 17, 1966 SCRANTON, PA.
49- 68 QUINN, FRANK WILLIAM	OLD ADD: 530 SW 27TH WAY - BOYNTON BEACH FL 33435
11-138 QUINN, JOHN EDWARD PICK	D. APRIL 9, 1956 MARLBORO, MASS.
41- 92 QUINN, WELLINGTON HUNT 'WIMPY'	D. SEPTEMBER 1, 1954 LOS ANGELES, CAL.
83-115 QUINONES, LUIS RAUL	URB STA TERESITA CALLE 1 AE11-PONCE PR 00731
74-107 QUINTANA, LUIS JOAQUIN	CASCRIO CATONI ED 12 #57 - VEGA BAJA PR 00763
62-109 QUIRK, ARTHUR LINCOLN	27 PIPPIN DR - GLASTONBURY CT 06033
75- 94 QUIRK, JAMES PATRICK 'JAMIE'	16263 E SKAGWAY ST - WHITTIER CA 90603
79- 87 QUISENBERRY, DANIEL RAYMOND	12208 BUENA VISTA - LEAWOOD KS 66209
82- 99 RABB, JOHN ANDREW	1321 W 106TH ST - LOS ANGELES CA 90014
22-113 RABBITT, JOSEPH PATRICK	D. DECEMBER 5, 1969 NORWALK, CONN.
57- 72 RABE, CHARLES HENRY	7725 LINDEN AVE - DARIEN IL 60559
40- 72 RACHUNOK, STEPHEN STEPANOVICH	2660 W. BALL RD #1 - ANAHEIM CA 92805
47- 70 RACKLEY, MARVIN EUGENE	3314 COVINGTON DR - DECATUR GA 30030
62-110 RADATZ, RICHARD RAYMOND	830 W. CHESTNUT ST - BROCKTON MA 02401
34- 88 RADCLIFF, RAYMOND ALLEN 'RIP'	D. MAY 23, 1962 ENID, OKLA.
11-139 RADEBAUGH, ROY	D. JANUARY 17, 1945 CEDAR RAPIDS, IA.
71- 84 RADER, DAVID MARTIN	2114 OAKWOOD DR - BAKERSFIELD CA 93304
13-146 RADER, DONALD RUSSELL	D. JUNE 26, 1983 WALLA WALLA, WASH.
67- 88 RADER, DOUGLAS LEE	112-7 CEDAR POINT - STUART FL 33494
21- 84 RADER, DREW LEON	D. JUNE 5, 1975 CATSKILL, N. Y.
36- 77 RADTKE, JACK WILLIAM	289 S LOCUST - TWIN FALLS ID 83301
54- 88 RAETHER, HAROLD HERMAN	5920 MEROLD DR - EDINA MN 55436
39- 93 RAFFENSBERGER, KENNETH DAVIS	669 CHESTNUT ST-YORK PA 17403
69-139 RAFFO, ALBERT MARTIN	BOX 866 - JASPER TN 37347
32- 68 RAGLAND, FRANK ROLAND	D. JULY 28, 1959 PARIS, MISS.
71- 85 RAGLAND, THOMAS	20201 GREENLAWN ST - DETROIT MI 48224
75- 95 RAICH, ERIC JAMES	OLD ADD: 1625 WOODRUFF #45 - BELL CA 90201
57- 73 RAINES, LAWRENCE GLENN HOPE	D. JANUARY 28, 1978 LANSING, MICH.
79- 88 RAINES, TIMOTHY	2316 AIRPORT BLVD - SANFORD FL 32771
79- 89 RAINEY, CHARLES DAVID	3498 LADY HILL RD - SAN DIEGO CA 92130
78-103 RAJSICH, DAVID CHRISTOPHER	5324 NORTH SIXTH ST - PHOENIX AZ 85012
82-100 RAJSICH, GARY LOUIS	5324 N 6TH ST - PHOENIX AZ 85012
60- 84 RAKOW, EDWARD CHARLES	12259 HILLMAN CIR - LAKE PARK FL 33403
10-123 RALSTON, SAMUEL BERYL 'DOC'	D. AUGUST 29, 1950 LANCASTER, PA.
46- 86 RAMAZOTTI, ROBERT LOUIS	1111 SOUTH 26TH ST - ALTOONA PA 16602
39- 94 RAMBERT, ELMER DONALD 'PEP'	D. NOVEMBER 16, 1974 WEST PALM BEACH, FLA.
26- 67 RAMBO, WARREN DAWSON 'PETE'	CROWN POINT RD - THOROFARE NJ 08086
83-116 RAMIREZ, DANIEL ALLAN	2806 ERWIN - VICTORIA TX 77901

```
80-107 RAMIREZ, MARIO (TORRES)              RR 2 BOX 7 - YAUCO PR 00768
70-110 RAMIREZ, MILTON                      7 TULIO LARRINAGA ST - MAYAGUEZ PR 00708
74-108 RAMIREZ, ORLANDO                     TORICES PASO ABADIO #1325-CARTAGENA COLOMBIA S.A.
80-108 RAMIREZ, RAFAEL EMILIO               M.P. GAZETT #8,ENS. PRIMAVERA-SAN PEDRO DE MACORIS D.R.
55- 97 RAMOS , PEDRO                        3222 NW 7TH ST - MIAMI FL 33125
78-104 RAMOS, DOMINGO ANTONIO               CARR DUARTE KM 8 1/2,LICEY AL MEDIO-SANTIAGO DOM. REP.
44-108 RAMOS, JESUS MANUEL GARCIA 'CHUCHO'  AVE SANTADER, LAPINTA #4 - EL PARAISO VENEZ
78-105 RAMOS, ROBERTO                       3202 SW FIRST AVE - MIAMI FL 33129
47- 71 RAMSDELL, JAMES WILLARD 'WILLIE'     D. OCTOBER 8, 1969 WICHITA, KAN.
78-106 RAMSEY, MICHAEL JEFFREY              2900 CEDAR KNOLL DR - ROSWELL GA 30076
45- 83 RAMSEY, WILLIAM THRACE               769 ROSEBANK RD - MEMPHIS TN 38116
53- 73 RAND, RICHARD HILTON                 18518 JEFFREY AVE - CERRITOS CA 90701
76- 79 RANDALL, ROBERT LEE                  308 OPAL CIR - AMES IA 50010
71- 86 RANDLE, LEONARD SHENOFF              1700 N ELVA AVE - COMPTON CA 90222
75- 96 RANDOLPH, WILLIE LARRY               648 JUNIPER PL - FRANKLIN LAKES NJ 07417
62-111 RANEW, MERRITT THOMAS                BOX 448 - REDDICK FL 32686
49- 69 RANEY, FRANK ROBERT DONALD 'RIBS'    11242 CHARLES DR - WARREN MI 48093
81-102 RANSOM, JEFFERY DEAN                 2131 CURTIS ST - BERKELEY CA 94702
49- 70 RAPP, EARL WELLINGTON                9 EAST AVE - SWEDESBORO NJ 08085
21- 85 RAPP, JOSEPH ALOYSIUS 'GOLDIE'       D. JULY 1, 1966 LAMESA, CALIF.
77-118 RAPP, VERNON FRED                    14800 N. LOWELL BLVD - BLOOMFIELD CO 80020
46- 87 RASCHI, VICTOR JOHN ANGELO           1255 W WESTLAKE RD - CONESUS NY 14435
83-103 RASMUSSEN, DENNIS LEE                2208 CYPRESS BEND DR #3-203 - POMPANO BEACH FL 33069
75- 97 RASMUSSEN, ERIC RALPH                8829 NORTHWEST AVE - RACINE WI 53406
15-131 RASMUSSEN, HENRY FLORIAN             D. JANUARY 1, 1949 CHICAGO, ILL.
68- 82 RATH, FRED HELSHER                   OLD ADD: 200 N. MIDLAND - LITTLE ROCK AR 72202
65- 89 RATLIFF, KELLY EUGENE 'GENE'         3403 MILLERFIELD RD - MACON GA 31201
63- 96 RATLIFF, PAUL HAWTHORNE              234 N KENWOOD #304 - GLENDALE CA 91206
80-109 RATZER, STEVEN WAYNE                 %C.EILERT,5310 HOLDER AVE-BALTIMORE MD 21214
72- 86 RAU, DOUGLAS JAMES                   RR 1 BOX 154-A - COLUMBUS TX 78934
72- 87 RAUCH, ROBERT JOHN                   OLD ADD: 1149 OLIVE RD - VIRGINIA BEACH VA 23462
```

SHANE RAWLEY
SeattleMariners

```
66- 73 RAUDMAN, ROBERT JOYCE 'SHORTY'       15657 ROMAN ST - SEPULVEDA CA 91343
77-119 RAUTZHAN, CLARENCE GEORGE 'LANCE'    RR 4 BOX 4454 - POTTSVILLE PA 17901
78-107 RAWLEY, SHANE WILLIAM                7859 SADDLE CREEK TR - SARASOTA FL 33583
14-174 RAWLINGS, JOHN WILLIAM               D. OCTOBER 16, 1972 INGLEWOOD, CALIF.
15-132 RAY, CARL GRADY                      D. APRIL 3, 1970 WALNUT COVE, N.C.
65- 90 RAY, JAMES FRANCIS                   OLD ADD:1911 FOUNTAIN VIEW #1-HOUSTON TX
81-103 RAY, JOHN CORNELIAS                  RR 1 BOX 64 - CHAUTEAU OK 74337
82-101 RAY, LARRY DOYLE                     OLD ADD: RR 3 - VEVAY IN 47043
10-124 RAY, ROBERT HENRY 'FARMER'           D. MARCH 11, 1963 ELECTRA, TEX.
58- 74 RAYDON, CURTIS LOWELL                1515 SOUTH BUNN ST - BLOOMINTON IL 61701
80-110 RAYFORD, FLOYD KINNARD               2518 HUDSPETH ST - INGLEWOOD CA 90303
59- 67 RAYMOND, JOSEPH CLAUDE               OLD ADD: 584 BLVD. GOVIN #4 - SAINT JEAN QUEBEC
19- 66 RAYMOND, LOUIS ANTHONY               D. MAY 2, 1979 ROCHESTER, N. Y.
73- 99 RAZIANO, BARRY JOHN                  1315 4TH ST - KENNER LA 70062
83-118 READY, RANDY MAX                     OLD ADD: 350 FRANCISCAN CT #18 - FREMONT CA 94538
69-140 REAMS, LEROY                         1638 85TH AVE - OAKLAND CA 94621
79- 90 REARDON, JEFFREY JAMES               4 MARLWOOD LN - PALM BEACH GARDENS FL 33410
38- 79 REBEL, ARTHUR ANTHONY                1726 W FORE DR-TAMPA FL 33610
68- 83 REBERGER, FRANK BEALL                1790 HILL RD - BOISE ID 83702
12-161 REDDING, PHILIP HAYDEN               D. MARCH 30, 1929 GREENWOOD, MISS.
32- 69 REDER, JOHN ANTHONY                  BOX 1892 - FALL RIVER MA 02722
28- 77 REDFERN, GEORGE HOWARD 'BUCK'        D. SEPTEMBER 8, 1964 ASHEVILLE, N. C.
76- 80 REDFERN, PETER IRVINE                15131 PADDOCK - SYLMAR CA 91342
74-109 REDMON, GLENN VINCENT                BETHESDA BAPTIST CHURCH - BROWNSBURG IN 46112
65- 91 REDMOND, HOWARD WAYNE                OLD ADD: 24514 WILLOUGHBY - EAST DETROIT MI
35- 92 REDMOND, JACKSON MCKITTRICK          D. JULY 28, 1969 GARLAND, TEX.
82-102 REDUS, GARY EUGENE                   BOX 202 - TANNER AL 35671
78-108 REECE, ROBERT SCOTT                  1906 WEST 23RD ST - LOVELAND CO 80537
58- 75 REED, HOWARD DEAN                    D. DECEMBER 7, 1984 CORPUS CHRISTI, TEX.
84- 92 REED, JEFF SCOTT                     OLD ADD: 901 CASSIE DR - JOLIET IL 60435
81-104 REED, JERRY MAXWELL                  21 GRANDVIEW RD - ASHEVILLE NC 28806
61- 87 REED, JOHN BURWELL                   BOX 97 - SILVER CITY MS 39166
11-140 REED, MILTON D.                      D. JULY 27, 1938 ATLANTA, GA.
15-133 REED, RALPH EDWIN 'TED'              D. FEBRUARY 16, 1959 BEAVER, PA.
69-141 REED, ROBERT EDWARD                  OLD ADD: 6224 KING ARTHUR-SCHWARTZ CREEK MI
66- 74 REED, RONALD LEE                     OLD ADD: 2613 CLIFFVIEW DR - LILBURN GA 30247
52- 83 REED, WILLIAM JOSEPH                 11807 MARRS - HOUSTON TX 77065
49- 71 REEDER, WILLIAM EDGAR                BOX 812 - WHITNEY TX 76692
18- 62 REES, STANLEY MILTON                 D. AUGUST 29, 1937 LEXINGTON, KY.
27- 73 REESE, ANDREW JACKSON                D. JANUARY 10, 1966 TUPELO, MISS.
40- 73 REESE, HAROLD HENRY 'PEE WEE'        3211 BEALS BRANCH RD-LOUISVILLE KY 40206
30- 65 REESE, JAMES HERMAN                  10797 ASHTON AVE - LOS ANGELES CA 90024
```

64- 89 REESE, RICHARD BENJAMIN	OLD ADD: 4210 DEVONSHIRE CT - NORTHBROOK IL 60062
26- 68 REEVES, ROBERT EDWIN	702 BELVOIR AVE - CHATTANOOGA TN 37412
54- 89 REGALADO, RUDOLPH VALENTINO	5122 LOS ALTOS COURT - SAN DIEGO CA 92109
17- 66 REGAN, MICHAEL JOHN	D. MAY 23, 1961 ALBANY, N. Y.
60- 85 REGAN, PHILIP RAYMOND	1375 108TH ST - BYRON CENTER MI 49315
26- 69 REGAN, WILLIAM WRIGHT	D. JUNE 11, 1968 PITTSBURGH, PA.
24- 87 REGO, ANTONE	D. JANUARY 6, 1978 TULSA, OKLA.
12-162 REHG, WALTER PHILLIP	D. AUGUST 5, 1946 BURBANK, CALIF.
33- 53 REIBER, FRANK BERNARD	BOX 6284 - SARASOTA FL 33578
49- 72 REICH, HERMAN CHARLES	3779 PALA MESA DR - FALLBROOK CA 92028
64- 90 REICHARDT, FREDERIC CARL 'RICK'	2605 NW 90TH TER - GAINESVILLE FL 32606
22-114 REICHLE, RICHARD WENDELL	D. JUNE 13, 1967 ST. LOUIS, MO.
46- 88 REID, EARL PERCY	D. MAY 11, 1984 CULLMAN, ALA.
69-142 REID, SCOTT DONALD	5112 TONIKO DR - PHOENIX AZ 85044
17- 67 REILLY, ARCHER EDWIN	D. NOVEMBER 29, 1963 COLUMBUS, O.
19- 67 REILLY, HAROLD J.	
74-110 REINBACH, MICHAEL WAYNE	% CREAMER, 9459 SLOPE ST - SANTEE CA 92071
19- 68 REINHART, ARTHUR CONRAD	D. NOVEMBER 11, 1946 HOUSTON, TEX.
28- 78 REINHOLZ, ARTHUR AUGUST	D. DECEMBER 29, 1980 NEWPORT RICHEY, FLA.
15-134 REINICKER, WALTER JOSEPH	D. APRIL 18, 1957 PITTSBURGH, PA.
11-141 REIS, HARRIE CRANE 'JACK'	D. JULY 20, 1939 CINCINNATI, O.
31- 73 REIS, ROBERT JOSEPH THOMAS	D. MAY 1, 1973 ST. PAUL, MINN.
38- 80 REIS, THOMAS EDWARD	41 HOLLY LN - FORT THOMAS KY 41075
40- 74 REISER, HAROLD PATRICK 'PETE'	D. OCTOBER 25, 1981 PALM SPRINGS, CALIF.
11-142 REISIGL, JACOB 'BUGGS'	D. FEBRUARY 24, 1957 AMSTERDAM, N.Y.
32- 70 REISS, ALBERT ALLEN	474 TARPON SPRINGS RD - ODESSA FL 33556
72- 88 REITZ, KENNETH JOHN	5644 RHODES - ST. LOUIS MO 63109
79- 91 REMMERSWAAL, WILHELMUS ABRAHAM	DOKTOR VAN PRAAG ST 16 - WASSENAAR HOLL.
12-163 REMNEAS, ALEXANDER NORMAN	D. AUGUST 27, 1975 PHOENIX, ARIZ.
75- 98 REMY, GERALD PETER	5 DENNIS DR - WESTPORT MA 02790
13-147 RENFER. ERWIN ARTHUR	D. OCTOBER 26. 1957 SYCAMORE. ILL.
59- 68 RENFROE, MARSHALL DALTON	D. DECEMBER 10, 1970 PENSACOLA, FLA.
68- 84 RENICK, WARREN RICHARD 'RICK'	RR4 - LONDON OH 43140
61- 88 RENIFF, HAROLD EUGENE	424 STAFFORD - SCRANTON PA 18505
38- 81 RENINGER, JAMES DAVID	RR 1 S-18 - LEES SUMMIT MO 64063
69-143 RENKO, STEVEN	10347 ALHAMBRA - OVERLAND PARK KS 66207
53- 74 RENNA, WILLIAM BENEDITTO	1476 LESHER CT - SAN JOSE CA 95125
30- 66 RENSA, GEORGE ANTHONY 'TONY'	28 NORTH MEADE ST - WILKES-BARRE PA 18702
39- 95 REPASS, ROBERT WILLIS	169 BRIMFIELD RD-WETHERSFIELD CT 06109
78-109 REPLOGLE, ANDREW DAVID	1115 YELLOWWOOD CIR - NOBLESVILLE IN 46060
64- 91 REPOZ, ROGER ALLEN	1106 IRVING ST - BELLINGHAM WA 98225
53- 75 REPULSKI, ELDON JOHN 'RIP'	1541 8TH AVE N - ST CLOUD MN 56301
43-114 RESCIGNO, XAVIER FREDERICK	10613 LABONNE VIE DR - EAST PATCHOGUE NY 11772
49- 73 RESTELLI, DINO PAUL	1860 SAN CARLOS AVE - SAN CARLOS CA 94070
68- 85 RETTENMUND, MERVIN WELDON	16670 ESPOLA RD - POWAY CA 92064
22-115 RETTIG, ADOLPH JOHN 'OTTO'	D. JUNE 16, 1977 STUART, FLA.
61- 89 RETZER, KENNETH LEO	1554 PLANTATION WAY - EL CAJON CA 92020
75- 99 REUSCHEL, PAUL RICHARD	RR 1 BOX 76 - CAMP POINT IL 62320
72- 89 REUSCHEL, RICK EUGENE	618 EAST MAUDE - ARLINGTON HEIGHTS IL 60004
69-144 REUSS, JERRY	1000 ELYSIAN AVE - LOS ANGELES CA 90012
78-110 REVERING, DAVID ALVIN	1601 N. TAMARISK - CHANDLER AZ 85224
83-119 REYES, GILBERTO ROLANDO	CALLE 2DA. #7 LOS MAMEYES - SANTO DOMINGO DOM. REP.
43-115 REYES, NAPOLEON AGUILERA	2203 NW 33RD ST - MIAMI FL 33142
42- 82 REYNOLDS, ALLIE PIERCE	2525 CASHION PL-OKLAHOMA CITY OK 73112
68- 86 REYNOLDS, ARCHIE EDWARD	601 PHEASANT RUN - BURLESON TX 76028
27- 74 REYNOLDS, CARL NETTLES	D. MAY 29, 1978 HOUSTON, TEX.
45- 84 REYNOLDS, DANIEL VANCE	BOX 55 - SCOTTS NC 28699
78-111 REYNOLDS, DONALD EDWARD	2605 SOUTHEAST RYAN - CORVALLIS OR 97330
75-100 REYNOLDS, GORDON CRAIG	4607 FOUNTAINHEAD - HOUSTON TX 77066
83-120 REYNOLDS, HAROLD CRAIG	2605 SE RYAN ST - CORVALLIS OR 97330
70-111 REYNOLDS, KENNETH LEE	OLD ADD: 53 COMMONWEALTH AVE - MARLBORO MA 01752
69-145 REYNOLDS, ROBERT ALLEN	32304 FOURTH PL #R12 - FEDERAL WAY WA 98003
83-121 REYNOLDS, ROBERT JAMES	7076 EL SORENO CIR - SACRAMENTO CA 95831
82-103 REYNOLDS, RONN DWAYNE	820 MANSFIELD DR - WICHITA KS 67207
14-175 REYNOLDS, ROSS ERNEST	D. JUNE 23, 1970 ADA, OKLA.
63- 97 REYNOLDS, THOMAS D	1577 SAN ALTOS - LEMON GROVE CA 92045
13-148 REYNOLDS, WILLIAM DEE	D. JUNE 5, 1924 CARNEGIE, OKLA.
47- 72 RHAWN, ROBERT JOHN	D. JUNE 9, 1984 DANVILLE, PA.
14-176 RHEAM, KENNETH JOHNSTON 'CY'	D. OCTOBER 23, 1947 PITTSBURGH, PA.
24- 88 RHEM, CHARLES FLINT	D. JULY 30, 1969 COLUMBIA, S. C.
29- 86 RHIEL, WILLIAM JOSEPH	D. AUGUST 16, 1946 YOUNGSTOWN, O.
74-111 RHODEN, RICHARD ALAN	5640 NOBLE AVE - VAN NUYS CA 91411
52- 84 RHODES, JAMES LAMAR "DUSTY"	245 DIXON AVE - STATEN ISLAND NY 10303
29- 87 RHODES, JOHN GORDON	D. MARCH 22, 1960 LONG BEACH, CAL.

RHOMBERG

RITTWAGE

82-104	RHOMBERG, KEVIN JAY	5786 BEACH DR - MENTOR ON THE LAKE OH 44060
26- 70	RHYNE, HAROLD J.	D. JANUARY 7, 1971 ORANGEVALE, CAL.
64- 92	RIBANT, DENNIS JOSEPH	601 PARKCENTER DR #200 - SANTA ANA CA 92705
76- 81	RICCELLI, FRANK JOSEPH	311 SCHAEFFER AVE - SYRACUSE NY 13206
45- 85	RICE, DELBERT W	D. JANUARY 26, 1983 BUENA PARK, CALIF.
15-135	RICE, EDGAR CHARLES 'SAM'	D. OCTOBER 13, 1974 ROSSMOR, MD.
48- 84	RICE, HAROLD HOUSTON	%RON RICE,1008 W. HAINES AVE-MUNCIE IN 47303
23-108	RICE, HARRY FRANCIS 'SAM'	D. JANUARY 1, 1971 PORTLAND, ORE.
74-112	RICE, JAMES EDWARD	RR 8 BOX 686 - ANDERSON SC 29621
44-109	RICE, LEONARD OLIVER	BOX 54 - ARNOLD CA 95223
26- 71	RICE, ROBERT TURNBULL	D. FEBRUARY 20, 1986 ELIZABETHTOWN, PA.
39- 96	RICH, WOODROW EARL	D. APRIL 18, 1983 MORGANTON, N.C.
71- 87	RICHARD, JAMES RODNEY	10235 SAGEDALE - HOUSTON TX 77089
71- 88	RICHARD, LEE EDWARD 'BEE BEE'	1621 E 14TH ST - PORT ARTHUR TX 77640
60- 86	RICHARDS, DUANE LEE	BOX 54 - PALESTINE OH 45352
77-120	RICHARDS, EUGENE	2 WOODSPRING CT - COLUMBIA SC 29210
51- 80	RICHARDS, FRED CHARLES	1760 DODGE NW - WARREN OH 44485
32- 71	RICHARDS, PAUL RAPIER	BOX 545 - WAXAHACHIE TX 75165
29- 88	RICHARDSON, CLIFFORD NOLEN	D. SEPTEMBER 25, 1951 ATHENS, GA.
64- 93	RICHARDSON, GORDON CLARK	RR 3 BOX 217 - COLQUITT GA 31737
15-136	RICHARDSON, JOHN WILLIAM	D. JANUARY 18, 1970 MARION, ILL.
42- 83	RICHARDSON, KENNETH FRANKLIN	3456 CENTINELA #24 - LOS ANGELES CA 90066

55- 98	RICHARDSON, ROBERT CLINTON	47 ADAMS - SUMTER SC 29150
17- 68	RICHARDSON, THOMAS MITCHELL	D. NOVEMBER 15, 1939 ONAWA, IA.
80-111	RICHARDT, MICHAEL ANTHONY	3555 WEST BULLARD - FRESNO CA 93711
21- 86	RICHBOURG, LANCE CLAYTON	D. SEPTEMBER 10, 1975 CRESTVIEW, FLA.
62-112	RICHERT, PETER GERARD	5932 PARADISE PLAZA - PALM SPRINGS CA 92264
33- 54	RICHMOND, BERYL JUSTICE	D. APRIL 24, 1980 CAMERON, W. VA.
41- 93	RICHMOND, DONALD LESTER	D. MAY 24, 1981 ELMIRA, N. Y.
20- 99	RICHMOND, RAYMOND SINCLAIR	D. OCTOBER 21, 1969 DESOTO, MO.
51- 81	RICHTER, ALLEN GORDON	BOX 4 - VIRGINIA BEACH VA 23458
11-143	RICHTER, EMIL HENRY 'REGGIE'	D. AUGUST 3, 1934 CHICAGO, ILL.
42- 84	RICKERT, MARVIN AUGUST	D. JUNE 3, 1978 OAKVILLE, WASH.
63- 98	RICKETTS, DAVID WILLIAM	717 SEWARD ST - ROCHESTER NY 14611
59- 65	RICKETTS, RICHARD JAMES	2 LEPERE DR - PITTSFORD NY 14534
69-146	RICO, ALFREDO CRUZ 'FRED'	5207 TEESDALE - NORTH HOLLYWOOD CA 91607
16- 70	RICO, ARTHUR RAYMOND	D. JANUARY 3, 1919 BOSTON, MASS.
23-109	RICONDA, HARRY PAUL	D. NOVEMBER 15, 1958 MAHOPAC, N. Y.
39- 97	RIDDLE, ELMER RAY	D. MAY 14, 1984 COLUMBUS, GA.
30- 67	RIDDLE, JOHN LUDY	851 INDIGO WAY #A - INDIANAPOLIS IN 46260
70-112	RIDDLEBERGER, DENNIS MICHAEL	OLD ADD: 5613 SPRINGWOOD AVE - NORFOLK VA
14-177	RIDGWAY, JACOB A. 'JOHN'	D. FEBRUARY 23, 1928 PHILADELPHIA, PA.
50- 81	RIDZIK, STEPHEN GEORGE	4825 PONDEROSA DR - ANNANDALE VA 22003
42- 85	RIEBE, HARVEY DONALD 'HANK'	28031 LAKE SHORE BLVD-CLEVELAND OH 44132
10-125	RIEGER, ELMER JAY	D. OCTOBER 21, 1959 LOS ANGELES, CALIF.
11-144	RIGGERT, JOSEPH ALOYSIUS	D. DECEMBER 10, 1973 KANSAS CITY, MO.
34- 89	RIGGS, LEWIS SIDNEY	D. AUGUST 12, 1975 DURHAM, N. C.
79- 92	RIGHETTI, DAVID ALLAN	1574 KOCH LN - SAN JOSE CA 95125
22-116	RIGNEY, EMORY ELMO 'TOPPER'	D. JUNE 6, 1972 SAN ANTONIO, TEX.
37- 90	RIGNEY, JOHN DUNGAN	D. OCTOBER 21, 1984 LOMBARD, ILL.
46- 89	RIGNEY, WILLIAM JOSEPH	3136 ROUND HILL RD - ALAMO CA 94507
84- 93	RIJO, JOSE ANTONIO	CENTRAL CABRAL #66 - SAN CRISTOBAL DOMINICAN REP.
41- 94	RIKARD, CULLEY	50 HWY 304 - OLIVE BRANCH MS 38654
85- 97	RILES, EARNEST	RR 1 BOX 38 - WHIGHAM GA 31797
79- 93	RILEY, GEORGE MICHAEL	2737 S. SHERIDAN ST - PHILADELPHIA PA 19148
10-126	RILEY, JAMES JOSEPH	D. MARCH 25, 1949 BUFFALO, N.Y.
21- 87	RILEY, JAMES NORMAN	D. MAY 25, 1969 SEQUIN, TEXAS
44-110	RILEY, LEON FRANCIS	D. SEPTEMBER 13, 1970 SCHENECTADY, N. Y.
80-112	RINCON, ANDREW JOHN	5425 LOS TOROS - PICO RIVERA CA 90660
79- 94	RINEER, JEFFREY ALAN	RR 1 BOX 81A - PEQUEA PA 17565
17- 69	RING, JAMES JOSEPH	D. JULY 2, 1965 NEW YORK, N. Y.
50- 82	RINKER, ROBERT JOHN	10 NORTH MADISON - MCADOO PA 18237
69-147	RIOS, JUAN	OLD ADD: PASO TABLA 9-SAN SEBASTIAN PR
85- 98	RIPKEN, CALVIN EDWIN, SR.	410 CLOVER ST - ABERDEEN MD 21001
81-105	RIPKEN, CALVIN EDWIN, JR.	410 CLOVER ST - ABERDEEN MD 21001
78-112	RIPLEY, ALLEN STEVENS	BOX 349 %A. COOPER - NORTH ATTLEBORO MA 02760
35- 93	RIPLEY, WALTER FRANKLIN	55 WEST ST - NORTH ATTLEBORO MA 02760
62-113	RIPPELMEYER, RAYMOND ROY	BOX 28 - VALMEYER IL 62295
44-111	RIPPLE, CHARLES DAWSON	D. MAY 6, 1979 WILMINGTON, N. C.
36- 78	RIPPLE, JAMES ALBERT	D. JULY 16, 1959 GREENSBURG, PA.
17- 70	RISBERG, CHARLES AUGUST 'SWEDE'	D. OCTOBER 13, 1975 RED BLUFF, CAL.
64- 94	RITCHIE, JAY SEAY	1108 TERRACE DR - SALISBURY NC 28144
12-164	RITTER, WILLIAM HERBERT 'HANK'	D. SEPTEMBER 3, 1964 AKRON, O.
70-113	RITTWAGE, JAMES MICHAEL	23931 COLUMBUS RD - BEDFORD HEIGHTS OH 44146

83-122	RIVERA, GERMAN (DIAZ)	VIA LETICIA #4E-S4,V.FONTANA - CAROLINA PR 00630
75-101	RIVERA, JESUS MANUEL 'BOMBO'	G#2 AMALIA MARIN - PONCE PR 00732
52- 85	RIVERA, MANUEL JOSEPH 'JIM'	RR 5 BOX 90 - ANGOLA IN 46703
70-114	RIVERS, JOHN MILTON 'MICKEY'	350 NW 48TH ST - MIAMI FL 33127
21- 88	RIVIERE, ARTHUR BERNARD 'TINK'	D. SEPTEMBER 27, 1965 LIBERTY, TEX.
12-165	RIXEY, EPPA	D. FEBRUARY 28, 1963 TERRACE PARK, O.
38- 82	RIZZO, JOHN COSTA	D. DECEMBER 4, 1977 HOUSTON, TEX.
41- 95	RIZZUTO, PHILIP FRANCIS	912 WESTMINSTER AVE-HILLSIDE NJ 07205
53- 76	ROACH, MELVIN EARL	106 W 30TH ST - RICHMOND VA 23225
10-127	ROACH, WILBUR CHARLES 'ROXY'	D. DECEMBER 26, 1947 BAY CITY, MICH.
61- 90	ROARKE, MICHAEL THOMAS	11 ROSEVIEW DR - CRANSTON RI 02910
79- 95	ROBBINS, BRUCE DUANE	3518 HIGHFIELD CT #B - INDIANAPOLIS IN 46222
33- 55	ROBELLO, THOMAS VARDASCO 'TONY'	3504 WESLEY AV - FT WORTH TX 76111

79- 96	ROBERGE, BERTRAND ROLAND	184 BROAD ST - AUBURN ME 04210
41- 96	ROBERGE, JOSEPH ALBERT ARMAND 'SKIPPY'	173 CRAWFORD - LOWELL MA 01854
43-116	ROBERTS, CHARLES EMORY 'RED'	RR2 #109 - CARROLLTON GA 30117
13-149	ROBERTS, CLARENCE ASHLEY 'SKIPPER'	D. DECEMBER 24, 1963 LONG BEACH, CALIF.
54- 90	ROBERTS, CURTIS BENJAMIN	D. NOVEMBER 14, 1969 OAKLAND, CALIF.
67- 89	ROBERTS, DALE	206 BERRY AVE - VERSAILLES KY 40383
69-148	ROBERTS, DAVID ARTHUR	18003 RAVENFIELD DR - HOUSTON TX 77084
62-114	ROBERTS, DAVID LEONARD	17510 MAYALL ST - NORTHRIDGE CA 91324
72- 90	ROBERTS, DAVID WAYNE	2663 NW BLUEBELL - CORVALLIS OR 97330
24- 89	ROBERTS, JAMES NEWSOM	D. JUNE 24, 1984 COLUMBUS, MISS.
74-113	ROBERTS, LEON KAUFFMAN	3200 TRANQUILITY - ARLINGTON TX 76016
19- 69	ROBERTS, RAYMOND	D. JANUARY 30, 1962 CRUGER, MISS.
48- 85	ROBERTS, ROBIN EVAN	504 TERRACE HILL DR - TEMPLE TERRACE FL 33617
54- 91	ROBERTSON, ALFRED JAMES 'JIM'	3342 AYITA CIR - LAS VEGAS NV 89109
81-106	ROBERTSON, ANDRE LEVETT	2229 CROSS LN ST - ORANGE TX 77360
19- 70	ROBERTSON, CHARLES CULBERTSON	D. AUGUST 23, 1984 FORT WORTH, TEX.
62-115	ROBERTSON, DARYL BERDINE	755 PRINCTON DR - MIDVALE UT 84047
12-166	ROBERTSON, DAVIS AYDELOTRE	D. NOVEMBER 5, 1970 VIRGINIA BEACH, VA.
54- 92	ROBERTSON, DONALD ALEXANDER	422 DOGWOOD ST - PARK FOREST IL 60466
19- 99	ROBERTSON, EUGENE EDWARD	D. OCTOBER 21, 1981 FALLON, NEV.
69-149	ROBERTSON, JERRY LEE	3251 PLASS - TOPEKA KS 66611
13-150	ROBERTSON, PRESTON	D. OCTOBER 2, 1944 NEW ORLEANS, LA.
66- 75	ROBERTSON, RICHARD PAUL	20060 RODRIGUES AVE #A - CUPERTINO CA 95014
67- 90	ROBERTSON, ROBERT EUGENE	RR 1 SHINNAMON DR - LAVALE MD 21502
40- 75	ROBERTSON, SHERRARD ALEXANDER	D. OCTOBER 23, 1970 HOUGHTON, S. D.
85- 99	ROBIDOUX, WILLIAM JOSEPH 'BILLY JOE'	RR BOX 148 - WARE MA 01082
43-117	ROBINSON, AARON ANDREW	D. MARCH 9, 1966 LANCASTER,O.
55- 99	ROBINSON, BROOKS CALBERT	1506 SHERBROOK RD - LUTHERVILLE MD 21093
78-113	ROBINSON, BRUCE PHILLIP	3968 SAN AUGUSTINE WAY - SAN DIEGO CA 92130
72- 91	ROBINSON, CRAIG GEORGE	OLD ADD: 1096 PIEDMONT AVE NE #11 - ATLANTA GA 30309
70-115	ROBINSON, DAVID TANNER	6140 CAMINO DEL RINSON - SAN DIEGO CA 92120
79- 97	ROBINSON, DEWEY EVERETT	1733 W ARTHUR AVE - CHICAGO IL 60626
78-114	ROBINSON, DON ALLEN	2012 POPLAR ST - KENOVA WV 25530
58- 76	ROBINSON, EARL JOHN	LANEY COLLEGE,900 PATTON ST-OAKLAND CA 94609
60- 87	ROBINSON, FLOYD ANDREW	5837 MARKET - SAN DIEGO CA 92114
56- 73	ROBINSON, FRANK	15557 AQUA VERDE DR - LOS ANGELES CA 90077
55-100	ROBINSON, HUMBERTO VALENTINO	1695 BROOKLYN AVE - BROOKLYN NY 11210
47- 73	ROBINSON, JACK ROOSEVELT	D. OCTOBER 24, 1972 STAMFORD, CONN.
84- 94	ROBINSON, JEFFREY DANIEL	27802 POLLENSA - MISSION VIEJO CA 92692
49- 74	ROBINSON, JOHN EDWARD	11 WINDING WAY - CEDAR GROVE NJ 07009
11-145	ROBINSON, JOHN HENRY 'HANK'	D. JULY 3, 1965 NORTH LITTLE ROCK, ARK.
84- 95	ROBINSON, RONALD DEAN	473 PINE ST - WOODLAKE CA 93286
42- 86	ROBINSON, WILLIAM EDWARD 'EDDIE'	6104 CHOLLA DR - FORT WORTH TX 76102
66- 76	ROBINSON, WILLIAM HENRY	RR 3 BOX 179A - SEWELL NJ 08080
69-150	ROBLES, RAFAEL RADAMES	INGENIO QUISQUEYA-SAN PEDRO DE MACORIS DOM. REP.
72- 92	ROBLES, SERGIO	ESCOBEDO #402 - MAGDALENA SONORA MEX.
74-114	ROBSON, THOMAS JAMES	OLD ADD: 4502 N. 35TH PLACE - PHOENIX AZ 85018

STEVE ROGERS

43-118	ROCCO, MICHAEL DOMINICK 'MICKEY'	868 WEST IOWA AVE - ST PAUL MN 55117
45- 86	ROCHE, ARMANDO BAEZ	OLD ADD: AVE LOS PINOS - HAVANA CUBA
14-178	ROCHE, JOHN JOSEPH	D. MARCH 31, 1983 PEORIA, ARIZ.
14-179	ROCHEFORT, BENNETT HAROLD	D. APRIL 2, 1981 RED BANK, N. J.
44-112	ROCHELLI, LOUIS JOSEPH	501 RATTON - VICTORIA TX 77901
36- 79	ROCK, LESTER HENRY	1027 OLIVE DR #6 - DAVIS CA 95616
76- 82	ROCKETT, PATRICK EDWARD	1335 VIEWRIDGE - SAN ANTONIO TX 78213
83-123	RODAS, RICHARD MARTIN	2514 FOOTHILL LANE - BREA CA 92621
57- 74	RODGERS, KENNETH ANDRE IAN	BOX N386 - NASSAU BAHAMAS W.I.
61- 91	RODGERS, ROBERT LEROY	5181 WEST KNOLL DR - YORBA LINDA CA 92686
15-137	RODGERS, WILBUR KINCAID	D. DECEMBER 24, 1978 GOLIAD, TEX.
44-113	RODGERS, WILLIAM SHERMAN	1433 NAUDAIN - HARRISBURG PA 17104
54- 93	RODIN, ERIC CHAPMAN	947 GARFIELD AVE - BRIDGEWATER TOWNSHIP NJ 08807
67- 91	RODRIGUEZ, AURELIO HUARTE	ROSENDO 6 CASTRO #112 - LOS MOCHIS SONORA MEX.
73-100	RODRIGUEZ, EDUARDO	URB CATALINA CALLE 4E-34-BARCELONETA PR 00617
82-105	RODRIGUEZ, EDWIN (MORALES)	JARDINES CARIBE 28 ST #Z-3 - PONCE PR 00731
68- 87	RODRIGUEZ, ELISEO C.'ELLIE'	LAGO VISTA #2 BLDG 29 #C - LEVITTOWN LAKES PR 00619
58- 77	RODRIGUEZ, FERNANDO PEDRO 'FREDDY'	OLD ADD: 555 MAYIA RODRIGUEZ - HAVANA CUBA
52- 86	RODRIGUEZ, HECTOR ANTONIO	OLD ADD: %A.CANIZARES,CERT. 99-A COL. POSTAL-MEXICO DF
16- 71	RODRIGUEZ, JOSE	D. MARCH 23, 1948 HAVANA, CUBA
67- 92	RODRIGUEZ, ROBERTO MUNOZ	CORTIJITO DESARRIAS,8 CJN RECOBE 30 - CARACAS VENEZ
84- 96	RODRIGUEZ, VICTOR MANUEL	APTO. 464K., BO MAIZALES - NAGUABO PR 00718
38- 83	ROE, ELWIN CHARLES 'PREACHER'	204 WILDWOOD TER - WEST PLAINS MO 65775
23-110	ROE, JAMES CLAY	D. APRIL 3, 1956 CLEVELAND, MISS.
55-101	ROEBUCK, EDWARD JACK	3434 WARWOOD RD - LAKEWOOD CA 90712
76- 83	ROENICKE, GARY STEVEN	1017 W SERVICE AVE - WEST COVINA CA 91790
81-107	ROENICKE, RONALD JON	1017 W SERVICE - WEST COVINA CA 91790
23-111	ROETTGER, OSCAR FREDERICK LOUIS	11566 POGGEMOELLER LANE - ST. LOUIS MO 63138
27- 75	ROETTGER, WALTER HENRY	D. SEPTEMBER 14, 1951 CHAMPAIGN, ILL.
29- 89	ROETZ, EDWARD BERNARD	D. MARCH 16, 1965 PHILADELPHIA, PA.
38- 84	ROGALSKI, JOSEPH ANTHONY	D. NOVEMBER 20, 1951 ASHLAND, WIS.
25- 88	ROGELL, WILLIAM GEORGE	1700 GARNET DR #206-NEWPORT RICHEY FL 33552
14-180	ROGERS, JAY LOUIS	D. JULY 18 1964 CARLISLE, PA.
38- 85	ROGERS, LEE OTIS	4920 HAWTHORNE RD-LITTLE ROCK AR 72207
35- 94	ROGERS, ORLIN WOODROW 'BUCK'	RR ONE BOX 222 - BLAIRS VA 24527
38- 86	ROGERS, STANLEY FRANK 'PACKY'	964 WALNUT ST-ELMIRA NY 14901
73-101	ROGERS, STEPHEN DOUGLAS	2335 E BERKELEY - SPRINGFIELD MO 65804
17- 71	ROGERS, THOMAS ANDREW	D. MARCH 7, 1936 NASHVILLE, TENN.
15-138	ROGGE, FRANCIS CLINTON	D. JANUARY 6, 1969 MOUNT CLEMENS, MICH.
63- 99	ROGGENBURK, GARRY EARL	19686 LORRAINE RD - CLEVELAND OH 44126
73-102	ROGODZINSKI, MICHAEL GEORGE	7 TICONDEROGA - LAUREL SPRINGS NJ 08021
49- 75	ROGOVIN, SAUL WALTER	420 W 24TH DR - NEW YORK NY 10011
83-124	ROHN, DANIEL JAY	9247 WEST LONG LAKE RD - ALPENA MI 49707
67- 93	ROHR, LESLIE NORVIN	1340 WICKS LANE - BILLINGS MT 59105
67- 94	ROHR, WILLIAM JOSEPH	700 W THIRD #309B - SANTA ANA CA 92701
21- 89	ROHWER, RAY	BOX 331 - DIXON CA 95620
53- 77	ROIG, ANTON AMBROSE	23310 INLET DR #12 - LIBERTY LAKE WA 99019
66- 77	ROJAS, MINERVINO ALEJANDRO 'MINNIE'	7101A PLASKA - HUNTINGTON PARK CA 90255

62-116	ROJAS, OCTAVIO 'COOKIE'	15245 MELROSE DR - STANLEY KS 66221
42- 87	ROJEK, STANLEY ANDREW	895 PAYNE AVE - NORTH TONAWANDA NY 14120
62-117	ROLAND, JAMES IVAN	47 SHADY OAKS DRIVE - FRANKLIN NC 28734
31- 74	ROLFE, ROBERT ABIAL 'RED'	D. JULY 8, 1969 GILFORD, N. H.
12-167	ROLLINGS, RAYMOND COPELAND	D. AUGUST 25, 1966 ST.PAUL, MINN.
27- 76	ROLLINGS, WILLIAM RUSSELL 'RED'	D. DECEMBER 31, 1964 MOBILE, ALA.
61- 92	ROLLINS, RICHARD JOHN	2751 E WALLINGS RD - BROADVIEW HGTS OH 44147
84- 97	ROMAN, JOSE RAFAEL	VISTA ALEGRE #10 SANCHES LUPERON-PUERTO PLATA DOM. REP.
64- 95	ROMAN, WILLIAM ANTHONY	OLD ADD: 4318 FAWN CT - CROSS PLAINS WI 53528
84- 98	ROMANICK, RONALD JAMES	4221 135TH PL SE - BELLEVUE WA 98006
50- 83	ROMANO, JAMES KING	233 BURLINGTON AVE - DEER PARK NY 11729
58- 78	ROMANO, JOHN ANTHONY	7 TANGLEWOOD HOLLOW - UPPER SADDLE RIVER NJ 07458
54- 94	ROMBERGER, ALLEN IRVING	D. MAY 26, 1983 WEIKERT, PA.
77-121	ROMERO, EDGARDO	OLD ADD: CALLE 6 BLOQUE 2 #6 - SABANA GARDENS PR 00630
84- 99	ROMERO, ROMAN	CLE ULISES ESPAILLOT #60-SAN PEDRO DE MACORIS DOM. REP.
85-100	ROMINE, KEVIN ANDREW	8750 ROGUE RIVER AVE - FOUNTAIN VALLEY CA 92708
20-100	ROMMEL, EDWIN AMERICUS	D. AUGUST 26, 1970 BALTIMORE, MD.
77-122	ROMO, ENRIQUE	AVENIDA S N CARLOS #923 - TORREON COAHUILA MEX.
68- 88	ROMO, VICENTE	CALLE 32 AVENIDA 17 #45 - GUAYMAS SONORA MEX.
53- 78	ROMONOSKY, JOHN	5090 BIXBY ROAD - GROVEPORT OH 43125
13-151	RONDEAU, HENRI JOSEPH	D. MAY 28 1943 WOONSOCKET, R.I.
76- 84	RONDON, GILBERT	1836 WATSON AVE #3E - BRONX NY 10472
81-108	ROOF, EUGENE LAWRENCE	RR 10 BOX 223 - PADUCAH KY 42001
61- 93	ROOF, PHILLIP ANTHONY	RR 1 BOX 402 - BOAZ KY 42027
68- 89	ROOKER, JAMES PHILIP	1684 CITATION DR - LIBRARY PA 15129
14-181	ROONEY, FRANK	D. APRIL 6, 1977 BESSEMER, MICH.
81-109	ROONEY, PATRICK EUGENE	925 S WALNUT - ARLINGTON HEIGHTS IL 60005
23-112	ROOT, CHARLES HENRY	D. NOVEMBER 5, 1970 HOLLISTER, CAL.
70-116	ROQUE, JORGE	BO SAN ANTON #135 - PONCE PR 00731
77-123	ROSADO, LUIS (ROBLES)	CALLE 508 B-213 #13 5TH-CAROLINA PR 00630
39- 98	ROSAR, WARREN VINCENT 'BUDDY'	733 EGGERT RD-BUFFALO NY 14215
71- 89	ROSARIO, ANGEL RAMON	CALLE 1 #421 HERNANDES DAVILA-BAYAMON PR00619
65- 92	ROSARIO, SANTIAGO	OLD ADD: VILLA GRILLASCA D.5B - PONCE PR
71- 90	ROSE, DONALD GARY	1133 HUNTINGDON - SAN JOSE CA 95129
63-100	ROSE, PETER EDWARD	1203 NEEB RD - CINCINNATI OH 45238

57- 75	ROSEBORO, JOHN JUNIOR	1703 VIRGINIA RD - LOS ANGELES CA 90019
55-102	ROSELLI, ROBERT EDWARD	1548 HEMLOCK AVE - SAN MATEO CA 94401
72- 93	ROSELLO, DAVID	PAZ 160 - BO PARIS - MAYAGUEZ PR 00708
47- 74	ROSEN, ALBERT LEONARD	BOX 24308 - SAN FRANCISCO CA 94124
37- 91	ROSEN, GOODWIN GEORGE	120 SHELBURNE AVE #1205 - TORONTO ONTARIO CAN.
30- 68	ROSENBERG, HARRY	23 MEADOWBROOK DR - SAN FRANCISCO CA 94127
23-113	ROSENBERG, LOUIS C	320 ALEMANY BLVD - SAN FRANCISCO CA 94110
31- 75	ROSENFELD, MAX	D. MARCH 10, 1969 MIAMI, FLA.
36- 80	ROSENTHAL, LAWRENCE JOHN	1335 WHITE BEAR AVE - ST. PAUL MN 55106
25- 89	ROSENTHAL, SIMON	D. APRIL 7, 1969 BOSTON, MASS.
44-114	ROSER, EMERSON COREY 'STEVE'	CAMP ROAD, CEDAR LAKE - CLAYVILLE NY 13322
22-118	ROSER, JOHN JOSEPH 'BUNNY'	D. MAY 6, 1979 ROCKY HILL, CONN.
24- 90	ROSS, CHESTER FRANKLIN 'BUSTER'	D. APRIL 24, 1982 MAYFIELD, KY.
39- 99	ROSS, CHESTER JAMES	OLD ADD: VA HOSP,3495 BAILEY AVE - BUFFALO NY 14215
54- 95	ROSS, CLIFFORD DAVID	2581 ROSEWOOD - ROSLYN PA 19001
38- 87	ROSS, DONALD RAYMOND	416 S OLD RANCH RD-ARCADIA CA 91006
50- 84	ROSS, FLOYD ROBERT 'BOB'	2245 E VERMONT - ANAHEIM CA 92806
68- 90	ROSS, GARY DOUGLAS	OLD ADD: 7985 LABRUSCA WAY - CARLSBAD CA 92008
18- 63	ROSS, GEORGE SIDNEY	D. APRIL 22, 1935 AMITYVILLE, N. Y.
36- 81	ROSS, LEE RAVON 'BUCK'	D. NOVEMBER 23, 1978 CHARLOTTE, N . C.
82-106	ROSS, MARK JOSEPH	7951 GLENHEATH - HOUSTON TX 77061
52- 87	ROSSI, JOSEPH ANTHONY	934 STANNAGE AVE - ALBANY CA 94706
44-115	ROSSO, FRANCIS JAMES	65 BROZ TERRACE - FEEDING HILLS MA 01030
48- 86	ROTBLATT, MARVIN JOSEPH	180 N LASALLE ST - CHICAGO IL 60601
14-182	ROTH, ROBERT FRANK 'BRAGGO'	D. SEPTEMBER 11, 1936 CHICAGO, ILL.
45- 87	ROTHEL, ROBERT BURTON	D. MAY 21, 1984 HURON, O.
25- 90	ROTHROCK JOHN HOUSTON	D. FEBRUARY 2, 1980 SAN BERNARDINO, CALIF.
81-110	ROTHSCHILD, LAWRENCE LEE	1136 BREABURN ST - FLOSSMOR IL 60422
70-117	ROUNSAVILLE, VIRL GENE	2901 LONE TREE WAY #A - ANTIOCH CA 94509
13-152	ROUSH, EDD J	122 39TH STREET CT NW - BRADENTON FL 33505
11-146	ROWAN, DAVID	D. JULY 30, 1955 TORONTO, ONT.
84-100	ROWDON, WADE LEE	OLD ADD: 12929 SW 64TH CT - MIAMI FL 33156
63-101	ROWE, DONALD HOWARD	19791 SCENIC BAY LN-HUNTINGTON BEACH CA 92648
16- 72	ROWE, HARLAND STIMSON	D. MAY 26, 1969 SPRINGVALE, ME.
63-102	ROWE, KENNETH DARRELL	365 NORTH ROGERS - NORTHVILLE MI 48167
33- 56	ROWE, LYNWOOD THOMAS 'SCHOOLBOY'	D. JANUARY 8, 1961 EL DORADO, ARK.
39-100	ROWELL, CARVEL WILLIAM 'BAMA'	RR 1 BOX 456 - CITRONELLE AL 36522
23-114	ROWLAND, CHARLIE LELAND	HIGHWAY 64 RR 2 - WENDELL NC 27591
15-139	ROWLAND, CLARENCE HENRY 'PANTS'	D. MAY 17, 1969 CHICAGO, ILL.

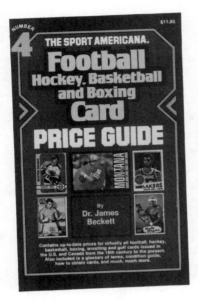

1985 SPORT AMERICANA FOOTBALL, HOCKEY, BASKETBALL & BOXING CARD PRICE GUIDE

$ 11.95 plus postage & handling

This 4th edition has just been released and is the biggest and best yet. Over 400 pages of prices, illustrations and descriptions of all but a few of the football, hockey, basketball and boxing cards in existence. In a format similar to the Baseball Card Price Guide, this book is complete through the 1985 Topps football card issue. It is the definitive book on cards of these sports. American and Canadian issues are included.

THE SPORT AMERICANA MEMORABILIA & AUTOGRAPH PRICE GUIDE

$ 8.95 plus postage and handling

THE ONE EVERYONE HAS AWAITED
The Baseball Memorabilia Price Guide has taken over a year to produce. Now you can find the current values for your programs, yearbooks, press pins, souvenirs, pins and coins, baseball statues, Exhibit or arcade cards, baseball envelopes, bubble gum paper inserts, magazines, autographed balls, photos and cards, and much, more more.

By Dr. James Beckett and Dennis W. Eckes

YEARBOOKS — All teams, all years
PROGRAMS — World Series & All-Star
PRESS PINS — World Series & All-Star
COINS & PINS — Topps, Salada, Armour, many, many more
ENVELOPES — Baseball Commemorative
ANNUALS — Street & Smith, Dell, many more
EXHIBITS — All
BREAD LABELS — Tip Top, Northland, more
CARD PREMIUMS — Wide Pens, Fine Pens, large R Cards, Sporting Life, etc.
WRAPPERS — All baseball 1933-1982
HARTLAND STATUES — All baseball
OBSCURE BASEBALL CARDS — Obaks, etc.
BASEBALL CARD PAPER INSERTS & STAMPS — Topps posters, tatoos, stamps, etc.
POSTCARDS — Significant baseball issues(Dormand, Rose, Burke, Bill & Bob, Sporting News, etc.)
AUTOGRAPHED TEAM BALLS — 1901-1981 all pennant winners, divisional winners, first year teams, last year teams, All-Star teams, etc.
AUTOGRAPHS — Values for almost all big league players on various media(3 x 5's, Photos, etc.)
RECENT MEMORABILIA — The treasures of the future, Gateway, Perez-Steele, quasi-legitimate issues

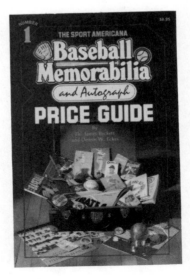

80-113 ROWLAND, MICHAEL EVAN	OLD ADD: 6425 EAST VIRGINIA - SCOTTSDALE AZ 85257
33- 57 ROY, EMILE ARTHUR	SOUTH COUNTRY CLUB RD - CRYSTAL RIVER FL 32629
46- 90 ROY, JEAN PIERRE	BOX 500, STATION "M" - MONTREAL QUEBEC H1V 3P2 CAN.
24- 91 ROY, LUTHER FRANKLIN	D. JULY 24, 1963 GRAND RAPIDS, MICH.
50- 85 ROY, NORMAN BROOKS	53 CENTRAL ST - WEST CONCORD MA 01781
73-103 ROYSTER, JERON KENNIS	18858 BERNARDO TRAILS DR - SAN DIEGO CA 92128
81-111 ROYSTER, WILLIE ARTHUR	229 55TH ST NE - WASHINGTON DC 20019
50- 86 ROZEK, RICHARD LOUIS	BOX 249 - CEDAR RAPIDS IA 52406
77-124 ROZEMA, DAVID SCOTT	856 BERKSHIRE RD - DETROIT MI 48203
64- 96 ROZNOVSKY, VICTOR JOSEPH	1686 W BULLARD - FRESNO CA 93711
40- 76 RUBELING, ALBERT WILLIAM	3054 OAK FOREST DR-BALTIMORE MD 21234
69-151 RUBERTO, JOHN EDWARD 'SONNY'	3264 ACACIA DR - INDIANAPOLIS IN 46224
66- 78 RUBIO, JORGE JESUS	1001 LERDO AVE - MEXICALI BAJA CALIF. MEX.
27- 77 RUBLE, WILLIAM ARTHUR	D. NOVEMBER 1, 1983 MARYVILLE, TENN.
81-112 RUCKER, DAVID MICHAEL	P.O. BOX 559 - PINION HILLS CA 92372
40- 77 RUCKER, JOHN JOEL	D. AUGUST 7, 1985 MOULTRIE, GA.
67- 95 RUDI, JOSEPH ODEN	RR 1 BOX 66 - BAKER OR 97814
45- 88 RUDOLPH, ERNEST WILLIAM	RR 2 BOX 14A - BLACK RIVER FALLS WI 54615
57- 76 RUDOLPH, FREDERICK DONALD 'DON'	D. SEPTEMBER 12, 1968 ENCINO, CAL.
69-152 RUDOLPH, KENNETH VICTOR	OLD ADD: 11815 KINGSFORT PL #1-FLORISSANT MO
10-128 RUDOLPH, RICHARD	D. OCTOBER 20, 1949 BRONX, N.Y.
15-140 RUEL, HEROLD DOMINIC 'MUDDY'	D. NOVEMBER 13, 1963 PALO ALTO, CALIF.
17- 72 RUETHER, WALTER HENRY 'DUTCH'	D. MAY 16, 1970 PHOENIX, ARIZ.
49- 76 RUFER, RUDOLPH JOSEPH	649 CORNWELL AVE - MALVERNE NY 11565
24- 92 RUFFING, CHARLES HERBERT 'RED'	D. FEBRUARY 17, 1986 MAYFIELD HEIGHTS, O.
74-115 RUHLE, VERNON GERALD	%MEKULEN,1802 BEDFORD LN #A19 - SUN CITY FL 33570

Babe Ruth (signature)

64- 97 RUIZ, HIRALDO SABLON 'CHICO'	D. FEBRUARY 9, 1972 SAN DIEGO, CALIF.
78-115 RUIZ, MANUEL 'CHICO'	TAPIA 267 - SANTUCE PR 00912
43-119 RULLO, JOSEPH VINCENT	D. OCTOBER 28, 1969 PHILADELPHIA, PA.
14-183 RUMLER, WILLIAM GEORGE	D. MAY 26, 1966 LINCOLN, NEB.
81-113 RUNGE, PAUL WILLIAM	646 DELAWARE AVE - KINGSTON NY 12401
85-101 RUNNELLS, THOMAS WILLIAM	2530 NINTH AVENUE COURT - GREELEY CO 80631
51- 82 RUNNELS, JAMES EDWARD 'PETE'	1106 WILMA-LOIS ST - PASADENA TX 77502
25- 91 RUSH, JESS HOWARD 'ANDY'	D. MARCH 16, 1969 FRESNO, CAL.
48- 87 RUSH, ROBERT RANSOM	1358 E 1ST PLACE - MESA AZ 85201
15-141 RUSSELL, ALLAN E.	D. OCTOBER 20, 1972 BALTIMORE, MD.
10-129 RUSSELL, CLARENCE DICKSON 'LEFTY'	D. JANUARY 22, 1962 BALTIMORE, MD.
13-153 RUSSELL, EWELL ALBERT 'REB'	D. SEPTEMBER 30, 1973 INDIANAPOLIS, IND.
39-101 RUSSELL, GLEN DAVID 'RIP'	D. SEPTEMBER 26, 1976 LOS ANGELES CAL.
14-184 RUSSELL, HARVEY HOLMES	D. JANUARY 8, 1980 ALEXANDRIA, VA.
26- 72 RUSSELL, JACK ERWIN	BOX 748 - CLEARWATER FL 33515
42- 88 RUSSELL, JAMES WILLIAM	RR TWO - BELLE VERNON PA 15012
83-125 RUSSELL, JEFFREY LEE	28 BRANDYWINE DR - CINCINNATI OH 45246
17- 73 RUSSELL, JOHN ALBERT	D. NOVEMBER 19, 1930 ELY, NEV.
84-101 RUSSELL, JOHN WILLIAM	412 FOREMAN AVE - NORMAN OK 73069
38- 88 RUSSELL, LOYD OPAL	D. MAY 24, 1968 WACO, TEX.
69-153 RUSSELL, WILLIAM ELLIS	6037 E. 106TH ST - TULSA OK 74137
39-102 RUSSO, MARIUS UGO	27 NORFOLK DR - ELMONT NY 11003
66- 79 RUSTECK, RICHARD FRANK	OLD ADD: 6315 SW PEYTON RD-PORTLAND OR 97219
44-116 RUSZKOWSKI, HENRY ALEXANDER	8815 HARVARD AVE - CLEVELAND OH 44105
14-185 RUTH, GEORGE HERMAN 'BABE'	D. AUGUST 16, 1948 NEW YORK, N.Y.

10-130 RUTHERFORD, JAMES HOLLIS	D. SEPTEMBER 18, 1956 LAKEWOOD, O.
52- 88 RUTHERFORD, JOHN WILLIAM	16100 WOODLAND DR - DEARBORN MI 48120
73-104 RUTHVEN, RICHARD DAVID	39779 BENEVENTE AVE - FREMONT CA 94538
47- 75 RUTNER, MILTON MICKEY	14 SHOTGUN LN - LEVITTOWN NY 11756
82-107 RYAL, MARK DWAYNE	BOX 291 - DEWAR OK 74431
42- 89 RYAN, CORNELIUS JOSEPH 'CONNIE'	626 BEAU CHENE N - MANDERVILLE LA 70448
12-168 RYAN, JOHN BUDD	D. JULY 9, 1956 SACRAMENTO, CALIF.
30- 69 RYAN, JOHN COLLINS 'BLONDY'	D. NOVEMBER 28, 1959 SWAMPSCOTT, MASS.
29- 90 RYAN, JOHN FRANCIS	D. SEPTEMBER 2, 1967 ROCHESTER, MINN.
66- 80 RYAN, LYNN NOLAN	719 DEZZO DR - ALVIN TX 77511
64- 98 RYAN, MICHAEL JAMES	126 NORTH MAIN ST - PLAISTOW NH 03865
19- 71 RYAN, WILFRED PATRICK DOLAN 'ROSY'	D. DECEMBER 10, 1980 PHOENIX, ARIZ.
35- 95 RYBA, DOMINIC JOSEPH 'MIKE'	D. DECEMBER 13, 1971 SPRINGFIELD, MO.
31- 76 RYE, EUGENE RUDOLPH	D. JANUARY 21, 1980 PARK RIDGE, ILL.
72- 94 RYERSON, GARY LAWRENCE	1059 TERRACE CREST - EL CAJON CA 92020

84-102 SABERHAGEN, BRET WILLIAM	19229 ARMINTA ST - RESEDA CA 91335
36- 82 SABO, ALEXANDER	816 ANCHOR DR - FORKED RIVER NJ 08731
51- 83 SACKA, FRANK	968 SYCAMORE ST - WYANDOTTE MI 48192
60- 88 SADECKI, RAYMOND MICHAEL	7710 EVERETT - KANSAS CITY KS 66112
73-105 SADEK, MICHAEL GEORGE	6632 SPRUCE LANE - DUBLIN CA 94568
60- 89 SADOWSKI, EDWARD ROMAN	11181 CLARISSA ST - GARDEN GROVE CA 92640
74-116 SADOWSKI, JAMES MICHAEL	914 HANSEN - PITTSBURGH PA 15209
63-103 SADOWSKI, ROBERT F.	4053 ASHENTREE DR - CHAMBLEE GA 30341
60- 90 SADOWSKI, ROBERT FRANK	1204 KNOLLHAVEN #A - MANCHESTER MO 63011
60- 91 SADOWSKI, THEODORE	196 ALMA ST - PITTSBURGH PA 15223
49- 77 SAFFELL, THOMAS JUDSON	11 SUNSET DR #501 - SARASOTA FL 33577
11-147 SAIER, VICTOR SYLVESTER	D. MAY 14, 1967 EAST LANSING, MICH.
42- 90 SAIN, JOHN FRANKLIN	2 SOUTH 707 AVENUE LATOUR - OAKBROOK IL 60521
51- 84 SAINTCLAIRE, EDWARD JOSEPH 'EBBA'	D. AUGUST 22, 1982 WHITEHALL, N. Y.
84-103 SAINTCLAIRE, RANDY ANTHONY	52 CHAMPLAIN AVE - WHITEHALL NY 12887
77-125 SAKATA, LENN HARUKI	27 ARVERNE CT - TIMONIUM MD 21093
84-104 SALAS, MARK BRUCE	330 BARCA AVE - LAPUENTE CA 91744
83-126 SALAZAR, ARGENIS ANTONIO	RODRIGUEZ DOMINGUES MANZANA G#7-VARINA VENEZ
80-114 SALAZAR, LUIS ERNESTO	PRINC. DE HUACARAPA 34-HUARENAS MIRANDA VENEZ
24- 93 SALE, FREDERICK LINK	D. MAY 27, 1956 HERMOSA BEACH, CAL.
45- 89 SALKELD, WILLIAM FRANKLIN	D. APRIL 22, 1967 LOS ANGELES, CAL.
12-169 SALMON, ROGER ELLIOTT	D. JUNE 17, 1974 BELFAST, ME.
64- 99 SALMON, RUTHERFORD EDUARDO 'CHICO'	OLD ADD: 3422 SYLVANHURST-CLEVELAND OH
32- 72 SALTZGAVER, OTTO HAMLIN 'JACK'	D. FEBRUARY 2, 1978 KEOKUK, IA.
33- 58 SALVESON, JOHN THEODORE	D. DECEMBER 28, 1974 NORWALK, CALIF.
39-103 SALVO, MANUEL	3541 WOODBROOK DR - NAPA CA 94558
76- 85 SAMBITO, JOSEPH CHARLES	9041 BAYWOOD PARK DR - SEMINOLE FL 33543
51- 85 SAMCOFF, EDWARD WILLIAM	8153 MADEIRA PORT LN - FAIR OAKS CA 95628
54- 96 SAMFORD, RONALD EDWARD	1325 W CANTERBURY CT - DALLAS TX 75208
78-116 SAMPLE, WILLIAM AMOS	10 PASCACK RD - WASHINGTON NJ 07675
62-118 SAMUEL, AMADO RUPERTO	1931 YALE DR - LOUISVILLE KY 40205
83-127 SAMUEL, JUAN MILTON	CALLE I #22 RESTAURACION-SAN PEDRO DE MACORIS DOM. REP.
30- 70 SAMUELS, JOSEPH JONES	9 HOWELL - BATH NY 14810
23-115 SANBERG, GUSTAVE E.	D. FEBRUARY 3, 1930 LOS ANGELES, CAL.
82-108 SANCHEZ, ALEJANDRO	BOCA CHICA GATEY GAUTIR-SANTO DOMINGO DOMINICAN REP.
72- 95 SANCHEZ, CELERINO	MUTUALISMO #222-A - CELAYA GUANAJUATO MEX.
81-114 SANCHEZ, LUIS MERCEDES	CALLE SAN FELIPE 11-CARIACO,EST. SUCRE VENEZ
81-115 SANCHEZ, ORLANDO	BOX SAN ISODRO P-52 - CANOVANAS PR 00629
52- 89 SANCHEZ, RAUL GUADALUPE	17821 NW 56TH AVE - CORAL CITY FL 33054
23-116 SAND, JOHN HENRY 'HEINIE'	D. NOVEMBER 3, 1958 SAN FRANCISCO, CAL.
81-116 SANDBERG, RYNE DEE	106 1/2 FIRST ST SW - BREWSTER WA 98812
45- 90 SANDERS, DEE WILMA	1312 COUNTRY CLUB RD - MCALESTER OK 74501
65- 93 SANDERS, JOHN FRANK	6112 SOUTH 25TH ST - LINCOLN NE 68512
64-100 SANDERS, KENNETH GEORGE	12141 PARKVIEW LN - HALES CORNERS WI 53130
42- 91 SANDERS, RAYMOND FLOYD	D. OCTOBER 28, 1983 WASHINGTON, MO.
74-117 SANDERS, REGINALD JEROME	5281 NEWPORT - DETROIT MI 48213
17- 74 SANDERS, ROY GARVIN	D. JANUARY 17, 1950 KANSAS CITY, MO.
18- 64 SANDERS, ROY L.	OLD ADD: 525 S THIRD ST - LOUISVILLE KY 40202
78-117 SANDERSON, SCOTT DOUGLAS	OLD ADD: 1271 WENDY DR - NORTHBROOK IL 60062
42- 92 SANDLOCK, MICHAEL JOSEPH	18 ROCK LAND PL-OLD GREENWICH CT 06870
67- 96 SANDS, CHARLES DUANE	2250 LONI CERA WAY - CHARLOTTESVILLE VA 22906
75-102 SANDT, THOMAS JAMES	9800 BOLSA AVE #8 - WESTMINSTER CA 92683
40- 78 SANFORD, JOHN DOWARD	1001 KINON ST-WILSON NC 27893
43-120 SANFORD, JOHN FREDERICK 'FRED'	1046 WEST 600 NORTH - SALT LAKE CITY UT 84116
56- 74 SANFORD, JOHN STANLEY 'JACK'	2300 PRESIDENTIAL WAY - WEST PALM BEACH FL 33401
67- 97 SANGUILLEN, MANUEL DE JESUS	1200 FEDERAL HWY #204 - BOCA RATON FL 33432
49- 78 SANICKI, EDWARD ROBERT	12 BARTON RD - OLD BRIDGE NJ 08857
29- 91 SANKEY, BENJAMIN TURNER	RR 3 BOX 603B - WASHINGTON GA 30673

```
83-128  SANTANA, RAFAEL FRANCISCO           VILLA PEREYRA CALLE IRA #99 - LAROMANA DOMINICAN REP.
54- 97  SANTIAGO, JOSE GUILLERMO            56-SE-NO. 1167 - RIO PIEDRAS PR 00921
63-104  SANTIAGO, JOSE RAFAEL               YOGRAMO 2-12,ARECIBO HEIGHTS - CAROLINA PR 00630
60- 92  SANTO, RONALD EDWARD                1303 SOMERSET - GLENVIEW IL 60025
79- 98  SANTODOMINGO, RAFAEL                BOX 277 - OROCOVIS PR 00720
68- 91  SANTORINI, ALAN JOEL                RR 2, ARTHUR RD - BELLE MEADE NJ 08502
21- 90  SARGENT, JOSEPH ALEXANDER           D. JULY 5, 1950 ROCHESTER, N. Y.
76- 86  SARMIENTO, MANUEL EDUARDO           AVE DIAZ MORENO #90-13-VALENCIA CARABOBO VENE
51- 86  SARNI, WILLIAM FLORINE              D. APRIL 15, 1983 CREVE COEUR, MO.
61- 94  SATRIANO, THOMAS VICTOR             4816 LOS FELIZ BLVD - LOS ANGELES CA 90027
51- 87  SAUCIER, FRANCIS FIELD              1615 BRYAN PL #9 - AMARILLO TX 79102
78-118  SAUCIER, KEVIN ANDREW               1604 AIRPORT BLVD - PENSACOLA FL 32504
43-121  SAUER, EDWARD                       8625 FENWICK #21 - SUNLAND CA 91040
41- 97  SAUER, HENRY JOHN                   207 VALLEJO CT - MILLBRAE CA 94030
70-118  SAUNDERS, DENNIS JAMES              OLD ADD: 19971 AVE DEL REY-ROWLAND HEIGHTS CA
27- 78  SAUNDERS, RUSSELL COLLIER 'RUSTY'   D. NOVEMBER 24, 1967 DOVER TWP.,OCEAN CO,N.J.
44-117  SAVAGE, DONALD ANTHONY              D. DECEMBER 25, 1961 MONTCLAIR, N. J.
12-170  SAVAGE, JAMES HAROLD                D. JUNE 26, 1940 NEW CASTLE, PA.
42- 93  SAVAGE, JOHN ROBERT 'BOB'           296 HOWARD ST - BERLIN NH 03570
62-119  SAVAGE, THEODORE EPHESIAN           OLD ADD: 3127 CLARENCE AVE - ST.LOUIS MO 63115
59- 70  SAVERINE, ROBERT PAUL               228 SLICE DR - STAMFORD CT 06907
29- 92  SAVIDGE, DONALD SNYDER              OLD ADD: 7979 W NORTON AVE #4 - LOS ANGELES
54- 98  SAVRANSKY, MORRIS 'MOE'             2178 CEDARVIEW DR - CLEVELAND OH 44121
15-142  SAWYER, CARL EVERETT                D. JANUARY 17, 1957 LOS ANGELES, CALIF.
48- 89  SAWYER, EDWIN MILBY                 BOX 296 - VALLEY FORGE PA 19481
74-118  SAWYER, RICHARD CLYDE               3219 KAIBAB - BAKERSFIELD CA 93306
82-109  SAX, DAVID JOHN                     2980 SAGEMILL WAY - SACRAMENTO CA 95833
28- 79  SAX, ERIK OLIVER 'OLLIE'            D. MARCH 21, 1982 NEWARK, N. J.
81-117  SAX, STEPHEN LOUIS                  11 WESTPORT - MANHATTAN BEACH CA 90266
39-104  SAYLES, WILLIAM NISBETH             2830 NE LAKE DR - LINCOLN CITY OR 97367
48- 90  SCALA, GERARD DANIEL                19 BERNADOTTE CT - PERRY HALL MD 21128
39-105  SCALZI, FRANK JOSEPH                D. AUGUST 25, 1984 PITTSBURGH, PA.
31- 77  SCALZI, JOHN ANTHONY                D. SEPTEMBER 27, 1962 PORT CHESTER, N. Y.
74-119  SCANLON, JAMES PATRICK 'PAT'        7400 PORTLAND AVE S - RICHFIELD MN 55423
56- 75  SCANTLEBURY, PATRICIO ATHELSTAN     47 WOODLAND AVE - MONTCLAIR NJ 07042
79- 99  SCARBERY, RANDY JAMES               5010 EAST LEWIS - FRESNO CA 93727
42- 94  SCARBOROUGH, RAY WILSON             D. JULY 1, 1982 MOUNT OLIVE NC
72- 96  SCARCE, GUERRANT MCCURDY 'MAC'      1708 BROADMOOR DR - RICHMOND VA 23221
29- 93  SCARRITT, RUSSELL MALLORY           429 POU STATION RD - PENSACOLA FL 32507
35- 96  SCARSELLA, LESLIE GEORGE            D. DECEMBER 26, 1958 SAN FRANCISCO, CAL.
64-101  SCHAAL, PAUL                        416 N IRONWOOD DR - MESA AZ 85201
19- 72  SCHACHT, ALEXANDER                  D. JULY 14, 1984 WATERBURY, CONN.
50- 87  SCHACHT, SIDNEY                     783 NW 30TH AVE - DELRAY BEACH FL 33445
45- 91  SCHACKER, HAROLD                    4609 NORTH MATANZAS AVE - TAMPA FL 33614
52- 90  SCHAEFFER, HARRY EDWARD             412 WHEATLAND AVE - SHILLINGTON PA 19607
72- 97  SCHAEFFER, MARK PHILIP              18261 PARTHENIA ST - NORTHRIDGE CA 91324
61- 95  SCHAFFER, JIMMIE RONALD             655 BIRCH TER - COOPERSBURG PA 18036
59- 71  SCHAFFERNOTH, JOSEPH ARTHUR         20 MARIAN AVE - BERKLEY HEIGHTS NJ 07922
58- 79  SCHAIVE, JOHN EDWARD                RR 2 BOX 55 - DAWSON IL 62520
32- 73  SCHALK, LEROY JOHN                  OLD ADD: 1840 E. BROADWAY - GAINESVILLE TX
```

12-171 SCHALK, RAYMOND WILLIAM	D. MAY 19, 1970 CHICAGO, ILL.
11-148 SCHALLER, WALTER 'BIFF'	D. OCTOBER 9, 1939 EMERYVILLE, CALIF.
51- 88 SCHALLOCK, ARTHUR LAWRENCE	155 CREST RD - NOVATO CA 94947
14-186 SCHANG, ROBERT MARTIN	D. AUGUST 29, 1966 SACRAMENTO, CALIF.
13-154 SCHANG, WALTER HENRY	2217 MEER WAY - SACRAMENTO CA 95822
44-118 SCHANZ, CHARLEY MURRELL	D. MARCH 6, 1965 ST. LOUIS, MO.
11-149 SCHARDT, WILBURT	D. JULY 20, 1964 VERMILION, O.
32- 74 SCHAREIN, ARTHUR OTTO	D. JULY 3, 1969 SAN ANTONIO, TEX.
37- 92 SCHAREIN, GEORGE ALBERT	D. DECEMBER 22, 1981 DECATUR, ILL.
81-118 SCHATTINGER, JEFFERY CHARLES	1322 W SAN MADELE - FRESNO CA 93711
77-126 SCHATZEDER, DANIEL ERNEST	33 E MADISON ST - VILLA PARK IL 60181
13-155 SCHAUER, ALEXANDER JOHN 'RUBE'	D. APRIL 15, 1957 MINNEAPOLIS, MINN.
13-156 SCHEER, ALLAN G.	D. MAY 6, 1959 LOGANSPORT, IND.
22-119 SCHEER, HENRY 'HEINIE'	D. MARCH 21, 1976 NEW HAVEN, CONN.
14-187 SCHEEREN, FREDERICK 'FRITZ'	D. JUNE 17, 1973 OIL CITY, PA.
43-122 SCHEETZ, OWEN FRANKLIN	275 ROBIN LN - REYNOLDSBURG OH 43068
41- 98 SCHEFFING, ROBERT BODEN	D. OCTOBER 26, 1985 PHOENIX, ARIZ.
12-172 SCHEGG, (GILBERT EUGENE PRICE) 'LEFTY	D. FEBRUARY 27, 1965 NILES, O.
43-123 SCHEIB, CARL ALVIN	2922 OLD RANCH RD - SAN ANTONIO TX 78217
65- 94 SCHEINBLUM, RICHARD ALAN 'RICHIE'	10141 OLD RANCH CIR - VILLA PARK CA 92667
54- 99 SCHELL, CLYDE DANIEL 'DANNY'	D. MAY 11, 1972 MAYVILLE, MICH.
39-106 SCHELLE, GERARD ANTHONY 'JIM'	7501 FAR HILLS DR - BALTIMORE MD 21204
23-117 SCHEMANSKE, FREDERICK GEORGE	D. FEBRUARY 18, 1960 DETROIT, MICH.
45- 92 SCHEMER, MICHAEL "LEFTY"	D. APRIL 22, 1983 MIAMI, FLA.
13-157 SCHENEBERG, JOHN BLUFORD	D. SEPTEMBER 7, 1950 HUNTINGTON, W. VA.
46- 91 SCHENZ, HENRY LEONARD	4055 LANSDOWNE AVE - CINCINNATI OH 45236
19- 73 SCHEPNER, JOSEPH MARTIN	D. JULY 25, 1959 MOBILE, ALA.
50- 88 SCHERBARTH, ROBERT ELMER	4858 N 61ST ST - MILWAUKEE WI 53218
69-154 SCHERMAN, FREDERICK JOHN	11546 STECK RD RT#1 - BROOKVILLE OH 45309
82-110 SCHERRER, WILLIAM JOSEPH	7166 CASCADE ST - SPRING HILL FL 33526
31- 78 SCHESLER, CHARLES 'DUTCH'	D. NOVEMBER 19, 1953 HARRISBURG, PA.
10-131 SCHETTLER, LOUIS MARTIN	D. MAY 1, 1960 YOUNGSTOWN, O.
17- 75 SCHICK, MAURICE FRANCIS	D. OCTOBER 25, 1979 HAZEL CREST, ILL.
61- 96 SCHILLING, CHARLES THOMAS	8 VILLAGE WAY - SMITHTOWN NY 11787
22-120 SCHILLINGS, ELBERT ISAIAH 'RED'	D. JANUARY 7, 1954 OKLAHOMA CITY, OKLA.
20-101 SCHINDLER, WILLIAM GIBBONS	D. FEBRUARY 6, 1979 PERRYVILLE, MO.
84-105 SCHIRALDI, CALVIN DREW	2102 SAN JUAN - AUSTIN TX 78746
14-188 SCHIRICK, HARRY ERNEST 'DUTCH'	D. NOVEMBER 12, 1968 KINGSTON, N.Y.
65- 95 SCHLESINGER, WILLIAM CORDES	5708 ABELIA COURT - CINCINNATI OH 45213
23-118 SCHLIEBNER, FREDERICK PAUL 'DUTCH'	D. APRIL 15, 1975 TOLEDO, O.
71- 91 SCHLUETER, JAYD	5467 E. LUPINE AVE - SCOTTSDALE AZ 85254
38- 89 SCHLUETER, NORMAN JOHN	4205 ATLANTIC #F-4-NEW SMYRNA BEACH FL 32069
15-143 SCHMANDT, RAYMOND HENRY	D. FEBRUARY 1, 1969 ST. LOUIS, MO.
52- 91 SCHMEES, GEORGE EDWARD	2803 MONTE CRESTA WAY - SAN JOSE CA 95132
67- 98 SCHMELZ, ALAN GEORGE	3730 EAST CORTEZ - PHOENIX AZ 85028
81-119 SCHMIDT, DAVID FREDERICK	26636 PORTALES - MISSION VIEJO CA 92675
81-120 SCHMIDT. DAVID JOSEPH	2300 BALSAM DR #G204 - ARLINGTON TX 76006
44-119 SCHMIDT, FREDERICK ALBERT	1940 WINFIELD ST - EMMAUS PA 18049
13-158 SCHMIDT, HERMAN FREDERICK 'PETE'	D. NOVEMBER 11, 1973 PEMBROKE, ONT.
72- 98 SCHMIDT, MICHAEL JACK	24 LAKEWOOD DR - MEDIA PA 19063
58- 80 SCHMIDT, ROBERT BENJAMIN	9 HARDWOOD ST - ST CHARLES MO 63301
16- 73 SCHMIDT, WALTER JOSEPH	D. JULY 4, 1973 CERES, CALIF.
52- 92 SCHMIDT, WILLARD RAYMOND	1242 LOMA DRIVE - NORMAN OK 73069
41- 99 SCHMITZ, JOHN ALBERT	526 E UNION AVE-WAUSAU WI 54401
43-124 SCHMULBACH, HENRY ALRIVES	29 DALE ALLEN DR - BELLEVILLE IL 62223
14-189 SCHMUTZ, CHARLES OTTO	D. JUNE 27, 1962 SEATTLE, WASH.
72- 99 SCHNECK, DAVID LEE	3891 LEHIGH DR - NORTHAMPTON PA 18067
10-132 SCHNEIBERG, FRANK FREDERICK	D. MAY 18, 1948 MILWAUKEE, WIS.
63-105 SCHNEIDER, DANIEL LOUIS	11315 E MICHELLE LN - TUCSON AZ 85715
81-121 SCHNEIDER, JEFFERY THEODORE	2340 41ST - ROCK ISLAND IL 61201
14-190 SCHNEIDER, PETER JOSEPH	D. JUNE 1, 1957 LOS ANGELES, CALIF.
22-121 SCHNELL, KARL OTTO	130 MELVILLE AVE - PALO ALTO CA 94301
68- 92 SCHOEN, GERALD THOMAS	OLD ADD: 8588 DE INDIAN SCHOOL-SCOTTSDALE AZ
45- 93 SCHOENDIENST, ALBERT FRED 'RED'	331 LADUE WOODS CT - CREVE COEUR MO 63141
53- 79 SCHOFIELD, JOHN RICHARD 'DICK'	138 CIRCLE DR - SPRINGFIELD IL 62703
83-129 SCHOFIELD, RICHARD CRAIG	138 CIRCLE DRIVE - SPRINGFIELD IL 62703
55-103 SCHOONMAKER, JERALD LEE	8343 SCHREIDER AVE - MUNSTER IN 46321
15-144 SCHORR, EDWARD WALTER	D. SEPTEMBER 12, 1969 ATLANTIC CITY, N.J.
35- 97 SCHOTT, ARTHUR EUGENE	OLD ADD: 703 WARD CIR - TAMPA FL 33619
53- 80 SCHRAMKA, PAUL EDWARD	4155 NORTH 40TH ST - MILWAUKEE WI 53216
11-150 SCHREIBER, DAVID HENRY 'BARNEY'	D. OCTOBER 6, 1964 CHILLICOTHE, O.
14-191 SCHREIBER, HENRY WALTER	D. FEBRUARY 23, 1968 INDIANAPOLIS, IND.
22-122 SCHREIBER, PAUL FREDERICK	D. JANUARY 28, 1982 SARASOTA, FLA.
63-106 SCHREIBER, THEODORE HENRY	144 JEROME ROAD - STATEN ISLAND NY 10305
65- 96 SCHRODER, ROBERT JAMES	4 DELOND PL - HATTIESBURG MS 39401
83-130 SCHROEDER, ALFRED WILLIAM 'BILL'	116 EXTONVILLE ROAD - TRENTON NJ 08620

JOHN ALBERT SCHMITZ
(JOHNNY)

58- 81	SCHROLL, ALBERT BRINGHURST	3031 ASBER - ALEXANDRIA LA 71301
80-115	SCHROM, KENNETH MARVIN	425 "G" IRONDALE - EL PASO TX 79912
84-106	SCHU, RICHARD SPENCER	4607 CHARLESTON DR - CARMICHAEL CA 95608
27- 79	SCHUBLE, HENRY GEORGE 'HEINIE'	1802 FLORIDA ST - BAYTOWN TX 77520
72-100	SCHUELER, RONALD RICHARD	646 SWEET COURT - LAFAYETTE CA 94549
79-100	SCHULER, DAVID PAUL	OLD ADD: 4575 SUNSTONE RD #119 - MURRAY UT 84107
31- 79	SCHULMERICH, EDWARD WESLEY 'WES'	D. JUNE 26, 1985 CORVALLIS, ORE.
53- 81	SCHULT, ARTHUR WILLIAM	231 EAST LANTANA RD - LANTANA FL 33462
27- 80	SCHULTE, FRED WILLIAM	D. MAY 20, 1983 BELVIDERE, ILL.
40- 79	SCHULTE, HERMAN JOSEPH	1655 S RIVER RD-SAINT CHARLES MO 63301
23-119	SCHULTE, JOHN CLEMENT	D. JUNE 28, 1978 ST. LOUIS, MO.
44-120	SCHULTE, LEONARD WILLIAM	5517 BARTON DRIVE - ORLANDO FL 32807
75-103	SCHULTZ, CHARLES BUDD	4919 E.PARADISE DR - SCOTTSDALE AZ 85254
55-104	SCHULTZ, GEORGE WARREN 'BARNEY'	790 WOODLANE RD - BEVERLY NJ 08010
43-125	SCHULTZ, HOWARD HENRY	741 N LEXINGTON - ST PAUL MN 55104
12-173	SCHULTZ, JOSEPH CHARLES SR	D. APRIL 13, 1941 COLUMBIA, S.C.
39-107	SCHULTZ, JOSEPH CHARLES	838 COALPORT - ST LOUIS MO 63141
51- 89	SCHULTZ, ROBERT DUFFY	D. MARCH 31, 1979 NASHVILLE, TENN.
24- 94	SCHULTZ, WEBB CARL	211 N SECOND ST #4 - DELAVAN WI 53115
47- 76	SCHULTZ, WILLIAM MICHAEL 'MIKE'	502 ROBY AVE - EAST SYRACUSE NY 13057
12-174	SCHULZ, ALBERT CHRISTOPHER	D. DECEMBER 13, 1931 TOLEDO, O.
20-102	SCHULZ, WALTER FREDERICK	D. FEBRUARY 27, 1928 PRESCOTT, ARIZ.
83-131	SCHULZE, DONALD ARTHUR	313 EAST PINE - ROSELLE IL 60172
31- 80	SCHUMACHER, HAROLD HENRY	90 SOUTH MAIN ST - DOLGEVILLE NY 13329
13-159	SCHUPP, FERDINAND MAURICE	D. DECEMBER 16, 1971 LOS ANGELES, CALIF.
64-102	SCHURR, WAYNE ALLEN	RR ONE - HUDSON IN 46747
37- 93	SCHUSTER, WILLIAM CHARLES	12700 ELLIOTT AVE #224 - EL MONTE CA 91732
61- 97	SCHWALL, DONALD BERNARD	2000 LAKE MARSHALL DR - GIBSONIA PA 15044
48- 91	SCHWAMB, RALPH RICHARD 'BLACKIE'	1974 ADD: 1348 PINE AVE - LONG BEACH CA 90813
65- 97	SCHWARTZ, DOUGLAS RANDALL 'RANDY'	757 EL RANCHO DR - EL CAJON CA 92021
14-192	SCHWARZ, WILLIAM DEWITT	D. JUNE 24, 1949 JACKSONVILLE BEACH, FLA.
13-160	SCHWENK, HAROLD EDWARD	D. SEPTEMBER 3, 1955 KANSAS CITY, MO.
14-193	SCHWERT, PIUS LOUIS	D. MARCH 11, 1941 WASHINGTON, D.C.
12-175	SCHWIND, ARTHUR EDWIN	D. JANUARY 13, 1968 SULLIVAN, ILL.
55-105	SCHYPINSKI, GERALD ALBERT	10830 BALFOR AVE - DETROIT MI 48224
80-116	SCIOSCIA, MICHAEL LORRI	810 MANCHESTER COURT - CLAREMONT CA 91711
36- 83	SCOFFIC, LOUIS	600 W 5TH ST-JOHNSTON CITY IL 62951
13-161	SCOGGINS, JAMES LYNN	D. AUGUST 16, 1923 COLUMBIA, S.C.
81-122	SCONIERS, DARYL ANTHONY	16787 MILLER AVE #B2 - FONTANA CA 92335
55-106	SCORE, HERBERT JUDE	RADIO STATION WWWE - CLEVELAND OH 44101
73-106	SCOTT, ANTHONY	1526 DIXMONT AVE - CINCINNATI OH 45207
83-132	SCOTT, DONALD MALCOLM	OLD ADD: 705 W. HENRY - TAMPA FL 33604
26- 73	SCOTT, FLOYD JOHN 'PETE'	D. MAY 3, 1953 DALY CITY, CAL.
66- 81	SCOTT, GEORGE	1316 GOODRICH ST - GREENVILLE MS 38701
20-103	SCOTT, GEORGE WILLIAM	OLD ADD: CORSICANA TX 75110
14-194	SCOTT, JAMES WALTER	D. MAY 12, 1972 SOUTH PASADENA, FLA.
74-120	SCOTT, JOHN HENRY	1766 E 111TH PLACE - LOS ANGELES CA 90059
16- 74	SCOTT, JOHN WILLIAM	D. NOVEMBER 30 1959 DURHAM, N. C.
39-108	SCOTT, LEGRANT EDWARD	RR 1 BOX 2168 - SHELBY AL 35143
14-195	SCOTT, LEWIS EVERETT	D. NOVEMBER 2, 1960 FORT WAYNE, IND.
45- 94	SCOTT, MARSHALL 'LEFTY'	D. MARCH 3, 1964 HOUSTON, TEX.
79-101	SCOTT, MICHAEL WARREN	5417 WEST 134TH PLACE - HAWTHORNE CA 90250
72-101	SCOTT, RALPH ROBERT 'MICKEY'	1134 VESTAL AVE - BINGHAMTON NY 13903
63-107	SCOTT, RICHARD LEWIS	124 SHORTLEAF PL - THOMASVILLE GA 31792
75-104	SCOTT, RODNEY DARRELL	4206 PRISCILLA - INDIANAPOLIS IN 46226
84-107	SCRANTON, JAMES DEAN	27500 HAMMACK AVE - PERRIS CA 92370
75-105	SCRIVENER, WAYNE ALLISON	3012 WOODHOME AVE - BALTIMORE MD 21234
80-117	SCURRY, RODNEY GRANT	11 EAST "L" ST - SPARKS NV 89431
64-103	SEALE, JOHNNIE RAY	1941 COUNTY RD 207 - DURANGO CO 81301
79-102	SEAMAN, KIM MICHAEL	4212 KREOLE AVE - MOSS POINT MS 39563
81-123	SEARAGE, RAYMOND MARK	4114 NORTH CASS AVE - WESTMONT IL 60559
43-126	SEARS, KENNETH EUGENE	D. JULY 17, 1968 BRIDGEPORT, TEX.
12-176	SEATON, THOMAS GORDON	D. APRIL 10, 1940 ELPASO, TEX.
40- 80	SEATS, THOMAS EDWARD	2655 45TH AVE-SAN FRANCISCO CA 94116
67- 99	SEAVER, GEORGE THOMAS 'TOM'	LARKSPUR LN - GREENWICH CT 06830
85-102	SEBRA, ROBERT BUSH	60 MANHASSET TRAIL - MEDFORD LAKES CA 90805
40- 81	SECORY, FRANK EDWARD	3026 MILITARY ST - PORT HURON MI 48060
69-155	SECRIST, DONALD LAVERN	104 N LEONARD - DUQUOIN IL 62832
21- 91	SEDGEWICK, HENRY KENNETH 'DUKE'	D. DECEMBER 4, 1982 CLEARWATER, FLA.
19- 74	SEE, CHARLES HENRY	D. JULY 19, 1948 BRIDGEPORT, CONN.
30- 71	SEEDS, ROBERT IRA	STAR RT BOX 152-A - GRAFORD TX 76045
71- 92	SEELBACH, CHARLES FREDERICK	20715 BEACHCLIFF BLVD - ROCKY RIVER OH 44116
43-127	SEEREY, JAMES PATRICK 'PAT'	9256 LEAMONT - ST LOUIS MO 63136

82-111 SEGELKE, HERMAN NEILS
52- 93 SEGRIST, KAL HILL
62-120 SEGUI, DIEGO PABLO
79-103 SEIBERT, KURT ELLIOTT
15-145 SEIBOLD, HARRY 'SOCKS'
80-118 SEILHEIMER, RICKY ALLEN
34- 90 SELKIRK, GEORGE ALEXANDER
22-123 SELL, ELWOOD LESTER 'EPP'
85-103 SELLERS, JEFFREY DOYLE
10-133 SELLERS, OLIVER 'RUBE'
72-102 SELLS, DAVID WAYNE
65- 98 SELMA, RICHARD JAY
29- 94 SELPH, CAREY ISOM
77-128 SEMBER, MICHAEL DAVID
65- 99 SEMBERA, CARROLL WILLIAM
43-128 SEMINICK, ANDREW WASIL
58- 82 SEMPROCH, ROMAN ANTHONY 'RAY'
52- 94 SENERCHIA, EMANUEL ROBERT 'SONNY'
82-112 SENTENEY, STEVE LEONARD
77-127 SEOANE, MANUEL MODESTO
42- 95 SEPKOWSKI, THEODORE WALTER
49- 79 SERENA, WILLIAM ROBERT
81-124 SERNA, PAUL DAVID
77-129 SERUM, GARY WAYNE
41-100 SESSI, WALTER ANTHONY
28- 80 SETTLEMIRE, EDGAR MERLE
65-100 SEVCIK, JOHN JOSEPH
11-151 SEVERAID, HENRY LEVAI
69-156 SEVERINSEN, ALBERT HENRY
70-119 SEVERSON, RICHARD ALLEN
43-129 SEWARD, FRANK MARTIN
21- 92 SEWELL, JAMES LUTHER 'LUKE'
20-104 SEWELL, JOSEPH WHEELER
27- 81 SEWELL, THOMAS KEVIN
32- 75 SEWELL, TRUETT BANKS 'RIP'
48- 92 SEXAUER, ELMER GEORGE
77-130 SEXTON, JIMMY DALE
63-108 SEYFRIED, GORDON CLAY
14-196 SHAFER, RALPH NEWTON
65-101 SHAMSKY, ARTHUR LOUIS
73-107 SHANAHAN, PAUL GREGORY 'GREG'
23-120 SHANER, WALTER DEDAKER
70-129 SHANK, HARVEY TILLMAN
70-120 SHANK, HARVEY TILLMAN
12-177 SHANKS, HOWARD SAMUEL
12-178 SHANLEY, HENRY ROOT 'DOC'
20-105 SHANNER, WILFRED WILLIAM
15-146 SHANNON, JOSEPH ALOYSIUS
15-147 SHANNON, MAURICE JOSEPH 'RED'
62-121 SHANNON, THOMAS MICHAEL 'MIKE'
59- 72 SHANNON, WALTER CHARLES
49- 80 SHANTZ, ROBERT CLAYTON
54-100 SHANTZ, WILMER EBERT 'BILLY'
17- 76 SHARMAN, RALPH EDWARD
73-108 SHARON, RICHARD LOUIS
73-109 SHARP, WILLIAM HOWARD
22-124 SHAUTE, JOSEPH BENJAMIN
17- 77 SHAW, BENJAMIN NATHANIEL
67-100 SHAW, DONALD WELLINGTON
13-162 SHAW, JAMES ALOYSIUS
57- 77 SHAW, ROBERT JOHN

384 HEATHER WAY - SOUTH SAN FRANCISCO CA 94080
3813 55TH ST - LUBBOCK TX 79413
OLD ADD: 10422 PARALLEL ST - KANSAS CITY KS
2608 BOEING DR - MIDLAND TX 79701
D. SEPTEMBER 21, 1965 PHILADELPHIA, PA.
2400 STONEHOLLOW #510 - BRENHAM TX 77833
405 N OCEAN BLVD - POMPANO BEACH FL 33062
D. FEBRUARY 20, 1961 READING, PA.
1506 E. POINSETTIA ST - LONG BEACH CA 90805
D. JANUARY 14, 1952 PITTSBURGH, PA.
3233 EAST GREENLEAF - BREA CA 92621
1493 N. DELMAR AVE - FRESNO CA 93728
D. FEBRUARY 24, 1976 HOUSTON, TEX.
6N041 LINDEN AVE - MEDINAH IL 60157
BOX 1103 - SHINER TX 77984
1920 S PARK AVE - MELBOURNE FL 32901
4220 BUECHNER AVE - CLEVELAND OH 44109
805 SHORE RD - SPRING LAKE HEIGHTS NJ 07762
7001 ROLLINGWOOD BLVD-CITRUS HEIGHTS CA 95610
4703 N ROME AVE - TAMPA FL 33603
128 INVERNESS RD - SEVERNA PARK MD 21146
26777 CALAROGA AVE - HAYWARD CA 94541
777 PICO #24 - EL CENTRO CA 92243
3912 VINCENT AVE SOUTH - MINNEAPOLIS MN 55410
351 WEST ST - MOBILE AL 36604
603 IROQUOIS - BELLEFONTAINE OH 43311
5321 GOLDEN VLY RD - GOLDEN VALLEY MN 55422
D. DECEMBER 17, 1968 SAN ANTONIO, TEX.
1032 ARCHER PL - BALDWIN NY 11510
15218 LINCOLN CIR - OMAHA NE 68131
117 LARCHMONT RD - ELMIRA NY 14905
722 SUNNYSIDE AV - AKRON OH 44303
1618 DEARING PL - TUSCALOOSA AL 35401
D. JULY 30, 1956 MONTGOMERY, ALA.
827 RUSSELL DR - PLANT CITY FL 33566
1005 RICHWOOD DR - DANVILLE IN 46122
RR 2 BOX 187-B - WILMER AL 36587
832 STANLEY AVE - LONG BEACH CA 90804
D. FEBRUARY 5, 1950 AKRON, O.
OLD ADD: 315 E. 69TH ST - NEW YORK NY 10021
240 W HAWTHORNE ST - EUREKA CA 95501
370 E. WINDMILL - LAS VEGAS NV 89123
10001 NORTH 7TH ST #118 - PHOENIX AZ 85012
5458 EAST OAKHURST WAY - SCOTTSDALE AZ 85254
D. JULY 30, 1941 MONACA, PA.
D. DECEMBER 14, 1934 ST. PETERSBURG, FLA.
4316 PENNINGTON AVE - EVANSVILLE IN 47712
D. JULY 28, 1955 JERSEY CITY, N.J.
D. APRIL 12, 1970 JERSEY CITY, N.J.
1 MEMORIAL DRIVE - ST. LOUIS MO 63102
416 TWIN CREEK RD - CREVE COEUR MO 63141
152 MOUNT PLEASANT AVE - AMBLER PA 19002
3430 NW 40TH CT - FT LAUDERDALE FL 33309
D. MAY 24, 1918 CAMP SHERIDAN, ALA.
P.O. BOX 709 - DILLON MT 59725
6147 NORTH SHERIDAN RD - CHICAGO IL 60660
D. FEBRUARY 21, 1970 SCRANTON, PA.
D. MARCH 16, 1959 AURORA, O.
12228 POGGEMOELLER - ST. LOUIS MO 63138
D. JANUARY 27, 1962 WASHINGTON, D.C.
31 SADDLE BACK RD - JUPITER FL 33458

13-163 SHAWKEY, JAMES ROBERT
16- 75 SHAY, ARTHUR JOSEPH 'MARTY'
47- 77 SHEA, FRANCIS JOSEPH 'SPEC'
28- 81 SHEA, JOHN MICHAEL JOSEPH
27- 82 SHEA, MERVYN DAVID JOHN
18- 65 SHEA, PATRICK HENRY
68- 93 SHEA, STEVEN FRANCIS
28- 82 SHEALY, ALBERT BERLEY
57- 78 SHEARER, RAY SOLOMON
12-179 SHEARS, GEORGE PENFIELD
36- 84 SHEEHAN, JAMES THOMAS
20-106 SHEEHAN, JOHN THOMAS

D. DECEMBER 31, 1980 SYRACUSE, N. Y.
D. FEBRUARY 20, 1971 WORCESTER, MASS.
72 JOHNSON - NAUGATUCK CT 06770
D. NOVEMBER 30, 1956 MALDEN, MASS.
D. JANUARY 27, 1953 SACRAMENTO, CAL.
D. NOVEMBER 17, 1981 STAFFORD, CONN.
OLD ADD: RR 1, JUNIPER DR - AMHERST NH
D. MARCH 7, 1967 HAGERSTOWN, MD.
D. FEBRUARY 21, 1982 YORK, PA.
D. NOVEMBER 12, 1978 LOVELAND, COLO.
107 ROBERT DR - EAST HAVEN CT 06512
360 PALMETTO ST - WEST PALM BEACH FL 33405

15-148	SHEEHAN, THOMAS CLANCY	D. OCTOBER 29, 1982 CHILLICOTHE, O.
21- 93	SHEELY, EARL HOMER	D. SEPTEMBER 16, 1952 SEATTLE, WASH.
51- 90	SHEELY, HOLLIS KIMBALL 'BUD'	D. OCTOBER 17, 1985 SACRAMENTO, CALIF.
36- 85	SHEERIN, CHARLES JOSEPH	158 FAIRFIELD ST - VALLEY STREAM NY 11581
84-108	SHEETS, LARRY KENT	BOX 277 - POCONOKE MD 21851
81-125	SHELBY, JOHN T	711 HEADLEY AVE - LEXINGTON KY 40508
74-121	SHELDON, BOB MITCHELL	BOX 4993 - CANYON LAKE CA 92380
61- 98	SHELDON, ROLAND FRANK	614 NE CORONADO - LEES SUMMIT MO 64063
18- 66	SHELLENBACK, FRANK VICTOR	D. AUGUST 17, 1969 NEWTON, MASS.
66- 82	SHELLENBACK, JAMES PHILIP	BOX 614 - BAKER OR 97814
35- 98	SHELLEY, HUBERT LENEIRRE 'HUGH'	D. JUNE 16, 1978 BEAUMONT, TEX.
15-149	SHELTON, ANDREW KEMPER 'SKEETER'	D. JANUARY 9, 1954 HUNTINGTON, W. VA.
44-121	SHEMO, STEPHEN MICHAEL 'STAN'	RR 1 BOX 290A - MADISON NC 27025
53- 82	SHEPARD, JACK LEROY	2450 EL CAMINO RD #108 - PALO ALTO CA 94306
68- 94	SHEPARD, LAWRENCE WILLIAM	1716 PINEDALE - LINCOLN NE 68520
45- 95	SHEPARD, ROBERT EARL 'BERT'	8014 BANGOR AVE - HESPERIA CA 92345
24- 95	SHEPHARDSON, RAYMOND FRANCIS	D. NOVEMBER 8, 1975 LITTLE FALLS, N. Y.
84-109	SHEPHERD, RONALD WAYNE	RR 2 BOX 53X - KILGORE TX 75662
18- 67	SHERDEL, WILLIAM HENRY	D. NOVEMBER 14, 1968 MCSHERRYSTOWN, PA.
29- 95	SHERID, ROYDEN RICHARD	D. FEBRUARY 28, 1982 PARKER FORD, PA.
18- 68	SHERIDAN, EUGENE ANTHONY 'RED'	D. NOVEMBER 25, 1975 QUEENS VILLAGE, N. Y.
48- 93	SHERIDAN, NEILL RAWLINS	150 CHAUCER DR - PLEASANT HILL CA 94523
81-126	SHERIDAN, PATRICK ARTHUR	31654 TAFT - WAYNE MI 48184
24- 96	SHERLING, EDWARD CREECH	D. NOVEMBER 16, 1965 ENTERPRISE, ALA.
30- 72	SHERLOCK, JOHN CLINTON 'MONK'	D. NOVEMBER 26, 1985 BUFFALO, N. Y.
35- 99	SHERLOCK, VINCENT THOMAS	237 SUMMIT AVE-BUFFALO NY 14214
14-197	SHERMAN, DANIEL L. 'BABE'	OLD ADD: 1146 LEEDS ST - UTICA NY 13501
15-150	SHERMAN, JOEL POWERS	5318 MALALUKA CT - CAPE CORAL FL 33904
78-119	SHERRILL, DENNIS LEE	OLD ADD: 240 SW 63RD CT - MIAMI FL 33144
11-152	SHERRY, FRED PETER	D. JULY 27, 1975 HONESDALE, PA.
58- 83	SHERRY, LAWRENCE	27181 ARENA LN - MISSION VIEJO CA 92675
59- 73	SHERRY, NORMAN BURT	10767 S. D. MISSION RD #313 - SAN DIEGO CA 92108
59- 74	SHETRONE, BARRY STEVAN	6353 COLBY WAY - VIRGINIA BEACH VA 23464
30- 73	SHEVLIN, JAMES CORNELIUS	D. OCTOBER 30, 1974 FORT LAUDERDALE, FLA.
24- 97	SHIELDS, BENJAMIN COWAN	D. JANUARY 24, 1982 WOODRUFF, S. C.
15-151	SHIELDS, FRANCIS LEROY 'PETE'	D. FEBRUARY 11, 1961 JACKSON, MISS.
85-104	SHIELDS, STEPHEN MACK	LYNDA AVE, RR 11 - GADSDEN AL 35903
24- 98	SHIELDS, VINCENT WILLIAM	D. NOVEMBER 24, 1952 PLASTER ROCK, NEB.
57- 79	SHIFFLETT, GARLAND JESSIE	1095 CODY - LAKEWOOD CO 80215
39-109	SHILLING, JAMES ROBERT	OLD ADD: 1849 N INDIANAPOLIS - TULSA OK
21- 94	SHINAULT, ENOCH ERSKINE 'GINGER'	D. DECEMBER 29, 1930 DENVER, COLO.
83-133	SHINES, ANTHONY RAYMOND 'RAZOR'	OLD ADD: 1129 MERRICK #16 - DURHAM NC 27707
22-125	SHINNERS, RALPH PETER	D. JULY 23, 1962 MILWAUKEE, WIS.
85-105	SHIPANOFF, DAVID NOEL	3 SALINA DRIVE - SAINT ALBERT, ALBERTA CAN.
58- 84	SHIPLEY, JOSEPH CLARK	OLD ADD: 29 HONEY LOCUST #7 - ST CHARLES MO
28- 83	SHIRES, CHARLES ARTHUR 'ART'	D. JULY 13, 1967 ITALY, TEX.
20-107	SHIREY, CLAIR LEE 'DUKE'	D. SEPTEMBER 1, 1962 HAGERSTOWN, MD.
41-101	SHIRLEY, ALVIS NEWMAN 'TEX'	314 LAWRENCE ROAD - RED OAK TX 75154
64-104	SHIRLEY, BARTON ARVIN	4602D CEDAR PASS - CORPUS CHRISTI TX 78413
24- 99	SHIRLEY, ERNEST RAEFORD 'MULE'	D. AUGUST 3, 1955 GOLDSBORO, N. C.
77-131	SHIRLEY, ROBERT CHARLES	3838 CAMINO DEL RIO N #252-SAN DIEGO CA 92108
82-113	SHIRLEY, STEVEN BRIAN	9200 JAMES PLACE NE - ALBUQUERQUE NM 87111
31- 81	SHIVER, IVEY MERWIN	D. AUGUST 31, 1972 SAVANNAH, GA.
16- 76	SHOCKER, URBAN JAMES	D. SEPTEMBER 9, 1928 DENVER, COLO.
64-105	SHOCKLEY, JOHN COSTEN	405 WALTER ST - GEORGETOWN DE 19947
61- 99	SHOEMAKER, CHARLES LANDIS	2310 FAIRVIEW AVE - MOUNT PENN PA 19606
29- 96	SHOFFNER, MILBURN JAMES 'MILT'	D. JANUARY 19, 1978 MADISON, O.
47- 78	SHOFNER, FRANK STRICKLAND 'STRICK'	620 HEWITT DT #34 - HEWITT TX 76643
41-102	SHOKES, EDWARD CHRISTOPHER	381 MILLWOOD AVE-WINCHESTER VA 22601
16- 77	SHOOK, RAYMAND CURTIS	D. SEPTEMBER 16, 1970 SOUTH BEND, IND.
59- 75	SHOOP, RONALD LEE	BOX 92 - RURAL VALLEY PA 16249
67-101	SHOPAY, THOMAS MICHAEL	17923 SW 77TH CT - MIAMI FL 33157
12-180	SHORE, ERNEST GRADY	D. SEPTEMBER 24, 1980 WINSTON-SALEM, N.C.
46- 92	SHORE, RAYMOND EVERETT	675 SILVER LEDGE LN - CINCINNATI OH 45231
28- 84	SHORES, WILLIAM DAVID	D. FEBRUARY 19, 1984 PURCELL, OKLA.
59- 76	SHORT, CHRISTOPHER JOSEPH	1609 BARNABY ST - NEWARK DE 19702
40- 82	SHORT, DAVID ORVIS	D. NOVEMBER 22, 1983 SHREVEPORT, LA.
60- 93	SHORT, WILLIAM ROSS	2975 57TH ST - SARASOTA FL 33580
15-152	SHORTEN, CHARLES HENRY 'CHICK'	D. OCTOBER 23, 1965 SCRANTON, PA.
35-100	SHOUN, CLYDE MITCHELL	D. MARCH 20, 1968 MOUNTAIN HOME, TENN.
11-153	SHOVLIN, JOHN JOSEPH	D. FEBRUARY 16, 1976 BETHESDA, MD.
81-127	SHOW, ERIC VAUGHN	11777 PETIRROJO CT - SAN DIEGO CA 92124
22-126	SHRIVER, HARRY GRAYDON	D. JANUARY 21, 1970 MORGANTOWN, W. VA.

BOB SHIRLEY

48- 94 SHUBA, GEORGE THOMAS	3421 BENT WILLOW LN - YOUNGSTOWN OH 44511
11-154 SHULTZ, WALLACE LUTHER 'TOOTS'	D. JANUARY 30, 1959 MCKEESPORT, PA.
42- 96 SHUMAN, HARRY	7402 MALVERN AVE - PHILADELPHIA PA 19151
45- 96 SHUPE, VINCENT WILLIAM	D. APRIL 5, 1962 CANTON, O.
16- 78 SICKING, EDWARD JOSEPH	D. AUGUST 30, 1978 CINCINNATI, O.
56- 76 SIEBERN, NORMAN LEROY	4951 N. TAMIAMI TR #6 - NAPLES FL 33940
74-122 SIEBERT, PAUL EDWARD	4804 WEST 70TH ST - EDINA MN 55135
32- 76 SIEBERT, RICHARD WALTHER	D. DECEMBER 9, 1978 MINNEAPOLIS, MINN.
64-106 SIEBERT, WILFRED CHARLES 'SONNY'	2583 BRUSH CREEK - ST LOUIS MO 63129
63-109 SIEBLER, DWIGHT LEROY	231 SOUTH WESGAYE - GRETNA NE 68028
25- 92 SIEMER, OSCAR SYLVESTER	D. DECEMBER 5, 1959 ST. LOUIS, MO.
49- 81 SIEVERS, ROY EDWARD	11505 BELLEFONTAINE RD-SPANISH LAKE MO 63138
26- 74 SIGAFOOS, FRANCIS LEONARD	D. APRIL 12, 1968 INDIANAPOLIS, IND.
14-198 SIGLIN, WESLEY PETER 'PADDY'	D. AUGUST 5, 1956 OAKLAND, CALIF.
29- 97 SIGMAN, WESLEY TRIPLETT 'TRIPP'	D. MARCH 8, 1971 AUGUSTA, GA.
43-130 SIGNER, WALTER DONALD ALOYSIUS	D. JULY 23, 1974 GREENWICH, CONN.
37- 94 SILBER, EDWARD JAMES	D. OCTOBER 26, 1976 DUNEDIN, FLA.
19- 75 SILVA, DANIEL JAMES	D. APRIL 4, 1974 HYANNIS, MASS.
55-107 SILVERA, AARON ALBERT 'AL'	723 N SIERRA DR - BEVERLY HILLS CA 90210
48- 95 SILVERA, CHARLES ANTHONY RYAN	1240 MANZANITA DR - MILLBRAE CA 94030
78-120 SILVERIO, LUIS PASCUAL	CLE NUMA SILVERIO#7 VIL GONZALEZ-STO DOMINGO DOM. REP.
70-121 SILVERIO, TOMAS ROBERTO	CALLE 9#14 COLINAS - SANTO DOMINGO DOMINICAN REP.
39-110 SILVESTRI, KENNETH JOSEPH	3328 W LAKE SHORE DR - TALLAHASEE FL 32303
50- 89 SIMA, ALBERT	813 CENTER ST - BRANDON FL 33511
24-100 SIMMONS, ALOYSIUS HARRY	D. MAY 26, 1956 MILWAUKEE, WIS.
47- 79 SIMMONS, CURTIS THOMAS	200 PARK RD - PROSPECTVILLE PA 19002
10-134 SIMMONS, GEORGE WASHINGTON 'HACK'	D. APRIL 26, 1942 ARVERNE, N.Y.
49- 82 SIMMONS, JOHN EARL	9 LEE DR - FARMINGDALE NY 11735
84-110 SIMMONS, NELSON BERNARD	209 CEDARIDGE DR - SAN DIEGO CA 92114
28- 85 SIMMONS, PATRICK CLEMENT	D. JULY 3, 1968 ALBANY, N. Y.
68- 95 SIMMONS, TED LYLE	BOX 26 - CHESTERFIELD MO 63017
23-121 SIMON, SYLVESTER ADAM	D. FEBRUARY 28, 1973 CHANDLER, IND.
31- 82 SIMONS, MELBERN ELLIS	D. OCTOBER 11, 1974 PADUCAH, KY.
51- 91 SIMPSON, HARRY LEON	D. APRIL 3, 1979 AKRON, O.
75-106 SIMPSON, JOE ALLEN	OLD ADD: 1311 DORCHESTER - NORMAN OK 73069
62-122 SIMPSON, RICHARD CHARLES	696 SAN JUAN AVE - VENICE CA 90291
72-103 SIMPSON, STEVEN EDWARD	5031 SW 26TH TER - TOPEKA KS 66614
53- 83 SIMPSON, THOMAS LEO	22640 JAMESON DR - WOODLAND HILLS CA 91364
70-122 SIMPSON, WAYNE KIRBY	330 COLLAMER DR - CARSON CA 90744
15-153 SIMS, CLARENCE 'PETE'	D. DECEMBER 2, 1968 DALLAS, TEX.
64-107 SIMS, DUANE B. 'DUKE'	101 ROSEWOOD AVE - POCATELLO ID 83201
66- 83 SIMS, GREGORY EMMETT	4540 11TH AVE - SACRAMENTO CA 95820
81-128 SINATRO, MATTHEW STEPHEN	68 MONTRE SQUARE NW - ATLANTA GA 30327
64-108 SINGER, WILLIAM ROBERT	1410 WEST BAY AVE - NEWPORT BEACH CA 92663
45- 97 SINGLETON, BERT ELMER	2489 NORTH 4425 WEST - OGDEN UT 84404
22-127 SINGLETON, JOHN EDWARD	D. OCTOBER 23, 1937 DAYTON, O.
70-123 SINGLETON, KENNETH WAYNE	5 TREMBLANT CT - LUTHERVILLE MD 21093
34- 91 SINGTON, FREDERIC WILLIAM	2017 5TH AVE N - BIRMINGHAM AL 35203
45- 98 SIPEK, RICHARD FRANCIS	1611 JACKSON ST - QUINCY IL 62301
69-157 SIPIN, JOHN WHITE	328 HERMAN AVE - WATSONVILLE CA 95076
82-114 SISK, DOUGLAS RANDALL	1408 BENCH DR NE - TACOMA WA 98422
62-123 SISK, TOMMIE WAYNE	3292 MOHAWK CIR - PROVO UT 84601
56- 77 SISLER, DAVID MICHAEL	11 HACIENDA DR - ST LOUIS MO 63124
15-154 SISLER, GEORGE HAROLD	D. MARCH 26, 1973 ST. LOUIS, MO.
46- 93 SISLER, RICHARD ALLEN	2315 ABBOTT MARTIN RD - NASHVILLE TN 37212
39-111 SISTI, SEBASTIAN DANIEL 'SIBBY'	39 CLIFFORD HEIGHTS - AMHERST NY 14226
36- 86 SIVESS, PETER	RR 1 BOX 555 - ST. MICHAELS MD 21663
82-115 SIWY, JAMES GERARD	103 DARLING ST - CENTRAL FALLS RI 02863
69-158 SIZEMORE, TED CRAWFORD	OLD ADD: 1059 FRUIT TREE LN - CREVE COEUR MO 63141
35-101 SKAFF, FRANCIS MICHAEL	2449 SPRINGLAKE DR - TIMONIUM MD 21093
77-132 SKAGGS, DAVID LINDSEY	911 DAUGHERTY RD - NORCO CA 91760
57- 80 SKAUGSTAD, DAVID WENDALL	1113 N. MAR-LES DR - SANTA ANA CA 92706
10-135 SKEELS, DAVID	D. DECEMBER 2, 1926 SPOKANE, WASH.
42- 97 SKETCHLEY, HARRY CLEMENT 'BUD'	D. DECEMBER 19, 1979 LOS ANGELES, CALIF.
70-124 SKIDMORE, ROBERT ROE	815 S STONE - DECATUR IL 62521
21- 95 SKIFF, WILLIAM FRANKLIN	D. DECEMBER 25, 1976 BRONXVILLE, N. Y.
22-128 SKINNER, ELISHA HARRISON 'CAMP'	D. AUGUST 4, 1944 DOUGLASVILLE, GA.
83-134 SKINNER, JOEL PATRICK	1576 DIAMOND ST - SAN DIEGO CA 92109
54-101 SKINNER, ROBERT RALPH	1576 DIAMOND ST - SAN DIEGO CA 92109
56- 78 SKIZAS, LOUIS PETER	2101 W WHITE - CHAMPAIGN IL 61821
73-110 SKOK, CRAIG RICHARD	1906 TREE CORNERS PKWY - NORCROS GA 30092
54-102 SKOWRON, WILLIAM JOSEPH 'MOOSE'	1118 BEACHCOMBER DR - SCHAUMBURG IL 60193
82-116 SKUBE, ROBERT JACOB	3569 GREENVILLE DR - SIMI VALLEY CA 93063

TED SIZEMORE

DAVE SKAGGS

30- 74	SLADE, GORDON LEIGH	D. JANUARY 2, 1974 LONG BEACH, CALIF.
79-104	SLAGLE, ROGER LEE	536 W THIRD ST - LARNED KS 67550
10-136	SLAGLE, WALTER JENNINGS	D. JUNE 17, 1974 SAN GABRIEL, CALIF.
11-155	SLAPNICKA, CYRIL CHARLES	D. OCTOBER 20, 1979 CEDAR RAPIDS, IA.
20-108	SLAPPEY, JOHN HENRY	D. JUNE 10, 1957 MARIETTA, GA.
71- 93	SLATON, JAMES MICHAEL	43515 28TH ST W - LANCASTER CA 93534
15-155	SLATTERY, PHILIP RYAN	D. MARCH 2, 1968 LONG BEACH, CAL9F.
82-117	SLAUGHT, DONALD MARTIN	5420 MEADOWDALE LN - RANCHO PALOS VD CA 90274
10-137	SLAUGHTER, BYRON ATKINS 'BARNEY'	D. MAY 17, 1961 PHILADELPHIA PA.
38- 90	SLAUGHTER, ENOS BRADSHER	RR 2-ROXBORO NC 27573
64-109	SLAUGHTER, STERLING FEORE	2530 S. EVERGREEN RD - TEMPE AZ 85282
26- 75	SLAYBACK, ELBERT 'SCOTTIE'	D. NOVEMBER 30, 1979 CINCINNATI, O.
72-104	SLAYBACK, WILLIAM GROVER	4918 CECILVILLE - LACRESCENTA CA 91214
28- 86	SLAYTON, FOSTER HERBERT 'STEVE'	D. DECEMBER 20, 1984 MANCHESTER, N. H.
50- 90	SLEATER, LOUIS MORTIMER	515 BROOK RD - TOWSON MD 21204
44-122	SLOAN, BRUCE ADAMS	D. SEPTEMBER 24, 1973 OKLAHOMA CITY, OKLA.
13-164	SLOAN, YALE YEASTMAN 'TOD'	D. SEPTEMBER 12, 1956 AKRON, O.
48- 96	SLOAT, DWAIN CLIFFORD	2101 E 5TH ST - ST PAUL MN 55119
69-159	SLOCUM, RONALD REECE	OLD ADD: 5715 BALTIMORE DR #82 - LAMESA CA 92041
30- 75	SMALL, CHARLES ALBERT	D. JANUARY 14, 1953 LEWISTON, ME.
78-121	SMALL, GEORGE HENRY 'HANK'	P.O. BOX 763 - MOUNT PLEASANT SC 29464
55-108	SMALL, JAMES ARTHUR	RR 1 - STANWOOD MI 49346
48- 97	SMALLEY, ROY FREDERICK JR	534 W ARBOR VITAE - INGLEWOOD CA 90301
75-107	SMALLEY, ROY FREDERICK III	6414 GLEASON COURT - EDINA MN 55436
17- 78	SMALLWOOD, WALTER CLAYTON	D. APRIL 29, 1967
46- 94	SMAZA, JOSEPH PAUL	D. MAY 30, 1979 ROYAL OAK, MICH.
34- 92	SMITH, ALFRED JOHN	D. APRIL 28, 1977 BROWNSVILLE, TEX.
26- 76	SMITH, ALFRED KENDRICKS	23928 GREEN HAVEN - RAMONA CA 92065
53- 84	SMITH, ALPHONSE EUGENE	8440 INDIANA 3RD FLOOR - CHICAGO IL 60619
12-182	SMITH, ARMSTRONG FREDERICK 'KLONDIKE'	D. NOVEMBER 15, 1959 SPRINGFIELD, MASS.
32- 77	SMITH, ARTHUR LAIRD	73 OENOKE RIDGE #307 - NEW CANAAN CT 06840
75-108	SMITH, BILLY EDWARD	5439 TIMBER POST - SAN ANTONIO TX 78250
81-129	SMITH, BILLY LAVERN	8407 NEFF - HOUSTON TX 77036
57- 81	SMITH, BOBBY GENE	3009 NORTH 22ND - TACOMA WA 98406
81-130	SMITH, BRYN NELSON	812 E FELSER - SANTA MARIA CA 93454
70-125	SMITH, CALVIN BERNARD 'BERNIE'	BOX 513 - LUTCHER LA 70071
66- 84	SMITH, CARL REGINALD 'REGGIE'	6157 ELLENVIEW - WOODLAND HILLS CA 91367
23-122	SMITH, CARR E	731 SHIRLEY AV - NORFOLK VA 23517
60- 94	SMITH, CHARLES WILLIAM	3060 SPROUT WAY - SPARKS NV 89431
81-131	SMITH, CHRISTOPHER WILLIAM	4817 E. CHOLLA - SCOTTSDALE AZ 85254
13-165	SMITH, CLARENCE OSSIE	D. FEBRUARY 16, 1924 SWEETWATER, TEX.
38- 91	SMITH, CLAY JAMIESON	RR 1 BOX 9 - CAMBRIDGE KS 67023
38- 92	SMITH, DAVID MERWIN	BOX 671-WHITEVILLE NC 28472
80-119	SMITH, DAVID STANLEY	2143 VIA MARVALLE - DEL MAR CA 92014
84-111	SMITH, DAVID WAYNE	16330 JERSEY DR - HOUSTON TX 77040
12-181	SMITH, DOUGLASS WELDON	D. SEPTEMBER 18, 1973 GREENFIELD, MASS.
55-109	SMITH, EARL CALVIN	2764 N LEONARD - FRESNO CA 93727
16- 79	SMITH, EARL LEONARD	D. MARCH 14, 1943 PORTSMOUTH, O.
19- 76	SMITH, EARL SUTTON	D. JUNE 8, 1963 LITTLE ROCK, ARK.
36- 87	SMITH, EDGAR	RT 130 KINKOVER - BORDENTOWN NJ 08505
45- 99	SMITH, EDWARD MAYO	D. NOVEMBER 24, 1977 BOYNTON BEACH, FLA.
14-199	SMITH, ELMER JOHN	D. AUGUST 3, 1984 COLUMBIA, KY.
26- 77	SMITH, ELWOOD HOPE 'MIKE'	D. MAY 31, 1981 CHESAPEAKE, VA.
30- 76	SMITH, ERNEST HENRY	D. APRIL 6, 1973 BROOKLYN, N. Y.
50- 91	SMITH, FRANK THOMAS	120 89TH AVE - ST PETERSBURG FL 33702
13-166	SMITH, FREDERICK VINCENT	D. MAY 28, 1961 CLEVELAND, O.
16- 80	SMITH, GEORGE ALLEN	D. JANUARY 7, 1965 GREENWICH, CONN.
63-110	SMITH, GEORGE CHARLES	OLD ADD: 2728 LAKEVIEW AVE - ST PETERSBURG FL 33712
26- 78	SMITH, GEORGE SELBY	D. MAY 26, 1981 RICHMOND, VA.
32- 78	SMITH, HAROLD LAVERNE	5200 N. OCEAN BLVD #612 - FORT LAUDERDALE FL 33308
56- 79	SMITH, HAROLD RAYMOND	6602 WINKLEMAN - HOUSTON TX 77083
55-110	SMITH, HAROLD WAYNE	1317 B POST OAK PARK - HOUSTON TX 77027
12-183	SMITH, HARRISON M	D. JULY 26, 1964 DUNBAR, NEB.
10-138	SMITH, HENRY JOSEPH 'HAP'	D. FEBRUARY 26, 1961 SAN JOSE, CALIF.
62-124	SMITH, JACK HATFIELD	621 TAHOE CIR - STONE MOUNTAIN GA 30083
11-156	SMITH, JACOB G	B. DUBOIS, PA.
11-157	SMITH, JAMES CARLISLE 'RED'	D. OCTOBER 11, 1966 ATLANTA, GA.
14-200	SMITH, JAMES HARRY	D. APRIL 1, 1922 CHARLOTTE, N.C.
14-201	SMITH, JAMES LAWRENCE	D. JANUARY 1, 1974 PITTSBURGH, PA.
82-118	SMITH, JAMES LORNE	4452 MISTY WAY - YORBA LINDA CA 92686
15-156	SMITH, JOHN	D. MAY 2, 1972 WESTCHESTER, ILL.
31- 83	SMITH, JOHN MARSHALL	OLD ADD: COCKEYSVILLE MD 21030
13-167	SMITH, JOHN WILLIAM 'CHICK'	D. OCTOBER 11, 1935 DAYTON, KY.

77-133 SMITH, KEITH LAVARNE	OLD ADD: 522 11TH ST NORTH - PALMETTO FL 33561
81-132 SMITH, KENNETH EARL	100 LANDSDOWNE BLVD - YOUNGSTOWN OH 44506
20-109 SMITH, LAWRENCE PATRICK 'PADDY'	2738 N MILITARY TRAIL #109-WEST PALM BEACH FL 33409
80-120 SMITH, LEE ARTHUR	4170 N. MARINE DR #4L - CHICAGO IL 60613
84-112 SMITH, LEROY PURDY 'ROY'	472 GRAMATON AVE - MOUNT VERNON NY 10552
78-122 SMITH, LONNIE	231 RIVER FOREST DR - INMAN SC 29349
83-135 SMITH, MARK CHRISTOPHER	OLD ADD: 711 SOUTH 19TH ST - ARLINGTON VA 22202
25- 93 SMITH, MARVIN HAROLD 'RED'	D. FEBRUARY 19, 1961 LOS ANGELES, CAL.
84-113 SMITH, MICHAEL ANTHONY	3226 LIVINGSTON RD - JACKSON MS 39213
55-111 SMITH, MILTON	5007 HAWAIIAN TER - CINCINNATI OH 45223
62-125 SMITH, NATHANIEL BEVERLY	OLD ADD: 5303 ENNIS ST - HOUSTON TX 77004
78-123 SMITH, OSBORNE EARL 'OZZIE'	8004 HILLANDALE - SAN DIEGO CA 92120
84-114 SMITH, PATRICK KEITH	19537 CHADWAY ST - CANYON COUNTRY CA 91351
53- 85 SMITH, PAUL LESLIE	27 RAVENSWORTH RD - CONROE TX 77301
16- 81 SMITH, PAUL STONER	D. JULY 3, 1958 DECATUR, ILL.
62-126 SMITH, PETER LUKE	OLD ADD: 52 FAIRVIEW AVE - NATICK MA 01762
81-133 SMITH, RAYMOND EDWARD	OLD ADD: 1063 OAK DR - VISTA CA 92083
63-111 SMITH, RICHARD ARTHUR	OLD ADD: 1196 SW OXFORD DR - LAKE OSWEGO OR
51- 92 SMITH, RICHARD HARRISON	1926 NORWOOD LN - STATE COLLEGE PA 16801
69-160 SMITH, RICHARD KELLY	3110 HICKORY HILL DR - SANFORD NC 27330
27- 83 SMITH, RICHARD PAUL 'RED'	D. MARCH 8, 1978 TOLEDO, O.
13-169 SMITH, ROBERT ASHLEY	1914 ADD: HARDWICK VT
23-123 SMITH, ROBERT ELDRIDGE	BAPTIST VILLAGE RETIREMENT HOME - WAYCROSS GA 31501
55-112 SMITH, ROBERT GILCHRIST	47 FERNWOOD - TEXARKANA TX 75503
58- 85 SMITH, ROBERT WALKAY 'RIVERBOAT'	CLARENCE MO 63437
27- 84 SMITH, RUFUS FRAZIER	BOX 473 - NEW ELLENTON SC 29809
13-168 SMITH, SALVATORE GIUSEPPE 'JOE'	D. JANUARY 12, 1974 YONKERS, N. Y.
11-158 SMITH, SHEROD MALONE	D. SEPTEMBER 12, 1949 REIDSVILLE, GA.
73-111 SMITH, TOMMIE ALEXANDER	1299 EAST CANNON AVE - ALBEMARLE NC 28001
41-103 SMITH, VINCENT AMBROSE	D. DECEMBER 14, 1979 VIRGINIA BEACH, VA.
11-159 SMITH, WALLACE H.	D. JUNE 10, 1930 FLORENCE, ARIZ.
17- 79 SMITH, WILLARD JEHU 'RED'	D. JULY 17, 1972 NOBLESVILLE, IND.
58- 86 SMITH, WILLIAM GARLAND	OLD ADD: 5110 LOGAN ST SE - WASHINGTON DC 20028
63-112 SMITH, WILLIE	607 BRADFORD ST - HOBSON CITY AL 36201
84-115 SMITH, ZANE WILLIAM	RR 4 BOX 138-C1 - NORTH PLATTE NE 69101
82-119 SMITHSON, BILLY MIKE	BOX 204 - CENTERVILLE TN 37033
40- 83 SMOLL, CLYDE HETRICK	D. AUGUST 31, 1985 QUAKERTOWN, PA.
12-184 SMOYER, HENRY NEITZ	D. FEBRUARY 28, 1958 DUBOIS, PA.
16- 82 SMYKAL, FRANK JOHN	D. AUGUST 11, 1950 CHICAGO, ILL.
44-123 SMYRES, CLARENCE MELVIN 'CLANCY'	11470 ORCAS AVE - SAN FERNANDO CA 91342
15-157 SMYTH, JAMES DANIEL 'RED'	D. APRIL 14, 1958 INGLEWOOD, CALIF.
29- 98 SMYTHE, WILLIAM HENRY 'HARRY'	D. AUGUST 28, 1980 AUGUSTA, GA.
12-185 SNELL, CHARLES ANTHONY	1033 AMITY ST - READING PA 19604
84-116 SNELL, NATHANIEL	RR 2 BOX 42 - HOLLY HILL SC 29059
13-170 SNELL, WALTER HENRY	D. JULY 23, 1980 PROVIDENCE, R. I.
47- 80 SNIDER, EDWIN LAKEMONT 'DUKE'	3037 LAKEMONT DR - FALLBROOK CA 92028
23-124 SNIPES, WYATT EURE 'ROXY'	D. MAY 1, 1941 FAYETTEVILLE, N. C.
73-112 SNOOK, FRANK WALTER	OLD ADD: RR2 - WHITEHOUSE STATION NJ
19- 77 SNOVER, COLONEL LESTER	D. APRIL 30, 1969 ROCHESTER, N. Y.
35-102 SNYDER, BERNARD AUSTIN	2415 WAVERLY - PHILADELPHIA PA 19146
85-106 SNYDER, BRIAN ROBERT	14834 WOOD HOME ROAD - CENTERVILLE VA 22020
59- 77 SNYDER, EUGENE WALTER	1960 N SHERMAN ST - YORK PA 17402
12-186 SNYDER, FRANK ELTON	D. JANUARY 5, 1962 SAN ANTONIO, TEX.
61-100 SNYDER, JAMES ROBERT	1060 WEST ADDISON ST - CHICAGO IL 60613
52- 95 SNYDER, JERRY GEORGE	2420 GULFCREST BLVD - PEARLAND TX 77581
14-202 SNYDER, JOHN WILLIAM	D. DECEMBER 13, 1981 REDSTONE TWP., PA.
59- 78 SNYDER, RUSSELL HENRY	BOX 114 - NELSON NE 68961
19- 78 SNYDER, WILLIAM NICHOLAS	D. OCTOBER 8, 1934 VICKSBURG, MICH.
37- 95 SODD, WILLIAM	3845 DIAMON LOCK W - FT WORTH TX 76118
71- 94 SODERHOLM, ERIC THANE	10 SOUTH 360 HAMPSHIRE LN W - HINSDALE IL 60521
79-105 SOFIELD, RICHARD MICHAEL	ATH. DEPT. U. SOUTH CAROLINA - COLUMBIA SC 29208
68- 96 SOLAITA, TOLIA 'TONY'	317 ALTA VISTA DR-SOUTH SAN FRANCISCO CA94080
83-136 SOLANO, JULIO CESAR	VILLA ESPANA C.O. 31 - LAROMANA DOMINICAN REP.
58- 87 SOLIS, MARCELINO	OLD ADD: CALLE VIDREA 8370 - MONTEREY MEXICO
73-113 SOLOMON, EDDIE 'BUDDY'	D. JANUARY 12, 1986 MACON, GA.
23-125 SOLOMON, MOSES H.	D. JUNE 25, 1966 MIAMI, FLA.
34- 93 SOLTERS, JULIUS JOSEPH 'MOOSE'	D. SEPTEMBER 28, 1975 PITTSBURGH, PA.
10-139 SOMERLOTT, JOHN WESLEY 'JOCK'	D. APRIL 21, 1965 BUTLER, IND.
12-187 SOMMERS, RUDOLPH	D. MARCH 18, 1949 LOUISVILLE,KY.
50- 92 SOMMERS, WILLIAM DUNN	44 POLO RD - MASSAPEQUA NY 11758
24-101 SONGER, DON	D. OCTOBER 3, 1962 KANSAS CITY, MO.
77-134 SORENSON, LARY ALAN	23610 MYRTLE DR - MOUNT CLEMENS MI 48043
28- 87 SORRELL, VICTOR GARLAND	D. MAY 4, 1972 RALEIGH, N. C.
65-102 SORRELL, WILLIAM	%A.WINTON,16476 BERNARDO CTR DR - SAN DIEGO CA 92128
22-129 SORRELLS, RAYMOND EDWIN 'CHICK'	D. JULY 20, 1983 TERRELL, TEXAS
72-105 SOSA, ELIAS	35 ESTE #25,ENS. LUPERON - SANTO DOMINGO DOMINICAN REP.
75-109 SOSA, JOSE YNOCENCIO	HAINA KM12 CARRETERA SANCHEZ - SANTO DOMINGO DOM. REP.
26- 79 SOTHERN, DENNIS ELWOOD	D. DECEMBER 7, 1977 DURHAM, N. C.
14-203 SOTHORON, ALLEN SUTTON	D. JUNE 17, 1939 ST. LOUIS, MO
77-135 SOTO, MARIO MELVIN	JOACHS LACHAUSTEGUI #42 SUR - BANI DOMINICAN REP.
46- 95 SOUCHOCK, STEPHEN	441 SW 55TH TER - FORT LAUDERDALE FL 33314
11-160 SOUTHWICK, CLYDE AUBRA	D. OCTOBER 14, 1961 FREEPORT, ILL.
64-110 SOUTHWORTH, WILLIAM FREDERICK	320 DOBBEN RD - WEBSTER GROVES MO 63119
13-171 SOUTHWORTH, WILLIAM HARRISON	D. NOVEMBER 15, 1969 COLUMBUS, O.
80-121 SOUZA, KENNETH MARK	2317 BRITTAN - SAN CARLOS CA 94070
42- 98 SPAHN, WARREN EDWARD	RR 2 - HARTSHORNE OK 74547
27- 85 SPALDING, CHARLES HARRY 'DICK'	D. FEBRUARY 3, 1950 PHILADELPHA, PA.
59- 79 SPANGLER, ALBERT DONALD	27202 AFTON WAY - HUFFMAN TX 77336
64-111 SPANSWICK, WILLIAM HENRY	10 ST THOMAS STREET - ENFIELD CT 06082
64-112 SPARMA, JOSEPH BLASE	767 1/2 11TH ST SE -MASSILLON OH 44646
55-113 SPEAKE, ROBERT CHARLES	4742 SW URISH RD - TOPEKA KS 66604
24-102 SPEECE, BYRON FRANKLIN	D. SEPTEMBER 29, 1974 ELGIN, ORE.
75-110 SPEED, HORACE ARTHUR III	1301 BANKERS DR - CARSON CA 90744
43-131 SPEER,VERNIE FLOYD	D. MARCH 22, 1969 LITTLE ROCK, ARK.
71- 95 SPEIER, CHRIS EDWARD	226 CHAMONIX LE CHANTECLER - ST. ADELE QUEBEC CAN.
69-161 SPEIER, JOHN ROBERT 'BOB'	2521 SAN MARCOS - SAN DIEGO CA 92104
40- 84 SPENCE, STANLEY ORVILLE	D. JANUARY 9, 1983 KINSTON, N. C.
52- 96 SPENCER, DARYL DEAN	2740 LARKIN DRIVE - WICHITA KS 67216

12-188	SPENCER, FRED CALVIN	D. FEBRUARY 5, 1969 ST. ANTHONY, MINN.
50- 93	SPENCER, GEORGE ELWELL	8160 HICKORY AVE - GALENA OH 43021
28- 88	SPENCER, GLENN EDWARD	D. DECEMBER 30, 1958 BINGHAMTON, N. Y.
78-124	SPENCER, HUBERT THOMAS 'TOM'	132 PINE ST - GALLIOPOLIS OH 45631
68- 97	SPENCER, JAMES LLOYD	725A OLD BANFIELD RD - SEVERNA PARK MD 21146
13-172	SPENCER, LLOYD BENJAMIN	D. SEPTEMBER 1, 1970 FINKSBURG, MD.
25- 94	SPENCER, ROY HAMPTON	D. FEBRUARY 8, 1973 PORT CHARLETTE, FLA.
20-110	SPENCER, VERNON MURRAY	D. JUNE 3, 1971 WIXOM, MICH.
20-111	SPERAW, PAUL BACHMAN	D. FEBRUARY 22, 1962 CEDAR RAPIDS, IA.
24-103	SPERBER, EDWIN GEORGE	D. JANUARY 5, 1976 CINCINNATI, O.
74-123	SPERRING, ROBERT WALTER	4515 MEREDITH WOOD - SAN ANTONIO TX 78249
36- 88	SPERRY, STANLEY KENNETH	D. SEPTEMBER 27, 1962 EVANSVILLE,WIS.
55-114	SPICER, ROBERT OBERTON	423 MCPHEE DR - FAYETTEVILLE NC 28305
64-113	SPIEZIO, EDWARD WAYNE	5620 N. BARRINGTON RD - MORRIS IL 60450
72-106	SPIKES, LESLIE CHARLES 'CHARLIE'	10921 KINNEIL RD - NEW ORLEANS LA 70127
74-124	SPILLNER, DANIEL RAY	111 SW 307TH ST - FEDERAL WAY WA 98003
78-125	SPILMAN, WILLIAM HARRY	RURAL ROUTE 4 BOX 36 - DAWSON GA 31742
39-112	SPINDEL, HAROLD STEWART	12816 EL MORO AVE-LA MIRADA CA 90638
69-162	SPINKS, SCIPIO RONALD	34 NE 66TH - OKLAHOMA CITY OK 73105
70-126	SPLITTORFF, PAUL WILLIAM	4204 HICKORY LN - BLUE SPRING MO 64015
32- 79	SPOGNARDI, ANDREA ETTORE	4394 WASHINGTON ST - ROSLINDALE MA 02131
28- 89	SPOHRER, ALFRED RAY	D. JULY 21, 1972 CARMEL, N. Y.
54-103	SPOONER, KARL BENJAMIN	D. APRIL 10, 1984 VERO BEACH, FLA.
30- 77	SPOTTS, JAMES RUSSELL	D. JUNE 15, 1964 MEDFORD, N. J.
47- 81	SPRAGINS, HOMER FRANK	BOX 113 - MINTER CITY MS 38944
68- 98	SPRAGUE, EDWARD NELSON	19544 YUMA ST - CASTRO VALLEY CA 94546
11-161	SPRATT, HENRY LEE 'JACK'	D. JULY 3, 1969 WASHINGTON, PA.
65-103	SPRIGGS, GEORGE HERMAN	282 W BAY FRONT RD - LOTHIAN MD 20820
55-115	SPRING, JACK RUSSELL	8506 EAST DALTON - SPOKANE WA 99206
25- 95	SPRINGER, BRADFORD LOUIS	D. JANUARY 4, 1970 BIRMINGHAM, MICH.
30- 78	SPRINZ, JOSEPH CONRAD	1359 33RD AVE - SAN FRANCISCO CA 94122
45-100	SPROULL, CHARLES WILLIAM	D. JANUARY 13, 1980 ROCKFORD, ILL.
61-101	SPROUT, ROBERT SAMUEL	2858 FLEETWOOD DR - LANCASTER PA 17601
78-126	SPROWL, ROBERT JOHN	114 E 144TH AVE - TAMPA FL 33612
24-104	SPURGEON, FRED	D. NOVEMBER 5, 1970 KALAMAZOO, MICH.
75-111	SQUIRES, MICHAEL LYNN	2815 RANDOM RD - KALAMAZOO MI 49004
80-122	STABLEIN, GEORGE CHARLES	9839 LA AMAPOLA AVE - FOUNTAIN VLY CA 92708
10-140	STACK, WILLIAM EDWARD	D. AUGUST 28, 1958 CHICAGO, ILL.
64-114	STAEHLE, MARVIN GUSTAVE	570 CHECKER DR - BUFFALO GROVE IL 60090
60- 95	STAFFORD, BILL CHARLES	6108 COURTLAND - PLYMOUTH MI 48170
16- 83	STAFFORD, HENRY ALEXANDER 'HEINIE'	D. JANUARY 29, 1972 LAKE WORTH, FLA.
77-136	STAGGS, STEPHEN ROBERT	16722 MONTE CRISTO - CERRITOS CA 90701
64-115	STAHL, LARRY FLOYD	314 S. JULIA ST (BOX 36) - SMITHTON IL 62285
75-112	STAIGER, ROY JOSEPH	4630 SOUTH DARLINGTON #80 - TULSA OK 74135
34- 94	STAINBACK, GEORGE TUCKER 'TUCK'	1000 ELYSIAN AVE - LOS ANGELES CA 90012
25- 96	STALEY, GEORGE GAYLORD 'GALE'	1935 GOLDEN RAIN RD - WALNUT CREEK CA 94529
47- 82	STALEY, GERALD LEE	2600 NE 99TH ST - VANCOUVER WA 98665
60- 96	STALLARD, EVAN TRACY	HCO5 BOX 316 - COEBURN VA 24230
47- 83	STALLCUP, THOMAS VIRGIL	PLEASANTDALE CIRCLE, RR 6 - GREENVILLE SC 29607
43-132	STALLER, GEORGE WALBORN	321 N 67TH ST - HARRISBURG PA 17111
41-104	STANCEU, CHARLES	D. APRIL 3, 1969 CANTON, O.
25- 97	STANDAEART, JEROME JOHN	D. AUGUST 4, 1964 CHICAGO, ILL.
11-162	STANDRIDGE, ALFRED PETER	D. AUGUST 2, 1963 SAN FRANCISCO, CALIF.
63-113	STANEK, AL	96 ALLYN ST - HOLYOKE MA 01070
79-106	STANFIELD, KEVIN BRUCE	7565 NEWCOMB ST - SAN BERNARDINO CA 92410
61-102	STANGE, ALBERT LEE	148 VISTA DEL PARQUE - REDONDO BEACH CA 90277
72-107	STANHOUSE, DONALD JOSEPH	5956 SHERRY LANE #1000 - DALLAS TX 75225
59- 80	STANKA, JOE DONALD	15810 ROLLING TIMBERS - HOUSTON TX 77084
43-133	STANKY, EDWARD RAYMOND	2100 SPRING HILL RD - MOBILE AL 36607
69-163	STANLEY, FREDRICK BLAIR	OLD ADD: BOX 6181 - SCOTTSDALE AZ 85255
14-204	STANLEY, JAMES F.	B. 1889
11-163	STANLEY, JOHN LEONARD 'BUCK'	D. AUGUST 13, 1940 NORFOLK, VA.
64-116	STANLEY, MITCHELL JACK 'MICKEY'	28545 ORCHARD LAKE RD #B - FARMINGTON HILLS MI 48018
77-137	STANLEY, ROBERT WILLIAM	WM. FAIRFIELD DR - WENHAM MA 01984
18- 69	STANSBURY, JOHN JAMES	D. DECEMBER 26, 1970 EASTON, PA.
31- 84	STANTON, GEORGE WASHINGTON 'BUCK'	401 WINDING WAY DR - SAN ANTONIO TX 78232
70-127	STANTON, LEROY BOBBY	1751 NORWOOD LN - FLORENCE SC 29501
75-113	STANTON, MICHAEL THOMAS	BOX 2573 - PHENIX CITY AL 36867
80-123	STAPLETON, DAVID LESLIE	RR 1 BOX 600 - LOXLEY AL 36551
62-127	STARGELL, WILVER DORNEL 'WILLIE'	7232 THOMAS BLVD - PITTSBURGH PA 15208
32- 80	STARR, RAYMOND FRANCIS	D. FEBRUARY 9, 1963 BAYLISS, ILL.
47- 84	STARR, RICHARD EUGENE	613 N CRESCENT DR - KITTANNING PA 19201
35-103	STARR, WILLIAM 'CHICK'	666 UPAS ST #1801 - SAN DIEGO CA 92103

63-114 STARRETTE, HERMAN PAUL	208 HERMITAGE RD - STATESVILLE NC 28677
72-108 STATON, JOSEPH	1433 33CD AVE - SEATTLE WA 98122
19- 79 STATZ, ARNOLD JOHN 'JIGGER'	2506 WAVE CREST DR - CORONA DEL MAR CA 92625
63-115 STAUB, DANIEL JOSEPH 'RUSTY'	1271 3RD AVE - NEW YORK NY 10021
23-126 STAUFFER, CHARLES EDWARD 'ED'	D. JULY 2, 1979 ST PETERSBURG, FLA.
74-125 STEARNS, JOHN HARDIN	2649 S PEORIA - AURORA CO 80232
16- 84 STEELE, ROBERT WESLEY	D. JANUARY 27, 1962 OCALA, FLA.
10-141 STEELE, WILLIAM MITCHELL	D. OCTOBER 19, 1949 OVERLAND, MO.
12-189 STEEN, WILLIAM JOHN	D. MARCH 13, 1979 SIGNAL HILL, CALIF.
24-105 STEENGRAFE, MILTON HENRY	D. JUNE 2, 1977 OKLAHOMA CITY, OKLA.
62-128 STEEVENS, MORRIS DALE	527 GENERAL KRUEGER - SAN ANTONIO TX 78213
83-137 STEFERO, JOHN ROBERT	529 MICHELLE ROAD - ODENTON MD 21113
78-127 STEGMAN, DAVID WILLIAM	316 EAST OAK - LOMPOC CA 93436
32- 81 STEIN, IRVIN MICHAEL	D. JANUARY 7, 1981 COVINGTON, LA.
38- 93 STEIN, JUSTIN MARION	1915 GRAPE AVE - ST LOUIS MO 63136
72-109 STEIN, WILLIAM ALLEN	2433 LEGAY ST - COCOA FL 32922
78-128 STEIN, WILLIAM RANDOLPH	1540 PALMER ST - POMONA CA 91766
37- 96 STEINBACHER, HENRY JOHN	D. APRIL 3, 1977 SACRAMENTO, CALIF.
12-190 STEINBRENNER, WILLIAM GASS	D. APRIL 25, 1970 PITTSBURGH, PA.
31- 85 STEINECKE, WILLIAM ROBERT	311 ST GEORGE ST - ST AUGUSTINE FL 32084
23-127 STEINEDER, RAYMOND	D. AUGUST 25, 1982 VINELAND, N. J.
45-101 STEINER, BENJAMIN SAUNDERS	205 BLACKBURN RD - NOKOMIS FL 33555
45-102 STEINER, JAMES HARRY 'RED'	17700 S WESTERN AVE - GARDENA CA 90248
82-120 STEIRER, RICKY FRANCIS	2646 DULANY - BALTIMORE MD 21223
16- 85 STELLBAUER, WILLIAM JENNINGS	D. FEBRUARY 16, 1974 HOUSTON, TEX.
71- 96 STELMASZEK, RICHARD FRANCIS	2734 E 97TH ST - CHICAGO IL 60617
80-124 STEMBER, JEFFREY ALAN	330 W JERSEY ST - ELIZABETH NJ 07202
12-191 STENGEL, CHARLES DILLON 'CASEY'	D. SEPTEMBER 29, 1975 GLENDALE, CAL.
62-129 STENHOUSE, DAVID ROTCHFORD	70 WOODBURY RD - CRANSTON RI 02905
82-121 STENHOUSE, MICHAEL S	70 WOODBURY RD - CRANSTON RI 02905
71- 97 STENNETT, RENALDO ANTONIO	OLD ADD: BOCA RATON FL 33432
68- 99 STEPHEN, LOUIS ROBERTS 'BUZZ'	308 N PARKVIEW - PORTERVILLE CA 93257
47- 85 STEPHENS, BRYAN MARIS	10222 WESLEY CIR - HUNTINGTON BEACH CA 92646
52- 97 STEPHENS, GLEN EUGENE 'GENE'	5804 N BILLEN ST - OKLAHOMA CITY OK 73112
41-105 STEPHENS, VERNON DECATUR	D. NOVEMBER 4, 1968 LONG BEACH, CAL.
71- 98 STEPHENSON, CHESTER EARL	RR 1 BOX 295D - ANGIER NC 27501
21- 96 STEPHENSON, JACKSON RIGGS	D. NOVEMBER 15, 1985 TUSCALOOSA, ALA.
63-116 STEPHENSON, JERRY JOSEPH	1425 MARELEN DR - FULLERTON CA 92635
64-117 STEPHENSON, JOHN HERMAN	105 BELLEWOOD - HAMMOND LA 70401
43-134 STEPHENSON, JOSEPH CHESTER	822 JADE WAY - ANAHEIM CA 92805
55-116 STEPHENSON, ROBERT LOYD	1518 BROOKHAVEN BLVD - NORMAN OK 73069
35-104 STEPHENSON, WALTER MCQUEEN	3160 REISOR RD-SHREVEPORT LA 71108
74-126 STERLING, RANDALL WAYNE	2516 LINDA AVE - KEY WEST FL 33040

DAVE STER

ROYLE STILLMAN

12-192 STERRETT, CHARLES HURLBUT 'DUTCH'	D. DECEMBER 9, 1965 BALTIMORE, MD.
41-106 STEVENS, CHARLES AUGUSTUS	12062 VALLEY VIEW #211-GARDEN GROVE CA 92645
45-103 STEVENS, EDWARD LEE	5610 BRAESVALLEY - HOUSTON TX 77035
14-205 STEVENS, JAMES ARTHUR	D. SEPTEMBER 25, 1966 BALTIMORE, MD.
58- 88 STEVENS, R. C.	1405 MOUND ST - DAVENPORT IA 52803
31- 86 STEVENS, ROBERT JORDAN	803 ROXBORO RD - ROCKVILLE MD 20850
13-173 STEWART, CHARLES EUGENE 'TUFFY'	D. NOVEMBER 18, 1934 CHICAGO, ILL.
78-129 STEWART, DAVID KEITH	2512 HAVENSCOURT BLVD - OAKLAND CA 94605
41-107 STEWART, EDWARD PERRY	5501 W 119TH ST-INGLEWOOD CA 90304
27- 86 STEWART, FRANK	RR 1 BOX 290 - SAINT JOSEPH WI 54082
40- 85 STEWART, GLEN WELDON	60 S ALICIA-MEMPHIS TN 38112
63-117 STEWART, JAMES FRANKLIN	RR 1 BOX 298 - LAFAYETTE AL 38622
16- 86 STEWART, JOHN FRANKLIN 'STUFFY'	D. DECEMBER 30, 1980 LAKE CITY, FLA.
13-174 STEWART, MARK	D. JANUARY 17, 1942 MEMPHIS, TENN.
78-130 STEWART, SAMUEL LEE	107 SCENIC VIEW DR - SWANNANOA NC 28778
52- 98 STEWART, VESTON GOFF 'BUNKY'	RAY MCCOTTER REALTY CO - NEW BERN NC28560
21- 97 STEWART, WALTER CLEVELAND 'LEFTY'	D. SEPTEMBER 26, 1974 KNOXVILLE, TENN.
40- 86 STEWART, WALTER NESBITT	5260 ROBERTS MILL RD, RR 5 - LONDON OH 43140
44-124 STEWART, WILLIAM MACKLIN 'MACK'	D. MARCH 21, 1960 MACON, GA.
55-117 STEWART, WILLIAM WAYNE	2484 PONTIAC DR - SYLVAN LAKE MI 48053
79-107 STIEB, DAVID ANDREW	160 SHEFFIELD CIR EAST - PALM HARBOR FL 33563
29- 99 STIELY, FRED WARREN	D. JANUARY 6, 1981 VALLEY VIEW, PA.
60- 97 STIGMAN, RICHARD LEWIS	12914 5TH AVE S - BURNSVILLE MN 55337
30- 79 STILES, ROLLAND MAYS	10161 SAKURA DR - ST. LOUIS MO 63128
75-114 STILLMAN, ROYLE ELDON	5201 HARTFORD WAY - WESTMINSTER CA 92683
61-103 STILLWELL, RONALD ROY	1417 DOVER - THOUSAND OAKS CA 91360
80-125 STIMAC, CRAIG STEVEN	OLD ADD: 1603 ROBINHOOD LN - LAGRANGE IL 60525
23-128 STIMSON, CARL REMUS	D. NOVEMBER 9, 1936 OMAHA, NEB.
34- 95 STINE, LEE ELBERT	1939 CALLE PASITO - HEMET CA 92343
69-164 STINSON, GORRELL ROBERT 'BOB'	10663 NE 133RD PLACE - KIRKLAND WA 98033

43-135	STIRNWEISS, GEORGE HENRY 'SNUFFY'	D. SEPTEMBER 15, 1958 NEWARK, N. J.
47- 86	STOBBS, CHARLES KLEIN	5150 HONORE AVE - SARASOTA FL 33583
13-175	STOCK, MILTON JOSEPH	D. JULY 16, 1977 MONTROSE, ALA.
59- 81	STOCK, WESLEY GAY	5917 FRANCES AVE NE - TACOMA WA 98422
81-134	STODDARD, ROBERT LYLE	15760 SUNNYSIDE AVE - MORGAN HILL CA 95037
75-115	STODDARD, TIMOTHY PAUL	3928 E BUTTERNUT ST - EAST CHICAGO IN 46312
25- 98	STOKES, ALBERT JOHN	55 CAVALRY HILL RD - WILTON CT 06897
25- 99	STOKES, ARTHUR MELTON	D. JUNE 3, 1962 TITUSVILLE, PA.
45-104	STONE, CHARLES RICHARD 'DICK'	D. FEBRUARY 18, 1980 OKLAHOMA CITY, OKLA.
53- 86	STONE, DARRAH DEAN	1221 7TH AVE CT - SILVIS IL 61282
13-176	STONE, DWIGHT ELY	D. JULY 3, 1976 GLENDALE, CALIF.
23-129	STONE, EDWIN ARNOLD 'ARNIE'	D. JULY 29, 1948 HUDSON FALLS N. Y.
69-165	STONE, EUGENE DANIEL	STAR RT 1 BOX 136 - COULEE CITY WA 99115
67-102	STONE, GEORGE HEARD	OLD ADD: BOX 260 - RUSTON LA 71270
66- 85	STONE, HARRY RONALD 'RON'	3870 FERRY ST - EUGENE OR 97405
83-138	STONE, JEFFREY GLEN	RR 1 BOX 94C - HAYTI MO 63851
28- 90	STONE, JOHN THOMAS	D. NOVEMBER 30, 1955 SHELBYVILLE, TENN.
43-136	STONE, JOHN VERNON 'ROCKY'	9462 BEVAN - WESTMINSTER CA 92685
71- 99	STONE, STEVEN MICHAEL	OLD ADD: 4333 N. BROWN AVE - SCOTTSDALE AZ 85251
23-130	STONE, WILLIAM ARTHUR 'TIGE'	D. JANUARY 1, 1960 JACKSONVILLE, FLA.
33- 59	STONEHAM, JOHN ANDREW	7201 OAK HILL DR - HOUSTON TX 77017
67-103	STONEMAN, WILLIAM HAMBLY	OLD ADD: RR 3 - GEORGETOWN ONTARIO L4F 5G5 CAN.
22-130	STONER, ULYSSES SIMPSON GRANT 'LIL'	D. JUNE 26, 1966 ENID, OKLA.
31- 87	STORIE, HOWARD EDWARD	D. JULY 27, 1968 PITTSFIELD, MASS.
30- 80	STORTI, LINDO IVAN	D. JULY 24, 1982 ONTARIO, CALIF.
64-118	STOTTLEMYRE, MELVIN LEON	5804 W CHESTNUT - YAKIMA WA 98908
31- 88	STOUT, ALLYN MCCLELLAND	D. DECEMBER 22, 1974 SIKESTON, MO.
38- 94	STOVIAK, RAYMOND THOMAS	2501 S OCEAN BLVD #208 - BACON RATON FL 33432
60- 98	STOWE, HAROLD RUDOLPH	RR 3 BOX 281 - GASTONIA NC 28052
70-128	STRAHLER, MICHAEL WAYNE	2501 38TH AVE - SACRAMENTO CA 95822
54-104	STRAHS, RICHARD BERNARD	OLD ADD: 1334 W. TOUHY AVE - CHICAGO IL 60626
79-108	STRAIN, JOSEPH ALLAN	1781 SOUTH FOREST - DENVER CO 80222
72-110	STRAMPE, ROBERT EDWIN	BOX 672 - WASHTUCNA WA 99371
13-177	STRAND, PAUL EDWARD	D. JULY 2, 1974 SALT LAKE CITY, UT.
15-158	STRANDS, JOHN LAWRENCE	D. JANUARY 19, 1957 FOREST PARK, ILL.
15-159	STRANDS, LEWIS	
34- 96	STRANGE, ALAN COCHRANE	8239 41ST AVE NE - SEATTLE WA 98115
34- 97	STRATTON, MONTY FRANKLIN PIERCE	D. SEPTEMBER 29, 1982 GREENVILLE, TEXAS
83-139	STRAWBERRY, DARRYL EUGENE	1419 RED BLUFF COURT - SAN DIMAS CA 91773
28- 91	STRELECKI, EDWARD HAROLD	D. JANUARY 9, 1968 NEWARK, N. J.
54-105	STREULI, WALTER HERBERT	1107 WESTMINSTER - GREENSBORO NC 27410
50- 94	STRICKLAND, GEORGE BEVAN	6328 CONSTANCE ST - NEW ORLEANS LA 70118
71-100	STRICKLAND, JAMES MICHAEL	179 PRYCE ST - SANTA CRUZ CA 95060
37- 97	STRICKLAND, WILLIAM GOSS	4444 US HWY 98 NORTH #532 - LAKELAND FL 33805
59- 82	STRIKER, WILBUR SCOTT 'JAKE'	120 SCHELL AVE - BUCYRUS OH 44820
40- 87	STRINCEVICH, NICHOLAS MIHAILOVICH	1308 CAMELOT MANOR - PORTAGE IN 46368
41-108	STRINGER, LOUIS BERNARD	207 CALLE FELICIDAD - SAN CLEMENTE CA 92672
28- 92	STRIPP, JOSEPH VALENTINE	1001 W. NEW HAMPSHIRE - ORLANDO FL 32804
72-111	STROM, BRENT TERRY	1628 WHITSETT DR - EL CAJON CA 92020
39-113	STROMME, FLOYD MARVIN	3029 SHERIDAN - NORTH BEND OR 97459
29-100	STRONER, JAMES M.	D. NOVEMBER 16, 1971 CHICAGO, ILL.
66- 86	STROUD, EDWIN MARVIN	1696 OAK ST - WARREN OH 44485
10-142	STROUD, RALPH VIVIAN 'SAILOR'	D. APRIL 11, 1970 STOCKTON, CALIF.
82-122	STROUGHTER, STEPHEN LOUIS	323 NE 2ND - VISALIA CA 93277
34- 98	STRUSS, CLARENCE HERBERT 'STEAMBOAT'	D. SEPTEMBER 12, 1985 GRAND RAPIDS, MICH.
24-106	STRYKER, STERLING ALPA 'DUTCH'	D. NOVEMBER 5, 1964 RED BANK, N. J.
22-131	STUART, JOHN DAVIS	D. MAY 13, 1970 CHARLESTON, W. VA.
21- 98	STUART, LUTHER LANE 'LUKE'	D. JUNE 15, 1947 WINSTON-SALEM, N. C.
49- 83	STUART, MARLIN HENRY	RR 1 BOX 133 - PARAGOULD AR 72450
58- 89	STUART, RICHARD LEE	%THOMAS GEORGE,202 E. MAIN ST - HUNTINGTON NY 11743
84-117	STUBBS, FRANKLIN LEE	RR 1 BOX 521C - HAMLET NC 28345
67-104	STUBING, LAWRENCE GEORGE	10627 QUEZADA - EL PASO TX 79935
21- 99	STUELAND, GEORGE ANTON	D. SEPTEMBER 9, 1964 ONAWA, IA.
50- 95	STUFFEL, PAUL HARRINGTON	11000 JULIE NE - ALLIANCE OH 44601
57- 82	STUMP, JAMES GILBERT	939 WESTON - LANSING MI 48906
31- 89	STUMPF, GEORGE FREDERICK	222 STAFFORD AV - NEW ORLEANS LA 70124
12-193	STUMPF, WILLIAM FREDRICK	D. FEBRUARY 14, 1966 CROWNSVILLE, MD.
82-123	STUPER, JOHN ANTON	116 WEITZEL RD - BUTLER PA 16001
55-118	STURDIVANT, THOMAS VIRGIL	805 SW 32ND - OKLAHOMA CITY OK 73109
27- 87	STURDY, GUY R.	D. MAY 4, 1965 MARSHALL, TEX.
40- 88	STURGEON, ROBERT HARWOOD	3903 LEWIS AVE-LONG BEACH CA 90807
14-206	STURGIS, DEAN DONNELL	D. JUNE 4, 1950 UNIONTOWN, PA.
41-109	STURM, JOHN PETER JOSEPH	3840 FRENCH CT-ST LOUIS MO 63116

STUTZ

SWENTOR

26- 80 STUTZ, GEORGE — D. DECEMBER 29, 1930 PHILADELPHIA, PA.
19- 80 STYLES, WILLIAM GRAVES 'LENA' — D. MARCH 14, 1956 HUNTSVILLE, ALA.
66- 87 SUAREZ, KENNETH RAYMOND — 1301 FINDLAY DR - ARLINGTON TX 76012
44-125 SUAREZ, LUIS ABELARDO — OLD ADD: AGUILA #4 - HAVANA CUBA
70-130 SUCH, RICHARD STANLEY — 3110 HICKORY HILL DR - SANFORD NC 27330
38- 95 SUCHE, CHARLES MORRIS — D. FEBRUARY 11, 1984 SAN ANTONIO, TEXAS
50- 96 SUCHECKI, JAMES JOSEPH — RR 2 - ZIMMERMAN MN 55398
68-100 SUDAKIS, WILLIAM PAUL — 4352 PICKWICK CIR #204 - HUNTINGTON BEACH CA 92649
41-110 SUDER, PETER — 903 ROOSEVELT AVE - ALIQUIPPA PA 15001
30- 81 SUHR, AUGUST RICHARD — 341 HAZEL AVE - MILLBRAE CA 94030
26- 81 SUKEFORTH, CLYDE LEROY — RR 3 BOX 123 - WALDOBORO ME 04572
64-119 SUKLA, EDWARD ANTHONY — 16 PERCH - IRVINE CA 92714
80-126 SULARZ, GUY PATRICK — 19602 WATERBURY LN - HUNTINGTON BEACH CA 92646
36- 89 SULIK, ERNEST RICHARD — D. MAY 31, 1963 OAKLAND, CAL.
44-126 SULLIVAN, CARL MANUEL 'JACK' — %V.CROWDER,602 BARNES ST - MCKINNEY TX 75069
28- 93 SULLIVAN, CHARLES EDWARD — D. MAY 28, 1935 MAIDEN, N. C.
53- 87 SULLIVAN, FRANKLIN LEAL — BOX 1873 - LIHUE HI 96766
55-119 SULLIVAN, HAYWOOD COOPER — FENWAY PARK - BOSTON MA 02215
21-100 SULLIVAN, JAMES RICHARD — D. FEBRUARY 12, 1972 BURTONSVILLE, MD.
35-105 SULLIVAN, JOE — D. APRIL 8, 1985 SEQUIM, WASH.
19- 81 SULLIVAN, JOHN JEREMIAH — D. APRIL 1, 1966 UNION CO., PA.
20-112 SULLIVAN, JOHN LAWRENCE — 9539 PRAIRIE AVE - HIGHLAND IN 46322
42- 99 SULLIVAN, JOHN PATRICK — 24 HIGHLAND ST - DANSVILLE NY 14437
63-118 SULLIVAN, JOHN PETER — 134 SPRING LN - CANTON MA 02021
82-124 SULLIVAN, MARC COOPER — 6602 N 82ND WAY - SCOTTSDALE AZ 85253
39-114 SULLIVAN, PAUL THOMAS 'LEFTY' — 1701 HILL-N-DALE DR - FREDERICKSBURG VA 22401
51- 93 SULLIVAN, RUSSELL GUY H — D. SEPTEMBER 23, 1962 WEST ROXBURY, MASS.
22-132 SULLIVAN, THOMAS AUGUSTIN — D. AUGUST 16, 1944 SEATTLE, WASH.
25-100 SULLIVAN, THOMAS BRANDON — 7957 N. TAMIAMI TRAIL - SARASOTA FL 33580
31- 90 SULLIVAN, WILLIAM JOSEPH JR — D. JANUARY 29, 1966 LOS ANGELES, CAL.
20-113 SUMMA, HOMER WAYNE — 3955 HONEYCUTT #105 - SAN DIEGO CA 92109
74-127 SUMMERS, JOHN JUNIOR 'CHAMP' — 18 WINTERSET DR - CHATHAM MA 02633
28- 94 SUMNER, CARL RINGDAHL — 4610 RIVERFOREST DR - ARLINGTON TX 76017
74-128 SUNDBERG, JAMES HOWARD — 1427 MARLIN DR - NAPLES FL 33962
56- 80 SUNDIN, GORDON VINCENT — D. MARCH 23, 1952 CLEVELAND, O.
36- 90 SUNDRA, STEPHEN RICHARD — RR 6-PARIS IL 61944
37- 98 SUNKEL, THOMAS JACOB — 239 PURCHASE ST - RYE NY 10580
85-107 SURHOFF, RICHARD CLIFFORD — 94 BROOKDALE BLVD - PAWTUCKET RI 02861
49- 84 SURKONT, MATTHEW CONSTANTINE 'MAX' — 1117 68TH AVENUE DR W - BRADENTON FL 33507
29-101 SUSCE, GEORGE CYRIL METHODIUS SR. — 12 JARVIS CIRCLE - NEEDHAM MA 02192
55-120 SUSCE, GEORGE DANIEL JR — D. MAY 22, 1978 JACKSONVILLE, FLA.
34- 99 SUSKO, PETER JONATHAN — 33 MALVEY ST-FALL RIVER MA 02720
38- 96 SUTCLIFFE, CHARLES INIGO 'BUTCH' — 313 NW NORTH SHORE DR - PARKVILLE MO 64151
76- 87 SUTCLIFFE, RICHARD LEE 'RICK' — 3445 LAS PALMAS AVE - GLENDALE CA 91208
64-120 SUTHERLAND, DARRELL WAYNE — 338 N OAK CLIFF - MONROVIA CA 91016
66- 88 SUTHERLAND, GARY LYNN — D. MAY 11, 1972 PORTLAND, ORE.
21-101 SUTHERLAND, HARVEY SCOTT 'SUDS' — D. AUGUST 26, 1979 WASHINGTON, D.C.
49- 85 SUTHERLAND, HOWARD ALVIN 'DIZZY' — 2237 S. OERTLEY DR - ANAHEIM CA 92802
80-127 SUTHERLAND, LEONARDO CANTIN — 1368 HAMILTON RD - KENNESAW GA 30144
76- 88 SUTTER, HOWARD BRUCE — 25442 GALLUP CIR - LAGUNA HILLS CA 92653
66- 89 SUTTON, DONALD HOWARD — RR 1 BOX 857 - DESOTO TX 75115
77-138 SUTTON, JOHNNY IKE

JIM SUNDBERG

83-140 SWAGGERTY, WILLIAM DAVID — OLD ADD: 3542 TERRACE HILL #204 - RANDALLSTOWN MD 21133
73-114 SWAN, CRAIG STEVEN — 72 ROCKWOOD LN - GREENWICH CT 06830
14-207 SWAN, HARRY GORDON 'DUCKY' — D. MAY 9, 1946 PITTSBURGH, PA.
55-121 SWANSON, ARTHUR LEONARD — 15718 WENDY GLEN - HOUSTON TX 77095
29-102 SWANSON, ERNEST EVAR — D. JULY 17, 1973 GALESBURG, ILL.
28- 95 SWANSON, KARL EDWARD — 212 HILLCREST DR - AVON PARK FL 33825
71-101 SWANSON, STANLEY LAWRENCE — 2515 HWY 93 SOUTH - HAMILTON MT 59840
14-208 SWANSON, WILLIAM ANDREW — D. OCTOBER 14, 1954 NEW YORK, N.Y.
47- 87 SWARTZ, SHERWIN MERLE — 1937 N BEVERLY DR - BEVERLY HILLS CA 90210
20-114 SWARTZ, VERNON MONROE 'DAZZY' — D. JANUARY 13, 1980 GERMANTOWN, O.
48- 88 SWATASKI, CARL ERNEST — 10201 MARKHAM ST WEST #214 - LITTLE ROCK AR 72205
14-209 SWEENEY, CHARLES FRANCIS — D. MARCH 13, 1955 PITTSBURGH, PA.
44-127 SWEENEY, HENRY LEON — D. MAY 6, 1980 COLUMBIA, TENN.
28- 96 SWEENEY, WILLIAM JOSEPH — D. APRIL 18, 1957 SAN DIEGO, CAL.
78-131 SWEET, RICHARD JOE 'RICK' — 16127 SE 46TH WAY - BELLEVUE WA 98006
27- 88 SWEETLAND, LESTER LEO — D. MARCH 4, 1974 MELBOURNE, FL.
22-133 SWENTOR, AUGUST WILLIAM — D. NOVEMBER 10, 1969 WATERBURY, CONN.

29-103	SWETONIC, STEPHEN ALBERT	D. APRIL 22, 1974 CANONSBURG, PA.
40- 89	SWIFT, ROBERT VIRGIL	D. OCTOBER 17, 1966 DETROIT, MICH.
85-108	SWIFT, WILLIAM CHARLES	170 PICKETT ST - SOUTH PORTLAND ME 04106
32- 82	SWIFT, WILLIAM VINCENT	D. FEBRUARY 23, 1969 BARTOW, FLA.
39-115	SWIGART, OADIS VAUGHN	ARCHIE MO 64725
17- 80	SWIGLER, ADAM WILLIAM	D. FEBRUARY 58 1975 PHILADELPHIA, PA.
11-164	SWINDELL, JOSHUA ERNEST	D. MARCH 19, 1969 FRUITA, COLO.
74-129	SWISHER, STEVEN EUGENE	825 CLUBVIEW BLVD N - WORTHINGTON OH 43085
65-104	SWOBODA, RONALD ALAN	603 EAST LAMARCHE - PHOENIX AZ 85022
77-139	SYKES, ROBERT JOSEPH	509 WEST MAIN ST - CARMI IL 62821
53- 88	SZEKELY, JOSEPH	3260 ALLEN - PARIS TX 75460
70-131	SZOTKIEWICZ, KENNETH JOHN	1709 BEECH ST - WILMINGTON DE 19805
76- 89	TABB, JERRY LYNN	4700 POLO PARKWAY #161 - MIDLAND TX 79705
26- 82	TABER, EDWARD TIMOTHY 'LEFTY'	D. NOVEMBER 5, 1983 LINCOLN, NEB.
81-135	TABLER, PATRICK SEAN	OLD ADD: 1023 NIMITZ LN - CINCINNATI OH
38- 97	TABOR, JAMES REUBIN	D. AUGUST 22, 1953 SACRAMENTO, CAL.
13-178	TAFF, JOHN GALLATIN	D. MAY 15, 1961 HOUSTON, TEX.
28- 97	TAITT, DOUGLAS JOHN	D. DECEMBER 12, 1970 PORTLAND, ORE.
63-119	TALBOT, FREDERICK LEALAND	770 LUNSEFORD LN - FALLS CHURCH VA 22043
53- 89	TALBOT, ROBERT DALE	608 W KAWEAH - VISALIA CA 93277
43-137	TALCOTT, LEROY EVERETT	5060 SW 82ND AVE - MIAMI BEACH FL 33143
66- 90	TALTON, MARION LEE 'TIM'	RR2 BOX 156A - PIKEVILLE NC 27863
76- 90	TAMARGO, JOHN FELIX	1425 E PARIS - TAMPA FL 33604
34-100	TAMULIS, VITAUTIS CASIMIRUS	D. MAY 5, 1974 NASHVILLE, TENN.
73-115	TANANA, FRANK DARYL	129 38TH - NEWPORT BEACH CA 92660
25-101	TANKERSLEY, LAWRENCE WILLIAM 'LEO'	D. SEPTEMBER 18, 1980 DALLAS, TEXAS
85-109	TANNER, BRUCE MATTHEW	34 MAITLAND LANE EAST - NEW CASTLE PA 16101
55-122	TANNER, CHARLES WILLIAM	34 MAITLAND LN E - NEW CASTLE PA 16101
54-106	TAPPE, ELVIN WALTER	2424 SPRING ST - QUINCY IL 62301
50- 97	TAPPE, THEODORE NASH	203 MARR - WENATCHEE WA 98801
14-221	TAPPEN, WALTER VAN DORN	D. DECEMBER 19, 1967 LYNWOOD, CALIF.
27- 89	TARBERT, WILBER ARLINGTON 'ARLIE'	D. NOVEMBER 27, 1946 CLEVELAND, O.
84-118	TARTABULL, DANILO	3912 WALNUT ST - TAMPA FL 33607
62-130	TARTABULL, JOSE	4105 NW 185TH ST - CORAL CITY FL 33055
58- 90	TASBY, WILLIE	1486 12TH ST - OAKLAND CA 94607
46- 96	TATE, ALVIN WALTER	739 WEST 3400 S - BOUNTIFUL UT 84010
24-107	TATE, HENRY BENNETT 'BENNIE'	D. OCTOBER 27, 1973 FRANKFORT, ILL.
58- 91	TATE, LEE WILLIE	6905 PRATT - OMAHA NE 68131
75-116	TATE, RANDALL LEE	6909 DENWOOD RD SE - KNOXVILLE TN 37920
68-101	TATUM, JARVIS	727 SOUTH ARTHUR - FRESNO CA 93706
69-166	TATUM, KENNETH RAY	340 WOODWARD RD - BIRMINGHAM AL 35228
41-111	TATUM, THOMAS VEE TEE	4929 PATE AVE-OKLAHOMA CITY OK 73112
35-106	TAUBY, FRED JOSEPH	D. NOVEMBER 23, 1955 CONCORDIA, CAL.
28- 98	TAUSCHER, WALTER EDWARD	2600 WESTERN PARKWAY - ORLANDO FL 32803
58- 92	TAUSSIG, DONALD FRANKLIN	BOX 225 - LONG BEACH NY 11561
21-102	TAVENER, JOHN ADAM	D. SEPTEMBER 14, 1969 FT. WORTH, TEX.
76- 91	TAVERAS, ALEJANDRO ANTONIO 'ALEX'	A. MONSANTO 8 TAMBORIL - SANTIAGO DOMINICAN REP.
71-102	TAVERAS, FRANKLIN CRISOSTOMO	CALLE 31 #16 LOS COLINOS - SANTIAGO DOMINICAN REP.
58- 93	TAYLOR, ANTONIO	7 ROBIN RD - YEADON PA 19051
21-103	TAYLOR, ARLAS WALTER	D. SEPTEMBER 10, 1958 DADE CITY, FLA.
12-194	TAYLOR, BENJAMIN HARRISON	D. NOVEMBER 3, 1946 MARTIN COUNTY, IND.
77-140	TAYLOR, BRUCE BELL	8 HIGHLAND PARK RD - RUTLAND MA 01543

25-102	TAYLOR, C. L. 'CHINK'	D. JULY 7, 1980 TEMPLE, TEXAS
68-102	TAYLOR, CARL MEANS	OLD ADD: 530 S VENICE BY-PASS - VENICE FL
69-167	TAYLOR, CHARLES GILBERT	1619 GEORGETOWN LN - MURFREESBORO TN 37130
26- 83	TAYLOR, DANIEL TURNEY	D. OCTOBER 11, 1972 LATROBE, PA.
26- 84	TAYLOR, EDWARD JAMES	BOX 2237 - CHULA VISTA CA 92012
51- 94	TAYLOR, EUGENE BENJAMIN 'BEN'	12677 COULSON - HOUSTON TX 77015
50- 98	TAYLOR, FREDERICK RANKIN	3144 DRRBY RD - COLUMBUS OH 43221
69-168	TAYLOR, GARY WILLIAM	OLD ADD: 827 N. MARTHA - DEARBORN MI 48128
57- 83	TAYLOR, HARRY EVANS	2125 COOKS LN - FORT WORTH TX 76112
32- 83	TAYLOR, HARRY WARREN	D. APRIL 27, 1969 TOLEDO, O.
46- 97	TAYLOR, JAMES HARRY	RR 13 BOX 3 - WEST TERRE HAUTE IN 47885
20-115	TAYLOR, JAMES WREN 'ZACK'	D. SEPTEMBER 19, 1974 ORLANDO, FLA.
54-107	TAYLOR, JOE CEPHUS	705 WATT LN - PITTSBURGH PA 15219
23-131	TAYLOR, LEO THOMAS	D. MAY 20, 1982 SEATTLE, WASH.
11-165	TAYLOR, PHILIP WILEY	D. JULY 9, 1954 TOPEKA, KAN.
57- 84	TAYLOR, ROBERT DALE 'HAWK'	RR 5 BOX 897 - MURRAY KY 42071
70-132	TAYLOR, ROBERT LEE	27 SUNNYBROOK RD - SPRINGFIELD MA 01109
62-131	TAYLOR, RONALD WESLEY	75 BANFF ROAD - TORONTO ONTARIO M4S 2V6 CAN.
58- 94	TAYLOR, SAMUEL DOUGLAS	1255 SHERIDAN ST - CHICOPEE MA 01022
24-108	TAYLOR, THOMAS LIVINGSTONE CARLTON	D. APRIL 5, 1956 GREENVILLE, MISS.
52- 99	TAYLOR, VERNON CHARLES 'PETE'	823 CEDARCROFT DR - MILLERSVILLE MD 21108
54-108	TAYLOR, WILLIAM MICHAEL	BOX 146 - ACTON CA 93510

30- 82 TEACHOUT, ARTHUR JOHN 'BUD'	D. MAY 11, 1985 LAGUNA BEACH, CALIF.
36- 91 TEBBETTS, GEORGE ROBERT 'BIRDIE'	229 OAK AVE-ANNA MARIA FL 33501
14-211 TEDROW, ALLEN SEYMOUR	D. JANUARY 23, 1958 WESTERVILLE, O.
53- 90 TEED, RICHARD LEROY	128 CUSTER DR - WINDSOR CT 06095
74-130 TEKULVE, KENTON CHARLES	1531 SEQUOIA - PITTSBURGH PA 15241
79-109 TELLMANN, THOMAS JOHN	W160 S7131 DAISY DR - MUSKEGO WI 53150
52-100 TEMPLE, JOHN ELLIS	RR 2 BOX 293C - IRMO SC 29063
55-123 TEMPLETON, CHARLES SHERMAN	BOX 457 - WYOMING MN 55092
76- 92 TEMPLETON, GARRY LEWIS	13552 DEL POMONTE RD - POWAY CA 92064
69-169 TENACE, FURY GENE	15368 MARKER RD - POWAY CA 92064
29-104 TENNANT, JAMES MCDONNELL	D. APRIL 16, 1967 TRUMBULL, CONN.
12-195 TENNANT, THOMAS FRANCIS	D. FEBRUARY 16, 1955 SAN CARLOS, CALIF.
67-105 TEPEDINO, FRANK RONALD	95 DAVIS ST - HAUPPAUGE NY 11787
46- 98 TEPSIC, JOSEPH JOHN	RR3 BOX 164 - TYRONE PA 16686
72-112 TERLECKI, ROBERT JOSEPH	760 NORWAY AVE - TRENTON NJ 08629
75-117 TERLECKY, GREGORY JOHN	1042 E GROVECENTER ST - WEST COVINA CA 91790
74-131 TERPKO, JEFFREY MICHAEL	RR 1 BOX 156 - SAYRE PA 18840
82-125 TERRELL, CHARLES WALTER 'WALT'	2915 BLACKISTON MILL RD-JEFFERSONVILLE IN 47130
73-116 TERRELL, JERRY WAYNE	1301 SUNNY CREEK LN - BLUE SPRINGS MO 64015
40- 90 TERRY, LANCELOT YANK	D. NOVEMBER 4, 1979 BLOOMINGTON, IND.

DERREL THOMAS

56- 81 TERRY, RALPH WILLARD	801 PARK - LARNED KS 67550
23-132 TERRY, WILLIAM HAROLD	BOX 2177 - JACKSONVILLE FL 32203
16- 87 TERRY, ZEBULON ALEXANDER	300 S HIGHLAND AVE - LOS ANGELES CA 90036
32- 84 TERWILLIGER, RICHARD MARTIN	D. JANUARY 21, 1969 GREENVILLE, MICH.
49- 86 TERWILLIGER, WILLARD WAYNE	7617 NOREAST DR - FORT WORTH TX 76118
15-160 TESCH, ALBERT JOHN	D. AUGUST 3, 1947 JERSEY CITY, N.J.
12-196 TESREAU, CHARLES MONROE 'JEFF'	D. SEPTEMBER 24, 1946 HANOVER, N.H.
58- 95 TESTA, NICHOLAS	2544 LURTING AVE - BRONX NY 10469
55-124 TETTELBACH, RICHARD MORLEY	7 BEACHWOOD RD - WOODRIDGE CT 06525
84-119 TETTLETON, MICKEY LEE	10405 LESTER LANE - OKLAHOMA CITY OK 73101
83-141 TEUFEL, TIMOTHY SHAWN	37 BYRAM TERRACE DR - GREENWICH CT 06830
14-212 TEXTOR, GEORGE	D. MARCH 11, 1954 MASSILLON, O.
58- 96 THACKER, MORRIS BENTON 'MOE'	10206 BLUFFSPRINGS TRACE - LOUISVILLE KY 40223
78-132 THAYER, GREGORY ALLEN	1000 3RD ST N - SAUK RAPIDS MN 56379
20-116 THEIS, JOHN LOUIS	D. JULY 6, 1941 GEORGETOWN, O.
77-141 THEISS, DUANE CHARLES	2761 RIDGEWOOD CT - MARIETTA OH 45750
71-103 THEOBALD, RONALD MERRILL	9 FLEUTI - MORAGA CA 94556
73-117 THEODORE, GEORGE BASIL	734 SOUTH 13TH EAST - SALT LAKE CITY UT 84102
44-128 THESENGA, ARNOLD JOSEPH 'JUG'	3907 COUNTRYSIDE PLAZA - WICHITA KS 67218
24-109 THEVENOW, THOMAS JOSEPH	D. JULY 28, 1957 MADISON, IND.
52-101 THIEL, MAYNARD BERT	RR2 - MARION WI 54950
63-120 THIES, DAVID ROBERT	6140 ARCTIC WAY - MINNEAPOLIS MN 55436
54-109 THIES, VERNON ARTHUR 'JAKE'	4 CORNFLOWER COURT - FLORISSANT MO 63033
67-106 THOENEN, RICHARD CRISPIN	51 N PEACH ST - MEDFORD OR 97501
26- 85 THOMAS, ALPHONSE 'TOMMY'	RR 1 - DALLASTOWN PA 17313
85-110 THOMAS, ANDRES PERES	35 DUARTE #35 - BOCA CHICA DOMINICAN REP.
11-166 THOMAS, BLAINE M.	D. AUGUST 21, 1915 PAYSON, ARIZ.
60- 99 THOMAS, CARL LESLIE	5850 E ORANGE BLOSSOM LN - PHOENIX AZ 85018
12-197 THOMAS, CHESTER DAVID 'PINCH'	D. DECEMBER 24, 1953 MODESTO, CALIF.
25-103 THOMAS, CLARENCE FLETCHER 'LEFTY'	D. MARCH 21, 1952 CHARLOTTESVILLE, VA.
16- 88 THOMAS, CLAUDE ALFRED	D. MARCH 6, 1946 SULPHUR, OKLA.
76- 93 THOMAS, DANNY LEE	D. JUNE 12, 1980 MOBILE, ALA.
71-104 THOMAS, DERREL OSBON	236 W. 73RD ST - LOS ANGELES CA 90003
27- 90 THOMAS, FAY WESLEY	10526 ANDORA AVE - CHATSWORTH CA 91311
51- 95 THOMAS, FRANK JOSEPH	118 DORAY DR - PITTSBURGH PA 15237
18- 70 THOMAS, FRED HARVEY	RR 1 BOX 183 - BIRCHWOOD WI 54817
57- 85 THOMAS, GEORGE EDWARD	12733 PORTLAND AVE S - BURNSVILLE MN 55337
24-110 THOMAS, HERBERT MARK	818 W PRATT ST - STARKE FL 32071
73-118 THOMAS, JAMES GORMAN	759 TALLWOOD RD - CHARLESTON SC 29412
61-104 THOMAS, JAMES LEROY 'LEE'	50 E CARDIGAN - ST LOUIS MO 63135
51- 96 THOMAS, JOHN TILLMAN 'BUD'	2607 STEPHENSON ST - SEDALIA MO 65301
52-102 THOMAS, KEITH MARSHALL 'KITE'	12F CYPRESS GROVE APTS - WILMINGTON NC 28401
50- 99 THOMAS, LEO RAYMOND	2024 SANDCREEK WAY - ALAMEDA CA 94501
32- 85 THOMAS, LUTHER BAXTER 'BUD'	RR 1 BOX 400 - NORTH GARDEN VA 22959
26- 86 THOMAS, MYLES LEWIS	D. DECEMBER 12, 1963 TOLEDO, O.
38- 98 THOMAS, RAYMOND JOSEPH	607 W VANCE ST - WILSON NC 27893
21-104 THOMAS, ROBERT WILLIAM 'RED'	D. MARCH 29, 1962 FREMONT, O.
77-142 THOMAS, ROY JUSTIN	4055 HIDDEN VALLEY LN - SAN JOSE CA 95127
74-132 THOMAS, STANLEY BROWN	17484 NE 40TH PLACE - REDMOND WA 98052
57- 86 THOMAS, VALMY	BOX 9184 - SANTURCE PR 00908
10-143 THOMASEN, ARTHUR WILSON	D. MAY 2, 1944 KANSAS CITY, MO.
74-133 THOMASON, MELVIN ERSKINE	405 S BROAD ST - CLINTON SC 29325
72-113 THOMASSON, GARY LEAH	4515 E ONYX ST - PHOENIX AZ 85028
78-133 THOMPSON, BOBBY LARUE	OLD ADD: 3106 CAPITOL DR #2 - CHARLOTTE NC 28208

54-110 THOMPSON, CHARLES LEMOINE 'TIM'	536 SUMMIT DR - LEWISTOWN PA 17044
70-133 THOMPSON, DANNY LEON	D. DECEMBER 10, 1976 ROCHESTER, MINN.
48- 98 THOMPSON, DAVID FORREST	D. FEBRUARY 26, 1979 CHARLOTTE, N. C.
49- 87 THOMPSON, DONALD NEWLIN	87 E EUCLID PKWY - ASHEVILLE NC 28804
39-116 THOMPSON, EUGENE EARL	8731 E CAMELBACK RD-SCOTTSDALE AZ 85252
20-117 THOMPSON, FRANK E.	D. JUNE 27, 1940 MINERAL TWP., MO.
11-167 THOMPSON, FULLER WEIDNER	D. FEBRUARY 19, 1972 LOS ANGELES, CALIF.
19- 82 THOMPSON, HAROLD	D. FEBRUARY 14, 1951 RENO, NEV.
47- 88 THOMPSON, HENRY CURTIS	D. SEPTEMBER 30, 1969 FRESNO, CAL.
14-213 THOMPSON, JAMES ALFRED 'SHAG'	101 SECOND ST - BLACK MOUNTAIN NC 28711
76- 94 THOMPSON, JASON DOLPH	26351 SORRELL - LAGUNA HILLS CA 92653
21-105 THOMPSON, JOHN DUDLEY 'LEE'	D. FEBRUARY 17, 1965 SANTA BARBARA, CAL.
48- 99 THOMPSON, JOHN SAMUEL 'JOCKO'	10 BEL PRE CT - ROCKVILLE MD 20853
25-104 THOMPSON, LAFAYETTE FRESCO	D. NOVEMBER 20, 1968 FULLERTON, CAL.
71-105 THOMPSON, MICHAEL WAYNE	7565 TURNER DR - DENVER CO 80221
84-120 THOMPSON, MILTON BERNARD	RR 2 BOX 95 - NINETY SIX SC 29666
85-111 THOMPSON, RICHARD NEIL	7 CHAMBERS COURT - HUNTINGTON STATION NY 11746
33- 60 THOMPSON, RUPERT LUCKHART 'TOMMY'	D. MAY 24, 1971 AUBURN, CAL.
12-198 THOMPSON, THOMAS CARL	D. JANUARY 16, 1963 LAJOLLA, CALIF.
12-199 THOMPSON, THOMAS HOMER	D. SEPTEMBER 19, 1957 ATLANTA, GA.
78-134 THOMPSON, VERNON SCOT	110 BEACON RD - RENFREW PA 16053
46- 99 THOMSON, ROBERT BROWN	122 SUNLIT DR - WATCHUNG NJ 07060
79-110 THON, RICHARD WILLIAM 'DICKIE'	HB-12 LOMBARDIA ST - RIO PIEDRAS CA 00924
17- 81 THORMAHLEN, HERBERT EHLER 'HANK'	D. FEBRUARY 6, 1955 LOS ANGELES, CALIF.
77-143 THORMODSGARD, PAUL GAYTON	6531 EAST CYPRESS - SCOTTSDALE AZ 85257
73-119 THORNTON, ANDRE	BOX 395 - CHAGRIN FALLS OH 44022
85-112 THORNTON, LOUIS	115 MCLEAN ROAD - HOPE HULL AL 36043
73-120 THORNTON, OTIS BENJAMIN	BOX 164 - DOCENA AL 35060
51- 97 THORPE, BENJAMIN ROBERT 'BOB'	BOX 46 - WAVELAND MS 39576
13-179 THORPE, JAMES FRANCIS	D. MARCH 28, 1953 LOMITA, CALIF.
55-125 THORPE, ROBERT JOSEPH	D. MARCH 17, 1960 SAN DIEGO, CAL.
16- 89 THRASHER, FRANK EDWARD 'BUCK'	D. JUNE 12, 1938 CLEVELAND, TENN.
55-126 THRONEBERRY, MARVIN EUGENE	12102 MACON RD - COLLIERVILLE TN 38017
52-103 THRONEBERRY, MAYNARD FAYE	12016 MACON RD - COLLIERVILLE TN 38017
75-118 THROOP, GEORGE LYNFORD	672 W HIGHLAND AVE - SIERRA MADRE CA 91024
39-117 THUMAN, LOUIS CHARLES FRANK	6117 EDLYNNE RD - BALTIMORE MD 21212
55-127 THURMAN, ROBERT BURNS	8415 E. GILBERT - WICHITA KS 67207
83-142 THURMOND, MARK ANTHONY	4706 MISTY SHADOWS DR - HOUSTON TX 77041
23-133 THURSTON, HOLLIS JOHN 'SLOPPY'	D. SEPTEMBER 14, 1973 LOS ANGELES, CAL.
64-121 TIANT, LUIS CLEMENTE	2495 STARMOUNT WAY - EL DORADO HILLS CA 95630
84-121 TIBBS, JAY LINDSEY	216 REDSTONE WAY - BIRMINGHAM AL 35215
72-114 TIDROW, RICHARD WILLIAM	3903 WOODRIDGE - LEES SUMMIT MO 64063
52-104 TIEFENAUER, BOBBY GENE	300 S LINCOLN - DESLOGE MO 63603
62-132 TIEFENTHALER, VERLE MATHEW	1852 QUINT AVE - CARROLL IA 51401
20-118 TIERNEY, JAMES ARTHUR 'COTTON'	D. APRIL 18, 1953 KANSAS CITY, MO.
33- 61 TIETJE, LESLIE WILLIAM	RR 2 BOX 107 - KASSON MN 55944
57- 87 TIGHE, JOHN THOMAS	20 SALADO ROAD - ST. AUGUSTINE FL 32084
15-161 TILLMAN, JOHN LAWRENCE	D. APRIL 7, 1964 HARRISBURG, PA.
62-133 TILLMAN, JOHN ROBERT 'BOB'	403 WADERBROOK DR - GALLATIN TN 37066
82-126 TILLMAN, KERRY JEROME 'RUSTY'	130 JACKSON RD - ATLANTIC BEACH FL 32233
67-107 TILLOTSON, THADDEUS ASA	870 DONNA DR - MERCED CA 95340
69-170 TIMBERLAKE, GARY DALE	HIGHWAY 11 - LACONIA IN 47135
69-171 TIMMERMAN, THOMAS HENRY	720 NORTH WALNUT - BREESE IL 62230
14-214 TINCUP, AUSTIN BEN	D. JULY 5, 1980 CLAREMORE, OK.
82-127 TINGLEY, RONALD IRVIN	OLD ADD: 1830 GREENBRAE - SPARKS NV 89431
32- 86 TINNING, LYLE FORREST 'BUD'	D. JANUARY 17, 1961 EVANSVILLE, IND.
15-162 TIPPLE, DANIEL E	D. MARCH 26, 1960 OMAHA, NEB.
39-118 TIPTON, ERIC GORDON	125 NINA LN - WILLIAMSBURG VA 23185
48-100 TIPTON, JOSEPH JOHN	1129 2ND AVE - PLEASANT GROVE AL 35127
69-172 TISCHINSKI, THOMAS ARTHUR	2607 NE 68TH TER - GLADSTONE MO 64119
36- 92 TISING, JOHNNIE JOSEPH	D. SEPTEMBER 5, 1967 LEADVILLE, COLO.
78-135 TOBIK, DAVID VANCE	4852 S SEDGEWICK RD - LYNDHURST OH 44124
37- 99 TOBIN, JAMES ANTHONY	D. MAY 19, 1969 OAKLAND, CAL.
32- 87 TOBIN, JOHN MARTIN	D. AUGUST 8, 1983 RHINEBECK, N. Y.
45-105 TOBIN, JOHN PATRICK	D. JANUARY 18, 1982 OAKLAND, CALIF.
14-215 TOBIN, JOHN THOMAS	D. DECEMBER 10, 1969 ST. LOUIS, MO.
41-112 TOBIN, MARION BROOKS 'PAT'	D. JANUARY 21, 1975 SHREVEPORT, LA.
32- 88 TODD, ALFRED CHESTER	931 GRAND CENTRAL AV - HORSEHEADS NY 14845
77-144 TODD, JACKSON A	4527 E 25TH PL - TULSA OK 74114
74-134 TODD, JAMES RICHARD JR.	8630 E PAWNEE DR - PARKER CO 80134
24-111 TODT, PHILIP JULIUS	D. NOVEMBER 15, 1973 ST. LOUIS, MO.
47- 89 TOENES, WILLIAM HARRELL 'HAL'	5119 BRANCH AVE - TAMPA FL 33603
65-105 TOLAN, ROBERT	6988 CAMINO AMERO - SAN DIEGO CA 92111
84-122 TOLIVER, FREDDIE LEE	27470 STRATFORD ST - HIGHLAND CA 92346

BOB THURMAN
Cincinnati Redlegs

81-136 TOLLESON, JIMMY WAYNE	OLD ADD: RR 10 PEACH VALLEY DR-SPARTANBURG SC
81-137 TOLMAN, TIMOTHY LEE	121 HART AVE - SANTA MONICA CA 90405
25-105 TOLSON, CHESTER JULIUS 'CHICK'	D. APRIL 16, 1965 WASHINGTON, D. C.
53- 91 TOMANEK, RICHARD CARL	165 DUFF DR - AVON LAKE OH 44012
49- 88 TOMASIC, ANDREW JOHN	230 7TH ST - WHITEHALL PA 18052
13-180 TOMER, GEORGE CLARENCE	D. DECEMBER 15, 1984 PERRY, IOWA
72-115 TOMLIN, DAVID ALLEN	RR 1 - MANCHESTER OH 45144
12-200 TOMPKINS, CHARLES HERBERT	D. SEPTEMBER 20, 1975 PRESCOTT, ARK.
65-106 TOMPKINS, RONALD EVERETT	188 E "J" ST - CHULA VISTA CA 92010
75-119 TOMS, THOMAS HOWARD	GREENWOOD VA 22943
11-168 TONEY, FRED ALEXANDRA	D. MARCH 11, 1953 NASHVILLE, TENN.
11-169 TONNEMAN, CHARLES RICHARD 'TONY'	D. AUGUST 7, 1951 PRESCOTT, ARIZ.
11-170 TOOLEY, ALBERT	D. AUGUST 17, 1976 MARSHALL, MICH.
21-106 TOPORCER, GEORGE 'SPECS'	30 TEED ST - HUNTINGDON STATION NY 11747
62-134 TOPPIN, RUPERTO	OLD ADD: 601 CROWN ST - BROOKLYN NY 11213
64-122 TORBORG, JEFFREY ALLEN	1375 CHAPEL HILL - MOUNTAINSIDE NJ 07092
47- 90 TORGESON, CLIFFORD EARL	2121 RUCKER - EVERETT WA 98201
17- 82 TORKELSON, CHESTER LEROY 'RED'	D. SEPTEMBER 22, 1964 CHICAGO, ILL.
20-119 TORPHY, WALTER ANTHONY 'RED'	D. FEBRUARY 11, 1980 FALL RIVER, MASS.
56- 82 TORRE, FRANK JOSEPH	%RAWLINGS,2300 DELMAR BLVD-ST LOUIS MO 63166
60-100 TORRE, JOSEPH PAUL	3088 GREENFIELD DR - MARIETTA GA 30067
75-120 TORREALBA, PABLO ARNOLDO	AVE PTE.MEDINA,MARIO 50,PISO 19-CARACAS VENEZ
77-145 TORRES, ANGEL RAFAEL	CALLE 16 DE AGOSTO #19 - AZUA DOMINICAN REP.
40- 91 TORRES, DON GILBERTO NUNEZ 'GIL'	D. JANUARY 11, 1983 REGLA, HAVANA, CUBA
62-135 TORRES, FELIX	RR 3 BOX 105 - SANTA ISABEL PR 00757
68-103 TORRES, HECTOR EPITACIO	RR 3 BOX 950 - EFFINGHAM SC 29541
20-120 TORRES, RICARDO J.	D. HAVANA, CUBA
71-106 TORRES, ROSENDO 'RUSTY'	151-34 136TH AVE - JAMAICA NY 11434
67-108 TORREZ, MICHAEL AUGUSTINE	208 N LAKE ST - TOPEKA KS 66616
42-100 TOST, LOUIS EUGENE	D. FEBRUARY 22,1967 SANTA CLARA, CAL.
62-136 TOTH, PAUL LOUIS	6538 SUDER - ERIE MI 48133
28- 99 TOUCHSTONE, CLAYLAND MAFFITT	D. APRIL 28, 1949 BEAUMONT, TEX.
65-107 TOVAR, CESAR LEONARDO	CALLE REAL PRADO MARIA #58 - CARACAS VENEZ
20-121 TOWNSEND, IRA DANCE	D. JULY 21, 1965 SCHULENBERG, TEX.
20-122 TOWNSEND, LEO ALPHONSE	D. DECEMBER 3, 1976 MOBILE, ALA.
84-123 TRABER, JAMES JOSEPH	10387 GREEN MOUNTAIN CIR - COLUMBIA MD 21044
62-137 TRACEWSKI, RICHARD JOHN	5 FLORA DR - PECKVILLE PA 18452
80-128 TRACY, JAMES EDWIN	4785 CELADON AVE - FAIRFIELD OH 45014
13-181 TRAGESSER, WALTER JOSEPH	D. DECEMBER 14, 1970 LAFAYETTE, IND.
40- 92 TRAMBACK, STEPHEN JOSEPH 'RED'	D. DECEMBER 28, 1979 BUFFALO, N. Y.
77-146 TRAMMELL, ALAN STUART	4797 QUITO CT - SAN DIEGO CA 92124
15-163 TRAUTMAN, FREDERICK ORLANDO	D. FEBRUARY 15, 1964 BUCYRUS, O.
12-201 TRAVERS, ALOYSIUS JOSEPH 'ALLAN'	D. APRIL 21, 1968 PHILADELPHIA, PA.
74-135 TRAVERS, WILLIAM EDWARD	10 SHORELINE DR - FOXBORO MA 02035
33- 62 TRAVIS, CECIL HOWELL	2260 HWY 138 - RIVERDALE GA 30296
20-123 TRAYNOR, HAROLD JOSEPH 'PIE'	D. MARCH 16, 1972 PITTSBURGH, PA.
30- 83 TREADAWAY, EDGAR RAYMOND 'RAY'	D. OCTOBER 12, 1935 CHATTANOOGA, TENN.
44-129 TREADWAY, THADFORD LEON 'RED'	750 DALRYMPLE RD NW #D-3 - ATLANTA GA 30328
37-100 TRECHOCK, FRANK ADAM	4600 29TH AVE S. - MINNEAPOLIS MN 55406
13-182 TREKELL, HARRY ROY	D. NOVEMBER 4, 1963 SPOKANE, WASH.
34-101 TREMARK, NICHOLAS JOSEPH	1906 LAUREL DR - HARLINGEN TX 78550
54-111 TREMEL, WILLIAM LEONARD	315 E 23RD AVE - ALTOONA PA 16601
27- 91 TREMPER, CARLTON OVERTON	15777 BOLESTA RD #143 - CLEARWATER FL 33520
38- 99 TRESH, MICHAEL	D. OCTOBER 1, 1966 DETROIT, MICH.
61-105 TRESH, THOMAS MICHAEL	4206 E WING RD, RR 6-MOUNT PLEASANT MI 48858
78-136 TREVINO, ALEJANDRO	ALONDRA #103,CUACHTEMOC-MONTERREY NUEVO LAREDO MEX.
68-104 TREVINO, CARLOS CASTRO 'BOBBY'	ALONDRA #102, CUAUHTEMOC - MONTERREY NUEVO LAREDO MEX.
53- 92 TRIANDOS, CONSTANDIN GUS	1207 WOODLAWN AVE - SAN JOSE CA 95128
53- 93 TRICE, ROBERT LEE	RR 2 BOX 25-R-9 - WEIRTON WV 26062
73-121 TRILLO, JESUS MANUEL 'MANNY'	CENTRO RES. HUMBOLDT #1B - PRADOS DEL ESTE CARACAS VENE
55-128 TRIMBLE, JOSEPH GERARD	71 ARBOR DR - PROVIDENCE RI 02903
43-138 TRINKLE, KENNETH WAYNE	D. MAY 10, 1976 PAOLI, ILL.
38-100 TRIPLETT, HERMAN COAKER	RR 1 BOX 72-C - BOONE NC 28607
73-122 TROEDSON, RICHARD LAMONTE	505 CHURCHILL PARK DR - SAN JOSE CA 95136
58- 97 TROSKY, HAROLD ARTHUR JR	1919 HAMILTON ST SW - CEDAR RAPIDS IA 52404
33- 63 TROSKY, HAROLD ARTHUR SR	D. JUNE 18, 1979 CEDAR RAPIDS, IOWA
37-101 TROTTER, WILLIAM FELIX	D. AUGUST 26, 1984 ARLINGTON, MASS.
52-105 TROUPPE, QUINCY THOMAS	P.O. BOX 1551 - HATTIESBURG MS 39401
39-119 TROUT, PAUL HOWARD 'DIZZY'	D. FEBRUARY 28, 1972 HARVEY, ILL.
78-137 TROUT, STEVEN RUSSELL	719 RIVERVIEW DR - SOUTH HOLLAND IL 60473
56- 83 TROWBRIDGE, ROBERT	D. APRIL 3, 1980 HUDSON, N. Y.
12-202 TROY, ROBERT 'BUN'	D. OCTOBER 7, 1918 MEUSE, FRANCE
41-113 TRUCKS, VIRGIL OLIVER 'FIRE'	RR 3 #5 GREENVALLEY - LEEDS AL 35094
10-144 TRUESDALE, FRANK DAY	D. AUGUST 27, 1943 ALBUQUERQUE, N. M.
85-113 TRUJILLO, MICHAEL ANDREW	2636 SOUTH STUART WAY - DENVER CO 80219
57- 88 TSITOURIS, JOHN PHILIP	5207 AUSTIN ROAD - MONROE NC 28110
27- 92 TUCKER, OSCAR DINWIDDIE	D. JULY 13, 1940 RADIANT, VA.
42-101 TUCKER, THURMAN LOWELL	OLD ADD: GORDON TX
79-111 TUDOR, JOHN THOMAS	14 FOREST ST - PEABODY MA 01960
18- 71 TUERO, OSCAR MONZON	D. OCTOBER 21, 1960 HOUSTON, TEXAS
81-138 TUFTS, ROBERT MALCOLM	27 WING RD - LYNNFIELD MA 01940
82-128 TUNNELL, BYRON LEE	5905 RISING HILLS DR - AUSTIN TX 78759
35-107 TURBEVILLE, GEORGE ELKINS	D. OCTOBER 5, 1983 SALISBURY, N. C.
43-139 TURCHIN, EDWARD LAWRENCE	D. FEBRUARY 8, 1982 BROOKHAVEN, N. Y.
23-134 TURGEON, EUGENE JOSEPH 'PETE'	D. JANUARY 24, 1977 WICHITA FALLS, TEX.
22-134 TURK, LUCAS NEWTON	BOX 168 - HOMER GA 30547
51- 98 TURLEY, ROBERT LEE	2035 OLD DOMINION RD - DUNWOODY GA 30338
48-101 TURNER, EARL WILLIAM	OLD ADD: 7 SULLIVAN DR - LENOX MA
37-102 TURNER, JAMES RILEY	1004 WOODMONT BLVD-NASHVILLE TN 37204
74-136 TURNER, JOHN WEBBER 'JERRY'	807 CALIFORNIA - VENICE CA 90291
67-109 TURNER, KENNETH CHARLES	4913 NEBLINA DR - CARLSBAD CA 92008
77-162 TURNER, ROBERT EDWARD 'TED'	1018 PEACHTREE ST NW - ATLANTA GA 30309
20-124 TURNER, THEODORE HOLTOP	D. FEBRUARY 4, 1958 LEXINGTON, KY.
15-164 TURNER, THOMAS LOVATT 'TINK'	D. FEBRUARY 25, 1962 PHILADELPHIA, PA.
40- 93 TURNER, THOMAS RICHARD	6110 W. WILLOW AVE - GLENDALE AZ 85304
52-106 TUTTLE, WILLIAM ROBERT	115 HARLEM RD #155 - KANSAS CITY MO 64116
11-171 TUTWEILER, GUY ISBELL	D. AUGUST 15, 1930 ANNISTON, ALA.
28-100 TUTWILER, ELMER STRANGE	D. MAY 3, 1976 PENSACOLA, FLA.
16- 90 TWINING, HOWARD EARLE 'TWINK'	D. JUNE 14, 1973 LANSDALE, PA.

JIM UMBARGER

JOSE VALDIVIELSO, P   Minnesota Twins

70-134	TWITCHELL, WAYNE LEE	7129 SW 33RD PL - PORTLAND OR 97219
80-129	TWITTY, JEFFREY DEAN	1734 C AVENUE - NORTH COLUMBIA SC 29169
20-125	TWOMBLY, CLARENCE EDWARD 'BABE'	D. NOVEMBER 23, 1974 SAN CLEMENTE, CALIF.
21-107	TWOMBLY, EDWIN PARKER 'CY'	D. DECEMBER 3, 1974 SAVANNAH, GA.
14-216	TWOMBLY, GEORGE FREDERICK	D. FEBRUARY 17, 1975 LEXINGTON, MASS.
43-140	TYACK, JAMES FRED	2901 MANOR AVE - BAKERSFIELD CA 93308
14-217	TYLER, FREDERICK FRANKLIN	D. OCTOBER 14, 1945 DERRY, N.H.
10-145	TYLER, GEORGE ALBERT 'LEFTY'	D. SEPTEMBER 29, 1953 LOWELL, MASS.
34-102	TYLER, JOHN ANTHONY	D. JULY 11, 1972 MOUNT PLEASANT, PA.
14-218	TYREE, EARL CARLTON	D. MAY 17, 1954 RUSHVILLE, ILL.
62-138	TYRIVER, DAVID BURTON	680 BOYD STREET - OSHKOSH WI 54901
72-116	TYRONE, JAMES VERNON	484 WEST MONTANA - PASADENA CA 91103
76- 95	TYRONE, OSCAR WAYNE	2301 NW 10TH AVE - MIAMI FL 33127
26- 87	TYSON, ALBERT THOMAS 'TY'	D. AUGUST 16, 1953 BUFFALO, N. Y.
44-130	TYSON, CECIL WASHINGTON 'TURKEY'	RR 1 BOX 202, TYSON LN - ELM CITY NC 27822
72-117	TYSON, MICHAEL RAY	479 THUNDERHEAD CANYON DR-BALDWIN MO 63011
26- 88	UCHRINSKO, JAMES EMERSON	204 WATER ST - WEST NEWTON PA 15089
62-139	UECKER, ROBERT GEORGE	N60W15734 HAWTHORNE DR - MENOMONEE FALLS WI 53051
34-103	UHALT, BERNARD BARTHOLOMEW 'FRENCHY'	231 CROSS RD - OAKLAND CA 94618
65-108	UHLAENDER, THEODORE OTTO	BOX 1355 - MCALLEN TX 78502
19- 83	UHLE, GEORGE ERNEST	D. FEBRUARY 26, 1985 LAKEWOOD, O.
38-101	UHLE, ROBERT ELLWOOD	8721 LANCASTER DR - ROHNERT PARK CA 94928
14-219	UHLER, MAURICE W.	D. MAY 4, 1918 BALTIMORE, MD.
34-104	UHLIR, CHARLES	OLD ADD: 11 S LASALLE - CHICAGO IL
80-130	UJDUR, GERALD RAYMOND	3312 BERKELEY RD - DULUTH MN 55811
45-106	ULISNEY, MICHAEL EDWARD	1405 NW 4TH AVE - FT LAUDERDALE FL 33311
83-143	ULLGER, SCOTT MATTHEW	9 BETH LANE - PLAINVIEW NY 11803
44-131	ULLRICH, CARLOS SANTIAGO CASTELLO	3671 NW 15TH ST - MIAMI FL 33125
25-106	ULRICH, FRANK W. 'DUTCH'	D. FEBRUARY 11, 1929 BALTIMORE, MD.
64-123	UMBACH, ARNOLD WILLIAM	655 SOUTH DEAN RD - AUBURN AL 36830
75-121	UMBARGER, JAMES HAROLD	181 EAST 56TH AVE #200 - DENVER CO 80216
59- 83	UMBRICHT, JAMES	D. APRIL 8, 1964 HOUSTON, TEX.
53- 94	UMPHLETT, THOMAS MULLEN	RR 2 BOX 17C - AHOSKIE NC 27910
27- 93	UNDERHILL, WILLIE VERN	D. OCTOBER 26, 1970 BAY CITY, TEXAS
79-112	UNDERWOOD, PATRICK JOHN	420 N BERKLEY RD - KOKOMO IN 46901
74-137	UNDERWOOD, THOMAS GERALD	420 NORTH BERKLEY RD - KOKOMO IN 46901
42-102	UNSER, ALBERT BERNARD	2096 N UNION-DECATUR IL 62526
68-105	UNSER, DELBERT BERNARD	495 FERNWOOD DR - MORAGA CA 94556
35-108	UPCHURCH, JEFFERSON WOODROW 'WOODY'	D. OCTOBER 23, 1971 BUIES CREEK, N. C.
67-110	UPHAM, JOHN LESLIE	1502 PIERRE AVE - WINDSOR ONTARIO CAN.
15-165	UPHAM, WILLIAM LAWRENCE	D. SEPTEMBER 14, 1959 NEWARK, N.J.
53- 95	UPRIGHT, R. T. 'DIXIE'	2118 LANE ST - KANNAPOLIS NC 28081
66- 91	UPSHAW, CECIL LEE	709 BURNT CREEK DR - LILBURN GA 30247
78-138	UPSHAW, WILLIE CLAY	BOX 395 - BLANCO TX 78606
50-100	UPTON, THOMAS HERBERT	4638 LARWIN - CYPRESS CA 90630
54-112	UPTON, WILLIAM RAY	BOX 3441 - LAMESA CA 92041
57- 89	URBAN, JACK ELMER	8607 FOWLER - OMAHA NE 68134
27- 94	URBAN, LOUIS JOHN 'LUKE'	D. DECEMBER 7, 1980 SOMERSET, MASS.
31- 91	URBANSKI, WILLIAM MICHAEL	D. JULY 12, 1973 PERTH AMBOY, N. J.
84-124	URIBE, JOSE ALTAGRACIA	CLE D#9 SAB. GRANDE DE PALENQUE - JUAN BARON DOM REP.
77-147	URREA, JOHN GODBY	12540 YOSEMITE - CERRITOS CA 90701
46-100	USHER, ROBERT ROYCE	1022 N FIFTH ST - SAN JOSE CA 95112
25-107	USSAT, WILLIAM AUGUST 'DUTCH'	D. MAY 29, 1959 DAYTON, O.
25-108	VACHE, ERNEST LEWIS 'TEX'	D. JUNE 11, 1953 LOS ANGELES, CALIF.
75-122	VAIL, MICHAEL LEWIS	3253 HARVESTMOON DR - PALM HARBOR FL 33563
44-132	VALDES, ARMANDO VIERA	OLD ADD: AS 1E, DES 16 - CARDENAS CUBA
57- 90	VALDES, RENE GUTIERREZ	AVENIDA 7A, 14511 ALTURAS-MANANA, HAVANA CUBA
65-109	VALDESPINO, HILARIO BORRATO 'SANDY'	17920 NW 43RD AVE - CAROL CITY FL 33054
80-131	VALDEZ, JULIO JULIAN CASTILLO	MAXIMO GAHEZ #4, NIZAO - BANI DOMINICAN REP.
55-129	VALDIVIELSO, JOSE LOPEZ	14 RITA DR - MOUNT SINAI NY 11766
75-123	VALENTINE, ELLIS CLARENCE	4905 PARKGLEN AVE - LOS ANGELES CA 90043
59- 84	VALENTINE, FRED LEE	4838 BLAGDEN AVE NW - WASHINGTON DC 20011
54-113	VALENTINE, HAROLD LEWIS 'CORKY'	RR 1, OLD BIRMINGHAM RD - CANTON GA 30114
69-173	VALENTINE, ROBERT JOHN	791 NORTH ST - WHITE PLAINS NY 10605
54-114	VALENTINETTI, VITO JOHN	271 SUMMIT AVE - MOUNT VERNON NY 10552
58- 98	VALENZUELA, BENJAMIN BELTRAN	BAHIA SAN ESTEBAN #267 SUR - LOS MOCHIS SINOLOA MEX.
80-132	VALENZUELA, FERNANDO	3004 N. BEACHWOOD DR - HOLLYWOOD CA 90068
84-125	VALLE, DAVID	20947 34TH ROAD - FLUSHING NY 11361
65-110	VALLE, HECTOR JOSE	URB. CATONI #7 - VEGA BAJA PR 00763
40- 94	VALO, ELMER WILLIAM	571 COLUMBIA AVE-PALMERTON PA 18071
50-101	VAN CUYK, CHRISTIAN GERALD	14405 AMY LANE - HUDSON FL 33562
27- 95	VANALSTYNE, CLAYTON EMERY	D. JANUARY 5, 1960 HUDSON, N. Y.
33- 64	VANATTA, RUSSELL	BOX 201 - LAFAYETTE NJ 07848

VANBRABANT

VOLLMER

```
65-111  VONHOFF, BRUCE FREDERICK              423 RIVER HILLS DR - TEMPLE TERRACE FL 33617
14-222  VONKOLNITZ, ALFRED HOLMES 'FRITZ'     D. MARCH 18, 1948 MOUNT PLEASANT, S.C.
83-145  VONOHLEN, DAVID                       11-06 128TH STREET - COLLEGE POINT NY 11356
30- 84  VOSMIK, JOSEPH FRANKLIN               D. JANUARY 27, 1962 CLEVELAND, O.
65-112  VOSS, WILLIAM EDWARD                  5882 SIERRA SIENA - IRVINE CA 92650
29-105  VOYLES, PHILIP VANCE                  D. NOVEMBER 3, 1972 MARLBORO, MASS.
75-124  VUCKOVICH, PETER DENNIS               6080 S 118TH ST - HALES CORNER WI 53130
80-135  VUKOVICH, GEORGE STEPHEN              421 N HARVARD AVE - ARLINGTON HEIGHTS IL60005
70-136  VUKOVICH, JOHN CHRISTOPHER            11 SHERI WAY - PINE HILL NJ 08021
17- 84  WACHTEL, PAUL HORINE                  D. DECEMBER 15, 1964 SAN ANTONIO, TEX.
84-126  WADDELL, THOMAS DAVID                 47 FIFTH STREET - CLOSTER NJ 07624
31- 93  WADDEY, FRANK ORUM                    RR 13 BOX 261 - GRAY TN 37615
48-103  WADE, BENJAMIN STYRON                 1165 MEDFORD RD - PASADENA CA 91107
55-133  WADE, GALEARD LEE                     RR 1 BOX 766 - NEBO NC 28761
36- 93  WADE, JACOB FIELDS                    WILDWOOD NC 28588
23-136  WADE, RICHARD FRANK 'RIP'             D. JUNE 15, 1957 SANDSTONE, MINN.
38-102  WAGNER, CHARLES THOMAS                1523 LINDEN ST-READING PA 19604
65-113  WAGNER, GARY EDWARD                   RR 4 BOX 480 - JACKSON NJ 08527
37-104  WAGNER, HAROLD EDWARD                 D. AUGUST 7, 1979 RIVERSIDE NJ
15-168  WAGNER, JOSEPH BERNARD                D. NOVEMBER 15, 1948 BRONX, N.Y.
58-100  WAGNER, LEON LAMAR 'DADDY WAGS'       1010 GOLDEN GATE AVE - SAN FRANCISCO CA 94115
76- 97  WAGNER, MARK DUANE                    1616 NEW HAVEN DR - ASHTABULA OH 44004
13-184  WAGNER, WILLIAM GEORGE 'BULL'         D. OCTOBER 2, 1967 MUSKEGON, MICH.
14-223  WAGNER, WILLIAM JOSEPH                D. JANUARY 11, 1951 WATERLOO, IA.
44-137  WAHL, KERMIT EMERSON                  7570 EAST SPEEDWAY BLVD - TUCSON AZ 85712
```

Greetings from   vous salue!
TOM WALKER

```
41-114  WAITKUS, EDWARD STEPHEN               D. SEPTEMBER 15, 1972 BOSTON, MASS.
73-127  WAITS, MICHAEL RICHARD 'RICK'         2329 BONNER RD - EAST POINT GA 30344
41-115  WAKEFIELD, RICHARD CUMMINGS           D. AUGUST 26, 1985 REDFORD TWP., WAYNE CO., MICH.
64-125  WAKEFIELD, WILLIAM SUMNER             %KRANSCO,P.O. BOX 884866 - SAN FRANCISCO CA 94188
23-137  WALBERG, GEORGE ELVIN 'RUBE'          D. OCTOBER 27, 1978 TEMPE, ARIZ.
45-108  WALCZAK, EDWIN JOSEPH                 544 NEW LONDON - NORWICH CT 06360
17- 85  WALDBAUER, ALBERT CHARLES 'DOC'       D. JULY 16, 1969 YAKIMA, WASH.
12-207  WALDEN, THOMAS FRED                   D. SEPTEMBER 27, 1955 JEFFERSON BARRACKS, MO.
80-136  WALK, ROBERT VERNON                   %C.SHIELDS,BOX 954 - FRAZIER PARK CA 93225
48-104  WALKER, ALBERT BLUFORD 'RUBE'         342 CUMBERLAND WAY - SMYRNA GA 30080
17- 86  WALKER, CHARLES FRANKLIN              D. SEPTEMBER 16, 1974 BRISTOL, TENN.
11-172  WALKER, CLARENCE WILLIAM 'TILLY'      D. SEPTEMBER 21, 1959 UNICOI, TENN.
80-137  WALKER, CLEOTHA 'CHICO'               B. NOVEMBER 25, 1957 JACKSON, MISS.
82-133  WALKER, DUANE ALLEN                   3108 GRANT ST - PASADENA TX 77503
13-185  WALKER, ERNEST ROBERT                 D. APRIL 1, 1965 PELL CITY, ALA.
31- 94  WALKER, FRED "DIXIE"                  D. MAY 17, 1982 BIRMINGHAM, ALA.
10-146  WALKER, FREDERICK MITCHELL            D. FEBRUARY 1, 1958 OAK PARK, ILL.
31- 95  WALKER, GERALD HOLMES 'GEE'           D. MARCH 20, 1981 WHITFIELD, MISS.
82-134  WALKER, GREGORY LEE                   422 E. JEFFERSON ST - DOUGLAS GA 31533
40- 96  WALKER, HARRY WILLIAM                 RR 2 BOX 145 - LEEDS AL 35094
31- 96  WALKER, HARVEY WILLOS 'HUB'           D. NOVEMBER 26, 1982 SAN JOSE, CALIF.
65-114  WALKER, JAMES LUKE                    3308 FCI ROAD - TEXARKANA TX 75501
12-208  WALKER, JAMES ROY                     D. FEBRUARY 10, 1962 NEW ORLEANS, LA.
57- 91  WALKER, JERRY ALLEN                   2015 COLLINS BLVD - ADA OK 74820
19- 85  WALKER, JOHN MILES                    D. AUGUST 19, 1976 HOLLYWOOD, FLA.
23-138  WALKER, JOSEPH RICHARD                D. JUNE 20, 1959 WEST MIFFLIN, PA.
28-102  WALKER, MARTIN VAN BUREN              D. APRIL 24, 1978 PHILADELPHIA, PA.
72-118  WALKER, ROBERT THOMAS 'TOM'           234 MONTCLAIR AVE - PITTSBURGH PA 15229
19- 86  WALKER, WILLIAM CURTIS 'CURT'         D. DECEMBER 9, 1955 BEEVILLE, TEX.
27- 96  WALKER, WILLIAM HENRY                 D. JUNE 14, 1966 EAST ST. LOUIS, ILL.
34-106  WALKUP, JAMES ELTON                   HAVANA AR 72842
27- 97  WALKUP, JAMES HUEY                    1111 GRAND - DUNCAN OK 73533
50-103  WALL, MURRAY WESLEY                   D. OCTOBER 8, 1971 LONE OAK, TEXAS
75-125  WALL, STANLEY ARTHUR                  9907 E. 80TH ST - RAYTOWN MO 64138
15-169  WALLACE, CLARENCE EUGENE 'JACK'       D. OCTOBER 15, 1960 WINNFIELD, LA.
73-128  WALLACE, DAVID WILLIAM                63 STONEHEDGE LN - ATTLEBORO MA 02703
67-111  WALLACE, DONALD ALLEN                 23 KRIS LN - MANITOU SPRINGS CO 80829
19- 87  WALLACE, FREDERICK RENSHAW 'DOC'      D. DECEMBER 31, 1964 HAVERFORD TWP, PA.
12-209  WALLACE, HARRY CLINTON 'HUCK'         D. JULY 9, 1951 CLEVELAND, O.
42-105  WALLACE, JAMES HAROLD 'LEFTY'         D. JULY 28, 1982 EVANSVILLE, IND.
73-129  WALLACE, MICHAEL SHERMAN              RR 1 BIX 176AA - MIDLAND VA 22728
80-138  WALLACE, TIMOTHY CHARLES              14742 FEATHERHILL RD - TUSTIN CA 92680
40- 97  WALLAESA, JOHN                        30 MACYWOOD LN - EASTON PA 18042
45-109  WALLEN, NORMAN EDWARD                 3429 NORTH WEIL - MILWAUKEE WI 53212
80-139  WALLER, ELLIOTT TYRONE 'TY'           5146 LAPAZ DR - SAN DIEGO CA 92114
75-126  WALLING, DENNIS                       BOX 1312 - WAYNESBORO VA 22980
75-127  WALLIS, HAROLD JOSEPH 'JOE'           1195 CHEYENNE DR - FLORISSANT MO 63033
52-108  WALLS, RAYMOND LEE                    3002 N. 70TH ST - SCOTTSDALE AZ 85251
27- 98  WALSH, AUGUST                         2004 5TH AVE - SAN RAFAEL CA 94901
```

14-224 WALSH, AUSTIN EDWARD   D. JANUARY 26, 1955 GLENDALE, CALIF.
28-103 WALSH, EDWARD ARTHUR   D. OCTOBER 31, 1937 MERIDEN, CONN.
12-210 WALSH, JAMES CHARLES   D. JULY 3, 1962 SYRACUSE, N.Y.
46-101 WALSH, JAMES GERALD   RR 1, LAYTON RD - OLYPHANT PA 18447
21-108 WALSH, JAMES THOMAS   D. MAY 13, 1967 BOSTON, MASS.
10-147 WALSH, JOSEPH FRANCIS   D. JANUARY 6, 1967 BUFFALO, N.Y.
38-103 WALSH, JOSEPH PATRICK 'TWEET'   7 ST.LUKE'S RD - ALLSTON MA 02134
13-186 WALSH, LEO THOMAS 'DEE'   D. JULY 14, 1971 ST. LOUIS, MO.
10-148 WALSH, MICHAEL TIMOTHY 'JIMMY'   D. JANUARY 21, 1947 BALTIMORE, MD.
20-127 WALSH, WALTER WILLIAM   D. JANUARY 15, 1966 NEPTUNE, N. J.
85-114 WALTER, GENE WINSTON   6042 SOUTH MONITOR - CHICAGO IL 60638
30- 85 WALTER, JAMES BERNARD 'BERNIE'   BOX 121 - DOVER TN 37058
15-170 WALTERS, ALFRED JOHN 'ROXY'   D. JUNE 3, 1956 ALAMEDA, CALIF.
69-175 WALTERS, CHARLES LEONARD   12387 PASEO VERANO - YUMA AZ 85365
45-110 WALTERS, JAMES FREDERICK 'FRED'   D. FEBRUARY 1, 1980 LAUREL, MISS.
60-101 WALTERS, KENNETH ROGERS   9545 BELLE MEADE DR - SAN RAMON CA 94583
83-146 WALTERS, MICHAEL CHARLES   80119 PALM CIRCLE DR - INDIO CA 92201
31- 97 WALTERS, WILLIAM HENRY 'BUCKY'   515 FOX RD - GLENSIDE PA 19038
68-106 WALTON, DANIEL JAMES   BOX 626 - LOS ALAMOS NM 87544
80-140 WALTON, REGINALD SHERARD   1142 S CARSON AVE - LOS ANGELES CA 90019
14-225 WAMBSGANSS, WILLIAM ADOLPH   D. DECEMBER 8, 1985 LAKEWOOD, O.

Bill Wambsganss

27- 99 WANER, LLOYD JAMES   D. JULY 22, 1982 OKLAHOMA CITY, OKLA.
26- 90 WANER, PAUL GLEE   D. AUGUST 29, 1965 SARASOTA, FLA.
25-110 WANNINGER, PAUL LOUIS 'PEE WEE'   D. MAY 7, 1981 NORTH AUGUSTA, S. C.
65-115 WANTZ, RICHARD CARTER   D. MAY 13, 1965 INGLEWOOD, CAL.
17- 87 WARD, AARON LEE   D. JANUARY 30, 1961 NEW ORLEANS, LA.
17- 88 WARD, CHARLES WILLIAM   D. APRIL 4, 1969 ST. PETERSBURG, FLA.
72-119 WARD, CHRIS GILBERT   17469 VIA LA JOLLA - SAN LORENZO CA 94580
85-115 WARD, COLIN NORVAL   356 VISTA BONITA ST - AZUSA CA 91702
79-116 WARD, GARY LAMELL   318 W RAYMOND ST - COMPTON CA 90220
63-122 WARD, JOHN FRANCIS 'JAY'   OLD ADD: RR 3 BOX 112-MOUNTAIN GROVE MO
12-211 WARD, JOSEPH NICHOLAS 'HAP'   D. SEPTEMBER 13, 1979 ELMER, N. J.
62-141 WARD, PETER THOMAS   575 SOUTHWEST "G" - LAKE OSWEGO OR 97034
48-105 WARD, PRESTON MEYER   4371 DESILVA PL - LAS VEGAS NV 89101
34-107 WARD, RICHARD OLE   D. JUNE 1, 1966 FREELAND, WASH.
68-107 WARDEN, JONATHAN EDGAR   770 QUAILWOODS DR - LOVELAND OH 45140
84-127 WARDLE, CURTIS RAY   30886 CURZULLA ROAD - WINCHESTER CA 92396
13-187 WARES, CLYDE ELLSWORTH 'BUZZY'   D. MAY 26, 1964 SOUTH BEND, IND.
16- 91 WARMOTH, WALLACE WALTER 'CY'   D. JUNE 20, 1957 MOUNT CARMEL, ILL.
30- 86 WARNEKE, LONNIE   D. JUNE 23, 1976 HOT SPRINGS, ARK.
12-212 WARNER, EDWARD EMORY   D. FEBRUARY 2, 1954 FITCHBURG, MASS.
16- 92 WARNER, HOKE HAYDEN 'HOOKS'   D. FEBRUARY 19, 1947 SAN FRANCISCO, CAL.
62-142 WARNER, JACK DYER   239 EAST ST. JOHNS - PHOENIX AZ 85022
66- 96 WARNER, JOHN JOSEPH   512 E LEADORA - GLENDORA CA 91740
25-111 WARNER, JOHN RALPH   D. MARCH 13, 1986 MOUNT VERNON, ILL.
35-112 WARNOCK, HAROLD CHARLES   BOX 871 - TUCSON AZ 85702
39-123 WARREN, BENNIE LOUIS   3708 NW 18TH ST-OKLAHOMA CITY OK 73107
83-147 WARREN, MICHAEL BRUCE   12342 BROWNING RD - GARDEN GROVE CA 92640
44-138 WARREN, THOMAS GENTRY   D. JANUARY 2, 1968 TULSA, OKLA.
14-226 WARREN, WILLIAM HACKNEY   D. JANUARY 28, 1960 WHITEVILLE, TENN.
30- 87 WARSTLER, HAROLD BURTON 'RABBIT'   D. MAY 31, 1964 NORTH CANTON,O.
75-128 WARTHEN, DANIEL DEAN   6336 N 38TH ST - OMAHA NE 68111
61-106 WARWICK, CARL WAYNE   14102 BONNEY BRIER - HOUSTON TX 77069
21-109 WARWICK, FIRMAN NEWTON 'BILL'   D. DECEMBER 19, 1984 SAN ANTONIO, TEXAS
37-105 WASDELL, JAMES CHARLES   D. AUGUST 6, 1983 NEWPORT RICHEY, FLA.
37-106 WASEM, LINCOLN WILLIAM   D. MARCH 6, 1979 SOUTH LAGUNA, CALIF.
41-116 WASHBURN, GEORGE EDWARD   D. JANUARY 5, 1979 BATON ROUGE, LA.
69-176 WASHBURN, GREGORY JAMES   1685 E. STELLON ST - COAL CITY IL 60416
61-107 WASHBURN, RAY CLARK   16309 JUANITA WOODVILLE WAY NE - BOTHELL WA 98011
74-138 WASHINGTON, CLAUDELL   12 CHARLES HILL RD - ORINDA CA 94563
74-139 WASHINGTON, HERBERT   642 E AUSTIN ST - FLINT MI 48505
78-139 WASHINGTON, LARUE   709 WEST PLUM ST - COMPTON CA 90222
77-148 WASHINGTON, RONALD   1900 ALLEN ST - NEW ORLEANS LA 70116
35-113 WASHINGTON, SLOANE VERNON 'GEORGE'   RR 2 - LINDEN TX 75563
77-149 WASHINGTON, U. L.   BOX 164 - STRINGTOWN OK 74569
67-112 WASLEWSKI, GARY LEE   MCKENZIE DR - SOUTHINGTON CT 06489
76- 98 WATERBURY, STEVEN CRAIG   710 N. GARFIELD - MARION IL 62958

55-134 WATERS, FRED WARREN	1350 EAST AVERY - PENSACOLA FL 32503
76- 99 WATHAN, JOHN DAVID	1401 DEER RUN TRAIL - BLUE SPRINGS MO 64015
69-177 WATKINS, DAVID ROGER	1502 ROOSEVELT RD - OWENSBORO KY 42301
30- 88 WATKINS, GEORGE ARCHIBALD	D. JUNE 1, 1970 HOUSTON, TEX.
69-178 WATKINS, ROBERT CECIL	1205 S ACACIA - COMPTON CA 90220
53- 97 WATLINGTON, JULIUS NEAL	BOX 418 - YANCEYVILLE NC 27379
14-227 WATSON, ARTHUR STANHOPE	D. MAY 9, 1950 BUFFALO, N. Y.
13-188 WATSON, CHARLES JOHN 'DOC'	D. DECEMBER 30, 1949 SAN DIEGO, CALIF.
18- 72 WATSON, JOHN REEVES 'MULE'	D. AUGUST 25, 1949 SHREVEPORT, LA.
30- 89 WATSON, JOHN THOMAS	D. APRIL 29, 1965 HUNTINGTON, W. V.
16- 93 WATSON, MILTON WILSON	D. APRIL 10, 1962 PINE BLUFF, ARK.
66- 97 WATSON, ROBERT JOSE	215 BOLLING RD - ATLANTA GA 30305
20-128 WATT, ALBERT BAILEY	D. MARCH 15, 1968 NORFOLK, VA.
66- 98 WATT, EDDIE DEAN	BOX 7 - NORTH BEND NE 68649
31- 98 WATT, FRANK MARION	D. AUGUST 31, 1956 GLEN COVE, MD.
29-106 WATWOOD, JOHN CLIFFORD	D. MARCH 1, 1980 GOODWATER, ALA.
52-109 WAUGH, JAMES ELDEN	3109 OAKRIDGE - CORSICANA TX 75110
27-100 WAY, ROBERT CLINTON	D. JUNE 20, 1974 PITTSBURGH, PA.
24-114 WAYENBERG, FRANK	D. APRIL 16, 1975 ZANESVILLE, O.
36- 94 WEAFER, KENNETH ALBERT	66 RYCKMAN AVE - ALBANY NY 12208
36- 95 WEATHERLY, CYRIL ROY 'STORMY'	1175 DENTON DRIVE - BEAUMONT TX 77707
62-143 WEAVER, DAVID FLOYD	RR 1 BOX 579 - POWDERLY TX 75473
68-108 WEAVER, EARL SIDNEY	19016 W LAKE DR - HIALEAH FL 33015
12-213 WEAVER, GEORGE DANIEL 'BUCK'	D. JANUARY 31, 1956 CHICAGO, ILL.
15-171 WEAVER, HARRY ABRAHAM	D. MAY 30, 1983 ROCHESTER, N. Y.
67-113 WEAVER, JAMES BRIAN	276 RHODA DR - LANCASTER PA 17601
28-104 WEAVER, JAMES DEMENT	D. DECEMBER 12, 1983 LAKELAND, FLA.
85-116 WEAVER, JAMES FRANCIS	212 77TH STREET - HOLMES BEACH FL 33510
31- 99 WEAVER, MONTGOMERY MORTON	826 S LAKE ADAIR BLVD - ORLANDO FL 32804
10-149 WEAVER, ORLIE FOREST	D. NOVEMBER 28, 1970 NEW ORLEANS, LA.
80-141 WEAVER, ROGER EDWARD	BOX 15 - SAINT JOHNSVILLE NY 13452
10-150 WEBB, CLEON EARL 'LEFTY'	D. JANUARY 12, 1958 CIRCLEVILLE, O.
72-120 WEBB, HENRY GAYLON	38 HARBOR OAKS CIR - SAFETY HARBOR FL 33572
32- 90 WEBB, JAMES LEVERNE 'SKEETER'	4118 POPLAR SPRING DR - MERIDIAN MS 39303
48-106 WEBB, SAMUEL HENRY 'RED'	5609 35TH PL - HYATTSVILLE MD 20782
25-112 WEBB, WILLIAM EARL	D. MAY 22, 1965 JAMESTOWN, TENN.
43-141 WEBB, WILLIAM FREDERICK	3758 SHARON DR - POWDER SPRINGS GA 30073
17- 89 WEBB, WILLIAM JOSEPH	D. JANUARY 12, 1943 CHICAGO, ILL.
42-106 WEBBER, LESTER ELMER	1645 S MCCLELLAND - SANTA MARIA CA 93454
83-148 WEBSTER, MITCHELL DEAN	322 WEST 6TH STREET - LARNED KS 67550
67-114 WEBSTER, RAMON ALBERTO	BOX 1340 - COLON PAN.
59- 86 WEBSTER, RAYMOND GEORGE	410 CENTER ST - YUBA CITY CA 95991
11-173 WEEDEN, CHARLES ALBERT	D. JANUARY 7, 1939 NORTHWOOD, N.H.
62-144 WEEKLY, JOHN	D. NOVEMBER 24, 1974 WALNUT CREEK, CAL.
69-179 WEGENER, MICHAEL DENIS	%M.A. WEGENER,2230 E. NOBLES - DENVER CO 80201
85-117 WEGMAN, WILLIAM EDWARD	5368 PLOVER LANE - CINCINNATI OH 45238
30- 90 WEHDE, WILBUR 'BIGGS'	D. SEPTEMBER 21, 1970 SIOUX FALLS,S.D.
45-111 WEHMEIER, HERMAN RALPH	D. MAY 21, 1973 DALLAS, TEX.
76-100 WEHRMEISTER, DAVID THOMAS	4216 DUBBE CT - CONCORD CA 94521
46-102 WEIGEL, RALPH RICHARD	1404 WHEATON RD - MEMPHIS TN 38117
48-107 WEIK, RICHARD HENRY	17532 70TH CT - TINLEY PARK IL 60477
40- 98 WEILAND, EDWIN NICHOLAS	D. JULY 12, 1972 CHICAGO, ILL.
28-105 WEILAND, ROBERT GEORGE	5518 W. MELROSE - CHICAGO IL 60641
12-214 WEILMAN, CARL WOOLWORTH	D. MAY 25, 1924 HAMILTON, O.
19- 88 WEINERT, PHILLIP WALTER 'LEFTY'	D. APRIL 17, 1973 ROCKLEDGE, FLA.
45-112 WEINGARTNER, ELMER WILLIAM	13604 LORAIN - CLEVELAND OH 44111
33- 65 WEINTRAUB, PHILIP	2091 CALIENTE - PALM SPRINGS CA 92262
36- 96 WEIR, WILLIAM FRANKLIN 'ROY'	1521 W CRIS PLACE - ANAHEIM CA 92802
62-145 WEIS, ALBERT JOHN	902 SOUTH POPLAR - ELMHURST IL 60126
22-136 WEIS, ARTHUR JOHN 'BUTCH'	209 KINGSVILLE CT - WEBSTER GROVES MO 63119
15-172 WEISER, HARRY BUDSON 'BUD'	D. JULY 31, 1961 SHAMOKIN, PA.
80-142 WEISS, GARY LEE	RR 1 BOX 80 - BRENHAM TX 77833
15-173 WEISS, JOSEPH HAROLD	D. JULY 7, 1967 CEDAR RAPIDS, IA.
39-124 WELAJ, JOHN LUDWIG	1519 COLLEGE ST #103 - ARLINGTON TX 76010
19- 89 WELCH, FRANK TIGUER	D. JULY 25, 1957 BIRMINGHAM, ALA.
25-113 WELCH, HERBERT M.	D. APRIL 13, 1967 MEMPHIS, TENN.
26- 91 WELCH, JOHN VERNON	D. SEPTEMBER 2, 1940 ST. LOUIS, MO.
45-113 WELCH, MILTON EDWARD	2860 TAYLOR ST - EUGENE OR 97405
78-140 WELCH, ROBERT LYNN	4150 DELPHI CIR - HUNTINGTON BEACH CA 92649
14-228 WELCH, THEODORE	B. 1893
82-135 WELCHEL, DONALD RAY	10327 GARWOOD DR - DALLAS TX 75238
11-174 WELCHONCE, HARRY MONROE	D. FEBRUARY 26, 1977 ARCADIA, CALIF.
16- 94 WELF, OLIVER HENRY	D. JUNE 25, 1967 CLEVELAND, O.

82-136 WELLMAN, BRAD EUGENE	18081 JOSEPH DR - CASTRO VALLEY CA 94546
48-108 WELLMAN, ROBERT JOSEPH	2321 ADAMS AVE - NORWOOD OH 45212
23-139 WELLS, EDWIN LEE	2085 MYRTLEWOOD DR - MONTGOMERY AL 36111
81-139 WELLS, GREGORY DEWAYNE 'BOOMER'	RR 1 BOX 98 - MCINTOSH AL 36553
44-139 WELLS, JOHN FREDERICK	3115 1/2 WEST STATE RD - OLEAN NY 14760
42-107 WELLS, LEO DONALD	1755 HIGHLAND PKWY - ST PAUL MN 55116
81-140 WELSH, CHRISTOPHER CHARLES	8760 APPLEKNOLL LN - CINCINNATI OH 45236
25-114 WELSH, JAMES DANIEL	D. OCTOBER 30, 1970 OAKLAND, CAL.
48-109 WELTEROTH, RICHARD JOHN	122 ELDRED ST - WILLIAMSPORT PA 17701
26- 92 WELZER, ANTON FRANK	D. MARCH 18, 1971 MILWAUKEE, WIS.
15-174 WENDELL, LEWIS CHARLES	D. JULY 11, 1953 BRONX, N. Y.
43-142 WENSLOFF, CHARLES WILLIAM 'BUTCH'	8 RYAN AVE - MILL VALLEY CA 94941
45-114 WENTZEL, STANLEY AARON	2900 OLEY TURNPIKE RD #J8 - READING PA 19606
68-109 WENZ, FREDERICK CHARLES	1 CIRCLE DR - SOMERVILLE NJ 08876
27-101 WERA, JULIAN VALENTINE	D. DECEMBER 12, 1975 ROCHESTER, MINN.
30- 91 WERBER, WILLIAM MURRAY	350 NEPTUNES BIGHT - NAPLES FL 33940
64-126 WERHAS, JOHN CHARLES	7420 STONE CREEK LANE - ANAHEIM CA 92807
49- 89 WERLE, WILLIAM GEORGE	833 W 28TH AVE - SAN MATEO CA 94403
56- 85 WERLEY, GEORGE WILLIAM	16429 HORSESHOE RIDGE - CHESTERFIELD MO 63017
75-129 WERNER, DONALD PAUL	19 FAIRWAY CT - APPLETON WI 54915
63-123 WERT, DONALD RALPH	RR 1 BOX 288 - NEW PROVIDENCE PA 17560
79-117 WERTH, DENNIS DEAN	BOX 8 - MOUNT PULASKI IL 62548
14-229 WERTZ, DWIGHT LEWIS 'DEL'	B. 1891
26- 93 WERTZ, HENRY LEVI 'JOHNNY'	1704 NANCE ST - NEWBERRY SC 29108
47- 92 WERTZ, VICTOR WOODROW	D. JULY 7, 1983 DETROIT, MICH.
79-118 WESSINGER, JAMES MICHAEL	504 KINGSTON RD - UTICA NY 13502
38-104 WEST, MAX EDWARD	507 SIERRA KEYS DR-SIERRA MADRE CA 91024
38-105 WEST, RICHARD THOMAS	RR ONE, WILDWOOD ISLE - LEESBURG IN 46538
27-102 WEST, SAMUEL FILMORE	1919 34TH ST #25 - LUBBOCK TX 79411
28-106 WEST, WALTER MAXWELL 'MAX'	D. APRIL 25, 1971 HOUSTON, TEX.
44-140 WEST, WELDON EDISON 'LEFTY'	D. JULY 23, 1979 HENDERSONVILLE, N. C.
55-135 WESTLAKE, JAMES PATRICK	909 SEAMAS AVE - SACRAMENTO CA 95801
47- 93 WESTLAKE, WALDON THOMAS	3800 61ST - SACRAMENTO CA 95820
29-107 WESTON, ALFRED JOHN	1 ALPINE TER - NEEDHAM MA 02192
47- 94 WESTRUM, WESLEY NOREEN	645 REVOLTA CIR - MESA AZ 85208
27-103 WETZEL, CHARLES EDWARD 'BUZZ'	D. MARCH 7, 1941 GLOBE, ARIZ.
20-129 WETZEL, FRANKLIN BURTON 'BUZZ'	D. MARCH 5, 1942 BURBANK, CAL.
82-137 WEVER, STEFAN MATTHEW	2240 LOMBARD ST #202 - SAN FRANCISCO CA 94123
23-140 WHALEY, WILLIAM CARL	D. MARCH 3, 1943 INDIANAPOLIS, IND.
13-189 WHALING, ALBERT JAMES	D. JANUARY 21, 1965 LOS ANGELES, CALIF.
54-116 WHEAT, LEROY WILLIAM	6125 PINE TER - FT LAUDERDALE FL 33317
15-175 WHEAT, MCKINLEY DAVIS 'MACK'	D. AUGUST 14, 1979 LOS BANOS, CALIF.
12-215 WHEATLEY, CHARLES	D. DECEMBER 10, 1982 TULSA, OKLA.
43-143 WHEATON, ELWOOD PIERCE	%H.R.WHEATON,1135 WABANK-LANCASTER PA 17603
49- 90 WHEELER, DONALD WESLEY	8127 COLFAX AVE S - MINNEAPOLIS MN 55420
45-115 WHEELER, EDWARD RAYMOND	OLD ADD: 135 N EUCALYPTUS ST - INGLEWOOD CA
21-110 WHEELER, FLOYD CLARK 'RIP'	D. SEPTEMBER 18, 1968 MARION, KY.
10-151 WHEELER, GEORGE HARRISON	D. JUNE 14, 1918 CLINTON, IND.
18- 73 WHEELER, RICHARD	D. FEBRUARY 12, 1962 LEXINGTON, MASS.
76-101 WHEELOCK, GARY RICHARD	15446 SE 20TH PL - BELLEVUE WA 98007
13-190 WHELAN, JAMES FRANCIS	D. NOVEMBER 29, 1929 DAYTON, O.
20-130 WHELAN, THOMAS JOSEPH	D. JUNE 26, 1957 BOSTON, MASS.
71-107 WHILLOCK, JACK FRANKLIN	2007 EDGEBROOK CT - ARLINGTON TX 76015
52-110 WHISENANT, THOMAS PETER 'PETE'	218 W GRACE ST - PUNTA GORDA FL 33950
77-150 WHISENTON, LARRY	2507 SLATTERY ST - ST LOUIS MO 63106
77-151 WHITAKER, LOUIS RODMAN	803 PIPE - MARTINSVILLE VA 24112
66- 99 WHITAKER, STEVE EDWARD	OLD ADD: 2501 N. OCEAN DR - HOLLYWOOD BEACH FL 33019
64-127 WHITBY, WILLIAM EDWARD	RR 1 BOX 1060 - HUNTERSVILLE NC 28078
45-116 WHITCHER, ROBERT ARTHUR	156 GRAHAM RD - CUYAHOGA FALLS OH 44223
37-107 WHITE, ADEL 'ABE'	D. OCTOBER 1, 1978 ATLANTA, GA.
40- 99 WHITE, ALBERT EUGENE 'FUZZ'	RR 1 BOX 1049 - BRANSON MO 65616
54-117 WHITE, CHARLES	OLD ADD: 8167 HUDSON ST - VANCOUVER BC
85-118 WHITE, DEVON MARKES	474 WEST 158TH ST #42 - NEW YORK NY 10032
48-110 WHITE, DONALD WILLIAM	3488 DON LORENZO DR - CARLSBAD CA 92008
55-136 WHITE, EDWARD PERRY	309 AZALEA ST - LAKELAND FL 33803
62-146 WHITE, ELDER LAFAYETTE	919 COLONY AVE - AHOSKIE NC 27910
40-100 WHITE, ERNEST DANIEL	D. MAY 22, 1974 AUGUSTA, GA.
73-130 WHITE, FRANK	8925 LAMBERT DR - LEES SUMMIT MO 64063
41-117 WHITE, HAROLD GEORGE	612 BIRD BAY DR #113C - VENICE FL 33595
74-140 WHITE, JEROME CARDELL	1255 ALICANTE DR - PACFICA CA 94044
27-104 WHITE, JOHN PETER	D. JUNE 19, 1971 FLUSHING, N. Y.
32- 91 WHITE, JOYNER CLIFFORD 'JO-JO'	40 THUNDERBIRD WAY SW #M8 - TACOMA WA 98498
63-124 WHITE, JOYNER MICHAEL 'MIKE'	1820 284TH EAST - ROY WA 98580

83-149 WHITE, LARRY DAVID	11240 DEHAVEN AVENUE - POLOMA CA 91331
78-141 WHITE, MYRON ALAN	3201 SOUTH DEEGAN DR - SANTA ANA CA 92704
65-116 WHITE, ROY HILTON	30 ASPEN WAY - UPPER SADDLE RIVER NJ 07458
51-101 WHITE, SAMUEL CHARLES	BOX 121 - HANALEI HI 96714
19- 90 WHITE, SAMUEL LAMBETH	D. NOVEMBER 11, 1929 PHILADELPHIA, PA.
12-216 WHITE, STEPHEN VINCENT	D. JANUARY 29, 1975 BRAINTREE, MASS.
45-117 WHITE, WILLIAM BARNEY	3721 DARRELL LN - TYLER TX 75701
56- 86 WHITE, WILLIAM DEKOVA	71 CALLOWHILL RD - CHALFONT PA 18914
33- 66 WHITEHEAD, BURGESS URQUHART	206 KING ST - WINDSOR NC 27983
35-114 WHITEHEAD, JOHN HENDERSON	D. OCTOBER 20, 1964 BONHAM, TEX.
23-141 WHITEHILL, EARL OLIVER	D. OCTOBER 22, 1954 OMAHA, NEB.
14-231 WHITEHOUSE, CHARLES EVIS	D. JULY 19, 1960 INDIANAPOLIS, IND.
12-217 WHITEHOUSE, GILBERT ARTHUR	D. FEBRUARY 14, 1926 BREWER, ME.
81-141 WHITEHOUSE, LEONARD JOSEPH	1874 NORTH AVE - BURLINGTON VT 05401
62-147 WHITFIELD, FRED DWIGHT	RR 1 BOX 91 - VANDIVER AL 35176
74-141 WHITFIELD, TERRY BERTLAND	2729 CARMEN DR - LOS ANGELES CA 90046
46-103 WHITMAN, DICK CORWIN	184 PETER DR - CAMPBELL CA 95008
46-104 WHITMAN, WALTER FRANKLIN 'FRANK'	44 BELLEVUE #5 - COLLINSVILLE IL 62234
80-143 WHITMER, DANIEL CHARLES	823 ROBINHOOD LN - REDLANDS CA 92373
28-107 WHITNEY, ARTHUR CARTER 'PINKY'	518 W KINGS HWY - SAN ANTONIO TX 78212
77-152 WHITSON, EDDIE LEE	127 YELTON ST - ERWIN TN 37650
76-102 WHITT, ERNEST LEO	18330 13 MILE RD - ROSEVILLE MI 48066
16- 95 WHITTAKER, WALTER ELTON	D. AUGUST 7, 1965 PEMBROKE, MASS.
12-218 WHITTED, GEORGE BOSTIC 'POSSUM'	D. OCTOBER 16, 1962 WILMINGTON, N.C.
68-110 WICKER, FLOYD EULISS	RR 2 BOX 166A - SNOW CAMP NC 27349
36- 97 WICKER, KEMP CASWELL	D. JUNE 11, 1973 KERNERSVILLE, N. C.
60-102 WICKERSHAM, DAVID CLIFFORD	9118 W 104TH TER - OVERLAND PARK KS 66204
13-191 WICKLAND, ALBERT	D. MARCH 14, 1980 PORT WASHINGTON, WISC.
47- 95 WIDMAR, ALBERT JOSEPH	3919 SOUTH OSWEGO AV - TULSA OK 74135
58-101 WIEAND, FRANKLIN DELANO ROOS. 'TED'	216 WALNUT ST - SLATINGTON PA 18080
34-108 WIEDEMEYER, CHARLES JOHN	D. OCTOBER 27, 1979 LAKE GENEVA, FLA.
79-119 WIEDENBAUER, THOMAS JOHN	618 N KEEN PL - TUCSON AZ 85710
81-142 WIEGHAUS, THOMAS ROBERT	RR 1 BOX 169 - GRANT PARK IL 60940
21-111 WIENEKE, JOHN	D. MARCH 16, 1933 PLEASANT RIDGE, MICH.
51-102 WIESLER, ROBERT GEORGE	2325 INDIAN CUP DR - FLORISSANT MO 63031
39-125 WIETELMANN, WILLIAM FREDERICK 'WHITEY'	7712 GOLFCREST DR - SAN DIEGO CA 92119
81-143 WIGGINS, ALAN ANTHONY	125 EAST WOODBURY RD - ALTADENA CA 91001
46-105 WIGHT, WILLIAM ROBERT	6247 MEADOW VISTA DR - CARMICHAEL CA 95608
23-142 WIGINGTON, FREDERICK THOMAS	D. MAY 8, 1980 MESA, ARIZ.
79-120 WIHTOL, ALEXANDER AMES 'SANDY'	2120 SURREY PLACE - CAMPBELL CA 95008
46-106 WILBER, DELBERT QUENTIN	513 WOODLEAF CT - KIRKWOOD MO 63122
40-101 WILBORN, CLAUDE EDWARD	RR 1-ROXBORO NC 27573
79-121 WILBORN, THADDEAUS IGLEHART 'TED'	6429 SURFSIDE WAY - SACRAMENTO CA 95831
70-137 WILCOX, MILTON EDWARD	OLD ADD: 6405 RAINTREE DR - CANTO MI 48187
77-153 WILES, RANDALL E	2421 PARK PLACE - GRETNA LA 70053
75-130 WILEY, MARK EUGENE	4444 71ST ST - LAMESA CA 92041
77-154 WILFONG, ROBERT DONALD	16246 BENBOW - COVINA CA 91722
53- 98 WILHELM, CHARLES ERNEST 'SPIDER'	1490 SANDERLING DR - ENGLEWOOD FL 33533
52-111 WILHELM, JAMES HOYT	BOX 2217 - SARASOTA FL 33578
78-142 WILHELM, JAMES WEBSTER	BOX 99 - BELVEDERE CA 94920
16- 96 WILHOIT, JOSEPH WILLIAM	D. SEPTEMBER 25, 1930 SANTA BARBARA, CALIF.
73-131 WILHUSEN, TERRY WAYNE	1207 E. 222ND ST - CARSON CA 90745
11-175 WILIE, DENNEY EARNEST	D. JUNE 20, 1966 HAYWARD, CALIF.
27-105 WILKE, HENRY JOSEPH 'HARRY'	1002 HARMON AV - HAMILTON OH 45011
83-150 WILKERSON, CURTIS VERNON	RR 1 BOX 191 - SUTHERLAND VA 23885
41-118 WILKIE, ALDON JAY	P.O. BOX 364, 902 W. 1ST ST - NEWBERG OR 97132
79-122 WILKINS, ERIC LAMOINE	2233 E MILLER - SEATTLE WA 98112
44-141 WILKINS, ROBERT LINWOOD	CADDO PARISH COURT HOUSE-SHREVEPORT LA 71101
11-176 WILKINSON, EDWARD HENRY	D. APRIL 9, 1918 TUCSON, ARIZ.
18- 74 WILKINSON, ROY HAMILTON	D. JULY 2, 1956 LOUISVILLE, KY.
85-119 WILKINSON, WILLIAM CARL	7919 SOUTH POPLAR WAY - ENGLEWOOD CO 80112
44-142 WILKS, TEDDY	5531 MCCORMICK - HOUSTON TX 77023
57- 92 WILL, ROBERT LEE	410 N MICHIGAN AVE - CHICAGO IL 60611
84-128 WILLARD, GERALD DUANE	806 THAYER LANE - PORT HUENEME CA 93041
58-102 WILLEY, CARLTON FRANCIS	BOX 64 - CHERRYFIELD ME 04622
63-125 WILLHITE, JON NICHOLAS 'NICK'	OLD ADD: 1800 16TH ST #H106 - NEWPORT BEACH CA 92660
80-144 WILLIAMS, ALBERT HAMILTON	PEARL LAGOON, DEPOT ZELOYA - NICARAGUA,C.A. NICA.
37-108 WILLIAMS, ALMON EDWARD	D. JULY 19, 1969 GROVES, TEX.
11-177 WILLIAMS, ALVA MITCHEL 'RIP'	D. JULY 23, 1933 KEOKUK, IA.
11-178 WILLIAMS, AUGUST JOSEPH	D. APRIL 16, 1964 STERLING, ILL.
70-138 WILLIAMS, BERNARD	861 47TH ST - OAKLAND CA 94608
59- 87 WILLIAMS, BILLY LEO	586 PRINCE EDWARD RD - GLEN ELLYN IL 60137
71-108 WILLIAMS, CHARLES PROSEK	259-04 KENSINGTON PL - GREAT NECK NY 11021

TERRY WHITFIELD

ERIC WILKINS   CLEVELAND INDIANS

WILLIAMS   # WILSON

13-192 WILLIAMS, CLAUD PRESTON 'LEFTY'   D. NOVEMBER 4, 1959 LAGUNA BEACH, CALIF.
81-144 WILLIAMS, DALLAS MCKINLEY   2301 NW 10TH AVE - MIAMI FL 33127
49- 91 WILLIAMS, DAVID CARLOUS   4645 COUNTRY CREEK #1101 - DALLAS TX 75236
13-193 WILLIAMS, DAVID CARTER 'MUTT'   D. MARCH 30, 1962 FAYETTEVILLE, ARK.
44-143 WILLIAMS, DEWEY EDGAR   720 13TH STREET W - WILLISTON ND 58801
58-103 WILLIAMS, DONALD FRED   11405 ROKEBY AVE - GARRETT PARK MD 20766
63-126 WILLIAMS, DONALD REID   5546 CHATEAU DR - SAN DIEGO CA 92117
28-108 WILLIAMS, EARL BAXTER   D. MARCH 10, 1958 KNOXVILLE, TENN.
70-139 WILLIAMS, EARL CRAIG   OLD ADD: 2900 CAMP CREEK PKWY - COLLEGE PARK GA

Billy Williams

30- 92 WILLIAMS, EDWIN DIBRELL 'DIB'   BOX 43 - GREENBRIER AR 72058
21-112 WILLIAMS, EVON DANIEL 'DENNY'   D. MARCH 24, 1929 LOS ANGELES CO., CAL.
84-129 WILLIAMS, FRANK LEE   OLD ADD: 12215 NE 128TH #113 - KIRKLAND WA 98033
45-118 WILLIAMS, FRED 'PAP'   1120 46TH AVE - MERIDIAN MS 39305
12-219 WILLIAMS, FREDERICK 'CY'   D. APRIL 23, 1974 EAGLE RIVER, WIS.
61-108 WILLIAMS, GEORGE   4267 TYLER ST - DETROIT MI 48238
13-194 WILLIAMS, HARRY PETER   D. DECEMBER 20, 1963 HAYWOOD, CALIF.
69-180 WILLIAMS, JAMES ALFRED   16350 HARBOR BLVD #2512 - SANTA ANA CA 92704
66-100 WILLIAMS, JAMES FRANCIS   2205 WEBB AVE - DUNEDIN FL 33528
14-232 WILLIAMS, JOHN BRODIE   D. SEPTEMBER 8, 1963 LONG BEACH, CALIF.
15-176 WILLIAMS, KENNETH ROY   D. JANUARY 22, 1959 GRANTS PASS, ORE.
26- 94 WILLIAMS, LEON THEO   626 OLD IVY RD NE - ATLANTA GA 30305
77-155 WILLIAMS, MARK WESTLEY   15 CONTINENTAL RD - CORNWALL NY 12518
16- 97 WILLIAMS, MARSHALL MCDIARMID   D. FEBRUARY 22, 1935 TUCSON, ARIZ.
83-151 WILLIAMS, MATTHEW EVAN   110 COTTONWOOD - LAKE JACKSON TX 77566
14-233 WILLIAMS, REES GEPHARDT 'STEAMBOAT' D. JUNE 29, 1979 DEER RIVER, MINN.
85-120 WILLIAMS, REGINALD DEWAYNE   1490 SINGING TREES AVE - MEMPHIS TN 38116
78-143 WILLIAMS, RICHARD ALLEN   1217 WESSMITH - MADERA CA 93638
51-103 WILLIAMS, RICHARD HIRSCHFIELD   50 BLUE ANCHOR CAY RD - CORONADO CA 92118
14-234 WILLIAMS, RINALDO LEWIS   D. APRIL 24, 1966 COTTONWOOD, ARIZ.
11-179 WILLIAMS, ROBERT ELIAS   D. AUGUST 6, 1962 NELSONVILLE, O.
40-102 WILLIAMS, ROBERT FULTON 'ACE'   OLD ADD: CROSS ST - MARSHFIELD MA 02050
58-104 WILLIAMS, STANLEY WILSON   4702 HAYTER AVE - LAKEWOOD CA 90712
39-126 WILLIAMS, THEODORE SAMUEL   BOX 481 - ISLAMORADA FL 33036
64-128 WILLIAMS, WALTER ALLEN   2417 MONTEREY DR - BROWNWOOD TX 76801
69-181 WILLIAMS, WILLIAM   3227 RANDOLPH AVE - OAKLAND CA 94602
38-106 WILLIAMS, WOODROW WILSON   PAMPLIN VA 23958
28-109 WILLIAMSON, NATHANIEL HOWARD 'HOWIE' D. AUGUST 15, 1969 TEXARKANA, ARK.
28-110 WILLIAMSON, SILAS ALBERT   D. NOVEMBER 29, 1978 HOT SPRINGS, ARK.
30- 93 WILLINGHAM, THOMAS HUGH   412 S MACOMB ST - EL RENO OK 73036
84-130 WILLIS, CARL BLAKE   RR 1 BOX 274 - YANCEYVILLE NC 27379
25-115 WILLIS, CHARLES WILLIAM 'LEFTY'   D. MAY 10, 1962 BETHESDA, MD.
63-127 WILLIS, DALE JEROME   1110 ESTATEWOOD DR - BRANDON FL 33511
53- 99 WILLIS, JAMES GLADDEN   BOX 35 - BOYCE LA 71409
11-180 WILLIS, JOSEPH DENK   D. DECEMBER 3, 1966 IRONTON, O.
47- 96 WILLIS, LESTER EVANS   D. JANUARY 22, 1982 JASPER, TEXAS
77-156 WILLIS, MICHAEL HENRY   3081 OAKVIEW DR - PALM HARBOR FL 33563
66-101 WILLIS, RONALD EARL   D. NOVEMBER 21, 1977 MEMPHIS, TENN.
25-116 WILLOUGHBY, CLAUDE WILLIAM   D. AUGUST 14, 1973 MCPHERSON, KAN.
71-109 WILLOUGHBY, JAMES ARTHUR   198 PARK ST - WEST ROXBURY MA 02132
77-157 WILLS, ELLIOTT TAYLOR 'BUMP'   3178 MANDA DR - SAN JOSE CA 95124
83-152 WILLS, FRANK LEE   733 GEN. PERSHING ST - NEW ORLEANS LA 70115
59- 88 WILLS, MAURICE MORNING   245 FOWLING - PLAYA DEL REY CA 90291
59- 89 WILLS, THEODORE CARL   524 CLOVIS AVE - CLOVIS CA 93612
18- 75 WILLSON, FRANK HOXIE 'KID'   D. APRIL 17, 1964 UNION GAP, WASH.
34-109 WILSHERE, VERNON SPRAGUE 'WHITEY' D. MAY 23, 1985 COOPERSTOWN, N. Y.
51-104 WILSON, ARCHIE CLIFTON   1620 WOODLAND ST SE - DECATUR AL 35601
51-105 WILSON, ARTHUR LEE   2226 NE 10TH AVE - PORTLAND OR 97212
31-100 WILSON, CHARLES WOODROW   D. DECEMBER 19, 1970 ROCHESTER, N. Y.
66-102 WILSON, DONALD EDWARD   D. JANUARY 5, 1975 HOUSTON, TEX.
58-105 WILSON, DUANE LEWIS   501 BUTLER - VALLEY CENTER KS 67147
59- 90 WILSON, EARL LAWRENCE   BOX 662 - PONCHATOULA LA 70454
36- 98 WILSON, EDWARD FRANCIS   D. APRIL 11, 1979 HAMDEN, CONN.
14-235 WILSON, FINIS ELBERT   D. MARCH 9, 1959 CORAL GABLES, FLA.
24-115 WILSON, FRANCIS EDWARD   D. NOVEMBER 25, 1974 LEICESTER, MASS.
79-123 WILSON, GARY STEVEN   RURAL ROUTE 2 BOX 644 - CAMDEN AR 71701
11-181 WILSON, GEORGE FRANCIS 'SQUANTO'   D. MARCH 26, 1967 WINTHROP, ME.
34-110 WILSON, GEORGE PEACOCK 'ICEHOUSE' D. OCTOBER 13, 1973 MORAGA, CAL.
52-112 WILSON, GEORGE WASHINGTON   D. OCTOBER 29, 1974 GASTONIA, N.C.
82-138 WILSON, GLENN DWIGHT   OLD ADD: BOX 787 - CHANNELVIEW TX 77530
24-116 WILSON, GOMER RUSSELL 'TEX'   D. SEPTEMBER 15, 1946 SULPHUR SPRINGS, TEX.
48-111 WILSON, GRADY HERBERT   5512 ORCHARD DR - COLUMBUS GA 31904
23-143 WILSON, JAMES   D. JUNE 1, 1947 PALMETTO, FLA.
45-119 WILSON, JAMES ALGER   2701 VISTA UMBROSA - NEWPORT BEACH CA 92660

85-121 WILSON, JAMES GEORGE
34-111 WILSON, JOHN FRANCIS 'JACK'
13-195 WILSON, JOHN NICODEMUS
27-106 WILSON, JOHN SAMUEL
11-182 WILSON, LESTER WILBUR
23-144 WILSON, LEWIS ROBERT 'HACK'
40-103 WILSON, MAX
83-153 WILSON, MICHAEL "TACK"
58-106 WILSON, ROBERT
51-106 WILSON, ROBERT JAMES 'RED'
28-111 WILSON, ROY EDWARD
60-103 WILSON, SAMMY O'NEIL 'NEIL'
21-113 WILSON, SAMUEL MARSHALL 'MIKE'
14-236 WILSON, THOMAS C.
45-120 WILSON, WALTER WOOD
20-131 WILSON, WILLIAM CLARENCE 'MUTT'
50-104 WILSON, WILLIAM DONALD
69-182 WILSON, WILLIAM HARLAN
80-145 WILSON, WILLIAM HAYWOOD 'MOOKIE'
76-103 WILSON, WILLIE JAMES
26- 95 WILTSE, HAROLD JAMES
56- 87 WINCENIAK, EDWARD JOSEPH
59- 91 WINDHORN, GORDON RAY
28-112 WINDLE, WILLIS BREWER
60-104 WINE, ROBERT PAUL
29-108 WINEAPPLE, EDWARD
30- 94 WINEGARNER, RALPH LEE
73-132 WINFIELD, DAVID MARK
32- 92 WINFORD, JAMES HEAD
24-117 WINGARD, ERNEST JAMES
23-145 WINGFIELD, FREDERICK DAVIS 'TED'
19- 91 WINGO, ABSALOM HOLBROOK 'AL'
20-132 WINGO, EDMOND ARMAND
11-183 WINGO, IVEY BROWN
73-133 WINKLES, BOBBY BROOKS
19- 92 WINN, GEORGE BENJAMIN
83-154 WINN, JAMES FRANCIS
84-131 WINNINGHAM, HERMAN SON
30- 95 WINSETT, JOHN THOMAS 'TOM'
33- 67 WINSTON, HENRY RUDOLPH
24-118 WINTERS, CLARENCE JOHN
19- 93 WINTERS, JESSE FRANKLIN
78-144 WIRTH, ALAN LEE
21-114 WIRTS, ELWOOD VERNON 'KETTLE'
32- 93 WISE, ARCHIBALD EDWIN
30- 96 WISE, HUGH EDWARD
57- 93 WISE, KENDALL COLE 'CASEY'
64-129 WISE, RICHARD CHARLES 'RICK'
44-144 WISE, ROY OGDEN
19- 94 WISNER, JOHN HENRY
64-130 WISSMAN, DAVID ALVIN
34-112 WISTERT, FRANCIS MICHAEL 'WHITEY'
14-230 WISTERZIL, GEORGE JOHN 'TEX'
40-104 WITEK, NICHOLAS JOSEPH 'MICKEY'
20-133 WITHROW, FRANK BLAINE
63-128 WITHROW, RAYMOND WALLACE 'CORKY'
57- 94 WITT, GEORGE ADRIAN
16- 98 WITT, LAWTON WALTER 'WHITEY'
81-145 WITT, MICHAEL ATWATER
46-107 WITTE, JEROME CHARLES
38-107 WITTIG, JOHN CARL
74-142 WOCKENFUSS, JOHN BILTON
23-146 WOEHR, ANDREW EMIL
72-121 WOHLFORD, JAMES EUGENE
62-148 WOJCIK, JOHN JOSEPH
54-118 WOJEY, PETER PAUL
85-122 WOJNA, EDWARD DAVID
12-220 WOLF, ERNEST A
27-107 WOLF, RAYMOND BERNARD
69-183 WOLF, WALTER BECK
21-115 WOLF, WALTER FRANCIS 'LEFTY'
23-147 WOLFE, CHARLES HENRY
52-113 WOLFE, EDWARD ANTHONY
17- 90 WOLFE, HAROLD

202 SW 9TH - CORVALLIS OR 97333
4111 164TH ST SW #62 - LYNNWOOD WA 98037
D. SEPTEMBER 23, 1954 ANNAPOLIS, MD.
D. AUGUST 27, 1980 CHATTANOOGA, TENN.
D. APRIL 4, 1969 EDMONDS, WASH.
D. NOVEMBER 23, 1948 BALTIMORE, MD.
D. JANUARY 2, 1977 GREENSBORO, N. C.
1832 EAST 15TH STREET - OAKLAND CA 94606
627 COVE HOLLOW DR - DALLAS TX 75224
806 CABOT LN - MADISON WI 53711
D. DECEMBER 3, 1969 CLARION, IA.
RR1 BOX 285 - LEXINGTON TN 38351
D. MAY 16, 1978 BOYNTON BEACH, FLA.
D. MARCH 7, 1953 SAN PEDRO, CALIF.
RR 1 - GLENN GA 30219
D. AUGUST 31, 1962 WILDWOOD, FLA.
11121 AGNES PL - CERRITOS CA 90701
10108 S. 198TH EAST AVE - BROKEN ARROW OK 74012
OLD ADD: 150 HIGHLAND AVE - STATEN ISLAND NY 10301
OLD ADD: 5 GLENWOOD PL - SUMMIT NJ
D. NOVEMBER 2, 1983 BUNKIE, LA.
10828 S AVE "O" - CHICAGO IL 60617
145 BENT CREEK RD - DANVILLE VA 24540
D. DECEMBER 8, 1981 CORPUS CHRISTI TX.
2612 WOODLAND AVE - NORRISTOWN PA 19401
960 PARK AVE - NEW YORK NY 10028
245 S. WICHITA ST - BENTON KS 67017
367 W. FOREST - TEANECK NJ 07666
D. DECEMBER 16, 1970 MIAMI, OKLA.
D. JANUARY 17, 1977 PRATTVILLE, ALA.
D. JULY 18, 1975 JOHNSON CITY, TENN.
D. OCTOBER 9, 1954 DETROIT, MICH.
D. DECEMBER 5, 1964 LACHINE, QUE.
D. MARCH 1, 1941 NORCROSS, GA.
1608 E ELM - ANAHEIM CA 92805
D. NOVEMBER 1, 1969 ROBERTA, GA.
RURAL ROUTE 1 - CLEVER MO 65631
1542 BELLEVILLE RD - ORANGEBURG SC 29115
3320 HIGHLAND PARK - MEMPHIS TN 38111
D. FEBRUARY 7, 1974 JACKSONVILLE, FLA.
D. JUNE 29, 1945 DETROIT, MICH.
2142 S. TENTH ST - ABILENE TX 79605
1012 WEST MOUNTAIN VIEW - MESA AZ 85201
D. JULY 12, 1968 SACRAMENTO, CAL.
D. FEBRUARY 2, 1978 WAXAHACHIE, TEX.
8931 N. NEW RIVER CANAL #1F - PLANTATION FL 33324
3631 RUM ROW - NAPLES FL 33940
RR 2 BOX 317 - HILLSBORO OR 97123
11841 MELODY LN DR - GARDEN GROVE CA 92640
D. DECEMBER 15, 1981 JACKSON, MICH.
20 WELLINGTON ST - SHELBURNE FALLS MA 01370
D. APRIL 23, 1985 PAINESVILLE, OHIO
D. JUNE 27, 1964 SAN ANTONIO, TEX.
30 WEST RIDGE ST - SHAVERTOWN PA 18708
D. SEPTEMBER 5, 1966 OMAHA, NEB.
1730 QUEENSWAY CT - OWENSBORO KY 42301
2209 CATALINA ST - LAGUNA BEACH CA 92651
RR 1 BOX 522 - WOODSTOWN NJ 08098
8042 SAN LEON CIR DR - BUENA PARK CA 90620
7515 OAK VISTA - HOUSTON TX 77087
163 STAFFORD STREET - BALTIMORE MD 21227
14 PETER CHRISTOPHER DR - LANDENBURG PA 19350
1215 W. FOSTER PKWY - FORT WAYNE IN 46807
13895 EL CAMINO REAL - ATASCADERO CA 93422
33 HAMILTON ST - BUFFALO NY 14207
2359 S BUENA DR - MOBILE AL 36605
48 WILLIAMSBURG DR - MONROE CT 06468
D. MAY 23, 1964 ATLANTIC HIGHLANDS, N.J.
D. OCTOBER 6, 1979 FORT WORTH, TEXAS
17711 TRAIL VIEW - YORBA LINDA CA 92686
D. SEPTEMBER 25, 1971 NEW ORLEANS, LA.
D. NOVEMBER 27, 1957 SCHELLSBURG, PA.
520 STONEHAM CIR - MEDFORD OR 97501
D. JULY 28, 1971 FORT WAYNE, IND.

77-158 WOLFE, LAURENCE MARCY	2616 SARDA WAY - RANCHO CORDOVA CA 95670
12-221 WOLFE, ROY CHAMBERLAIN 'POLLY'	D. NOVEMBER 21, 1938 MORRIS, ILL.
41-119 WOLFF, ROGER FRANCIS	1307 KNOTT-CHESTER IL 62233
14-237 WOLFGANG, MELDON JOHN	D. JUNE 30, 1947 ALBANY, N.Y.
66-103 WOMACK, HORACE GUY 'DOOLEY'	119 CENTURY DR - COLUMBIA SC 29210
26- 96 WOMACK, SIDNEY KIRK	D. AUGUST 8, 1958 JACKSON, MISS.
30- 97 WOOD, CHARLES ASHER 'SPADES'	3901 E. ELM - WICHITA KS 67208
23-148 WOOD, CHARLES SPENCER 'DOC'	D. NOVEMBER 3, 1974 NEW ORLEANS, LA.
61-109 WOOD, JACOB	851 MAGNOLIA AVE - ELIZABETH NJ 07201
44-145 WOOD, JOE FRANK	BOX 53 - CLINTON CT 06413
08 WOOD, JOSEPH 'SMOKEY JOE'	D. JULY 27, 1985 WEST HAVEN, CONN.
43-144 WOOD, JOSEPH PERRY	D. MARCH 25, 1985 HOUSTON, TEXAS
48-112 WOOD, KENNETH LANIER	6337 TERESA AVE - CHARLOTTE NC 28214
13-196 WOOD, ROY WINTON	D. APRIL 6, 1974 FAYETTEVILLE, ARK.
61-110 WOOD, WILBUR FORRESTER	8 WACHUSETT DR - LEXINGTON MA 02173
20-134 WOODALL, CHARLES LAWRENCE 'LARRY'	D. MAY 6, 1963 NEWTON, MASS.
78-145 WOODARD, DARRELL LEE	1227 EAST 69TH ST - LOS ANGELES CA 90001
85-123 WOODARD, MICHAEL CARY	P.O. BOX 35 - MAYWOOD IL 60153
11-184 WOODBURN, EUGENE STEWART	D. JANUARY 18, 1961 SANDUSKY, O.
44-146 WOODEND, GEORGE ANTHONY	D. FEBRUARY 6, 1980 HARTFORD, CONN.
56- 88 WOODESHICK, HAROLD JOSEPH	803 WYCLIFFE DR - HOUSTON TX 77079
43-145 WOODLING, EUGENE RICHARD	926 REMSEN RD - MEDINA OH 44256
14-239 WOODMAN, DANIEL COURTENAY	D. DECEMBER 14, 1962 TOPSFIELD, MASS.
77-159 WOODS, ALVIS	2518 60TH AVE - OAKLAND CA 94605
14-238 WOODS, CLARENCE COFIELD	D. JULY 2, 1969 RISING SUN, IND.
76-104 WOODS, GARY LEE	6701 E. 38TH - TUCSON AZ 85730
43-146 WOODS, GEORGE ROWLAND 'PINKY'	D. OCTOBER 30, 1982 LOS ANGELES, CALIF.
57- 95 WOODS, JAMES JEROME	151 ROSS WAY - SAN BRUNO CA 94066
24-119 WOODS, JOHN FULTON	D. OCTOBER 4, 1946 NORFOLK, VA.
69-184 WOODS, RONALD LAWRENCE	413 PLYMOUTH ST - INGLEWOOD CA 90302
69-185 WOODSON, RICHARD LEE	3416 LONESOME TRAIL - GEORGETOWN TX 78626
18- 76 WOODWARD, FRANK RUSSELL	D. JUNE 11, 1961 NEW HAVEN, CONN.
85-124 WOODWARD, ROBERT JOHN	15 PLEASANT ST - WEST LEBANON NH 03784
63-129 WOODWARD, WILLIAM FREDERICK 'WOODY'	13 LAMBERT DR - SPARTA NJ 07871
55-137 WOOLDRIDGE, FLOYD LEWIS	214 BARBER ST - GREENFIELD MO 65661
47- 97 WOOTEN, EARL HAZELL	702 WILLIAMS ST - WILLIAMSTON SC 29697
14-240 WORDEN, FRED B	D. NOVEMBER 9, 1941 ST. LOUIS, MO.
38-108 WORKMAN, CHARLES THOMAS	D. JANUARY 3, 1953 KANSAS CITY, MO.
24-120 WORKMAN, HARRY HALL 'HOGE'	D. MAY 20, 1972 FORT MYERS, FLA.
50-105 WORKMAN, HENRY KILGARIFF	307 19TH ST - SANTA MONICA CA 90402
85-125 WORRELL, TODD ROLAND	306 HARVARD DRIVE - ARCADIA CA 91006
78-146 WORTHAM, RICHARD COOPER	10302 TIMBERCREST LN - AUSTIN TX 78750
53-100 WORTHINGTON, ALLAN FULTON	LIBERTY BAPTIST COL - LYNCHBURG VA 24506
31-101 WORTHINGTON, ROBERT LEE 'RED'	D. DECEMBER 8, 1963 LOS ANGELES, CAL.
16- 99 WORTMAN, WILLIAM LEWIS 'CHUCK'	D. AUGUST 19, 1977 LAS VEGAS, NEV.
83-155 WOTUS, RONALD ALLAN	CRESTVIEW DRIVE - COLCHESTER CT 06415
33- 68 WRIGHT, ALBERT EDGAR	OLD ADD: 156 JOHN ST - OAKLAND CA
35-115 WRIGHT, ALBERT OWEN 'AB'	407 S. PAYNE ST - STILLWATER OK 74074
16-100 WRIGHT, CEYLON	D. NOVEMBER 7, 1947 HINES, ILL.
66-104 WRIGHT, CLYDE	528 JEANINE AVE - ANAHEIM CA 92806
24-121 WRIGHT, FOREST GLENN	D. APRIL 6, 1984 OLATHE, KAN.
82-139 WRIGHT, GEORGE DEWITT	4228 NE 18TH ST - OKLAHOMA CITY OK 73121
45-121 WRIGHT, HENDERSON EDWARD 'ED'	827 LAKE ROAD - DYERSBURG TN 38024
27-108 WRIGHT, JAMES	D. APRIL 12, 1963 OAKLAND, CAL.
78-147 WRIGHT, JAMES CLIFTON	439 HARRISON ST - COOPERSVILLE MI 49404
81-146 WRIGHT, JAMES LEON	2822 SOUTH 29TH - ST. JOSEPH MO 64503
82-140 WRIGHT, JAMES RICHARD	3605 W. HOUSTON - PARIS TX 75460
70-140 WRIGHT, KENNETH WARREN	1416 WISTERIA AVE - PENSACOLA FL 32507
54-119 WRIGHT, MELVIN JAMES	D. MAY 16, 1983 HOUSTON, TEX.
15-177 WRIGHT, ROBERT CASSIUS	5757 CYPRESS AVE #207 - CARMICHAEL CA 95608
56- 89 WRIGHT, ROY EARL	331 PINEHURST CIR - CHICKAMAUGA GA 30707
38-109 WRIGHT, TAFT SHEDRON	D. OCTOBER 22, 1981 ORLANDO, FLA.
48-113 WRIGHT, THOMAS EVERETT	RR 2 BOX 45 - SHELBY NC 28150
17- 91 WRIGHT, WAYNE BROMLEY 'RASTY'	D. JUNE 12, 1948 COLUMBUS, O.
15-178 WRIGHT, WILLIAM JAMES 'DICK'	D. JANUARY 24, 1952 BETHLEHEM, PA.
20-135 WRIGHTSTONE, RUSSELL GUY	D. MARCH 1, 1969 HARRISBURG, PA.
29-109 WUESTLING, GEORGE 'YATS'	D. APRIL 26, 1970 ST. LOUIS, MO.
44-147 WURM, FRANK JAMES	OLD ADD: 7 CLINTON ST - GLENS FALLS NY 12801
61-111 WYATT, JOHN	3439 BELLEFONTAINE - KANSAS CITY MO 64128
29-110 WYATT, JOHN WHITLOW 'WHIT'	BUCHANAN GA 30113
24-122 WYATT, LORAL JOHN 'JOE'	D. DECEMBER 5, 1970 OBLONG, ILL.
13-197 WYCKOFF, JOHN WELDON	D. MAY 8, 1961 SHEBOYGAN FALLS, WIS.
76-105 WYNEGAR, HAROLD DELANO 'BUTCH'	528 SPRING CREEK DR - LONGWOOD FL 32779

39-127 WYNN, EARLY	BOX 218 - NOKOMIS FL 33551
63-130 WYNN, JAMES SHERMAN	OLD ADD: 932 1/2 E. 41ST PL - LOS ANGELES CA 90053
83-156 WYNNE, MARVELL	8052 SOUTH CALUMET - CHICAGO IL 60619
67-115 WYNNE, WILLIAM VERNON	3945 CHESTWOOD AVE - JACKSONVILLE FL 32211
42-108 WYROSTEK, JOHN BARNEY	2749 N 44TH ST - EAST SAINT LOUIS IL 62201
42-109 WYSE, HENRY WASHINGTON	1133 SE 14TH ST- PRYOR OK 74361
30- 98 WYSONG, HARLIN 'BIFF'	D. AUGUST 8, 1951 XENIA, O.
72-122 YANCY, HUGH	BOX 9064 - SARASOTA FL 33578
42-110 YANKOWSKI, GEORGE EDWARD	164 CHAPMAN ST-WATERTOWN MA 02172
12-222 YANTZ, GEORGE WEBB	D. FEBRUARY 26, 1967 LOUISVILLE, KY.
26- 97 YARNELL, WALDO WILLIAM 'RUSTY'	D. OCTOBER 9, 1985 LOWELL, MASS.
22-137 YARRISON, BYRON WARDSWORTH 'RUBE'	D. APRIL 22, 1977 WILLIAMSPORT, PA.
21-116 YARYAN, CLARENCE EVERETT 'YAM'	D. NOVEMBER 16, 1964 BIRMINGHAM, ALA.
61-112 YASTRZEMSKI, CARL MICHAEL	4621 S OCEAN BLVD - HIGHLAND BEACH FL 33431
71-110 YATES, ALBERT ARTHUR	OLD ADD: 11613 W YUMA CT - NEW BERLIN WI
24-123 YDE, EMIL OGDEN	D. DECEMBER 4, 1968 LEESBURG, FLA.
19- 95 YEABSLEY, ROBERT WATKINS 'BERT'	D. FEBRUARY 8, 1961 PHILADELPHIA, PA.
72-123 YEAGER, STEPHEN WAYNE	5225 - 4 WHITE OAK - ENCINO CA 91316
22-138 YEARGIN, JAMES ALMOND	D. MAY 8. 1937 GREENVILLE, S. C.
17- 92 YELLE, ARCHIE JOSEPH	D. MAY 2, 1983 WOODLAND, CALIF.
63-131 YELLEN, LAWRENCE ALAN	OLD ADD: 67-30 CLYDE ST - FOREST HILLS NY 11375
21-117 YELLOWHORSE, MOSES J. 'CHIEF'	D. APRIL 10, 1964 PAWNEE, OKLA.
27-109 YERKES, CHARLES CARROLL	D. DECEMBER 20, 1950 OAKLAND, CAL.
85-126 YETT, RICHARD MARTIN	11860 BUTTERFIELD - CHINO CA 91710
57- 96 YEWCIC, THOMAS	31 CHEORKEE RD - ARLINTON MA 02174
11-185 YINGLING, EARL HERSHEY	D. OCTOBER 2, 1962 COLUMBUS, O.
51-107 YOCHIM, LEONARD JOSEPH	316 NELSON DR - NEW ORLEANS LA 70123
48-114 YOCHIM, RAYMOND AUSTIN ALOYSIUS	3728 45TH ST - METAIRIE LA 70001
19- 96 YORK, JAMES EDWARD 'LEFTY'	D. APRIL 9, 1961 YORK, PA.
70-141 YORK, JAMES HARLAN	10957 E HOLBECK AVE - NORWALK CA 90650
34-113 YORK, RUDOLPH PRESTON	D. FEBRUARY 5, 1970 ROME, GA.
44-148 YORK, TONY BATTEN	D. APRIL 18, 1970 HILLSBORO, TEXAS
80-146 YOST, EDGAR FREDERICK 'NED'	23 CASTLEWOOD DR - PLEASANTON CA 94566
44-149 YOST, EDWARD FRED JOSEPH	35 CROWN RIDGE RD - WELLESLEY MA 02181
21-118 YOTER, ELMER ELLSWORTH	D. JULY 26, 1966 CAMP HILL, PA.
85-127 YOUMANS, FLOYD EVERETT	591 LANCEWOOD - RIALTO CA 92376
15-179 YOUNG, CHARLES	D. MAY 12, 1952 RIVERSIDE, N. J.
83-157 YOUNG, CURTIS ALLEN	2614 APPOLO DRIVE - SAGINAW MI 48602
37-109 YOUNG, DELMER EDWARD	D. DECEMBER 8, 1979 SAN FRANCISCO, CALIF.
65-117 YOUNG, DONALD WAYNE	OLD ADD: 1350 TRENTON ST - DENVER CO 80220
13-198 YOUNG, GEORGE JOSEPH	D. MARCH 13, 1950 BRIGHTWATERS, N.Y.
11-186 YOUNG, HERMAN JOHN	D. DECEMBER 13, 1966 IPSWICH, MASS.
71-111 YOUNG, JOHN THOMAS	124 W 57TH ST - LOS ANGELES CA 90037
78-148 YOUNG, KIP LANE	RR 2 BOX 113-C - WINCHESTER OH 45697
33- 69 YOUNG, LEMUEL FLOYD 'PEP'	D. JANUARY 14, 1962 JAMESTOWN, N. C.
83-158 YOUNG, MATTHEW JOHN	6143 139TH PL SE - BELLEVUE WA 98006
82-141 YOUNG, MICHAEL DARREN	3250 SUNNYBROOK CT - HAYWARD CA 94541
36- 99 YOUNG, NORMAN ROBERT 'BABE'	D. DECEMBER 25, 1983 EVERETT, MASS.
13-199 YOUNG, RALPH STUART	D. JANUARY 24, 1965 PHILADELPHIA, PA.
51-108 YOUNG, RICHARD ENNIS	OLD ADD: 6923 189TH - LYNNWOOD WA 98036
48-115 YOUNG, ROBERT GEORGE	D. JANUARY 28, 1985 BALTIMORE, MD.
31-102 YOUNG, RUSSELL CHARLES	D. MAY 13, 1984 ROSEVILLE, CALIF.
22-139 YOUNGBLOOD, ARTHUR CLYDE 'CHIEF'	D. JULY 6, 1968 AMARILLO, TEX.
76-106 YOUNGBLOOD, JOEL RANDOLPH	4309 HARBY ST - HOUSTON TX 77023
17- 93 YOUNGS, ROSS MIDDLEBROOK	D. OCTOBER 22, 1927 SAN ANTONIO, TEX.
37-110 YOUNT, FLOYD EDWIN 'EDDIE'	D. OCTOBER 26, 1973 NEWTON, N. C.
14-241 YOUNT, HERBERT MACON 'DUCKY'	D. MAY 9, 1970 WINSTON-SALEM, N. C.

KIP YOUNG

MATT YOUNG

Seattle Mariners

71-112	YOUNT, LAWRENCE KING	4304 N HUNT CLUB LN - WESTLAKE VLG CA 91360
74-143	YOUNT, ROBIN R	8140 E. SANDS DR, BOX 545 - SCOTTSDALE AZ 85255
24-124	YOWELL, CARL COLUMBUS	D. JULY 27, 1985 JACKSONVILLE, TEXAS
52-114	YUHAS, JOHN EDWARD 'EDDIE'	3732 HEATHROW DR - WINSTON SALEM NC 27107
78-149	YURAK, JEFFREY LYNN	16244 16TH AVE SW - SEATTLE WA 98166
47- 98	YVARS, SALVADOR ANTHONY	1 ALLEN ST - VALHALLA NY 10595
45-122	ZABALA, ADRIAN RODRIGUEZ	11243 ANDREA DR - JACKSONVILLE FL 32218
13-200	ZABEL, GEORGE WASHINGTON 'ZIP'	D. MAY 31, 1970 BELOIT, WIS.
44-150	ZACHARY, ALBERT MYRON 'CHINK'	426 LORRAINE AVE - UTICA NY 13502
18- 77	ZACHARY, JONATHAN THOMPSON WALTON	D. JANUARY 24, 1969 GRAHAM, N. C.
63-132	ZACHARY, WILLIAM CHRIS	6825 COCHISE DR - HALLS CROSS ROADS TN 37918
10-152	ZACHER, ELMER HENRY	D. DECEMBER 20, 1944 BUFFALO, N.Y.
76-107	ZACHRY, PATRICK PAUL	3400 BRANNON - WACO TX 76710
11-187	ZACKERT, GEORGE CARL	D. FEBRUARY 18, 1977 BURLINGTON, IA.
73-134	ZAHN, GEOFFREY CLAYTON	7141 E MOCKINGBIRD WAY - ANAHEIM CA 92807
23-149	ZAHNISER, PAUL VERNON	D. SEPTEMBER 26, 1964 KLAMATH FALLS, ORE.
44-151	ZAK, FRANK THOMAS	D. FEBRUARY 6, 1972 PASSAIC, N.J.
13-201	ZAMLOCH, CARL EUGENE	D. AUGUST 19, 1963 SANTA BARBARA, CALIF.
74-144	ZAMORA, OSCAR JOSE	OLD ADD: 2201 BRICKELL AVE #82 - MIAMI FL 33129
58-107	ZANNI, DOMINICK THOMAS	7 SUSSEX AVE N - MASSAPEQUA NY 11758
33- 70	ZAPUSTAS, JOSEPH JOHN	16 VESEY RD - RANDOLPH MA 02368
45-123	ZARDON, JOSE ANTONIO SANCHEZ	7825 SW 18TH TER - MIAMI FL 33155
43-147	ZARILLA, ALLEN LEE 'ZEKE'	431 NAHUA ST #705 - HONOLULU HI 96815
84-132	ZASKE, LLOYD JEFFREY 'JEFF'	16731 68TH AVE W - LYNNWOOD WA 98037
51-109	ZAUCHIN, NORBERT HENRY 'NORM'	818 N MONTEZ DR - THOMAS ACRES AL 35020
77-160	ZDEB, JOSEPH EDWARD	6802 ACUFF - SHAWNEE KS 66215
77-161	ZEBER, GEORGE WILLIAM	9722 RAVENSCROFT RD - SANTA ANA CA 92705
10-153	ZEIDER, ROLLIE HUBERT	D. SEPTEMBER 12, 1967 AUBURN, IND.
14-242	ZEISER, MATTHEW J.	D. JUNE 10, 1942 NORWOOD PARK, ILL.
70-142	ZELLER, BARTON WALLACE	5112 IMPERIAL DR - RICHTON PARK IL 60471
69-186	ZEPP, WILLIAM CLINTON	35430 BROOKVIEW DR - LIVONIA MI 48152
49- 92	ZERNIAL, GUS EDWARD	521 WEST POLSON - CLOVIS CA 93612
54-120	ZICK, ROBERT GEORGE	1355 E 93RD ST - CHICAGO IL 60619
41-120	ZIENTARA, BENEDICT JOSEPH	D. APRIL 16, 1985 LAKE ELSINORE, CALIF.
54-121	ZIMMER, DONALD WILLIAM	10124 YACHT CLUB DR - ST PETERSBURG FL 33706
61-113	ZIMMERMAN, GERALD ROBERT	13650 FERNRIDGE - MILWAUKIE OR 97222
45-124	ZIMMERMAN, ROY FRANKLIN	24 NORTH ST - TREMONT PA 17981
15-180	ZIMMERMAN, WILLIAM H.	D. OCTOBER 4, 1952 NEWARK, N.J.
21-119	ZINK, WALTER NOBLE	D. JUNE 12, 1964 QUINCY, MASS.
11-188	ZINN, GUY	D. OCTOBER 6, 1949 CLARKSBURG, W. VA.
19- 97	ZINN, JAMES EDWARD	5614 APPLEWOOD DR - NORTH LITTLE ROCK AR72118
44-152	ZINSER, WILLIAM FREDERICK	OLD ADD: 177 CALDWELL DR #1J - CINCINNATI OH 45216
61-114	ZIPFEL, MARION SYLVESTER 'BUD'	57 WHITESIDE DR - BELLEVILLE IL 62221
71-113	ZISK, RICHARD WALTER	OLD ADD: 1411 MEADOWLARK DR - PITTSBURGH PA 15243
19- 98	ZITZMANN, WILLIAM ARTHUR	D. MAY 29, 1985 PASSAIC, N. J.
10-154	ZMICH, EDWARD ALBERT	D. AUGUST 20, 1950 CLEVELAND, O.
44-153	ZOLDAK, SAMUEL WALTER	D. AUGUST 25, 1966 MINEOLA, N. Y.
36-100	ZUBER, WILLIAM HENRY	D. NOVEMBER 2, 1982 CEDAR RAPIDS, IA.
57- 97	ZUPO, FRANK JOSEPH	2824 MARIPOSA DR - BURLINGAME CA 94010
82-142	ZUVELLA, PAUL	1396 LASSEN AVE - MILPITAS CA 95305
51-110	ZUVERINK, GEORGE	1721 ELLIS DR - TEMPE AZ 85282
10-155	ZWILLING, EDWARD HARRISON 'DUTCH'	D. MARCH 27, 1978 LA CRESCENTA, CALIF.

DON ZIMMER
Cincinnati Reds

Bill Zuber's Dugout Restaurant Homestead, Iowa

149

UMPIRES DEBUTING FROM 1910 TO 1985

U14- 1	ANDERSON, OLIVER O	D. JULY 7, 1945 LOS ANGELES, CALIF.
U70- 1	ANTHONY, GEORGE MERLYN	OLD ADD: 2361 WILMPALA ST - MESA AZ 85203
U66- 1	ASHFORD, EMMETT LITTLETON	D. MARCH 1, 1980 MARINA DEL REY, CALIF.
U69- 1	AVANTS, NICK R	5805 WOODLAWN - LITTLE ROCK AR 72205
U36- 1	BALLANFANT, EDWARD LEE	7018 CASA LOMA - DALLAS TX 75214
U40- 1	BARLICK, ALBERT JOSEPH	RR 2 - RIVERTON IL 62561
U68- 1	BARNETT, LAWRENCE ROBERT	6464 HUGHES RD - PROSPECT OH 43342
U31- 1	BARR, GEORGE MCKINLEY	D. JULY 26, 1974 SULPHUR, OKLA.
U28- 1	BARRY, DANIEL	D.
U36- 2	BASIL, STEPHEN JOHN	D. JUNE 24, 1962 GILCHRIST, TEX.
U42- 1	BERRY, CHARLES FRANCIS	PLAYER DEBUT 1925
U76- 1	BETCHER, RALPH	153 PARKFEL AVE - PITTSBURGH PA 15237
U22- 4	BIERHALTER	
U70- 2	BLANDFORD, FRED	1123 CHARLES ST - ELMIRA NY 14904
U44- 1	BOGGESS, LYNTON ROSS 'DUSTY'	D. JULY 8, 1968 DALLAS, TEX.
U44- 2	BOYER, JAMES MURRY	D. JULY 25, 1959 FINKSBURG, MD.
U17- 1	BRANSFIELD, WILLIAM EDWARD 'KITTY'	D. MAY 1, 1947 WORCESTER, MASS.
U74- 1	BREMIGAN, NICHOLAS GREGORY	1602 SOLWAY - LEWISVILLE TX 75067
U15- 1	BREWER,	
U73- 1	BRINKMAN, JOSEPH NORBERT	1021 INDIAN RIVER DR - COCOA FL 32922
U79- 1	BROCKLANDER, FRED	123-40 83RD AVE #7C - KEW GARDENS NY 11415
U57- 1	BURKHART, WILLIAM KENNETH 'KEN'	PLAYER DEBUT 1945
U11- 1	BUSH, GARNET C.	D. DECEMBER 30, 1919 ST. LOUIS, MO.
U13- 1	BYRON, WILLIAM J. 'LORD'	D. DECEMBER 27, 1955 YPSILANTI, MICH.
U28- 2	CAMPBELL, WILLIAM M	OLD ADD: 676 S BELVEDERE - MEMPHIS TN
U61- 1	CARRIGAN, HERVE SAMUEL 'SAM'	OLD ADD: 651 MCKINSTRY AVE - CHICOPEE FALLS MA 01020
U14- 2	CHILL, OLIVER P. 'OLLIE'	OLD ADD: MAJESTIC HOTEL - KANSAS CITY MO
U54- 1	CHYLAK, NESTOR	D. FEBRUARY 17, 1982 DUNMORE, PA.
U76- 2	CLARK, ALAN MARSHALL	16 INDEPENDENCE PL - NEWTOWN PA 18940
U30- 1	CLARKE, ROBERT M	
U82- 1	COBLE, GEORGE DREW	RR 3 BOX 368 - GRAHAM NC 27253
U15- 2	COCKILL, GEORGE W	D. NOVEMBER 2, 1937 STEELTOWN, PA.
U76- 3	COHEN, ALFRED	1026 N HIGHLAND AVE - PITTSBURGH PA 15206
U10- 1	COLLIFLOWER, JAMES HARRY	D. AUGUST 14, 1961 WASHINGTON, D. C.
U68- 2	COLOSI, NICHOLAS	68-17 54TH AVE - MASPETH NY 11378
U41- 1	CONLAN, JOHN BERTRAND 'JOCKO'	PLAYER DEBUT 1934
U75- 1	COONEY, TERRANCE JOSEPH	4860 N. WOODROW #101 - FRESNO CA 93726
U14- 3	CORCORAN, THOMAS WILLIAM	D. JUNE 25, 1960 PLAINFIELD, CONN.
U83- 1	COSTELLO, PERRY	901 WEST BARNES - LANSING MI 48910
U79- 2	COUSINS, DERRYL	702 4TH ST - HERMOSA BEACH CA 90254
U76- 4	CRAWFORD, GERALD JOSEPH	1 PINZON AVE - HAVERTOWN PA 19083
U56- 1	CRAWFORD, HENRY CHARLES 'SHAG'	1530 VIRGINIA AVE - HAVERTOWN PA 19083
U14- 4	CROSS, MONTFORD MONTGOMERY	D. JUNE 21, 1934 PHILADELPHIA, PA.
U71- 1	DALE, JERRY PARKER	428 W. HUNTINGTON SR #4 - ARCADIA CA 91006
U48- 1	DASCOLI, FRANK	BOX 75 - DANIELSON CT 06239
U69- 2	DAVIDSON, DAVID LEONARD 'SATCH'	2400 WESTHEIMER ST #209W - HOUSTON TX 77098
U82- 2	DAVIDSON, ROBERT	2405 TRAILS END - ALTOONA IA 50009
U83- 2	DAVIS, GERALD	616 CAMELLIA LN - APPLETON WI 54915
U70- 3	DEEGAN, WILLIAM EDWARD JOHN	1289 104 EAST GRAND AVE - ESCONDIDO CA 92027
U56- 2	DELMORE, VICTOR	D. JUNE 10, 1960 SCRANTON, PA.
U83- 3	DEMUTH, DANA	859 N. MOUNTAIN AVE #124 - UPLAND CA 91786
U69- 3	DENKINGER, DONALD ANTON	132 WOODSTOCK RD - WATERLOO IA 50701
U66- 2	DEZELAN, FRANK JOHN	1314 WOOD ST - PITTSBURGH PA 15221
U63- 1	DIMURO, LOUIS JOHN	D. JUNE 7, 1982 ARLINGTON, TEX.
U53- 1	DIXON, HAL HAYWORTH	D. JULY 28, 1966 CHURNEE, S.C.
U50- 1	DONATELLI, AUGUST JOSEPH	4681 FIRST ST NE - ST PETERSBURG FL 33703
U31- 2	DONNELLY, CHARLES H	D. DECEMBER 13, 1968 LAKE WORTH, FLA.
U30- 2	DONOHUE, MICHAEL R	D. AUGUST 7, 1968 ST. LOUIS, MO.
U11- 2	DOYLE, JOHN JOSEPH 'DIRTY JACK'	D. DECEMBER 31, 1958 HOLYOKE, MASS.
U63- 2	DOYLE, WALTER JAMES	OLD ADD: 3314 HENDERSON BLVD - TAMPA FL 33609
U60- 1	DRUMMOND, CALVIN TROY	D. MAY 2, 1970 DES MOINES, IOWA
U51- 1	DUFFY, JAMES FRANCIS	165 2ND ST - PAWTUCKET RI 02861
U39- 1	DUNN, THOMAS PATRICK	D. JANUARY 20, 1976 PRINCE GEORGES CO., MD.
U14- 5	ELDRIDGE, CLARENCE E	
U65- 1	ENGEL, ROBERT ALLEN	3500 HARMONY LN - BAKERSFILED CA 93306
U52- 1	ENGELN, WILLIAM RAYMOND	D. APRIL 17, 1968 PALO ALTO, CALIF.
U72- 1	EVANS, JAMES BREMOND	1801 ROGGE LANE - AUSTIN TX 78723
U13- 2	FERGUSON, CHARLES AUGUSTUS	D. MAY 17, 1931 SAULT SAINTE MARIE, MICH.
U79- 3	FIELDS, STEVE	216 E GLENDALE #2 - ALEXANDRIA VA 22301
U11- 3	FINNERAN, WILLIAM F	D. JULY 30, 1961 ERIE, PA.
U79- 4	FITZPATRICK, MICHAEL	262 LODGE LANE - KALAMAZOO MI 49009
U53- 2	FLAHERTY, JOHN FRANCIS 'RED'	9 FOWLER LN - FALMOUTH MA 02540
U75- 2	FORD, ROBERT DALE	RR 7 BOX 114- JONESBORO TN 37659
U61- 2	FORMAN, ALLEN SANFORD	61 WASHINGTON AVE - MORRISTOWN NJ 07960
U69- 4	FRANTZ, ARTHUR FRANK	OLD ADD: 276 LYCEUM ST - ROCHESTER NY
U11- 4	FRARY, RALPH	D. NOVEMBER 10, 1925 ABERDEEN, WASH.
U20- 1	FRIEL, WILLIAM EDWARD	D. DECEMBER 24, 1959 ST. LOUIS, MO.
U71- 2	FROEMMING, BRUCE NEAL	5045 ELK CT - MILWAUKEE WI 53223
U52- 2	FROESE, GROVER A	D. JULY 20, 1982 BAY SHORE NY
U15- 3	FYFE, LOUIS	
U75- 3	GARCIA, RICHARD RAUL	2633 FIRESTONE DR - CLEARWATER FL 33519
U25- 1	GEISEL, HARRY CHRISTIAN	D. FEBRUARY 20, 1966 INDIANAPOLIS, IND.
U14- 6	GOECKEL, E	
U36- 3	GOETZ, LAWRENCE JOHN	D. OCTOBER 31, 1962 CINCINNATI, O.
U68- 3	GOETZ, RUSSELL LOUIS	1010 VERMONT ST - GLASSPORT PA 15045
U46- 1	GORE, ARTHUR JOSEPH	BOX 154 - MIRROR LAKE NH 03853
U51- 2	GORMAN, THOMAS DAVID	PLAYER DEBUT 1939
U77- 1	GREGG, ERIC VANAN DALE	2635 MIMI CIR - PHILADELPHIA PA 19131
U38- 1	GRIEVE, WILLIAM TURNER	D. AUGUST 17, 1979 YONKERS, N. Y.
U70- 4	GRIMSLEY, JOHN WILLIAM	204 RAVENWOOD DR - GREENVILLE NC 27834
U83- 4	GRINDER, SCOTT	128 NORTH VIEW DR - ZELIONOPLE PA 16063
U14- 7	GROOM, ROBERT	D. FEBRUARY 19, 1948 BELLEVILLE, ILL.
U70- 5	GRYGIEL, GEORGE	OLD ADD: BOX 401 - SOUTH BEND IN
U76- 5	GUCKERT, ELMER	590 CRANE AVE - PITTSBURGH PA 15216
U52- 3	GUGLIELMO, ANGELO AUGIE	183 JERSEY ST - WATERBURY CT 06706
U13- 3	GUTHRIE, WILLIAM J	D. MARCH 6, 1950 CHICAGO, ILL
U61- 3	HALLER, WILLIAM EDWARD	2013 SOUTH LAKE DR - VANDALIA IL 62471

U83- 8	RIPPLEY, T. STEVE	2889 WHISPERING DR #17/13 - LARGO FL 33541
U47- 2	ROBB, DOUGLAS W. 'SCOTTY'	D. APRIL 10, 1969 MONTCLAIR, N.J.
U53- 3	ROBERTS, LEONARD WYATT	OLD ADD: 5505 SPRUCE VIEW - DALLAS TX 75232
U74- 3	RODRIGUEZ, ARMANDO HUMBERTO	OLD ADD: INDEPENCIA 1375 - VERACRUZ VERACRUZ MEXICO
U80- 1	ROE, JOHN 'ROCKY'	2846 TAMWOOD CT - MILFORD MI 48042
U38- 3	ROMMEL, EDWIN AMERICUS	PLAYER DEBUT 1920
U23- 4	ROWLAND, CLARENCE HENRY	D. MAY 17, 1969 CHICAGO, ILL.
U38- 4	RUE, JOSEPH WILLIAM	D. DECEMBER 1, 1984 LAGUNA HILLS, CALIF.
U54- 2	RUNGE, EDWARD PAUL	4949 CRESITA DR - SAN DIEGO CA 92115
U72- 3	RUNGE, PAUL EDWARD	649 CALLE DE LA SIERRA - EL CAJON CA 92021
U46- 3	RYAN, WALTER	D. JUNE 16, 1981
U62- 2	SALERNO, ALEX JOSEPH	1913 TILDEN AVE - NEW HARTFORD NY 13413
U70- 8	SATCHELL, DAROLD L	OLD ADD: 1613 N DUKE ST - DURHAM NC 27701
U60- 4	SCHWARTS, HARRY CLARK	D. FEBRUARY 22, 1963 CLEVELAND, O.
U30- 4	SCOTT, JAMES 'DEATH VALLEY JIM'	D. APRIL 7, 1957 PALM SPRINGS, CALIF.
U34- 1	SEARS, JOHN WILLIAM 'ZIGGY'	D. DECEMBER 16, 1956 HOUSTON, TEX.
U52- 5	SECORY, FRANK EDWARD	PLAYER DEBUT 1940
U14-15	SHANNON, WILLIAM PORTER 'SPIKE'	D. MAY 16, 1940 MINNEAPOLIS, MINN.
U79-11	SHULOCK, JOHN	3175 62ND AVE - VERO BEACH FL 32960
U57- 2	SMITH, VINCENT AMBROSE	PLAYER DEBUT 1941
U60- 5	SMITH, WILLIAM ALARIC 'AL'	609 DELHI ST - BOSSIER CITY LA 71111
U50- 2	SOAR, ALBERT HENRY 'HANK'	60 CONCH RD - NARRAGANSETT RI 02882
U77- 7	SPENN, FREDERICK CHARLES	6905 11TH AVE NW - BRADENTON FL 33505
U66- 4	SPRINGSTEAD, MARTIN JOHN	5 BRUCE CT - SUFFERN NY 10901
U28- 3	STARK, ALBERT D. 'DOLLY'	D. AUGUST 24, 1968 NEW YORK, N.Y.
U61- 6	STEINER, MELVIN JAMES	1701 HARBOR WAY - SEAL BEACH CA 90740
U68- 7	STELLO, RICHARD JACK	10800 US HWY 19 #111 - PINELLAS PARK FL 33565
U48- 2	STEVENS, JOHN WILLIAM	D. SEPTEMBER 9, 1981 PHILADELPHIA PA.
U41- 3	STEWART, ERNEST DRAPER	107 SAN MARCOS - DEL RIO TX 78840
U59- 1	STEWART, ROBERT WILLIAM	D. 1982 WOONSOCKET RI
U33- 2	STEWART, WILLIAM JOSEPH	D. FEBRUARY 18, 1964 JAMAICA PLAIN, MASS.
U15- 9	STOCKDALE, M. J.	OLD ADD: 314 W 42ND ST - NEW YORK NY
U57- 3	SUDOL, EDWARD LAWRENCE	415 REVILO BLVD - DAYTONA BEACH FL 32014
U33- 3	SUMMERS, WILLIAM REED	D. SEPTEMBER 12, 1966 UPTON, MASS.
U24- 2	SWEENEY, JAMES M	D. JANUARY 29, 1950 TYLER, TEX.
U56- 3	TABACCHI, FRANK TULE	D. OCTOBER 26, 1983 HOBOKEN, N. J.
U73- 3	TATA, TERRY ANTHONY	8 PROMONTORY DR - CHESHIRE CT 06410
U70- 9	TREMBLAY, RICHARD HENRY	RR 2 - WHITEFIELD NH 03598
U54- 3	UMONT, FRANK WILLIAM	2116 NE 63RD CT - FORT LAUDERDALE FL 33308
U63- 4	VALENTINE, WILLIAM TERRY	BOX 5599 - LITTLE ROCK AR 72215
U27- 2	VAN GRAFLAN, ROY	D. SEPTEMBER 4, 1953 ROCHESTER, N. Y.
U14-16	VAN SICKLE, CHARLES F	D. 1950
U60- 6	VARGO, EDWARD PAUL	101 FREEDOM RD - BUTLER PA 16001
U57- 4	VENZON, ANTHONY	D. SEPTEMBER 20, 1971 PITTSBURGH PA
U77- 8	VOLTAGGIO, VITO HENRY 'VIC'	646 BRENTWOOD DR - VINELAND NJ 08360
U22- 3	WALSH, EDWARD AUGUSTIN 'BIG ED'	D. MAY 26, 1959 POMPANO BEACH, FLA.
U61- 7	WALSH, FRANCIS D.	D. 1985 SAN ANTONIO, TEX.
U49- 2	WARNEKE, LONNIE	PLAYER DEBUT 1930
U43- 1	WEAFER, HAROLD LEON	7726 GRANITE HALL AVE - RICHMOND VA 23225
U83- 9	WELKE, TIMOTHY	31004 US 12 BOX 9 - STURGIS MI 49091
U66- 5	WENDELSTEDT, HARRY HUNTER	88 S ST ANDREWS - ORMOND BEACH FL 32074
U76-10	WEST, JOSEPH HENRY	8601 BROADWAY #1097 - HOUSTON TX 77061
U11- 6	WESTERVELT, FREDERICK E	D. MAY 4, 1955 DREXEL HILL, PA.
U61- 8	WEYER, LEE HOWARD	3001 NW 48TH AVE,BLD 6,#444 - LAUDERDALE LAKES FL 33313
U63- 5	WILLIAMS WILLIAM GEORGE	RR 2 BOX 822 #0-29 - POMPANO BEACH FL 33067
U72- 4	WILLIAMS, ARTHUR	D. FEBRUARY 8, 1979 BAKERSFIELD, CALIF.
U78- 1	WILLIAMS, CHARLES H.	5020 SOUTH LAKE DR #1715 - CHICAGO IL 60615
U21- 1	WILSON, FRANK	D. JUNE, 1928 BROOKLYN, N. Y.
U83-10	YOUNG, LARRY	8320 44TH ST N - PINELLAS PARK FL 33565

COACHES WITH NO MAJOR LEAGUE PLAYING OR MANAGERIAL EXPERIENCE DEBUTING FROM 1910 TO 1985

C67- 1	BERINGER, CARROLL JAMES 'C.B.'	4917 GRANITE SHOALS - FORT WORTH TX 76103
C64- 1	BLACKBURN, WAYNE CLARK	1414 OFFNERE ST - PORTSMOUTH OH 45662
C74- 1	BLOOMFIELD, GORDON LEIGH 'JACK'	1310 IRIS - MCALLEN TX 78501
C67- 2	BRAGAN, JAMES ALTON	1059 MARTINWOOD LN - BIRMINGHAM AL 35235
C69- 1	CAMACHO, JOSEPH GOMES	48 MASSASOIT AVE - FAIRHAVEN MA 02719
C70- 1	CARNEVALE, DANIEL JOSEPH	161 DORCHESTER RD - BUFFALO NY 14213
C59- 1	CARTER, RICHARD JOSEPH	D. SEPTEMBER 11, 1969 PHILADELPHIA, PA.
C77- 1	CLEAR, ELWOOD ROBERT 'BOB'	120 E 234TH ST - CARSON CA 90745
C79- 2	CLUCK, ROBERT	6065 MISSION GORGE RD #91 - SAN DIEGO CA 92120
C85- 1	CONNOR, MARK P.	1113 BURTON RD - KNOXVILLE TN 37919
C77- 2	CRESSE, MARK EMERY	3840 GOLDENROD ST - SEAL BEACH CA 90740
C79- 1	DEWS, ROBERT WALTER	423 AUDUBON - ALBANY GA 31707
C80- 1	DONNELLY, RICHARD FRANCIS	1902 GREEN MEADOW CT - ARLINGTON TX 76010
C61- 1	DOUGLAS, OTIS W	HAGUE VA 22469
C69- 2	DUNLOP, HARRY ALEXANDER	7470 29TH ST - SACRAMENTO CA 95820
C83- 1	DUSAN, EUGENE	61174 CONCHO ST - BEND OR 97701
C83- 2	EZELL, GLENN WAYNE	1504 LAUREL DR - ARLINGTON TX 76012
C47- 1	FITZGERALD, JOSEPH PATRICK	D. AUGUST 29, 1967 ORLANDO, FLA.
C53- 1	FITZPATRICK, JOHN ARTHUR	1728 E COMMONWEALTH #102-FULLERTON CA 92631
C85- 2	GALANTE, MATTHEW J.	177 CROSSFIELD AVE - STATEN ISLAND NY 10312
C82- 1	HARMON, THOMAS HAROLD	2635 BARTON HILLS DR - AUSTIN TX 78704
C84- 1	HINES, BEN THORNTON	2709 SECOND ST - LAVERNE CA 91750
C84- 2	HOLMQUIST, DOUGLAS LEONARD	981 ARDEN ST - LONGWOOD FL 32750
C48- 1	HOLT, GOLDEN DESMOND 'GOLDIE'	4937 STERN AVE - SHERMAN OAKS CA 91423
C68- 1	HOSCHEIT, VERNARD ARTHUR	BOX 36 - PLAINVIEW NE 68769
C55- 1	KAHN, LOUIS	916 TIFT ST - ALBANY GA 31701
C30- 1	KELLY, BERNARD FRANCIS	D. OCTOBER 23, 1968 INDIANAPOLIS, IND.
C69- 3	KISSELL, GEORGE MARSHALL	OLD ADD: 658 MOUNT OAK DR NE - ST PETERSBURG FL 33702
C71- 1	KITTLE, HUBERT MILTON 'HUB'	RR 6 BOX 255E - YAKIMA WA 98902
C70- 2	KOENIG, FRED CARL	6721 E 51ST ST - TULSA OK 74145
C57- 1	LEVY, LEONARD HOWARD	%J.SNELSON,324 COLTART ST-PITTSBURGH PA 15213
C82- 2	LEYLAND, JAMES RICHARD	213 W. INDIANA AVE - PERRYSBURG OH 43551
C84- 3	LEYVA, NICHOLAS T.	1042 EAST YALE - ONTARIO CA 91764

LOBE   WEST

C51- 1	LOBE, WILLIAM CHARLES	D. JANUARY 7, 1969 CLEVELAND, O.
C72- 1	LOWE, Q. V.	1118 NE 31ST ST - OCALA FL 32670
C85- 3	MAZZONE, LEO DAVID	RR 3 BOX 278X - RAWLINGS MD 21557
C51- 2	MCDONNELL, ROBERT 'MAJE'	7423 REVERE ST - PHILADELPHIA PA 19152
C85- 4	MERRILL, CARL HARRISON 'STUMP'	18 MERRYMEETING RD - TOPSHAM ME 04086
C77- 3	MOZZALI, MAURICE JOSEPH 'MO'	5802 STONE BLUFF RD - LOUISVILLE KY 40291
C85- 5	MULL, JACK LEROY	1041 WILSON AVE - CHAMBERSBURG PA 17201
C83- 3	NAPOLEON, EDWARD G.	1312 73RD ST NW - BRADENTON FL 33529
C83- 4	NOTTLE, EDWARD WILLIAM	6612 PINEHURST DR - EVANSVILLE IN 47711
C58- 1	OCEAK, FRANK JOHN	D. MARCH 19, 1983 JOHNSTOWN, PA.
C62- 1	ONEIL, JOHN B. 'BUCK'	3049 E 32ND ST - KANSAS CITY MO 64128
C63- 1	OSBORN, DONALD EDWIN	D. MARCH 23, 1979 TORRANCE, CALIF.
C74- 2	PACHECO, ANTONIO ARISTIDES 'TONY'	401 NW 56TH AVE - MIAMI FL 33126
C61- 2	PAEPKE, JACK	DRAWER CE - CRESTLINE CA 92325
C84- 4	PETERSON, ERIC HARDING 'RICK'	P.O. BOX 1359 - BRADENTON FL 33506
C69- 4	PLAZA, RONALD EDWARD	2050 68TH AVE S - ST PETERSBURG FL 33712
C66- 1	RESINGER, GROVER S.	D. JANUARY 11, 1986 ST. LOUIS, MO.
C81- 1	REYES, BENJAMIN 'CANANEA'	MATAMOROS Y CACATFCAS - HERMOSILLO SONORA MEX.
C66- 2	ROBINSON, WARREN GRANT 'SHERIFF'	OLD ADD: 305 OAKLEY ST - CAMBRIDGE MD
C73- 1	ROSENBAUM, GLEN OTIS	BOX 1 - UNION MILLS IN 46382
C72- 2	ROWE, RALPH EMANUEL	308 ESPLANADE ST - CHARLOTTE NC 28213
C76- 2	SAUL, JAMES ALLEN	2405 OSBORNE ST - BRISTOL VA 23201
C70- 3	SCHERGER, GEORGE RICHARD	701 ST JULIEN - CHARLOTTE NC 28205
C84- 5	SMITH, BILLY FRANKLIN	109 POTTER DR - JAMESTOWN NC 27282
C85- 6	SNITKER, BRIAN GERALD	1105 TREE MOUNTAIN PKWY - STONE MOUNTAIN GA 30083
C85- 7	TORCHIA, ANTHONY L.	5229 SW ELEVENTH AVE - CAPE CORAL FL 33904
C84- 6	TREBELHORN, THOMAS JOHN	4344 SE 26TH AVE - PORTLAND OR 97202
C81- 2	VAN ORNUM, JOHN CLAYTON	6624 N HAZEL ST - FRESNO CA 93711
C43- 1	VINCENT, ALBERT LINDER	260 MANOR AVE - BEAUMONT TX 77706
C61- 3	WALKER, VERLON LEE 'RUBE'	D. MARCH 24, 1971 CHICAGO, ILL.
C73- 2	WALTON, JAMES ROBERT	BOX 787 - SHATTUCK OK 73858
C77- 5	WARNER, HARRY CLINTON	106 BELFAIR - REEDERS PA 18352
C77- 6	WILLIAMS, DONALD ELLIS	205 FOXFIRE - PARAGOULD AR 72450
C81- 3	WILLIAMS, JAMES BERNARD	61 PURDUE ST - PUEBLO CO 81005
C32- 1	WOLGAMOT, CLIFTON EARL	D. APRIL 25. 1970 INDEPENDENCE. IA.

LATE ADDITIONS, CORRECTIONS & DEATHS

63- 3	ALLEN, RICHARD ANTHONY	P.O. BOX 204 - SELLERSVILLE PA 18960
63- 4	ALLEY, LEONARD EUGENE 'GENE'	OLD ADD: RR 1 BOX 225D - ROCKVILLE VA 23146
63- 11	BLOOMFIELD, CLYDE STALCUP 'BUD'	RR 8 BOX 592 - ROGERS AR 72756
64- 9	BORK, FRANK BERNARD	OLD ADD: 725 FAIRWAY BLVD - COLUMBUS OH 43227
67- 14	CAREW, RODNEY CLINE	5144 EAST CRESCENT DR - ANAHEIM CA 92807
66- 21	CLOSTER, ALAN EDWARD	2325 MAURY ST - RICHMOND VA 23224
77- 31	COLLINS, DONALD EDWARD	BOX 208 - LYONS GA 30436
15- 30	DANNER, HENRY FREDERICK 'BUCK'	D. SEPTEMBER 21, 1949 BOSTON, MASS.
16- 20	DRISCOLL, MICHAEL COLUMBUS	D. MARCH 22, 1953 FOXBORO, MASS.
63- 37	EGAN, RICHARD WALLIS	BOX 266 - MINDEN NV 89423
18- 19	FAHEY, FRANCIS RAYMOND	D. MARCH 19, 1954 BOSTON, MASS.
38- 27	FEINBERG, EDWARD	D. APRIL 20, 1986 HOLLYWOOD, FLA.
84- 36	FRANCO, JOHN ANTHONY	54 BAY 46TH ST - BROOKLYN NY 11214
67- 35	GASTON, CLARENCE EDWIN 'CITO'	65 HILTON AVE - TORONTO ONTARIO M5R 3E5 CAN.
27- 41	GRAMPP, HENRY ERCHARDT	D. MARCH 24, 1986 NEW YORK, N. Y.
23- 54	GRANT, JAMES RONALD	D. NOVEMBER 30, 1985 DES MOINES, IOWA
61- 43	HARKNESS, THOMAS WILLIAM 'TIM'	222 PEARSON RD #42 - OSHAWA ONTARIO L1G 7C6 CAN.
63- 54	HART, JAMES RAY	322 CAMARITAS AVE - SOUTH SAN FRANCISCO CA 94080
53- 36	JABLONSKI, RAYMOND LEO	D. NOVEMBER 25, 1985 CHICAGO, ILL.
66- 50	JOHNSTONE, JOHN WILLIAM 'JAY'	1300 WENTWORTH AVE - PASADENA CA 91106
24- 58	KAMP, ALPHONSE FRANCIS	D. FEBRUARY 25, 1955 BOSTON, MASS.
22- 67	KETCHUM, AUGUST FRANKLIN 'GUS'	D.
19- 47	KIMMICK, WALTER LYONS	OLD ADD: 3333 NE 34TH ST #320 - FT LAUDERDALE FL 33308
75- 63	LACORTE, FRANK JOSEPH	1667 EL DORADO DR - GILROY CA 95020
36- 49	LUBY, HUGH MAX	D. MAY 5, 1986 EUGENE, ORE.
61- 71	MACKENZIE, HENRY GORDON 'GORDY'	OLD ADD: RR 1 BOX 411C - LEESBURG FL 32748
50- 66	MCGHEE, WARREN EDWARD 'ED'	D. FEBRUARY 13, 1986 MEMPHIS, TENN.
41- 70	MILLER, ROLLAND ARTHUR 'RONNIE'	7511 LILA - HAZELWOOD MO 63042
78- 88	MURA, STEPHEN ANDREW	5105 CRAIG AVE - KENNER LA 70065
35- 88	PATTON, GEORGE WILLIAM	D. MARCH 16, 1986 PHILADELPHIA, PA.
70-108	PITLOCK, LEE PATRICK THOMAS 'SKIP'	11047 SUE AVE - LYNWOOD CA 90262
32- 71	RICHARDS, PAUL RAPIER	D. MAY 5, 1986 WAXAHACHIE, TEXAS
73-101	ROGERS, STEPHEN DOUGLAS	2718 SOUTH UTICA - TULSA OK 74114
39- 99	ROSS, CHESTER JAMES	VA HOSPITAL,3495 BAILEY AVE - BUFFALO NY 14215
43-127	SEEREY, JAMES PATRICK 'PAT'	D. APRIL 28, 1986 JENNINGS, MO.
64-112	SPARMA, JOSEPH BLASE	D. MAY 14, 1986 COLUMBUS, O.
74-124	SPILLNER, DANIEL RAY	27535 SE 154TH - ISSAQUAH WA 98027
15-159	STRANDS, LEWIS	DELETE
18- 70	THOMAS, FREDERICK HARVEY	D. JANUARY 15, 1986 RICE LAKE, WISC.
81-137	TOLMAN, TIMOTHY LEE	8601 E. FAIRMOUNT PLACE - TUCSON AZ 85715
67-110	UPHAM, JOHN LESLIE	1100 HURON CHURCH RD - WINDSOR ONTARIO N9C 2K7 CAN.
81-140	WELSH, CHRISTOPHER CHARLES	4112 PLUMOSA TER - BRADENTON FL 33507
27-102	WEST, SAMUEL FILMORE	D. NOVEMBER 23, 1985 LUBBOCK, TEXAS

GLOSSARY

The definitions presented in this glossary are definitions as they are interpreted by autograph collectors. For example, PHOTO refers to an autographed photo and HOFer refers to the autograph of a HOFer. Some of the definitions may appear self-explanatory and hence unnecessary; however, they are included for completeness.

ALL STAR BALL—A ball autographed by most or all members of a particular baseball all star game.

AUTOPEN—A mechanical device used to affix a signature on a document, letter or other paper medium. Autopen autographs are not considered collectible.

BALL POINT—A type of pen through which the ink is delivered by means of a revolving ball tip.

BASEBALL COMMEMORATIVE ENVELOPE—A stamped envelope postmarked on the date of a significant event in baseball history. The envelope contains some graphic or illustrative identification of the event. These envelopes autographed by a participant of the event are quite attractive and popular with autograph collectors. These envelopes should not be confused with first day covers popular with stamp collectors, although a hybrid first day cover/baseball commemorative envelope does exist. (This envelope contains the 1969 commemorative stamp of baseball's first hundred years and is cacheted with many different baseball superstars.)

CARD—A card autographed by the player portrayed on the card. Cards are normally autographed on the front; however, cards autographed on the back still qualify under this definition.

CHECK—A cancelled check or bank note containing the autograph of a ball player. Checks are quite often obtained from the estate of deceased ball players. Official ball club checks in many cases contain more than one autograph.

CLUB ISSUED POSTCARDS—Postcard size pictures of ball players, the older ones normally being in black and white with modern postcards being predominantly in color. They are usually blank backed, sold at ballparks and make excellent autograph media. Many players send autographed copies of these postcards to fans requesting autographs.

CONTRACT—A legal document, for any purpose, including agreements concerning players and management, equipment or other product manufacturers, or personal agreements signed by the sports personality.

CUT—An autograph that has been "cut" from a larger piece of paper, photo, letter or other written or printed matter.

DATED—An autograph which contains both the signature and the date when the signature was written.

DEBUT YEAR—The year in which a player first appeared in a game in the big leagues. For a manager or coach with no player experience the debut year refers to the year he first appeared as a manager or coach.

DEBUT YEAR NUMBER—Within a particular debut year the number for a player obtained by placing in alphabetical order all players who debuted that particular year and placing a number on each, from 1 to "the total number of players debuting that year," based on this alphabetical order.

FACSIMILE—A copy of an original signature. Facsimile autographs are not considered collectible.

FELT TIP—A type of pen which has a felt tip and which provides a smooth unbroken signature.

HOFer—The autograph of a member of baseball's Hall of Fame.

LETTER—A typed or handwritten communication with a heading listing to whom the letter is written and a closing autographed by a sports personality.

ORIGINAL ART—A unique drawing, painting or other piece of artwork portraying a personality or an event and bearing the signature of a participant of the event or the personality portrayed.

PENCIL—A signature in pencil by a sports personality. Pencil signatures predominated during the early parts of this century and are sometimes the only types of signatures available of certain sports personalities. Care should be taken with pencil signatures as they smear quite easily.

PLACQUE—Postcard pictures of the bronzed placques of Hall of Fame baseball players in the Baseball Hall of Fame in Cooperstown, NY. Through the years there have been several different color placques issued by the Hall of Fame, including black and white types.

PERSONALIZED—An autograph which contains a reference to the person for whom the autograph was written.

PHOTO—A glossy picture, normally 5" X 7" or 8" X I0," which contains an autograph of the player portrayed on the photo.

SASE—Self-addressed stamped envelope. When requesting autographs, SASE's should be sent to insure that returned autographs will be sent to the proper place and to provide the autograph giver a convenient means of returning autographed material.

SHARPIE—A brand of ink pen very popular with autograph collectors because of its broad stroke and its rapid drying characteristics on almost any surface.

STAMP—A signature affixed by means of a rubber or wooden device which contains a facsimile of the sports personality's autograph. Stamped signatures are not considered collectible.

TEAM BALL—A ball autographed by most or all members of a particular team.

TEAM SHEET—A single sheet of paper containing the autographs of most or all members of a particular team during a particular year. Many team sheets are on club stationery.

3 X 5—An index card, either lined or unlined, which many collectors use for obtaining autographs. The 3 X 5 refers to the approximate dimensions of the card. 3 X 5's usually contain only one signature.

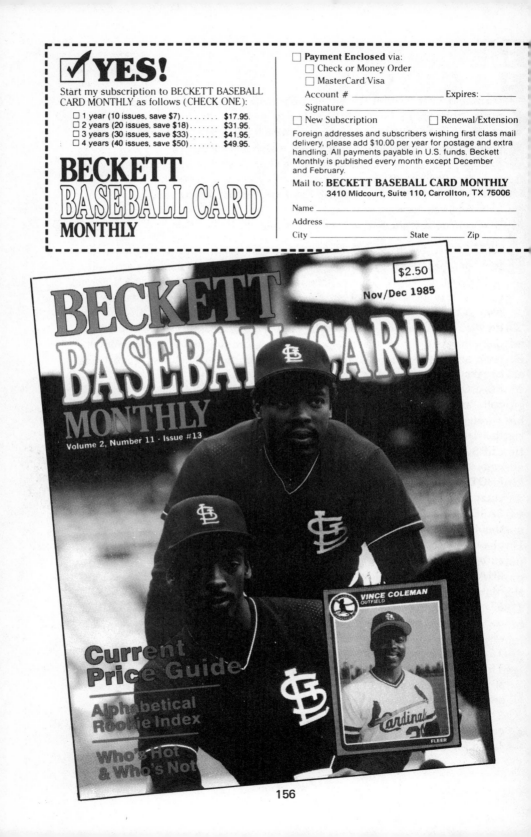